ASSET MARKETS, EXCHANGE RATES, AND ECONOMIC INTEGRATION

ASSET MARKETS, EXCHANGE RATES, AND ECONOMIC INTEGRATION

A SYNTHESIS

POLLY REYNOLDS ALLEN
UNIVERSITY OF CONNECTICUT

PETER B. KENEN
PRINCETON UNIVERSITY

CAMBRIDGE UNIVERSITY PRESS

CAMBRIDGE

LONDON   NEW YORK   NEW ROCHELLE
MELBOURNE   SYDNEY

Published by the Press Syndicate of the University of Cambridge
The Pitt Building, Trumpington Street, Cambridge CB2 1RP
32 East 57th Street, New York, NY 10022, USA
296 Beaconsfield Parade, Middle Park, Melbourne 3206, Australia

© Cambridge University Press 1980

First published 1980

Printed in the United States of America
Typeset by Progressive Typographers, Inc., Emigsville, Pa.
Printed and bound by Halliday Lithograph Corp., West Hanover, Mass.

Library of Congress Cataloging in Publication Data
Allen, Polly Reynolds.
Asset markets, exchange rates, and economic integration
Includes index.
1. International finance–Mathematical models.
2. Foreign exchange–Mathematical models.
3. International economic integration–Mathematical models.
I. Kenen, Peter B., 1932– joint author. II. Title.
HG3881.A447   332.4′5   79-16874
ISBN 0 521 22982 0

FOR ROBERT TRIFFIN
who continues to ask the interesting questions

Contents

x   **Contents**

Preface

The origins and aims of this book are described at length in Chapter 1. In 1973–4, one of us was working on the conduct of monetary policy in a monetary union; the other was working on the role of asset-market integration in the process of balance-of-payments adjustment. We decided to join forces. At first, we planned to write a monograph built on a simple two-country model designed to explore the relationships between market integration on the one hand and policy unification on the other. Two years later, however, we were still at work. It was not sufficient, we discovered, to build a conventional two-country model. We had instead to follow the path taken by customs-union theory – to allow for trade in goods and bonds between each country and the outside world. One cannot study the effects of a customs union without asking what it does to its members' trade with third countries. One cannot study the effects of a monetary or fiscal union without asking how its policies influence its joint balance of payments or common external exchange rate. The construction and solution of the model came to be quite complicated.

When we presented the first version of our monograph, moreover, at a seminar in Princeton in the fall of 1976, we were told to be more ambitious. Our model was more general than many others, containing larger numbers of commodities and assets and allowing for partial as well as perfect market integration. It could be used to present, extend, and qualify many propositions in the theory of the balance of payments and exchange-rate determination. We had done most of the hard work, we were told, and should harvest the whole of the crop we had sown. We would not need more than a year to finish the job.

The advice was good, but the forecast was far off. We have used two years, not one, and would not find it hard to spend another on issues we have set aside. But we are not sorry. The first half of this book is much more comprehensive than the draft from which it grew. It is, we believe, a rigorous presentation of modern international monetary theory – the so-called asset-market approach – and the whole of it is based on a single, general model from which we can derive many special cases. At the same time, the first half serves as the foundation for the new work we present in the second half–our contribution to the theory of economic integration.

During the five years that we have spent on this project, much has happened to our subject. Many findings that seemed new when we came upon them will by now be thoroughly familiar to our readers. We have, of course, attempted to give credit to those who have anticipated our results, and we apologize sincerely to anyone whose work we have slighted. It is hard to read and write at the same time.

We have incurred many debts in the course of our work–material and intellectual. Our research was supported by the John Simon Guggenheim Foundation, the Ford Foundation, and the International Finance Section at Princeton University. Our efforts were encouraged–and criticized–by many colleagues.

We have made joint presentations in seminars at New York University, the University of Pennsylvania, Princeton University, and Rutgers University, and individual presentations at Brown University, the University of Chicago, Columbia University, Harvard University, and the University of Pittsburgh. Early versions of our work on certain topics have appeared in the *American Economic Review,* the *European Economic Review, Rivista Internazionale di Scienze Economiche e Commerciali, Weltwirtschaftliches archiv,* and in an occasional paper published by the Center of Planning and Economic Research in Athens, and we have had useful comments from referees and readers.

We are grateful to colleagues who read and gave us comments on draft chapters, especially to Alan Blinder, Stephen Goldfeld, and Dwight Jaffee of Princeton, Jacob Frenkel and the late Harry Johnson of the University of Chicago, Rudiger Dornbusch of MIT, and Ralph Bryant of the Brookings Institution, and we owe a special debt to Willem Buiter and Jonathan Eaton of Princeton and to Marina Whitman of the University of Pittsburgh, who read and criticized the entire manuscript. Finally, we thank Howard Kaufold of Princeton, who worked his way through every proof and sentence, ferreting out errors. He has spared us much embarrassment and our readers much confusion.

Polly Reynolds Allen
Peter B. Kenen

March 1980

PART I

Introduction

1

An agenda

The point of departure

When we began this book, our aim was rather modest. We sought to reassess the effectiveness of national monetary and fiscal policies when capital markets are closely integrated and to use our findings in appraising the costs and benefits of economic unions, especially monetary unions. One of us had been working on the implications of capital mobility for the effectiveness of national policies.[1] The other had been working on the problems of monetary unification.[2] It looked as though we might put our work together once we had constructed a macroeconomic model that would be receptive to our questions. As we went along, however, we grew more ambitious. Encouraged by our colleagues and by each other, we came to believe that our model could be put to more extensive use. It was indeed becoming a synthesis of recent research on the theory of the balance of payments and exchange-rate determination. What had started as a monograph was becoming a treatise and might even be able to respond to Haberler's suggestion: "What would be welcome," he wrote recently, "is an updated version of Meade's classic treatise."[3]

The reader will have to decide if our response has been successful. First, however, we have to explain in what ways we have tried to "update" Meade, for we have not followed Haberler's prescription. He called for a marriage of Meade's approach to balance-of-payments theory, which stresses the roles of price and expenditure effects, to the "valid elements" of the monetary approach rehabilitated by Johnson and others, which stresses the requirements of long-run equilibrium in the money

---

[1] P. B. Kenen, *Capital Mobility and Financial Integration: A Survey*, Princeton Studies in International Finance 39, Princeton University, Princeton, N.J., 1976.

[2] P. R. Allen, *Organization and Administration of a Monetary Union*, Princeton Studies in International Finance 38, Princeton University, Princeton, N.J., 1976.

[3] G. Haberler, "Review of *The Monetary Approach to the Balance of Payments*," *Journal of Economic Literature*, 14 (December 1976), p. 1328. The reference, of course, is to J. E. Meade, *The Balance of Payments*, Oxford University Press, London, 1951.

market.[4] We have sought instead to marry Meade's analysis of price and expenditure effects to a broad approach to asset-market equilibrium that looks at money *and* bond markets, one we believe to be much richer than the monetary approach and less doctrinaire in its implications. We build and use a model that borrows its treatment of goods markets from Meade, its treatment of saving and wealth from Metzler,[5] and its treatment of financial markets from Markowitz and Tobin.[6]

A marriage of Meade's model to the modern monetary model would be an unhappy union. The partners would be incompatible. One of them, indeed, wants nothing to do with the other. In a paper published shortly after his death, Johnson defined the monetary approach in these terms:[7]

> The central propositions of the monetary approach are, first, that the balance of payments is a monetary phenomenon and requires analysis with the tools of monetary theory and not barter or "real" trade theory; second, that money is a stock, whereas real theory traditionally deals with flows, so that an adequate balance-of-payments theory must integrate stocks and flows; and third, that the money stock can be changed in two alternative ways, through domestic credit creation or destruction and through international reserve flows, the policy choice being important for balance-of-payments analysis.

[4] See, e.g., J. A. Frenkel and H. G. Johnson, eds., *The Monetary Approach to the Balance of Payments,* University of Toronto Press, Toronto, 1975, especially the editors' introductory essay and the papers by Johnson, Mundell, Frenkel, Dornbusch, and Rodriguez; also H. G. Johnson, "The Monetary Approach to Balance of Payments Theory: A Diagrammatic Analysis," *The Manchester School,* 43 (September 1975), pp. 220–74, and "The Monetary Approach to the Balance of Payments: A Nontechnical Guide," *Journal of International Economics,* 7 (August 1977), pp. 251–68, and J. A. Frenkel, "Adjustment Mechanisms and the Monetary Approach to the Balance of Payments: A Doctrinal Perspective," in E. Claassen and P. Salin, eds., *Recent Issues in International Monetary Economics,* North-Holland, Amsterdam, 1976, pp. 29–48. Other important contributions include R. Dornbusch, "Currency Depreciation, Hoarding, and Relative Prices," *Journal of Political Economy,* 81 (July/August 1973), pp. 893–915, R. A. Mundell, "The Optimum Balance of Payments Deficit," in E. Claassen and P. Salin, eds., *Stabilization Policies in Interdependent Economies,* North-Holland, Amsterdam, 1972, pp. 69–86, and R. Komiya, "Economic Growth and the Balance of Payments: A Monetary Approach," *Journal of Political Economy,* 77 (January/February 1969), pp. 35–48. For critical reviews of monetary models, see M. v. N. Whitman, "Global Monetarism and the Monetary Approach to the Balance of Payments," *Brookings Papers in Economic Activity,* 1975(3), pp. 121–66, and F. H. Hahn, "The Monetary Approach to the Balance of Payments," *Journal of International Economics,* 7 (August 1977), pp. 231–49.

[5] L. A. Metzler, "Wealth, Saving and the Rate of Interest," *Journal of Political Economy,* 59 (April 1951), pp. 930–46.

[6] H. M. Markowitz, *Portfolio Selection,* Wiley, New York, 1959, and J. Tobin, "Liquidity Preference as Behavior Toward Risk," in D. D. Hester and J. Tobin, eds., *Risk Aversion and Portfolio Choice,* Wiley, New York, 1967, pp. 1–26, and "A General Equilibrium Approach to Monetary Theory," *Journal of Money, Credit and Banking,* 1 (February 1969), pp. 15–30.

[7] Johnson, "A Nontechnical Guide," p. 251.

Models fashioned in accordance with these tenets sometimes deny altogether the relevance of price and expenditure effects – the ingredients of "real" trade theory – that figure strategically in Meade's treatise. They focus single mindedly on monetary equilibrium in the never-never land of the stationary state, and they are constructed expressly to affirm the neutrality of money, which is to say that they assume it. The economy is dichotomized completely into real and monetary sectors.

Adherents of the monetary approach are right to remind us that the exchange rate is the relative price of money – the price at which one currency is sold for another. But they then go on to draw the dubious inference that the exchange rate is determined in and by the money market. The monetary theory of the balance of payments is crafted to explain endogenous adjustments in the money supply when the exchange rate is pegged. The monetary theory of exchange-rate determination is crafted to explain endogenous adjustments in the "price" of money when the rate is flexible. Both theories are simplified drastically in order to focus symmetrically and narrowly on behavior in the money market.

Our approach is different in all of these respects. Although we are concerned to amend Meade's analysis by adding the requisite stock-flow relationships and portfolio constraints, we do not look mainly at their long-run implications. We examine the effects of disturbances and policies from start to finish, stressing the behavior over time of saving, wealth, and asset holdings and their effects on trade and capital flows. We show how an economy adapts to the requirements of long-run equilibrium, including money-market equilibrium, and how its adaptations are affected by the exchange-rate regime and the strength of the connections between home and foreign markets, especially the degree of substitutability between domestic and foreign bonds. Thus, we integrate the analysis of relative prices and expenditure with an analysis of changes in aggregate demand (absorption) brought about by changes in interest rates, exchange rates, and wealth, rather than subordinating all of those effects to the study of money-market effects.

We do not dichotomize our model. Money is not necessarily neutral in the model, even in the long run, so that monetary phenomena, including changes in the "price" of money, can influence real economic activity. Many restrictive assumptions are required to impose neutrality, and some of them may blind us to important insights. We shall see, for example, that money is not neutral when there is more than one exogenous variable denominated in nominal terms. To impose neutrality, it is thus necessary to limit the number of outside assets held by an economy or to endow those assets with characteristics that trivialize the problem of portfolio selection; doing so, we can suppress asset-market processes that have an important influence on exchange-rate behavior.[8] Readers may decide that we go too far in the opposite direction by insisting that exchange-rate determination is dominated in the short run by wealth holders' choices between home-currency and foreign-currency assets, but our model may be more realistic in this regard than models that rule out this possibility in the attempt to impose classical neutrality.

The exchange rate is treated as the "price" of money, but it is not determined in and by the money market. Although the exchange rate is the price that *clears* the money market it is determined jointly with other variables, including interest rates, by interactions between money and bond markets. Over time and in the long run, moreover, the exchange rate comes to conform with the requirements of equilibrium in the goods markets, not only in the bond and money markets. A decrease in the "price" of the home currency (a devaluation of a pegged exchange rate) is not equivalent in the long run to an increase in the quantity of money (an open-market purchase by the central bank).

In the preface to his book, Meade acknowledges indebtedness to Keynes and to Machlup, Metzler, and Nurkse, who were among the first to use Keynesian methods in balance-of-payments analysis. He also acknowledges a debt, however, to Robinson and others for their work on price effects and what we have now come to call the elasticities approach to exchange-rate theory.[9] It was Meade's chief contribution to synthesize Keynesian expenditure theory and neoclassical price theory.[10]

Meade is sometimes criticized, indeed, for devoting excessive attention to price elasticities and thereby neglecting the effects of changes in expenditure–for failing to emphasize the need for changes in absorption to validate a change in the exchange rate. True, he fails to allow for the possibility of endogenous changes in absorption, whether they be those invoked by Laursen and Metzler, Alexander, or Dornbusch.[11] But Meade

---

[8] The formulation here, and in Chapter 5, draws on the discussion in P. Isard, *Exchange-Rate Determination: A Survey of Popular Views and Recent Models,* Princeton Studies in International Finance 42, Princeton University, Princeton, N.J., 1978, pp. 25–6, Isard, in turn, cites D. Roper, "Two Ingredients of Monetarism in an International Setting," Seminar Paper 46, Institute for International Economic Studies, Stockholm, 1975.

[9] Meade, *The Balance of Payments,* pp. ix–x.

[10] The following discussion is adapted from P. B. Kenen, "Flexible Exchange Rates and National Autonomy," *Rivista Internazionale di Scienze Economiche e Commerciali,* 23, 1976(2), pp. 106–12.

[11] S. Laursen and L. A. Metzler, "Flexible Exchange Rates and the Theory of Employment," *Review of Economics and Statistics,* 32 (November 1950), pp. 281–99, S. S. Alex-

does not neglect the policy problem posed by students of the absorption approach. In effect, he assigns monetary and fiscal policies to the regulation of aggregate demand – to the task of making the changes in absorption required to validate a change in the exchange rate. Meade was among the first to warn that a devaluation cannot improve the balance of payments of a fully employed economy if the government does not engineer a reduction in absorption or if labor will not countenance a cut in the real wage.

Meade's use of price elasticities is not in the partial-equilibrium tradition of Robinson and others who were the first to use them. On the contrary, it evokes Edgeworth's warning about the deceptive simplicity of offer-curve analysis. Offer curves, said Edgeworth, are like the hands of a clock. There is much machinery concealed behind them. Similarly, much machinery is moving behind the foreign-exchange market in Meade's model.

Meade's book, moreover, deals with many of the issues that are in vogue today, and says things that economists are saying now as though they had never been said before. His chapter on nontraded goods, for example, tells us much that we have been learning anew from Dornbusch, Jones and Corden, and Krueger,[12] and much that will be found in this book too. It tells us how substitution in production and consumption determines the extent to which effects of changes in exchange rates spread out from the markets for traded goods to influence activity and prices in markets for nontraded goods. It does so, moreover, without making the small-country assumption that is so popular today – without pretending that adjustments in internal prices are the only ones that matter. In a chapter that compares international with interregional payments adjustment, Meade anticipates many statements made by Mundell, Ingram, and others concerning the roles of labor and capital mobility in the adjustment process.[13] And Meade's chapter on speculation in the foreign-exchange

ander, "Effects of a Devaluation on a Trade Balance," *International Monetary Fund Staff Papers*, 2 (April 1952), pp. 263–78, and Dornbusch, "Currency Depreciation, Hoarding, and Relative Prices."

[12] R. Dornbusch, "Devaluation, Money, and Nontraded Goods," in Frenkel and Johnson, eds., *The Monetary Approach to the Balance of Payments*, pp. 168–86, R. W. Jones and W. M. Corden, "Devaluation, Non-flexible Prices, and the Trade Balance for a Small Country," *Canadian Journal of Economics*, 9 (February 1976), pp. 150–61, and A. O. Krueger, "The Role of Home Goods and Money in Exchange Rate Adjustments," in W. Sellekaerts, ed., *International Trade and Finance: Essays in Honour of Jan Tinbergen*, Macmillan, London, 1974, pp. 139–61.

[13] R. A. Mundell, "A Theory of Optimum Currency Areas," *American Economic Review*, 51 (December 1961), pp. 657–65, and J. C. Ingram, *The Case for European Monetary Integration*, Essays in International Finance 98, Princeton University, Princeton, N.J., 1973.

market is superior pedagogically to Friedman's famous article,[14] because Meade is careful to articulate fully the assumptions one must make in order to establish that private speculation will help to stabilize a flexible exchange rate.

Meade does not neglect capital movements in his account of balance-of-payments adjustment, and his model includes a well-defined money market. When capital movements appear in his examples, however, they serve mainly to supplement movements of goods. Look in particular at Chapter XV of *The Balance of Payments*, where Meade compares adjustment under a gold standard with adjustment under a flexible exchange rate. One could delete all references to capital movements without altering substantially Meade's major conclusions. And though the stock of money appears in his model, it does not constrain economic behavior. In most of his book, Meade instructs the central bank to maintain a constant interest rate; the bank's open-market operations offset changes in the supply of money caused by movements of reserves and offset changes in the demand for money caused by movements in domestic income.[15]

What is most important from our standpoint, Meade does not connect capital movements with behavior in bond markets. Demands for claims on foreigners are added to his model; they are not extracted from the model as excess demands for bonds. There are, in fact, no bond markets in Meade's model and thus no way to link flow demands for bonds with the level of saving or to link stock demands with the level of wealth.

Meade's book appeared just 15 years after Keynes's *General Theory*, years in which there was intermittent warfare between two Cambridge Colleges. At Kings, Keynes maintained that the rate of interest depends on the demand for money, reflecting liquidity preference. At Trinity, Robertson maintained that it depends on the demand for loanable funds, reflecting thrift or saving. The skirmishing ended only when the two sides had digested Hicks's *Value and Capital*, reminding them of Walras's law, and came to understand that excess demand in one market implies excess supply in another. When the markets for goods and money clear, the market for bonds must also clear. The truce between the Colleges, however, led many to believe that they were free to concentrate on the demand for money, neglecting the demand for bonds, and this is what Meade did. The method is permissible, but it can be hazardous. When we

[14] M. Friedman, *Essays in Positive Economics*, University of Chicago Press, Chicago, 1953, pp. 157–203.

[15] On money and monetary policy in Meade's model, see S. C. Tsiang, "The Role of Money in Trade Balance Stability," *American Economic Review*, 51 (December 1961), pp. 912–36.

write out an equation to describe the money market, we make important statements about the bond market, and we should write them out too, if only to be sure that we are content with the statements we have made about the money market. When we work with open systems, moreover, in which goods and asset markets are connected with their counterparts in other countries, it is absolutely essential that we do so.

To bring Meade's treatise up to date, it is therefore necessary to specify fully and explicitly the requirements of equilibrium in each and every asset market – along with the relationships between demands for stocks of assets and the flows by which those stocks are altered through time. Furthermore, holdings of assets, including money, must be constrained by wealth. Saving must be made to add to wealth. And wealth must be allowed to influence the level of saving and therefore to influence aggregate expenditure.

The need to include and exploit stock-flow relationships is, of course, a major tenet of the monetary approach to the balance of payments. Even in the simplest of monetary models, where money is the only asset, hoarding (saving) adds to money holdings (wealth), and the level of those holdings affects the rate of hoarding.[16] But stock-flow relationships appeared for the first time in modern balance-of-payments analysis in a different context – in attempts to show why some of us had failed to prove statistically that capital flows are sensitive to interest rates.[17] They came to be included in general open-economy models when wealth and portfolio-balance constraints were invoked to modify Mundell's conclusions regarding the optimum policy mix and the assignment problem.[18]

[16] See, e.g., Dornbusch, "Currency Depreciation, Hoarding, and Relative Prices."

[17] See, e.g., W. H. Branson, *Financial Capital Flows in the U.S. Balance of Payments,* North-Holland, Amsterdam, 1968, and N. C. Miller and M. v. N. Whitman, "The Outflow of Short-term Funds from the United States: Adjustments of Stocks and Flows," in F. Machlup et al., eds., *International Mobility and Movement of Capital,* Columbia University Press for the National Bureau of Economic Research, New York, 1972, pp. 253–86.

[18] The first of the general models was, we believe, the one in R. I. McKinnon and W. E. Oates, *The Implications of International Economic Integration for Monetary, Fiscal, and Exchange-Rate Policies,* Princeton Studies in International Finance 16, Princeton University, Princeton, N.J., 1966. On the development of the approach, see J. Myhrman, "Balance-of-Payments Adjustment and Portfolio Theory: A Survey," in Claassen and Salin, eds., *Recent Issues in International Monetary Economics,* pp. 203–37. See also T. Scitovsky, *Money and the Balance of Payments,* Rand McNally, Chicago, 1969, especially chap. 7, which anticipates subsequent contributions. On the reformulation of Mundell's conclusions, see M. v. N. Whitman, *Policies for Internal and External Balance,* Special Papers in International Economics 9, Princeton University, Princeton, N.J., 1970, pp. 23–30, and the sources cited there; also W. H. Branson and T. D. Willett, "Policy Toward Short-term Capital Movements: Some Implications of the Portfolio Approach," in Machlup et al., eds., *International Mobility and Movement of Capital,* pp. 287–310.

The earliest of these portfolio models were quite simple–too simple to deal with many issues studied in this book. Typically, they focused on wealth holders' choices between the domestic money and a single bond, and they did not always specify the currency in which the bond was denominated.[19] Progress in this field has been rapid, however, and the model used throughout this book, although new when we began to build it, is not new today. Inspired by concern about the implications of asset-market integration for national autonomy, especially monetary autonomy, model builders have included foreign and domestic bonds, so as to define asset-market integration by the degree of substitutability between pairs of securities.[20] Inspired by concern about the amplitude of exchange-rate fluctuations after rates began to float, model builders have included home-currency and foreign-currency assets, so as to explain exchange-rate behavior by shifts between the two.[21]

[19] See, e.g., McKinnon and Oates, *The Implications of International Economic Integration,* and R. I. McKinnon, "Portfolio Balance and International Payments Adjustment," in R. A. Mundell and A. K. Swoboda, eds., *Monetary Problems of the International Economy,* University of Chicago Press, Chicago, 1969, pp. 199–234; also P. R. Allen, "A Portfolio Approach to International Capital Flows," *Journal of International Economics,* 3 (May 1973), pp. 135–60, P. B. Kenen, "International Capital Movements and the Integration of Capital Markets," in F. Machlup, ed., *Economic Integration: Worldwide, Regional, Sectoral,* Macmillan, London, 1976, pp. 187–200, and P. R. Allen and P. B. Kenen, "Portfolio Adjustment in Open Economies: A Comparison of Alternative Specifications," *Weltwirtschaftliches archiv,* 112, 1976(1), pp. 34–71. Some models appear to be richer than our own because they include equities, but they are not truly so, as equities and bonds are made to be too much alike. See, e.g., R. Dornbusch, "A Portfolio Balance Model of the Open Economy," *Journal of Monetary Economics,* 1 (January 1975), pp. 3–20, where bonds are indexed in terms of the consumption good, and "Capital Mobility, Flexible Exchange Rates, and Macroeconomic Equilibrium," in Claassen and Salin, eds., *Recent Issues in International Monetary Economics,* pp. 261–78, where there are two countries, two equities, and two bonds, but all four assets are defined in real terms and are assumed to be perfect substitutes. For models in which equities appear alone, see J. E. Floyd, "Portfolio Equilibrium and the Theory of Capital Movements," in Machlup et al., eds., *International Mobility and Movement of Capital,* pp. 91–124, and J. E. Frenkel and C. A. Rodriguez, "Portfolio Equilibrium and the Balance of Payments: A Monetary Approach," *American Economic Review,* 65 (September 1975), pp. 674–88.

[20] See, e.g., W. H. Branson, "Stocks and Flows in International Monetary Analysis," in A. Ando et al., eds., *International Aspects of Stabilization Policies,* Federal Reserve Bank of Boston and International Seminar in Public Economics, Boston, 1975, pp. 27–50, where there are domestic equities and foreign bonds, and "Portfolio Equilibrium and Monetary Policy with Foreign and Nontraded Assets," in Claassen and Salin, eds., *Recent Issues in International Monetary Economics,* pp. 241–50, where there are domestic bonds and equities as well as foreign bonds.

[21] See L. Girton and D. Henderson, "Central Bank Operations in Foreign and Domestic Assets Under Fixed and Flexible Exchange Rates," in P. Clark et al., eds., *The Effects of Exchange Rate Adjustments,* U.S. Treasury, Washington, D.C., 1977, pp. 151–78, and "Financial Capital Movements and Central Bank Behavior in a Two-Country, Short-Run

The plan of the book

The model built and used in Part II, where we address ourselves to these concerns, contains two bonds, one of which is denominated in foreign currency. The model describes a single country whose residents (households) hold domestic money issued by the central bank, a home-currency bond issued by the government, and a foreign-currency bond issued by the outside world. The domestic assets are held at home, not traded, and the interest rate on the domestic bond is determined endogenously. The foreign bond is held at home and abroad and is traded freely; it can in fact be bought or sold in unlimited quantities at a fixed (exogenous) foreign interest rate. (The country represented by the model is thus a net foreign creditor and is also a foreign-currency creditor. The outside world is therefore a net foreign debtor, but it is not a foreign-currency debtor, because its debts are in its own currency. This distinction must be borne in mind when interpreting our work. It may at first appear that our model has very limited applicability, because it deals only with a foreign-currency creditor. But countries can be foreign-currency creditors even when they are net foreign debtors. In fact, all countries can be foreign-currency creditors simultaneously, even though some must be net foreign creditors and others must be net foreign debtors. One has only to assume, as in our model, that countries hold claims in foreign currency but do not issue debts in foreign currency.)

The model includes three goods as well as three assets, but only one of them is nontraded. The country produces and consumes two commodities, an export good and a nontraded good, and it consumes in addition an

Portfolio Balance," *Journal of Monetary Economics,* 2 (January 1976), pp. 33–61; also R. Dornbusch, "Capital Mobility and Portfolio Balance," in R. Z. Aliber, ed., *The Political Economy of Monetary Reform,* Allanheld, Osmun and Co., Montclair, N.J., 1977, pp. 106–25, H. Genberg and H. Kierzkowski, "Short Run, Long Run, and Dynamics of Adjustment Under Flexible Exchange Rates," Graduate Institute of International Studies, Geneva, 1975 (mimeo), and R. S. Boyer, "Commodity Markets and Bond Markets in a Small Fixed-Exchange-Rate Economy," *Canadian Journal of Economics,* 8 (February 1975), pp. 1–23, and "Devaluation and Portfolio Balance," *American Economic Review,* 67 (March 1977), pp. 54–63. The models used by Genberg and Kierzkowski and by Boyer are much like our own, and anticipate many of our findings. Some of those findings are also anticipated by models that contain no bonds but make wealth holders choose between home and foreign currencies. See, e.g., C. Chen, "Diversified Currency Holdings and Flexible Exchange Rates," *Quarterly Journal of Economics,* 87 (February 1973), pp. 96–111, P. J. K. Kouri, "The Exchange Rate and the Balance of Payments in the Short Run and in the Long Run: A Monetary Approach," *Scandinavian Journal of Economics,* 78, 1976(2), pp. 280–304, and G. Calvo and C. A. Rodriguez, "A Model of Exchange Rate Determination Under Currency Substitution and Rational Expectations," *Journal of Political Economy,* 85 (June 1977), pp. 617–25.

import good that can be purchased in unlimited quantities at a fixed (ex-ogenous) foreign-currency price. Thus, our model differs from some others, in that our country is not small in all foreign markets. It is, we said, a price taker in the market for the foreign bond and also in the market for the foreign (import) good. But it is not a price taker in the market for its export good; it faces a downward-sloping foreign demand curve, and its terms of trade are not exogenous. (It is for this reason, inci-dentally, that we are able sometimes to delete the nontraded good. We do not need it to produce endogenous changes in relative prices. The home-currency price of the export good is endogenous, and the process of adjustment to exogenous disturbances can therefore involve endogenous price changes even when there is no nontraded good.)

The model is set out algebraically in Chapter 2 and is solved in Chapter 3. Thereafter, we interpret the results, stressing the effects of asset-market integration and exchange-rate behavior on the way in which the economy adjusts to exogenous disturbances and changes in domestic poli-cies. In Chapters 4 and 5 we deal with comparative statics, looking first at impact or short-run effects, before saving has had time to affect the stock of wealth, and then at steady-state or long-run effects, when saving has been driven to zero. In Chapter 6 we deal with dynamics, focusing on con-nections among the basic wealth-saving relationship, portfolio effects on capital flows, and expenditure (absorption) effects on the trade balance.

The solutions in Chapter 3 and discussions in subsequent chapters deal with responses to goods-market disturbances, including shifts in ag-gregate domestic demand between domestic goods (the export and non-traded goods), shifts in domestic and foreign demand between traded goods, and changes in the foreign-currency price of the foreign (import) good. We deal also with asset-market disturbances, represented by an ex-ogenous increase in the foreign interest rate. We concentrate, however, on policy changes – on balanced-budget changes in government spending, on cuts in lump-sum taxes that cause budget deficits and add to the supply of domestic bonds, and on open-market operations by the central bank.

In Chapter 4, dealing with goods-market disturbances, and Chapter 5, dealing with other disturbances, we analyze disturbances and policies one at a time, examining impact and steady-state effects and asking in each in-stance how outcomes are affected by the exchange-rate regime. We also pause to comment on differences between the *form* in which results are cast in our model, where most things are measured in nominal terms, and the form in which results are cast in monetarist models, where most things are measured in real terms. In Chapter 6, dealing with dynamics, we look first at the process of adjustment with a pegged exchange rate, concentrating on a handful of disturbances, then look at the process with a flexible rate. We organize this chapter differently because of our finding in earlier chapters that the nature of the process of adjustment depends primarily on the exchange-rate regime, not on the disturbance or policy change.

It is, of course, the main aim of these chapters to explain in economic terms the formal solutions supplied in Chapter 3, but that is not the only aim. We pause to comment on a number of issues germane to the choice between exchange-rate regimes. Is it true, for example, that a flexible exchange rate can insulate a single national economy from disturbances coming from abroad? If so, how rapidly and how completely? Is it true. that a flexible exchange rate enhances the effectiveness of monetary policy and reduces the effectiveness of fiscal policy? If so, for what reasons and to what extent? In this same vein, we ask how asset-market integration affects the way in which an economy responds to disturbances and policy changes.

Although the domestic bond is not traded in our model, and the domestic interest rate is determined endogenously, it is not hard to measure asset-market integration–the degree to which the domestic bond market is connected with the foreign bond market. Scitovsky defines asset-market integration as a function of the transferability of bonds between asset holders in various places:[22]

Indeed, the unresponsiveness of an asset's price to selling in one and buying in another region is the best index of the degree to which its market is integrated. The unresponsiveness of asset prices as a whole to asset transfers and attempted asset transfers of this sort indicates the extent of integration of asset markets in general.

But assets can be transferred without changing their prices only when they are perfect substitutes. If wealth holders in one region want to hold more of one asset and wealth holders in a second want to hold less of another, there will be changes in the prices of both assets unless the excess demand for the first can be satisfied by the excess supply of the second. Transferability and thus integration, as Scitovsky defines it, are functions of substitutability. There must, of course, be at least one tradable asset for markets to be integrated; when there are prohibitive barriers to trade in each and every asset, the prices of assets are not connected, and the

[22] Scitovsky, *Money and the Balance of Payments*, p. 90.

markets for assets cannot be integrated.[23] But it is not necessary that all assets be tradable, only that there be some substitutability between those that are tradable and those that are not.

When households look on the domestic (nontraded) bond as a close substitute for the foreign (traded) bond, the interest rate on the domestic bond will not vary freely, even though it is determined endogenously. When they look on the two bonds as perfect substitutes, the domestic interest rate cannot change at all unless there is a change in the foreign interest rate; the two bond markets will be perfectly integrated. To put the point formally, the extent of asset-market integration is measured in this book by the sizes of the relevant cross-elasticities – the elasticity of demand for the domestic bond with respect to the foreign interest rate and the elasticity of demand for the foreign bond with respect to the domestic interest rate – and perfect integration is said to prevail in the limiting case of infinite cross-elasticities.[24]

We have said that we subscribe to the new view that exchange rates are determined in the short run by behavior in the money and bond markets – the chief dictum of the asset-market approach. How do we represent this supposition formally? We are not free to follow those who do so by assuming that the money and bond markets clear much faster than the goods markets. All markets in our model clear continuously; there are no disequilibria, even momentarily. Furthermore, we cannot say that the demands for foreign and domestic assets are governed exclusively or dominated by wealth holders' expectations about exchange-rate changes, which has by now become the most popular approach.[25] Throughout Part

[23] When markets are efficient in the sense that prices respond instantaneously to new information, sets of markets may appear to be connected even if there is no trade between them. This would be the case, for example, if movements in nominal interest rates reflected common expectations about changes in inflation rates. But trade in assets is required to maintain connections between markets in the face of changes in supplies of assets, including those arising from budget deficits and open-market operations. On the use of the notion of market efficiency to define and measure asset-market integration, see D. E. Logue, M. A. Salant, and R. J. Sweeney, "International Integration of Financial Markets: Survey, Synthesis, and Results," in C. H. Stem et al., eds., *Eurocurrencies and the International Monetary System,* American Enterprise Institute, Washington, D.C., 1976, pp. 91–137; for comments and criticism, see Kenen, *Capital Mobility and Financial Integration,* pp. 8–20.

[24] We also use cross-elasticities to measure integration between goods markets. By imposing perfect integration (substitutability) on various pairs of goods, we show that our three-product model can be made to replicate well-known conclusions drawn from various two-product models.

[25] See, e.g., Kouri, "The Exchange Rate and the Balance of Payments," R. Dornbusch, "Expectations and Exchange Rate Dynamics," *Journal of Political Economy,* 84 (December 1976), pp. 1161–76, and W. Ethier, "Expectations and Asset-Market Theories of

II and in most of the rest of the book, expectations are stationary. Wealth holders do not act with perfect certainty; if they did, they would not hold all assets simultaneously. But they do not *forecast* changes in exchange rates.

To build an asset-market view into our model, we have therefore adopted a series of assumptions to segregate asset markets from goods markets, at least in the short run, and two of those assumptions should be mentioned here:

1. Although asset markets and goods markets clear continuously, the *ways* in which they clear are different. In goods markets, prices adjust continuously to equate flow demands with flow supplies. Saving adapts to gradual changes in the interest rate and stock of wealth, and aggregate demand (absorption) must also adapt gradually. In asset markets, prices adjust continuously to equate stock demands with stock supplies. Households are able to alter immediately their holdings of money and bonds, subject only to the accounting requirement that their holdings of all assets add up to their wealth. There are no observable discrepancies between actual and optimal portfolios. This assumption is extreme but may be more realistic than the assumption sometimes made that portfolio adjustment takes place gradually – an assumption under which wealth holders would be seen to hold unwanted stocks of bonds or money. In Foley's words:[26]

Asset markets are in fact among the best organized of markets; information about prices of many (especially financial) assets is disseminated widely and rapidly, and the great bulk of the total in industrial capitalist economies is held in very large portfolios for which fixed transaction costs will be negligible in relation to portfolio shifts. These observations suggest that the vision of stock equilibrium may be a good approximation to the real situation.

To put this first assumption in different terms, the goods markets in our model are structured to distribute commodity flows from producers to consumers, whereas the bond and money markets are structured to dis-

the Exchange Rate," Discussion Paper 346, Department of Economics, University of Pennsylvania, Philadelphia, 1976. Asset holders' expectations also play important roles in models that explain exchange-rate behavior by invoking interest parity or purchasing-power parity; see, e.g., J. A. Frenkel, "A Monetary Approach to the Exchange Rate: Doctrinal Aspects and Empirical Evidence," *Scandinavian Journal of Economics,* 78, 1976(2), pp. 200–24, and the discussion in Isard, *Exchange-Rate Determination,* pp. 24–5, 30–4.

[26] D. K. Foley, "On Two Specifications of Asset Equilibrium in Macroeconomic Models," *Journal of Political Economy,* 83 (April 1975), p. 319 (cited also in Isard, *Exchange-Rate Determination,* p. 22).

tribute stocks of assets from wealth holders wanting to reduce their holdings to wealth holders wanting to enlarge their holdings.[27]

2. In most macroeconomic models, the demand for money is made to depend on interest rates and income. In this one, it is made to depend on interest rates and wealth. The demands for money, the domestic bond, and the foreign bond are alike in form, apart from the signs of their partial derivatives with respect to interest rates. As a result, the money and bond markets are not affected instantaneously by changes in goods prices or aggregate demand, and the exchange rate is determined in the short run by the money and bond markets, jointly with the interest rate on the domestic bond.

There is thus an asymmetry in our model. Goods markets are affected immediately by disturbances and policies that impinge in the first instance on asset markets, but asset markets are affected only gradually by disturbances and policies that impinge in the first instance on goods markets. In goods markets, demands and supplies respond immediately to changes in goods prices, including those that testify to exchange-rate changes caused by asset-market disturbances and policies. Furthermore, the level of aggregate demand (absorption) depends in part on the exchange rate, as well as on the interest rate. A depreciation or devaluation of the domestic currency raises the home-currency price of the foreign-currency bond, adding to household wealth measured in home currency, and an increase in nominal wealth depresses the incentive to save, raising nominal consumption and aggregate demand. In asset markets, by contrast, changes in goods prices and aggregate demand caused by goods-market disturbances and policies affect the interest rate and exchange rate, but only with the passage of time. By altering incomes and saving, they lead eventually to changes in the stock of wealth and, therefore, to changes in demands for assets.

Readers who work carefully through Part II will want answers to a number of questions concerning our assumptions about the demand for money, expectations, and tax policies. How would exchange-rate behavior be affected were we to abandon our assumption that the demand for money depends on wealth but not on income? How would it be affected if households could anticipate the rate of change of the exchange rate? How would the performance of our model as a whole be altered if the govern-

---

[27] For a comparison between instantaneous and gradual portfolio adjustments (between markets that deal in stocks and those that deal in flows), see Allen and Kenen, "Portfolio Adjustment."

ment relied on an income tax rather than the lump-sum tax used in Part II, and how would this change in specification modify our findings concerning the effects of fiscal policies?

Answers to these questions are given in Part III, where we experiment sequentially with several changes in specification, using a simplified version of our model. We begin in Chapter 7 by reviewing briefly the strategic assumptions made in Part II and some of the reasons for making them. We go on in Chapter 8 to show what happens when the demand for money depends on income as well as wealth. Next, in Chapter 9, we introduce anticipations and speculation. We do not allow wealth holders to anticipate disturbances or changes in monetary policies. We do endow them with sufficient foresight to predict long-run effects on the exchange rate and price level.[28] We then cause the demands for assets to depend in part on wealth holders' forecasts of the rate of change of the exchange rate – on the speed with which it is expected to approach its long-run equilibrium after a disturbance or policy change, and we cause saving to depend on real interest rates (which depend in turn on wealth holders' forecasts of the rates of change of goods prices).

Finally, in Chapter 10, we digress to study the effects of using an income tax rather than a lump-sum tax, following Blinder and Solow, Turnovsky, and Branson.[29] We find, of course, that the balancing of the government budget becomes an endogenous process and has important consequences for the evolution of the current-account balance. Concomitantly, the size of the government debt (the stock of domestic bonds) becomes an endogenous variable, and its behavior has important consequences for the evolution of the capital account.

The small-country assumption is helpful in Parts II and III, where we seek to synthesize balance-of-payments theories and investigate the consequences of asset-market integration for the conduct of monetary and fiscal policies. But we must alter our approach when we turn to our third task, which is to study economic interdependence and the costs and benefits of economic unions.

[28] A similar assumption is used by Dornbusch ("Expectations and Exchange Rate Dynamics," p. 1163).

[29] A. S. Blinder and R. M. Solow, "Does Fiscal Policy Matter?," *Journal of Public Economics,* 2 (November 1973), pp. 319–37, S. J. Turnovsky, "The Dynamics of Fiscal Policy in an Open Economy," *Journal of International Economics,* 6 (May 1976), pp. 115–42, and W. H. Branson, "The Dual Role of the Government Budget and the Balance of Payments in the Movement from Short-Run to Long-Run Equilibrium," *Quarterly Journal of Economics,* 90 (August 1976), pp. 345–68.

In much of what is written on this subject, "integration" and "interdependence" are used almost interchangeably.[30] In this book, we seek to distinguish between the two. We have already employed "integration" to denote the closeness of connections between national markets and have identified it with the degree of substitutability between pairs of goods or assets. We employ "interdependence" to denote the extent to which disturbances originating in one country, including and especially changes in its policies, affect another country sufficiently to produce endogenous and policy responses that impinge in turn on the first country. Going further, we distinguish between two types of interdependence. The first is structural interdependence, the degree to which events in one country affect private or market behavior in another country. The second is policy interdependence, the degree to which events in one country give rise to changes in another country's policies. It is, of course, our aim to stress policy interdependence, but its character and strength clearly depend on the degree of structural interdependence.[31]

Under these definitions, there is no necessary relationship between economic size and the degree of economic integration. The markets of a small open economy can be loosely or closely connected to foreign markets. In Part II, for example, we study a country that is a price taker in the market for foreign bonds but has its own bond market too, and we show that the domestic interest rate can vary independently of the foreign rate when the domestic and foreign bonds are not close substitutes. It is impossible, however, for a small economy to be interdependent with other economies. It is too small by definition to influence the prices of other countries' outputs, their incomes, interest rates, and stocks of wealth. In the language used above, smallness rules out structural interdependence and, therefore, policy interdependence.

To study economic interdependence, we must therefore abandon the small-country assumption, and this is what we do in Part IV. We build and solve a multicountry model that is designed expressly to pave the way for the investigation in Part V, where we weigh the costs and benefits of an economic union and show how they are influenced by market integration and policy interdependence.

When economists abandon the small-country assumption, they usually

[30] See, e.g., R. N. Cooper, *The Economics of Interdependence*, McGraw-Hill, New York, 1968, chap. 1, and M. v. N. Whitman, "International Interdependence and the U.S. Economy," in W. Fellner, ed., *Contemporary Economic Problems 1976*, American Enterprise Institute, Washington, D.C., 1976, pp. 183–223.

[31] A similar distinction is drawn in R. C. Bryant, *Money and Monetary Policy in Interdependent Nations*, The Brookings Institution, Washington, D.C., 1980, chap. 10.

move on to a two-country model in which each country is sufficiently large to influence the other. They introduce structural interdependence and, therefore, the possibility of policy interdependence. In a two-country model, however, the nature of structural interdependence is narrowly limited. Each country tends to be the mirror image of the other. When one country gains reserves, for example, the other loses them. Furthermore, a simple two-country model cannot be used to study many of the problems of an economic union. One can study the effects of merging the two central banks and following a common monetary policy. The effects that one can measure in this context, however, may not be those that are decisive for a comprehensive cost-benefit analysis or for the success of a monetary union. Using a two-country model, we cannot ask what happens when a monetary union allows its common external exchange rate to float; there is no common external exchange rate. We cannot ask how the degree of integration with external asset markets impinges on the union's monetary policy; there are no external markets.[32]

To examine these and other issues, we present in Chapter 11 a model that contains two countries, North and South, that deal with each other but also with the outside world. The two countries resemble in many ways the single small economy of Part II. In fact, we construct our two-country model by setting a second small economy alongside the one described in Chapter 2, omitting the nontraded goods, and allowing each country to buy the other's export good and to hold the other's bond. Each country is a price taker in the market for the good it imports from the outside world and also in the market for the outside world's bond. Like the small economy of Part II, however, it is not a price taker in its export market, and because each country trades with the other, their goods markets are interdependent. Finally, the fact of reciprocal bond holdings (with no world demand for either country's bond) means that their bond markets are interdependent.

In two interdependent economies, connected to a third economy, the signs and sizes of reactions to disturbances depend on many national parameters. Unless additional assumptions are made about those parameters – about the relative sizes of demand and supply responses in goods and asset markets – the usual result obtains. Anything can happen.

[32] We have come across only one other model that can deal with these issues; see S. W. Arndt, "Joint Balance: Capital Mobility and the Monetary System of a Currency Area," in H. G. Johnson and A. K. Swoboda, eds., *The Economics of Common Currencies,* Harvard University Press, Cambridge, Mass., 1973, pp. 196–209. It is, however, a simple flow model with fixed prices, a pegged exchange rate, and perfect asset-market integration between the members of the union.

By imposing certain similarities and symmetries, however, we can isolate dominant responses and thus ascertain the signs of many reactions. In Chapter 12, then, we impose a series of restrictions on demand conditions in the North and South. We assume, for example, that Northern households hold more Northern bonds than Southern or world bonds, while Southern households hold more Southern bonds, and we go on to assume that each country's behavior is more markedly affected by its own domestic interest rate than by its partner's rate or the world rate.

Finally, in Chapter 13, we solve our model for the effects of various exogenous disturbances and changes in Northern and Southern policies. We do so, however, for a limited number of exchange-rate regimes. In a model with two countries and an outside world, there are four possibilities: (1) Each country's currency can float freely against the world's currency and, therefore, against its partner's currency. (2) One currency can be pegged to the world's currency, and the other can float freely. (3) One currency can be pegged directly to the other, and the two can then float jointly against the world's currency. (4) Each country's currency can be pegged to the world's currency and, therefore, to its partner's currency. We solve our model for the third and fourth regimes, under which the bilateral (North–South) exchange rate is pegged, but the common external exchange rate can float freely or be pegged. These regimes provide the most convenient starting points for the study of monetary and fiscal unions.[33]

Our discussion of economic unions in Part V begins with a survey of the relevant literature in Chapter 14, stressing the major analytical issues and the ways in which they have been studied heretofore. We then devote two chapters to monetary policies and monetary unions and two chapters to fiscal policies and fiscal unions.

In Chapter 15 we examine systematically the uses of monetary policy in one country (the North), asking what it can accomplish when the Northern currency is pegged to the Southern currency, when the Northern bond market is integrated with the Southern and world markets, and when the South responds to Northern initiatives. Going a step fur-

---

[33] Because we do not deal with cases 1 and 2, in which the bilateral exchange rate can float, we cannot assess the consequences of policy interdependence or the costs and benefits of policy unification from the standpoint of a country that is free to choose a fully flexible exchange rate. In effect, our analysis begins after there has been a political decision to peg the North–South rate. The reasons are partly analytical; our model is hard to solve for a floating bilateral rate and the solutions are not easy to interpret. But there are other reasons too, having to do with the political and economic circumstances under which two countries are likely to elect the formation of an economic union. We return to this subject in Chapter 14.

ther, we ask how the degree of asset-market integration between North
and South affects the sizes of Southern policy responses and their impact
on the North.

In Chapter 16 we use the results of this anaiysis to assess the consequences for the North of forming a monetary union with the South. Such a
union requires an agreement between North and South on the choice of an
external exchange-rate regime and, if they choose to peg the external rate,
an agreement on the pooling of reserves. Furthermore, each country must
agree to allow the union's central bank to enter its bond market in order to
conduct open-market operations. Most important, however, monetary
unification calls for an agreement between North and South on the targets
that the union's central bank should pursue. Should the bank be guided by
aggregates and averages, such as the sum of Northern and Southern incomes, or should it also be concerned with the ways in which its policies
affect the two countries separately? Much will turn on what the bank is
told to do and what it is capable of doing, given the degrees of market integration and the external exchange-rate regime.

Turning next to fiscal policies, we start in Chapter 17 with a systematic
study of Northern policies–of changes in deficit spending, balanced-
budget changes in government spending, and tax reductions–to measure
the effects of market integration and structural interdependence on policy
interdependence. Thereafter, in Chapter 18, we take up a series of questions that have been asked more often than they have been answered.
When two countries form a monetary union, is there scope or need for national autonomy in the conduct of the members' fiscal policies? Or is a
fiscal union the necessary twin to a monetary union? Our model is well
suited to the study of these questions. It distinguishes between fiscal policies that operate primarily in goods markets, such as balanced-budget
changes in government spending, and those that operate in asset markets
too, such as tax cuts that give rise to budget deficits and changes in supplies of bonds. Finally, it allows us to describe the implications of asset-
market integration for the distribution of an increase in one country's
debt–its effects on interest rates, incomes, and wealth in the member
countries of the monetary union.

PART II

Modeling an open economy

2

The structure of the model

An overview

To study interactions between national economies and between national economic policies, we have first to describe in some detail the structure of a single national economy, then to show how it responds to exogenous disturbances and changes in domestic policies.

This chapter is devoted to the first task. It presents an algebraic model of a small economy that serves as the cornerstone of this book. The remaining chapters of Part II are devoted to the second task. They show how the economy responds instantaneously to disturbances and policy changes, how it adapts dynamically, and how the disturbances and policy changes affect it permanently. They also show how the economy's behavior is affected by the exchange-rate regime, by substitutability between traded and nontraded goods, and by substitutability between domestic and foreign assets. Throughout, we emphasize the roles of asset markets in the determination of a flexible exchange rate and in the determination of the balance of payments when the exchange rate is pegged.

In Part III, we relax some of the assumptions adopted in this chapter to simplify the presentation and solution of the model. We examine alternative specifications of the demand for money and of fiscal policies and the influence of expectations on the behavior of a flexible exchange rate. Finally, in Parts IV and V, the same small-country model is used as an ingredient of a larger model – the one we employ to analyze policy interdependence and economic unions.

The model in this chapter has five classes of actors: (1) Firms buy factor services to produce and sell commodities. (2) Households sell factor services and buy commodities. They also save, pay taxes, and manage portfolios containing bonds and money. (3) The central bank is the supplier of money; it regulates the supply by open-market operations in the domestic bond. It also intervenes in the foreign-exchange market when the exchange rate is to be pegged. (4) The government is the supplier of domestic bonds. It is also a consumer of domestic goods and, of course, the tax collector. (5) Foreigners buy and sell goods and also supply the foreign-currency bond that is included in household portfolios.

Firms and factor-service markets are represented in a rudimentary way. We model the labor market explicitly, but neglect all others. The labor market, however, is described in terms that allow us to explore the implications of classical and Keynesian assumptions concerning the supply of labor and the money wage rate.

There are three goods markets in the model—one for the foreign good and two for the domestic goods. The foreign good is supplied to the small economy at a constant foreign-currency price. The domestic goods are consumed at home by households and the government, but one (the export good) is also sold to foreigners, whereas the other (the nontraded good) is sold only at home.

There are three asset markets in the model—two for bonds and one for money. The first bond is issued in the outside world; it is denominated in foreign currency and is supplied to the small country at a constant interest rate. The second bond is issued by the country's own government; it is denominated in domestic currency and is not held by foreigners.[1] Money is issued by the central bank and is held exclusively by the country's households; it is not held by foreigners.

The existence of a foreign-exchange market is implied, and we refer to it from time to time when describing the behavior of the model. When the other asset markets clear, however, the foreign-exchange market must also clear, and it does not have to be included explicitly in the description of the model. There is no forward foreign-exchange market.[2]

---

[1] To model goods and asset markets more symmetrically, we could assume that foreigners hold the domestic bond. To do so, however, would complicate the algebra without altering the behavior of the model, except at one important point noted in Chapter 3. Furthermore, we do allow for one such possibility in Chapter 11; each of the two countries represented there holds bonds issued by the other. The specification employed in this chapter resembles the one in W. H. Branson, "Portfolio Equilibrium and Monetary Policy with Foreign and Non-Traded Assets," in E. Claassen and P. Salin, eds., *Recent Issues in International Monetary Economics*, North-Holland, Amsterdam, 1976, pp. 241–50.

[2] This might seem to be a serious omission, as we cannot invoke the covered interest-parity condition to constrain or analyze the relationship between the interest rates on the two bonds. But one would not expect that condition to hold in the context of our model. A forward foreign-exchange contract can be used to hedge against exchange risk, and the households in our model are risk averse. A forward contract, however, is not free of risk. There is the nonnegligible possibility of default by the other party. It is thus simplistic to assume that interest parity must always hold, even when the foreign and domestic bonds are perfect substitutes apart from exchange risk. It would hold only if forward contracts were risk free or the parties to the contracts were risk neutral. We *will* come across the open interest-parity condition (the one involving the expected change in the spot exchange rate rather than the forward premium or discount) when we study expectations and speculation in Chapter 9.

In the literature on currency areas, country size is often measured by the degree of dependence on foreign markets. A country is said to be small if it exports a large fraction of its output and imports a large fraction of its consumption. Its economy is specialized, not diversified, and is therefore especially vulnerable to external disturbances.[3] In the literature on the problems we shall study, country size is measured differently, by invoking the distinction between a price taker and a price maker. A country is said to be small if it is a price taker in world markets – if its purchases and sales are not large enough to influence the prices of traded goods and assets.

On this definition of economic size, however, a country can be small in every world market or small in some and large in others, and we have adopted the second supposition. The country described below is too small to influence the prices of the things it buys. It cannot affect the foreign-currency price of its import good, and it cannot affect the interest rate on the foreign bond. But it is large enough to influence the prices of the things it sells, notably the price of its export good.

This approach is less restrictive than one which assumes that a country is small in every world market.[4] It does not fix the terms of trade and does not rule out any type of product-market substitution. Thus, we encounter substitution between the two traded goods and between each traded good and the nontraded good.

More important for our purposes, our approach is less restrictive than the most common treatment of trade in securities. Many models used to study capital mobility contain a single bond and interest rate. This specification is not too simple for some purposes, but when it is combined with the small-country assumption, it works to polarize the analysis. There has either to be no capital mobility, so that the interest rate is determined domestically and endogenously, or "perfect" capital mobility, so that the interest rate is determined internationally and exogenously. The one-bond, small-country model precludes consideration of the realistic intermediate case of partial or "imperfect" capital mobility, in which the domestic interest rate is endogenous but is also affected directly by the

---

[3] See, e.g., M. v. N. Whitman, *International and Interregional Payments Adjustment: A Synthetic View*, Princeton Studies in International Finance 19, Princeton University, Princeton, N.J., 1967, and "Economic Openness and International Financial Flows," *Journal of Money, Credit and Banking*, 1 (November 1969), pp. 727–49; also P. B. Kenen, "The Theory of Optimum Currency Areas: An Eclectic View," in R. A. Mundell and A. K. Swoboda, eds., *Monetary Problems of the International Economy*, University of Chicago Press, Chicago, 1969, pp. 41–60.

[4] The standard small-country case is examined thoroughly in M. F. J. Prachowny, *Small Open Economies*, Lexington Books, Lexington, Mass., 1975.

foreign interest rate. Furthermore, the one-bond, small-country combination implies an economic absurdity. It says that a small country can issue large quantities of debt on international capital markets without suffering a deterioration in its credit rating and an increase in the cost of borrowing.[5]

Working with two bonds, we are able to avoid both of these anomalies. We can deal with partial or "imperfect" mobility by assuming that the foreign and domestic bonds are imperfect substitutes. The domestic interest rate will vary independently of the foreign rate but will also be affected by the foreign rate. We can also deal with "perfect" mobility by assuming that the two bonds are perfect substitutes; the domestic interest rate cannot then vary independently of the foreign rate.[6] And we need not make unrealistic suppositions concerning the small country's credit rating; domestic debt is held at home in our model, and the demand is not perfectly elastic.

We are thus able to examine many special cases without altering the structure of our model. We can represent various degrees of international capital mobility–what we describe as asset-market integration–merely by altering the degree of substitutability between the domestic and foreign bonds. We can represent several special situations in the three goods markets by altering the degrees of substitutability between pairs of goods. This technique allows us to compare our own results with those obtained from other, less general models.

Many international financial models assume that a country produces two traded goods, an export and an import-competing good.[7] To replicate

[5] This implication could be avoided by assuming that the one bond in the model is issued by a foreigner, not by the small economy itself. In that instance, however, the government of the small economy would not be able to engage in bond-financed deficit spending. There is no plausible way to analyze fiscal policy in a one-bond, small-country model.
[6] Unless, of course, actual substitution is carried to the point at which households cease to hold foreign bonds, but we rule out "corner solutions" of this and other types.
[7] This is the specification used in models designed to incorporate supply effects into the elasticities analysis of changes in the terms of trade. See, e.g., G. Haberler, "The Market for Foreign Exchange and the Stability of the Balance of Payments," *Kyklos,* 3 (1949), pp. 193–218, R. W. Jones, "Stability Conditions in International Trade: A General Equilibrium Analysis," *International Economic Review,* 2 (May 1961), pp. 199–209, and E. Sohmen, *Flexible Exchange Rates,* University of Chicago Press, Chicago, 1969, chap. 1; also M. Mussa, "Tariffs and the Balance of Payments: A Monetary Approach," in J. A. Frenkel and H. G. Johnson, eds., *The Monetary Approach to the Balance of Payments,* University of Toronto Press, Toronto, 1976, pp. 187–221. The same approach is taken in many other models where the demand for imports is defined or implied to be the difference between the total domestic demand for the imported good and the domestic supply of the good; see, e.g., R. Dornbusch, "Currency Depreciation, Hoarding, and Relative Prices," *Journal of Political Economy,* 81 (July/August 1973), pp. 893–915.

the chief results obtained from models of this type, we have only to assume that the nontraded and import goods are perfect substitutes in consumption; for all practical purposes, the two goods become a single composite commodity, as their prices cannot vary independently, and domestic production of the nontraded good is equivalent to domestic production of the import good. Other models assume that a country produces only one commodity, an export good.[8] We can replicate most of their conclusions by assuming that the nontraded and export goods are perfect substitutes in consumption or production; the two goods become a single composite commodity. Finally, there are models that include a nontraded good and a composite traded good.[9] We can replicate results obtained from models of this type by assuming that the two traded goods are perfect substitutes at home or abroad; the terms of trade are then fixed, so that the only endogenous price changes involve the composite traded good and the nontraded good.

Having listed ways in which our model is general, we must also emphasize ways in which it is quite special.

When dealing as we do in Chapter 3 with the effects of disturbances and policies on the single, small economy, we have to solve no fewer than four market-clearing equations.[10] Later in this book, moreover, the number of countries is doubled, and we have to solve larger numbers of equations. To do so simultaneously is very difficult, and it is not easy to interpret the solutions. Therefore, we have sought to simplify the structure and behavior of the single, small economy to make the mathematics somewhat more manageable. We have tried to do so, however, in ways that also highlight some of the phenomena that distinguish our approach, especially the roles of asset markets in determining exchange rates.

[8] This is the approach followed by Meade in most of his treatise, but much of the *Mathematical Supplement* uses a three-product model resembling the one developed in this chapter; see J. E. Meade, *The Balance of Payments* (and *Mathematical Supplement*), Oxford University Press, London, 1951. The production side of Meade's model is examined in M. J. Flanders, "The Balance of Payments Adjustment Mechanism: Some Problems in Model-Building," *Kyklos*, 16 (1963), pp. 395–414.

[9] See e.g., R. Dornbusch, "Devaluation, Money, and Nontraded Goods," in Frenkel and Johnson, eds., *The Monetary Approach to the Balance of Payments*, pp. 168–86, and "Exchange Rates and Fiscal Policy in a Popular Model of International Trade," *American Economic Review*, 65 (December 1975), pp. 859–71. The same approach is used implicitly by authors who employ the small-country assumption to fix the terms of trade, then investigate the effects of changes in the price of the nontraded good relative to prices of traded goods; see, e.g., D. J. Mathieson, "Traded Goods, Nontraded Goods, and the Balance of Payments," *International Economic Review*, 14 (October 1973), pp. 615–24.

[10] There are six market-clearing equations in the model, but two of them are cleared by quantities of goods and bonds supplied by the outside world, not by domestic variables.

First, we build our model in a way that will allow us to partition it. Under the assumptions we impose on the demand for money, on the determination of domestic output, on the state of expectations, and on the definition of household wealth, it is possible to separate asset markets from goods markets and thus to solve the model in two steps. Partitionability is an aid to mathematical manageability but also serves an important economic purpose. It allows us to represent algebraically a notion that is central to recent thinking about the behavior of a flexible exchange rate. A disturbance or policy change affects the exchange rate immediately only if it is one that impinges directly on the bond and money markets. Its influence by way of the goods markets occurs only gradually, as the disturbance or policy change begins to affect domestic saving (absorption) and the current-account balance.

Second, we build our model in a way that will allow us to classify disturbances according to the markets in which they arise. Under the assumptions we adopt concerning fiscal policies, disturbances affecting prices and incomes will not necessarily alter the government's receipts or payments. In consequence, they will not necessarily affect the size of the government's surplus or deficit, the level of borrowing, or the stock of debt. We can thus distinguish clearly between goods-market and asset-market disturbances.

Third, we build our model in a way that will allow us to simplify the presentation and analysis of dynamic processes. Under our assumptions concerning fiscal policies, the model will contain a single endogenous stock-flow relationship–the one that connects saving and wealth. The proof of stability is straightforward, and it will not be hard to identify the processes that drive the economy to its steady state.

We say more about these simplifications and the assumptions that enable us to make them as we build our model and again in Part III, where we relax some of the assumptions.

The framework and notation

Markets and actors in this model exhibit familiar characteristics. All markets are perfectly competitive. They are not encumbered by transactions costs, and they are assumed to clear continuously. All actors are able always to achieve their aims. Desired and actual quantities are never different. In brief, there are no disequilibria and no disappointments.

Households and other actors believe that prices of goods and assets will remain unchanged, but they do not hold their views with certainty. Thus, there are no differences between real and nominal interest rates. Nevertheless, households will be impelled to diversify their holdings of bonds and money to hedge against the possibility of changes in asset prices. They are risk averse.

Finally, wealth holders are assumed to adjust their portfolios instantaneously in response to changes in rates of return, and asset markets are structured to accommodate large shifts in the households' holdings of bonds and money. (They must also accommodate flow demands for assets–demands that reflect saving or dissaving. In continuous-time models like this one, however, changes in these flow demands are too small, by definition, to affect the levels of the market-clearing variables.)

Unless otherwise indicated, all variables are measured in nominal terms and denominated in domestic currency. Those that carry an asterisk, such as $*E$, are quantities desired (demanded); those that carry a bar, such as $\bar{E}$, are exogenous or policy determined. (The variables used in this and other chapters dealing with the one-country model are listed with brief definitions in Section I of the Glossary that appears at the end of this book.)

We begin the formal presentation of the model by looking at production and the labor market. We turn next to saving and the households' demands for goods, then to government and foreign demands, and to the market-clearing equations for goods. Thereafter, we define the households' demands for money and for bonds, the roles of the central bank in the money, bond, and foreign-exchange markets, the role of the government in the bond market, and the market-clearing equations for money and bonds.

Production and the labor market

Two goods are produced domestically, a traded good 1 and a nontraded good N. The output of each good depends uniquely on the quantity of labor employed, and production is subject to diminishing returns:

$$(2.1) \quad Q_1 = Q_1(E_1) \qquad Q_{1E} > 0 \qquad Q_{1EE} < 0$$

$$(2.2) \quad Q_N = Q_N(E_N) \qquad Q_{NE} > 0 \qquad Q_{NEE} < 0$$

where Q_1 and Q_N are physical outputs, and E_1 and E_N are physical inputs of labor. Nominal gross domestic product (income from production) is therefore defined by

$$(2.3) \quad Y = p_1 Q_1 + p_N Q_N$$

where p_1 and p_N are the prices of the traded and nontraded goods.

As firms are competitive and maximize profits, the quantities of labor they desire, $*E_1$ and $*E_N$, are those that equate the marginal value product of labor to the money wage rate:

(2.4) $w = p_1 Q_{1E}(*E_1)$

(2.5) $w = p_N Q_{NE}(*E_N)$

and there are no differences between desired and actual quantities:

(2.6) $E_1 = *E_1$

(2.7) $E_N = *E_N$

As all markets clear continuously, aggregate employment, E, is always equal to the total demand for labor:

(2.8) $*E_1 + *E_N - E = 0$

In the classical variant of the model, the supply of labor is perfectly inelastic:

(2.9a) $E = \bar{E}$

and Eq. (2.8) determines the wage rate. In the Keynesian variant of the model, the supply of labor is perfectly elastic at a fixed money wage:

(2.9b) $w = \bar{w}$

and Eq. (2.8) determines the level of employment.

The assumption of diminishing returns to labor is normally taken to imply that an additional factor of production, land or machinery, is used in each industry. But we do not say much about it. We assume, in effect, that the stocks of the second factor are specific to each industry, are fixed forever in supply, and are owned by households, and that the claims to ownership (equities) are not transferable. By fixing the sizes of the stocks, we rule out real capital formation and streamline the goods markets; all demands for goods are final demands. By giving them to households, we simplify the definitions of income and saving; households are the claimants to the whole of gross domestic product. And by ruling out the transferability of claims, we simplify our next task–the definition and analysis of household wealth.

Wealth, saving, and the households' demands for goods

Domestic wealth, W^h, is held in three forms–in money, domestic bonds denominated in domestic currency, and foreign bonds denominated in foreign currency. Each bond is a bill and is a promise to pay one unit of the currency in which it is issued. Thus,

$$(2.10) \quad W^h = L_1^h + B_1^h + \pi B_0^h$$

where L_1^h is the stock of money held by households; B_1^h is the number of domestic bonds; B_0^h is the number of foreign bonds; and π is the price of the foreign currency in units of the home currency (the spot exchange rate).

When bonds are bills as they are here, rather than long-term securities, changes in bond prices caused by changes in interest rates have no effects on wealth. To allow for these effects by working with long-term bonds would not alter substantially the solutions shown in Chapter 3; it would merely complicate the algebra.[11] When bonds are bills, however, it is not easy to explain why households invest simultaneously in all three financial assets, even when those households are risk averse. Uncertainty about the exchange rate explains why they hold both bonds but not why they hold both bonds and money in the absence of transactions costs. One must attach some other source of uncertainty to the returns on bonds. The possibility of default comes to mind, although that possibility may be remote when the domestic bond is issued by the government.

If claims to the ownership of land or machinery were transferable, Eq. (2.10) would have to include the present values of the corresponding income streams. At the highest level of aggregation, wealth would have to include total nonlabor income, Y less wE, divided by a discount rate. But if this term were added, we would have also to add a market-clearing equation in order to determine the discount rate.[12] Furthermore, changes

---

[11] See Appendix B, where we rework a sample of results for the case in which bonds are consols (perpetual annuities).

[12] The market value of the claims would be $K = (Y - wE)/r_k$, where r_k is the discount rate; the demand for them would be $^*K = K(r_0, r_1, r_k, W^h)$, where r_0 and r_1 are the interest rates on the two bonds; and the new market-clearing equation would be $^*K - K = 0$. The equation for $^*K$ has the same form as the demand equations for money and bonds shown later in this chapter (but those equations would also have to be modified to include r_k). The omission of equities from Eq. (2.10) does not necessarily imply that households disregard their claims to nonlabor incomes when they decide how much to save. Let households be alike in that each of them has title to an equal amount of labor income (human capital) and of nonlabor income (tangible capital). Suppose that they employ a (subjective) discount rate, r_k, to capitalize the income streams from the two forms of capital, and that $r_k = k(r_0, r_1)$, $k_0, k_1 > 0$. If there are no markets for the claims to the two forms of capital, there is no need to include those claims in Eq. (2.10). One would have to account for them, however, when asking how the households' wealth affects desired saving, and this might be done by modifying Eq. (2.13) below, defining desired saving. It can be rewritten as $^*S = S'(r_0, r_1, Y^d, W^{h'})$, where $W^{h'} = W^h + (Y^d/r_k)$. Desired saving is made to depend on holdings of bonds and money, W^h, and on an approximation to the present value of the income streams furnished by holdings of human and tangible capital. Differentiating totally the

in gross domestic product and the wage bill would then come to have immediate effects on asset markets. They would do so directly by affecting the discounted value of nonlabor incomes and, therefore, the new market-clearing equation. They would do so indirectly by affecting wealth and, therefore, the households' demands for money and bonds, as well as their demands for claims to nonlabor incomes. Wealth would depend on Y and wE, and these in turn depend on p_1 and p_N. Goods and asset markets would be interdependent, and we would not be able to partition our model.

Household wealth can be altered by two processes – by saving out of current income, S, and by changes in asset prices (i.e., exchange-rate changes). The structure and strategy developed below require us to distinguish carefully between them. We must therefore define the totality of wealth accumulated through time T in consequence of household saving:

$$(2.11) \quad W^{hs} = \int_0^T S \, dt$$

so that the time derivative of W^{hs} is

$$(2.11a) \quad \dot{W}^{hs} = S$$

We can then write household wealth as the sum of the histories of saving and of changes in asset values:

$$(2.12) \quad W^h = W^{hs} + \int_0^T [(B_0^h)\dot{\pi}] \, dt$$

Desired saving is an increasing function of interest rates and income; it is a decreasing function of household wealth:

$$(2.13) \quad *S = S(r_0, r_1, Y^d, W^h) \qquad S_0 > 0, \, S_1 > 0, \, 0 < S_Y < 1, \, S_W < 0$$

where r_0 and r_1 are the interest rates on the foreign and domestic bonds

---

equation for desired saving and replacing dr_k with $k_0 \, dr_0 + k_1 \, dr_1$, we have

$$d*S = [S_0' - S_W'(Y^d/r_k^2)k_0] \, dr_0 + [S_1' - S_W'(Y^d/r_k^2)k_1] \, dr_1$$
$$+ [S_Y' + (S_W'/r_k)] \, dY^d + S_W' \, dW^h$$

Thus, the results obtained in subsequent chapters using Eq. (2.13) can be deemed to allow for the influence of holdings of human and tangible capital. One need only treat the partial derivatives of that equation as proxies for the ones above: $S_W = S_W' < 0$, $S_i = [S_i' - S_W'(Y^d/r_k^2)k_i] > 0$ for $i = 0, 1$, and $S_Y = [S_Y' + (S_W'/r_k)] > 0$ (provided that $r_k S_Y' > -S_W'$). It must be noted, however, that the omission of equities from the definition of W^h has an additional implication. It says that the households' nonmarketable claims to nonlabor incomes do not affect their demands for bonds and money; W^h is the measure of wealth used in Eqs. (2.30) through (2.32) below, defining those demands.

(strictly speaking, the discount rates at which they are issued) and stand for the real rates as well, because price expectations are stationary, and where Y^d is disposable income. The saving function is assumed to be homogeneous of first degree in disposable income and wealth.[13] Disposable income is

(2.14) $Y^d = Y + r_0 \pi B_0^h + r_1 B_1^h - T^h$

It is the sum of gross domestic product and interest income *less* lump-sum tax payments, T^h, from households to government.[14]

The households' demands for domestic goods, $*C_N$ and $*C_1$, and for foreign goods, $*C_0$, are defined in physical terms. They depend on the

[13] Taken together with the assumptions below, that the demands for money and bonds are homogeneous of degree one in wealth and that the demands for goods are homogeneous of degree zero in prices and total nominal consumption, the homogeneity of Eq. (2.13) banishes money illusion from household behavior in the asset and goods markets. (There is, of course, money illusion in the Keynesian variant of the model, where the supply of labor is perfectly elastic at a fixed money wage rate, and money illusion is built into the government's demands for goods, described below.) By assuming that $*S$ is homogeneous of first degree in nominal income and wealth, we avoid the need to use a price index (we do not have to translate from nominal to real terms). Note in passing that Eq. (2.13) implies that households have well-defined notions about desired wealth (the level that is reached in the steady state, when saving goes to zero). It would be possible indeed to write Eq. (2.13) in familiar stock-adjustment form, as $*S = \lambda(*W^h - W^h)$, where $*W^h = W(r_0, r_1, Y^d)$, and λ would be $-S_W$. Note also that the inclusion of B_1^h in the definition of W^h and the inclusion of the latter in Eq. (2.13) amounts to the assertion that government debt is deemed to be net wealth. For the opposite view, see R. J. Barro, "Are Government Bonds Net Wealth?," *Journal of Political Economy*, 82 (November/December 1974), pp. 1095–1117, where it is argued that bond-financed deficit spending does not add to wealth because bond holders anticipate the increase in their taxes that will be needed to pay interest on the new bonds and treat the present value of the increase in taxes as an offset to the increase in their holdings of bonds.

[14] Some would perhaps prefer to include in Y^d the households' capital gains and losses on the foreign bond–to add to Eq. (2.14) the current change, if any, in the home-currency value of households' holdings of the foreign bond. If this were done, of course, saving would have to be redefined as *any* increase in wealth, inclusive of capital gains, and Eqs. (2.11) and (2.11a) would have to be rewritten as $W^h = \int_0^T S\, dt$, and $\dot{W}^h = S$, respectively. By implication, Eq. (2.12) would define W^{hs} as the difference between the integrals of saving and of capital gains. Furthermore, Eq. (2.13) would have to be rewritten in terms of W^{hs} rather than W^h, to avoid doublecounting of capital gains. Under this alternative specification, a depreciation of the home currency would raise saving (by raising Y^d) rather than reducing it (by raising W^h), but the saving would include the capital gains conferred by the depreciation. Consumption (absorption) would rise in any case (because $0 < S_Y < 1$). The time path of wealth might be different following a depreciation or devaluation, but the direction would not be reversed. Wealth would rise through time under both definitions of Y^d and $*S$, and saving would fall in response, causing the economy to approach its new steady state.

prices of the three goods and on total desired nominal consumption:

(2.15) $*C_N = C_N(p_N, p_1, p_0, *C)$

(2.16) $*C_1 = C_1(p_N, p_1, p_0, *C)$

(2.17) $*C_0 = C_0(p_N, p_1, p_0, *C)$

where

(2.17a) $*C = p_N*C_N + p_1*C_1 + p_0*C_0$

Desired consumption is defined by

(2.18) $*C = Y^d - *S$

The demand equations (2.15) through (2.17) are assumed to have these important properties:

1. The functions are homogeneous of degree zero in all prices and consumption, so that

$$e_{ii} - \sum_j e_{ij} = e_{ic}   i, j = 0, 1, N   j \neq i$$

where $e_{ii} = -p_i(C_{ii}/*C_i)$, and $e_{ij} = p_j(C_{ij}/*C_i)$, the own- and cross-price elasticities of demand, whereas $e_{ic} = *C(C_{ic}/*C_i)$, the consumption elasticity.

2. The three goods are gross substitutes in consumption, so that $e_{ii} > 0$, and $e_{ij} > 0$.

3. The consumption elasticities, e_{ic}, are unity.
From the definition of total consumption, Eq. (2.17a), it follows in addition that

$$\sum_i m_i = 1   i = 0, 1, N$$

where $m_i = p_i C_{ic}$, the marginal (and average) propensity to spend on the ith commodity. Furthermore, assumption 3 implies that[15]

$$p_i*C_i e_{ij} = p_j*C_j e_{ji}   i \neq j$$

We use this result extensively below.

---

[15] In proof, write the derivative of $*C_i$ with respect to p_j as the sum of a substitution effect, C_{ij}, and the corresponding expenditure effect, $C_{ic}*C_j$, or $C_{ij} = C'_{ij} - C_{ic}*C_j = C'_{ij} - e_{ic}(*C_i/*C)*C_j$. Under assumption 3, however, $e_{ic} = 1$, whereas $C'_{ij} = C'_{ji}$, because they are pure substitution terms. Therefore, $C_{ij} = C'_{ij} - (*C_i/*C)*C_j = C'_{ji} - (*C_j/*C)*C_i = C_{ji}$, or $p_i*C_i(p_j C_{ij}/*C_i) = p_i*C_i e_{ij} = p_j*C_j(p_i C_{ji}/*C_j) = p_j*C_j e_{ji}$.

Government and foreign consumption

The government consumes both of the domestic goods, and its spending decisions are policy determined in nominal rather than real terms:

(2.19) $*G_1 = \bar{G}_1$

(2.20) $*G_N = \bar{G}_N$

The foreign demand for the traded domestic good is defined in physical terms and is assumed to depend on foreign prices and foreign consumption expressed in foreign currency:

(2.21) $*C_1^f = C_1^f(p_N^f, p_1^f, p_0^f, *C^f)$

It has the same properties as its domestic counterparts, so that

$$e_{11}^f - e_{1N}^f - e_{10}^f = e_{1c}^f = 1$$

where $e_{11}^f = -p_1^f(C_{11}^f/*C_1^f) > 0,$ $e_{1N}^f = p_N^f(C_{1N}^f/*C_1^f) > 0,$ $e_{10}^f = p_0^f(C_{10}^f/*C_1^f) > 0,$ and $e_{1c}^f = *C^f(C_{1c}^f/*C_1^f).$

Under our version of the small-country assumption, total foreign consumption is exogenous, and so is the foreign-currency price of the foreign nontraded good:

(2.22) $*C^f = \bar{C}^f$

(2.23) $p_N^f = \bar{p}_N^f$

Arbitrage between goods markets is assumed to align the foreign- and domestic-currency prices of each traded good:

(2.24) $p_0 = \pi p_0^f$

(2.25) $p_1 = \pi p_1^f$

The goods markets

Invoking once again our version of the small-country assumption, the foreign supply of the import good is perfectly elastic at a fixed foreign-currency price:

(2.26) $p_0^f = \bar{p}_0^f$

Quantities supplied adjust instantaneously to satisfy changes in domestic demand, $*C_0$, clearing the market continuously.

The markets for the two domestic goods are also assumed to clear continuously. In those markets, however, changes in the prices p_1 and p_N keep excess demands at zero. The market-clearing equations are

(2.27) $*C_1 + (*G_1/p_1) + *C_1^f - Q_1 = 0$

(2.28) $*C_N + (*G_N/p_N) - Q_N = 0$

Finally, we assume that all economic actors (households, foreigners, and the government) are able to obtain the quantities that they demand, so that there can be no involuntary saving:

(2.29) $S = *S$

Household demands for money and bonds

To partition our model for mathematical manageability, for distinguishing between types of disturbances, and for portraying exchange-rate determination in the asset markets, we have had to omit claims on nonlabor incomes from the definition of household wealth. We must now make a second simplification for the same set of reasons. Income does not affect the demand for money, and there is, therefore, no reason for it to affect the demands for bonds. Instead, the demands for the three financial assets are made to depend on interest rates and household wealth. Working in nominal terms,

(2.30) $*L_1^h = L_1(r_0, r_1, W^h)$ $L_{10} < 0, L_{11} < 0, 0 < L_{1W} < 1$

(2.31) $\pi*B_0^h = B_0(r_0, r_1, W^h)$ $B_{00} > 0, B_{01} < 0, 0 < B_{0W} < 1$

(2.32) $*B_1^h = B_1(r_0, r_1, W^h)$ $B_{10} < 0, B_{11} > 0, 0 < B_{1W} < 1$

These demands are constrained by household wealth:

(2.32a) $W^h = *L_1^h + *B_1^h + \pi*B_0^h$

so that

$$B_{00} + B_{10} + L_{10} = 0$$
$$B_{01} + B_{11} + L_{11} = 0$$
$$B_{0W} + B_{1W} + L_{1W} = 1$$

Finally, we assume that the two bonds are gross substitutes, so that $B_{00} > -B_{01}$ and $B_{11} > -B_{10}$, and that the demand for each asset is homogeneous of first degree in nominal wealth (that each wealth elasticity is unity).[16]

The central bank and monetary policy

The domestic money stock, L_1, is issued by the central bank. There are no commercial banks.[17] The assets of the central bank are domestic (non-traded) bonds and (nonnegative) foreign-exchange reserves. Its balance sheet is

(2.33) $L_1 + W^c = B^c_1 + \pi R$

where W^c is the central bank's net worth, B^c_1 is its inventory of domestic bonds, and R is its inventory of foreign-exchange reserves measured in units of foreign currency. The central bank does not save; its net worth at time T reflects the history of changes in the home-currency value of its reserves:

(2.34) $W^c = \displaystyle\int_0^T (R\dot{\pi})\, dt$

The central bank's demand for domestic bonds is determined in accordance with its policy objectives:

(2.35) $^*B^c_1 = \bar{B}^c_1$

Its demand for foreign-exchange reserves is determined by its exchange-rate policy. Under a flexible exchange rate, the central bank ab-

---

[16] On gross substitutability between bonds, see J. Tobin, "A General Equilibrium Approach to Monetary Theory," *Journal of Money, Credit and Banking,* 1 (February 1969), pp. 15–30. The assumption of gross substitutability is not drastically restrictive. Invoking the wealth-constrained relationships in the text above, $(B_{11} + B_{10}) + (B_{00} + B_{01}) = -(L_{10} + L_{11}) > 0$. If, then, we were to assume that $B_{11} < -B_{10}$, we would have to assume that $B_{00} > -B_{01}$, which is arbitrarily asymmetrical. [It would, of course, be possible to obtain the same relationship between B_{11} and B_{10} by replacing B_{11} with $-(B_{01} + L_{10})$ and assuming that $B_{10} = B_{01}$, and this can be shown to be true for certain utility functions; see M. Parkin, "Discount House Portfolio and Debt Selection," *Review of Economic Studies,* 37 (October 1970), pp. 469–97. But no essential purpose is served by making this stronger assumption.] The assumption of homogeneity is the one cited in note 13, above, on the absence of money illusion in the asset markets. It is tantamount to writing the demand for any asset, $^*A_j$, as $^*A_j = A_j(r_0, r_1)W^h$.

[17] The inclusion of fractional-reserve commercial banks would have no significant qualitative impact on the behavior of the model. See, for example, P. B. Kenen, *Capital Mobility and Financial Integration: A Survey,* Princeton Studies in International Finance 39, Princeton University, Princeton, N.J., 1976, especially the appendix.

stains entirely from intervention in the foreign-exchange market, and its holdings of reserves cannot vary:

(2.36a) $R = \bar{R}$

Under a pegged exchange rate, the central bank intervenes sufficiently to guarantee that the rate remains at its policy-determined level:

(2.36b) $\pi = \bar{\pi}$

and its holdings of reserves vary accordingly.

As foreign-exchange reserves are assumed to earn no interest, the total income of the central bank is $r_1 B_1^c$, and it is paid over to the government.

The government and fiscal policy

Our treatment of household behavior was affected heavily by the desire for partitionability. Our treatment of government behavior is affected just as heavily by the desire for a clear distinction between goods-market and asset-market disturbances and for tractable dynamics.

Government receipts include taxes from households, T^h, and the interest income of the central bank, $r_1 B_1^c$. They also include transfers from foreigners, T^f. Government outlays include spending on domestic goods, $\bar{G}_1$ and $\bar{G}_N$. They also include interest payments on the public debt, $r_1 B_1$. The government's deficit, D, is therefore defined by

(2.37) $D = \bar{G}_1 + \bar{G}_N + r_1 B_1 - T^h - T^f - r_1 \bar{B}_1^c$

Deficits are financed by issuing new bonds:[18]

(2.38) $\dot{B}_1 = D$

so that

(2.38a) $B_1 = \int_0^T D \, dt$

If we were now to adopt the familiar supposition that tax receipts depend on income, the size of the deficit, D, would likewise depend on income, and any disturbance or policy change affecting income would affect the volume of government borrowing and the flow supply of domestic bonds. It would then be impossible to distinguish disturbances impinging on goods markets from disturbances impinging on asset markets. A dis-

---

[18] For deficits financed by issuing money, see Appendix D.

turbance affecting the level of income would impinge directly on asset markets too, by altering gradually the supply of bonds, B_1. When tax receipts depend on income, moreover, the proof of stability and study of dynamics become quite complicated. The flow supply of bonds, $\dot{B}_1$, is endogenous, and we have to work with two dynamic relationships–the one represented by Eqs. (2.11a) and (2.13a), connecting $\dot{W}^{hs}$ to disposable income, interest rates, and wealth, and the other represented by Eqs. (2.37) and (2.38), connecting $\dot{B}_1$ to the endogenous variables appearing in the government budget.

For these reasons and for others set forth in Chapter 10, we adopt a different view of fiscal policy. The size of the nominal deficit will be policy determined:

$$(2.39) \quad D = \bar{D}$$

Deficits, however, are not allowed to last forever. At some point in time, $t = k$, the government balances its budget, and $\dot{B}_1$ goes to zero, limiting the cumulative change in B_1. To put the point operationally, the government adjusts the lump-sum tax, T^h, continuously, in order to align D with $\bar{D}$, where $\bar{D} = 0$ at and after time $t = k$. Furthermore, the time $t = k$ is policy determined, so that the cumulative change in B_1 can be regarded as a policy instrument–the steady-state counterpart of the budget deficit.[19]

We make an analogous assumption with regard to transfers from foreigners. They are regulated in a way that offsets exactly and continuously the flow of interest income earned from foreigners:

$$(2.40) \quad T^f = -r_0(\pi B_0^h)$$

As the interest-income term is positive, T^f must be negative, which is to say that the government makes grants to foreigners (instead of receiving them) and adjusts those grants continuously to satisfy Eq. (2.40).[20]

This last supposition is arbitrary but very powerful. First, it will remove the interest-income term, $r_0(\pi B_0^h)$, from the current-account balance, and that balance will then equal the trade balance. Second, it will remove the

---

[19] If the change in B_1 were not bounded, the model could not reach a steady state. To treat the change in B_1 as a policy instrument, however, it must be possible to choose time $t = k$ so that the cumulative effects of a budget deficit give the desired change in debt. The treatment of taxation outlined here resembles the one employed in D. K. Foley and M. Sidrauski, *Monetary and Fiscal Policy in a Growing Economy*, Macmillan, New York, 1971, p. 56. In Chapter 10 we show what happens when an income tax is used instead of a lump-sum tax (and when we drop the transfer term discussed below).

[20] The definition of T^f as a transfer *from* the foreigner anticipates its use in the two-country model of Parts IV and V, where it can be positive for one country.

interest-income term from the definition of disposable income. To see that this is so, substitute Eqs. (2.40) and (2.39) into Eq. (2.37) and solve for the lump-sum tax:

(2.37a) $T^h = \bar{G}_1 + \bar{G}_N + r_0(\pi B_0^h) + r_1(B_1 - \bar{B}_1^c) - \bar{D}$

Then substitute the argument of Eq. (2.37a) into the definition of disposable income:

(2.14a) $Y^d = Y + \bar{D} - \bar{G}_1 - \bar{G}_N$

In other words, we have no need to distinguish between gross domestic product, Y, and gross national product. (The latter, in turn, is equal in this model to national income, and we use "income" synonymously with "gross domestic product" when we refer to Y.)[21]

The asset markets

Under our version of the small-country assumption, the supply of foreign bonds is perfectly elastic at a constant foreign interest rate:

(2.41) $r_0 = \bar{r}_0$

The market for the foreign bond is cleared continuously by instantaneous variations in the quantity supplied.

The markets for the two domestic assets, nontraded bonds and money, are cleared by variations in the domestic interest rate and in the exchange rate or stock of central-bank reserves.

As households and the central bank are the only holders of domestic bonds, the market-clearing equation is

(2.42) $^*B_1^h + ^*B_1^c - B_1 = 0$

---

[21] Our assumptions concerning T^f and T^h, taken together, say that households do not earn any income after tax from their holdings of the foreign bond. Taxes finance transfers that offset the flow of interest income. This does not mean, however, that households will decline to hold the foreign bond. It is the only available foreign-currency asset (and, therefore, the vehicle for speculation when, in Chapter 9, expectations are not stationary). Furthermore, households may not expect to be taxed in proportion to the increase in T^f that can be ascribed directly to their own investments in the foreign bond. To hold that expectation, they would have to behave in a Kantian fashion–to refrain from buying a foreign bond because it would be pointless to do so if every other household bought one too. On Kantian behavior and its implications, see J. J. Laffont, "Macroeconomic Constraints, Economic Efficiency and Ethics: An Introduction to Kantian Economics," *Economica*, 42 (November 1975), pp. 430–7. We are indebted to Elhanan Helpman for calling this point to our attention.

As households are the only holders of domestic money, the market-clearing equation is

(2.43) $*L_1^h - L_1 = 0$

Once again, moreover, we assume that all actors can carry out their plans:

(2.44) $*B_1^c = B_1^c$

(2.45) $*B_1^h = B_1^h$

(2.46) $*L_1^h = L_1^h$

Taken together with Eqs. (2.10) and (2.32a), these conditions also say that $*B_0^h = B_0^h$.

Summary

The 46 equations set out above allow us to solve for all of the endogenous variables contained in our one-country model.[22] After several substitutions, however, we can write it more compactly. Focusing on the market-clearing equations for domestic goods and domestic assets,

(2.27a) $C_1(p_N, p_1, \pi \bar{p}_0^f, Y^d - *S) + C_1^f\left(\bar{p}_N^f, \dfrac{p_1}{\pi}, \bar{p}_0^f, \bar{C}^f\right)$

$$+ (\bar{G}_1/p_1) - \theta_1(p_N, p_1) = 0$$

(2.28a) $C_N(p_N, p_1, \pi \bar{p}_0^f, Y^d - *S) + (\bar{G}_N/p_N) - \theta_N(p_N, p_1) = 0$

(2.42a) $B_1(\bar{r}_0, r_1, W^h) + \bar{B}_1^c - B_1 = 0$

(2.43a) $L_1(\bar{r}_0, r_1, W^h) - (\bar{B}_1^c + \pi R - W^c) = 0$

where the functions $\theta_1(p_N, p_1)$ and $\theta_N(p_N, p_1)$ stand for the domestic outputs Q_1 and Q_N, reflecting the fact that $*E_1$ and $*E_N$ can be expressed as functions of the prices p_1 and p_N, using the labor-market equations.[23]

Saving depends on the interest rates, disposable income, and wealth. But disposable income is a function of gross domestic product and three policy-determined variables, as shown by Eq. (2.14a), and gross domestic product is itself a function of the two domestic prices:

(2.3a) $Y = p_N \theta_N(p_N, p_1) + p_1 \theta_1(p_N, p_1)$

Furthermore, W^h and W^c can be treated as functions of W^{hs} and π, using

[22] These are the variables listed in Section I of the Glossary.
[23] See Appendix A.

Eqs. (2.12) and (2.34). Therefore, the four market-clearing equations can be solved for four market-clearing variables, p_1, p_N, r_1, and π or R (depending on the exchange-rate regime), given the exogenous variables $\bar{p}_0^f$, $\bar{p}_N^f$, $\bar{r}_0$, $\bar{C}^f$, and $\bar{w}$ or $\bar{E}$; the policy-determined variables $\bar{B}_1^c$, $\bar{G}_1$, $\bar{G}_N$, $\bar{D}$, and $\bar{R}$ or $\bar{\pi}$; and the histories of household saving, W^{hs}, and of government deficits, B_1. The dynamic equations for W^{hs} and B_1 are

(2.11b) $\dot{W}^{hs} = S(r_0, r_1, Y^d, W^h)$

(2.38b) $\dot{B}_1 = \bar{D}$

But $\bar{D}$ is zero after time $t = k$, so that the model reaches a steady state when W^{hs} comes to be constant (when $\dot{W}^{hs}$ goes to zero).

The remaining chapters of Part II examine the behavior of this model. In Chapter 3, we solve it algebraically. In Chapters 4 and 5, we interpret the solutions, paying particular attention to the implications of substitutability in goods and asset markets, and dealing with a number of limiting cases mentioned at the start of this chapter. In Chapter 6, we look at the dynamics involved, concentrating on the differences between adaptations under pegged and flexible exchange rates.

3

Solving the model

The small-country model presented in Chapter 2 has three classes of solutions. For each disturbance or policy change, we must first obtain the impact or instantaneous effects on goods prices, income, the interest rate, and the exchange rate or reserves (depending on the choice of exchange-rate regime). Thereafter, we must prove stability and solve for the dynamic effects of the disturbances–effects that depend on the way in which disturbances influence the level of saving or the current-account balance. Finally, we must solve for the change in the stock of wealth that results from the saving or dissaving that takes place on the way to the new steady state. Two sets of solutions are required at each stage–one for a flexible exchange rate and another for a pegged exchange rate.

We make no attempt to interpret our results in this chapter. The signs of the responses to disturbances and policies are summarized in tables, but economic explanations are deferred to Chapters 4, 5, and 6. In Chapters 4 and 5 we study in detail comparative statics, looking at disturbances and policies one at a time and contrasting the effects of flexible and pegged exchange rates. In Chapter 6 we examine the dynamics of our model to show how it converges eventually to a stationary state and to illustrate the crucial role of the exchange-rate regime in determining the path of the economy. Some readers may therefore prefer to scan this chapter quickly, to understand our strategy, and pass to a more careful reading of the next three chapters where we explain our findings with the help of diagrams describing the behavior of goods and asset markets.

Solving for impact effects

Because we are able to partition our model, the first part of our task is relatively simple. As income does not affect the demands for assets, and claims on nonlabor incomes do not figure in the definition of household wealth, the bond and money markets are not influenced at once by events in the goods markets. We can solve the market-clearing equations for money and for bonds before we solve those for the two domestic goods. At this first stage, moreover, the histories of saving and of government borrowing, W^{hs} and B_1, are deemed to be constant.[1] They can change only gradually through time, in accordance with Eqs. (2.11b) and (2.38b). (Nevertheless, we shall show solutions for the changes in these stocks, δW^{hs} and δB_1, because they will be needed later to study the dynamics of the model.)

Impact effects in asset markets

Differentiating totally Eqs. (2.42a) and (2.43a) and using Eqs. (2.12) and (2.34) to replace the derivatives of W^c and W^h wherever they appear, we obtain two equations in δr_1, $\delta \pi$, δR, and in $\delta \bar{B}_1^c$, $\delta \bar{r}_0$, δW^{hs}, and δB_1.[2] These are the equations we require to solve for asset-market responses to financial disturbances, but we must do so separately for flexible and pegged exchange rates.

The flexible-rate case. When the exchange rate is flexible, $\delta \pi$ is endogenous and δR is zero; the central bank does not intervene in the foreign-exchange market, and its holdings of reserves do not change. Therefore, the two total derivatives can be written as[3]

$$(3.1a)\quad \begin{bmatrix} -B_{11} & -B_{1W} \\ -L_{11} & -L_{1W} \end{bmatrix} \begin{bmatrix} \delta r_1 \\ V_\pi \left(\dfrac{\delta \pi}{\pi} \right) \end{bmatrix}$$

$$= \begin{bmatrix} 1 & B_{10} \\ -1 & L_{10} \end{bmatrix} \begin{bmatrix} \delta \bar{B}_1^c \\ \delta \bar{r}_0 \end{bmatrix} + \begin{bmatrix} B_{1W} & -1 \\ L_{1W} & 0 \end{bmatrix} \begin{bmatrix} \delta W^{hs} \\ \delta B_1 \end{bmatrix}$$

where

$$V_\pi = \pi B_0^h$$

denoting the effect on household wealth of the change in the home-currency value of the foreign bond brought about by a change in the exchange rate.

The determinant of this system is denoted by H_π, where

$$H_\pi = (B_{11}L_{1W} - B_{1W}L_{11}) > 0$$

[1] The values of stocks of wealth, W^c and W^h, are not constant, however, because they are affected instantaneously whenever there are changes in the exchange rate.
[2] Throughout this book, the operator δ is used to denote an impact effect, and the operator d is used to denote a steady-state (permanent) effect.
[3] Throughout Chapter 3, equations numbered a and b relate to flexible and pegged rates, respectively. Equations without suffixes apply to both regimes.

Table 3.1A. *Impact effects under a flexible exchange rate*

Disturbance	δπ	δr₁	δp_N	δp₁	δY	δY^d	δw or E	δW^h
				Effect				
$\delta\bar{r}_0$	+	?	?	?	?	?	?	+
$\delta\bar{B}_1^c$	+	−	+	+	+	+	+	+
$\delta\bar{D}$	0	0	+	+	+	+	+	0
$\delta\bar{G}$	0	0	?	?	?	−	?	0
$\delta\bar{p}_0^f$	0	0	+	+	+	+	+	0
δc_{N1}	0	0	+	−	?	?	?	0
$\delta c_1^f - \delta c_{01}$	0	0	+	+	+	+	+	0
δW^{hs}	−	0	−	−	−	−	−	xx
δB_1	+	+	?ᵃ	?ᵃ	?ᵃ	?ᵃ	?ᵃ	xx

Some signs shown here are different from those shown for the limiting cases considered in Chapters 4 and 5. Certain effects go to zero or unity; others become unambiguous.
ᵃ Positive when $S_w L_{11} > L_{1W} S_1$ (i.e., when there is no crowding out); see Chapter 5.

Solving for the instantaneous responses of the interest rate and the exchange rate,

$$(3.2a) \qquad \delta r_1 = (1/H_\pi)[(B_{1W}L_{10} - B_{10}L_{1W})\, \delta\bar{r}_0 - (L_{1W} + B_{1W})\, \delta\bar{B}_1^c + (L_{1W})\, \delta B_1 + (0)\, \delta W^{hs}]$$

$$(3.3a) \qquad \left(\frac{\delta\pi}{\pi}\right) = (1/V_\pi H_\pi)[(B_{10}L_{11} - B_{11}L_{10})\, \delta\bar{r}_0 - (B_{01})\, \delta\bar{B}_1^c - (L_{11})\, \delta B_1 - (H_\pi)\, \delta W^{hs}]$$

An open-market purchase of the domestic bond, $\delta\bar{B}_1^c$, causes the home currency to depreciate and reduces the domestic interest rate.[4] An increase in the foreign interest rate, $\delta\bar{r}_0$, also causes the home currency to depreciate but has an ambiguous effect on the domestic interest rate (because each of the two terms $B_{1W}L_{10}$ and $B_{10}L_{1W}$ is negative). The signs of these effects and the others that take place with a flexible exchange rate are shown in Table 3.1A. (Question marks in this and other tables say that an outcome is ambiguous, given our assumptions, not that we have given up the attempt to learn the sign.)

[4] The coefficient of δB_1^c in Eq. (3.3a) is obtained from the fact that $(B_{11} + L_{11}) = -B_{01}$; similar substitutions occur frequently below.

The pegged-rate case. When the exchange rate is pegged, δR is endogenous and $\delta \pi$ is $\delta \bar{\pi}$, a policy-determined devaluation or revaluation. The total derivatives can be written as

$$(3.1b) \quad \begin{bmatrix} -B_{11} & 0 \\ L_{11} & -1 \end{bmatrix} \begin{bmatrix} \delta r_1 \\ \pi \delta R \end{bmatrix}$$

$$= \begin{bmatrix} 1 & B_{10} \\ 1 & -L_{10} \end{bmatrix} \begin{bmatrix} \delta \bar{B}_1^c \\ \delta \bar{r}_0 \end{bmatrix} + \begin{bmatrix} B_{1W} & -1 \\ -L_{1W} & 0 \end{bmatrix} \begin{bmatrix} V_\pi \left(\dfrac{\delta \bar{\pi}}{\bar{\pi}} \right) + \delta W^{hs} \\ \delta B_1 \end{bmatrix}$$

The determinant is $B_{11} > 0$.

Solving for the instantaneous responses of the interest rate and the stock of reserves,

$$(3.2b) \quad \delta r_1 = (1/B_{11}) \left[(-B_{10}) \, \delta \bar{r}_0 - (1) \, \delta \bar{B}_1^c - (B_{1W} V_\pi) \left(\frac{\delta \bar{\pi}}{\bar{\pi}} \right) \right.$$

$$\left. + (1) \, \delta B_1 - (B_{1W}) \, \delta W^{hs} \right]$$

$$(3.3b) \quad \bar{\pi} \, \delta R = (1/B_{11}) \left[-(B_{10} L_{11} - B_{11} L_{10}) \, \delta \bar{r}_0 + (B_{01}) \, \delta \bar{B}_1^c \right.$$

$$\left. + (H_\pi V_\pi) \left(\frac{\delta \bar{\pi}}{\bar{\pi}} \right) + (L_{11}) \, \delta B_1 + (H_\pi) \, \delta W^{hs} \right]$$

An open-market purchase by the central bank reduces reserves, and it depresses the interest rate, just as it did with a flexible rate. An increase of the foreign interest rate also reduces the stock of reserves; here, moreover, it raises the domestic interest rate (there is no ambiguity). Finally, a devaluation of the home currency ($\delta \bar{\pi} > 0$) causes an immediate increase in reserves, and because an increase in reserves adds to the supply of money, the interest rate declines. The signs of these and other effects are shown in Table 3.1B.

Before moving on to the goods markets, we draw attention to an important difference between the systems (3.1a) and (3.1b), for flexible and pegged exchange rates. Under a flexible rate, there are no zeros in the asset-market matrix; the interest rate and the exchange rate are determined jointly by behavior in the bond and money markets. Under a pegged rate, by contrast, there is one zero in the asset-market matrix; the interest rate and the stock of central-bank reserves are determined sequentially in the bond and money markets. This comparison affirms formally what we said in Chapter 1 concerning the monetary approach to the

Table 3.1B. *Impact effects under a pegged exchange rate*

Disturbance	$\bar{\pi}\,\delta R$	δr_1	δp_N	δp_1	δY	δY^d	δw or δE	δW^h	$\pi\,\delta B_0^h$
					Effect				
$\delta\bar{r}_0$	−	+	−	−	−	−	−	0	+
$\delta\bar{\pi}$	+	−	+	+	+	+	+	+	−
$\delta\bar{B}_1^c$	−	−	+	+	+	+	+	0	+
$\delta\bar{D}$	0	0	+	+	+	+	+	0	0
$\delta\bar{G}$	0	0	?	?	?	−	?	0	0
$\delta\bar{p}_0^f$	0	0	+	+	+	+	+	0	0
δc_{N1}	0	0	+	−	?	?	?	0	0
$\delta c_1^f - \delta c_{01}$	0	0	+	+	+	+	+	0	0
δW^{hs}	+	−	+	+	+	+	+	xx	xx
δB_1	−	+	−	−	−	−	−	xx	xx

Some signs shown here are different from those shown for the limiting cases considered in Chapters 4 and 5. Certain effects go to zero or unity; others become unambiguous.

balance of payments. Its basic tenet is not wrong when it is stated carefully. Under a pegged exchange rate, the stock of reserves is determined in and by the money market, given the responses of all other markets. But that tenet cannot be extended to describe determination of a flexible exchange rate. The demands for assets, including the demand for money, depend in part on wealth, and the stock of wealth depends on the exchange rate when that stock includes foreign-currency assets. Therefore, the exchange rate affects and is affected by bond-market behavior. A flexible exchange rate is not determined in and by the money market, even though one may regard it as the price that clears that market. There is a fundamental difference between the determination of the stock of reserves (the quantity of money) when the exchange rate is pegged and the determination of the exchange rate (the "price" of money) when that rate is flexible.

Impact effects in goods markets

Possessing solutions for δr_1 and $\delta\pi$, we can go on to solve for the responses of goods prices and of certain other goods-market variables that are functions of those prices. Furthermore, the equations for the two domestic goods can be arranged in the same fashion for flexible and pegged exchange rates, although we shall have to interpret them differently under the two regimes. Their total derivatives can be written as[5]

(3.4)

$$
\begin{bmatrix}
-\{u_{0N} + u_{1N} + u_E + [1 - m_N(1 - S_Y)]\sigma_N\} \\
[u_{1N} + u_E + m_1(1 - S_Y)\sigma_N]
\end{bmatrix}
$$

$$
\begin{bmatrix}
[u_{1N} + u_E + m_N(1 - S_Y)\sigma_1] \\
-\{u_t + u_{1N}^f + u_{1N} + u_E + [1 - m_1(1 - S_Y)]\sigma_1\}
\end{bmatrix}
\begin{bmatrix}
\left(\dfrac{\delta p_N}{p_N}\right) \\
\left(\dfrac{\delta p_1}{p_1}\right)
\end{bmatrix}
$$

$$
=
\begin{bmatrix}
[m_N S_W V_\pi - u_{0N}] & m_N S_1 \\
[m_1 S_W V_\pi - (u_t + u_{1N}^f + p_1^* C_1^f)] & m_1 S_1
\end{bmatrix}
\begin{bmatrix}
\left(\dfrac{\delta \pi}{\pi}\right) \\
\delta r_1
\end{bmatrix}
$$

$$
+
\begin{bmatrix}
m_N S_0 & m_N S_W \\
m_1 S_0 & m_1 S_W
\end{bmatrix}
\begin{bmatrix}
\delta r_0 \\
\delta W^{hs}
\end{bmatrix}
$$

$$
+
\begin{bmatrix}
-1 & 0 & -u_{0N} \\
1 & -1 & -u_t
\end{bmatrix}
\begin{bmatrix}
\delta c_{N1} \\
\delta c_1^f - \delta c_{01} \\
\left(\dfrac{\delta \bar{p}_0^f}{\bar{p}_0^f}\right)
\end{bmatrix}
$$

$$
+
\begin{bmatrix}
-m_N(1 - S_Y) & -[1 - m_N(1 - S_Y)] \\
-m_1(1 - S_Y) & m_1(1 - S_Y)
\end{bmatrix}
$$

$$
\begin{bmatrix}
m_N(1 - S_Y) \\
-[1 - m_1(1 - S_Y)]
\end{bmatrix}
\begin{bmatrix}
\delta \bar{D} \\
\delta \bar{G}_N \\
\delta \bar{G}_1
\end{bmatrix}
$$

The first vector on the right-hand side of this system contains the changes in the exchange rate, defined by Eq. (3.3a) or by a decision to devalue, and the change in the interest rate, defined by Eq. (3.2a) or (3.2b). An exchange-rate change affects the goods markets by way of its effects on foreign and domestic prices and by way of its effect on domestic saving (via its effect on wealth). An interest-rate change affects the goods markets by way of its effect on saving. The second vector on the right-hand side contains the exogenous changes in $\bar{r}_0$ and W^{hs}. They affect saving directly, but also influence saving and goods markets indirectly by affecting the exchange rate and the interest rate. (Changes in $\bar{B}_1^c$ and B_1 do not appear in this or any other vector but appear in the solutions shown below because they affect the exchange rate and the interest rate.) The third vector contains an exogenous change in the foreign-currency price

[5] Here, Eq. (2.12) is used to replace δW^h, and Eq. (A.3c) in Appendix A is used to replace the changes in supplies of goods (δQ_1 and δQ_N).

of the import good and three terms that have not been encountered before: δc_{N1} is a shift of domestic demand from the export good to the nontraded good (a shift that does not affect the domestic demand for the import good); δc_{01} is a shift of domestic demand from the export good to the import good (a shift that does not affect the domestic demand for the nontraded good); and δc_1^f is an exogenous increase in the foreign demand for the domestic export good (which can represent a shift in the pattern of foreign demand or an increase in the level of foreign consumption, $\delta \bar{C}^f$).[6] The final vector on the right-hand side contains three fiscal variables: an increase in the budget deficit reflecting a tax cut, a balanced-budget increase in government spending on the nontraded good, and a balanced-budget increase in government spending on the export good.[7]

There are several new symbols in this system, and they require definition. The terms u_{ij} and u_{ij}^f are value-weighted price elasticities:

$$u_{ij} = p_i^* C_i e_{ij} \qquad u_{ij}^f = p_i^* C_i^f e_{ij}^f \qquad i, j = 0, 1, N$$

The system itself is written in terms of cross-price elasticities ($i \neq j$) to focus on the implications of substitutability in consumption.[8] The term u_t is the sum of u_{10} and u_{10}^f, the value-weighted cross-price elasticities of demands for the two traded goods. The terms u_E and σ_i ($i = 1, N$) come from the supply side of the model. The former stands for substitution in production when employment is fixed and the wage rate is flexible (the classical case); it vanishes when the wage rate is fixed (the Keynesian case). The σ_i measure the effects of an increase in the price p_i on the value of the output of the ith domestic good; to be precise, $\sigma_i = p_i Q_i$ in the classical case, and $\sigma_i = (1 + a_i)p_i Q_i$, $a_i > 0$, in the Keynesian case.[9]

---

[6] The shifts in domestic demand are defined as follows: Attach an autonomous increase, δC_i^a, to the total derivative of the ith demand equation ($i = 0, 1, N$), and invoke the consumption constraint to write $\sum_i p_i \, \delta C_i^a = 0$. The disturbance $\delta c_{N1} > 0$ is therefore the case in which $p_0 \, \delta C_0^a = 0$ and $p_N \, \delta C_N^a = -p_1 \, \delta C_1^a > 0$; the disturbance $\delta c_{01} > 0$ is the case in which $p_N \, \delta C_N^a = 0$ and $p_0 \, \delta C_0^a = -p_1 \, \delta C_1^a > 0$.

[7] The disturbances $\delta \bar{G}_1$ and $\delta \bar{G}_N$ are balanced-budget changes, because T^h is varied continuously to offset changes in all other budgetary items; see Eq. (2.37a).

[8] Under our assumptions concerning the demand equations, $u_{ii} = \sum_j u_{ij} + p_1^* C_i$, and $u_{ij} = u_{ji}$, for $i, j = 0, 1, N$, and $j \neq i$. These relations are employed to write in terms of cross-price elasticities, the u_{ij}, all of the expressions in the differentiation of Eqs. (2.27a) and (2.28a).

[9] The a_i are not zero in the classical case. They are supply responses that play important roles in the Keynesian and classical cases alike. In the latter, however, their influence is represented by the term u_E, not in the terms σ_i. For details, see Appendix A.

The determinant of the system (3.4) is denoted by N_s, where

$$N_s = (u_t + u_{1N}^f)(u_{0N} + u_{1N} + u_E) + u_{0N}(u_{1N} + u_E) + N_0 N_Y$$
$$+ u_{0N}[1 - m_1(1 - S_Y)]\sigma_1 + (u_t + u_{1N}^f)[1 - m_N(1 - S_Y)]\sigma_N > 0$$

because

$$N_0 = (u_{1N} + u_E)(\sigma_1 + \sigma_N) + \sigma_1 \sigma_N > 0$$
$$N_Y = S_Y + m_0(1 - S_Y) > 0$$

the latter being the sum of the marginal propensities to save and import out of disposable income. As several terms in N_s appear separately below, it will be useful to identify them from the start. To this end, we rewrite N_s as

$$N_s = N_w + S_Y N_u$$

where

$$N_w = (u_t + u_{1N}^f)[(u_{0N} + u_{1N} + u_E) + (1 - m_N)\sigma_N]$$
$$+ u_{0N}[(u_{1N} + u_E) + (1 - m_1)\sigma_1] + m_0 N_0$$
$$N_u = \sigma_N N_{NU} + \sigma_1 N_{1U}$$
$$N_{NU} = m_N(u_t + u_{1N}^f + \sigma_1) + (1 - m_0)(u_{1N} + u_E)$$
$$N_{1U} = m_1(u_{0N} + \sigma_N) + (1 - m_0)(u_{1N} + u_E)$$

so that N_s, N_w, and N_u are always positive.

The solutions for the instantaneous changes in p_1 and p_N are presented in two parts. We deal first with the effects of goods-market disturbances ($\delta \bar{D}$, $\delta \bar{G}_1$, $\delta \bar{G}_N$, δc_{N1}, δc_{01}, δc_1^f, and $\delta \bar{p}_0^f$), those that do not have instantaneous effects on the exchange rate or domestic interest rate. Thereafter, we deal with the changes in p_1 and p_N that take place on account of financial disturbances and on account of exogenous changes in W^{hs} and B_1, and must then work separately with flexible and pegged exchange rates.

Effects of goods-market disturbances. Solving for the instantaneous impact of the goods-market disturbances,

(3.5) $$\left(\frac{\delta p_N}{p_N}\right) = (1/N_s)[(1 - S_Y)N_{NU}]\,\delta \bar{D}$$
$$+ (1/N_s)\{(u_t + u_{1N}^f)[g_N - m_N(1 - S_Y)]$$
$$+ (u_{1N} + u_E + g_N \sigma_1)N_Y\}\,\delta \bar{G}$$
$$+ (1/N_s)[u_t + u_{1N}^f + N_Y \sigma_1]\,\delta c_{N1}$$
$$+ (1/N_s)[u_{1N} + u_E + m_N(1 - S_Y)\sigma_1](\delta c_1^f - \delta c_{01})$$
$$+ (1/N_s)\{(u_t + u_{0N})[u_{1N} + u_E + m_N(1 - S_Y)\sigma_1]$$
$$+ u_{0N}(u_t + u_{1N}^f + N_Y \sigma_1)\} \left(\frac{\delta \bar{p}_0^f}{\bar{p}_0^f}\right)$$

$$(3.6) \quad \left(\frac{\delta p_1}{p_1}\right) = (1/N_s)[(1 - S_Y)N_{1U}] \, \delta \bar{D}$$
$$+ (1/N_s)\{u_{0N}[g_1 - m_1(1 - S_Y)]$$
$$+ (u_{1N} + u_E + g_1 \sigma_N)N_Y\} \, \delta \bar{G}$$
$$- (1/N_s)[u_{0N} + N_Y \sigma_N] \, \delta c_{N1}$$
$$+ (1/N_s)\{(u_{0N} + u_{1N} + u_E)$$
$$+ [1 - m_N(1 - S_Y)]\sigma_N\}(\delta c_1^f - \delta c_{01})$$
$$+ (1/N_s)\{(u_t + u_{0N})[u_{1N} + u_E + m_1(1 - S_Y)\sigma_N]$$
$$+ u_t(u_{0N} + N_Y \sigma_N)\} \left(\frac{\delta \bar{p}_0^f}{\bar{p}_0^f}\right)$$

The new term, $\delta \bar{G}$, in these equations is the sum of changes in government spending on the two domestic goods (i.e., $\delta \bar{G}_N = g_N \, \delta \bar{G}$, and $\delta \bar{G}_1 = g_1 \, \delta \bar{G}$, where $g_N + g_1 = 1$).

As indicated in Tables 3.1A and 3.1B, the price effects of $\delta \bar{D}$, δc_1^f, and $\delta \bar{p}_0^f$ are uniformly and unambiguously positive, and those of δc_{01} are negative. Furthermore, the effects of δc_{N1} are positive on p_N and negative on p_1. The only effects that are inherently ambiguous are those of balanced-budget changes in government spending. One cannot be sure that an increase of $\delta \bar{G}$ will raise the price p_i unless the fraction of the change in government spending allocated to the ith commodity, g_i, exceeds the households' marginal propensity to spend on that commodity, $m_i(1 - S_Y)$.[10]

Effects of financial disturbances under a flexible rate. To obtain expressions for responses to financial disturbances under a flexible exchange rate, we must solve the system (3.4) for the effects of δr_1 and $\delta \pi$, together with those of $\delta \bar{r}_0$ and δW^{hs}, then substitute the arguments of Eqs. (3.2a) and (3.3a) for δr_1 and $\delta \pi$. Doing so, we obtain

$$(3.7a) \quad \left(\frac{\delta p_N}{p_N}\right) = (1/N_s H_\pi V_\pi)\{[V_\pi N_{NU}H_0 + N_{N\pi}(B_{10}L_{11} - B_{11}L_{10})] \, \delta \bar{r}_0$$
$$+ [V_\pi N_{NU}(L_{1W} + B_{1W})S_1 - B_{01}(N_{N\pi} - S_W V_\pi N_{NU})] \, \delta \bar{B}_1^c$$
$$+ [V_\pi N_{NU}(S_W L_{11} - L_{1W}S_1) - N_{N\pi}L_{11}] \, \delta B_1$$
$$- (N_{N\pi}H_\pi) \, \delta W^{hs}\}$$

---

[10] This condition reflects the fact that the increase $\delta \bar{G}$ is a balanced-budget change that has to be matched by an increase in taxes and, therefore, reduces disposable income. When, of course, $\delta \bar{G}$ is allocated to a single commodity, its price has to rise (and the sign of the change in the price of the other is ambiguous). Note, finally, that both prices can rise simultaneously. This is because $g_N + g_1 = 1$, and $m_N(1 - S_Y) + m_1(1 - S_Y) = (1 - m_0)(1 - S_Y) < 1$. Households save some part of any change in their incomes and spend some of the rest on the imported good; the government, by contrast, spends only on domestic goods.

(3.8a) $\left(\dfrac{\delta p_1}{p_1}\right) = (1/N_s H_\pi V_\pi)\{[V_\pi N_{1U} H_0 + N_{1\pi}(B_{10}L_{11} - B_{11}L_{10})]\,\delta \bar{r}_0$
$+ [V_\pi N_{1U}(L_{1W} + B_{1W})S_1 - B_{01}(N_{1\pi} - S_W V_\pi N_{1U})]\,\delta \bar{B}_1^c$
$+ [V_\pi N_{1U}(S_W L_{11} - L_{1W}S_1) - N_{1\pi}L_{11}]\,\delta B_1$
$- (N_{1\pi}H_\pi)\,\delta W^{hs}\}$

Here,

$$H_0 = B_{1W}(L_{11}S_0 - L_{10}S_1) + B_{11}(S_W L_{10} \div L_{1W}S_0)$$
$$- B_{10}(S_W L_{11} - L_{1W}S_1)$$

which is thoroughly ambiguous until we impose more restrictive assumptions. Furthermore,

$$N_{N\pi} = u_\pi[u_{1N} + u_E + m_N(1 - S_Y)\sigma_1] + u_{0N}(u_t + u'_{1N} + N_Y\sigma_1)$$
$$N_{1\pi} = u_\pi[u_{1N} + u_E + m_1(1 - S_Y)\sigma_N]$$
$$+ (u_t + u'_{1N} + p_1^*C'_1)(u_{0N} + N_Y\sigma_N)$$

where

$$u_\pi = u_t + u'_{1N} + u_{0N} + p_1^*C'_1 > 0$$

so that $N_{N\pi}$ and $N_{1\pi}$ are unambiguously positive.[11] It follows that the price effects of an open-market purchase are positive, whereas those of an increase in $\bar{r}_0$ are uncertain. (The effects of δB_1 are likewise ambiguous, unless and until we are willing to restrict the relative sizes of $S_W L_{11}$ and $L_{1W}S_1$, both of which are positive. The effects of δW^{hs} are negative.)

Effects of financial disturbances under a pegged exchange rate. It is easier to solve for the responses to financial disturbances when π is pegged. Because exchange-rate changes are exogenous, we need only replace δr_1 with the argument of Eq. (3.2b) in the solution of the system (3.4):

(3.7b) $\left(\dfrac{\delta p_N}{p_N}\right) = (N_{NU}/N_s B_{11})[(S_1 B_{10} - S_0 B_{11})\,\delta \bar{r}_0 + (S_1)\,\delta \bar{B}_1^c - (S_1)\,\delta B_1$
$+ (S_1 B_{1W} - S_W B_{11})\,\delta W^{hs}]$
$+ (1/N_s)[N_{N\pi} + N_{NU}(V_\pi/B_{11})(S_1 B_{1W} - S_W B_{11})]\left(\dfrac{\delta \bar{\pi}}{\bar{\pi}}\right)$

[11] The new term u_π is the familiar Marshall-Lerner-Robinson condition:

$$u_\pi = p_1^*C'_1(e'_{10} + e'_{1N} + 1) + p_0^*C_0(e_{01} + e_{0N}) = p_1^*C'_1 e'_{11} + p_0^*C_0 e_{00} - p_0^*C_0$$

Thus, the Marshall-Lerner-Robinson condition must always be satisfied when, as here, all cross-price elasticities are positive and income elasticities of demand are unity. For demonstrations couched in similar terms, see R. W. Jones, "Stability Conditions in International Trade: A General Equilibrium Analysis," *International Economic Review*, 2 (May 1961), pp. 199–209, F. Hahn, "The Balance of Payments in a Monetary Economy," *Review of Economic Studies*, 26 (February 1959), pp. 110–25, and T. Negishi, "Approaches to the Analysis of Devaluation," *International Economic Review*, 9 (June 1968), pp. 218–27.

(3.8b) $\left(\dfrac{\delta p_1}{p_1}\right) = (N_{1U}/N_s B_{11})[\ldots]$
$\qquad + (1/N_s)[N_{1\pi} + N_{1U}(V_\pi/B_{11})(S_1 B_{1W} - S_W B_{11})]\left(\dfrac{\delta\bar{\pi}}{\bar{\pi}}\right)$

where ellipses denote sets of arguments identical to those contained in Eq. (3.7b). Here, again, an open-market purchase raises p_N and p_1 instantaneously. So does a devaluation. With a pegged exchange rate, moreover, an increase in the foreign interest rate reduces domestic prices. No outcome is ambiguous.

Other impact effects

Tables 3.1A and 3.1B list the signs of the instantaneous responses of other variables. A brief explanation is in order.

The signs of the changes in gross domestic product, Y, depend on the signs of the changes in goods prices; so do those of w and E, the wage rate and employment, in the classical and Keynesian cases, respectively. When the two domestic prices rise or fall together, δY, δw, and δE take their signs from the price changes. When those prices move in opposite directions, we cannot attach signs to δY, δw, or δE without placing additional restrictions on the relative sizes of various parameters, especially on the supply responses σ_1 and σ_N.[12]

The signs of changes in disposable income, Y^d, can differ from the signs of the changes in Y only when there is a change in the budget deficit or government spending. In these instances,[13]

(3.9) $\delta Y^d = (1/N_s)\{[N_g + N_0 + \sigma_1 u_{0N} + \sigma_N(u_t + u_{1N}^f)]\,\delta\bar{D}$
$\qquad - [N_g + g_N\sigma_1 u_{0N} + g_1\sigma_N(u_t + u_{1N}^f)]\,\delta\bar{G}\}$

where

$\qquad N_g = (u_t + u_{1N}^f)(u_{0N} + u_{1N} + u_E) + u_{0N}(u_{1N} + u_E) > 0$

Thus, a tax reduction, raising $\bar{D}$, raises disposable income, whereas a balanced-budget increase in government spending reduces it (because it involves an increase in taxes).

The signs of the changes in household wealth are obtained by differentiating Eq. (2.12):

(3.10) $\delta W^h = V_\pi\left(\dfrac{\delta\pi}{\pi}\right) + \delta W^{hs}$

[12] See Appendix A, especially Eqs. (A.1a), (A.1b), and (A.4c).
[13] These results are obtained from Eq. (2.14a) and Eq. (A.4c) in Appendix A, using the changes in goods prices given by Eqs. (3.5) and (3.6); they apply equally to flexible and pegged exchange rates.

The changes in holdings of the foreign bond, δB_0^h, listed in Table 3.1B for a pegged exchange rate, are obtained by differentiating Eq. (2.31) and replacing δW^h with the argument of Eq. (3.10):

$$(3.11) \quad \pi \, \delta B_0^h = (B_{00}) \, \delta \bar{r}_0 + (B_{01}) \, \delta r_1 - (1 - B_{0W}) V_\pi \left(\frac{\delta \pi}{\pi}\right)$$

We omit the instantaneous effects of δW^{hs} and δB_1, because they are not true disturbances. Replacing δr_1 with the argument of Eq. (3.2b) and setting $\delta \pi = \delta \bar{\pi}$,

$$(3.11b) \quad \bar{\pi} \, \delta B_0^h = (1/B_{11}) \left[(B_{10} L_{11} - B_{11} L_{10}) \, \delta \bar{r}_0 - (B_{01}) \, \delta \bar{B}_1^c \right.$$

$$\left. - (H_\pi) V_\pi \left(\frac{\delta \bar{\pi}}{\bar{\pi}}\right) \right]$$

which is equal absolutely but opposite in sign to the corresponding change in reserves, $\bar{\pi} \, \delta R$, given by Eq. (3.3b). Thus, the instantaneous adjustment of portfolios is accomplished by exchanging money (reserves) for foreign bonds. Under a flexible exchange rate, no such instantaneous adjustment is possible. As $\pi \, \delta R$ is zero, $\pi \, \delta R_0^h$ must also be zero. This result can be confirmed by replacing δr_1 and $\delta \pi$ in Eq. (3.11) with the arguments of Eqs. (3.2a) and (3.3a).

Under a pegged exchange rate, the central bank stands ready to supply unlimited quantities of foreign currency, including the amounts required to satisfy an instantaneous increase in the demand for the foreign bond. Under a flexible rate, by contrast, no one is prepared to accommodate passively an increase in demand for foreign currency. The currency required to buy foreign bonds can come only from a surplus in the current-account balance, and that balance is a flow; it cannot shift abruptly in the manner required to satisfy an increase in the stock demand for the foreign bond. With a pegged exchange rate, a small economy can alter its portfolio of foreign assets instantaneously; it can swap foreign money for foreign bonds, using the reserves of the central bank. With a flexible exchange rate, no such swap is possible.[14]

Solving for dynamic effects

We deal next with two tasks—proving dynamic stability and showing how various exogenous disturbances influence the time paths of the market-clearing variables, including the balance of payments.

[14] If there were a second traded bond in the model, there could be instantaneous portfolio adjustments under a flexible exchange rate; one bond could be traded for the other. This is

The proof of stability

Although our model has two dynamic relationships, Eqs. (2.11b) and (2.38b), it is not difficult to prove dynamic stability. Under our assumptions about fiscal policy, $\bar{D}$ goes to zero at time $t = k$, and $\dot{B}_1$ goes to zero too. The stock of debt, B_1, is stabilized thereafter. Thus, the stability of the model depends on the properties of Eq. (2.11b), defining the behavior of $\dot{W}^{hs}$. It is necessary and sufficient to prove that

$$(3.12) \quad \frac{\delta \dot{W}^{hs}}{\delta W^{hs}} = S_1 \left(\frac{\delta r_1}{\delta W^{hs}} \right) + S_Y \left(\frac{\delta Y^d}{\delta W^{hs}} \right) + S_W \left(\frac{\delta W^h}{\delta W^{hs}} \right) < 0$$

Under a flexible rate, we can show that[15]

$$(3.12a) \quad \frac{\delta \dot{W}^{hs}}{\delta W^{hs}} = -(S_Y/V_\pi)(N_t/N_s) < 0$$

because

$$N_t = (\sigma_N N_{N\pi} + \sigma_1 N_{1\pi})$$
$$= u_\pi N_0 + u_{0N}[(u_t + u_{1N}^f)\sigma_N + (u_t + u_{1N}^f + p_1^* C_1^f)\sigma_1] > 0$$

Under a pegged exchange rate,[16]

$$(3.12b) \quad \frac{\delta \dot{W}^{hs}}{\delta W^{hs}} = -(N_w/N_s B_{11})[S_1 B_{1W} + S_W(L_{11} + B_{01})] < 0$$

because, as shown above,

$$N_w = N_s - S_Y N_u > 0$$

The model is stable under both regimes.

Extending this procedure, we can obtain the effect of any exogenous disturbance, z_j, on $\dot{W}^{hs}$. Differentiating Eq. (2.11b) with respect to any such disturbance and using Eq. (3.10),

$$(3.13) \quad \frac{\delta \dot{W}^{hs}}{\delta z_j} = S_Y \left(\frac{\delta Y^d}{\delta z_j} \right) + S_0 \left(\frac{\delta r_0}{\delta z_j} \right) + S_1 \left(\frac{\delta r_1}{\delta z_j} \right) + S_W V_\pi \left(\frac{\delta \pi}{\pi \, \delta z_j} \right)$$

where $(\delta r_0/\delta z_j) = 1$ for $z_j = \bar{r}_0$ and zero otherwise.

the single instance mentioned in Chapter 2, in which our results depend importantly on the assumption that the domestic bond is not held by foreigners.

[15] From Eq. (3.2a), $(\delta r_1/\delta W^{hs}) = 0$. Furthermore, Eqs. (3.3a) and (3.10) give $(\delta W^h/\delta W^{hs}) = 0$. Finally, we can use Eqs. (3.7a) and (3.8a), together with Eq. (A.4c) of Appendix A, to show that $(\delta Y^d/\delta W^{hs}) = (\delta Y/\delta W^{hs}) = -(1/N_s V_\pi)(\sigma_N N_{N\pi} + \sigma_1 N_{1\pi})$.

[16] From Eqs. (3.2b) and (3.10), $S_1(\delta r_1/\delta W^{hs}) + S_W(\delta W^h/\delta W^{hs}) = -(1/B_{11})(B_{1W}S_1 - S_W B_{11})$. Furthermore, we can use Eqs. (3.7b) and (3.8b), together with Eq. (A.4c) of Appendix A, to show that $S_Y(\delta Y^d/\delta W^{hs}) = S_Y(\delta Y/\delta W^{hs}) = (S_Y/N_s B_{11})(B_{1W}S_1 - S_W B_{11})N_u$.

Table 3.2A. *Dynamic effects under a flexible exchange rate*

Disturbance	$\delta\dot{\pi}$	$\delta\dot{r}_1$	$\delta\dot{p}_N$	$\delta\dot{p}_1$	$\delta\dot{Y}$ and $\delta\dot{Y}^d$	$\delta\dot{W}$ or $\delta\dot{E}$	$\delta\dot{W}^{hs}$	$\delta\dot{F}$
$\delta\bar{r}_0$	?	0	?	?	?	?	?	?
$\delta\bar{B}^c_1$	?	0	?	?	?	?	?	?
$\delta\bar{D}$	?	+	?	?	?	?	+	−
$\delta\bar{G}$	+	0	+	+	+	+	−	−
$\delta\bar{p}^f_0$	−	0	−	−	−	−	+	+
δc_{N1}	?	0	?	?	?	?	?	?
$\delta c^f_1 - \delta c_{01}$	−	0	−	−	−	−	+	+

Some signs shown here are different from those shown for the limiting cases considered in Chapter 6. Certain effects go to zero or unity; others become unambiguous.

When z_j is a goods-market disturbance ($\delta\bar{D}$, $\delta\bar{G}_N$, $\delta\bar{G}_1$, $\delta\bar{p}^f_0$, δc_{N1}, δc_{01}, or δc^f_1), all terms except $(\delta Y^d/\delta z_j)$ are zero under either a flexible or pegged exchange rate; goods-market disturbances have no immediate effects on the interest rate or exchange rate. In these cases, then, the sign of $(\delta\dot{W}^{hs}/\delta z_j)$ depends only on the sign of $(\delta Y^d/\delta z_j)$, and it is shown in Tables 3.1A and 3.1B. This is how we obtain the goods-market effects on $\dot{W}^{hs}$ listed in Tables 3.2A and 3.2B. When δz_j is a financial disturbance, the outcomes depend on the exchange-rate regime.

Under a flexible exchange rate,[17]

$$(3.13a) \quad \delta\dot{W}^{hs} = (1/N_s H_\pi V_\pi)\{[S_Y N_t(B_{10}L_{11} - B_{11}L_{10}) - V_\pi N_w H_0]\,\delta\bar{r}_0$$
$$+ [S_Y N_t(-B_{01}) - S_1(L_{1W} + B_{1W})V_\pi N_w - S_W B_{01} V_\pi N_w]\,\delta\bar{B}^c_1$$
$$- [L_{11}S_Y N_t + V_\pi N_w(S_W L_{11} - L_{1W}S_1)]\,\delta B_1\}$$

All of these expressions are ambiguous (because V_π appears in some terms of each argument and does not appear in others of opposite sign).

Under a pegged exchange rate,

$$(3.13b) \quad \delta\dot{W}^{hs} = (N_w/N_s B_{11})[(S_0 B_{11} - S_1 B_{10})\,\delta\bar{r}_0 - (S_1)\,\delta\bar{B}^c_1 + (S_1)\,\delta B_1]$$

$$+ (1/N_s B_{11})[S_Y N_t B_{11} - N_w V_\pi(S_1 B_{1W} - S_W B_{11})]\left(\frac{\delta\dot{\pi}}{\bar{\pi}}\right)$$

The effects of $\delta\bar{r}_0$ and δB_1 are positive, that of $\delta\bar{B}^c_1$ is negative, and that of $\delta\dot{\pi}$ is ambiguous (because V_π appears again in one of the two terms).

[17] This solution uses Eq. (3.3a) to replace $(\delta\pi/\pi\delta z_j)$ and Eq. (3.2a) to replace $(\delta r_1/\delta z_j)$. In the pegged-rate case below, $(\delta\pi/\pi\delta z_j) = 1$ for $z_j = \bar{\pi}$ and is zero otherwise, and Eq. (3.2b) is used to replace $(\delta r_1/\delta z_j)$. In both cases, $(\delta Y^d/\delta z_j)$ is obtained as it was above to solve for $(\delta\dot{W}^{hs}/\delta W^{hs})$.

Table 3.2B. *Dynamic effects under a pegged exchange rate*

					Effect				
Disturbance	$\bar{\pi}\,\delta\bar{R}$	$\delta\dot{r}_1$	$\delta\dot{p}_N$	$\delta\dot{p}_1$	$\delta\dot{Y}$ and $\delta\dot{Y}^d$	$\delta\dot{w}$ or $\delta\dot{E}$	$\delta\dot{W}^{hs}$	$\delta\dot{F}$	$\delta(p_1^*C_1^f - p_0^*C_0)$
$\delta\bar{r}_0$	$+$	$-$	$+$	$+$	$+$	$+$	$+$	$+$	$+$
$\delta\bar{\pi}$	?	?	?	?	?	?	?	?	?
$\delta\bar{B}_1^c$	$-$	$+$	$-$	$-$	$-$	$-$	$-$	$-$	$-$
$\delta\bar{D}$	?	$+$	?	?	?	?	$+$	?	$-$
$\delta\bar{G}$	$-$	$+$	$-$	$-$	$-$	$-$	$-$	$-$	$-$
$\delta\bar{p}_0^f$	$+$	$-$	$+$	$+$	$+$	$+$	$+$	$+$	$+$
δc_{N1}	?	?	?	?	?	?	?	?	?
$\delta c_1^f - \delta c_{01}$	$+$	$-$	$+$	$+$	$+$	$+$	$+$	$+$	$+$

Some signs shown here are different from those shown for the limiting cases considered in Chapter 6. Certain effects go to zero or unity; others become unambiguous.

In certain circumstances, however, some of these ambiguities can be banished. Because the demands for assets are homogeneous of first degree in W^h, the term V_π can be written as $B_{0W}W^h$. And when the economy is in a steady state initially, so that saving is zero, $W^h = -(S_Y/S_W)Y^d$, because the saving function is homogeneous of first degree in W^h and Y^d. Accordingly, $V_\pi = -B_{0W}(S_Y/S_W)Y^d$. Returning to Eq. (3.13a), the impact of an increase in B_1 can then be written as

$$\delta\dot{W}^{hs} = -(S_Y/S_W)N_t(1/N_sH_\pi V_\pi)\{S_W L_{11}[1 - B_{0W}(N_w Y^d/N_t)] + L_{1W}S_1[B_{0W}(N_w Y^d/N_t)]\}\,\delta B_1$$

It can be shown, moreover, that $N_t \gtrless N_w Y^d$,[18] and we know that $B_{0W} < 1$. By implication, an increase of B_1 will have the effect of raising $\dot{W}^{hs}$. This method cannot be employed to banish other ambiguities in Eqs. (3.13a) and (3.13b), but we shall have occasion to use it again.

The time paths of market-clearing variables

At any point in time, the values of the market-clearing variables depend on the stocks W^{hs} and B_1. Their time paths, then, depend on the rates of change $\dot{W}^{hs}$ and $\dot{B}_1$. Therefore,

$$(3.14) \quad \frac{\delta\dot{x}}{\delta z_j} = \left(\frac{\delta x}{\delta W^{hs}}\right)\left(\frac{\delta\dot{W}^{hs}}{\delta z_j}\right) + \left(\frac{\delta x}{\delta B_1}\right)\left(\frac{\delta\dot{B}_1}{\delta z_j}\right)$$

[18] See Appendix C.

where x is any market-clearing variable, and where $(\delta \dot{B}_1/\delta z_j) = 1$ for $z_j = \bar{D}$ and zero otherwise. The derivatives $(\delta x/\delta W^{hs})$ and $(\delta x/\delta B_1)$ are, of course, the instantaneous effects shown by Eqs. (3.2a) through (3.8b) and summarized in Tables 3.1A and 3.1B.

It is therefore easy to determine the directions in which the time paths $\dot{x}$ begin to change immediately after an exogenous disturbance. When it does not involve a change in $\bar{D}$, we need only examine the signs of the terms $(\delta x/\delta W^{hs})$ and those of the changes in the time paths of $\dot{W}^{hs}$ implied by Eqs. (3.13) through (3.13b). When the disturbance does involve a change in $\bar{D}$, we must also examine the signs of the terms $(\delta x/\delta B_1)$, but this complication does not pose great difficulties. The signs of the $\delta \dot{x}$ obtained in this fashion are shown in Tables 3.2A and 3.2B, for flexible and pegged exchange rates, respectively.[19]

The solutions for $\bar{\pi} \, \delta \dot{R}$ in Table 3.2B have particular importance. They describe the evolution of the balance of payments under a pegged exchange rate. To show that this is so, we derive a balance-of-payments equation from the households' balance sheet and goods-market equations:[20]

$$(3.15) \quad S - \bar{D} - \bar{\pi}\dot{B}_0^h - \bar{\pi}\dot{R} = (p_1^*C_1^f - p_0^*C_0) - \dot{F} - \bar{\pi}\dot{R} = 0$$

where $(p_1^*C_1^f - p_0^*C_0)$ is the trade balance, $\dot{F}$ is the capital outflow measured in home currency, $\bar{\pi}\dot{B}_0^h$, and both are flows through time.

---

[19] It should be noted that $\delta\dot{x}$ is the very short-run change in the time path of the variable x; it does not define the entire time path. Of course, if the model begins in a steady state (so that $\dot{W}^{hs} = \dot{B}_1 = 0$ to start), one can make stronger statements. This is what we shall do in Chapter 6, where we shall interpret Eq. (3.14) as an approximation to the rate of change in x itself:

$$\dot{x} = \left(\frac{\delta x}{\delta W^{hs}}\right) \dot{W}^{hs} + \left(\frac{\delta x}{\delta B_1}\right) \dot{B}_1$$

and Eqs. (3.17b) and (3.18b), below, will be written as

$$\bar{\pi}\dot{R} = (H_\pi/B_{11})\dot{W}^{hs} + (L_{11}/B_{11})\bar{D}$$
$$\dot{F} = [(B_{11} - H_\pi)/B_{11}]\dot{W}^{hs} + (B_{01}/B_{11})\bar{D}$$

One must still bear in mind, however, that these statements hold only in the neighborhood of the initial steady state. Note, finally, that goods-market disturbances will affect the time paths of r_1 and π or R, even though they do not have immediate effects on the levels of those variables; this is because they start at once to influence W^{hs} and B_1.

[20] This result is obtained in two steps. First, we combine Eqs. (2.10), (2.33), and (2.42) through (2.46) to rewrite household wealth as $W^h = B_1 + \pi B_0^h + \pi R - W^c$, then take its total time derivative. Second, we use Eqs. (2.14a), (2.17a), (2.18), (2.27), and (2.28) to derive the familiar national-income relationship, $S - \bar{D} = p_1^*C_1^f - p_0^*C_0$. Our assumptions concerning T^h and T^f, which cause all interest-income terms to vanish from the definition of disposable income, eliminate the foreign interest-income term, $\bar{r}_0(\pi B_0^h)$, from the balance-of-payments equation.

Using Eqs. (3.15) and (2.11a), we write the change in the trade balance as

(3.16) $\delta(p_1{}^*C_1^f - p_0{}^*C_0) = \delta\dot{W}^{hs} - \delta\bar{D}$

This statement is true for both exchange-rate regimes. For disturbances other than $\delta\bar{D}$, then, the change in the trade balance is equal to the corresponding change in saving, $\delta\dot{W}^{hs}$. For $\delta\bar{D}$, it equals $-(1 - S_Y) \times (N_w/N_s)\,\delta\bar{D}$. An increase in the budget deficit reduces the trade surplus (increases the trade deficit).

Under a flexible exchange rate, of course, $\dot{R}$ is always zero, so that the change in the home-currency capital outflow, $\delta\dot{F}$, must always equal the change in the trade balance. Under a pegged exchange rate, however, the change in the trade balance is the *sum* of $\delta\dot{F}$ and $\bar{\pi}\,\delta\dot{R}$. To solve for $\delta\dot{F}$ and $\bar{\pi}\,\delta\dot{R}$ separately, we must use Eqs. (3.3b), (3.14), (3.15), and (3.16) together:

$$(3.17b) \quad \bar{\pi}\,\delta\dot{R} = \left(\frac{\bar{\pi}\,\delta R}{\delta\,W^{hs}}\right)\delta\dot{W}^{hs} + \left(\frac{\bar{\pi}\,\delta R}{\delta B_1}\right)\delta\bar{D}$$

$$= [H_\pi/B_{11}]\,\delta\dot{W}^{hs} + (L_{11}/B_{11})\,\delta\bar{D}$$

$$(3.18b) \quad \delta\dot{F} = [(B_{11} - H_\pi)/B_{11}]\,\delta\dot{W}^{hs} + [B_{01}/B_{11}]\,\delta\bar{D}$$

where $(B_{11} - H_\pi) = -[L_{11}B_{0w} + (1 - L_{1w})B_{01}] > 0$. Thus, for disturbances other than $\delta\bar{D}$, the change in saving that results will be divided between holdings of domestic money and of foreign bonds, fostering changes of the same signs in $\bar{\pi}\dot{R}$ and $\dot{F}$. Any disturbance that stimulates saving will enlarge the balance-of-payments surplus even though it also leads to a capital outflow. (By implication, it must strengthen the trade balance by more than it stimulates the capital outflow.) When the disturbance is an increase in the budget deficit, saving will increase, but the signs of $\bar{\pi}\,\delta\dot{R}$ and $\delta\dot{F}$ are uncertain. The trade balance will deteriorate, as shown before, but $\dot{F}$ can rise or fall, and it is not impossible to witness an improvement in the overall balance of payments.

Solving for steady-state effects

Having shown that our model is stable, we are entitled to assume that it will converge to a steady state, and we can ask how various disturbances will influence its steady-state values.

We must solve anew the market-clearing equations for the two domestic goods, the domestic bond, and money, but we shall do so differently than when we were concerned with impact effects. Instead of replacing disposable income with Eq. (2.14a) and wealth with Eq. (2.12), we shall obtain the changes in Y^d and W^h directly from the relevant steady-state equations. Once again, moreover, we shall partition the model, but we shall do so differently from before and differently also for flexible and pegged exchange rates.

Steady-state effects under a flexible rate

Here, it is convenient to write the model in this form and order:

(2.42a) $B_1(\bar{r}_0, r_1, W^h) + \bar{B}_1^c - \bar{B}_1 = 0$

(2.43a) $L(\bar{r}_0, r_1, W^h) - (\bar{B}_1^c + \pi\bar{R} - W^c) = 0$

(2.11a) $S(\bar{r}_0, r_1, Y^d, W^h) = 0$

(2.27a) $C_1(p_N, p_1, \pi\bar{p}_0^f, Y^d) + (\bar{G}_1/p_1) + C_1^f\left(\bar{p}_N^f, \dfrac{p_1}{\pi}, \bar{p}_0^f, \bar{C}^f\right)$
$$- \theta_1(p_N, p_1) = 0$$

(2.28a) $C_N(p_N, p_1, \pi\bar{p}_0^f, Y^d) + (\bar{G}_N/p_N) - \theta_N(p_N, p_1) = 0$

(2.14b) $Y^d + \bar{G}_1 + \bar{G}_N - [p_N\theta_N(p_N, p_1) + p_1\theta_1(p_N, p_1)] = 0$

Equations (2.42a) and (2.43a), relating to the bond and money markets, are written as they were before, apart from designating R and B_1 as exogenous variables. (The latter, we have said, is the long-run counterpart of the policy-determined budget deficit, which must be eliminated from the model before it can start to move to a steady state.) As p_1, p_N, π, and Y^d do not appear in those equations, they can be solved separately for the long-run changes in r_1 and W^h.[21] Equation (2.11a) is written to reflect the fact that $*S = 0$ in the steady state. It can be solved separately for the change in Y^d, given the changes in r_1 and W^h. Equations (2.27a) and (2.28a) are different than they were before only in that $*S$ has vanished from households' demands for goods. Those equations can be used with Eq. (2.14b) to solve for the changes in p_1, p_N, and π, given the changes in Y^d.[22] Finally, we can use Eq. (2.12) and the changes in π, r_1, and W^h to solve for the change in accumulated saving, W^{hs}.

[21] The exchange rate does appear in Eq. (2.43a), but when we differentiate, it will be canceled by the corresponding term in the derivative of W^c.

[22] Equation (2.14b) is obtained from Eqs. (2.3a) and (2.14a); it differs from earlier definitions of disposable income because $\bar{D}$ has disappeared (there being no government deficit in the steady state). The supply-side terms are obtained, as before, from Appendix A.

Although this strategy differs from the one employed above to solve for the impact effects of disturbances, the procedure and notation are similar, and we move at once to the results:

$$(3.19a) \quad dr_1 = (1/H_\pi)[(L_{10}B_{1W} - L_{1W}B_{10})\,d\bar{r}_0 - (L_{1W} + B_{1W})\,d\bar{B}_1^c + (L_{1W})\,d\bar{B}_1]$$

$$(3.20a) \quad dW^h = (1/H_\pi)[(B_{10}L_{11} - B_{11}L_{10})\,d\bar{r}_0 - (B_{01})\,d\bar{B}_1^c - (L_{11})\,d\bar{B}_1]$$

$$(3.21a) \quad dY^d = (1/H_\pi S_Y)\{(H_0)\,d\bar{r}_0 + [S_1(L_{1W} + B_{1W}) + S_W B_{01}]\,d\bar{B}_1^c + (S_W L_{11} - L_{1W}S_1)\,d\bar{B}_1\}$$

$$(3.22a) \quad \left(\frac{dp_N}{p_N}\right) = (1/N_t)\{[u_\pi(u_{1N} + u_E + g_N\sigma_1) + u_{0N}(u_t + u_{1N}^f)]\,d\bar{G}$$
$$+ [u_{0N}(u_{1N}^f + p_1^*C_1^f)\sigma_1]\left(\frac{d\bar{p}_0^f}{\bar{p}_0^f}\right)$$
$$+ (u_\pi\sigma_1)\,dc_{N1} - (u_{0N}\sigma_1)(dc_1^f - dc_{01}) + (N_{Nt})\,dY^d\}$$

$$(3.23a) \quad \left(\frac{dp_1}{p_1}\right) = (1/N_t)\{[u_\pi(u_{1N} + u_E + g_1\sigma_N)$$
$$+ u_{0N}(u_t + u_{1N}^f + p_1^*C_1^f)]\,d\bar{G}$$
$$- [u_{0N}(u_{1N}^f + p_1^*C_1^f)\sigma_N]\left(\frac{d\bar{p}_0^f}{\bar{p}_0^f}\right)$$
$$- (u_\pi\sigma_N)\,dc_{N1} + (u_{0N}\sigma_N)(dc_1^f - dc_{01}) + (N_{1t})\,dY^d\}$$

$$(3.24a) \quad \left(\frac{d\pi}{\pi}\right) = (1/N_t)\{[N_g + u_{0N}g_N\sigma_1 + (u_t + u_{1N}^f)g_1\sigma_N]\,d\bar{G}$$
$$- [u_{0N}(u_t + u_{1N}^f)\sigma_N + u_{0N}u_t\sigma_1 + (u_t + u_{0N})N_0]\left(\frac{d\bar{p}_0^f}{\bar{p}_0^f}\right)$$
$$- [(u_t + u_{1N}^f)\sigma_N - u_{0N}\sigma_1]\,dc_{N1}$$
$$- [u_{0N}\sigma_1 + N_0](dc_1^f - dc_{01}) + (N_w)\,dY^d\}$$

where

$$N_{Nt} = u_\pi(u_{1N} + u_E + m_N\sigma_1)' + u_{0N}(u_t + u_{1N}^f + m_0\sigma_1) > 0$$
$$N_{1t} = u_\pi(u_{1N} + u_E + m_1\sigma_N) + (u_{0N} + m_0\sigma_N)(u_t + u_{1N}^f + p_1^*C_1^f) > 0$$

The signs of the effects shown here are listed in Table 3.3A. The table also shows the signs of the changes in accumulated saving, obtained from Eq. (2.12), the changes in income and the wage rate or employment, obtained from the changes in goods prices, and the changes in domestic holdings of

Table 3.3A. *Steady-state effects under a flexible exchange rate*

Disturbance	$d\pi$	dr_1	dp_N	dp_1	dY	dY^d	dw or dE	dW^h	dW^{hs}	$\pi\,dB_0^h$
$d\bar{r}_0$	?	?	?	?	?	?	?	+	?	?
$d\bar{B}_1^c$	+	−	+	+	+	+	+	+	?	?
$d\bar{B}_1$	?ᵃ	+	?ᵃ	?ᵃ	?ᵃ	?ᵃ	?ᵃ	+	?	?
$d\bar{G}$	+	0	+	+	1	0	+	0	−	−
$d\bar{p}_0^f$	−	0	+	−	0	0	?	0	+	+
dc_{N1}	?	0	+	−	0	0	?	0	?	?
$dc_1^f - dc_{01}$	−	0	−	+	0	0	?	0	+	+

Some signs shown here are different from those shown for the limiting cases considered in Chapters 4 and 5. Certain effects go to zero or unity; others become unambiguous.
ᵃ Positive when $S_W L_{11} > L_{1W} S_1$ (i.e., when there is no crowding out); see Chapter 5.

the foreign bond. These last are obtained from the households' balance sheet,

$$(3.25) \quad \pi\,dB_0^h = dW^{hs} - dB_1 - \pi\,dR$$

and the fact that $\pi\,dR = 0$ when the exchange rate is flexible.

Before turning to solutions for the pegged-rate case, let us note one economic implication of the mathematical approach that we have just employed. When solving for the impact effects of disturbances, we saw that the exchange rate was unaffected by goods-market disturbances; it responded only to financial disturbances. In that shortest of short runs, the exchange rate was determined in the asset markets, independently of what was happening in the two goods markets. In the steady state, however, we find that the exchange rate *is* affected by events in the goods markets. In fact, the long-run level of the exchange rate is responsive to financial disturbances and policies only insofar as they affect the steady-state level of disposable income. In this longest of long runs, the exchange rate is determined in the goods markets. This is why we claimed that partitionability furnishes a formal representation of the casual observation that short-run fluctuations in flexible exchange rates appear to be determined by financial phenomena, including monetary policies, whereas long-term trends are governed by relative price trends and other "fundamental" goods-market phenomena.

Steady-state effects under a pegged rate

Here, it is convenient to list the equations in a slightly different order:

$$(2.27a)\quad C_1(p_N, p_1, \bar{\pi}\bar{p}_0^f, Y^d) + (\bar{G}_1/p_1) + C_1^f\left(\bar{p}_N^f, \frac{p_1}{\bar{\pi}}, \bar{p}_0^f, \bar{C}^f\right)$$
$$- \theta_1(p_N, p_1) = 0$$

$$(2.28a)\quad C_N(p_N, p_1, \bar{\pi}\bar{p}_0^f, Y^d) + (\bar{G}_N/p_N) - \theta_N(p_N, p_1) = 0$$

$$(2.14b)\quad Y^d + \bar{G}_1 + \bar{G}_N - [p_1\theta_1(p_N, p_1) + p_N\theta_N(p_N, p_1)] = 0$$

$$(2.11a)\quad S(\bar{r}_0, r_1, Y^d, W^h) = 0$$

$$(2.42a)\quad B_1(\bar{r}_0, r_1, W^h) + \bar{B}_1^c - \bar{B}_1 = 0$$

$$(2.43a)\quad L(\bar{r}_0, r_1, W^h) - [\bar{B}_1^c + \bar{\pi}R - W^c] = 0$$

These equations are identical to those shown for the flexible-rate case, apart from the designation of R as endogenous and π as exogenous. But they lend themselves to a different strategy. The first three equations can be solved for changes in p_1, p_N, and Y^d. The fourth and fifth can be solved for changes in r_1 and W^h, given the changes in Y^d. Finally, the sixth can be solved for changes in R, given the changes in r_1 and W^h. In economic terms, the steady-state levels of prices and expenditure are determined entirely by goods-market conditions. The interest rate and wealth are determined by bond-market conditions and by the requirement that saving be zero, given the level of disposable income. The stock of money is adjusted to the interest rate and wealth by cumulative changes in the stock of reserves.

The solutions furnished by this structure and strategy are

$$(3.21b)\quad dY^d = (1/N_w)\left\{(N_t)\left(\frac{d\bar{\pi}}{\bar{\pi}}\right)\right.$$
$$- [N_g + u_{0N}g_N\sigma_1 + (u_t + u_{1N}^f)g_1\sigma_N]\, d\bar{G}$$
$$+ [u_{0N}(u_t + u_{1N}^f)\sigma_N + u_{0N}u_t\sigma_1 + (u_t + u_{0N})N_0]\left(\frac{d\bar{p}_0^f}{\bar{p}_0^f}\right)$$
$$+ [(u_t + u_{1N}^f)\sigma_N - u_{0N}\sigma_1]\, dc_{N1}$$
$$+ [u_{0N}\sigma_1 + N_0](dc_1^f - dc_{01})\Big\}$$

Table 3.3B. *Steady-state effects under a pegged exchange rate*

Disturbance	$\bar{\pi}\,dR$	dr_1	dp_N	dp_1	dY	dY^d	dw or dE	dW^h	dW^{hs}	$\pi\,dB_0^h$
$d\bar{r}_0$	?	?	0	0	0	0	0	+	+	?
$d\bar{\pi}$	+	−	+	+	+	+	+	+	?	?
$d\bar{B}_1^c$	−	−	0	0	0	0	0	−	−	?
$d\bar{B}_1$	?^{a}	+	0	0	0	0	0	+	+	?
$d\bar{G}$	−	+	?	?	?	−	?	−	−	−
$d\bar{p}_0^f$	+	−	+	+	+	+	+	+	+	+
dc_{N1}	?	?	+	−	?	?	?	?	?	?
$dc_1^f - dc_{01}$	+	−	+	+	+	+	+	+	+	+

Some signs shown here are different from those shown for the limiting cases considered in Chapters 4 and 5. Certain effects go to zero or unity; others become unambiguous.

^{a} Negative when $S_W L_{11} > L_{1W} S_1$ (i.e., when no crowding out); see Chapter 5.

$$(3.22b) \quad \left(\frac{dp_N}{p_N}\right) = (1/N_w)\left\{(N_{Nt})\left(\frac{d\bar{\pi}}{\bar{\pi}}\right)\right.$$

$$+ \left[(u_t + u_{1N}^f)(g_N - m_N) + (u_{1N} + u_E + g_N\sigma_1)m_0\right] d\bar{G}$$

$$+ \left[(u_t + u_{0N})(u_{1N} + u_E + m_N\sigma_1)\right.$$

$$\left. + u_{0N}(u_t + u_{1N}^f + m_0\sigma_1)\right]\left(\frac{d\bar{p}_0^f}{\bar{p}_0^f}\right)$$

$$+ \left[u_t + u_{1N}^f + m_0\sigma_1\right] dc_{N1}$$

$$\left. + \left[u_{1N} + u_E + m_N\sigma_1\right](dc_1^f - dc_{01})\right\}$$

$$(3.23b) \quad \left(\frac{dp_1}{p_1}\right) = (1/N_w)\left\{(N_{1t})\left(\frac{d\bar{\pi}}{\bar{\pi}}\right)\right.$$

$$+ \left[u_{0N}(g_1 - m_1) + (u_{1N} + u_E + g_1\sigma_N)m_0\right] d\bar{G}$$

$$+ \left[(u_t + u_{0N})(u_{1N} + u_E + m_1\sigma_N)\right.$$

$$\left. + u_t(u_{0N} + m_0\sigma_N)\right]\left(\frac{d\bar{p}_0^f}{\bar{p}_0^f}\right)$$

$$- \left[u_{0N} + m_0\sigma_N\right] dc_{N1}$$

$$\left. + \left[u_{1N} + u_E + u_{0N} + (1 - m_N)\sigma_N\right](dc_1^f - dc_{01})\right\}$$

$$(3.19b) \quad dr_1 = (1/H_f)[(S_W B_{10} - S_0 B_{1W})\,d\bar{r}_0 + (S_W)\,d\bar{B}_1^c - (S_W)\,d\bar{B}_1$$

$$- (S_Y B_{1W})\,dY^d]$$

(3.20b) $dW^h = (1/H_f)[(S_0 B_{11} - S_1 B_{10})\, d\bar{r}_0 - (S_1)\, d\bar{B}_1^c + (S_1)\, d\bar{B}_1$
$+ (S_Y B_{11})\, dY^d]$

(3.24b) $\bar{\pi}\, dR = (1/H_f)\{(-H_0)\, d\bar{r}_0 - [S_1(B_{1W} + L_{1W}) + S_W B_{01}]\, d\bar{B}_1^c$
$- (S_W L_{11} - L_{1W} S_1)\, d\bar{B}_1 + (S_Y H_\pi)\, dY^d\}$

where

$$H_f = S_1 B_{1W} - S_W B_{11} > 0$$

The signs of these effects are shown in Table 3.3B, together with the signs of the changes in W^{hs}, Y, w or E, and πB_0^h, obtained just as they were in the flexible-rate case.

4

Comparative statics: goods-market disturbances

The mathematical analysis in Chapter 3 focused by turns on classes of responses. It dealt sequentially with impact, dynamic, and steady-state effects under flexible and pegged exchange rates. We have now to reorganize and interpret the results – to ask how each disturbance or policy change affects the economy, to explain the processes activated in each instance, and to study the role of the exchange-rate regime. We have also to ask how the various responses are influenced by economic structure and behavior in the goods and asset markets, especially to ask in what measure they depend on the degree of substitutability between pairs of goods and between domestic and foreign bonds.

To avoid excessive repetition, we split our task into two parts. In this chapter and the next, we study comparative statics. Looking at disturbances and policy changes one at a time, we ask how the economy adapts on impact and in the steady state and how its adaptations are affected by the exchange-rate regime and by degrees of substitutability in goods and asset markets. In Chapter 6 we look at behavior over time to see how the impact effects of a disturbance give way to the steady-state effects.

Under the assumptions adopted in Chapter 2, notably those that govern the demand for money, events in goods markets do not impinge immediately on asset markets. It is therefore possible to isolate a set of disturbances and policy changes that have no impact effects on the domestic interest rate, the exchange rate, or reserves, because they originate in the goods markets. They impinge gradually on asset markets, insofar as they affect saving and wealth, but even when we deal with their steady-state effects, we shall see that long-run outcomes are conditioned strongly by the ways in which goods markets are affected.

Six of these disturbances were defined in Chapter 3, and all of them are studied here. They are (1) an increase in $\bar{C}^f$, nominal foreign spending; (2) a shift of foreign demand from the import (foreign traded) good to the export (domestic traded) good; (3) a shift of domestic demand from the export good to the import good; (4) a shift of domestic demand from the

68

Table 4.1. *Shift of domestic or foreign demand from the import good to the export good*

Variable	Impact effect	Steady-state effect	
		Pegged rate	Flexible rate
p_N	+	+	−
p_1	+	+	+
p_1/p_N	?	?	+
Y^d	+	+	0
Y	+	+	0
r_1	0	$-^a$	0
$\bar{\pi}R$	0	+	0
π	0	0	−
W^h	0	+	0

Signs for $(\delta c_1^f - \delta c_{01}) > 0$ (where δc_1^f includes $\delta \bar{C}^f$).
[a] Goes to zero when domestic and foreign bonds are perfect substitutes.

export good to the nontraded good; (5) an increase in $\bar{p}_0^f$, the foreign-currency price of the import good; and (6) a balanced-budget increase in government spending.

We have seen, however, that the first three disturbances are sufficiently similar in character to be combined into a single trade-balance disturbance ($\delta c_1^f - \delta c_{01} > 0$ in the notation of Chapter 3) and can therefore consolidate their treatment here. When we have examined them carefully, moreover, and used them to introduce our methods and diagrams, it will be possible to analyze the others very briefly.

Shifts in demand between traded goods

In Table 4.1 we summarize the principal effects of a shift of foreign or domestic demand from the import good to the export good. They are culled from the tables in Chapter 3 and pertain to the general case in which all goods are gross substitutes in consumption but no good is a perfect substitute for any other. We deal first with this case, then with certain special cases.

Outcomes in the general case

The impact effects in Table 4.1 are the same for pegged and flexible exchange rates, as the shift in demand has not had time to influence the bond and money markets. The steady-state results are different, however, as asset markets are involved over the long run. On impact, the shift in demand raises the price of the export good and, by way of substitution, raises the price of the nontraded good. Income rises, households start to save, and the current-account balance shifts into surplus. Under a pegged exchange rate, reserves rise through time, and the two domestic prices also rise, raising income further. Under a flexible rate, by contrast, the home currency appreciates through time, and the two domestic prices fall, reducing income until it returns to its initial level.

Responses in goods markets. The impact effects of a shift in demand from the import good to the export good can be interpreted with the aid of Figure 4.1. There, curve nn is the locus of sets of domestic prices that clear the market for the nontraded good. Its slope is necessarily positive when goods are gross substitutes; an increase in p_1 raises the demand for the nontraded good, and an increase in p_N is needed to clear the market for that good. The position of nn depends on the home-currency price of the import good, on saving and taxes (which join with income to determine domestic consumption), and on the size and composition of government spending.[1] Similarly, curve tt is the locus of sets of points that clear the market for the export good. Its slope is positive too, and its position depends on the same set of variables. (Equations for the curves used in this and the next chapter are given in tables appended to this chapter.)

Any disturbance that induces excess demand for the nontraded good at initial prices will raise nn, because an increase in p_N is needed to clear the market for that good. Similarly, any disturbance that induces excess demand for the export good will shift tt to the right, because an increase in p_1 is needed to clear the market. By implication, a shift of demand from the import good to the export good does not affect nn; at the initial set of market-clearing prices, it does not cause excess demand or supply in the market for the nontraded good. It does affect tt, however, moving it to $t't'$, by causing excess demand for the export good. Goods-market equilibrium is displaced immediately from p to p', raising both domestic prices. There is an instantaneous increase of Y, nominal income, and an equal increase of Y^d, disposable income. When both prices rise, moreover, the wage rate rises in the classical case and employment rises in the

---

[1] Its position does not depend on income, which is itself determined by p_N and p_1, as shown by Eq. (2.3a). It does depend indirectly on interest rates and wealth (because they affect the level of saving). For a diagram similar to Figure 4.1, see R. A. Mundell, *Monetary Theory*, Goodyear, Pacific Palisades, Calif., 1971, chap. 11.

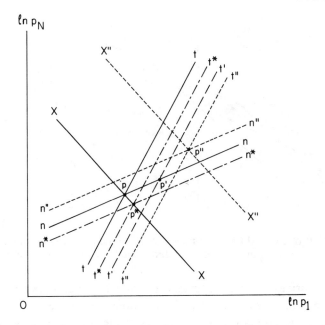

Figure 4.1 Shift of demand from the import good to the export good: impact and steady-state effects on goods markets under pegged and flexible exchange rates.

Keynesian case.[2] In the present instance, however, the sign of the change in relative prices is uncertain. From Eqs. (3.5) and (3.6),

$$\left(\frac{\delta p_1}{p_1}\right) - \left(\frac{\delta p_N}{p_N}\right) = (1/N_s)[u_{0N} + N_Y\sigma_N \\ + (1 - S_Y)(m_1\sigma_N - m_N\sigma_1)](\delta c_1^f - \delta c_{01})$$

and this expression is ambiguous (because we do not know the sizes of the relevant supply responses, σ_N and σ_1, relative to the expenditure effects, m_N and m_1).

The goods-market effects of this shift in demand can also be described with the aid of Figure 4.2, in which nominal income is plotted as a function of the exchange rate. Curve zz prevails instantaneously. Curve ZZ prevails in the steady state. To derive zz, we solve the market-clearing equations for the two domestic goods to obtain prices p_1 and p_N, given the exchange rate and other variables affecting the demands for goods, and

[2] When one price rises and the other falls, as happens in the steady state with a flexible exchange rate, we cannot know what happens to the wage rate or employment, even when there is no change in nominal income. (We return to this problem later, when we ask to what extent a flexible exchange rate can insulate an economy.)

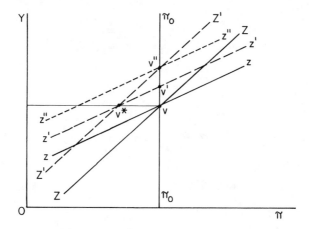

Figure 4.2 Shift of demand from the import good to the export good: impact and steady-state effects on nominal income under pegged and flexible exchange rates.

we use those prices to obtain nominal income, Y, which depends exclusively on p_1 and p_N. We come out with a relationship between Y and π that must prevail at all points in time, given the values of the other variables affecting the demands for goods. To derive ZZ, we repeat this procedure but impose the steady-state requirement that saving be zero. We come out with a relationship between Y and π that must prevail in the steady state, given the values of other relevant variables.

To prove that zz is upward sloping, one has only to show what a change in the exchange rate will do to curves nn and tt in Figure 4.1. Because an increase in π raises the home-currency price of the import good, it stimulates domestic demand for the nontraded good, shifting nn upward, and stimulates domestic and foreign demands for the export good, shifting tt rightward. It has thus to raise p_N and p_1, raising nominal income. It follows, of course, that the position of zz depends on the same parameters and variables that determine the positions of nn and tt. It likewise follows that a shift of demand to the export good raises zz to some such level as $z'z'$, because it raises p_N and p_1, thereby raising Y at the initial exchange rate.[3]

[3] The terms that define the shifts in zz, shown in the goods-market table at the end of this chapter, are the flexible-price analogues to the familiar Keynesian multipliers. They appear to be more complicated because they include the effects of changes in domestic prices. If we were to impound price changes, the terms would collapse into familiar Keynesian form. When a_N, $a_1 \rightarrow \infty$, so that σ_N, $\sigma_1 \rightarrow \infty$, the price changes go to zero (domestic supply elasticities are infinite), and the sizes of the shifts in zz come to depend on $(1/N_Y)$, where $N_Y = S_Y + m_0(1 - S_Y)$, the sum of the marginal propensities to save and import out of disposable income.

Curve ZZ is upward sloping for the same economic reasons. In the steady state, as well as on impact, demands for the domestic goods rise with π, raising the permanent levels of p_N and p_1 and thus raising the steady-state level of income. But ZZ is steeper than zz, because none of the income-raising effect of an increase in π is dissipated into saving. For this same reason, the shifts in ZZ resulting from goods-market disturbances are larger than the corresponding shifts in zz. This is shown in Figure 4.2, where the shift in demand to the export good displaces ZZ to $Z'Z'$, which lies above $z'z'$ at the initial exchange rate.[4]

Note, finally, that the position of zz depends in part on interest rates and wealth (because it depends on saving), and they are affected instantaneously by a change in the exchange rate. Accordingly, the slope of zz does not show the whole change in Y that takes place with a change in π. A depreciation of the home currency causes a rightward movement along zz, reflecting the "expenditure-switching" and output effects of the depreciation. It also causes an upward shift of zz, reflecting the "expenditure-changing" effect of the depreciation (the reduction in desired saving that takes place as wealth rises and the interest rate falls in response to the depreciation).[5] The slope of ZZ, by contrast, portrays the full effect of a change in the exchange rate on the long-run level of nominal income (because there is no saving in the steady state).

As the exchange rate cannot respond instantaneously to a shift in demand, the impact effects of the shift are the same in Figure 4.2 for pegged and flexible exchange rates. Goods-market equilibrium is displaced from v to v', where the short-run curve $z'z'$ intersects the exchange-rate schedule $\pi_0\pi_0$. Income rises by the distance vv'. But the steady-state effects differ fundamentally, for the reason invoked in Chapter 3.

Under a pegged exchange rate, goods-market disturbances have permanent effects on income, and its steady-state level can be said to be determined in the goods markets. Thus, steady-state equilibrium is established at v'' in Figure 4.2, the point at which $Z'Z'$ intersects the initial exchange-rate schedule $\pi_0\pi_0$. There is a permanent increase in income (the distance vv''). By inference, the short-run curve must move gradually

[4] Using the equations for zz and ZZ, it can be shown that the latter is steeper by $S_Y(N_u/N_s)(N_t/N_w)$, and that the shift in ZZ is bigger by $S_Y(N_u/N_s)[(N_0 + \sigma_1 u_{0N})/N_w]$.

[5] From the solution of Eq. (3.4), it can be shown that δY includes the term $(N_u/N_s)(-S_W)V_\pi(\delta\pi/\pi)$. The slope of zz does not include that term, however, because the term describes the effect of the change in wealth induced by an exchange-rate change. It appears as an expenditure-changing effect on the position of zz. The distinction between "expenditure-switching" and "expenditure-changing" effects is borrowed from H. G. Johnson, "Toward a General Theory of the Balance of Payments," *International Trade and Economic Growth*, Harvard University Press, Cambridge, Mass., 1961, pp. 153–68.

upward, from $z'z'$ to $z''z''$, as the economy travels to the new steady state.

Under a flexible exchange rate, by contrast, goods-market disturbances do not have permanent effects on income, as income is determined in the asset markets, given the requirement that saving to zero. It is instead the steady-state exchange rate that can be said to be determined in the goods markets. Thus, steady-state equilibrium is established at v^* in Figure 4.2, the point at which $Z'Z'$ intersects $z'z'$. Income returns to its initial level as the economy travels to the new steady state, and the home currency appreciates (by the distance vv^*) to clear the goods markets. It is, in fact, possible to generalize from this example. Any shift in the pattern of demand that causes a permanent increase in nominal income under a pegged exchange rate must cause a permanent appreciation of the home currency under a flexible rate.

Before turning to behavior in the asset markets, to explain the reasons for this difference between long-run outcomes, let us look more closely at adjustments in goods markets and at the changes in steady-state prices, using Figure 4.1. Curve XX, drawn through point p, is the locus of sets of prices that correspond to a constant level of nominal income. It is obtained from Eq. (2.3a). The slope of XX is thus governed by the steady-state relationship

$$\left(\frac{dp_N}{p_N}\right) = -(\sigma_1/\sigma_N)\left(\frac{dp_1}{p_1}\right)$$

and its position is defined by the market-clearing level of nominal income.

Under a pegged exchange rate, the gradual shift from $z'z'$ to $z''z''$ in Figure 4.2 reflects rising demands for both goods. It is matched in Figure 4.1 by outward shifts in both goods-market curves, from $t't'$ to $t''t''$ and from nn to $n''n''$. The two domestic prices are higher, which means that income must be higher too. The size of the long-run change in Y is denoted by the shift from XX to $X''X''$ (a shift that corresponds to the distance vv'' in Figure 4.2).

Under a flexible exchange rate, the domestic currency appreciates gradually, reducing the home-currency price of the import good. Because goods are gross substitutes in consumption, demands for both domestic goods decline, shifting $t't'$ backward to t^*t^* and shifting nn downward to n^*n^*. The shifts in these two curves, moreover, must cause them to intersect at some point on XX, such as p^*, because income must return to what it was initially. As n^*n^* lies below nn, p^* must lie to the southeast of p; the price of the export good comes to be higher and that of the nontraded

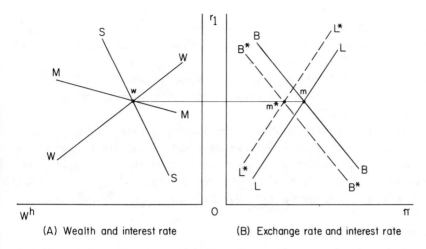

(A) Wealth and interest rate   (B) Exchange rate and interest rate

Figure 4.3 Shift of demand from the import good to the export good: steady-state effects on asset markets under a flexible exchange rate.

good comes to be lower. The change in relative prices is unambiguous in the long run, whereas it was ambiguous in the short run (and remains ambiguous in the long run under a pegged exchange rate).

Responses in asset markets. In Figure 4.3A, we draw three new curves. Curve SS is the locus of values of the domestic interest rate and wealth, r_1 and W^h, at which there is no saving, given the steady-state level of disposable income. Curve WW is the locus of values of r_1 and W^h that clear the market for the domestic bond, given the supply of bonds available to households. Curve MM is the locus of values that clear the money market, given the money supply.

Curve SS is upward sloping because an increase in wealth causes dissaving unless it is offset by an increase in the domestic interest rate. By implication, an increase in steady-state disposable income will shift SS downward, as an increase in Y^d will raise saving unless the interest rate is reduced. Curve WW is downward sloping because an increase in wealth raises the demand for the domestic bond and calls for a decrease in the interest rate to clear the bond market. (In other words, there is excess demand in the bond market above WW and excess supply below it.) It follows that an increase in the supply of bonds available to households, resulting from an interval of budget deficits or an open-market sale by the central bank, will shift WW upward, as there would be excess supply in the bond market at a constant interest rate. Finally, curve MM is upward sloping because an increase in wealth raises the demand for money and calls for an increase in the interest rate to clear the money market. (There is excess supply in the money market above *MM* and excess demand below it.) It follows that an increase in the money supply, resulting from an increase in central-bank holdings of bonds or reserves, will shift *MM* downward, as there would be excess supply in the money market at a constant interest rate.[6]

It is at once apparent from these definitions that asset markets can be in instantaneous equilibrium whenever *WW* and *MM* intersect. They can be in steady-state equilibrium, however, only when the three curves intersect, as they do at *w* in Figure 4.3A. The definitions of *SS*, *WW*, and *MM* hold equally for pegged and flexible exchange rates, but the curves behave quite differently. This is why goods-market outcomes differed in the long run in Figures 4.1 and 4.2.

Under a flexible exchange rate, asset markets are cleared instantaneously by the interest rate and exchange rate. The requisite changes in r_1 are recorded explicitly in Figure 4.3A as movements along *WW* and *MM;* the changes in π are recorded implicitly as movements along those curves, because a change in π alters home-currency holdings of the foreign bond and shows up as a change in wealth. The positions of *WW* and *MM* are not affected by market-clearing changes in r_1 and π. In fact, their positions are not affected by anything that happens as a result of the shift in demand to the export good. The location of the bond-market curve depends on the supply of bonds available to households (the total supply *less* central-bank holdings), and it is not altered by the shift in demand. The location of the money-market curve depends on the supply of money (central-bank holdings of bonds and reserves), and it is not altered either, because a flexible exchange rate precludes changes in the stock of reserves. Therefore, the disturbance examined here cannot affect the interest rate or wealth, even temporarily, under a flexible exchange rate. Asset-market equilibrium must remain at *w* in Figure 4.3A. In the steady state, moreover, *SS* must intersect the asset-market curves, and when they do not shift, *SS* cannot shift either. By implication, there can be no permanent change in disposable income–which means in turn that there can be no permanent change in total income (as *Y* is equal to Y^d *plus* $\bar{G}$ in the steady state). In brief, Figure 4.3A explains why the short-run income curve remains at *z'z'* in Figure 4.2 and why it intersects *Z'Z'* at the initial

[6] The positions of *SS*, *WW*, and *MM* depend in addition on the foreign interest rate, $\bar{r}_0$, but we can ignore its role until Chapter 5. Notice also that *MM* is drawn to be flatter than *SS*, which is not necessarily so. We return to this point too in Chapter 5.

level of income. With a flexible exchange rate, steady-state equilibrium can be reestablished only when income returns to its initial level.

We have said that the exchange rate affects household wealth by affecting the value of home-currency holdings of the foreign bond. We have also shown in Figure 4.2 that a shift in demand from the import good to the export good causes the home currency to appreciate. Yet we have just discovered in Figure 4.3A that wealth does not change, even momentarily, on account of the shift in demand. The resolution of this apparent paradox resides in the behavior of saving and the resulting changes in holdings of the foreign bond during the transition to the new steady state. The shift in demand to the export good induces saving and also generates a current-account surplus. Both of these are matched by purchases of the foreign bond–the only asset whose supply is not policy determined. But the appreciation of the home currency resulting from the current-account surplus can be shown to offset the growth in holdings of that bond. It keeps constant the home-currency value of those holdings, preventing any change in wealth.

To illustrate, we turn to Figure 4.3B, where the market-clearing equations for bonds and money are translated into two new curves. Curve BB is the locus of sets of values of r_1 and π that clear the bond market, given the supply of bonds available to households and the integral of saving. Curve LL is the locus of sets of values that clear the money market, given the supply of money and the integral of saving. Thus, BB is the counterpart of WW, whereas LL is the counterpart of MM, and the slopes of the new curves can be inferred from those of their counterparts. Because a depreciation of the home currency raises household wealth, it raises the demands for bonds and money. The interest rate must fall to clear the bond market (so that BB is downward sloping); the interest rate must rise to clear the money market (so that LL is upward sloping).

Point m in Figure 4.3B, where BB and LL intersect, defines values of r_1 and π that can clear both asset markets at a point in time, given the supplies of bonds and money and the integral of saving, W^{hs}. It follows, of course, that BB, LL, and point m will shift up and down with WW, MM, and point w in Figure 4.3A. But BB and LL have also to shift with changes in W^{hs}, and this does not happen to WW and MM. An interval of saving will raise W^{hs}, and this will drive BB and LL to the left by raising the demands for domestic bonds and money. Both curves will shift leftward at the same rate, moreover, keeping the domestic interest rate constant but causing the home currency to appreciate. The appreciation reduces the home-currency value of holdings of the foreign bond by just enough to offset the acquisitions of that bond that are the counterpart of saving. Thus, the appreciation shown in Figure 4.2 is seen to be consistent with asset-market equilibrium at w in Figure 4.3A, where wealth and the interest rate are constant.

It is the task of Chapter 6 to show that the path of saving is such as to produce the required acquisitions of the foreign bond and the appreciation of the home currency that brings income back to its initial level. Even at this juncture, however, we can show that the appropriate behavior of saving is implied by the sign of the short-run change in Y^d. We have seen that income rises on impact, raising disposable income by the same amount. We have also seen that there is no immediate change in the interest rate, exchange rate, or wealth. Therefore, saving must increase immediately in response to the shift of demand to the export good.

Under a pegged exchange rate, asset-market outcomes are described by Figure 4.4. We begin by drawing *SS, WW,* and *MM* just as we did before. When the exchange rate is pegged, however, asset markets behave differently and so does the diagram. (1) Because the exchange rate does not change, wealth cannot change instantaneously. The home-currency value of holdings of the foreign bond can be altered immediately only by buying or selling the bond in exchange for money (reserves), and these transactions do not alter wealth. Accordingly, changes in wealth can take place only gradually, as a result of saving or dissaving. (2) The position of the money-market curve *MM* becomes endogenous, because there can be changes in reserves that alter the supply of money. Shifts in *MM* can take place instantaneously, moreover, because households can shift freely between foreign bonds and domestic money. The central bank stands ready to buy or sell unlimited quantities of foreign currency.

These two differences have, in turn, two implications. Because the stock of wealth can change only gradually, momentary asset-market equilibrium is determined uniquely by the size of the existing stock of wealth and the position of the bond-market curve. The money-market curve shifts automatically to meet the bond-market curve where the latter intersects the initial level of wealth. Wealth and the supply of bonds available to households determine the interest rate. Wealth and the interest rate, in turn, determine the demand for money and, therefore, reserves. Furthermore, steady-state equilibrium is established where the appropriate *SS* curve intersects *WW,* as at point w' in Figure 4.4A, and *MM* moves to meet them there. The requirements that saving be zero and that the bond market clear combine to determine the steady-state levels of wealth and

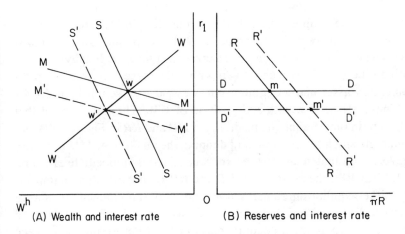

(A) Wealth and interest rate   (B) Reserves and interest rate

Figure 4.4 Shift of demand from the import good to the export good: steady-state effects on asset markets under a pegged exchange rate.

the interest rate. These together determine the demand for money and steady-state holdings of reserves.

We are able now to see how the shift in demand to the export good affects asset markets with a pegged exchange rate and what happens to wealth, the interest rate, and reserves. None of these variables changes instantaneously, because there is no immediate change in wealth and no change whatsoever in the variables affecting the position of WW. (The impact effects are thus the same as they were with a flexible exchange rate.) But asset markets must adjust eventually to accommodate events in the goods markets. Starting with Figure 4.2, we find that there must be a permanent increase in disposable income equal to the permanent increase in nominal income. Turning to Figure 4.4A, curve SS must shift to $S'S'$ because of the increase in disposable income and steady-state equilibrium must be established at w' (there being no shift in WW). Wealth rises and the interest rate declines. By implication, MM must move to $M'M'$, which tells us that reserves have risen.

The behavior of reserves is shown explicitly in Figure 4.4B, where the curves DD and RR are the loci of values of r_1 and $\bar{\pi}R$ that clear the bond and money markets, respectively. Curve DD is horizontal because the stock of reserves does not appear in the bond-market equation. Nevertheless, DD shifts up and down with WW because it responds to the same disturbances. It also shifts up with a decrease in W^{hs} and down with an increase. Curve RR is downward sloping because an increase in reserves adds to the money supply and calls for a reduction in the interest rate to clear the money market. Furthermore, RR shifts up and down with MM (unless the shifts in MM are due to changes in reserves). Finally, it shifts up with an increase in W^{hs} and down with a decrease.

Momentary asset-market equilibrium, we said, is given in Figure 4.4A by the initial stock of wealth and position of WW. The attributes of that equilibrium, in turn, define the positions of DD and RR in Figure 4.4B, determining the stock of reserves (and defining the position of MM in Figure 4.4A). As a shift in demand to the export good has no immediate effect on WW, MM, or W^{hs}, the positions of DD and RR are not affected on impact. Asset-market equilibrium remains at m, and there is no immediate change in reserves. But wealth rises through time, as shown in Figure 4.4A, and this means that there must be an increase in W^{hs} (that saving takes place on the way to the new steady state, just as it did in the flexible-rate case). Accordingly, DD drops to $D'D'$, and RR rises to $R'R'$. Asset-market equilibrium moves gradually to m', and there is a permanent increase in reserves.

When we studied the responses of goods and asset markets under a flexible exchange rate, we saw that a shift in demand between traded goods could not alter the location of w in Figure 4.3A, so that long-run equilibrium in Figure 4.2 had to be established at the initial income level. The endogeneity of the exchange rate made possible that outcome. Under a pegged exchange rate, it is the endogeneity of the money supply, resulting from changes in reserves, that permits the economy to achieve long-run equilibrium. Goods-market equilibrium must be established at v'' in Figure 4.2, where $Z'Z'$ intersects $\pi_0\pi_0$, because the exchange rate cannot change. Accordingly, there must be a permanent change in income, which means that SS must shift in Figure 4.4A. Asset-market equilibrium must be established at w', where $S'S'$ intersects WW. It is the endogeneity of the position of MM that makes possible this outcome.

Recall in this connection the points we made earlier about the determination of the balance of payments and the determination of a flexible exchange rate. In Chapter 1 we said that the monetary approach to balance-of-payments theory is valid to a first approximation for a pegged exchange rate; the stock of reserves is determined by the money market, given the level of income and the interest rate, which are determined in the goods and bond markets, respectively. It is not valid, however, for a flexible exchange rate; the exchange rate is determined in the short run by the bond and money markets jointly, and it is determined in the long run by the goods markets (but depends even then on the level of disposable income, which is determined by the bond and money markets and by the requirement that saving be zero). In Chapter 3 we called attention to these same propositions in a different context, showing that the bond-market and money-market equations can be solved sequentially with a pegged exchange rate but must be solved simultaneously with a flexible exchange rate.

The special goods-market cases

In Chapter 2 we claimed that our three-product model can generate a series of special goods-market cases. By assuming that certain pairs of goods are perfect substitutes in consumption, the model can be made to behave like some of the two-product models that have been used most frequently in balance-of-payments analysis. (1) When the nontraded good is assumed to be a perfect substitute for the import good, the model resembles an economy that produces two traded goods – an export good and an import-competing good. This is the traded-goods variant of the model. (2) When the export good is assumed to be a perfect substitute for the import good, the model resembles a conventional small economy that faces fixed terms of trade and produces two commodities – the nontraded good and a composite traded good. This is the composite-good variant. (3) When the nontraded good is assumed to be a perfect substitute for the export good, the model resembles an economy that is completely specialized in the production of a single export good. This is the single-good variant.

In the traded-goods and single-good variants, there is, in effect, no nontraded good, and relative price changes can take place only between traded goods. In the composite-good variant, they can take place only between traded and nontraded goods, as the terms of trade are determined exogenously.

To generate the traded-goods variant, we need merely assume that $u_{0N} \to \infty$. In this limiting case, curve nn in Figure 4.1 becomes perpendicular to the vertical axis. The price of the import-competing good (alias the nontraded good) cannot change unless there is a change in the foreign-currency price of the import good, $\bar{p}_0^f$, or in the exchange rate, π, at which that price is converted into home currency. On impact, when tt shifts to the right with the shift in demand to the export good, p_1 rises, p_N does not change, and the change in relative domestic prices, p_1/p_N, becomes unambiguously positive. (It is tantamount, moreover, to an improvement in the terms of trade, because $p_N = p_0$.) Gross domestic product rises, and so does disposable income, just as they did in the general case described by Table 4.1. But this result is due entirely to the increase in the value of the output of the export good; there is no change in the value of the output of the import-competing good.

In the steady state, the same things happen with a pegged exchange rate. Curve tt shifts to the right in Figure 4.1, and long-run equilibrium is established to the right of p. There is a permanent increase in the price of the export good, in nominal income, and in disposable income. Wealth rises, the interest rate declines, and there is an inflow of reserves. Under a flexible exchange rate, the appreciation of the home currency causes the shift to t^*t^* in Figure 4.1, but it also causes a downward shift in nn resembling the shift to n^*n^*. The appreciation reduces the home-currency price of the import good, and p_N must fall by the same amount. The new equilibrium point is to the southeast of p, just as it is in Figure 4.1, and there is no significant qualitative difference in the steady-state outcome.

To sum up, the character of the second domestic good–whether it is truly nontradable or is virtually tradable because it is a perfect substitute for the import good–has only one important implication for the results of a shift in demand between traded goods. In the traded-goods variant of the model, the sign of the change in relative domestic prices is never ambiguous (and is equivalent to a change in the terms of trade).

To generate the composite-good variant, we need merely assume that $u_{10} \to \infty$ (so that $u_t \to \infty$). In this limiting case, curve tt in Figure 4.1 becomes perpendicular to the horizontal axis. The price of the export good cannot change unless there is a change in the foreign-currency price of the import good or in the exchange rate. In this case, however, tt cannot respond to a shift in demand between traded goods, and there is no change whatsoever in any variable, not even temporarily. To put the point in different terms, it is not meaningful to talk of a shift in demand between traded goods when they are deemed to be perfect substitutes, and in the context of our model it does not matter whether they are so regarded at home, abroad, or globally.

To generate the single-good variant, we need merely assume that $u_{1N} \to \infty$. In this limiting case, however, Figure 4.1 cannot illustrate the outcomes. It serves only to remind us that p_N and p_1 cannot move independently–that relative domestic prices are fixed. (Curves nn and tt in Figure 4.1 come to be identical, and the slope of the new, single curve is exactly unity.) But when both prices move together, we can use Figure

4.2 instead. As $(dp_N/p_N) = (dp_1/p_1)$, the change in nominal income can be written as

$$dY = (\sigma_N + \sigma_1)\left(\frac{dp_1}{p_1}\right)$$

and the changes in the two domestic prices can be inferred from the changes in nominal income recorded in Figure 4.2. With a shift in demand to the export good, for example, the two domestic prices must rise immediately by the same amounts; they must rise further in the long run with a pegged exchange rate; and they must return to their initial levels with a flexible rate. Thus, this variant is the only one in which a flexible exchange rate is able to prevent any permanent change in the wage rate or employment; they have to return to their initial levels. In language we shall use at a later point, the flexible rate is able to insulate the labor market from the shift in demand, not merely to insulate nominal income. The reason here is trivial, however, because there is no scope for changes in relative domestic prices; the economy is completely specialized. We encounter a more interesting case below, when we study the effects of an increase in $\bar{p}_0^f$ using the composite-good variant.

One last point should be made about the single-good variant. The steady-state change in the exchange rate, obtained from Eq. (3.24a), reduces to

$$\left(\frac{d\pi}{\pi}\right) = -(1/u_\pi)(dc_1^f - dc_{01})$$

where u_π is the Marshall-Lerner-Robinson condition.[7]

Let us recapitulate. When a country produces two traded goods, with the foreign supply of the import good perfectly elastic, a shift in demand to the export good improves the terms of trade and, within the country, raises the price of the export good relative to that of the import-competing good. This is true on impact and in the long run, under both exchange-rate regimes. When a country produces only an export good, the shift in demand to that good raises its price initially and does so permanently too with a pegged exchange rate. With a flexible rate, however, income must return eventually to its initial level, and this means that the price of the export good must also return to its initial level, providing full insulation from the trade-balance disturbance. Finally, a shift of demand between traded

[7] See note 11 to Chapter 3.

goods has no economic meaning when a country produces a composite traded good and thus faces fixed terms of trade.

The special bond-market case

The degree of asset-market integration (capital mobility) is measured in our model by the extent of substitutability between the domestic bond and the foreign bond. It depends on the size of B_{10}, which measures the change in demand for the domestic bond induced by a change in the foreign interest rate, and the size of B_{01}, which measures the change in demand for the foreign bond induced by a change in the domestic interest rate. Furthermore, $B_{11} + B_{01} = -L_{11}$, and there is no reason to suppose that the interest sensitivity of the demand for money varies with the extent of substitutability between the two bonds. Therefore, an increase in $-B_{01}$ will be matched by an increase in B_{11}, and it has the effect of flattening the bond-market curve WW. With perfect substitutability, indeed, that curve becomes horizontal. By implication, an increase in substitutability enlarges the change in the domestic interest rate resulting from a change in the foreign rate but reduces the change in the domestic rate resulting from any other disturbance. In the limiting case of perfect substitutability, the domestic rate changes by the full amount of the change in the foreign rate and does not respond at all to any other disturbance. Let us see how perfect asset-market integration affects the outcomes in Table 4.1.

As goods-market disturbances do not impinge immediately on the bond and money markets, the degree of asset-market integration has no relevance for the impact effects of the shift in demand. Thereafter, moreover, its influence is limited. When foreign and domestic bonds are perfect substitutes, WW becomes horizontal in Figures 4.3A and 4.4A, and BB becomes horizontal in Figure 4.3B. Under a flexible exchange rate, however, the slope of WW does not matter, as none of the curves shifts in Figure 4.3A. Furthermore, the slope of BB does not influence the outcome in Figure 4.3B, as the size of the exchange-rate change comes from Figure 4.2, and the size of the shift in LL required to achieve that change in π is independent of the slope of BB. By inference, the degree of asset-market integration does not even influence the size of the change in W^{hs} (the amount of saving that has to occur on the way to the new steady state).

Under a pegged exchange rate, there are changes in the sizes of some outcomes, but no change in any sign. The magnitude of the shift from SS to $S'S'$ in Figure 4.4A is determined by the size of the change in income given by Figure 4.2. It is unaffected by asset-market integration. But when WW is horizontal, the shift in SS implies a larger increase in wealth and, therefore, a larger volume of saving during the transition to the steady state. Furthermore, the change in the location of w' affects the size of the shift in MM, and this affects the size of the increase in reserves. We cannot know with certainty, however, whether the increase is made larger or smaller. Because there is a larger increase in wealth, the shift of RR to $R'R'$ is larger in Figure 4.4B, and this tends to amplify the increase in reserves. But there is no downward shift in DD (no change in r_1), and this tends to limit the increase in reserves. Without more information, we cannot know which effect will dominate.[8]

To sum up, the degree of asset-market integration has no bearing on the impact effects of the shift in demand under either exchange-rate regime and no bearing on any of the steady-state effects when the exchange rate is flexible. When the rate is pegged, moreover, its influence is merely to limit the change in the domestic interest rate and, therefore, to alter the sizes of the changes in wealth and reserves. As these conclusions are perfectly general – they do not depend on the nature of the shift in demand – we shall not refer again to asset-market integration until Chapter 5, when we examine asset-market disturbances.

Other goods-market disturbances

Shifts in demand between domestic goods

The effects of a shift of domestic demand from the export good to the non-traded good are summarized in Table 4.2. The effects on goods markets are shown in Figure 4.5. A shift in demand from the export good to the nontraded good raises the price of the nontraded good immediately and lowers the price of the export good. The effect on nominal income is ambiguous, depending on whether the increase in the value of nontraded-good production exceeds the decrease in the value of export-good production. If income rises on impact, there will be saving and a current-account surplus. (Although imports rise with income, the reduc-

---

[8] Putting the point in terms of Figure 4.4A, the effect on the size of the steady-state increase in reserves depends on the slopes of SS and MM. If the former is steeper, as drawn, the increase in reserves will be smaller; when WW is horizontal, the shift from SS to $S'S'$ calls for a larger shift in MM. But SS can be flatter than MM, and in this case, the increase in reserves will be larger. We discuss these possibilities thoroughly in Chapter 5, when we come to analyze open-market operations; at that point, the slopes of SS and MM determine the influence of asset-market integration on the size of the change in income (i.e., the effectiveness of monetary policy).

Table 4.2. *Shift of domestic demand from the export good to the nontraded good*

Variable	Impact effect	Steady-state effect	
		Pegged rate	Flexible rate
p_N	+	+	+
p_1	−	−	−
p_1/p_N	−	−	−
Y^d	?	?	0
Y	?	?	0
r_1	0	?[a]	0
$\bar{\pi}R$	0	?	0
π	0	0	?
W^h	0	?	0

Signs for $\delta c_{N1} > 0$.
[a] Goes to zero when domestic and foreign bonds are perfect substitutes.

tion in p_1 generates a larger increase in exports.) Under a pegged exchange rate, reserves will rise through time, and income will rise further than it did on impact. Under a flexible exchange rate, the home currency will appreciate, causing income to decline until it returns to its initial level. Alternatively, if income falls on impact, there will be dissaving and a current-account deficit. (The fall in income tends to reduce imports, but this effect is swamped by a price effect; the increase in p_N induces substitution of the import for the nontraded good.) Under a pegged exchange rate, reserves and income will decline through time. Under a flexible rate, the home currency will depreciate, raising income until it returns to its initial level.

The general case. When all goods are partial substitutes, a shift in demand between domestic goods has clear-cut effects on both of the goods-market curves. In Figure 4.5, nn shifts upward to $n'n'$, reflecting the increase in demand for the nontraded good, and tt shifts backward to $t't'$, reflecting the decrease in demand for the export good. Goods-market equilibrium is displaced to p', which must lie to the northwest of the initial point p.[9] One price rises, the other falls, and the change in nominal income is ambiguous. (An increase in Y is shown at p' but is not a necessary consequence here. If income falls, the counterpart of p' lies below XX.)

[9] To prove that p' is northwest of p, one must prove that the vertical shift in tt exceeds the vertical shift in nn. This can be done with the equations for tt and nn given at the end of this chapter.

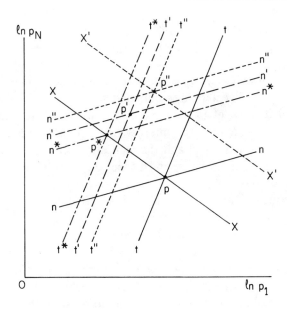

Figure 4.5 Shift of demand from the export good to the nontraded good: impact and steady-state effects on goods markets under pegged and flexible exchange rates.

Turning from impact to steady-state effects, the changes are ambiguous too. They depend on the direction of the change in income. If income rises on impact, households will start to save, and both goods-market curves will shift outward under a pegged exchange rate, enlarging the increase in income. This is the result depicted in Figure 4.5, where $t't'$ shifts to $t''t''$ and $n'n'$ to $n''n''$, and goods-market equilibrium is displaced from p' to p''. (In this case, wealth and reserves will rise and the interest rate will fall.) If income falls on impact, both goods-market curves will shift inward, enlarging the decrease in income. When income rises, as in Figure 4.5, the initial reduction in p_1 is partially reversed. When income falls, the initial increase in p_N is partially reversed. These reversals, however, cannot be large enough to cancel the impact effects. In the new steady state, p_N will be higher than it was initially, and p_1 will be lower.

Because we do not know what happens to income under a pegged exchange rate, we cannot predict the sign of the steady-state change in a flexible exchange rate. When income rises in the pegged-rate case, the home currency will appreciate in the flexible-rate case. This is what is shown in Figure 4.5, where $n'n'$ shifts back to $n*n*$, $t't'$ shifts back to $t*t*$, and the two curves intersect at $p*$. When income falls in the pegged-rate case, the home currency will depreciate in the flexible-rate case. In both instances, however, p^* will lie on XX and must be northwest of p, so that p_N must rise and p_1 must fall with a flexible exchange rate.

The special goods-market cases. This particular shift in demand is a good one for the study of the special cases obtained when pairs of goods are perfect substitutes. In two of those three cases, we can determine the signs of the changes in income, the interest rate, wealth, and reserves when the exchange rate is pegged and the sign of the change in the exchange rate when it is flexible. In the third case, the shift in demand has no effect on the economy.

In the traded-goods variant (where $u_{0N} \to \infty$), a shift in demand between domestic goods is indistinguishable from a shift in demand between traded goods. When the nontraded good is a perfect substitute for the import good, a shift in demand from the export good to the nontraded good is equivalent to a shift from the export good to the import good. In this particular limiting case, then, the effects of the disturbance under study here are identical absolutely but opposite in sign to those of the previous disturbance.[10] The domestic price of the import-competing good (alias the nontraded good) is tied to $\pi \bar{p}_0^f$, and nn becomes horizontal, as shown in Figure 4.6A. The shift in demand displaces equilibrium from p to p' on impact, the price of the export good declines, and nominal income falls. With a pegged exchange rate, steady-state equilibrium is established at p''; there is a permanent reduction in income, together with an increase in the interest rate, a decline in wealth, and a loss of reserves. With a flexible exchange rate, the home currency must depreciate; because p' lies below XX in Figure 4.6A, there must be an upward shift of nn to n^*n^* and an outward shift of $t't'$ to t^*t^* to establish equilibrium at some such point at p^*. (The shift to n^*n^* can take place even though that curve is horizontal, because an increase in π raises the home-currency price of the import good and calls for an identical increase in the price of the import-competing good.)

In the composite-good variant (where $u_{10} \to \infty$), the roles of prices are reversed, and so is the sign of the change in income. It is the home-currency price of the export good that is tied to $\pi \bar{p}_0^f$, so that tt becomes vertical in Figure 4.6B. The shift in demand displaces equilibrium from p to p', the price of the nontraded good rises, and so does income. Under a

---

[10] To prove that they are exactly equivalent, compare the results of the disturbances δc_{N1} and δc_{01} in Eqs. (3.5), (3.6), (3.22a), (3.23a), (3.24a), (3.21b), (3.22b), and (3.23b) when $u_{0N} \to \infty$. In Eq. (3.6), for example, the change in p_1 is given by $(1/N_s')[\delta c_{N1} - (\delta c_1^f - \delta c_{01})]$, where $N_s' = u_t + u_{1N}' + u_{1N} + u_E + [1 - m_1(1 - S_Y)]\sigma_1$.

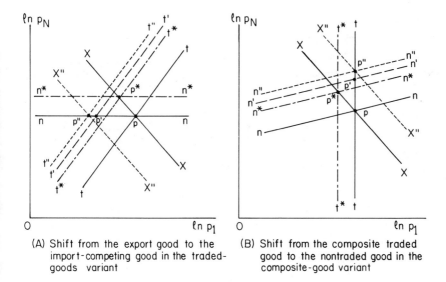

(A) Shift from the export good to the import-competing good in the traded-goods variant

(B) Shift from the composite traded good to the nontraded good in the composite-good variant

Figure 4.6 Shifts of demand in the special goods-market cases: impact and steady-state effects on goods markets under pegged and flexible exchange rates.

pegged exchange rate, then, $n'n'$ shifts to $n''n''$, and the economy moves to p''. There is an increase in steady-state income, together with a decline in the interest rate, and increases in wealth and reserves. Under a flexible exchange rate, the home currency must appreciate, causing the two curves to shift from $n'n'$ to $n*n*$ and from $t't'$ to $t*t*$, and displacing equilibrium to $p*$.

Finally, in the single-good variant (where $u_{1N} \to \infty$), there can be no economic meaning to a shift in demand between domestic goods, because the relevant goods are perfect substitutes. Therefore, no variable changes.

To sum up, we contrast the results obtained in the first and second limiting cases by looking at them from a different standpoint. When the nontraded good is a perfect substitute for the import good, the shift in demand under study here is tantamount to a shift in demand from a domestic good to a foreign good. The effect is thus deflationary under a pegged rate, and the home currency depreciates under a flexible rate. But when instead the export good is the perfect substitute for the import good, the same disturbance is tantamount to a shift in demand from a foreign good to a domestic good. The effect is thus inflationary under a pegged rate, and the home currency appreciates under a flexible rate.

Table 4.3. *Increase in the price of the import good*

Variable	Impact effect	Steady-state effect	
		Pegged rate	Flexible rate
p_N	+	+	+
p_1	+	+	−
p_1/p_N	?	?	−
Y^d	+	+	0
Y	+	+	0
r_1	0	$-^a$	0
$\bar{\pi}R$	0	+	0
π	0	0	−
W^h	0	+	0

Signs for $\delta\bar{p}_0^f > 0$.
[a] Goes to zero when domestic and foreign bonds are perfect substitutes.

A change in foreign prices

The effects of an increase in the foreign price $\bar{p}_0^f$ are summarized in Table 4.3, and the effects on goods markets are shown in Figure 4.7. The effects of this disturbance are similar in many ways to those of a shift in demand from the import good to the export good – not surprisingly, because it induces a similar shift of demand. In this instance, however, the shift is to the export good and to the nontraded good. On impact, the increase in $\bar{p}_0^f$ raises both domestic prices and nominal income. It induces saving and a current-account surplus. Under a pegged exchange rate, reserves rise through time, and so do domestic prices, raising income further. Under a flexible rate, the home currency appreciates through time, reducing both domestic prices relative to what they were on impact and bringing income back to its initial level. But the appreciation affects the demand for the export good strongly enough to reverse the short-run increase in p_1 while only offsetting partially the short-run increase in p_N. There is a permanent change in relative prices.

The general case. When all goods are partial substitutes, an increase in the foreign-currency price of the import good has three distinct effects on domestic goods markets: (1) an immediate increase in the domestic demand for the nontraded good, (2) a similar increase in the domestic demand for the export good, and (3) an increase in the foreign demand for the export good. The first effect is reflected in an upward shift of *nn* to

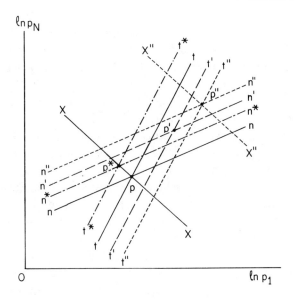

Figure 4.7 Increase in the price of the import good: impact and steady-state effects on goods markets under pegged and flexible exchange rates.

$n'n'$ in Figure 4.7. The second and third effects are reflected in an outward shift of tt to $t't'$. The economy moves at once from p to p', both domestic prices rise, and income rises too (but we cannot be sure about the change in relative domestic prices). The usual results ensue. Under a pegged exchange rate, both curves move outward, to $n''n''$ and $t''t''$, and equilibrium is displaced from p' to p''. There is a permanent increase in income, a decline in the interest rate, and increases in wealth and reserves. As the movement from p' to p'' involves an increase in both prices, the change in relative domestic prices is still ambiguous. Under a flexible exchange rate, the home currency must appreciate, shifting $n'n'$ to n^*n^* and $t't'$ to t^*t^*, until the two curves intersect at some such point as p^* lying on XX. The results are similar to those associated with a shift in demand between traded goods.

But something is peculiar here and calls for explanation. Curve t^*t^* lies to the left of tt in Figure 4.7, and n^*n^* lies above nn. Under a flexible exchange rate, there is a permanent increase in p_N and a decrease in p_1. This outcome reflects the fact that the change in the exchange rate is less than proportional to the change in the foreign-currency price of the import good (so that there is an increase in $\pi \bar{p}_0^i$, its price in home currency), and this fact reflects in turn the special character of the disturbance. Because we assume that $\bar{p}_0^f$ rises by itself (there is no increase in $\bar{p}_N^f$, the price of the foreign nontraded good, or in $\bar{C}^f$, total foreign expenditure), the price increase constitutes a real disturbance, affecting relative prices and real variables in the outside world, and it is able therefore to affect relative prices and real variables in the domestic economy.

The easiest way to prove these statements is to show why the exchange-rate change cannot be proportional to the change in $\bar{p}_0^f$. If it were proportional, $\pi\bar{p}_0^f$ would not change, and at unchanged domestic prices, p_1 and p_N, the domestic demand for the nontraded good would be what it was initially. Curves n^*n^* and nn would coincide, and steady-state equilibrium would have to be established at p, the original point on XX. For this to happen, however, t^*t^* would have to coincide with tt, and this cannot occur if the exchange-rate change is proportional to the change in $\bar{p}_0^f$. The domestic demand for the export good would be what it was initially, but the foreign demand would be smaller, and t^*t^* would lie to the left of tt. (If the change in π were proportional to the change in $\bar{p}_0^f$, foreigners would confront a change in relative prices. The prices of both traded goods would be higher than they were to start, but the price of the foreign nontraded good would be unchanged. The foreign demand for traded goods would thus have to fall.)

In brief, a change in the exchange rate that would preclude changes in domestic demands for domestic goods–the first and second changes mentioned at the start of this discussion–would reverse the sign of the change in the foreign demand for the export good–the third change in demand mentioned above. To reach equilibrium on the XX curve, it is thus necessary for the change in the exchange rate to be smaller absolutely than the change in $\bar{p}_0^f$. Curve n^*n^* must lie above nn, and this means that t^*t^* must lie to the left of tt (but by less than it would in the case of a proportional change in π).

For those who prefer algebra to diagrams, we supply a second, more general proof. It is obtained by writing out the total derivative of the foreign demand for the export good on the assumption that p_1 is constant:[11]

---

[11] Working with Eq. (2.21),

$$p_1\,dc_1^f = -u_{11}^f\left[\left(\frac{dp_1}{p_1}\right) - \left(\frac{d\pi}{\pi}\right)\right] + u_{10}^f\left(\frac{d\bar{p}_0^f}{\bar{p}_0^f}\right) + u_{1N}^f\left(\frac{d\bar{p}_N^f}{\bar{p}_N^f}\right) + (p_1 C_{1C}^f)\,d\bar{C}^f$$

But $C_{1C}^f = (C_1^f/C^f)$, because expenditure elasticities are unity, and $u_{11}^f = u_{10}^f + u_{1N}^f + p_1 C_1^f$, because demand functions are homogeneous of degree zero in prices and nominal expenditure. Substituting into the equation above and setting $(dp_1/p_1) = 0$, we obtain the expression in the text.

$$p_1 \, dC_1^f = u_{10}^f \left[\left(\frac{d\bar{p}_0^f}{\bar{p}_0^f} \right) + \left(\frac{d\pi}{\pi} \right) \right] + u_{1N}^f \left[\left(\frac{d\bar{p}_N^f}{\bar{p}_N^f} \right) + \left(\frac{d\pi}{\pi} \right) \right]$$

$$+ p_1 C_1^f \left[\left(\frac{d\bar{C}^f}{\bar{C}^f} \right) + \left(\frac{d\pi}{\pi} \right) \right]$$

and this equation makes two statements:

1. If there had been an equiproportional change in all foreign arguments ($\bar{p}_0^f$, $\bar{p}_N^f$, and $\bar{C}^f$), goods-market equilibrium would have been restored by a change in π identical in size but opposite in sign. That change would preclude any change in the foreign demand for the export good, as well as changes in domestic demands. (In Figure 4.7, n^*n^* would coincide with nn, t^*t^* would coincide with tt, and domestic prices would be what they were initially.)

2. When $\bar{p}_N^f$ and $\bar{C}^f$ do not change together with $\bar{p}_0^f$, a proportional change in π reduces the foreign demand for the export good. If $(d\pi/\pi) = -(d\bar{p}_0^f/\bar{p}_0^f)$, then

$$p_1 \, dC_1^f = -(u_{1N}^f + p_1 C_1^f) \left(\frac{d\bar{p}_0^f}{\bar{p}_0^f} \right)$$

which says that the exchange-rate change required to preclude changes in domestic demands for domestic goods cannot preclude a change in the foreign demand for the export good. (In Figure 4.7, t^*t^* must lie to the left of tt when n^*n^* coincides with nn.) By inference, the appreciation of the home currency must be smaller absolutely than the increase in the foreign-currency price of the import good, and this is what we find when we rearrange the relevant term in Eq. (3.24a):

$$\left(\frac{d\pi}{\pi} \right) = -[1 - (u_{1N}^f + p_1 C_1^f)(N_0 + u_{0N}\sigma_1)/N_t] \left(\frac{d\bar{p}_0^f}{\bar{p}_0^f} \right)$$

As N_t includes $(u_{1N}^f + p_1 C_1^f)(N_0 + u_{0N}\sigma_1)$, the exchange-rate change will be smaller absolutely than the change in $\bar{p}_0^f$.

The special goods-market cases. As a change in $\bar{p}_0^f$ will shift nn and tt, even when one of the two domestic goods is a perfect substitute for the import good, the limiting cases in which $u_{0N} \to \infty$ and $u_{10} \to \infty$ give results that do not differ importantly from those encountered in the general case. In the third special case, moreover, the outcome is trivial; when $u_{1N} \to \infty$, p_1 and p_N must move together. It is thus possible to deal quickly with these special cases.

In the traded-goods variant (where $u_{0N} \to \infty$), nn becomes horizontal, and the shift in nn caused by an increase in $\bar{p}_0^f$ must equal exactly the change in its home-currency counterpart, $\pi \bar{p}_0^f$. But the signs of the outcomes are no different from those shown in Table 4.3. Both domestic prices rise on impact, raising gross domestic product. Accordingly, there are permanent increases in p_N, p_1, and Y with a pegged exchange rate (together with a reduction in r_1 and increases in W^h and $\bar{\pi}R$), and there is a permanent appreciation of the home currency with a flexible exchange rate. In this particular case, moreover, the sign of the change in relative prices continues to be ambiguous with a pegged exchange rate, and the size of the change in a flexible exchange rate continues to be smaller than the change in $\bar{p}_0^f$ (so that there is a permanent increase in p_N and a reduction in p_1).

In the composite-good variant (where $u_{10} \to \infty$), tt becomes vertical but shifts to the right with an increase in $\bar{p}_0^f$. The signs of the impact effects are the same as those in the general case, and so are the signs of the steady-state effects under a pegged exchange rate. Under a flexible rate, however, the long-run change in the exchange rate *is* proportional to the change in $\bar{p}_0^f$, and domestic prices return to their initial levels. This is because the position of t^*t^* depends uniquely on the invariant relationship between p_1 and $\pi \bar{p}_0^f$, not on foreign and domestic demands for the export good. By implication, t^*t^* would lie to the right of tt, not to the left, if the exchange-rate change were smaller absolutely than the change in $\bar{p}_0^f$, and n^*n^* would lie below nn, not above it, if the exchange-rate change were larger than the change in $\bar{p}_0^f$. As the two curves cannot intersect on XX in either of these cases, one possibility remains: The curve n^*n^* must coincide with nn, which means that $\pi \bar{p}_0^f$ must return to what it was initially, taking p_1 with it, and t^*t^* must then come to coincide with tt. Goods-market equilibrium is restored at p.

Finally, in the single-good variant (where $u_{1N} \to \infty$), the two domestic prices have to move together. On impact, then, both prices rise, and under a pegged exchange rate, they are higher permanently. Under a flexible exchange rate, moreover, the only change in π that can restore goods-market equilibrium at the initial level of nominal income is the one that brings all prices back to what they were initially.[12]

---

[12] There is, of course, a permanent reduction in the foreign demand for the export good. It is needed to accommodate the increase in domestic demand. Because domestic consumers are indifferent between domestic goods, the reduction in their demand for the import good implies an increase in their demand for the composite domestic good, which means that there must be a reduction in the foreign demand for the export good.

Insulation under a flexible exchange rate

One claim made frequently for exchange-rate flexibility is that it can insulate the domestic economy from an external disturbance. It is generally agreed that a flexible rate affords more insulation than a pegged rate, and it is often said to do so instantaneously and completely.[13] In our model, however, insulation from a shift in the current-account balance is not instantaneous. Gross domestic product changes when there is a change in foreign demand for the export good or a change in the price of the import good. It returns to its initial level only when the domestic economy has returned to a steady state.[14]

To afford instantaneous insulation, the exchange rate must be free to adjust immediately and sufficiently to forestall any change in the current-account balance. Otherwise, income would have to change to clear goods markets. Two conditions must therefore be satisfied. First, disturbances affecting goods markets must have an immediate influence on asset markets. Second, a change in the exchange rate must not affect the capital-account balance directly.

The first condition does not hold in our model. The demands for money and bonds do not depend on income, and asset markets are cleared by the interest rate and the exchange rate. Therefore, a goods-market disturbance cannot produce immediate exchange-rate changes. With the passage of time, of course, the demand for money *is* affected, because changes in income cause saving or dissaving, altering demands for assets. But the corresponding change in the exchange rate cannot confer insulation until the steady state is reached, because the second condition is not satisfied. Any change in the exchange rate affects the home-currency value of the foreign bond and must therefore generate capital flows, as households buy or sell that bond to optimize their holdings. And when there is any net capital flow, the current account cannot be balanced. Accordingly, insulation cannot be complete until holdings of assets come to be constant, and capital flows go to zero.

[13] See, e.g., E. Tower and T. D. Willett, *The Theory of Optimum Currency Areas and Exchange-Rate Flexibility: A More General Framework*, Special Papers in International Economics 11, Princeton University, Princeton, N.J., 1976, pp. 51–7, and R. G. McTeer, "Economic Independence and Insulation through Flexible Exchange Rates," in N. A. Beadles and L. A. Drewry, eds., *Money, the Market, and the State*, University of Georgia Press, Athens, Ga., 1968, pp. 102–33.

[14] For similar results, see R. Dornbusch, "The Theory of Flexible Exchange Rate Regimes and Macroeconomic Policy," *Scandinavian Journal of Economics*, 78 (1976), pp. 255–75.

Recasting this argument in general terms, models that exhibit immediate insulation are those in which the only flows affected by exchange-rate changes are those that reflect demands for goods and services.[15] In asset-market models like the one used here, by contrast, exchange-rate determination is part of the process of portfolio adjustment, by which households' demands for stocks of assets are reconciled with available supplies at each point in time. In these models, the exchange rate required to stabilize the current-account balance in the face of an external goods-market disturbance can come to be consistent with the one required to clear asset markets only after households have had time to adjust their holdings of foreign-currency assets (foreign bonds in our model). Changes in those holdings are needed to offset changes in the values of those assets brought on by exchange-rate changes.

When the point is put this way, it can be seen that the deferral of insulation does not result entirely from our specification of the demand for money. Thus, in Chapter 8, where income does affect the demand for money, there is only partial insulation on impact. A change in the foreign demand for the export good alters the exchange rate immediately, but the alteration is not large enough to prevent the current-account balance from changing, and income is affected temporarily. The size of the exchange-rate change is influenced by the need to maintain equilibrium in the money and bond markets.

Taking the argument one step further, it is perhaps misleading to describe as "insulation" the stabilization of nominal income that does take place eventually. The same sort of insulation occurs in respect of certain domestic disturbances, not only foreign disturbances. We have seen, for example, that a flexible exchange rate prevents any permanent change in income (strictly, disposable income) when there is a shift of domestic demand between domestic goods. In the next chapter, moreover, we shall see that a flexible rate cannot prevent a permanent change in income

---

[15] These properties are characteristic of the models that Meade and Mundell used to study the behavior of a flexible exchange rate; see J. E. Meade, *The Balance of Payments*, Oxford University Press, London, 1951, chap. xii (and *Mathemetical Supplement*, sec. viii) and R. A. Mundell, *International Economics*, Macmillan, New York, 1968, chap. 17. They are likewise characteristic of models in which capital flows reflect stock adjustments in asset markets but all assets are denominated in home currency; see e.g., P. R. Allen and P. B. Kenen, "Portfolio Adjustment in Open Economies: A Comparison of Alternative Specifications," *Weltwirtschaftliches archiv*, 112, 1976(1), pp. 34–71. In some models, insulation is incomplete even in the steady state; see P. B. Kenen, *Capital Mobility and Financial Integration: A Survey*, Princeton Studies in International Finance 39, Princeton University, Princeton, N.J., 1976, especially Table A-II(b). In that paper, however, wealth changes arising from exchange-rate changes do not affect the demand for money because capital gains are never realized.

when there is a foreign financial disturbance, such as a change in the foreign interest rate.

Finally, it has to be noted that the stabilization of nominal income does not preclude a permanent change in real activity. All of the disturbances studied in this chapter lead to permanent changes in relative prices. These affect the composition of domestic output, even in the classical case, and the level of employment in the Keynesian case.[16] These real changes are ruled out completely only when the economy is completely specialized (the limiting case in which $u_{1N} \to \infty$) or when the goods-market disturbance is itself "monetary" (the case of equiproportional changes in $\bar{p}_0^f$, $\bar{p}_N^f$, and $\bar{C}^f$).

Balanced-budget changes in government spending

Under our assumptions concerning tax policy, changes in government expenditure, $\bar{G}$, are matched immediately and exactly by changes in lump-sum taxes, T^h. They are balanced-budget changes and can therefore be described as goods-market policies. They do not alter the supplies of bonds or money. Their effects are summarized in Table 4.4 (and in Figures 4.8 and 4.9), for the case in which the government's propensities to spend on the two domestic goods are larger than the households' propensities to spend on those same goods (i.e., $g_N > m_N$ and $g_1 > m_1$).[17] We leave the reader to work through other cases and also to pursue the implications of the three limiting goods-market cases.[18]

---

[16] The long-run change in employment in response to any disturbance is obtained from Eq. (A.1b) in Appendix A:

$$ w\, dE = (a_1 p_1 Q_1) \left(\frac{dp_1}{p_1} \right) + (a_N p_N Q_N) \left(\frac{dp_N}{p_N} \right) $$

With a flexible exchange rate and an increase in the foreign demand for the export good, Eqs. (3.22a) and (3.23a) give $(dp_1/p_1) = (u_{0N}\sigma_N/Nt)\, dc_1^f$, and $(dp_N/p_N) = -(u_{0N}\sigma_1/N_t)\, dc_1^f$, so that $w\, dE = (u_{0N}/N_t)(p_1 Q_1)(p_N Q_N)(a_1 - a_N)\, dc_1^f$, and $a_1 \gtrless a_N$. The sign of the change in employment is ambiguous.

[17] It will be remembered that $g_1 + g_N = 1$, whereas $m_1 + m_N = 1 - m_0$, so that $(g_1 + g_N) > (m_1 + m_N)$, which permits us to assume that $g_N > m_N$ and $g_1 > m_1$ simultaneously.

[18] One can create additional cases by assuming that a fraction of government expenditure is allocated to the import good. When this fraction is large, a balanced-budget increase in government spending can be deflationary; the additional government spending on domestic goods can no longer compensate for the tax-induced reduction in private consumption. An assumption of this sort would seem to underlie McKinnon's conclusion that deficit spending may have no significant influence on economic activity; see R. I. McKinnon, "The Limited Role of Fiscal Policy in an Open Economy," Banca Nazionale del Lavoro, *Quarterly Review*, 127 (June 1976), pp. 3–25; also E. Helpman, "Nontraded Goods and Macroeconomic Policy Under a Fixed Exchange Rate," *Quarterly Journal of Economics*, 91 (August 1977), pp. 469–80.

Table 4.4. *Balanced-budget increase in government spending*

Variable	Impact effect	Steady-state effect	
		Pegged rate	Flexible rate
p_N	+	+	+
p_1	+	+	+
p_1/p_N	?	?	?
Y^d	−	−	0
Y	+	+	+
r_1	0	$+^a$	0
$\bar{\pi}R$	0	−	0
π	0	0	+
W^h	0	−	0

Signs for $\delta\bar{G} > 0$ with $g_1 > m_1$ and $g_N > m_N$.
[a] Goes to zero when domestic and foreign bonds are perfect substitutes.

When these expenditure patterns prevail, the increase in the government's demand for domestic goods will exceed the tax-induced reduction in households' demand. In Figure 4.8, the short-run income curve shifts upward from zz to $z'z'$, and equilibrium is displaced instantaneously from v to v'. The steady-state income curve is shifted too, from ZZ to $Z'Z'$, but this shift is smaller. Although nominal income has risen at v', it has risen less than government spending and has therefore risen less than the lump-sum tax that finances the spending. By implication, disposable income has fallen, and dissaving is under way.[19]

When the exchange rate is pegged, the economy will move to steady-state equilibrium at v'', the only point consistent with the pegged exchange rate, and $z'z'$ must drop back to $z''z''$. Disposable income fell on impact and continues to fall, on account of the gradual decline in income

---

[19] Disposable income declines in the short run for *all* nonnegative values of g_1 and g_N. By definition, $\delta Y^d = \delta Y - \delta\bar{G}$, and it is not difficult to show that the immediate increase in Y is smaller than the increase in $\bar{G}$ when both of the government's propensities to spend are nonnegative. Beginning with the increase in income,

$$\delta Y = (1/N_s)\{u_{0N}[g_1 - m_1(1 - S_Y)]\sigma_1 + (u_t + u'_{1N})[g_N - m_N(1 - S_Y)]\sigma_N + N_Y N_0\}\,\delta\bar{G}$$

which is unambiguously positive when, as in the text, $g_i > m_i$, $i = 1, N$. But this expression can be combined with the one above to show that

$$\delta Y^d = -(1/N_s)\{u_{0N}[(u_{1N} + u_E) + (1 - g_1)\sigma_1] + (u_t + u'_{1N})[(u_{0N} + u_{1N} + u_E) + (1 - g_N)\sigma_N]\}\,\delta G$$

which is unambiguously negative whenever g_1 and g_N are nonnegative.

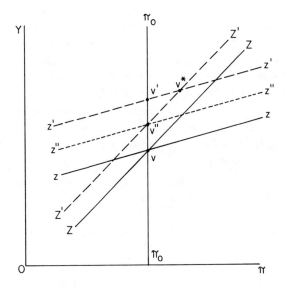

Figure 4.8 Balanced-budget increase in government spending: impact and steady-state effects on nominal income under pegged and flexible exchange rates.

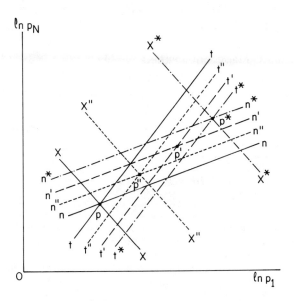

Figure 4.9 Balanced-budget increase in government spending: impact and steady-state effects on goods markets under pegged and flexible exchange rates.

that occurs on the way to the new steady state. From this result we can infer the asset-market outcomes. When there is a permanent reduction in disposable income, there must be a permanent increase in the domestic interest rate, a decline in wealth, and a loss of reserves.[20] (The outcome is exactly opposite to the one we saw in Figure 4.4. By interchanging SS with $S'S'$ and MM with $M'M'$, we switch the positions of w and w', raising the interest rate and reducing wealth. By interchanging DD with $D'D'$ and RR with $R'R'$, we switch m and m', reducing reserves.) The increase in the interest rate and decline in wealth account for the downward shift from $z'z'$ to $z''z''$ in Figure 4.8.

When the exchange rate is flexible, the economy moves eventually to v^* in Figure 4.8, the intersection of $z'z'$ and $Z'Z'$. The home currency depreciates, and there is a further increase in nominal income, rather than a partial decrease. This result is mandated by the asset markets. Because the supplies of money and bonds are unaffected (there is no government deficit), the positions of WW and MM cannot change. Therefore, SS cannot move, and disposable income must return to what it was initially. The home currency must thus depreciate until income has risen by the full amount of the increase in government spending. (Looking back at Figure 4.3B, the steady-state outcome can be described by interchanging BB with B^*B^* and LL with L^*L^*, switching the positions of m and m' so that π will rise. The requisite rightward shifts of BB and LL are implied by the decline in W^{hs} that results from the dissaving caused by the initial decline in Y^d.)

The effects on individual goods markets are shown in Figure 4.9. The balanced-budget increase in government spending shifts nn upward to $n'n'$ and tt rightward to $t't'$, raising p_N and p_1 immediately.[21] As is often the case in this chapter, however, the change in relative prices is ambiguous, and the ambiguity is not due entirely to our assumptions about the various propensities to spend. Using Eqs. (3.5) and (3.6),

$$\left(\frac{\delta p_1}{p_1}\right) - \left(\frac{\delta p_N}{p_N}\right) = (1/N_s)\{u_{0N}[g_1 - m_1(1 - S_Y)] - (u_t + u_{1N}^f)[g_N - m_N(1 - S_Y)] + N_Y(g_1\sigma_N - g_N\sigma_1)\}\,\delta\bar{G}$$

[20] The steady-state change in disposable income is obtained by replacing N_s with N_w in the expression for the instantaneous change given in the previous note. (The sign of the change in wealth can also be inferred from the sign of that expression. When Y^d falls on impact, there must be dissaving. Therefore, W^{hs} must start to fall, and its path is monotonic. The same inference is invoked in the text, below, to explain the shifts in LL and BB that take place with a flexible exchange rate.)

[21] The signs of the changes in p_N, p_1, and Y do not depend exclusively on our assumption about the propensities to spend. If g_N were smaller than $m_N(1 - S_Y)$, for example, nn

and the sign of this expression depends on the demand and supply elasticities lying behind u_{0N}, u_t, u_{1N}^f, σ_N, and σ_1, as well as on the various propensities to spend.

Turning to the steady-state changes in prices, both goods-market curves move inward with a pegged exchange rate, to $n''n''$ and $t''t''$, and the economy moves to p'' (the counterpart of v'' in Figure 4.8). Both curves move outward with a flexible rate, to n^*n^* and t^*t^*, and the economy moves to p^* (the counterpart of v^* in Figure 4.8). In the new steady state, however, p_N and p_1 are higher than they were initially, whether the exchange rate is pegged or flexible, and the change in relative prices remains ambiguous.

Under a flexible exchange rate, the "balanced-budget multiplier" turns out to be unity in the long run, and it is therefore larger with a flexible rate than with a pegged rate. But care must be taken in interpreting this outcome. It has nothing to do with Mundell's conclusions regarding the powers of fiscal policy under the two exchange-rate regimes,[22] because the fiscal policy considered here is not the one he analyzed. A balanced-budget increase in government spending does not involve any increase in the supply of bonds (which is why our result does not depend on the degree of asset-market integration). Furthermore, our "balanced-budget multiplier" is not the one obtained from a simple Keynesian model. When it is extracted from such a model, one has to impound changes in the interest rate. When it is extracted from our model, by contrast, one allows for changes in the interest rate, r_1, but finds that there are none with a flexible exchange rate.[23]

Notice, finally, that there are no uncertainties here about the effects of an increase in $\bar{G}$ on employment or the wage rate. Under pegged and flexible rates alike, both domestic prices rise, on impact and permanently, raising employment in the Keynesian case and raising the wage rate in the classical case.

----

would shift down. But the rightward shift of tt would be larger, and it would still be possible for p_N to rise. On the sign of the change in Y, see note 19, above.

[22] Mundell, *International Economics*, chaps. 17–18, where he says that fiscal policy will be more effective under a flexible rate when there is no capital mobility but more effective under a pegged rate when there is "perfect" mobility (i.e., perfect substitutability between domestic and foreign bonds).

[23] In Chapter 8, however, we show that the balanced-budget multiplier is smaller than unity when the demand for money depends on income. It is equal to unity, as it is here, only when the demand for money depends on disposable income.

Equations for the goods-market curves

The market for the nontraded good (Eq. 2.28a)
Impact version (*nn*):

$$\left(\frac{\delta p_N}{p_N}\right) = (1/v_N)[u_{1N} + u_E + m_N(1 - S_Y)\sigma_1]\left(\frac{\delta p_1}{p_1}\right) + (1/v_N)(u_{0N})\left(\frac{\delta \pi}{\pi}\right) - (1/v_N)(m_N S_1)\ \delta r_1$$

$$- (1/v_N)(m_N S_0)\ \delta \bar{r}_0 + (1/v_N)\ \delta c_{N1} + (0)(\delta c^f_1 - \delta c_{01}) + (1/v_N)(u_{0N})\left(\frac{\delta \bar{p}^f_0}{\bar{p}^f_0}\right)$$

$$+ (1/v_N)[g_N - m_N(1 - S_Y)]\delta \bar{G} + (1/v_N)m_N(1 - S_Y)\ \delta \bar{D} + (1/v_N)m_N(-S_W)\ \delta W^h$$

where $v_N = u_{0N} + u_{1N} + u_E + [1 - m_N(1 - S_Y)]\sigma_N$

The market for the export good (Eq. 2.27a)
Impact version (*tt*):

$$\left(\frac{\delta p_1}{p_1}\right) = (1/v_T)[u_{1N} + u_E + m_1(1 - S_Y)\sigma_1]\left(\frac{\delta p_N}{p_N}\right) + (1/v_T)[u_t + u^f_{1N} + p_1 C^f_1]\left(\frac{\delta \pi}{\pi}\right)$$

$$- (1/v_T)(m_1 S_1)\ \delta r_1 - (1/v_T)(m_1 S_0)\ \delta \bar{r}_0 - (1/v_T)\ \delta c_{N1} + (1/v_T)(\delta c^f_1 - \delta c_{01})$$

$$+ (1/v_T)(u_t)\left(\frac{\delta \bar{p}^f_0}{\bar{p}^f_0}\right) + (1/v_T)[g_1 - m_1(1 - S_Y)]\ \delta \bar{G} + (1/v_T)m_1(1 - S_Y)\ \delta \bar{D} + (1/v_T)m_1(-S_W)\ \delta W^h$$

where $v_T = u_t + u^f_{1N} + u_{1N} + u_E + [1 - m_1(1 - S_Y)]\sigma_1$

Gross domestic product in income and exchange-rate space (Eq. 3.4)
Impact version (*zz*):[a]

$$\delta Y = (N_t/N_s)\left(\frac{\delta \pi}{\pi}\right) - (N_u/N_s)(S_1\ \delta r_1 + S_0\ \delta \bar{r}_0) + (1/N_s)[(u_t + u^f_{1N})\sigma_N - u_{0N}\sigma_1]\ \delta c_{N1}$$

$$+ (1/N_s)(N_0 + u_{0N}\sigma_1)(\delta c^f_1 - \delta c_{01})$$

$$+ (1/N_s)\{(u_t + u_{0N})N_0 + u_{0N}[u_t + u^f_{1N})\sigma_N + u_t\sigma_1]\}\left(\frac{\delta \bar{p}^f_0}{\bar{p}^f_0}\right)$$

$$+ (1/N_s)\{N_Y N_0 + (u_t + u^f_{1N})[g_N - m_N(1 - S_Y)]\sigma_N + u_{0N}[g_1 - m_1(1 - S_Y)]\sigma_1\}\ \delta \bar{G}$$

where $N_u = \sigma_N N_{NU} + \sigma_1 N_{1U}$

Steady-state version (ZZ):[a]

$$dY = (N_t/N_w)\left(\frac{d\pi}{\pi}\right) + (1/N_w)[(u_t + u^f_{1N})\sigma_N - u_{0N}\sigma_1]\,dc_{N1} + (1/N_w)(N_0 + u_{0N}\sigma_1)(dc^f_1 - dc_{01})$$

$$+ (1/N_w)\{(u_t + u_{0N})N_0 + u_{0N}[(u_t + u^f_{1N})\sigma_N + u_t\sigma_1]\}\left(\frac{d\bar{p}^f_0}{\bar{p}^f_0}\right)$$

$$+ (1/N_w)[m_0 N_0 + (u_t + u^f_{1N})(g_N - m_N)\sigma_N + u_{0N}(g_1 - m_1)\sigma_1]\,d\bar{G}$$

Constant gross domestic product in product-price space (Eqs. 2.14a and 2.3a)

Steady-state version (XX):

$$\left(\frac{dp_N}{p_N}\right) = -(\sigma_1/\sigma_N)\left(\frac{dp_1}{p_1}\right) + (1/\sigma_N)\,dY^d + (1/\sigma_N)\,d\bar{G}$$

Unless otherwise indicated, the sign of each slope and shift coefficient is given by the sign (+ or −) preceding the coefficient. It is assumed throughout that $g_1 > m_1$ and $g_N > m_N$.

[a] Sign of shift coefficient for δc_{N1} (or dc_{N1}) ambiguous.

Equations for the asset-market curves

The steady-state requirement (*SS*) (Eq. 2.13 for $S = 0$)

$$dr_1 = (-S_W/S_1) \, dW^h - (S_Y/S_1) \, dY^a - (S_0/S_1) \, d\bar{r}_0$$

The market for the domestic bond (Eq. 2.42a)
In interest-rate and wealth space (*WW*):

$$dr_1 = -(B_{1W}/B_{11}) \, dW^h - (1/B_{11}) \, d\bar{B}_1^c + (-B_{10}/B_{11}) \, d\bar{r}_0 + (1/B_{11}) \, dB_1$$

In interest-rate and reserve (or exchange-rate) space (*DD* and *BB*):[a]

$$dr_1 = (0)\bar{\pi} \, dR - (B_{1W}/B_{11})V_\pi \left(\frac{d\pi}{\pi} \right) - (1/B_{11}) \, d\bar{B}_1^c + (-B_{10}/B_{11}) \, d\bar{r}_0 + (1/B_{11}) \, dB_1 - (B_{1W}/B_{11}) \, dW^{hs}$$

The market for domestic money (Eq. 2.43a)
In interest-rate and wealth space (*MM*):

$$dr_1 = [L_{1W}/(-L_{11})] \, dW^h - [1/(-L_{11})]\bar{\pi} \, dR - [1/(-L_{11})] \, d\bar{B}_1^c - (L_{10}/L_{11}) \, d\bar{r}_0$$

In interest-rate and reserve (or exchange-rate) space (*RR* and *LL*):[a]

$$dr_1 = -[1/(-L_{11})]\bar{\pi} \, dR + [L_{1W}/(-L_{11})]V_\pi \left(\frac{d\pi}{\pi} \right) - [1/(-L_{11})] \, d\bar{B}_1^c - (L_{10}/L_{11}) \, d\bar{r}_0 + [L_{1W}/(-L_{11})] \, dW^{hs}$$

The equations shown here are for the steady-state versions of the various curves, but the equations for the impact versions of *WW*, *DD*, *BB*, *MM*, *RR*, and *LL* differ only in that they omit the terms relating to dB_1 and dW^{hs}. The sign of each slope and shift coefficient is given by the sign (+ or −) preceding the coefficient.
[a] Under a pegged exchange rate, the coefficients of the change in reserves are the slopes of the curves *DD* and *RR* (and the coefficients of the change in the exchange rate describe the shifts of the curves resulting from a once-for-all devaluation or revaluation). Under a flexible exchange rate, the coefficients of the change in the exchange rate are the slopes of the curves *BB* and *LL*.

5

Comparative statics: asset-market and compound disturbances

In this chapter we continue to review disturbances and policies, using the diagrams developed in Chapter 4. We start with disturbances and policy changes that impinge directly only on the asset markets, then turn to those that have direct effects on both goods and asset markets.

Asset-market disturbances

It would be quite easy to define shifts in demands for assets analogous to the shifts in demands for goods analyzed in Chapter 4. We could ask what would happen, for example, if households sought to hold more foreign bonds and fewer domestic bonds. The consequences of such shifts, however, are captured by the two asset-market disturbances defined in Chapter 3. When the central bank purchases domestic bonds in the open market, it raises the total demand for those bonds and the supply of money. The effects resemble those that would occur if households sought to hold more bonds and less money. Similarly, an increase in the foreign interest rate raises the demand for the foreign bond and reduces the demand for the domestic bond. The effects resemble those that would occur with a shift in demand from domestic to foreign bonds. It will therefore suffice to analyze these two examples.

Open-market operations

As there are no commercial banks in this model, the central bank can alter the money supply only by altering its own assets. Open-market operations are the only instrument of monetary policy, and we shall examine them in some detail.[1] We begin with the general case in which all pairs of goods and assets are partial substitutes.

[1] In practice, of course, central banks can alter discount rates, ceilings on commercial-bank borrowing, and reserve requirements. But the conclusions we draw from our model are nevertheless quite general. One of us has pointed out elsewhere that the creation of inside money must by definition involve the exchange of money for another asset held by the

Table 5.1. *Open-market purchase of the domestic bond*

	Pegged rate		Flexible rate	
Variable	Impact effect	Steady-state effect	Impact effect	Steady-state effect
p_N	$+^a$	0	$+$	$+$
p_1	$+^a$	0	$+$	$+$
p_1/p_N	$?^a$	0	$?$	$?$
Y^d	$+^a$	0	$+$	$+$
Y	$+^a$	0	$+$	$+$
r_1	$-^a$	$-^a$	$-^a$	$-^a$
$\bar{\pi}R$	$-^b$	$-^b$	0	0
π	0	0	$+$	$+$
W^h	0	$-^a$	$+$	$+$

Signs for $\delta\bar{B}_i^c > 0$.
[a] Goes to zero when domestic and foreign bonds are perfect substitutes.
[b] Goes to $-\delta\bar{B}_i^c$ when domestic and foreign bonds are perfect substitutes.

The effects of an open-market purchase of the domestic bond are shown in Table 5.1. By raising the total demand for the domestic bond (or cutting the supply available to households), it reduces the domestic interest rate, immediately and permanently. By enlarging the supply of money, it causes a loss of reserves when the exchange rate is pegged and a depreciation of the home currency when the rate is flexible. On impact, moreover, it raises nominal income under both regimes. Under a pegged ex-

public, whether by the central bank or by commercial banks. (P. R. Allen, *Organization and Administration of a Monetary Union,* Princeton Studies in International Finance 38, Princeton University, Princeton, N.J., 1976, pp. 23–4.) As long as the assets bought by the banking system are not close substitutes for traded assets that have highly elastic demands or supplies in international markets, the central bank will enjoy some independence in conducting monetary policy, although only temporarily with a pegged exchange rate. The same point has been made by others; see, e.g., W. H. Branson, "Portfolio Equilibrium and Monetary Policy with Foreign and Non-traded Assets," in E. Claassen and P. Salin, eds., *Recent Issues in International Monetary Economics,* North-Holland, Amsterdam, 1976, pp. 241–50. Mathieson has gone further, pointing out that changes in reserve requirements can confer a degree of independence even when foreign and domestic assets are perfect substitutes (and open-market operations are ineffective); see D. J. Mathieson, "Monetary Policy in an Inside Money, Open Economy," *Quarterly Journal of Economics,* 89 (February 1975), pp. 81–102. Putting his point in our terms, when altering reserve requirements, the central bank is acting on the market for an asset (reserve money) that is not a perfect substitute for any other asset. (It would, of course, be possible for us to analyze open-market operations in the foreign bond, as has been done in papers cited later in this chapter. We shall not do so, however, until Part IV, where each central bank in our two-country model holds the other country's bond.)

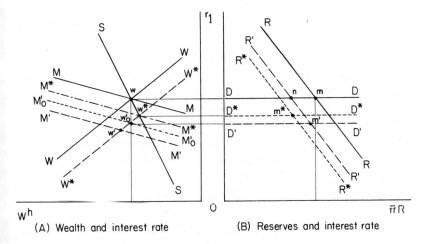

Figure 5.1 Open-market purchase of the domestic bond: impact and steady-state effects on asset markets under a pegged exchange rate.

change rate, however, income cannot increase permanently; it must return eventually to its initial level. And under a flexible rate, the permanent increase in income can be larger or smaller than the immediate increase.

Outcomes under a pegged rate. In Figure 5.1 the increase in demand for the domestic bond corresponding to the open-market purchase is represented by the downward shift in the bond-market curve from WW to W^*W^* and by an equal downward shift from DD to $D'D'$. These show the reduction in the domestic interest rate required to clear the bond market at the initial level of wealth. The increase in the money supply is represented by the downward shift of the money-market curve from MM to $M'M'$ and by an equal downward shift from RR to $R'R'$. These show the reduction in r_1 required to clear the money market. (The downward shift in RR is equivalent to a leftward shift by the distance mn, which measures the open-market purchase, δB_1^c, by measuring the excess supply of money that would emerge if wealth and the interest rate were constant.)

Because money and domestic bonds are not the only assets held by households (they hold foreign bonds too), the downward shifts in the money-market curves are larger than the downward shifts in the bond-market curves. The shifts in MM and RR are $(1/L_{11})\,\delta\bar{B}_1^c$, whereas the shifts in WW and DD are $-(1/B_{11})\,\delta\bar{B}_1^c$ or $[1/(L_{11} + B_{01})]\,\delta\bar{B}_1^c$. The former are larger because domestic and foreign bonds are partial substitutes

$(B_{01} \neq 0)$. Therefore, asset-market equilibrium is displaced from m to m' in Figure 5.1B, and there is an instantaneous loss of reserves. Households seek to buy foreign bonds with part of the increase in their money holdings, producing excess demand in the foreign-exchange market, because they need foreign currency to buy foreign bonds. The central bank must intervene to keep the exchange rate from changing. It must supply foreign currency from its reserves.[2] (Because m' lies to the right of n in Figure 5.1B, the loss of reserves is smaller than the open-market purchase. Households do not try to swap *all* of the new money for foreign bonds, because they want to hold some additional money at the new lower interest rate. We return to this point later.)

The loss of reserves shown explicitly in Figure 5.1B appears in Figure 5.1A as an upward shift in the money-market curve from $M'M'$ to $M'_0M'_0$. Asset-market equilibrium is displaced from w to w'_0 (not to w'), reflecting the change in the money supply caused jointly by the open-market purchase and the loss of reserves. The point w'_0 is vertically below the initial point w for the reason given in Chapter 4. Under a pegged exchange rate, wealth cannot change until households start to save or dissave.

The reduction in the domestic interest rate brought about by the open-market purchase has as its immediate goods-market effect a reduction in desired saving and, therefore, an increase in consumption (absorption). This effect is shown in Figure 5.2 by the shift of the short-run income curve from zz to $z'z'$. There is no shift, however, in the long-run curve ZZ, because saving must be zero at all points on that curve. We must therefore expect the long-run results to differ from those described in Chapter 4. The goods-market disturbances examined there had permanent effects on income with a pegged exchange rate and no such effects with a flexible rate. The asset-market disturbances examined in this chapter have permanent effects on income with a flexible rate and no such effects with a pegged rate.

---

[2] This immediate loss of reserves takes place in other models that feature instantaneous portfolio optimization. See, e.g., J. A. Frenkel and C. A. Rodriguez, "Portfolio Equilibrium and the Balance of Payments: A Monetary Approach," *American Economic Review*, 65 (September 1975), pp. 674–88; W. H. Branson, "Stocks and Flows in International Monetary Analysis," in A. Ando et al., eds., *International Aspects of Stabilization Policies*, Federal Reserve Bank of Boston and International Seminar in Public Economics, Boston, 1975, pp. 27–50; L. Girton and D. Henderson, "Central Bank Operations in Foreign and Domestic Assets Under Fixed and Flexible Exchange Rates," in P. Clark et al., eds., *The Effects of Exchange Rate Adjustments*, U.S. Treasury, Washington, D.C., 1977, pp. 151–78; and R. S. Boyer, "Commodity Markets and Bond Markets in a Small, Fixed-Exchange Rate Economy," *Canadian Journal of Economics*, 8 (February 1975), pp. 1–23.

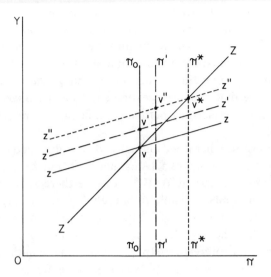

Figure 5.2 Open-market purchase of the domestic bond: impact and steady-state effects on nominal income under pegged and flexible exchange rates.

The shift in the short-run income curve from zz to $z'z'$ displaces the goods-market equilibrium from v to v', where $z'z'$ intersects the schedule $\pi_0\pi_0$, denoting the pegged exchange rate, and there is an instantaneous increase in income. But equilibrium cannot remain at v', because saving is not zero. When the government budget is balanced and short-run equilibrium is established at a point to the right of the intersection between the short-run and long-run income curves, there is a current-account surplus (absorption is less than income), and households start to save. When equilibrium is established at a point such as v', to the left of that intersection, there is a current account deficit (absorption exceeds income), and households start to dissave.[3] The current account is balanced and saving is zero

---

[3] To show that there is a current-account surplus or deficit whenever the short-run and long-run income curves do not coincide, we use the equations for those curves given at the end of Chapter 4. Take any set of changes in π, r_1, W^h, and $\bar{D}$, and ask how it affects the difference between the steady-state and instantaneous levels of Y when the economy is in momentary equilibrium (the difference that measures the vertical distance between the two income curves):

$$dY - \delta Y = \left[(N_t/N_w)\left(\frac{\delta\pi}{\pi}\right)\right] - \left[(N_t/N_s)\left(\frac{\delta\pi}{\pi}\right)\right]$$

$$+ (N_u/N_s)(S_1\,\delta r_1 + S_W\,\delta W^h) - (N_u/N_s)(1 - S_Y)\,\delta\bar{D}\Bigg]$$

$$= (N_u/N_s)\left[S_Y(N_t/N_w)\left(\frac{\delta\pi}{\pi}\right) - S_Y\,\delta Y^d + \delta^*S - (1 - S_Y)\,\delta\bar{D}\right]$$

only at the intersection of the two income curves. When the exchange rate is pegged, however, the only relevant intersection is the one at which ZZ also intersects $\pi_0\pi_0$. Thus, the economy must return eventually to v, which means that income must return to its initial level. In brief, Figure 5.2 replicates a familiar proposition. When the exchange rate is pegged and the economy is one that converges eventually to a stationary state, monetary policy cannot exercise any permanent influence on prices, output, or employment.

If income must return to what it was initially, disposable income must do so too, and the curve SS in Figure 5.1A cannot shift. Furthermore, the bond-market curve must remain at W^*W^*, because there is no further change in the supply of bonds available to households. Accordingly, the economy must come to rest at w^*, where SS and W^*W^* intersect. The stock of wealth declines, reflecting the process of dissaving, and there is a permanent reduction in the interest rate (but by less than the initial reduction). By implication, the stock of reserves has fallen further, as the money-market curve has had to shift from $M_0'M_0'$ to M^*M^*. (The same changes in the interest rate and reserves are shown in Figure 5.1B by the shift of $D'D'$ to D^*D^* and the shift of $R'R'$ to R^*R^*. These shifts reflect the decline in the integral of saving, W^{hs}, that takes place with dissaving and is equal in turn to the decline in wealth with a pegged exchange rate.) Anticipating momentarily the discussion of dynamics in Chapter 6, the dissaving that begins at v' in Figure 5.2 initiates a gradual decline in wealth, accompanied by a rise in the interest rate. These processes diminish the incentive to dissave, depressing absorption and shifting the short-run income curve downward from $z'z'$ until it comes to rest again at zz.

Although we can be sure that the loss of reserves is larger in the long run than on impact (that m^* lies to the left of m' in Figure 5.1B), we cannot know if it is large enough to reduce the money stock below its initial level (if m^* lies to the left of n). The steady-state change in the money stock is given by $dL_1 = \bar{\pi} \, dR + d\bar{B}_1^c$, and when we use Eq. (3.24b) to replace $\bar{\pi} \, dR$, we find that $dL_1 = (1/H_f)(S_W L_{11} - L_{1W} S_1) \, d\bar{B}_1^c$. But none of

because $S_1 \delta r_1 + S_W \delta W^h = \delta^* S - S_Y \delta Y^d$ and $N_w = N_s - S_Y N_u$. From Eq. (3.24a), however, $(N_t/N_w)(\delta\pi/\pi) = dY^d$. When $\bar{G}$ is constant, moreover, $dY^d = dY$, and $\delta Y^d = \delta Y + \delta \bar{D}$. Substituting and rearranging, $dY - \delta Y = (N_u/N_w)(\delta^* S - \delta \bar{D})$. We start, however, from a steady state, in which $^*S = \bar{D} = (p_1^* C_1^f - p_0^* C_0) = 0$. Therefore, the short-run curve will lie below the long-run curve (and short-run equilibrium will lie to the right of the intersection between zz and ZZ) whenever the current account is in surplus, and the converse is equally true. Furthermore, $\delta \bar{D} = 0$ in the present case, and we can make an additional statement: The short-run curve will lie below the long-run curve whenever there is saving, and above it, as in Figure 5.2, whenever there is dissaving.

the assumptions made thus far–not about behavior nor about stability–
tells us the sign of the difference between $S_W L_{11}$ and $L_{1W} S_1$. We shall meet
this difference frequently, however, and shall find that it has to be positive
to validate a number of familiar propositions. It is therefore convenient to
assume that $S_W L_{11} > L_{1W} S_1$ (which means in the present case that the
long-run reduction in reserves does not swamp the increase in the money
stock produced by the open-market purchase).

What interpretation can we give to this assumption? Geometrically, it
restricts the relationship between SS and MM in Figure 5.1A. The slope
of SS is $(-S_W/S_1)$; the slope of MM is $(-L_{1W}/L_{11})$; and SS must be
steeper then MM when $S_W L_{11} > L_{1W} S_1$. We have thus been invoking this
assumption all along. Analytically, the assumption says that saving (absorption) is comparatively sensitive to changes in wealth, whereas the demand for money is comparatively sensitive to changes in the interest rate.
Using language made popular by recent discussions of fiscal policy in a
closed economy, the assumption says that "crowding out" does not dominate, and this is the expression we shall use to invoke it hereafter.[4]

Outcomes under a flexible rate. In Figure 5.3 we show how an open-
market purchase affects the bond and money markets in the flexible-rate
case. Two characteristics of a flexible exchange rate are prominent here.
First, the stock of money becomes exogenous, because the central bank
does not intervene in the foreign-exchange market. Accordingly, the initial shift in the money-market curve, from MM to M^*M^*, is permanent;
the curve does not adjust endogenously, as it did in Figure 5.1. Second,
the level of wealth can change instantaneously, because an exchange-rate

---

[4] On crowding out and fiscal policy in a closed economy, see A. S. Blinder and R. M.
Solow, "Does Fiscal Policy Matter?," *Journal of Public Economics,* 2 (November 1973),
pp. 319–37. The form of the crowding-out condition is slightly different in their model, because interest-rate changes affect investment, not saving, and bonds are long term (so that
the effects of interest-rate changes include wealth effects of capital gains and losses).
But it has the same economic interpretation; crowding out does not dominate when the
ratio of wealth effects to interest-rate effects is larger absolutely with respect to the demand for goods than with respect to the demand for money. Monetarist critics of fiscal
policy argue that crowding out must dominate eventually, so that a bond-financed budget
deficit cannot stimulate the economy permanently; see, e.g., M. Friedman, "Comments
on the Critics," *Journal of Political Economy,* 80 (September/October 1972), p. 916.
Their case is based partly on the supposition that government borrowing does not increase
wealth; see R. J. Barro, "Are Government Bonds Net Wealth?," *Journal of Political
Economy,* 82 (November/December 1974), pp. 1095–117. (Unless otherwise indicated,
we shall always draw SS and MM to satisfy the assumption that crowding out does not
dominate, but the tables of signs in this chapter will not make that assumption. They will
record an ambiguity whenever crowding out is at issue. In the next chapter and Part III,
however, we shall assume from the start that $S_W L_{11} > L_{1W} S_1$ and shall revise signs accordingly.)

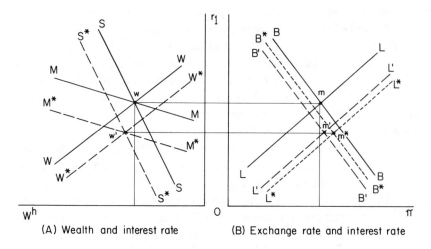

(A) Wealth and interest rate   (B) Exchange rate and interest rate

Figure 5.3 Open-market purchase of the domestic bond: impact and steady-state effects on asset markets under a flexible exchange rate.

change affects the home-currency value of the foreign-currency bond.

As the shift from *MM* to *M*M** in Figure 5.3A is just as large as the shift from *MM* to *M'M'* in Figure 5.1A, and the sizes of the shifts in the bond-market curves are likewise identical, the points *w'* are located identically in the two diagrams. With a flexible exchange rate, however, the economy moves to *w'* and stays there permanently. It cannot move to w_0' in the short run or to *w** in the long run, as it did with a pegged exchange rate, because reserves cannot change. Thus, *w'* defines the immediate and permanent effects of an open-market purchase on wealth and the interest rate. The change in the interest rate is necessarily larger than it was in the short run with a pegged exchange rate.

The instantaneous increase in wealth shown at *w'* in Figure 5.3A implies a depreciation of the home currency, and this is what we find in Figure 5.3B. With the central bank's purchase of the domestic bond, *BB* shifts downward to *B'B'*. With the corresponding increase in the supply of money, *LL* shifts downward to *L'L'*. The shift in the money-market curve, moreover, is larger than the shift in the bond-market curve (because *MM* shifts by more than *WW*), and asset-market equilibrium is displaced from *m* to *m'*. The price of foreign currency rises immediately. Households try to buy foreign bonds with some of the newly created money, just as they did when the exchange rate was pegged, and therefore try to buy foreign currency. But the central bank refuses to sell foreign currency, and there is thus no additional supply forthcoming.[5] The price of foreign currency has to rise immediately. Putting the point in different terms, the supply of foreign bonds is perfectly elastic at the foreign interest rate, but households have no access to that supply when they cannot buy the foreign currency they need. Hence, an increase of demand for the foreign bond can be satisfied immediately only by raising the home-currency value of foreign bonds already held domestically, and this is what happens when the home currency depreciates.[6]

The increase in income that takes place on impact is larger than the one obtained with a pegged exchange rate. The reduction in the interest rate is bigger in Figure 5.3 than in Figure 5.1, and there is an immediate increase in wealth on account of the depreciation of the home currency. Therefore, the increase in desired absorption has to be bigger too, and the short-run income curve shifts to $z''z''$ in Figure 5.2. Furthermore, the instantaneous change in the exchange rate, described by the shift of the exchange-rate schedule from $\pi_0\pi_0$ to $\pi'\pi'$, has an expenditure-switching effect, as well as an expenditure-changing effect. The economy moves along $z''z''$ until it reaches v''. A flexible exchange rate, then, enhances the short-run influence of monetary policy, and does so in two ways. First, the economy cannot "export" any of the money created by the central bank, and there must be a larger reduction in the interest rate, fostering a larger increase in desired absorption at the initial exchange rate. Second, the depreciation of the home currency augments the demand for domestic goods; it enlarges the increase in desired absorption by raising wealth, and it shifts domestic and foreign demands to domestic goods by altering relative prices.[7]

[5] There can be an instantaneous increase in the *flow* supply of foreign currency. This happens when there is an immediate improvement in the current-account balance, an increase in the net capital inflow, or a decrease in the net capital outflow. We pointed out in Chapter 2, however, that an increase in the flow supply is negligible, by definition, compared to an increase in the stock demand that takes place as households try to swap domestic money for foreign bonds.

[6] To make the point in yet another way, the increase in π has the effect of raising wealth, and the increase in W^h, together with the decrease in r_1, raises the demand for domestic currency, absorbing the excess supply of money. This explanation is closely consistent with the spirit of the convention adopted in Chapter 2, where we said that the exchange rate is the price that clears the money market. The explanations in the text, however, remind us that the markets for foreign bonds and foreign exchange are involved in the short-run determination of the exchange rate.

[7] This last effect is the one stressed in early work on monetary policy and exchange-rate flexibility; see R. A. Mundell, *International Economics*, Macmillan, New York, 1968, chap. 17, J. M. Fleming, *Essays in International Economics*, Harvard University Press, Cambridge, Mass., 1971, chap. 9, and E. Sohmen, *Flexible Exchange Rates*, University of Chicago Press, Chicago, 1969, chap. v.

Monetary policy must also be more effective in the long run with a flexible exchange rate. There is a permanent increase in income with a flexible rate, and there was none with a pegged rate. To prove that the increase in income is permanent, we need merely show that disposable income rises permanently, and this follows directly from the fact that the economy cannot depart from w' in Figure 5.3A. If long-run equilibrium is to obtain at w', SS must shift to S^*S^*, and this shift can occur only when there is a permanent increase in disposable income.

The steady-state increase in income implied by the shift from SS to S^*S^* occurs at v^* in Figure 5.2, where $z''z''$ intersects ZZ. Because wealth and the interest rate do not change after the initial impact effects of the open-market purchase, the short-run income curve cannot shift through time. For this very reason, however, the flexible exchange rate must adjust through time. In Figure 5.2, v'' is to the left of ZZ, and there is dissaving on the way to the new steady state. The integral of saving, W^{hs}, must therefore decline, shifting BB and LL to the right in Figure 5.3B. Asset-market equilibrium is displaced gradually from m' to m^*, and the home currency depreciates during the transition, clearing the bond and money markets at unchanging levels of the interest rate and wealth.[8]

But these are not the only possibilities. The instantaneous depreciation of the home currency can be large enough, compared to the shift from zz to $z''z''$, for v'' to lie to the right of ZZ in Figure 5.2. The subsequent movement to v^* must then be associated with a decline in income and an appreciation of the home currency, compared to the levels of Y and π obtaining on impact. When short-run equilibrium is established to the right of ZZ, households start to save, and W^{hs} begins to grow. (In Figure 5.3B, BB and LL move to the left, and the home currency appreciates gradually during the transition to the new steady state.)

There are thus several possible paths to long-run equilibrium under a flexible exchange rate. There can be "undershooting" initially, in that the immediate changes in Y and π fall short of those that must be reached eventually. This is what is shown to happen in Figure 5.2. But there can instead be "overshooting" initially, in that the changes in Y and π are larger than those that must be reached eventually. (The reasons for overshooting and undershooting are somewhat different here than in many other discussions of exchange-rate behavior. Elsewhere, they reflect the effects of expectations and speculation. Here, they reflect the effects of *unexpected* capital gains or losses on holdings of foreign-currency bonds. Expectations are stationary.)

---

[8] On the way that movements in BB and LL keep wealth from changing, see pp. 77–8.

A fuller explanation of these ambiguities is offered in Chapter 6, where we look at the dynamics involved, but a brief interpretation can be given here. An open-market purchase has conflicting effects on saving. On the one hand, the increase in wealth and reduction in the interest rate shown at w' in Figure 5.3A tend to depress saving; on the other, the increase in income shown at v'' in Figure 5.2 stimulates saving. If the wealth and interest-rate effects dominate, dissaving occurs on the way to the new steady state. The home currency must depreciate further to raise income (i.e., to eliminate the dissaving) and also to raise the home-currency value of holdings of the foreign bond (i.e., to hold wealth constant despite the dissaving). If the income effect dominates instead, saving occurs on the way to the steady state, and the home currency must appreciate to reduce income and also to reduce home-currency holdings of the foreign bond.

To sum up, an open-market purchase of the domestic bond always produces a permanent depreciation of the home currency and a permanent increase in income. We do not know with certainty, however, whether the short-run changes in π and Y will be smaller or larger than those that are needed for steady-state equilibrium—whether there is undershooting or overshooting in the short run.

Questions remain, moreover, about the character of the long-run increase in income. It has been asserted, for example, that an open-market purchase leads eventually to an increase in all domestic prices proportional to the increase in the stock of money, ruling out permanent changes in relative prices and in the output mix, let alone an increase in employment. It has also been asserted that the depreciation of the home currency will come to be proportional to the increase in the stock of money. This assertion is similar to one we shall encounter concerning devaluation—that it can have no permanent effect on real variables because the increase in the money supply resulting from the inflow of reserves will come to be proportional to the devaluation.[9] What does our model say about these assertions?

If there is no "money illusion" anywhere in the economy, an open-market operation will have no permanent effect on relative domestic prices; the long-run changes in p_N and p_1 will be proportional to the change in the exchange rate. But the change in the exchange rate will not be proportional to the change in the supply of money.

[9] See, e.g., R. Dornbusch, "Devaluation, Money, and Nontraded Goods," in J. A. Frenkel and H. G. Johnson, eds., *The Monetary Approach to the Balance of Payments,* University of Toronto Press, Toronto, 1976, pp. 168–86, and "Currency Depreciation, Hoarding, and Relative Prices," *Journal of Political Economy,* 81 (July/August 1973), pp. 893–915.

When the economy begins in a steady state, the long-run change in relative domestic prices can be written as[10]

$$\left(\frac{dp_1}{p_1}\right) - \left(\frac{dp_N}{p_N}\right) = -(1/N_t)[u_\pi(m_N N_{1k} - m_1 N_{Nk}) + m_0 u_{0N}(N_{Nk} + N_{1k})]\, dY^d$$

where

$$N_{ik} = a_i p_i Q_i + b_i G_i \qquad i = 1, N$$

and the new terms b_i are the fractions of government spending on the two domestic goods, G_N and G_1, that are policy determined in nominal rather than real terms. Thus, relative domestic prices are unaffected in the long run when the N_{ik} are zero, and this will happen when two conditions are satisfied. There can be no "money illusion" in the labor market (the a_i must vanish), and there can be no "money illusion" in government behavior (the b_i must vanish). Under these ultraclassical conditions, moreover, the long-run change in disposable income is proportional to the change in the price level (i.e., to the changes in p_N and p_1) and is likewise proportional to the exchange-rate change.[11] In brief, p_N, p_1, and π move together.

The change in the exchange rate, however, can be larger or smaller proportionally than the change in the supply of money. Under ultraclassical conditions,[12]

$$\left(\frac{d\bar{B}^c_1}{L_1}\right) - \left(\frac{d\pi}{\pi}\right) = -[(B_{1W} + L_{1W})/S_W][(S_W L_{11} - L_{1W} S_1)/H_\pi]\left(\frac{d\bar{B}^c_1}{L_1}\right)$$

which says that $(d\pi/\pi) < (d\bar{B}^c_1/L_1)$ when $S_W L_{11} > L_{1W} S_1$. The long-run change in the exchange rate will be less than proportional to the change in the stock of money when crowding out does not dominate, and monetary

[10] See Eq. (C.8a) in Appendix C.

[11] In the steady state, $dY^d = dY - dG_N - dG_1$. Under ultraclassical conditions, however, $dY = \sigma_N(dp_N/p_N) + \sigma_1(dp_1/p_1) = Y(dp_i/p_i)$ for $i = 1, N$, because $(dp_N/p_N) = (dp_1/p_1)$ and $\sigma_i = p_i Q_i$. Furthermore, $dG_i = G_i(dp_i/p_i)$ when government spending is fixed in real terms. Therefore, $dY^d = Y^d(dp_i/p_i)$, or $(dY^d/Y^d) = (dp_i/p_i)$. The proof that $(d\pi/\pi) = (dY^d/Y^d)$ is given in connection with Eq. (C.9) in Appendix C. (It follows from the proof that $N_t = Y^d N_w$ under ultraclassical conditions.)

[12] From Eq. (3.21a), $(dY^d/Y^d) = (1/H_\pi)[S_1(L_{1W} + B_{1W}) + S_W B_{01}](L_1/S_Y Y^d)(d\bar{B}^c_1/L_1)$. But $L_1 = L_{1W} W^h$, because demands for assets are homogeneous of first degree in nominal wealth, and $(W^h/S_Y Y^d) = -(1/S_W)$ in the initial steady state, because the saving function is homogeneous of first degree in Y^d and W^h. Finally, under ultraclassical conditions, $(dY^d/Y^d) = (d\pi/\pi)$. Making the appropriate substitutions and rearranging terms, we obtain the equation in the text.

policy will not be perfectly neutral, even when there is no money illusion in labor-market or government behavior.

There are several ways of looking at the statement made by this last equation. When p_N, p_1, and π move together, for example, the change in any one of them can be used to represent the change in the price level, and the left-hand side of the equation stands for the long-run change in real balances resulting from an open-market purchase. On this interpretation, the equation says that an open-market purchase will raise real balances when crowding out does not dominate, despite the depreciation of the home currency. In many models used to study flexible exchange rates, no such change occurs. In those models, however, money is the only home-currency asset or the only one denominated in that currency. In our model, by contrast, two assets are denominated in home currency— money and the domestic bond. Under a flexible exchange rate, moreover, the supplies of the two assets are determined exogenously, and relative supplies are altered exogenously by an open-market purchase. Thus, a change in the price level that prevents a change in the real supply of one asset cannot prevent a change in the real supply of the other. Furthermore, the domestic bond is not a perfect substitute for the foreign bond, which means that households cannot compensate for a change in the real supply of the domestic bond by purchasing or selling the foreign bond. The domestic interest rate must change together with the change in the price level.[13]

The cause of nonneutrality in our model–the presence of a second home-currency asset–is the one cited by Patinkin as the cause of nonneutrality in a closed economy.[14] We cite it once again when we study the effects of a devaluation and show that it will not be neutral either, even under ultraclassical conditions.

---

[13] When the two bonds in our model are perfect substitutes, $H_\pi \to \infty$, so that $(d\bar{B}_1^c/L_1) - (d\pi/\pi) \to 0$. The real supply of the composite bond can be adjusted endogenously at a constant interest rate, by purchases or sales of the foreign bond, and the price level (exchange rate) is free to rise sufficiently to prevent a change in real balances.

[14] D. Patinkin, *Money, Interest, and Prices*, Harper & Row, New York, 1965, pp. 288–94; also D. Roper, "Two Ingredients of Monetarism in an International Setting," Seminar Paper 46, Institute for International Economic Studies, Stockholm, 1975, cited in P. Isard, *Exchange-Rate Determination: A Survey of Popular Views and Recent Models*, Princeton Studies in International Finance 42, Princeton University, Princeton, N.J., 1978, pp. 25–6. Dornbusch argues that an open-market purchase of the *foreign* bond will be completely neutral, but he draws this conclusion from a model in which the domestic bond is denominated in real (not nominal) units; see R. Dornbusch, "A Portfolio Balance Model of the Open Economy," *Journal of Monetary Economics*, 1 (January 1975), pp. 3–20.

Implications of asset-market integration. The influence of asset-market integration on the functioning of monetary policy has been studied intensively in abstract and econometric models. Most analyses confirm the conclusions reached initially by Mundell, Fleming, and Sohmen. An increase in asset-market integration (capital mobility) reduces the effectiveness of monetary policy with a pegged exchange rate and enhances its effectiveness with a flexible rate.[15] We reaffirm this familiar conclusion but show that it depends in part on the assumption that crowding out does not dominate.[16]

When there is no substitutability between domestic and foreign bonds, $B_{01} = 0$, so that $B_{11} = -L_{11}$, and an open-market purchase of domestic bonds causes identical downward shifts in the asset-market curves. In Figure 5.1A, for example, the shift of the money-market curve from MM to $M'M'$ would be matched by an equal vertical shift of the bond-market curve (not shown). The two curves would intersect at the initial level of wealth, and asset-market equilibrium would be established without any change in reserves. (In Figure 5.1B the shifts in DD and RR would be identical, and the new equilibrium point would lie directly below m.) Desired saving would decrease, shifting the short-run income curve in Figure 5.2, and the shift would be bigger than the one from zz to $z'z'$, because the reduction in r_1 would be bigger. Equilibrium would be established above v', and the increase in income would be larger.

Reversing the analysis, we can therefore conclude that asset-market integration reduces the influence of monetary policy with a pegged exchange rate. It causes a larger loss of reserves, a smaller drop in the domestic interest rate, and a smaller increase in income. The argument, moreover, can be extended to the limiting case. With perfect substitutability between the two bonds, WW becomes horizontal and does not shift in response to an open-market purchase. By implication, the economy cannot depart from w in Figure 5.1A, and the money-market curve must

---

[15] See the citations in note 7. For surveys of subsequent research including econometric work, see R. C. Bryant, "Empirical Research on Financial Capital Flows," and J. Helliwell, "Adjustment Under Fixed and Flexible Exchange Rates," in P. B. Kenen, ed., *International Trade and Finance: Frontiers for Research*, Cambridge University Press, Cambridge, 1975, pp. 321–62, 379–410, and Z. Hodjera, "International Short-Term Capital Movements: A Survey of Theory and Empirical Analysis," *International Monetary Fund Staff Papers*, 20 (November 1973), pp. 683–740; also P. B. Kenen and Associates, *A Model of the U.S. Balance of Payments*, Lexington Books, Lexington, Mass., 1978, chap. 6.

[16] This result is anticipated in E. Katz, "The Efficacy of Fiscal and Monetary Policies Under Floating Exchange Rates: The Implications of Capital Mobility Reconsidered," Queen Mary College, London, 1977 (mimeograph).

return at once to its initial position. It is shifted to $M'M'$ by the open-market purchase but shifts back to MM immediately. The instantaneous loss of reserves must offset exactly the open-market purchase, so that there will be no net change in the stock of money. Households will buy foreign bonds to replace *all* of the domestic bonds sold to the central bank and will thus "export" all of the new money created by the open-market purchase. (In Figure 5.1B, BB will stay put, and equilibrium will be displaced at once from m to n.) With no change in the interest rate, moreover, desired saving cannot change, and income will be unaffected. Under a pegged exchange rate, perfect asset-market integration robs monetary policy of any influence over the economy, even in the short run.

These same findings are stated algebraically in Table 5.2. The first column shows how an increase in substitutability affects the increase in income, the loss of reserves with a pegged exchange rate, and the depreciation of the home currency with a flexible exchange rate. The second column shows what happens to the changes in those variables in the limiting case of perfect substitutability.[17] On the first line of the table, for example, we show that an increase in asset-market integration diminishes the short-run increase in income with a pegged exchange rate and that the increase goes to zero with perfect integration (when $-B_{01} \to \infty$). On the third line, we show that an increase in integration enlarges the short-run reserve loss and that it goes to -1 with perfect integration (i.e., that $\bar{\pi}\delta R \to -\delta\bar{B}_1^c$, so that $\delta L_1 \to 0$).

We have already seen that monetary policy cannot affect income permanently with a pegged exchange rate, which is why there are zeros in the second line of Table 5.2. It does cause a permanent loss of reserves, however, that is at least as large as the short-run loss. We saw earlier that the long-run loss of reserves is smaller than the open-market purchase when crowding out does not dominate. But the influence of crowding out, whether or not dominant, varies inversely with asset-market integration. Therefore, integration reduces the difference between reserve losses in the short run and the long run, and perfect integration reduces it to zero. To put the point another way, asset-market integration increases the reserve loss on impact and permanently, but more so on impact, so that the loss through time is smaller. (Mathematically, the limit $dL_1 \to 0$ is a lower limit when $S_W L_{11} > L_{1W} S_1$, because the loss of reserves increases with

[17] To illustrate the derivation of statements in this table, Eqs. (3.7b) and (3.8b) give us $(\delta Y / \delta \bar{B}_1^c) = (N_u / N_s)(S_1 / B_{11})$. Taking the derivative of this expression with respect to $-B_{01}$ (or B_{11}), we obtain the expression in the first row and column of Table 5.2. Taking the limit of the original expression as $-B_{01} \to \infty$, we obtain the limit (zero) in the first row and second column.

substitutability, but it is an upper limit in the opposite case, because the loss decreases with substitutability.)

To sum up for the pegged-rate case, asset-market integration reduces the short-run increase in income resulting from an open-market purchase and foreshortens the process by which it wears off. With perfect integration, indeed, the process is contained within a moment in time. An open-market purchase serves merely to alter instantaneously the mix of foreign and domestic bonds held by the economy. The central bank acquires domestic bonds and loses reserves. Households lose domestic bonds and acquire foreign bonds. Perfect integration turns our model into a simple, small-country construct. The two bonds become one, and the supply of the composite is perfectly elastic at the interest rate $\bar{r}_0$. The central bank has no policy autonomy, even in the short run.

The influence of asset-market integration is more pervasive under a flexible exchange rate, because it affects the size of the permanent increase in income resulting from an open-market purchase. But crowding out is decisive for the *direction* of that influence. If crowding out does not dominate, asset-market integration will enhance the influence of monetary policy in the short run and the long run. Otherwise, it may not do so in the short run and cannot do so in the long run. The influence of asset-market integration can be analyzed by using Figure 5.4, which depicts the country's asset markets in two limiting cases—with no integration ($B_{01} = 0$) and with perfect integration ($-B_{01} \rightarrow \infty$).

The downward-sloping curve WW is the one that obtains with no integration. In this case, an open-market purchase causes WW and MM to shift down by equal amounts, to W^*W^* and M^*M^*, respectively, and to intersect at w', directly below the initial point w. The reduction in the interest rate shown at w' is the largest that can be produced by an open-market purchase (and equals the reduction that occurs with a pegged exchange rate). There is no immediate change in the exchange rate or wealth, because households do not seek to substitute foreign for domestic bonds.

The horizontal curve W_iW_i is the one that obtains with perfect integration, and it is not shifted by an open-market purchase. Thus, asset-market equilibrium is displaced to w_i', directly to the left of w. Households do attempt to buy foreign bonds, but the instantaneous adjustment in portfolios comes about through the resulting depreciation of the home currency and increase in wealth. There is no change in the interest rate.

The relevance of these responses for the short-run change in income

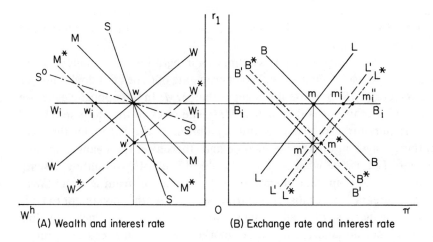

Figure 5.4 Effects of asset-market integration on responses to an open-market purchase: impact and steady-state effects on asset markets under a flexible exchange rate.

can be illustrated with the aid of Figure 5.2, interpreted appropriately. With no integration, the shift in the short-run income curve is produced by the reduction in the interest rate (there is no change in wealth), and there is no immediate change in the exchange rate. Denote this outcome by the shift from zz to $z'z'$ and the displacement of equilibrium from v to v', where $z'z'$ intersects the (unchanged) exchange-rate schedule $\pi_0\pi_0$. With perfect integration, there is again a shift in the short-run income curve, but it is produced by the increase in wealth (there is no change in the interest rate). Denote this effect by the shift from zz to $z''z''$. In this case, moreover, the home currency depreciates, shifting the exchange-rate schedule from $\pi_0\pi_0$ to $\pi'\pi'$, and moving the economy to v''.

Given this interpretation of Figure 5.2, the increase of income is clearly larger with perfect asset-market integration. Monetary policy is more effective. There are two reasons. First, the depreciation of the home currency has an expenditure-switching effect, denoted by the movement along $z''z''$. Second, the shift in the short-run income curve is larger. This second reason holds, however, only when crowding out does not dominate. The expenditure-raising effect of the increase in wealth (the movement from zz to $z''z''$ with perfect integration) is assumed to be larger than that of the decrease in the interest rate (the movement from zz to $z'z'$ with no integration). If crowding out did dominate, $z''z''$ could lie below $z'z'$, and the expenditure-switching effect might not be large enough to compensate for the smaller shift (income could be lower at the counterpart of v'' than it is at v').[18]

The steady-state effects of asset-market integration can be analyzed entirely by the use of Figure 5.4. When crowding out does not dominate, we use the curve SS, because it is steeper than MM. In the opposite case, we use S^0S^0, because it is flatter than MM. The sizes of the shifts in SS and S^0S^0 required to establish long-run equilibrium allow us to infer the sizes of the changes in disposable income and, therefore, the changes in total income. Let us see what SS and S^0S^0 do in each of two limiting cases.

With no asset-market integration, SS must travel from w to w'. With perfect integration, it must travel from w to w_i'. As the movement to w_i' is larger, the increase in steady-state income must be larger. When crowding out does not dominate, then, asset-market integration necessarily raises the effectiveness of monetary policy; our model reproduces the familiar result in the long run as well as the short run. The outcomes for S^0S^0, however, are reversed. The distance it must travel from w to w_i' is smaller than the distance it must travel from w to w', which says that the steady-state increase in income must be smaller too. When crowding out dominates, asset-market integration necessarily reduces the effectiveness of monetary policy in the long run.

These conclusions are reproduced in Table 5.2. The last four rows of the first column show that when $S_W L_{11} > L_{1W} S_1$, an increase of asset-market integration raises the increase in nominal income resulting from an open-market purchase and causes a larger depreciation of the home currency.[19]

---

[18] To make the same point algebraically, we use Eqs. (3.2a) and (3.3a) to measure the change in desired dissaving resulting from the change in r_1 and π (the shift in the short-run income curve): $-(\delta^* S/\delta \bar{B}_1^c)|_{\bar{\gamma}^d} = (1/H_\pi)[S_1(L_{1W} + B_{1W}) + S_W B_{01}]$. The derivative of this expression with respect to $-B_{01}$ is $(1/H_\pi^2)(S_W L_{11} - L_{1W} S_1)(B_{1W} + L_{1W})$. When crowding out does not dominate, an increase in substitutability enlarges desired dissaving and the upward shift in the short-run income curve. This is the result recorded in the fifth line of Table 5.2, where the derivative is positive whenever $V_\pi(S_W L_{11} - L_{1W} S_1) > (N_t/N_u)L_{11}$. Because a depreciation of the home currency serves also to switch expenditure to domestic goods, improving the current-account balance, it is sufficient but not necessary to assume that $S_W L_{11} > L_{1W} S_1$ in order to assert that asset-market integration raises the effectiveness of monetary policy in the short run.

[19] The conclusions with respect to the exchange rate are illustrated in Figure 5.4B. With no integration, asset-market equilibrium is displaced from m to m' in the short run and to m^* in the long run. With perfect integration, it is displaced from m to m_i' and then to m_i''. It can be shown, however, that m_i'' lies to the right of m^* (that there is a larger depreciation of the home currency with perfect integration) if and only if crowding out does not dominate.

Table 5.2. *Influence of capital mobility on the effectiveness of monetary policy*

Case	Result of increase in substitutability	Size of change with perfect substitutability
Pegged exchange rate		
Influence on size of change in income		
Impact effect	$-(1/B_{11})(S_1 N_u/B_{11}N_s) < 0$	0
Steady-state effect	0	0^b
Influence on size of change in reserves		
Impact effect	$(1/B_{11})(L_{11}/B_{11}) < 0$	-1
Steady-state effect	$(1/H_f)(S_W/H_f)(S_W L_{11} - L_{1W}S_1) < 0^a$	-1
Flexible exchange rate		
Influence on size of change in income		
Impact effect	$(1/V_\pi H_\pi)[N_u(1 - B_{0W})/N_s H_\pi][V_\pi(S_W L_{11} - L_{1W}S_1) - (N_t/N_u)L_{11}] > 0^a$	$(N_u/N_s V_\pi L_{1W})[(N_t/N_u) - S_W V_\pi] > 0$
Steady-state effect	$(1/H_\pi S_Y)[(1 - B_{0W})(S_W L_{11} - L_{1W}S_1)/H_\pi] > 0^a$	$-(S_W/L_{1W}S_Y) > 0$
Influence on size of change in exchange rate		
Impact effect	$-(1/V_\pi H_\pi)[L_{11}(1 - B_{0W})/H_\pi] > 0$	$(1/V_\pi L_{1W}) > 0$
Steady-state effect	$(1/H_\pi S_Y)[N_W(1 - B_{0W})(S_W L_{11} - L_{1W}S_1)/N_t H_\pi] > 0^a$	$-(N_W S_W/N_t L_{1W}S_Y) > 0$

^{a} On the assumption that crowding out does not dominate. ^{b} Regardless of degree of substitutability.

To sum up for the flexible-rate case, asset-market integration is likely to enlarge the short-run increase in income resulting from an open-market purchase. It will always do so when crowding out does not dominate, and it can even do so in the opposite case, because the expenditure-switching effect of a depreciation can swamp the expenditure-reducing effect that takes place in that instance. But the influence of asset-market integration on long-run outcomes depends entirely on the crowding-out effect. Asset-market integration will enlarge the steady-state increase in income if and only if crowding out does not dominate.

The special goods-market cases. When studying goods-market disturbances in Chapter 4, we found that the signs of many outcomes depended on the properties of the two domestic goods. Under a pegged exchange rate, for example, a shift in domestic demand from the export good to the nontraded good led to a permanent decrease in income in the traded-goods variant of the model (where $u_{0N} \to \infty$) but led to a permanent increase in the composite-good variant (where $u_{10} \to \infty$). The effects of asset-market disturbances are less sensitive to these permutations, for the reason that their influence on goods markets arises initially from their impact on the level of absorption, not on its distribution across commodities. Under a flexible exchange rate, moreover, the prices of the two domestic goods are not constrained to move in opposite directions, as income need not move back to its initial level.

When the exchange rate is pegged, the special goods-market cases are interesting only in the short run. In the steady state, all goods prices go back to their initial levels. Even in the short run, moreover, there are few major differences between the results obtained in the general case described by Table 5.1 and those obtained in the three special goods-market cases. In the traded-goods variant of the model (where $u_{0N} \to \infty$), an open-market purchase cannot cause a change in p_N, and all of the short-run increase in nominal income is due to the increase in p_1. In the composite-good variant (where $u_{10} \to \infty$), there can be no change in p_1, and all of the increase in income is due to the increase in p_N. Finally, in the single-good variant (where $u_{1N} \to \infty$), there can be no change in relative prices, and the increase in Y reflects an equiproportional increase in the two domestic prices. In all three variants, however, the wage rate rises in the classical case, and employment rises in the Keynesian case.

When the exchange rate is flexible, there are increases in p_N and p_1 in all goods-market variants, on impact and permanently, because the home currency depreciates immediately with an open-market purchase. In the traded-goods variant, there is an immediate increase in the price of the import-competing good (alias the nontraded good). In the composite-good variant, there is an immediate increase in the price of the export good. It follows directly that the increase in income resulting from an open-market purchase is always associated with an increase in the wage rate in the classical case and an increase in employment in the Keynesian case. (We have already derived an expression for the long-run change in relative domestic prices and seen that it is zero under ultraclassical conditions. When one of those conditions is violated, the change in p_1/p_N is negative in the traded-goods variant, ambiguous in the composite-good variant, and zero in the single-good variant.)

The results just summarized, moreover, hold also for a change in the foreign interest rate and for an increase in the budget deficit brought about by a reduction in lump-sum taxes. Thus, we shall not look again at these limiting goods-market cases until we examine the effects of a devaluation.

Changes in the foreign interest rate

In our work on the effects of goods-market disturbances, we were able to confirm a familiar proposition. When assets are traded together with goods, a flexible exchange rate cannot confer immediate insulation against an external disturbance.[20] Insulation obtains only in the steady state, when capital flows have come to an end. At that point, a flexible exchange rate clears goods markets by balancing the current account–by equating total expenditure on domestic goods with the value of domestic output. We come now to another important proposition. A flexible exchange rate cannot confer insulation, even in the long run, in the face of an external asset-market disturbance. When foreign bonds are held domestically and are partial substitutes for domestic bonds, a change in the foreign interest rate, the example we have chosen, has permanent effects on the domestic economy. It alters demands for domestic bonds and money and leads to a permanent change in income.

Under pegged and flexible exchange rates alike, however, there is uncertainty about the ways in which a change in $\bar{r}_0$ affects the economy. Table 5.3, summarizing our results, is littered with question marks. The

[20] See, e.g., R. G. McTeer, "Economic Independence and Insulation Through Flexible Exchange Rates," in N. A. Beadles and L. A. Drewry, eds., *Money, the Market and the State*, University of Georgia Press, Athens, Ga., 1968, pp. 102–33, and E. Tower and T. D. Willett, *The Theory of Optimum Currency Areas and Exchange-Rate Flexibility: A More General Framework*, Special Papers in International Economics 11, Princeton University, Princeton, N.J., 1976, pp. 51–4.

Table 5.3. *Increase in the foreign interest rate*

Variable	Pegged rate		Flexible rate	
	Impact effect	Steady-state effect	Impact effect	Steady-state effect
p_N	$-$	0	?[a]	?[a]
p_1	$-$	0	?[a]	?[a]
p_1/p_N	?	0	?	?
Y	$-$	0	?[a]	?[a]
Y^d	$-$	0	?[a]	?[a]
r_1	$+$[b]	?[b]	?[b]	?[b]
$\bar{\pi}R$	$-$	?[c]	0	0
π	0	0	$+$	?[a]
W^h	0	$+$	$+$	$+$

Sign for $\delta\bar{r}_0 > 0$.
[a] Positive when $H_0 > 0$.
[b] Goes to $\delta\bar{r}_0$ when domestic and foreign bonds are perfect substitutes.
[c] Negative when $H_0 > 0$.

main reason is uncertainty about the sign of an expression that appeared pervasively in Chapter 3:

$$H_0 = B_{1W}(L_{11}S_0 - L_{10}S_1) + B_{11}(S_W L_{10} - L_{1W}S_0) - B_{10}(S_W L_{11} - L_{1W}S_1)$$

When crowding out does not dominate with respect to either interest rate, the second and third terms in H_0 are positive. But we cannot be sure that H_0 is positive unless, in addition, $L_{11}S_0 \geqslant L_{10}S_1$, and we have not yet made any such assumption.[21] It is thus pointless to examine exhaustively the responses to a change in the foreign interest rate, and we shall confine ourselves to three tasks. We shall show why there are so many ambiguities in Table 5.3, why there are important differences between responses under pegged and flexible exchange rates, and why a flexible exchange rate cannot confer insulation.

Outcomes under a pegged rate. The immediate effects of an increase in the foreign interest rate are shown in Figure 5.5A. First, it reduces the demand for the domestic bond, creating excess supply in the bond market.

[21] When we assume that $L_{11}S_0 = L_{10}S_1$ (the special case considered below), it will be unnecessary to assume that crowding out does not dominate with respect to the foreign interest rate. Substituting $L_{11}(S_0/S_1)$ for L_{10}, we obtain $H_0 = [(B_{11}S_0 - B_{10}S_1)(S_W L_{11} - L_{1W}S_1)/S_1]$, so that $H_0 > 0$ when crowding out does not dominate with respect to the domestic interest rate.

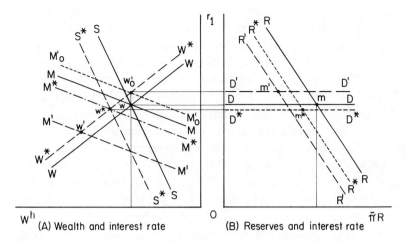

Figure 5.5 Increase in the foreign interest rate: impact and steady-state effects on asset markets under a pegged exchange rate.

At each and every level of wealth, an increase in r_1 is needed to offset the increase in $\bar{r}_0$, and the bond-market curve must shift upward from WW to W^*W^*. The size of the shift depends, of course, on the degree of substitutability between the two bonds; algebraically, it is $\delta r_1|_{\bar{w}^h} = -(B_{10}/B_{11})\,\delta\bar{r}_0$, as shown in the table at the end of Chapter 4. Second, the increase in the foreign interest rate reduces the demand for money, creating excess supply in the money market. But here, a decrease in r_1 is needed to offset the increase in $\bar{r}_0$, and the money-market curve must shift downward from MM to $M'M'$. The size of this shift is given by $\delta r_1|_{\bar{w}^h} = -(L_{10}/L_{11})\,\delta\bar{r}_0$.

As wealth cannot change instantaneously with a pegged exchange rate, momentary equilibrium is determined by initial wealth and the new position of the bond-market curve. It is established at w'_0, vertically above w, and the money-market curve shifts back from $M'M'$ to $M'_0M'_0$. The bond market is cleared by an increase in the domestic interest rate, there being no other way to clear it when the domestic bond is not traded and the supply is fixed. The money market is cleared by a loss of reserves that reduces the stock of money. As with an open-market purchase, there is an increase in demand for foreign currency, as households seek to buy foreign bonds, and the central bank supplies the foreign currency from its reserves.

In the present case, however, the households' offer of domestic money exceeds the initial excess supply, because $M'_0M'_0$ lies above MM. This is because the increase in r_1 required to clear the bond market enlarges the excess supply of money. The same point is made in Figure 5.5B, where the money-market curve shifts downward from RR to $R'R'$ (by as much as the shift from MM to $M'M'$), and the bond-market curve shifts upward from DD to $D'D'$ (by as much as the increase in r_1). Momentary equilibrium is displaced from m to m', and the reserve loss is larger than the leftward shift from RR to $R'R'$ (the initial excess supply of money).

When both interest rates rise, as they do here, households seek to save, and the short-run income curve is displaced from zz to $z'z'$ in Figure 5.6. Momentary equilibrium is established at v', and income is reduced instantaneously. But the long-run curve ZZ does not shift, which means that steady-state equilibrium must be restored at v. There can be no permanent change in nominal income or disposable income.

In previous examples, curve SS remained in place when there was no permanent change in disposable income, but that is not the case here. An increase in the foreign interest rate affects SS directly, because it affects desired saving. Specifically, an increase in $\bar{r}_0$ must be offset by a decrease in r_1, given the level of wealth, if there is to be no saving in the steady state, and it must therefore cause a downward shift in SS. Algebraically, $\delta r_1|_{\bar{w}^h} = -(S_0/S_1)\, \delta\bar{r}_0$. Accordingly, steady-state equilibrium will be established at w^* in Figure 5.5A, shifting the money-market curve from $M_0'M_0'$ to M^*M^*. The domestic interest rate must come to rest at a level lower than it was at w_0', but it can be either higher or lower than it was initially. (It is, in fact, drawn to be lower in Figure 5.5A.) The sign of the permanent change in reserves is likewise ambiguous. We can be sure that reserves will rise during the transition to the new steady state (the economy will run a balance-of-payments surplus), because M^*M^* must lie below $M_0'M_0'$. But we cannot know whether reserves will rise by more than they fell on impact—whether M^*M^* will lie below or above $M'M'$.

Uncertainty about the change in the domestic interest rate cannot be resolved by any simple supposition; the location of w^* depends on the slopes and shifts of W^*W^* and S^*S^*. We know only that the rate is less likely to decline, relative to its initial level, the greater is the degree of substitutability between the two bonds. (The greater the degree of substitutability, the flatter the bond-market curve and the larger the shift from WW to W^*W^*.) Uncertainty about the change in reserves, by contrast, can be resolved by invoking two assumptions: (1) that crowding out does not dominate, and (2) that $(S_0/S_1) = (L_{10}/L_{11})$.

We have already seen the need for the first assumption. It helped us to obtain a number of results bearing on the influence of monetary policy,

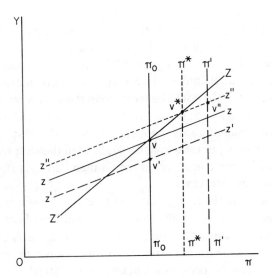

Figure 5.6 Increase in the foreign interest rate: impact and steady-state effects on nominal income under pegged and flexible exchange rates.

and it will help us to obtain important results bearing on the influence of fiscal policy. The second assumption is needed only when there is a change in the foreign interest rate (or when expectations are not stationary, as in Chapter 9). It is not hard to justify, however, in terms of household behavior. The terms S_0 and S_1 speak to the opportunity cost of consumption (the income foregone by not saving). The terms L_{10} and L_{11} speak to the opportunity cost of holding money (the income foregone by not holding bonds). Both costs should bear some relationship to the sizes of holdings of foreign and domestic bonds, which determine the weights that the two interest rates should be given in cost calculations, and the assumption of "proportionality" can be taken to assert that the weights are equal to the holdings (i.e., that they are proportional to the ratio B_{0W}/B_{1W}).

The two assumptions are employed in Figure 5.5A, where S^*S^* is steeper than M^*M^*, reflecting the first assumption, and the vertical shift from SS to S^*S^* is of the same size as the shift from MM to $M'M'$, reflecting the second. Algebraically, the assumptions guarantee that H_0 is positive. Diagrammatically, they guarantee that w^* will lie to the northeast of w' and that the gradual shift from $M_0'M_0'$ to M^*M^* will be smaller than the instantaneous shift from $M'M'$ to $M_0'M_0'$. The gradual increase in reserves on the way to the steady state will be smaller than the instantaneous reduction in reserves that took place when households shifted into foreign bonds. (To see why both assumptions play roles here, consider the effects of relaxing them sequentially. If crowding out dominated, $M'M'$ would be steeper than S^*S^* in Figure 5.5A, and the locations of w' and w^* would be reversed. If interest-rate responses were not proportional, the shift from SS to S^*S^* could be larger than the shift from MM to $M'M'$, and if it were large enough, it too could reverse the locations of w' and w^*. With the reversal of those points, however, the shift of the money-market curve from w'_0 to w^* would be larger than the shift from w' to w'_0, and the gradual increase in reserves would then be larger than the instantaneous decrease in reserves.)

To sum up, an increase in the foreign interest rate is deflationary in the short run with a pegged exchange rate. Nominal income falls because of the reduction in absorption caused by the exogenous increase in $\bar{r}_0$ and the endogenous increase in r_1. With the passage of time, however, income rises and r_1 falls, and when the economy reaches its new steady state, income is restored to its initial level, while r_1 may be higher or lower than it was before the increase in $\bar{r}_0$. The behavior of reserves is summarized in Figure 5.5B. There is a loss on impact (the movement from m to m') and a gain thereafter (the movement from m' to m^*). The net effect is uncertain. When crowding out does not dominate, however, and the responses of saving to changes in interest rates are proportional to the responses of the demand for money, there is a long-run loss (m^* is to the right of m' but to the left of m).

Outcomes under a flexible rate. Here, the effects of disturbance are more complicated, and ambiguities are more frequent in Table 5.3. The reason is that the sign of H_0 matters from the start, not only in the long run. To simplify matters, we shall therefore invoke immediately the assumptions used above to guarantee that H_0 is positive.

Looking at Figure 5.7A, the initial shifts in the asset-market curves are the same as those with a pegged exchange rate, but the curves do not shift again. Asset-market equilibrium is established at w', immediately and permanently. Thus, wealth rises instantaneously, because the home currency depreciates at once in response to an excess demand for the foreign bond, and the domestic interest rate changes too. But the sign of the change in r_1 is uncertain, even when H_0 is positive; it depends on both the relative shifts and relative slopes of WW and MM.

One outcome is certain, however, and it is important. Unless the two bonds in our model are perfect substitutes, the domestic interest rate cannot rise as much with a flexible exchange rate as it did with a pegged

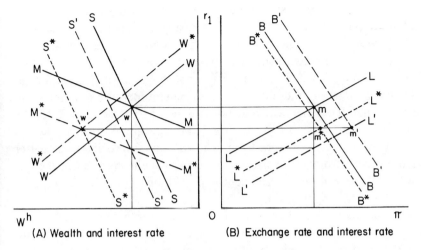

(A) Wealth and interest rate   (B) Exchange rate and interest rate

Figure 5.7 Increase in the foreign interest rate: impact and steady-state effects on asset markets under a flexible exchange rate.

rate (it can in fact decline, as it does in Figure 5.7A). For this reason, and because wealth rises immediately, saving does not fall as much, and the short-run income curve cannot fall as far as it did with a pegged exchange rate. When, indeed, H_0 is positive, the wealth effect dominates, causing the curve to rise rather than fall.[22] Thus, it shifts from zz to $z''z''$ in Figure 5.6. Finally, the depreciation of the home currency, denoted by the shift from $\pi_0\pi_0$ to $\pi'\pi'$, causes the economy to move along $z''z''$ to v''. Income cannot fall as far as with a pegged exchange rate, and when H_0 is positive, it rises instead.

Under a flexible exchange rate, of course, the short-run income curve does not shift again after moving from zz to $z''z''$. Therefore, the steady-state level of income is to be found at v^* in Figure 5.6, where $z''z''$ intersects ZZ. When H_0 is positive, income will rise permanently and the home currency will depreciate because of the upward shift in the short-run income curve. (The opposite result obtains when H_0 is negative, because of the downward shift in the short-run curve.) But the steady-state changes in Y and π will be smaller than the short-run changes. When $(S_0/S_1) = (L_{10}/L_{11})$, the change in π must be larger in the short run, and when π rises in the long run (because $H_0 > 0$), there must thus be "overshooting" in the short run, as shown in Figure 5.6.

These results are consistent with those in the asset markets, depicted in

[22] In proof, hold disposable income constant and calculate the change in desired saving, using the changes in r_1 and π given by Eqs. (3.2a) and (3.3a): $\delta^*S|_{\bar{y}^d} = -(H_0/H_\pi)\,\delta\bar{r}_0$. Desired saving falls and zz shifts upward when $H_0 > 0$.

Figure 5.7A. The steady-state requirement that saving be zero says that S^*S^* must pass through w'. When interest-rate responses are proportional, however, and crowding out does not dominate, the increase in $\bar{r}_0$ will not cause a sufficient shift. The exogenous increase in $\bar{r}_0$ produces a movement from SS to $S'S'$, and an additional shift is needed, from $S'S'$ to S^*S^*. By implication, there must be a permanent increase in nominal income to generate an increase in disposable income.[23] The behavior of the exchange rate is described by Figure 5.7B. The home currency depreciates at once (the movement from m to m') and appreciates thereafter (the movement from m' to m^*), but the permanent increase in income says that there will be a permanent depreciation of the home currency (that m^* is to the right of m).

To summarize our findings for the simple case in which crowding out does not dominate and interest-rate responses are proportional, an increase in the foreign interest rate is inflationary with a flexible exchange rate. Because the home currency depreciates on impact, there is an immediate increase in income. And though the home currency appreciates through time, causing income to decline, the impact effects are not reversed. Income is higher in the new steady state than it was initially, and π is higher too. But the change in the domestic interest rate is ambiguous, just as it was with a pegged exchange rate.

Implications of asset-market integration. We have already mentioned the principal effect of asset-market integration on responses to an increase in the foreign interest rate. The greater the degree of substitutability between the domestic and foreign bonds, the flatter is the curve WW and the larger the shift in WW with an increase in $\bar{r}_0$. When indeed the two bonds are perfect substitutes (when $-B_{01}$, $-B_{10} \to \infty$), WW becomes horizontal, and the vertical shift to W^*W^* measures the change in the foreign interest rate.[24] Inspection of Figures 5.5 and 5.7 reveals the main implication. Asset-market integration strengthens the connection between the two interest rates, and an increase in the foreign rate produces a larger increase (smaller decrease) in the domestic rate. Under the assumptions adopted above, moreover, it can be shown that asset-market integration enlarges the reductions in income and reserves under a pegged exchange

---

[23] If the shift from SS to $S'S'$ were larger than the shift from MM to M^*M^*, then $S'S'$ could meet W^*W^* below w'. If crowding out dominated, S^*S^* would lie below $S'S'$, given equal shifts to $S'S'$ and M^*M^*. In each instance, Y would have to fall to reduce Y^d.

[24] The shift in WW is $\delta r_1 = -(B_{10}/B_{11}) \delta \bar{r}_0$, and we have assumed that $B_{11} > -B_{10}$ when the latter is finite. When the two bonds become perfect substitutes, however, $-B_{10} \to \infty$, and $-B_{01} \to \infty$ (which means, in turn that $B_{11} \to \infty$). Thus, the shift in WW becomes $\delta r_1 = \delta \bar{r}_0$.

rate and enlarges the increase in income and the depreciation of the home currency under a flexible rate.[25]

In Figure 5.5A, closer integration will enlarge the shift to W^*W^*, lengthening the distance ww_0'. The instantaneous increase in r_1 will be bigger, together with the loss of reserves (the latter because of the increase in the shift from $M'M'$ to $M_0'M_0'$). By implication, desired saving will rise further, and the downward shift to $z'z'$ will be larger in Figure 5.6. Income will fall further. In the steady state, moreover, w^* will move to the northwest in Figure 5.5A, because W^*W^* is higher and flatter, which means that r_1 will be higher and the long-run loss of reserves will be larger (the latter because M^*M^* will lie further from $M'M'$ when crowding out does not dominate).

In Figure 5.7A, closer integration will move w' to the northwest, raising the increase in r_1 (reducing the decrease). Furthermore, the increase in wealth will be bigger, which says that the depreciation will be larger. In Figure 5.6, the upward shift to $z''z''$ will be larger when H_0 is positive. Therefore, income will rise further (because of the larger shift in the short-run income curve combined with the larger depreciation that makes for more movement along the curve). The larger the shift to $z''z''$, moreover, the larger the permanent increase in income and the larger the permanent depreciation of the home currency.

Compound disturbances

Heretofore, we have been able to exploit the sharp distinction between disturbances and policy changes that appear directly only in goods markets and those that appear directly only in asset markets. Goods-market disturbances have affected asset markets, but only by affecting income, saving, and wealth, thereby affecting endogenously the demands for assets. Similarly, asset-market disturbances have affected goods markets, but only by affecting the interest rate and exchange rate, thereby affecting endogenously domestic and foreign demands for goods.

We must now consider two disturbances that impinge directly on both sets of markets. A tax reduction does so sequentially. It starts as a goods-market disturbance but begins to have direct asset-market effects as the government issues bonds to finance its deficit. A devaluation of a

[25] Proofs of these assertions can be adduced by taking derivatives and limits analogous to those in Table 5.2 (and assuming that $\delta B_{01} = \delta B_{10} = -\delta B_{11}$). The same method can be used to prove the proposition in the text below that the effects of a larger increase in π swamp the effect of a larger increase in r_1. (One need only differentiate the expression for the change in desired saving in note 22.)

pegged exchange rate affects both sets of markets directly and simultaneously. It affects goods markets by switching expenditure from foreign to home goods and affects asset markets by conferring capital gains on holders of foreign-currency bonds and thus raising their demands for domestic bonds and money.

Temporary tax reductions and budget deficits

In Chapter 2 we introduced a lump-sum tax, T^h, and instructed the government to adjust it continuously to realize a budget deficit, $\bar{D}$, that would be its principal fiscal target. Thus far, however, we have assumed that the government has held its deficit at zero. The supply of domestic bonds, B_1, has been fixed. We must now investigate a different policy: Suppose that the government reduces the lump-sum tax T^h to generate a deficit (and adjusts T^h thereafter to stabilize that deficit). It issues bonds to finance the deficit, adding gradually to B_1. At some subsequent point in time, however, the government raises T^h to balance its budget and keeps it balanced thereafter. The stimulus afforded by the temporary tax cut disappears at that point, but the economy is left with a larger stock of domestic bonds.[26]

The comparative-static analysis of this new policy can be divided into two distinct parts. The first is concerned with the impact effects of the tax cut. They are confined to goods markets, as there has not yet been any discernible increase in the supply of bonds. The second is concerned with the steady-state effects of the increase in the supply of bonds and must therefore focus on asset markets. The temporary tax cut has long since been rescinded. The results obtained from this two-part analysis are shown in Table 5.4, which lists the impact effects of the temporary tax cut (the increase in $\bar{D}$) along with the steady-state effects of the permanent increase in B_1 resulting from the interval of budget deficits.[27]

[26] The analysis would not be very different if there were a temporary increase in government spending, rather than a tax cut. The goods-market effects would be stronger, as none of the direct fiscal stimulus could leak into saving or imports before it had affected the demands for domestic outputs. But the long-run effects would depend solely on the change in the supply of debt, just as they do here. (For budget deficits financed by issuing money, see Appendix D.)

[27] Until recently, research on the theory of fiscal policy in open economies has emphasized the first step, at which taxes are cut and bonds are issued, and attention has focused on capital flows resulting from sales of government bonds. See, for example, Mundell, *International Economics,* chaps. 17–18, Fleming, *Essays in International Economics,* chap. 9, and the subsequent literature surveyed in M. v. N. Whitman, *Policies for Internal and External Balance,* Special Papers in International Economics 9, Princeton University, Princeton, N.J., 1970. Papers dealing with the long-run increase in the stock of debt include R. I. McKinnon and W. E. Oates, *The Implications of International Economic*

Table 5.4. *Temporary tax reduction and budget deficit*

	Pegged rate		Flexible rate	
Variable	Impact effect	Steady-state effect	Impact effect	Steady-state effect
p_N	+	0	+	$?^b$
p_1	+	0	+	$?^b$
p_1/p_N	?	0	?	?
Y^d	+	0	+	$?^b$
Y	+	0	+	$?^b$
r_1	0	+	0	+
$\bar{\pi}R$	0	$?^a$	0	0
π	0	0	0	$?^b$
W^h	0	+	0	+

Impact effects for $\delta \bar{D} > 0$; steady-state effects for $dB_1 > 0$.
[a] Negative when $S_W L_{11} > L_{1W} S_1$.
[b] Positive when $S_W L_{11} > L_{1W} S_1$.

Impact effects of a tax reduction. On impact, we said, a tax cut is a pure goods-market disturbance. It cannot affect the interest rate, exchange rate, or stock of reserves, because it has not yet affected the supply of bonds, B_1, or integral of saving, W^{hs}. And because it does not alter the exchange rate immediately, its impact effects are the same with pegged and flexible exchange rates. These effects are shown in Figure 5.8. The short-run income curve is shifted from zz to $z'z'$, as households increase their consumption, and goods-market equilibrium is displaced from v to v'. Nominal income rises.

The location of v' would seem to indicate dissaving, but this is not the case. When dealing with a budget deficit, we cannot infer the sign of saving from our standard diagram. Although v' lies above ZZ (which em-

Integration for Monetary, Fiscal, and Exchange-Rate Policy, Princeton Studies in International Finance 16, Princeton University, Princeton, N.J., 1966, R. I. McKinnon, "Portfolio Balance and International Payments Adjustment," in R. A. Mundell and A. K. Swoboda, eds., *Monetary Problems of the International Economy,* University of Chicago Press, Chicago, 1969, pp. 199–234, D. J. Mathieson, "Fiscal and Financial Policies in the Open Economy: A Long-run Perspective," *Journal of International Economics,* 4 (April 1974), pp. 67–76, W. H. Branson, "The Dual Roles of the Government Budget and the Balance of Payments in the Movement from Short-Run to Long-Run Equilibrium," *Quarterly Journal of Economics,* 90 (August 1976), pp. 345–68, and S. J. Turnovsky, "The Dynamics of Fiscal Policy in an Open Economy," *Journal of International Economics,* 6 (May 1976), pp. 115–42. In Chapter 10 we adopt a specification that resembles the one used by Turnovsky.

bodies the double assumption that $S = \bar{D} = 0$), we know only that the difference between $\bar{D}$ and S has to be positive.[28] It can be shown, however, that households start to save. As there has been no time for any change in r_1, π, or W^{hs}, the sign of the change in saving is given by

$$\delta S = S_Y \, \delta Y^d = S_Y(\delta Y + \delta \bar{D}) = S_Y[(N_u/N_s)(1 - S_Y) + 1] \, \delta \bar{D}$$

which is unambiguously positive. Furthermore,

$$\delta \bar{D} - \delta S = (N_w/N_s)(1 - S_Y) \, \delta \bar{D}$$

which says that $\bar{D} > S > 0$ at v' (because $\bar{D} = S = 0$ at v).

Steady-state effects of an increase in the stock of debt. In Chapter 6 we look at the behavior of the economy under the joint influence of a budget deficit and the corresponding increase in the supply of bonds. We find that it can follow a number of paths, depending on the exchange-rate regime and the degree of asset-market integration. We also trace its behavior from the time that the budget deficit is ended to the new steady state. Our task here, however, is merely to examine the properties of that long-run equilibrium.

When the economy has adjusted fully to the increase in the supply of bonds, it must come to rest on the long-run income curve ZZ in Figure 5.8. Under a pegged exchange rate, then, it must return to v, restoring income to its original level. A temporary tax cut cannot have a permanent influence on income, even though it leaves behind a permanent increase in the supply of bonds. Once the budget deficit is ended, moreover, the relationship between Y and Y^d reverts to what it was before the tax cut, and disposable income must also return to its original level. Accordingly, in Figure 5.9A, curve SS cannot shift, and long-run asset-market equilibrium must be established at some point on that curve. But the bond-market curve is shifted gradually upward under the influence of the increase in the supply of bonds and comes to rest at W^*W^* when the government balances its budget. Steady-state equilibrium is established at w^*, where W^*W^* intersects SS. Wealth and the interest rate rise permanently.

As usual, the change in reserves must move the money-market curve from MM to M^*M^*, so as to pass through w^*, and the sign of the change in reserves depends on the strength of the crowding-out effect. An increase in wealth raises the demand for money, and an increase in the interest rate reduces it. When crowding out does not dominate, the interest-rate effect is stronger and the demand for money declines, re-

[28] See note 3.

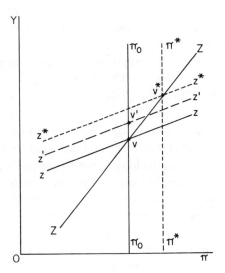

Figure 5.8 Temporary tax reduction and budget deficit: impact and steady-state effects on nominal income under pegged and flexible exchange rates.

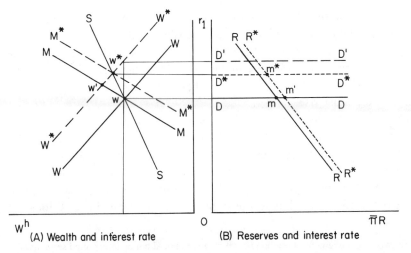

(A) Wealth and interest rate   (B) Reserves and interest rate

Figure 5.9 Temporary tax reduction and budget deficit: steady-state effects on asset markets under a pegged exchange rate.

ducing reserves. Diagrammatically, SS is steeper than MM in Figure 5.9A, and MM must move upward to pass through w^*.

The same statements are made in Figure 5.9B, where the increase in B_1 resulting from the budget deficit raises the bond-market curve from DD to

$D'D'$ (by the same distance as from WW to W^*W^*), but the gradual increase in W^{hs} implied by the increase in W^h lowers the bond-market curve from $D'D'$ to D^*D^* and also moves the money-market curve from RR to R^*R^*. Long-run equilibrium is displaced from m to m^*. There is a permanent loss of reserves when, as here, the wealth effect on the demand for money (the shift from RR to R^*R^*) is weaker than the interest-rate effect (the movement along R^*R^* from m' to m^*).[29]

Under a flexible exchange rate, the economy must come to rest on the same long-run income curve in Figure 5.8, but not at the point v when the exchange rate changes. To be precise, the long-run outcome in Figure 5.8 depends on the way in which the steady-state changes in wealth and the interest rate affect desired saving, given income. If their combined influence would cause dissaving, a permanent increase in Y^d is required for saving to be zero in the steady state, and income must then increase too. This case is the one depicted in Figure 5.8. The short-run income curve rises to z^*z^*, intersecting ZZ at v^* and thus at higher levels of Y and π than those obtained on impact.

The circumstance in which these things happen is described by Figure 5.10A. As in the pegged-rate case, the bond-market curve shifts from WW to W^*W^*, denoting the increase in B_1. But the money-market curve cannot shift when the exchange rate is flexible, and long-run equilibrium must be established at w^*, where W^*W^* intersects MM. Wealth and the interest rate rise, and SS must move to S^*S^*. When crowding out does not dominate, moreover, S^*S^* must lie below SS, which says that disposable income must rise.

The permanent depreciation of the home currency shown in Figure 5.8 is also shown in Figure 5.10B. The bond-market curve is shifted from BB to $B'B'$ because of the increase in B_1, but there is again an increase in W^{hs} that moves the bond-market curve from $B'B'$ to B^*B^* and also moves the money-market curve from LL to L^*L^*.[30] Equilibrium is displaced gradually from m to m^* and lies to the right of m when crowding out does not dominate.

---

[29] The two-step movement of the bond-market curve should not be interpreted sequentially. The shift from DD to $D'D'$ is the effect of the increase in B_1, the shift from $D'D'$ to D^*D^* is the effect of the increase in W^{hs}, but B_1 and W^{hs} change concurrently. (The change in W^{hs}, however, reflects in addition the saving or dissaving that takes place after the government has balanced its budget. For details, see Chapter 6.) The two-step movement of BB in Figure 5.10A will have to be interpreted analogously, as a way of disentangling the effects of changes in B_1 and W^{hs}.

[30] In the pegged-rate case, the increase in W^h shown by Figure 5.9A was proof of an increase in W^{hs}. In the flexible-rate case, we can draw no such inference. We cannot even draw it from the fact that there is saving at v' in Figure 5.8, for we shall see in Chapter 6 that

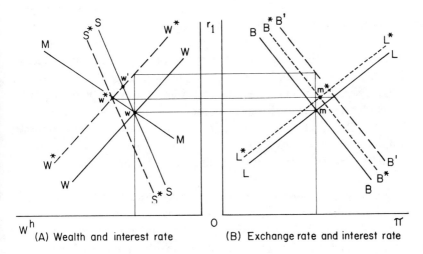

Figure 5.10 Temporary tax reduction and budget deficit: steady-state effects on asset markets under a flexible exchange rate.

There is no fixed relationship between the size of the short-run increase in income shown at v' in Figure 5.8 and the size of the long-run increase shown at v^*. The former depends only on the size of the temporary budget deficit. The latter depends on the size of the increase in B_1, which depends in turn on the duration of the deficit, as well as its size. An increase in B_1 sufficient to carry the economy to v^* could be due to a short period of large budget deficits or to a long period of small deficits.

The increase in income and depreciation of the home currency that occur in the flexible-rate case and the loss of reserves that occurs in the pegged-rate case are crucially dependent on our assumption that

saving can be followed by dissaving after the budget is balanced. To prove that there will be an increase in W^{hs} in the flexible-rate case, we must therefore write

$$\left(\frac{dW^{hs}}{dB_1}\right) = \left(\frac{dW^{h}}{dB_1}\right) - V_\pi\left(\frac{d\pi}{\pi\,dB_1}\right)$$

then replace the arguments on the right-hand side with terms from Eqs. (3.20a), (3.21a) and (3.24a):

$$\left(\frac{dW^{hs}}{dB_1}\right) = -(1/H_\pi)[L_{11} + (V_\pi/S_Y)(N_w/N_t)(S_w L_{11} - L_{1w}S_1)]$$

But $(V_\pi/S_Y) = -B_{0w}(Y^d/S_w)$ in the initial steady state, which says that

$$\left(\frac{dW^{hs}}{dB_1}\right) = -(L_{11}/H_\pi)[1 - B_{0w}(N_w Y^d/N_t) + B_{0w}(N_w Y^d/N_t)(L_{1w}S_1/L_{11}S_w)]$$

which is unambiguously positive, because $B_{0w} < 1$ and $(Y^d N_w/N_t) \le 1$ (see Appendix C).

crowding out does not dominate. There is thus a strong similarity between our results for the flexible-rate case and those obtained by others for a closed economy.[31] If crowding out were to dominate, our results would be reversed, with income falling and the home currency appreciating under a flexible rate and the stock of reserves rising under a pegged rate. (We can depict these perverse results in Figures 5.9A and 5.10A by switching MM and SS. Under a pegged exchange rate, the economy would move to w' in Figure 5.9A. Reserves would rise. Under a flexible rate, the economy would move to w' in Figure 5.10A. Disposable income would fall, so that z^*z^* would be below zz in Figure 5.8, and income would fall.)

Implications of asset-market integration. The large literature on fiscal policy has examined extensively interactions between the exchange-rate regime and asset-market integration. It is the common finding that close integration (high capital mobility) enhances the effectiveness of fiscal policy under a pegged exchange rate and diminishes its effectiveness under a flexible rate.[32] As asset-market integration strengthens the influence of the interest rate on capital flows, it allows the government to borrow from foreigners, directly or indirectly, and therefore to finance a budget deficit without much increase in the domestic interest rate. In other words, it diminishes the likelihood that a budget deficit will crowd out private domestic expenditure (that it will raise saving in our model, reducing absorption). But the capital inflow that is thus advantageous under a pegged exchange rate has a detrimental by-product under a flexible exchange rate. If large enough in relation to the budget deficit, it will cause the home currency to appreciate, switching expenditure away from domestic goods. It is indeed the conventional conclusion that perfect asset-market integration interacts with exchange-rate flexibility to dissipate completely the influence of fiscal policy–that a budget deficit cannot affect domestic activity.

Our comparative-static analysis distinguishes sharply between effects that occur before the exchange rate has had time to change and those that are visible only after the budget is balanced and capital flows have ceased. It is thus difficult to compare our results directly with those summarized above. The conventional conclusions pertain to the effects of an ongoing budget deficit on demands for goods and on the flow supply of bonds, and

[31] On the closed economy, see Blinder and Solow, "Does Fiscal Policy Matter?," and W. H. Buiter, "The Long-run Effects of Fiscal Policy," Econometric Research Program Research Memorandum 187, Princeton University, Princeton, N.J., October 1975 (mimeograph).

[32] See, for example, the works by Mundell, Fleming, and Whitman cited in note 27.

they come from models that are not designed to reach a stationary state. We can obtain similar results only in the context of Chapter 6, where we trace the evolution of goods markets, asset markets, and the balance of payments under the influence of an ongoing deficit. It is then possible to show that when crowding out does not dominate, our model reproduces the conventional conclusions. At this point, we pause merely to investigate the effects of asset-market integration on the comparative-static results shown in Table 5.4 and in Figures 5.8 through 5.10.

The impact effects of a tax cut are not affected by the exchange-rate regime or by the degree of asset-market integration. The location of v' in Figure 5.8 depends only on the size of the budget deficit. Furthermore, the increase in B_1 that is the permanent reflection of the deficit does not affect steady-state income under a pegged exchange rate, and this result does not depend on the degree of asset-market integration. It follows from the fact that our model is designed to reach a stationary state once the budget has been balanced and from the way in which it is constrained to do so with a pegged exchange rate.[33] There is thus only one comparative-static result that can be sensitive to asset-market integration. It is the long-run result with a flexible exchange rate.

To see how this result is affected, let us look at the size of the permanent increase in income that takes place when crowding out does not dominate and deal with two limiting cases—the one in which there is no substitutability between domestic and foreign bonds, and the other in which the bonds are perfect substitutes. (1) If there were no substitutability, WW would be steeper than in Figure 5.10A but would shift leftward by the same distance. By implication, the changes in wealth and the interest rate would be larger, and the shift from SS to S^*S^* would have to be larger too. Therefore, the shift from zz to z^*z^* would have to be bigger in Figure 5.8, enlarging the increase in income and the depreciation of the home currency. (2) If the two bonds were perfect substitutes, WW would be horizontal in Figure 5.10A and would not shift at all with an increase in the supply of bonds. Households would be willing to substitute domestic for foreign bonds at a constant interest rate. By implication, there would be no change in wealth, the interest rate, or disposable income in Figure 5.10A and no change in the position of the short-run income schedule in Figure 5.8. The economy would come to rest at v, where Y and π would be what they were initially.

---

[33] Thus, the same result is obtained by McKinnon and Oates, *The Implications of International Economic Integration,* and by others who employ models that converge to a stationary state.

Comparing these results with the general case, in which the two bonds are partial substitutes, we come to a conclusion that is at least analogous to the one we have described as the conventional result. An increase in the degree of asset-market integration (capital mobility) reduces the effectiveness of fiscal policy under a flexible exchange rate. It limits the size of the permanent increase in income that takes place when crowding out does not dominate.

Devaluation of a pegged exchange rate

We come at last to the disturbance that has been studied most thoroughly in analyses of open economies–a permanent but unanticipated devaluation of a pegged exchange rate. During the last three decades, contributions to the theory of devaluation have emphasized by turns (1) the role of changes in relative prices and the price elasticities required to improve the current-account balance; (2) the role of changes in absorption relative to income and the extent to which a devaluation can induce those changes endogenously, without support from other policies; (3) the role of the exchange rate in clearing the money market and the implications of money-market equilibrium for the effects of a devaluation; (4) the conditions under which a devaluation will be neutral in that it will not cause permanent changes in relative prices, resource allocation, or resource utilization; and (5) analogies between a devaluation and an open-market purchase of domestic bonds.[34]

[34] This is not the place to survey comprehensively the literature on each of these issues. We cite only a few important contributions. On elasticities, absorption, and related questions, see J. Robinson, "The Foreign Exchanges," *Essays in the Theory of Employment,* Blackwell, Oxford, 1947, pp. 134–55, G. Haberler, "The Market for Foreign Exchange and the Stability of the Balance of Payments," *Kyklos,* 3 (1949), pp. 193–218, A. C. Harberger, "Currency Depreciation, Income, and the Balance of Trade," *Journal of Political Economy,* 58 (February 1950), pp. 47–60, J. E. Meade, *The Balance of Payments,* Oxford University Press, London, 1951, chaps. xi–xvi, and S. S. Alexander, "Effects of a Devaluation on a Trade Balance," *International Monetary Fund Staff Papers,* 2 (April 1952), pp. 263–78; also S. C. Tsiang, "The Role of Money in Trade Balance Stability," *American Economic Review,* 51 (December 1961), pp. 912–36, H. G. Johnson, "Toward a General Theory of the Balance of Payments," *International Trade and Economic Growth,* Harvard University Press, Cambridge, Mass., 1961, pp. 153–68, L. A. Metzler, "The Process of International Adjustment Under Conditions of Full Employment," in R. E. Caves and H. G. Johnson, eds., *Readings in International Economics,* Richard D. Irwin, Homewood, Ill., 1968, pp. 465–86, and A. O. Krueger, "Balance of Payments Theory," *Journal of Economic Literature,* 7 (March 1969), pp. 1–26. On the monetary approach, neutrality, and related issues, see F. Hahn, "The Balance of Payments in a Monetary Economy," *Review of Economic Studies,* 27 (February 1959), pp. 110–25, R. A. Mundell, *Monetary Theory,* Goodyear, Pacific Palisades, Calif., 1971, chap. 9, and H. G. Johnson,

Our model permits us to comment briefly on each of these issues. Because it contains three commodities and is constructed to encompass several goods-market cases, we are able to investigate the responses of relative domestic prices and of the terms of trade and the restrictions one must place on price elasticities to obtain results produced by other models. Because income, interest rates, and wealth affect desired saving and, therefore, absorption, we are able to show how endogenous changes in absorption affect responses to a devaluation. Because our model includes money and bond markets, we are able to show what one can infer from the requirements of asset-market equilibrium about the changes in reserves resulting from a devaluation. Because it contains classical and Keynesian variants, we are able to show when and why a devaluation can be neutral in the long run. And because we have already studied the effects of an open-market operation, it is easy to draw the relevant analogies. Most important, however, our model is designed to segregate sharply three classes of responses – those that occur on impact, those that occur through time, and those that obtain only with respect to the stationary state. Hence, it is possible to ascertain which of the many statements made about devaluation pertain to one or more of these three types of responses.

We find that a devaluation raises the demand for money, which says that it will always cause a permanent increase in reserves. This is the irrefutable lesson taught by the monetary approach to the balance of payments. With international capital mobility, moreover, we find that reserves can also increase instantaneously. By implication, a devaluation can raise reserves without improving the current-account balance. As a matter of fact, a devaluation does not necessarily cause an improvement in the current-account balance, even though the familiar elasticities conditions are satisfied in our model. A devaluation can induce an increase in absorption larger than the increase in income, and when this happens, there will be dissaving and a current-account deficit.[35] We also show,

"The Monetary Approach to Balance-of-Payments Theory," in Frenkel and Johnson, eds., *The Monetary Approach to the Balance of Payments*, pp. 147–67; also Dornbusch, "Currency Depreciation, Hoarding, and Relative Prices," Frenkel and Rodriguez, "Portfolio Equilibrium," and H. G. Johnson, "The Monetary Approach to the Balance of Payments: A Nontechnical Guide," *Journal of International Economics*, 7 (August 1977), pp. 251–68.

[35] Other authors have also demonstrated that devaluation can produce a current-account deficit, absent "perverse" price elasticities, but for reasons different from those adduced below. In papers by Salop and by Brito and Richardson, for example, the current account moves into deficit because real wages fall, reducing the supply of labor and domestic output. See J. Salop, "Devaluation and the Balance of Trade Under Flexible Wages," in G.

Table 5.5. *Devaluation of a pegged
exchange rate*

Variable	Impact effect	Steady-state effect
p_N	+	+
p_1	+	+
p_1/p_N	?	?
Y^d	+	+
Y	+	+
r_1	−	−
$\bar{\pi}R$	+	+
W^h	+	+

Signs for $\delta\bar{\pi} > 0$.

however, that price elasticities are not irrelevant, not even to the size of
the long-run increase in reserves, unless we adopt the strictest classical
assumptions, ruling out any price rigidity. Finally, we find that the analogy between devaluation and an open-market operation has been over-
drawn. Although there are important resemblances between the two policies, the differences between them are not negligible.

We begin by looking at our general case – the one in which all pairs of
goods are gross substitutes but not perfect substitutes, foreign and domestic bonds are partial substitutes, and we have not ruled out "money illusion" in labor-market or government behavior. Thereafter, we look at
the implications of asset-market integration and the three goods-market
cases defined in Chapter 4. Finally, we study the effects of imposing strict
classical assumptions and deal in that context with the analogy between
devaluation and an open-market purchase.

Outcomes in the general case. The effects of a devaluation are summarized in Table 5.5 and in Figures 5.11 and 5.12, which deal with asset
and goods markets, respectively. Although the effects of a devaluation
are felt at once in both sets of markets, it is convenient to begin with the
asset markets and to look first at Figure 5.11B, which shows what
happens to reserves and the domestic interest rate.

Horwich and P. A. Samuelson, eds., *Trade, Stability, and Macroeconomics,* Academic
Press, New York, 1974, pp. 129–51, and D. L. Brito and J. D. Richardson, "Some Dis-
equilibrium Dynamics of Exchange-Rate Changes," *Journal of International Economics,*
5 (February 1975), pp. 1–14.

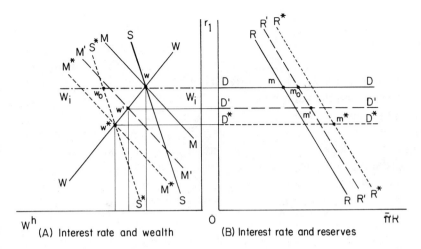

(A) Interest rate and wealth   (B) Interest rate and reserves

Figure 5.11 Devaluation of a pegged exchange rate: impact and steady-state effects on asset markets with saving induced by the change in absorption.

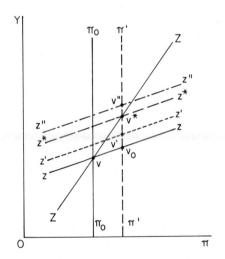

Figure 5.12 Devaluation of a pegged exchange rate: impact and steady-state effects on nominal income.

When households hold foreign bonds, a devaluation raises wealth immediately, thereby raising the demands for domestic bonds and money. The bond-market curve must shift from DD to $D'D'$, and the money-market curve must shift from RR to $R'R'$. Thus, equilibrium is displaced instantaneously from m to m', causing a reduction in the interest rate (which clears the bond market) and an increase in reserves (which clears the money market). Looking at events from a different standpoint, the devaluation enlarges abruptly home-currency holdings of the foreign bond by $V_\pi(\delta\bar{\pi}/\bar{\pi})$ but enlarges the demand by only $B_{0W}V_\pi(\delta\bar{\pi}/\bar{\pi})$, and households seek to sell some of their foreign bonds. As they do so and repatriate the proceeds, the central bank must intervene in the foreign-exchange market to keep the home currency from appreciating (to enforce the decision to devalue). It must buy foreign currency with newly issued domestic currency. The foreign currency is added to its reserves; the new home currency serves to satisfy the increase in the demand for money that is reflected in the shift of the money-market curve. (These same events show up in Figure 5.11A as an immediate movement from w to w', along WW. Wealth rises because of the capital gains conferred by the devaluation. The money-market curve moves from MM to $M'M'$, reflecting the increase in reserves.)

In Figure 5.12, describing the behavior of absorption and income, the exchange-rate schedule shifts from $\pi_0\pi_0$ to $\pi'\pi'$, reflecting directly the devaluation. The short-run income curve shifts upward, reflecting the reduction in desired saving (the increase in absorption) that is the result of the fall in the interest rate and the rise in wealth. But the change in saving *realized* at the new exchange rate is uncertain, and we show two possibilities.[36] The first is illustrated by the shift from zz to $z'z'$, which displaces equilibrium from v to v'. Income and absorption rise, but absorption by less than income. Households begin to save, and the current-account balance improves.[37] The second possibility is illustrated by the shift from zz to $z''z''$, which displaces equilibrium from v to v''. Absorption rises by more than income. Households begin to dissave, and the current-account balance deteriorates.

---

[36] The shift is given by $-(N_u/N_s)(S_1\,\delta r_1 + S_W\,\delta W^h)$, which is positive because $\delta r_1 < 0$ and $\delta W^h > 0$. But this shift does not give us the sign of the change in desired saving, which is what we shall need to know below. It is given by Eq. (3.13b):

$$\delta^*S = (N_t/N_sB_{11})[S_YB_{11} - (N_w/N_t)V_\pi(B_{1W}S_1 - S_WB_{11})]\left(\frac{\delta\bar{\pi}}{\bar{\pi}}\right)$$

which is ambiguous even when we start in a steady state, where $V_\pi = -B_{0W}(S_Y/S_W)Y^d$, and when we assume away money illusion, so that $Y^dN_w = N_t$.

[37] The proof that there will be a current-account surplus when saving is positive comes from Eq. (3.16). When, as here, $\bar{D} = 0$, then $\delta S = \delta(p_1C_1^f - p_0C_0)$, and under our assumptions concerning transfers to foreigners, T^f, the right-hand side of this expression *is* the change in the current-account balance. In the present instance, moreover, saving and the trade balance are zero initially, so that the increase in saving implies a current-account surplus. (We discuss the current-account balance more thoroughly in Chapter 6.)

In a moment, we shall trace the implications of these possibilities for the subsequent behavior of asset markets, the balance of payments, and the stock of reserves. Before doing so, however, let us see what must happen eventually in the goods market. As usual, long-term equilibrium must be established at the intersection of ZZ and the exchange-rate schedule, and this occurs at v^* in Figure 5.12. When short-term equilibrium occurs at v', then, the short-run income curve $z'z'$ must rise gradually to z^*z^*, and this will be achieved under the influence of the increase in W^{hs} that results from the saving that takes place at v'. When, instead, short-term equilibrium occurs at v'', the short-run income curve $z''z''$ must fall gradually to z^*z^*, and this will be achieved under the influence of the decrease in W^{hs} that results from the dissaving that takes place at v''. (In each instance, the effect of the change in W^{hs} will be reinforced by the change in r_1 that takes place on the way to the new steady state. It is explained below.) The main point to note here is that the change in the steady-state level of income (the increase from v to v^*) is determined uniquely by the size of the devaluation (the shift from $\pi_0\pi_0$ to $\pi'\pi'$) and the slope of ZZ. The latter, moreover, is (N_t/N_w), which means that the size of the permanent increase in income depends on price elasticities and other goods-market terms. We say more about them later.

Returning to the asset markets, let us trace the consequences of the two possibilities in Figure 5.12. When a devaluation induces saving, demands for all assets rise gradually with the corresponding increase in W^{hs}. The bond-market curve must continue to fall in Figure 5.11B, and the money-market curve must continue to rise. This is, in fact, the case that we have drawn. When saving goes to zero, the bond-market curve comes to rest at D^*D^*, below $D'D'$, and the money-market curve comes to rest at R^*R^*, above $R'R'$. Long-run equilibrium is established at m^*, which says that there has been an additional decline in the interest rate and an additional increase in reserves. By inference, the economy has run a balance-of-payments surplus during the transition from m' to m^*. Finally, Figure 5.11A has been drawn to reflect our findings about income and reserves. The economy comes to rest at w^*, where wealth is higher than it was at w', and the interest rate is lower. The position of WW has not changed, but SS has shifted to S^*S^*, reflecting the permanent increase in income shown at v^* in Figure 5.12, and the money-market curve has shifted from $M'M'$ to M^*M^*, reflecting the further increase in reserves shown at m^* in Figure 5.11B.

When there is dissaving rather than saving because of the initial

148   **Modeling an open economy**

changes in absorption and income, the movements of the curves are opposite to those in Figure 5.11B, and m' lies to the southeast of m^*. (In Figure
5.11A, $M'M'$ and w' lie to the southwest of M^*M^* and w^*.) The interest
rate rises during the transition from m' to m^*, and reserves decline. The
economy runs a balance-of-payments deficit during the passage to the
new steady state. But m^* must always lie to the southeast of the initial
point m. Reserves are higher and the interest rate lower than they were
before the devaluation.

To prove this last assertion, we need only note that the size of the shift
from SS to S^*S^* in Figure 5.11A is determined entirely by the parameters
of the saving function and by the size of the permanent change in income.
Thus, it depends on the location of v^* in Figure 5.12, which depends on
demand and supply elasticities in goods markets and on the various
marginal propensities to spend. Point w^* will always lie to the southwest
of w, and m^* will lie to the southeast of m. The direction from which the
economy approaches those points depends on the way in which asset
markets respond to the devaluation in the short run (on the size of the initial change in r_1) and on the way in which saving (absorption) responds to
the short-run changes in wealth and the interest rate.

Implications of asset-market integration. When domestic and foreign
bonds are perfect substitutes, DD cannot shift in Figure 5.11B, and devaluation displaces asset-market equilibrium from m to m_0. The immediate
increase in reserves is smaller than before. In this same case, moreover,
the short-run income curve shifts by less than it did with partial substitutability, because the domestic interest rate does not fall; devaluation
displaces equilibrium to a point between v_0 and v' in Figure 5.12. The increase in income is reduced, but the increase in absorption is reduced
more sharply, and we can be certain that households will save rather than
dissave. In different terms, the current-account balance is sure to improve, because the increase in domestic absorption due to the increase
in wealth cannot exceed the switch in expenditure (the "elasticities"
effect) built into the slope of the short-run income curve.[38]

But the size of the permanent increase in income is unaffected. When
saving goes to zero, the economy must reach v^* in Figure 5.12, regardless
of the degree of asset-market integration, and income has to rise through
time. By implication, perfect substitutability makes for a larger increase

---

[38] Returning to the equation for the change in desired saving given in note 36, replacing V_π
with its initial steady-state value, and taking the limit as $-B_{01} \to \infty$, $\delta^*S \to (N_t/N_s)S_Y[1 - B_{0W}(Y^dN_w/N_t)](\delta\bar{\pi}/\bar{\pi})$. Thus $\delta^*S > 0$, because $B_{0W}(Y^dN_w/N_t) < 1$.

in the integral of saving, W^{hs}, and thus for a larger increase in wealth, as there is no decline in the interest rate to reinforce the effect of the increase in wealth on the position of the short-run income curve.

Returning to our asset-market diagram, we can at once infer that the shift from $R'R'$ to R^*R^* will be larger than the one in Figure 5.11B, but we cannot know whether the new equilibrium point will be to the right or left of m^*, because the bond-market curve DD has not shifted. The demand for money is augmented by the larger wealth effect but diminished by the absence of an interest-rate effect. Consider, however, the situation in Figure 5.11A. When domestic and foreign bonds are perfect substitutes, the bond-market curve is W_iW_i, and long-run equilibrium is established at w_0 (because the size of the shift from SS to S^*S^* depends only on the permanent increase in disposable income). Hence, the size of the permanent increase in reserves depends on the strength of the crowding-out effect. When it does not dominate, as in Figure 5.11A, the money-market curve $M'M'$ will not have to shift as far to reach w_0 as it did to reach w^*, and perfect asset-market integration curtails the increase in reserves.

To summarize, let us state our findings in terms of the effects of an increase in asset-market integration: (1) The impact effects of a devaluation are reduced; the increase in reserves is smaller, together with the increase in nominal income. (2) We are more likely to see saving rather than dissaving, an improvement in the current-account balance, and thus a further inflow of reserves through time. (3) The permanent increase in income is unaffected, but the increase in wealth is amplified. (4) The permanent increase in reserves is reduced when crowding out does not dominate. One more finding needs to be repeated: With perfect asset-market integration, there cannot be dissaving and a current-account deficit in the wake of a devaluation. This may explain why many studies of devaluation make no mention of this perverse possibility. Two often, they look only at the limiting case of perfect substitutability.

Relative prices, the terms of trade, and the special goods-market cases. In early work on the elasticities approach to the analysis of devaluation, there was much discussion of the relationship between the change in the trade balance and the change in the terms of trade.[39] In subsequent work, it was shown that there can be an improvement in the trade balance even with fixed terms of trade; substitution between traded and nontraded

[39] See Haberler, "The Market for Foreign Exchange," Sohmen, *Flexible Exchange Rates,* pp. 13–20, and the survey in F. Machlup, "The Terms-of-Trade Effects of Devaluation upon Real Income and the Balance of Trade," *Kyklos,* 9 (1956), pp. 417–52.

goods can take the place of substitution between export and import-competing goods.[40]

In our model, of course, the long-run effects of a devaluation do not depend on the behavior of the trade balance. Furthermore, trade-balance behavior does not depend exclusively on the size or character of the switches in expenditure brought about by changes in relative prices, it depends in part on the change in absorption. It is worth pausing briefly, however, to ask how a devaluation will affect relative domestic prices and the terms of trade. We deal first with the general case in which all goods are partial substitutes, then turn to the three special goods-market cases defined in Chapter 4, but look only at the permanent price changes given by Eqs. (3.22b) and (3.23b).

The changes in relative domestic prices and in the terms of trade can be written as[41]

$$
\left(\frac{dp_1}{p_1}\right) - \left(\frac{dp_N}{p_N}\right) = -(1/N_w)[u_\pi(m_N N_{1k} - m_1 N_{Nk})
$$

$$
+ m_0 u_{0N}(N_{Nk} + N_{1k})] \left(\frac{d\bar{\pi}}{\bar{\pi}}\right)
$$

$$
\left(\frac{dp_1}{p_1}\right) - \left(\frac{dp_0}{p_0}\right) = -(1/N_w)[u_{0N}(m_N N_{1k} - m_1 N_{Nk}) + m_0(u_{1N}
$$

$$
+ u_E)(N_{Nk} + N_{1k}) + m_0 \sigma_N N_{1k}] \left(\frac{d\bar{\pi}}{\bar{\pi}}\right)
$$

where, as before, $N_{ik} = a_i p_i Q_i + b_i G_i$, with $i = 1, N$. Under ultraclassical conditions, then, a devaluation can have no permanent effect on relative domestic prices or the terms of trade and can thus have no permanent effect on resource use or allocation. When "money illusion" is banished from the labor market and from government behavior, the N_{ik} are zero, and the long-run changes in p_0, p_1, and p_N are proportional to the devaluation. When those ultraclassical conditions do not hold, there *can* be changes in relative domestic prices and the terms of trade.

[40] See W. E. G. Salter, "Internal and External Balance: The Role of Price and Expenditure Effects," *Economic Record,* 35 (August 1959), pp. 226–38, Dornbusch, "Devaluation, Money, and Nontraded Goods," and R. W. Jones and W. M. Corden, "Devaluation, Nonflexible Prices, and the Trade Balance for a Small Country," *Canadian Journal of Economics,* 9 (February 1976), pp. 150–61; also A. Amano, "Non-traded Goods and the Effects of Devaluation," *Economic Studies Quarterly,* 23 (August 1972), pp. 1–9, D. J. Mathieson, "Traded Goods, Nontraded Goods, and the Balance of Payments," *International Economic Review,* 14 (October 1973), pp. 615–24, and A. O. Krueger, "The Role of Home Goods and Money in Exchange Rate Adjustments," in W. Sellekaerts, ed., *International Trade and Finance,* Macmillan, London, 1974, pp. 141–61.
[41] For the derivation of these expressions, see Appendix C, Eqs. (C.8a) and (C.10a).

But the signs of the changes are ambiguous when all pairs of goods are partial substitutes, and they are also ambiguous in some of the special goods-market cases.

The traded-goods case (where $u_{0N} \to \infty$) most nearly resembles the model that was used in early work on the elasticities approach to the analysis of devaluation. The domestic economy can be deemed to produce two traded goods, an export and an import substitute (alias the nontraded good), and the two price ratios come to be the same. Thus,

$$\left(\frac{dp_1}{p_1}\right) - \left(\frac{dp_N}{p_N}\right) = \left(\frac{dp_1}{p_1}\right) - \left(\frac{dp_0}{p_0}\right) = (1/N_w^t)(m_1 N_{Nk} - m_N N_{1k})\left(\frac{d\bar{\pi}}{\bar{\pi}}\right)$$

where $N_w^t = [u_t + u_{1N}^f + u_{1N} + u_E + (1 - m_1)\sigma_1]$. But the sign of this expression is ambiguous. Devaluation need not cause a permanent deterioration in the terms of trade.

The single-good case (where $u_{1N} \to \infty$) can be viewed in this context as a variant of the traditional trade model. The economy can be deemed to be completely specialized in the production of an export good. In this instance, of course, the domestic price ratio is fixed, but the terms of trade are variable. In fact,

$$\left(\frac{dp_1}{p_1}\right) - \left(\frac{dp_0}{p_0}\right) = -(1/N_w^s)m_0(N_{Nk} + N_{1k})\left(\frac{d\bar{\pi}}{\bar{\pi}}\right)$$

where $N_w^s = [u_t + u_{1N}^f + u_{0N} + m_0(\sigma_N + \sigma_1)]$. As this expression is always negative when the N_{ik} are not zero, devaluation does imply a permanent deterioration in the terms of trade.[42]

The composite-good case (where $u_{10} \to \infty$) is the conventional small-country case that has been used to show how changes in relative prices can occur even with fixed terms of trade. When the two traded goods are perfect substitutes in domestic consumption, the economy behaves as if it were a pure price taker in all international markets. But relative domestic prices are not fixed. They change by

$$\left(\frac{dp_1}{p_1}\right) - \left(\frac{dp_N}{p_N}\right) = (1/N_w^c)(m_1 N_{Nk} - m_N N_{1k})\left(\frac{d\bar{\pi}}{\bar{\pi}}\right)$$

[42] Using the relationships developed in Appendix C, it can be shown that $N_w^s = u_\pi + m_0(N_{Nk} + N_{1k})$, so that the deterioration can be written as $-[u_h/(u_\pi + u_h)](d\bar{\pi}/\bar{\pi})$, where $u_h = m_0(N_{Nk} + N_{1k})$. Three findings follow: (1) The size of the deterioration varies inversely with u_π, which embodies the Marshall-Lerner-Robinson condition. (2) It varies directly with u_h, which is to say that it varies directly with the domestic supply elasticities embodied in u_h. (3) It approaches the size of the devaluation when the supply elasticities become very large ($u_h \to \infty$), because p_1 comes to be constant. All of these conclusions can be found in the traditional literature.

where $N_w^c = [(u_{0N} + u_{1N} + u_E) + (1 - m_N)\sigma_N]$. Once again, however, the outcome is ambiguous. Devaluation does not necessarily imply a permanent increase in the price of the composite traded good relative to that of the nontraded good.

Neutrality and all that. Under ultraclassical conditions, devaluation does not have any permanent influence on the real side of the economy. Relative prices return to what they were initially. Under those conditions, moreover,[43]

$$\left(\frac{\bar{\pi}\,dR}{L_1}\right) = -(S_W/L_{1W})[(L_{1W}B_{11} - L_{11}B_{1W})/H_f]\left(\frac{d\bar{\pi}}{\bar{\pi}}\right)$$

The steady-state change in the stock of reserves can be deduced from demands for assets and the requirement that saving go to zero.

Results of this type are found in many recent papers,[44] and they would appear to support Johnson's assertion:[45]

It should be emphasized that the analysis of the effects of a devaluation is completely independent of any critical-magnitude condition applying to the elasticities of international demand. The relevant stability condition is the monetary-theoretic one that a reduction in real balances produces a reduction in real expenditure from a given real income, and vice versa.

He goes on to say that elasticities conditions are "completely irrelevant" to a monetary economy because they are conditions for stability of exchange in a barter economy.[46]

But statements like these must be carefully qualified. They hold only for the long-run comparative-static effects of a devaluation and only for models that are thoroughly classical, in which the economy can be dichotomized ex post, for purposes of long-run analysis. Elasticities drop out of the equation shown above only because $Y^d N_w = N_t$ under ultraclassical conditions. Furthermore, the *evolution* of the balance of payments cannot be studied without reference to conditions of demand in goods markets. In our model, for example, the position and slope of the short-run income curve depend on the terms N_t, N_s, and N_w, which contain demand and

[43] From Eq. (3.21b), $(dY^d/Y^d) = (d\bar{\pi}/\bar{\pi})$ when $Y^d N_w = N_t$, and $L_1 = L_{1W}W^h = -(L_{1W}/S_W)S_Y Y^d$ when the economy begins in a steady state. These results are applied to Eq. (3.24b), defining the long-run change in reserves, to obtain the expression in the text.
[44] See, e.g., Dornbusch, "Currency Depreciation, Hoarding, and Relative Prices" and "Devaluation, Money, and Nontraded Goods," Frenkel and Rodriguez, "Portfolio Equilibrium," and Mundell, *Monetary Theory*, chap. 9.
[45] Johnson, "The Monetary Approach to Balance-of-Payments Theory," p. 275.
[46] Johnson, "The Monetary Approach to Balance-of-Payments Theory," p. 281. See also the passage quoted on p. 4, above.

supply elasticities and are made to be positive by assuming gross substitutability—a generalization of the Marshall-Lerner-Robinson condition for a successful devaluation. To put the point differently, dynamic stability does not depend exclusively on our assumption about the effect of wealth on saving—the counterpart of Johnson's "monetary-theoretic" assumption about the effect of real balances on expenditure. It depends in addition on assumptions about N_t, N_s, and N_w, which depend in turn on supply and demand elasticities. And it is improper to draw any inference about an economy from its long-run comparative-static properties unless one can be sure that it is stable—that it will in fact converge on the situation implied by its long-run properties.

This point leads us to another. The real-balance effect is not absent from our model, although it does not appear explicitly because we work entirely with nominal magnitudes and follow Metzler rather than Patinkin in stressing the connection between wealth and saving rather than the narrower connection between real balances and hoarding.[47] But the real-balance effect is not the only force that animates the model, and it cannot play the role to which it is assigned in the typical monetary model.

When money is the only home-currency asset and ultraclassical conditions prevail, the long-run increase in reserves resulting from a devaluation has a simple function. It raises the nominal money stock in proportion to the devaluation, thereby keeping real cash balances constant in the face of the increase in the price level that is itself proportional to the devaluation.[48] When there is a second home-currency asset, the results are different. Early in this chapter, we saw that the long-run change in a flexible exchange rate resulting from an open-market purchase will not be

[47] The references are to L. A. Metzler, "Wealth, Saving, and the Rate of Interest," *Journal of Political Economy*, 59 (April 1951), pp. 930–46, and Patinkin, *Money, Interest and Prices*, especially chap. ii. The use of nominal magnitudes, incidentally, does not cause major differences between the results obtained from our model and those obtained from monetary models. We have assumed that nominal saving is a function homogeneous of first degree in nominal income and nominal wealth. In the classical version of the model, moreover, price changes are equal to exchange-rate changes in the long run. Therefore, statements about long-run changes in nominal income and nominal wealth can be restated in real terms without significantly changing their meaning.

[48] Money is not the only home-currency asset in all monetary models, but assumptions are adopted that wash out the effects that crop up here. Some models include home-currency bonds, but the bonds can be traded at a fixed international interest rate. Other models index the domestic bonds. In both cases, the nominal quantity is adjustable on terms that do not alter the demand for money. See, e.g., Dornbusch, "A Portfolio Balance Model," where there is a foreign bond denominated in home currency, but it is indexed in terms of the consumption good. (In that paper, Dornbusch begins as we do, with a wealth-saving relationship similar to Metzler's, but he goes on to index *all* assets except money. The wealth-saving relationship becomes a simple real-balance effect.)

proportional to the increase in the nominal money stock. If it were proportional, real balances would not change, but there would be a decline in real holdings of the domestic bond. This decline cannot be offset automatically when nominal bond holdings are fixed by fiscal policy and the domestic bond is not a perfect substitute for the foreign bond.

The outcome of a devaluation is analogous, in that there is apt to be a permanent increase in real balances. When the change in the price level is proportional to the devaluation, the equation in the text above can be rearranged to define the long-run change in real balances:

$$\left(\frac{\bar{\pi}\, dR}{L_1}\right) - \left(\frac{d\bar{\pi}}{\bar{\pi}}\right) = (B_{1W}/L_{1W})[(S_W L_{11} - L_{1W} S_1)/H_f]\left(\frac{d\bar{\pi}}{\bar{\pi}}\right)$$

which is positive when crowding out does not dominate. The price increase that results from a devaluation reduces real wealth but by less than it reduces the real supply of the domestic bond.[49] There would thus be excess demand in the bond market if the domestic interest rate did not decline, and when it does decline, it raises the demand for real cash balances. When crowding out does not dominate, moreover, this increase in demand for real cash balances outweighs the decrease in demand associated with the reduction in real wealth. The increase in nominal cash balances brought about by the increase in reserves must be more than proportional to the devaluation.

We have just invoked the analogy between an open-market purchase of domestic bonds under a flexible exchange rate and a devaluation of a pegged exchange rate. It is, of course, tempting to do so. An open-market purchase of domestic bonds involves an exogenous increase in the money supply and an endogenous increase in the price of foreign currency. A devaluation involves an exogenous increase in the price of foreign currency and an endogenous increase in the money supply. But the analogy is imperfect when money is not the only home-currency asset.

Using equations given above for the changes in real balances brought about by an open-market purchase and by a devaluation, it is easy to define an open-market purchase, $d\hat{B}_1^c$, that alters the supply of real balances by the same amount as a devaluation, $(d\bar{\pi}/\bar{\pi})$, and thus to compare the sizes of the policy changes. In strict monetary models, they will be the same. In

---

[49] Using Eq. (3.20b) and ultraclassical assumptions, the long-run decline in real wealth can be written as $[(dW^h/W^h) - (d\bar{\pi}/\bar{\pi})] = [S_1 B_{1W}/(S_1 B_{1W} - S_W B_{11})](d\bar{\pi}/\bar{\pi})$, which is smaller than the devaluation and, therefore, smaller than the long-run decline in the real supply of the domestic bond.

our model, by contrast,

$$\left(\frac{d\hat{B}_1^c}{L_1}\right) = [B_{1W}/(B_{1W} + L_{1W})][(S_W B_{11} L_{1W}$$

$$- B_{1W} S_W L_{11})/(S_W B_{11} L_{1W} - B_{1W} L_{1W} S_1)] \left(\frac{d\bar{\pi}}{\bar{\pi}}\right)$$

In general, then, the policy-determined change in the nominal money stock will not equal the policy-determined change in the exchange rate when the two are standardized to have the same effect on real balances.[50]

To sum up, this analysis of devaluation has allowed us to identify some of the distinguishing characteristics of our model. We have shown, for example, that long-run changes in the terms of trade are unambiguous only in certain special goods-market cases and that the terms of trade have to be constant only in the ultraclassical case, when there is no "money illusion" in labor-market or government behavior. We have shown that inferences drawn from simple monetary models hold only in that same ultraclassical case and only in the longest of long runs and that it is improper to draw those inferences unless certain elasticities conditions are satisfied. Those elasticities conditions, however, do not tell us much about the evolution of the balance of payments, not even about the current account, as both depend in part on the behavior of absorption–on the size of the change in expenditure as well as the size of the switch in expenditure brought about by a devaluation. Finally, we have seen that the real-balance effect, so much stressed in monetary models, is not absent from our model, but it does not fully explain the behavior of the model. It does not even explain the size of the change in the stock of reserves when the economy settles down. The change in reserves does not restore the real money supply to its initial level, as it does in most monetary models.

[50] When the two bonds are not perfect substitutes and crowding out does not dominate, we cannot know whether $(d\hat{B}_1^c/L_1)$ will be larger or smaller than $(d\bar{\pi}/\bar{\pi})$. Although $B_{1W} < (B_{1W} + L_{1W})$, it is also true that $|S_W B_{11} L_{1W} - B_{1W} S_W L_{11}| > |S_W B_{11} L_{1W} - B_{1W} L_{1W} S_1|$ when $S_W L_{11} > L_{1W} S_1$. When the bonds are perfect substitutes, however, $(d\hat{B}_1^c/L_1) = [B_{1W}/(B_{1W} + L_{1W})](d\bar{\pi}/\bar{\pi})$, and the open-market purchase must be smaller than the devaluation for the two to have identical effects on real balances.

6

Dynamics under pegged and flexible exchange rates

Now that we have reviewed the impact and steady-state effects of various disturbances, we are ready to show how the economy travels from the one to the other and how its behavior over time is affected by the exchange-rate regime. We shall not do so however, for all of the disturbances studied in Chapters 4 and 5. Instead, we shall select examples that illustrate clearly the processes at work under the two exchange-rate regimes.

Comparative-static analysis has already revealed strong generic similarities between adjustments to the principal disturbances under a given exchange-rate regime, and it is one purpose of this chapter to stress those similarities. With a pegged exchange rate, for example, goods-market disturbances have permanent effects on income, and asset-market disturbances do not. With a flexible exchange rate, the pattern of outcomes is usually reversed. Therefore, we look first at dynamic responses to the principal disturbances under a pegged-rate regime, then at responses to the same disturbances under a flexible-rate regime.

To show how the economy behaves with a pegged exchange rate, we study two disturbances – a shift of demand between traded goods and an open-market operation in the domestic bond. We also study the responses to a devaluation. Thereafter, we examine the dynamics of adjustment under a flexible exchange rate, studying the same pair of disturbances. Finally, we consider the responses to a tax cut, the disturbance that produces the most complex reactions under both regimes, because it involves a budget deficit.

We do not modify our model at this stage. Throughout this chapter, however, we assume what was assumed from time to time in Chapter 5, that crowding out does not dominate. Algebraically, $S_W L_{11} > L_{1W} S_1$. Diagrammatically, curve MM is drawn to be flatter than curve SS whenever we employ them. In most of our work, moreover, we assume that foreign and domestic bonds are partial substitutes. We shall not pause to catalogue the effects of asset-market integration, as we did repeatedly in

156

Chapters 4 and 5, until we study tax reductions and budget deficits. At that point, it will be convenient and instructive to start with the limiting case of perfect integration.

Stability, saving, and the balance of payments

Before beginning to examine particular types of disturbances, let us recall important points made in Chapter 3. There, we were able to prove stability by showing that the level of saving must always decline in response to an increase in the integral of saving, W^{hs}, reducing the rate of change in W^{hs}. Saving goes to zero eventually, wealth comes to be constant, and the economy reaches a stationary state.[1] We also called attention to certain identities that hold at all times in our model:

1. Because there is no investment in the model, saving must always be lodged in some combination of three financial assets:

$$S = \dot{B}_1 + \pi \dot{B}_0^h + \bar{\pi}\dot{R}$$

where $\dot{B}_1$ is $\bar{D}$, the bond-financed budget deficit; $\pi \dot{B}_0^h$ is $\dot{F}$, the capital outflow measured in home currency; and $\bar{\pi}\dot{R}$ is the rate of increase in the money supply resulting from an inflow of reserves and serves also to measure the overall surplus or deficit in the balance of payments.

2. A current-account surplus must always be offset by some combination of changes in claims on foreigners:

$$[(p_1 C_1^f - p_0 C_0) + \bar{r}_0(\pi B_0^h) + T^f] - \dot{F} - \bar{\pi}\dot{R} = 0$$

But under our assumption that $T^f = -\bar{r}_0(\pi B_0^h)$, the current-account balance is always equal to the trade balance, so that

$$(p_1 C_1^f - p_0 C_0) - \dot{F} = \bar{\pi}\dot{R}$$

which must be zero with a flexible exchange rate.

3. The first and second statements say, in turn, that

$$S - \bar{D} = (p_1 C_1^f - p_0 C_0)$$

---

[1] This response is not unlike those built into other models that display instantaneous portfolio adjustment. See, e.g., W. H. Branson, "Stocks and Flows in International Monetary Analysis," in A. Ando et al., eds., *International Aspects of Stabilization Policies*, Federal Reserve Bank of Boston and International Seminar in Public Economics, Boston, 1975, pp. 27–50, R. Dornbusch, "A Portfolio Balance Model of the Open Economy," *Journal of Monetary Economics*, 1 (January 1975), pp. 3–20, and J. A. Frenkel and C. A. Rodriguez, "Portfolio Equilibrium and the Balance of Payments: A Monetary Approach," *American Economic Review*, 65 (September 1975), pp. 674–88.

When household saving exceeds the government's budget deficit, income exceeds absorption, and there must be a current-account surplus.[2] But no budget deficit is allowed to last forever. It is regulated by tax policy and is terminated exogenously when the government raises the lump-sum tax T^h to balance its budget. By implication, $\bar{D}$ cannot have any permanent influence on the behavior of the economy, and statement 3 must simplify eventually into an equality between saving and the current-account balance.

Setting aside temporarily the complications introduced by budget deficits, let us focus on the basic dynamic relationship between saving and wealth that guarantees stability in this model. Under both exchange-rate regimes, the effects of a disturbance or policy change on the path of the economy are determined by its impact on household saving and, by way of saving, on the path of wealth. A disturbance leads at once to saving and a current-account surplus or to dissaving and a current-account deficit. Its impact effect determines completely the subsequent path of the economy. That path must be monotonic, moreover, because the wealth-saving nexus is the only dynamic relationship in the model when the government's budget is balanced.

To emphasize these propositions, we illustrate responses to disturbances that lead at once to equal amounts of saving and show that they produce identical time paths. (The paths for disturbances that lead to dissaving are, of course, their mirror images.) We find it convenient, however, to look at those responses from different standpoints, depending on the exchange-rate regime under consideration.

When the exchange rate is pegged, it is convenient to focus on the influence of saving itself. It leads to a gradual increase in wealth and, therefore, in claims on the outside world–in holdings of the foreign bond and reserves. It also causes a decline in the domestic interest rate, because there can be no increase in the supply of bonds when the government's budget is balanced. As wealth rises through time and the interest rate falls, saving declines, raising absorption. Prices and income must therefore rise to clear the goods markets, causing the current-account surplus to decline apace with the level of saving. In brief, it is saving that drives the economy to its steady state.

When the exchange rate is flexible, by contrast, it is convenient to focus on the current-account surplus that is the counterpart of saving. It leads to

---

[2] This is the basic identity of national-income accounting, and it can be derived directly by adding Eqs. (2.27) and (2.28), the market-clearing equations for the two domestic goods, replacing $(p_N C_N + p_1 C_1)$ with $(Y^d - S - p_0 C_0)$, and replacing Y^d with $(p_N Q_N + p_1 Q_1) + \bar{D} - G_N - G_1$.

a gradual appreciation of the home currency that has two effects. First, the appreciation imposes capital losses on holders of the foreign bond. These offset additions to domestic holdings of those bonds that take place with saving and thus serve to hold wealth constant in the face of saving. When wealth is constant, moreover, the domestic interest rate is constant too. Second, the appreciation causes the current-account surplus to shrink, so that prices and income have to fall to clear the goods markets. As income falls, saving declines apace with the reduction in the current-account surplus. Thus, it is the current-account surplus and its influence on the flexible exchange rate that drive the economy to its steady state.

Dynamics under a pegged exchange rate

We begin by illustrating more extensively the interpretation suggested above. Suppose that the exchange rate is pegged, that the budget deficit is zero, and that households have begun to save under the influence of a disturbance. (Its nature does not matter for present purposes.) As portfolios are optimized continuously, statement 1, above, has a special meaning. Households will attempt to lodge a fraction of their saving in *each* of the financial assets–domestic money, domestic bonds, and foreign bonds. But supplies of the three assets will not be forthcoming at the requisite rates. In particular, $\dot{B}_1$ is zero when $\bar{D}$ is zero, and the domestic interest rate must therefore fall in order to reduce to zero the households' flow demand for the domestic bond. Taking the total time derivative of Eq. (2.32) and setting it at zero,

$$\dot{B}_1^h = B_{1W}\dot{W}^{hs} + B_{11}\dot{r}_1 = \dot{B}_1 = 0$$

so that

$$\dot{r}_1 = -(B_{1W}/B_{11})\dot{W}^{hs} < 0$$

In effect, the economy must move along WW in the asset-market diagrams of Chapters 4 and 5.

As this begins to happen, however, the flow demands for money and for foreign bonds, obtained from Eqs. (2.30) and (2.31), become[3]

$$\dot{L}_1^h = L_{1W}\dot{W}^{hs} - L_{11}(B_{1W}/B_{11})\dot{W}^{hs} = \bar{\pi}\dot{R},$$
$$\bar{\pi}\dot{B}_0^h = B_{0W}\dot{W}^{hs} - B_{01}(B_{1W}/B_{11})\dot{W}^{hs} = \dot{F}$$

[3] They can be rewritten as $\bar{\pi}\dot{R} = (H_\pi/B_{11})\dot{W}^{hs}$, and $\dot{F} = [(B_{11} - H_\pi)/B_{11}]\dot{W}^{hs}$, which have the same arguments as Eqs. (3.17b) and (3.18b) but deal in flows, not changes in flows. It must be remembered that equations of this type, like their counterparts in Chapter 3, are

so that $\bar{\pi}\dot{R} > 0$ and $\dot{F} > 0$ when $\dot{W}^{hs} > 0$. The sum of the two flow demands is

$$\bar{\pi}\dot{R} + \dot{F} = \dot{W}^{hs} = S = (p_1 C_1^f - p_0 C_0)$$

because $L_{11} + B_{01} = -B_{11}$. At every point in time, the decline in the interest rate will serve to keep the sum of flow demands for claims on foreigners equal to the current-account surplus that is the counterpart of saving.

Over time, moreover, the decline in the interest rate works jointly with the gradual increase in wealth to reduce the level of saving. Holding disposable income constant and working with Eq. (2.13),

$$\dot{S}|_{\bar{Y}^d} = S_1 \dot{r}_1 + S_W \dot{W}^{hs} = -[(S_1 B_{1W} - S_W B_{11})/B_{11}]\dot{W}^{hs} < 0$$

for $\dot{W}^{hs} > 0$. Absorption will rise gradually, given Y^d, stimulating aggregate demand and raising domestic prices. The current-account surplus will shrink apace with the decline in saving.[4]

The first of the disturbances considered in Chapter 4 furnishes the clearest view of these processes.

Shifts of demand between traded goods

Suppose, as in Chapter 4, that there is a permanent shift of foreign or domestic demand from the import good to the export good. The prices of domestic goods, p_N and p_1, rise instantaneously, as was shown in Figure 4.1, and there is an increase in nominal income. Households start to save. Correspondingly, the shift in demand generates a current-account surplus and a balance-of-payments surplus ($\bar{\pi}\dot{R} > 0$). There is a capital outflow ($\dot{F} > 0$), reflecting the flow demand for foreign bonds, but it is smaller than the current-account surplus.

Some of these same statements are made by Figure 6.1, which builds on the basic goods-market diagram developed in Chapter 4. In the upper right-hand panel, we reproduce Figure 4.2, plotting the level of nominal income, Y, against the (pegged) exchange rate, $\bar{\pi}$, and showing the initial positions of the income curves, zz and ZZ. The shift in demand to the ex-

---

linear approximations and strictly valid only in the neighborhood of the initial equilibrium (see also note 19 to Chapter 3).

[4] The increase in Y^d that comes about as prices rise will offset some of the reduction in desired saving denoted by $*\dot{S}|_{\bar{Y}^d}$ but cannot offset all of it. From Eqs. (3.7b) and (3.8b), $\dot{Y}^d = \dot{Y} = (N_u/N_s)[(S_1 B_{1W} - S_W B_{11})/B_{11}]\dot{W}^{hs}$, and the rate of change of actual saving must therefore be $\dot{S} = S_Y \dot{Y}^d + *\dot{S}|_{\bar{Y}^d} = -(N_w/N_s)[(S_1 B_{1W} - S_W B_{11})/B_{11}]\dot{W}^{hs}$, which is, of course, the argument of Eq. (3.12b) proving stability in the pegged-rate case.

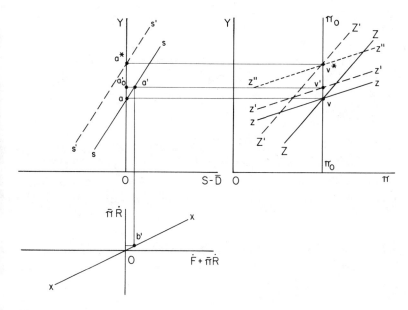

Figure 6.1 Shift of demand from the import good to the export good: adjustment under a pegged exchange rate.

port good is represented by a shift of the long-run curve from ZZ to $Z'Z'$ and by the smaller shift of the short-run curve from zz to $z'z'$. Goods-market equilibrium is displaced immediately from v to v', and the latter lies below $Z'Z'$. The instantaneous increase in income is larger than the corresponding increase in absorption, so there must be saving and a current-account surplus.

The difference between saving and the budget deficit is equal to the current-account balance (and is equal in this instance to saving itself, because $\bar{D} = 0$). It is shown explicitly in the upper left-hand panel of Figure 6.1. Curve ss treats saving as a function of income and is drawn to pass through the vertical axis opposite v, showing that saving is zero at initial income. The impact effect of the shift in demand is described by the movement along ss. (There is no shift of ss at this stage, because the other determinants of saving, W^h and r_1, do not change immediately in response to the shift in demand.) There is thus saving at a' on ss, the point corresponding to the income level given by v' in the right-hand panel. The amount of saving is $a'a'_0$.

In the lower panel of Figure 6.1, we replicate the statement made at the start of this chapter. The current-account surplus, measured by $S - \bar{D}$, is matched by the sum of flow demands for claims on foreigners–the flow demand for foreign bonds or capital outflow, $\dot{F}$, and the flow demand for money or inflow of reserves, $\bar{\pi}\dot{R}$. Curve xx plots the inflow of reserves against the current-account balance (measured by the corresponding asset flows). When, as here, there is no budget deficit, xx has to pass through zero, and its slope is positive but less than unity:

$$\bar{\pi}\dot{R} = [(L_{1W}B_{11} - L_{11}B_{1W})/B_{11}]\dot{W}^{hs} = (H_{\pi}/B_{11})S < S$$

At b', then, the balance of payments is in surplus.

In Chapter 4, we saw that wealth must increase gradually and the interest rate must fall as the economy moves to its steady state. (In Figure 4.4A, asset-market equilibrium was displaced through time from w to w'.) Under the influence of the increase in wealth and decline in the interest rate, there is a gradual reduction in desired saving at each and every level of disposable income (i.e., $*\dot{S}|_{\bar{Y}^d} < 0$). The saving curve shifts steadily to the left in Figure 6.1, and the short-run income curve moves steadily upward, reflecting the increase in absorption that corresponds to the decline in desired saving. Income rises, saving falls, and these movements continue until saving goes to zero. The saving curve will come to rest at $s's'$, when it intersects its vertical axis at a*, opposite the intersection of $z''z''$ and $Z'Z'$ at v^*. In the lower panel of the diagram, the inflow of assets declines to zero, along with the current-account surplus, and so does the overall balance-of-payments surplus.

Risking repetition, we emphasize the role of saving in the processes described by Figure 6.1. Whenever there is saving in an amount $a'a_0'$, and the exchange rate is pegged, wealth rises and the interest rate falls. Income rises by an amount $v'v^*$, because of the upward shift of the short-run income curve from $z'z'$ to $z''z''$, and saving goes gradually to zero, as the saving curve shifts from ss to $s's'$. The same processes follow in the wake of other disturbances, even those with different comparative-static effects, whenever they begin by inducing $a'a_0'$ of saving.

Tracing these events through time in Figure 6.2, income rises gradually, following the initial increase; it moves asymptotically toward the permanent level given by v^* in Figure 6.1. Saving and the current-account balance increase on impact, but return to zero thereafter. Under a pegged exchange rate, moreover, saving is the only influence on wealth, and positive saving leads to a gradual increase in wealth, comprising gradual increases in reserves and in domestic holdings of the foreign bond

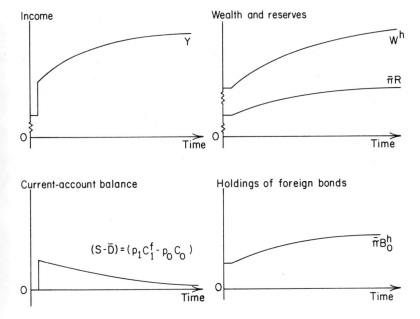

Figure 6.2 Shift of demand from the import good to the export good: time paths under a pegged exchange rate.

(the integrals of the inflow $\bar{\pi}\dot{R}$ and of the capital outflow $\dot{F}$, respectively).[5]

Open-market operations

In order to illustrate the similarity of dynamic processes in cases having different comparative-static results, we look next at an open-market *sale* of the domestic bond, a sale of a size that induces the same initial amount of saving as did the shift in demand examined above.

In Chapter 5, we showed that an open-market purchase reduces the interest rate immediately (asset-market equilibrium was displaced from w to w_0' in Figure 5.1A). There was dissaving, an increase in absorption, and an increase in income (goods-market equilibrium was displaced from v to v' in Figure 5.2). On the way to the new steady state, however, income returned to its initial level, the interest rate rose part way to its initial level,

[5] In this and subsequent diagrams, stocks of wealth and assets are drawn to a common scale (as are saving, budget deficits, and current-account balances where they appear separately). But income and the current-account balance are not drawn to a common scale.

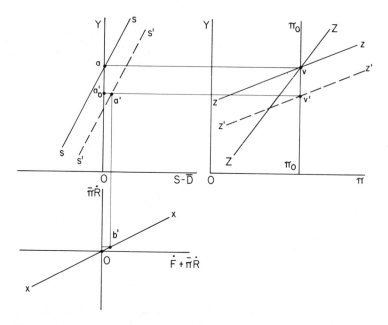

Figure 6.3 Open-market sale of domestic bonds: adjustment under a pegged exchange rate.

and dissaving reduced the level of wealth. With an open-market sale, these outcomes are reversed. The interest rate rises immediately, households start to save, absorption is reduced, and income falls. Thus, in Figure 6.3, the short-run income curve shifts downward from zz to $z'z'$, and income falls from v to v'.

The saving induced by the increase in the interest rate shifts the saving curve from ss to $s's'$, so that the new income level generates $a'a_0'$ of saving, the amount observed in the previous case. The current account moves into surplus, and there is an inflow of reserves, indicated at b' in the lower panel of Figure 6.3. The dynamic process that begins at this juncture is just like the one described above. Wealth rises gradually on account of saving, and the interest rate declines. The saving curve moves back through time from $s's'$ to ss, its original position; the short-run income curve moves back from $z'z'$ to zz. Income rises from v' to v as the economy reaches its new steady state, and saving goes to zero at a, the point corresponding to the long-run income level.

The comparative-static results of the two disturbances are quite different. The shift in demand to the export good raised income on impact and raised it further with the passage of time. The open-market sale re-

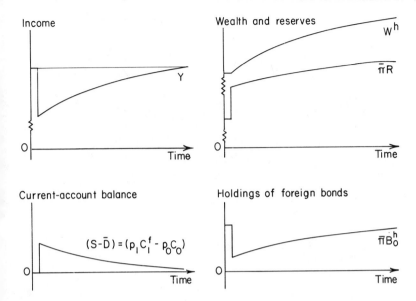

Figure 6.4 Open-market sale of domestic bonds: time paths under a pegged exchange rate.

duced income on impact but did not do so permanently. The shift in demand had no immediate effects on asset markets, but the interest rate declined on the way to the steady state. The open-market sale, by contrast, raised the interest rate immediately and raised its long-run level too (albeit by a smaller amount).

The two disturbances are similar, however, in that they generate the same amounts of saving on impact, causing identical dynamic responses. Compare the movement from v' to v^* in Figure 6.1 with the movement from v' to v in Figure 6.3. They are identical, even though they start and end in different positions. As a matter of fact, the gradual shifts in the income and saving curves are themselves identical, and the time paths shown in Figure 6.4 for the open-market sale are the same as the time paths shown in Figure 6.2, once the starting points are given.

Devaluation of a pegged exchange rate

Having examined a typical goods-market disturbance and a typical asset-market disturbance, we turn now to devaluation, a disturbance that has immediate effects on both sets of markets.

In Chapter 5, we showed that a devaluation can cause either saving or

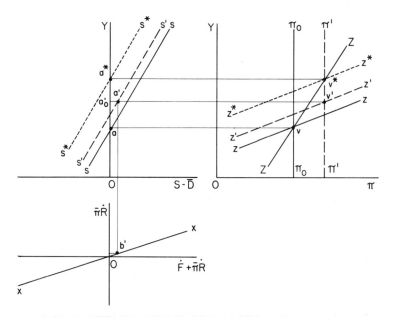

Figure 6.5 Devaluation of a pegged exchange rate when saving occurs.

dissaving on impact. By conferring capital gains on holders of the foreign bond, it raises wealth immediately and calls for a decline in the interest rate to clear the market for the domestic bond. There is an immediate increase in reserves to satisfy the increase in demand for money. The increase in wealth and reduction in the interest rate tend to reduce saving. In Figure 6.5, the short-run income curve shifts from zz to $z'z'$, and the saving curve shifts from ss to $s's'$. At the same time, however, the devaluation switches domestic and foreign demands to the export good. There is an income-increasing movement along $z'z'$ to goods-market equilibrium at v'. As this tends to raise saving, the net change in saving is uncertain. But Figure 6.5 is drawn to show saving, not dissaving, in the usual amount $a'a_0'$, so as to facilitate comparisons with earlier examples. The effect of the switch in expenditure, which increases saving by raising income, is assumed to dominate the effect of the shift in expenditure, which reduces saving by raising absorption.

Subsequent developments replicate those that we have seen before. Wealth rises gradually and the interest rate declines, so that the short-run income curve moves upward from $z'z'$ to $z*z*$, and the saving curve

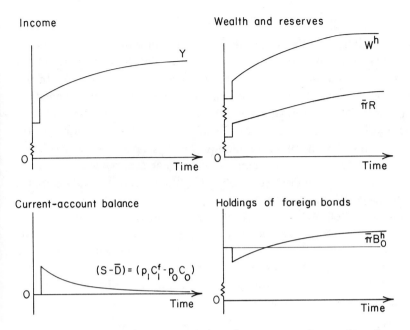

Figure 6.6 Devaluation of a pegged exchange rate: time paths when saving occurs.

moves leftward from $s's'$ to s^*s^*. Long-run equilibrium is established at v^*, and saving is zero at the corresponding point a^*. The usual time paths are shown in Figure 6.6.[6] They are, of course, opposite to those that would take place if the devaluation had produced dissaving. (Wealth would have fallen gradually, along with reserves and holdings of the foreign bond. The former, however, would not have fallen all the way to the initial level.)

[6] In Figure 6.6, holdings of foreign bonds, like holdings of reserves, are measured at the pre-devaluation exchange rate in order to identify the instantaneous adjustment of portfolios brought about by the devaluation. The steady-state change in holdings of the foreign bond is equal to the change in the home-currency value of those holdings measured at the current exchange rate *less* that part which represents the capital gain on initial holdings. The change measured at the current exchange rate is equal to $dW^h - \bar{\pi}\, dR$, and Eqs. (3.21b), (3.20b), and (3.24b) can be used to show that this amount is equal to $-(S_Y/H_f)(N_t/N_w)[L_{11}B_{0W} + (1 - L_{1W})B_{01}](d\bar{\pi}/\bar{\pi})$, and is positive. But the difference between this expression and the capital gain, $V_\pi(d\bar{\pi}/\bar{\pi})$ or $-B_{0W}(S_Y/S_W)Y^d(d\bar{\pi}/\bar{\pi})$ in the initial steady state, is ambiguous. (Home-currency holdings of foreign bonds measured at the current exchange rate increase even when devaluation induces dissaving, leading to a cumulative capital inflow – a reduction in holdings of the foreign bond measured at a constant exchange rate.)

Dynamics under a flexible exchange rate

When the exchange rate is flexible, the supply of money is policy determined. The flow supply of money is always zero because the central bank does not intervene in the foreign-exchange market (i.e. $\bar{\pi}R = 0$). In this case, then, the interest rate cannot play the role it did with a pegged exchange rate. To suppress the flow demand for bonds, $\dot{B}_1^h$, produced by household saving, the interest rate would have to fall. To suppress the corresponding flow demand for money, $\dot{L}_1^h$, it would have to rise. It is therefore the task of the exchange rate to clear the markets for home-currency assets, and it does so by offsetting the influence of saving on the flow demands for those assets.

Suppose, as before, that households are saving and that the government budget is balanced. There will be a current-account surplus and, therefore, a flow supply of foreign currency coming from the outside world. At the initial exchange rate, moreover, that supply will be larger than the flow demand for foreign currency that comes from the households' flow demand for the foreign bond. Algebraically,

$$(p_1 C_1^f - p_0 C_0) - \dot{F} = S - \dot{F} = \dot{W}^{hs} - B_{0W}\dot{W}^{hs}$$
$$= (1 - B_{0W})\dot{W}^{hs} > 0$$

when $\dot{W}^{hs} > 0$. The domestic currency must appreciate to clear the foreign-exchange market and will do so at this rate:

$$\left(\frac{\dot{\pi}}{\pi}\right) = -(1/V_\pi)\dot{W}^{hs}$$

because it is the rate of change that satisfies three conditions. (1) The rate of change of total wealth, $\dot{W}^h$, will be zero, because $\dot{W}^h = \dot{W}^{hs} + V_\pi(\dot{\pi}/\pi) = 0$. Capital losses on foreign bonds will offset current saving.[7] (2) When wealth does not change and the interest rate is constant, demands for domestic assets will be constant too. Accordingly, $\dot{L}_1^h = \bar{\pi}R = 0$, and $\dot{B}_1^h = \dot{B}_1 = \bar{D} = 0$. (3) When wealth is constant, the demand for home-currency holdings of the foreign bond is constant too, but there will be a positive flow demand for the foreign bond. Households will want to offset the capital losses imposed by the appreciation of the home currency. They will buy additional foreign bonds at the rate $\dot{F} =$

---

[7] We have thus reaffirmed an assertion made in earlier chapters. Under a flexible exchange rate, $\dot{r}_1 = \dot{W}^h = 0$, so that the steady-state changes in the interest rate and wealth will be the same as the instantaneous changes. This is what we saw in the asset-market diagrams of Chapters 4 and 5. (When the disturbance is a tax cut, however, $\dot{r}_1$ is not zero; the interest rate must rise through time to raise the demand for the domestic bond.)

$-V_\pi(\dot{\pi}/\pi) = \dot{W}^{hs} = S = (p_1 C_1^f - p_0 C_0)$. Thus, the third condition says that saving will be used to buy foreign bonds (which is, of course, the only way that it can be used when $\bar{D}$ is zero, the exchange rate is flexible, and there is no investment), and the capital outflow will equal the current-account surplus. The rate of appreciation of the home currency will clear the foreign-exchange market in the face of saving and a current-account surplus. (The appreciation can likewise be described as serving to suppress the flow demand for money generated by household saving. It does so by reducing the rate of change of wealth to zero. By looking at the matter from this standpoint, we link our approach with the one adopted in monetary explanations of exchange-rate changes.)

As the home currency appreciates, however, the current-account surplus shrinks through time. Domestic and foreign demands are diverted from home to foreign goods. Therefore, income will decline, and so will disposable income. As Y^d declines, moreover, saving does so too, and thus remains equal to the current-account surplus. In brief, the dynamics of the flexible-rate case can be described by the way in which the current-account balance and the flexible exchange rate interact to drive the economy to its steady state.[8]

We illustrate this process of adjustment by looking at the paths that will be followed after a shift of demand between traded goods and an open-market sale of the domestic bond, both scaled to induce identical current-account surpluses (saving).

Shifts of demand between traded goods

Recall the results obtained in Chapter 4. Because the exchange rate is not affected immediately by a goods-market disturbance, a shift of domestic or foreign demand to the export good raises income and shifts the current-account balance into surplus. Eventually, however, income returns to its initial level, and the current-account surplus goes to zero. These results are shown in Figure 6.7 and are explained in Figure 6.8.

In the upper right-hand panel of Figure 6.8, we show the shifts in the income curves. The long-run curve rises from ZZ to $Z'Z'$, the short-run curve rises from zz to $z'z'$, and income rises by vv'. (These outcomes are the same as those in Figure 6.1, which dealt with the pegged-rate case.)

---

[8] Under a flexible exchange rate, $*\dot{S}|_{\bar{F}^d} = 0$ (because $\dot{r}_1 = \dot{W}^h = 0$ without a budget deficit). Accordingly, $\dot{S} = S_Y \dot{Y}^d$, and from Eqs. (3.7a) and (3.8a), $\dot{Y}^d = \dot{Y} = -(N_t/N_s)(1/V_\pi)\dot{W}^{hs} = (N_t/N_s)(\dot{\pi}/\pi)$, because $\dot{W}^{hs} = -V_\pi(\dot{\pi}/\pi)$. Therefore, $\dot{S} = -S_Y(N_t/N_s)(1/V_\pi)\dot{W}^{hs}$, which is the argument of Eq. (3.12a), the proof of stability in the flexible-rate case. Alternatively, $\dot{S} = S_Y(N_t/N_s)(\dot{\pi}/\pi)$, which emphasizes the path of the exchange rate.

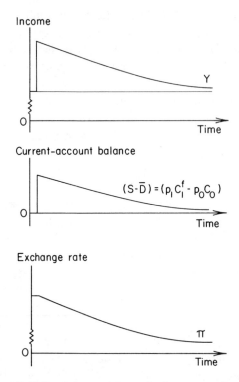

Figure 6.7 Shift of demand from the import good to the export good: time paths under a flexible exchange rate.

In the upper left-hand panel of Figure 6.8, we replace the saving curve with a current-account curve cc. The current-account balance is, of course, equal to $S - \bar{D}$, but it varies inversely with income, because the demand for imports rises with income. The slope of cc is negative, not positive, and thus opposite to that of ss. The economy is at u initially, where cc intersects its vertical axis at an income level corresponding to v in the income diagram. The shift of demand to the export good shifts cc to $c'c'$, and the economy moves at once from u to u', at an income level corresponding to v'. There is a current-account surplus equal to $u'u_0'$.

In the lower part of Figure 6.8, we make two statements. With a flexible exchange rate, the current-account surplus must always equal the capital outflow, $\dot{F}$, and that outflow is associated with an appreciation of the home currency ($\dot{\pi} < 0$). Curve qq is the flexible-rate counterpart of xx in our pegged-rate diagrams. It is defined by the statement above, that $\dot{F} = -V_\pi(\dot{\pi}/\pi)$. Thus, the current-account surplus at u' is matched by a capital outflow at g' and an appreciation of the home currency.

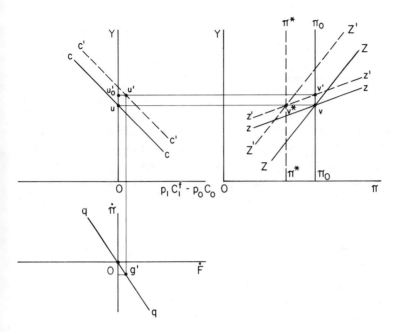

Figure 6.8 Shift of demand from the import good to the export good: adjustment under a flexible exchange rate.

In Chapter 4, we found that wealth and the interest rate do not change on impact or through time on account of a goods-market disturbance (that asset-market equilibrium remains at w in Figure 4.3A). The wealth-increasing effect of saving is offset exactly by capital losses on the foreign bond resulting from the gradual appreciation of the home currency. Accordingly, the short-run income curve remains at $z'z'$ in Figure 6.8. The appreciation, however, switches expenditure away from domestic goods, moving the economy along that curve from v' to v^*, where income returns to what it was initially. As a result, the current-account curve moves gradually back from $c'c'$ to cc on the left-hand side of Figure 6.8, as the appreciation worsens the current account at all income levels. The current-account surplus vanishes, and the exchange rate ceases to appreciate.

Open-market operations

In Chapter 5, we showed that an open-market purchase of the domestic bond reduces the domestic interest rate and causes the home currency to depreciate, but that the immediate effect on saving is uncertain. There can be dissaving and a current-account deficit, in which case the home currency continues to depreciate (there is undershooting initially). There can be saving and a current-account surplus, in which case the home currency begins to appreciate, reversing part of the instantaneous depreciation (there is overshooting initially).

The same sort of ambiguity arises with an open-market sale. The interest rate rises immediately and the home currency appreciates. But there can be saving and a current-account surplus or dissaving and a current-account deficit. We deal here with the first possibility in order to maintain comparability with the responses to a shift in demand and to an open-market sale under a pegged exchange rate. (The size of the sale, however, need not be the same as with the pegged rate, because the effects on saving and the current-account balance may not be identical under the two regimes.)

The impact effects of this disturbance are shown in the right-hand panel of Figure 6.9. The exchange-rate schedule shifts from $\pi_0 \pi_0$ to $\pi' \pi'$, denoting the immediate appreciation of the home currency, and the short-run income curve shifts downward from zz to $z'z'$, denoting the drop in absorption caused by the wealth-reducing effect of the appreciation and the immediate increase in the interest rate. Furthermore, the current-account curve shifts downward from cc to $c'c'$ in the left-hand panel, denoting the expenditure-switching effects of the appreciation. Income falls from the level defined by v to the one defined by v', and the current-account balance moves into surplus by $u'u_0'$ (the cut in income is assumed to improve the current-account balance by more than the appreciation worsens it). The home currency continues to appreciate at the speed defined by g' in the lower panel of the diagram.

Wealth and the interest rate do not change during the transition to the new steady state, and the short-run income curve remains in place. But the current-account curve moves from $c'c'$ to c^*c^*, under the influence of the appreciation shown by the shift in the exchange-rate schedule from $\pi' \pi'$ to $\pi^* \pi^*$. The economy moves from v' to v^*, reducing income to its steady-state level, and the current-account surplus is ended at u^*. The time paths of income, the current account, and the exchange rate are the same as those we traced in Figure 6.7, but the points of departure are different. There are abrupt reductions in Y and π, corresponding to the shift from v to v' in Figure 6.9. (If the open-market sale had produced a current-account deficit, the time paths would have been reversed. We would have seen overshooting initially, as Y and π would fall below their steady-state levels, then rise gradually through time.)

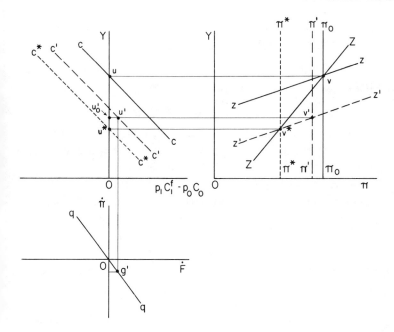

Figure 6.9 Open-market sale of domestic bonds: adjustment under a flexible exchange rate.

All of the disturbances analyzed thus far were calibrated to produce equal amounts of saving and, therefore, the same current-account surpluses. The impact and steady-state effects have differed from disturbance to disturbance, but all of them have had the same dynamic effects under a given exchange-rate regime. The fundamental difference between the two regimes can best be identified by looking once again at the saving curve for the pegged-rate regime and the current-account curve for the flexible-rate regime. In Figure 6.1, for example, the point of departure was a' on the saving curve ss, the process of adjustment with a pegged rate involved a gradual increase in income, and the terminal point was a^* on the saving curve $s's'$. The increase in income reflected the increase in absorption occurring on account of the increase in wealth brought about by saving. In Figure 6.8, by contrast, the point of departure was u' on the current-account curve $c'c'$, the process of adjustment with a flexible rate involved a gradual decrease in income, and the terminal point was u on the current-account curve cc. The decrease in income reflected the reduction in the current-account surplus occurring because of the switch in expenditure brought about by the appreciation of the home currency.

When saving and a current-account surplus emerge on impact, dynamic adjustments are expansionary with a pegged exchange rate and are contractionary with a flexible exchange rate.

A temporary tax reduction and budget deficit

Somewhat different processes are encountered when there is a temporary tax reduction resulting in a budget deficit. In Chapter 5, we studied a simple tax policy. It began when the government reduced the lump-sum tax T^h to generate a deficit, then adjusted T^h continuously to stabilize that deficit at the desired level $\bar{D}$. At some subsequent point in time, however, the government balanced its budget by raising the lump-sum tax and adjusted it to maintain a balanced budget. In the notation used below, the deficit is zero at time $t = 0$; it is $\bar{D} > 0$ in the interval of time $0 < t < k$; and it is zero again at and after time $t = k$.

No government is likely to adopt such a policy, for reasons that will soon be apparent. If it had the power to control its deficit exactly by adjusting taxes continuously, it would probably allow its deficit to fall gradually, rather than ending it abruptly at time $t = k$. But the dynamics of a simple, discontinuous tax policy are hard enough to analyze, and we shall not try to deal here with more realistic cases.

In Chapter 5, we showed that this simple tax policy begins as a pure goods-market disturbance. It causes an immediate increase of income, independent of the exchange-rate regime or degree of asset-market integration. But the long-run effects are determined by responses to the increase in the stock of debt that remains in the wake of the budget deficit. Under a pegged exchange rate, income returns to its initial level. Under a flexible rate, income is raised permanently when crowding out does not dominate, but the size of the permanent increase in income varies inversely with the degree of asset-market integration. Finally, recall one point stressed in Chapter 5. The sizes of effects of the deficit $\bar{D}$ bear no simple relationship to those of the permanent increase in the supply of bonds, as the size of the increase in B_1 depends on the duration of the deficit (on the date $t = k$ when the deficit is ended), not merely on its magnitude.

To trace the path of the economy under the influence of this particular disturbance, we ask two questions: (1) What is the path of the economy within the time interval $0 < t < k$, under the influence of an ongoing deficit? (2) What is its path after the time $t = k$, when the stock of debt comes to be constant and the economy starts to move to a new steady state? The first is more difficult to answer, because the supply of bonds is increasing steadily when $\bar{D} > 0$ and we must therefore study the effects of simultaneous changes in two stocks–in B_1 and W^h. The second is comparatively simple, because the processes involved were studied before.

Dynamics under a pegged exchange rate

When looking at responses to a shift in demand and an open-market operation under a pegged exchange rate, we were able to suppose that there would be no flow supply of bonds–that the government balanced its budget continuously. The path of the domestic interest rate, $\dot{r}_1$, was thus governed by the need to keep the flow demand for bonds at zero. In the present case, the path of the interest rate is governed by the need to balance the flow demand, $\dot{B}_1^h$, with the flow supply, $\dot{B}_1$, which must in turn equal $\bar{D}$ until time $t = k$. Accordingly,

$$\dot{r}_1 = -(B_{1W}/B_{11})\dot{W}^{hs} + (1/B_{11})\bar{D} = (1/B_{11})[(1 - B_{1W})\bar{D} - B_{1W}(S - \bar{D})]$$

But $\bar{D} > S > 0$ on impact, as was shown in Chapter 5, so that $\dot{r}_1 > 0$ initially (unless foreign and domestic bonds are perfect substitutes). On this finding, moreover, the flow demand for money and, therefore, $\bar{\pi}\dot{R}$ is given by

$$\bar{\pi}\dot{R} = (1/B_{11})[(B_{0W}L_{11} - L_{1W}B_{01})\bar{D} + H_{\pi}(S - \bar{D})]$$

which is ambiguous even when $\bar{D} > S > 0$. Furthermore,

$$\dot{F} = (1/B_{11})\{[B_{11}B_{0W} + B_{01}(1 - B_{1W})]\bar{D} + [B_{11}B_{0W} - B_{01}B_{1W}](S - \bar{D})\}$$

which is likewise ambiguous. Although there is a current-account deficit $(S - \bar{D} < 0)$, so that there must be an outflow of assets $(\dot{F} + \bar{\pi}\dot{R} < 0)$, the *composition* of that outflow is uncertain. If there is an outflow of bonds $(\dot{F} < 0)$, there must be a reserve gain $(\bar{\pi}\dot{R} > 0)$, and conversely. Thus, the outcome here is different from those that we encountered early in this chapter (where $\dot{F}$ and $\bar{\pi}\dot{R}$ had the same signs).

Most important, we cannot predict the movement of the short-run income curve under the influence of a budget deficit:

$$*\dot{S}|_{\bar{y}^d} = (1/B_{11})\{[B_{11}S_W + S_1(1 - B_{1W})]\bar{D} - [B_{1W}S_1 - S_W B_{11}](S - \bar{D})\}$$

and there is nothing we can say about the sign of the first term.

When domestic and foreign bonds are perfect substitutes, however, these ambiguities disappear. It is rather easy to trace the path of the economy under the influence of an ongoing deficit and the path that it will follow after the deficit has been ended. Using this case as a benchmark, moreover, we shall be able to infer the implications of asset-market integration for the effectiveness of fiscal policy, a matter studied briefly in Chapter 5 but deferred for further examination in this chapter.

The limiting case. When the two bonds in our model are perfect substitutes, $-B_{01} \to \infty$, so that $B_{11} \to \infty$, and $\dot{r}_1 \to 0$. Furthermore,

$$\bar{\pi}\dot{R} \to L_{1W}\bar{D} + L_{1W}(S - \bar{D}) = L_{1W}S > 0$$

$$\dot{F} \to -L_{1W}\bar{D} + (1 - L_{1W})(S - \bar{D}) = (1 - L_{1W})S - \bar{D} < 0$$

and

$$*\dot{S}|_{\bar{Y}^d} \to S_W\bar{D} + S_W(\bar{S} - \bar{D}) = S_W S < 0$$

Reserves will rise (the balance of payments will be in surplus) for as long as households continue to save under the influence of a budget deficit, but the rate of increase will decline if saving falls. There will be a capital inflow ($\dot{F} < 0$) initially, because $\bar{D} > S > 0$, and it will rise if saving falls (approaching $\bar{D}$ as S approaches zero). Finally, desired absorption will increase through time ($*\dot{S}|_{\bar{Y}^d} < 0$) for as a long as households continue to save.

Possessing this new information and what we learned in Chapter 5 about the immediate effects of a tax cut, we can trace the entire path of the economy, using Figure 6.10.

Before the tax cut and budget deficit, the economy will be at v on the short-run income curve zz (the one that passes through the long-run curve ZZ at the exchange rate given by $\pi_0\pi_0$); it will be at a on the saving curve ss; and it will be at zero on curve xx in the lower part of the diagram. When the government reduces lump-sum taxes, the short-run income curve will shift to $z'z'$. Curve ss, which measures $S - \bar{D}$, will shift to $s's'$, by the horizontal distance aa_0, which measures the budget deficit $\bar{D}$. And the balance-of-payments schedule will shift to $x'x'$, by the same horizontal distance ($0b'' = aa_0$).[9] Goods-market equilibrium will be displaced to v', raising income; the current account will move into deficit at a' on $s's'$; but the balance of payments will move into surplus ($\bar{\pi}\dot{R} > 0$) at b' on $x'x'$.

[9] The equation for xx is $\bar{\pi}\dot{R} = (1/B_{11})[(B_{01}L_{1W} - L_{11}B_{0W})\bar{D} + (B_{11}L_{1W} - L_{11}B_{1W})(\dot{F} + \bar{\pi}\dot{R})]$ With perfect substitutability, however, $\bar{\pi}\dot{R} = L_{1W}[\bar{D} + (\dot{F} + \bar{\pi}\dot{R})]$, or $(\dot{F} + \bar{\pi}\dot{R}) = (1/L_{1W})\bar{\pi}\dot{R} - \bar{D}$. An increase in $\bar{D}'$ shifts xx leftward by the amount of the budget deficit. Similarly, ss shifts leftward by the amount of the deficit, because W^h and r_1 are not affected immediately, and they are the other variables that determine its position.

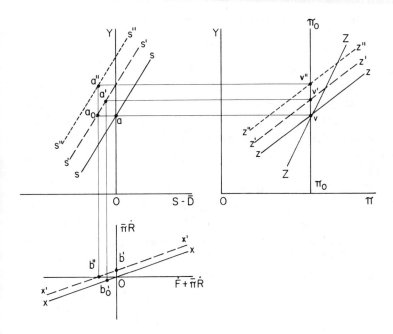

Figure 6.10 Temporary tax reduction and budget deficit: adjustment under a pegged exchange rate with perfect asset-market integration.

By implication, there will be a capital inflow ($\dot{F} < 0$) that is larger absolutely than the current-account deficit.

Although v' lies above ZZ, we know that households start to save and wealth begins to rise. Therefore, the short-run income curve must move gradually in the direction of $z''z''$, and $s's'$ must move gradually in the direction of $s''s''$. Under a pegged exchange rate, then, v' will tend to v'', a' will tend to a'', and b' will tend to b''. Income will rise through time, the current-account deficit will get larger, and the balance-of-payments surplus will get smaller.

Before asking what will happen at time $t = k$, when $\bar{D}$ is cut to zero, let us ask first what would happen if that day were deferred indefinitely, allowing the economy to adjust completely to an ongoing budget deficit. What are the properties of v'', a'', and b'', to which it would tend? We know that the short-run income curve can come to rest only when saving is driven to zero by the growth of wealth. When saving is zero, moreover, the current-account deficit must equal the budget deficit (as it does at a''), and the balance-of-payments surplus must go to zero (as it does at b'').

Thus, the economy would tend to what we shall describe as a quasi-stationary state. Income and wealth would come to be constant at levels higher than they were before the tax cut, and households would cease to add to their holdings of money and bonds. With perfect asset-market integration, however, households would be content to sell foreign bonds in order to buy additional domestic bonds. The government could continue to finance its deficit by issuing domestic bonds. The budget deficit and current-account deficit would both be covered by the capital inflow – the proceeds of the households' sales of foreign bonds. In effect, the government could borrow abroad indirectly, using households as intermediaries, and could do so until households ran out of foreign bonds. (It is, of course, this last possibility that distinguishes the situation at v'', a'', and b'' from a true stationary state. It cannot be perpetuated forever.)

Figure 6.11 is drawn to describe these tendencies. There is an instantaneous increase of income, and a further increase over time, tending to the upper limit corresponding to v'' in Figure 6.10. There is an immediate increase of saving, but it declines thereafter. There is a current-account deficit that is smaller at first than the budget deficit but grows gradually through time as saving declines. Wealth rises at a diminishing rate, and reserves rise with it. Holdings of domestic bonds grow steadily at the rate $\dot{B}_1 = \bar{D}$. Holdings of foreign bonds fall at an accelerating rate that tends finally to $-\dot{B}_1$ as the growth of wealth goes to zero. Households sell foreign bonds to make room for the domestic bonds issued by the government, and all other variables come to be constant.

When the government terminates its deficit, by raising lump-sum taxes at time $t = k$, the economy reverses direction. In most respects, indeed, it retraces its steps. The short-run income curve falls abruptly by as much as it rose initially (by a distance equal to vv'); the saving curve $s''s''$ shifts rightward by the amount of the reduction in $\bar{D}$; and curve $x'x'$ drops back to xx. At that juncture, however, income will be higher than it was before the tax cut and has to fall further. On the eve of the decision to balance the budget, goods-market equilibrium was somewhere between v' and v'', which means that the new equilibrium point must lie above v. There must thus be dissaving and a current-account deficit, and because there is no longer any budget deficit, the balance of payments must move into deficit too. (Prior to time $t = k$, there was saving at goods-market equilibria above v. At and after time $t = k$, however, there is dissaving at those equilibria. At v' and a', for example, there is a current-account deficit, which means that $S < 0$ when $\bar{D} = 0$, and the balance of payments is in

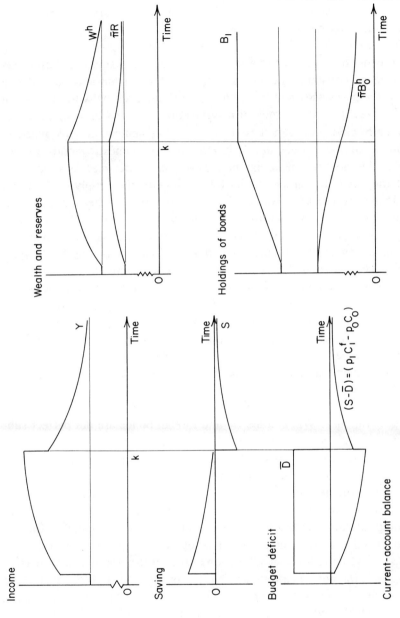

Figure 6.11 Temporary tax reduction and budget deficit: time paths under a pegged exchange rate with perfect asset-market integration.

deficit at b_0'. There is a capital inflow, but it is too small to offset the current-account deficit.)

The subsequent path of the economy is governed entirely by the basic relationship between wealth and saving, because the supply of bonds has come to be constant. Income, saving, and the current-account balance follow the paths shown in Figure 6.11, returning eventually to their initial levels. Wealth and the stock of reserves do so too, as dissaving and the balance-of-payments deficit reverse the movements that took place in response to the budget deficit.[10] Holdings of domestic bonds cannot change, but holdings of foreign bonds continue to decline. As a matter of fact, they have to fall eventually by as much as the supply of domestic bonds has grown; when wealth and reserves return to their initial levels, holdings of the two bonds taken together must also return to their initial level. There is thus a sense in which the budget deficit is *always* financed by borrowing from foreigners when asset markets are perfectly integrated. The budget deficit is larger than the concurrent capital inflow; the two would be equal in the quasi-stationary state, but this is one to which the economy tends, not one that it reaches in finite time. After time $t = k$, however, additional sales of foreign bonds close the gap between the integral of budget deficits and the integral of capital inflows. The time paths after the budget deficit is ended are those for the economy in the process of dissaving and gradually reverse the earlier outcomes (apart from those for B_1 and $\bar{\pi}B_0^h$).

The general case. When domestic and foreign bonds are not perfect substitutes, the steady-state outcomes are different from those shown in Figure 6.11. The economy must still wind up at v in Figure 6.10. There can be no permanent increase in income with a pegged exchange rate. But there will be a permanent increase in wealth and in the domestic interest rate, and reserves will be reduced when crowding out does not dominate. Holdings of domestic bonds must grow, of course, but holdings of foreign bonds need not be reduced when asset markets are not closely integrated.[11] In Figure 6.12, an adaptation of the asset-market diagram used in Chapter 5, the bond-market curve shifts from WW to W^*W^*, because the budget deficit raises the supply of domestic bonds. Steady-state equilibrium is established at w^*, where wealth is larger than it was initially and the interest rate is higher.

---

[10] When, as here, $-B_{01} \to \infty$, Eqs. (3.20b) and (3.24b) tell us that $dW^h = \bar{\pi}\, dR = 0$.

[11] From Eqs. (3.25), (3.20b), and (3.24b), $\bar{\pi}\, dB_0^h = (1/H_f)(S_1 B_{0W} - S_W B_{01})\, dB_1$, which can be positive or negative.

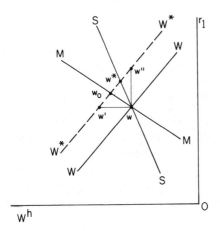

Figure 6.12 Temporary tax reduction and budget deficit: selected asset-market outcomes under a pegged exchange rate.

When the two bonds are not perfect substitutes, moreover, the economy can follow any one of many paths under the influence of a budget deficit. Therefore, it can reach any one of many points on the bond-market curve when that curve comes to rest at W^*W^*. It need not proceed directly to w^*. By implication, there are many paths that it can follow after time $t = k$, when the government balances its budget.

Having worked our way through these possibilities, we are tempted to describe them fully here. But the fiscal policy to which they correspond is unrealistically simple, and it would be foolish to examine all of the responses to it. Instead, we list briefly the principal features of the three classes of responses–classes corresponding to the three ways in which saving can evolve.

On impact, of course, the short-run income curve moves to $z'z'$ and the saving curve moves to $s's'$, just as they did in the limiting case described by Figure 6.10. Thereafter, the movements of the two curves are governed by

$$*S|_{\bar{Y}^d} = S_1 \dot{r}_1 + S_W \dot{W}^{hs}$$

At time $t = 0$, when the tax cut takes effect, $\dot{W}^{hs}$ is positive, and its size does not depend on substitutability between the two bonds. It depends on the location of a' in Figure 6.10 and is thus determined by the expenditure effects of the tax cut. As $\bar{D} > S > 0$ at that point, moreover, $\dot{r}_1$ is nonnegative. But the size of $\dot{r}_1$ does depend on the degree of substitutability (it varies directly with B_{01} and, therefore, inversely with B_{11}). Thus, there are these three possibilities at time $t = 0$:

1. When $\dot{r}_1/\dot{W}^{hs} < -(S_W/S_1)$, then $*\dot{S}|_{\bar{y}^d} < 0$. The saving curve will move to the left and the short-run income curve will rise after time $t = 0$. Income will rise, saving will fall, and the current-account deficit will get bigger, much as they did in the limiting case described by Figure 6.11.

2. When $\dot{r}_1/\dot{W}^{hs} = -(S_W/S_1)$, then $*\dot{S}|_{\bar{y}^d} = 0$. The saving curve will stay put and so will the short-run income curve. Income, saving, and the current-account deficit will stay at v' and a' in Figure 6.10.

3. When $\dot{r}_1/\dot{W}^{hs} > -(S_W/S_1)$, then $*\dot{S}|_{\bar{y}^d} > 0$. The saving curve will move to the right and the short-run income curve will fall. Income will fall, saving will rise, and the current-account deficit will get smaller, in the manner illustrated by Figure 6.13.

To carry the analysis further, consider first the implications of following path 2. That path will be self-perpetuating, because $\dot{r}_1$ is constant when saving and the budget deficit are constant. Furthermore, the ratio $\dot{r}_1/\dot{W}^{hs}$ will equal the slope of SS in Figure 6.12, which says that the economy moves along that curve until time $t = k$. Therefore, it will arrive directly at w^* when the government balances its budget and causes the bond-market curve to come to rest at W^*W^*. There will be no saving or dissaving after time $t = k$, no further change in the interest rate, and no further change in income. In other words, the short-run income curve will remain at $z'z'$ in Figure 6.10 until time $t = k$ and will then drop abruptly to zz. Income will be constant until time $t = k$ at the level reached on impact and will then fall abruptly to what it was before the tax cut. The economy will run a balance-of-payments deficit of constant size until time $t = k$, because the money-market curve MM in Figure 6.12 will travel steadily along SS with the movement from w to w^*. But there will be no deficit or surplus after time $t = k$ (reserves will be constant and lower than they were to start), because there is no further change in wealth or the interest rate.

If the economy sets out on path 1 or path 3, behavior will be more complicated, as the rates of change of wealth and the interest rate will vary over time. But the ratio $\dot{r}_1/\dot{W}^{hs}$ will tend eventually to $-(S_W/S_1)$, and the economy must therefore converge on a path that is exactly parallel to SS. If the economy starts out on path 1, it must arrive at a point between w' and w^* in Figure 6.12. Thereafter, wealth must fall (households must dissave) and the interest rate must rise, moving the economy to w^*. If the economy starts out on path 3, it must arrive at a point between

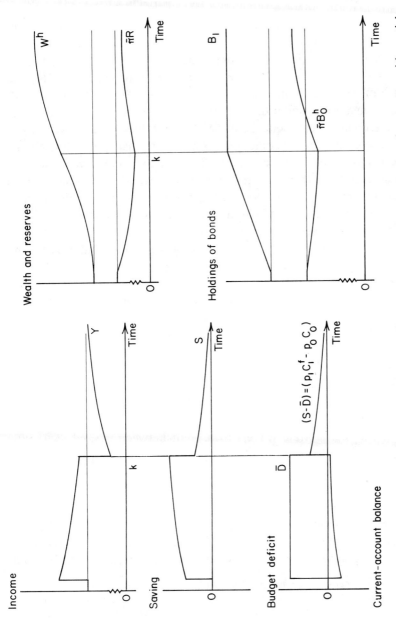

Figure 6.13 Temporary tax reduction and budget deficit: time paths under a pegged exchange rate with partial asset-market integration (illustrative outcomes for path 3).

w^* and w''. Thereafter, wealth must rise (households must save) and the interest rate must fall.[12]

Let us look more closely at events when the economy follows path 1. Saving must begin to fall after the fashion illustrated in Figure 6.11, and the rate of increase of the interest rate must rise. Thus, the ratio $\dot{r}_1/\dot{W}^{hs}$ grows through time, and if the budget deficit lasts long enough, that ratio must eventually equal the slope of SS. When it does so, however, it will be stabilized, as $\dot{W}^{hs}$ will come to be constant, so that $\dot{r}_1$ must come to be constant too. In other words, the short-run income curve will rise from $z'z'$ to a level lower than $z''z''$ in Figure 6.10 (lower than the one to which it tended when $\dot{r}_1$ was zero, and saving had to go to zero). Prior to time $t = k$, then, income, saving, and the current-account deficit will behave in ways resembling those in Figure 6.11. But income will tend to a limit lower than the one shown there, because saving will not fall to zero, and the current-account deficit will not get as large. At time $t = k$, when the government balances its budget, the short-run income curve will fall back by as much as it rose initially but will still be above zz. Income will fall immediately, but not all the way to what it was before the tax cut, and dis-saving will begin. After time $t = k$, then, income will fall further, much as it does in Figure 6.11.

Wealth will rise at a decreasing rate under the influence of the budget deficit and will fall thereafter at a decreasing rate; it will behave much as it does in Figure 6.11 (but will not fall all the way to what it was initially). The path of reserves, however, may differ from the one in Figure 6.11. If asset-market equilibrium travels to a point between w' and w_0 (below MM), reserves will be higher at time $t = k$ than before the tax cut and will have to fall thereafter. The balance of payments will be in surplus until time $t = k$ and in deficit thereafter, much as it was in Figure 6.11. (The integral of deficits, however, will be larger than the integral of surpluses, because w^* in Figure 6.12 lies above the money-market curve MM when crowding out does not dominate.) If instead asset-market equilibrium travels to a point between w_0 and w^* (above MM), reserves will be lower

---

[12] There would appear to be a paradox here. At time $t = 0$, saving is given by a' in Figure 6.10. In the interval $0 < t < k$, saving declines along path 1 and rises along path 3. Yet wealth is larger at all points between w' and w^* in Figure 6.12 than it is between w^* and w''. The resolution of the paradox resides in the fact that the choice between paths 1 and 3 depends in part on the size of B_{11}, and the same term affects the slope of the bond-market curve. The curve W^*W^* that corresponds to path 1 will be flatter than the curve that corresponds to path 3. Therefore, the level of wealth achieved at time $t = k$ will be lower when path 1 is followed than the level achieved when path 3 is followed.

at time $t = k$ and will fall further after the budget is balanced. There will be a balance-of-payments deficit for some or all of the interval $0 < t < k$, as well as after time $t = k$.[13]

If the economy follows path 3 instead of path 1, saving rises in the fashion illustrated by Figure 6.13, and the rate of increase of the interest rate must decline. The ratio $\dot{r}_1/\dot{W}^{hs}$ falls through time, until it is equal to the slope of SS. The short-run income curve will fall back from $z'z'$, and it will fall below zz at time $t = k$. Income will drop below what it was before the tax cut, as shown in Figure 6.13, which says that households go on saving after time $t = k$. Wealth will rise at an increasing rate prior to time $t = k$ and at a decreasing rate thereafter. The path of reserves, moreover, will look like the one in Figure 6.13. The balance of payments will be in deficit before time $t = k$ and in surplus thereafter.[14]

In Chapter 5, we asked how asset-market integration might influence the powers of a temporary tax cut under a pegged exchange rate. We found that it cannot affect the initial change in income (which depends entirely on events in goods markets) and cannot affect outcomes in the steady state (as income must return to its initial level). The results that we have just obtained, however, confirm the conventional conclusion that asset-market integration raises the effectiveness of fiscal policy. It adds to the increase in income within the interval $0 < t < k$.

When asset markets are perfectly integrated, the short-run income curve can rise all the way to $z''z''$ in Figure 6.10, and income can rise to the level denoted by v'', where saving goes to zero. When those markets are not perfectly integrated, the income curve can rise or fall. Even when it rises, however, it cannot go as far as $z''z''$, because saving cannot go to zero. The decline in saving is arrested when $\dot{r}_1/\dot{W}^{hs}$ comes to equal the slope of SS. With imperfect asset-market integration, then, income will be lower everywhere within the interval $0 < t < k$ than it is in Figure 6.11.

[13] As $\dot{F} = \dot{W}^{hs} - \bar{\pi}\dot{R} - \dot{B}_1 = -[(\bar{D} - S) + \bar{\pi}\dot{R}]$, it follows that $\dot{F} < 0$ when $\bar{\pi}\dot{R} > 0$, which will be the case when the economy goes to a point between w' and w_0. Furthermore, $\dot{F} < 0$ when $S < 0$ and $\dot{r}_1 > 0$, as will be the case after time $t = k$. Thus, a movement to a point between w' and w_0 implies a continuing decline in holdings of the foreign bond (a capital inflow). The outcome is similar to the one in Figure 6.11 (but with less of a loss in the end). But a movement to a point between w_0 and w^* or to one between w^* and w'' has uncertain implications for $\dot{F}$ prior to time $t = k$, which means that the final value of $\bar{\pi}B_0^h$ is uncertain too.

[14] The path shown in Figure 6.13 for holdings of foreign bonds is illustrative, not definitive. Holdings have to rise after time $t = k$ (because $S > 0$ and $\dot{r}_1 < 0$), but we cannot know what will happen earlier and cannot be sure that holdings will be higher in the end than they were before the tax cut.

Dynamics under a flexible exchange rate

Under a flexible exchange rate, the impact effects of a tax cut are the same as those in Figure 6.10 and are likewise independent of asset-market integration. But the steady-state effects are very different. Recall the results obtained in Chapter 5. When crowding out does not dominate and asset markets are not perfectly integrated, there will be a permanent increase in income and depreciation of the home currency, but their sizes are inversely related to the degree of substitutability.

Unfortunately, dynamics are not simpler here than in the pegged-rate case. As usual,

$$L_{11}\dot{r}_1 + L_{1W}\dot{W}^h = 0$$
$$B_{11}\dot{r}_1 + B_{1W}\dot{W}^h = \bar{D}$$

so that

$$\dot{r}_1 = (L_{1W}/H_\pi)\bar{D}$$

The domestic interest rate must rise for as long as the government runs a budget deficit, regardless of the state of the current-account balance. Furthermore,

$$\dot{W}^h = \dot{W}^{hs} + V_\pi\left(\frac{\dot{\pi}}{\pi}\right) = -(L_{11}/H_\pi)\bar{D}$$

and this says that

$$\left(\frac{\dot{\pi}}{\pi}\right) = (1/H_\pi V_\pi)[(L_{1W}B_{01} - B_{0W}L_{11})\bar{D} - H_\pi(S - \bar{D})]$$

The effect of a current-account deficit is clearly positive. The effect of a budget deficit per se is ambiguous.[15]

Our problem can be made more manageable, however, by following the strategy adopted in the pegged-rate case. We start with the case in which bonds are perfect substitutes, then turn to the case in which they are partial substitutes.

The limiting case. The immediate effect of a tax cut is, of course, to increase income. In Figure 6.14, the short-run income curve shifts from zz to $z'z'$, just as in the pegged-rate case, and income rises to the level

[15] The numerator of this expression is equal absolutely but opposite in sign to that of the expression for $\dot{\pi}\dot{R}$ in the pegged-rate case. We need not derive a new expression for $\dot{F}$, as it must equal the current-account surplus.

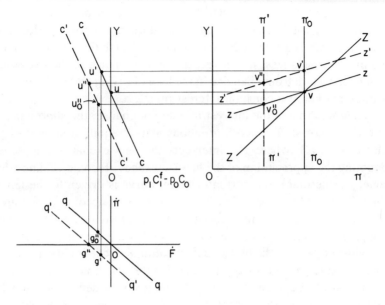

Figure 6.14 Temporary tax reduction and budget deficit: adjustment under a flexible exchange rate with perfect asset-market integration.

denoted by v', because there has been no time for a change in the exchange rate. We know, however, that this increase cannot be permanent – that income must fall back to its initial level because the domestic interest rate cannot change. Our task, then, is to trace the path by which it does so. Does it begin to fall immediately after time $t = 0$, or does it do so only after time $t = k$, when the government balances its budget?

To answer this question, we must first note that the tax cut generates a current-account deficit, for the reason that $\bar{D} > S > 0$. It is shown at u' on curve cc in Figure 6.14. (The curve itself does not shift, because the exchange rate and interest rate have not had time to change.) We must next note that qq shifts to $q'q'$, just like its pegged-rate counterpart in Figure 6.10, so that the exchange rate begins to appreciate at g'.[16] As households start to save, they demand domestic and foreign bonds at the rate $(1 - L_{1W})\dot{W}^{hs}$. But the supply of domestic bonds is rising faster, at the rate $\dot{B}_1$, and there is thus an excess flow supply of bonds amounting to $\dot{B}_1 - (1 - L_{1W})\dot{W}^{hs}$, or $(\bar{D} - S) + L_{1W}S$. Households will attempt to sell foreign bonds. The excess flow supply, moreover, is bigger than the

[16] When $-B_{01} \rightarrow \infty$ so that $B_{11} \rightarrow \infty$, the equation for $(\dot{\pi}/\pi)$ becomes $(\dot{\pi}/\pi) = -(1/V_\pi)[\bar{D} + (S - \bar{D})] = -(1/V_\pi)\dot{W}^{hs}$. The home currency appreciates whenever $S > 0$, and the position of $q'q'$ reflects this fact.

current-account deficit, so that the home currency must start to appreciate, reducing the home-currency value of the households' holdings of the foreign bonds and thus reducing the rate at which they want to sell them. As in other instances, moreover, the rate of change of the exchange rate will keep wealth from changing in the face of saving and will thus clear the money market at a constant interest rate.

When wealth and the interest rate do not change, the short-run income curve will not shift. Therefore, goods-market equilibrium moves gradually toward v'', where $z'z'$ intersects the new exchange-rate schedule, denoting the appreciation of the home currency. Income declines through time. Furthermore, the current-account curve is driven to the left under the influence of the appreciation, and the current-account deficit grows in the direction of u''. By implication, the level of saving declines.[17] Accordingly, the situation in Figure 6.14 resembles the one encountered in the pegged-rate case. If the budget deficit continued indefinitely, the economy would converge on a quasi-stationary state. At some such point as v'', saving would be zero, and the current-account deficit denoted by u'' would be equal to the budget deficit. The exchange rate would cease to appreciate at g'', and income would be stabilized at a level higher than it was before the tax cut but lower than the level at v'.

When the government balances its budget, $z'z'$ shifts back to zz, and income falls at once to the level denoted by v_0''. The economy moves down the current-account curve to u_0'', and g'' gives way to g_0''. Thereafter, the economy travels along zz. Income rises and the home currency depreciates. The current-account curve moves gradually back from $c'c'$ to cc, shrinking the current-account deficit. The economy returns eventually to v, the point at which it started. (The processes just described can be seen from another standpoint. In Figure 5.10A, the movement from initial asset-market equilibrium depended on the movement of the bond-market curve from WW to W^*W^*. When domestic and foreign bonds are perfect substitutes, however, that curve cannot move with an increase in B_1. Hence, wealth is constant at all times, and income must return eventually to its initial level. If wealth is constant, moreover, the home currency must appreciate prior to time $t = k$, when households are saving, and must depreciate thereafter, when households are dissaving. And if income must return to its initial level, the exchange rate must do so too, because the long-run income curve in Figure 6.14 is not shifted by the budget deficit or the elimination of that deficit.)

The time paths of income, the budget deficit, the current-account bal-

<hr>

[17] See note 8, which showed that $\dot{S} = S_Y \dot{Y}^d$ when $\dot{r}_1 = \dot{W}^h = 0$. [For proof that $\dot{W}^h = 0$, see note 16, which showed that $(\dot{\pi}/\pi) = -(1/V_\pi)\dot{W}^{hs}$.]

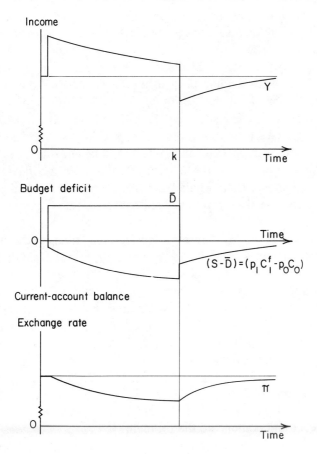

Figure 6.15 Temporary tax reduction and budget deficit: time paths under a flexible exchange rate with perfect asset-market integration.

ance, and the exchange rate are shown in Figure 6.15. During the interval of budget deficits, income declines from the level reached on impact, approaching asymptotically the lower limit corresponding to v'' in Figure 6.14. At time $t = k$, income is cut back abruptly below its initial level, then moves back gradually to that level, under the influence of the improvement in the current-account balance. The current account is in continuous deficit, but that deficit gets bigger until time $t = k$, because the home currency appreciates, and declines thereafter as the currency depreciates.[18] The appreciation takes place at a falling rate before time

[18] By implication, the economy is selling foreign bonds from time $t = 0$ until it returns to the stationary state. It can be shown, moreover, that these sales will sum up to the increase in

$t = k$, as the economy moves in the direction of g'' in Figure 6.14; the subsequent depreciation also takes place at a falling rate, as the economy travels to its steady state.

To sum up, the dynamics of this limiting case resemble in one way the dynamics of the corresponding pegged-rate case, but they differ in another. They are similar in that, prior to time $t = k$, the economy approaches a quasi-stationary state in which the budget deficit would be financed by borrowing from foreigners (the capital inflow would equal $\bar{D}$). In that state, moreover, the exchange rate would be constant, just as reserves would be constant in the pegged-rate case. With a flexible exchange rate, however, income falls back from the level reached on impact, whereas income rises with a pegged exchange rate.

The general case. When bonds are not perfect substitutes and crowding out does not dominate, π and Y will be higher in the steady state than they were before the tax cut. Returning to Figure 6.14, the economy must move eventually to a point on the long-run income curve ZZ that is northeast of v. But we have no way to know whether that point will be higher than v', and we cannot know precisely the time path to that point. Repeating what we have said several times, the impact effect of a tax cut (the location of v') is determined by conditions in goods markets; the steady-state effect of the increase in B_1 left behind the tax cut is determined by conditions in the asset markets. There is no easy way to connect the two effects. During the interval of deficits, moreover, goods and asset markets interact and complicate the problem.

One source of ambiguity is removed by a flexible exchange rate. We know what will happen to wealth and the interest rate during the interval $0 < t < k$. Because $L_{11}\dot{r}_{11} + L_{1W}\dot{W}^h = 0$, we know that $\dot{r}_1/\dot{W}^h = -(L_{1W}/L_{11})$. The economy must travel along MM in Figure 5.10A, because that curve cannot move endogenously when reserves are constant. After the government balances its budget, moreover, the economy remains at w^*. Wealth and the interest rate will be constant after time $t = k$ at higher levels than they were initially.

But the path of the exchange rate is ambiguous, and it affects the path of income. (The cause of ambiguity in the path of the exchange rate is, of course, the same as the cause of ambiguity in the path of reserves when the exchange rate is pegged. But the path of the exchange rate regulates

---

B_1, just as in the corresponding pegged-rate case. When wealth and reserves cannot change, the cumulative change in home-currency holdings of the foreign bond must exactly offset the cumulative increase in supply of the domestic bond.

the path of income, and the path of reserves does not–which again em-
phasizes the fundamental difference between the two exchange-rate
regimes.) In the present instance, moreover, there is no way to classify
the paths of π exhaustively.[19] These are the only simple statements we
can make:

1. If the home currency depreciates continuously before time $t = k$, income will rise. In this case, however, we cannot predict the level of
saving at time $t = k$, which means that we cannot predict the paths of π
and Y after the government balances its budget.

2. If the home currency appreciates continuously before time $t = k$, we
cannot predict the path of income under the influence of the budget deficit. It can rise or fall. In this case, however, we know enough about the
level of saving at time $t = k$ to predict the paths of π and Y after the government balances its budget. The home currency must depreciate and income must rise.[20]

3. At all points in time, before and after time $t = k$, income will be
higher than it was in Figure 6.15, pertaining to the case of perfect
asset-market integration. By implication, asset-market integration reduces the effectiveness of fiscal policy with a flexible exchange rate.

To prove statement 1, suppose that the exchange rate depreciates continuously under the influence of a budget deficit. This will happen if
$[(L_{1W}B_{01} - B_{0W}L_{11})/H_\pi]\bar{D} > (S - \bar{D})$, which says that it is more likely to
happen the lower the degree of asset-market integration.[21] To show that
income rises, we need only rewrite the relevant part of the equation for
the short-run income curve:

$$\dot{Y} = (1/N_s) \left[N_t \left(\frac{\dot{\pi}}{\pi} \right) - N_u(S_1 \dot{r}_1 + S_W \dot{W}^h) \right]$$

But the sign of $S_1 \dot{r}_1 + S_W \dot{W}^h$, or $*\dot{S}|_{\bar{Y}^d}$, is determined unambiguously by
the paths of the interest rate and wealth as the economy moves along the
money-market curve MM:

$$*\dot{S}|_{\bar{Y}^d} = -(1/H_\pi)(S_W L_{11} - L_{1W}S_1)\bar{D}$$

---

[19] The two possibilities listed below are not exhaustive, because the path of π may not be
monotonic when $0 < t < k$. If $\dot{\pi} < 0$, for example, we shall see that $\dot{S} < 0$. As saving
falls, however, $\dot{\pi}$ rises.
[20] If $\dot{\pi} < 0$ before time $t = k$, we can be sure that $\dot{\pi} > 0$ thereafter, without prior knowledge
of the sign of the current-account balance. When the economy reaches the new steady
state, π must be higher than it was before the tax cut.
[21] Differentiating the left-hand side of the inequality with respect to $-B_{01}$,
$(L_{11}/H_\pi)(L_{1W}/H_\pi)\bar{D} < 0$ for $\bar{D} > 0$. Thus, the inequality is the less likely to obtain the
higher the degree of substitutability between the two bonds.

It is negative before time $t = k$ (when $\bar{D} > 0$) and zero afterward (when $\bar{D} = 0$). Accordingly, income rises in the interval $0 < t < k$ when the home currency depreciates.

If income rises, however, the sign of the change in saving is ambiguous:

$$\dot{S} = S_Y \dot{Y}^d + {}^*\dot{S}|_{\bar{Y}^d} = S_Y(N_t/N_s)\left(\frac{\dot{\pi}}{\pi}\right) + (N_w/N_s){}^*\dot{S}|_{\bar{Y}^d}$$

so that $\dot{S} \gtreqless 0$ even when $(\dot{\pi}/\pi) > 0$, because ${}^*\dot{S}|_Y < 0$ when crowding out does not dominate. There are thus two ways in which the economy can move after the government balances its budget. If $\dot{S} > 0$ before time $t = k$, saving will be higher than it was at v' in Figure 6.14, and the elimination of the budget deficit does not reduce it to zero. The current account will be in surplus at time $t = k$, and the home currency will have to appreciate on the way to the steady state. Income falls from what it was at time $t = k$. If, instead, $\dot{S} < 0$ before time $t = k$, saving will be lower than it was at v', and it will give way to dissaving as soon as the budget is balanced. The current account will be in deficit thereafter, and the home currency will depreciate. Income rises from its level at time $t = k$.

To prove statement 2, we use the same equations for $\dot{Y}$ and $\dot{S}$. If the home currency appreciates with a budget deficit, as it did with perfect asset-market integration, income can rise or fall. But $\dot{S}$ will be negative, so that saving will be smaller at time $t = k$ than it was at v' in Figure 6.14. The current account will be in deficit after the government balances its budget, and the home currency will depreciate. Income rises on the way to the steady state. (The paths of the variables will resemble those in Figure 6.15. At time $t = k$, however, Y can be higher than it was before the tax cut, as $\dot{Y} \gtreqless 0$ in the interval $0 < t < k$, whereas π and Y will be higher in the new steady state than they were before the tax cut.)

To prove statement 3, that asset-market integration reduces the effectiveness of fiscal policy, it will suffice to prove that during the interval $0 < t < k$ the rate of change of income, $\dot{Y}$, varies inversely with the degree of substitutability between the two bonds. The path of income in the general case must then lie above the path in Figure 6.15. Income will be the same at time $t = 0$. It will be higher, however, when $0 < t < k$ and will be higher immediately after the budget is balanced, because the discontinuous decrease in income at time $t = k$ reverses the discontinuous increase at time $t = 0$. Therefore, income will be higher at all times, because we have already shown that it will be higher in the new steady state than it was initially unless the two bonds are perfect substitutes. The proof that $\dot{Y}$

varies inversely with substitutability is simple enough. Combining the equations for $(\dot{\pi}/\pi)$, $*\dot{S}|_{\bar{Y}^d}$ and Y,

$$\dot{Y} = (N_t/N_s)[(1/H_\pi V_\pi)(L_{1w}B_{01} - B_{0w}L_{11})\bar{D}$$
$$+ (N_u/N_t H_\pi)(S_w L_{11} - L_{1w}S_1)\bar{D} - (1/V_\pi)(S - \bar{D})]$$

Differentiating with respect to $-B_{01}$,[22]

$$(\delta\dot{Y}/\delta B_{11}) = -(L_{1w}/H_\pi)(N_t/N_S H_\pi)[(N_u/N_t)(S_w L_{11} - L_{1w}S_1)$$
$$- (L_{11}/V_\pi)]\bar{D}$$

which is unambiguously negative, so that $\dot{Y}$ does indeed vary inversely with the degree of substitutability when the government is running a deficit.

Asset-market integration, the exchange-rate regime, and the effectiveness of domestic policies

To pull together this analysis, we summarize the influence of asset-market integration, measured by its influence on the income changes resulting from an open-market purchase and from a cut in lump-sum taxes leading to an increase in government indebtedness.

Under a pegged exchange rate, both policies are powerless to raise income permanently. The steady-state level of income cannot differ from the initial level. But asset-market integration limits the reduction in the interest rate brought on by an open-market purchase, limiting the impact effect on income, and perfect asset-market integration prevents any increase in income whatsoever. Turning to the consequences of a tax cut, asset-market integration has no bearing on the size of the short-run change in income, because the tax cut starts as a goods-market disturbance. This finding is unconventional. Thereafter, however, asset-market integration makes for a smaller increase in the interest rate resulting from the issue of new government bonds and thus amplifies the increase in income that takes place while the government is running a deficit. In this sense, our model reaffirms results reported by Mundell and others – that asset-market integration (capital mobility) reduces the effectiveness of monetary policy but raises the effectiveness of fiscal policy. The effects

---

[22] Saving is held constant here because it is determined by the state of the economy at a point in time (by the levels of Y, π, and other variables), and we are concerned with the rate of change of income at that point in time (with the behavior of $\dot{Y}$, given Y).

are transitory with a pegged exchange rate, but they have the same signs that others have obtained.[23]

Under a flexible exchange rate, both policies have permanent effects on income. Furthermore, asset-market integration raises the effectiveness of monetary policy in the short run and the long run. The greater the degree of substitutability between the domestic and foreign bond, the larger the demand for the foreign bond and the larger the depreciation of the home currency. Thus, asset-market integration stimulates domestic and foreign demands for domestic output and amplifies the increase in income. Turning once again to the effects of a tax cut, asset-market integration does not affect the short-run increase in income but does affect the subsequent path of income. It enlarges the capital inflow, the appreciation of the home currency, and the current-account deficit, causing income to decline more rapidly through time. As a matter of fact, perfect integration precludes any permanent increase in income. Under a flexible exchange rate, then, asset-market integration enhances the effectiveness of monetary policy and reduces the effectiveness of fiscal policy, which again reaffirms the results obtained by others.

[23] See, e.g., R. A. Mundell, *International Economics,* Macmillan, New York, 1968, chaps. 17–18, and J. M. Fleming, *Essays in International Economics,* Harvard University Press, Cambridge, Mass., 1971, chap. 9. One must emphasize again, however, that many of the statements in this and the next paragraph hold only when crowding out does not dominate.

PART III

Extending the model

7

Claims, caveats, and simplifications

In Chapters 1 and 2 we made a number of claims for our model. We pointed out, however, that some of our assumptions restrict the generality of the strong conclusions drawn in subsequent chapters. As the same assumptions will be used to build the two-country model in Part IV, we pause here to examine some of them more closely.

In this chapter we review the principal claims made for the model and assess the extent to which our conclusions depend on restrictive assumptions. In addition, we make way for the relaxation of certain assumptions, one at a time, in the next three chapters. In Chapter 8 we relax the assumption that the demand for money does not depend on income. In Chapter 9 we relax the assumption that expectations are stationary. Finally, in Chapter 10 we relax the assumption that the government's receipts derive entirely from a lump-sum tax (and the assumption that transfers to foreigners offset the interest income earned on foreign bonds).

Claims

Six features of our model command attention at this point. We restate them briefly:

First, the demands for goods and bonds were written to allow for several types of substitution. There was substitution between traded goods, between each traded good and the nontraded good, and between traded and nontraded bonds. Furthermore, the supply side was constructed to encompass competing assumptions about the supply of labor—the "classical" assumption that the wage rate is flexible and the "Keynesian" assumption that the wage rate is rigid. Accordingly, we could examine many special cases without making ad hoc modifications or solving the model anew for each special case. In addition, we could study asset-market integration (capital mobility) as a matter of degree, by varying the degree of substitutability between the domestic and foreign bonds.

Second, we invoked the small-country assumption to simplify the

197

model but did so asymmetrically. The economy was deemed to be small in those foreign markets where it is a buyer, but not in markets where it is a seller. Used this way, the small-country assumption does not rule out endogenous changes in prices of domestic goods or assets. It serves merely to rule out foreign repercussions – changes in prices of foreign goods and assets and in the level of foreign expenditure resulting from events within the small economy.

Third, we used a simple relationship between wealth and saving to drive the economy through time, in order to facilitate dynamic analysis. At the same time, the time paths of prices, interest rates, asset holdings, and other variables are not chosen arbitrarily. They are determined endogenously within the model, by parameters of the wealth-saving relationship and of the domestic market-clearing equations. Furthermore, the stock-flow relationship governing dynamics in the model is more general than those in many other models. In a number of those models, for example, money is the only asset or the only one denominated in home currency, and time paths are determined by the stock-flow relationship between real balances and hoarding. In our model, by contrast, money, domestic bonds, and foreign bonds figure in wealth holdings, and we take account of changes in supplies of all three assets.

Fourth, the foreign bond is denominated in foreign currency. Therefore, exchange-rate changes affect household wealth directly by causing capital gains or losses on the foreign bond. As a result, they affect saving (absorption) directly, not merely by affecting trade flows and income. Capital flows are affected too, because the gain or loss on holdings of foreign bonds is larger than the corresponding change in the demand for them – the change due to the wealth effect of the gain or loss.

Fifth, our approach to stocks and flows has allowed us to define three sets of responses to disturbances and policies. Impact effects are those that occur before flows have had time to influence the corresponding stocks. Steady-state effects are those that occur when flows go to zero and the corresponding stocks come to be constant. Dynamic effects are those that take place as stocks change in response to flows and flows are affected by the changes in the stocks. We do not draw conclusions from one set of effects alone, as has been done too often recently, and we can be precise about certain propositions. Thus, "insulation" is depicted as a process that takes place through time. It does not occur completely within finite time, because full insulation is a steady-state phenomenon. Similarly, we have formulated carefully the statements we have made about the theory of policy. We have not said that monetary policy is ineffective with a pegged exchange rate. We have said instead that its influence wears off with time and that the speed at which it does so depends on the degree of asset-market integration.

Sixth, we have been able to partition our model so as to achieve three objectives. We can solve the model and its two-country counterpart in manageable blocks. We can classify disturbances according to the type of market in which they first appear. We can give rigorous representation to the "new view" of exchange-rate determination. On this view, asset markets dominate the behavior of a flexible exchange rate, because they adjust more rapidly than goods markets. In our model, of course, markets clear continuously, and there are no differences between short-run and long-run price responses (elasticities) in any market. There can thus be no differences between the speeds at which asset and goods markets adjust to disturbances. We are able nonetheless to take an asset-market view because of the *way* in which asset and goods markets are made to adjust.

By partitioning the model, we can treat the exchange rate as an asset-market variable. It is determined at all times by the requirements of equilibrium in the money and bond markets. In other words, we block the routes by which events in goods markets would otherwise impinge on the asset markets. Those events do affect income and saving, which means that they affect demands for assets by affecting wealth. But our stock-flow relationships defer these effects. Impact or short-run effects of disturbances are defined as those that take place before any flow has time to affect the corresponding stock. Therefore, asset-market variables, including the exchange rate, do not respond promptly to goods-market disturbances. Finally, portfolio optimization takes place instantaneously. Desired holdings of money and bonds are translated at once into stock demands, and the market-clearing equations for money and bonds are written in terms of those stock demands, not in terms of flow demands. In brief, our model guarantees that the exchange rate reacts promptly to events in asset markets but reacts only slowly to events in goods markets.

Caveats

Two groups of caveats go together with our claims. First, we must warn against errors in interpretation that may be made when trying to draw conclusions from our model. Second, we must warn against omissions and assumptions that help to make the model manageable but qualify severely some of our results.

Problems in interpretation

Although the distinction we have drawn between impact and steady-state effects is vital for clarity, it is also artificial and can cause one to make statements about short runs and long runs that may be misleading. As we have defined the short run, it may be too short to encompass some of the events described as impact or short-run effects. If saving cannot add to wealth and a budget deficit cannot add to the supply of bonds in what we call the short run, can one hope to witness the large changes in income, the interest rate, exchange rate, or stock of reserves generated by certain disturbances? The instantaneous changes in income, for example, reflect the full effects of the Keynesian multiplier for a small economy. (The term N_Y is the sum of the marginal propensities to save and to import, and it appears in M_s, which figures in the short-run solutions for income in Chapter 3.)

At the opposite extreme, the long run may be too long to be interesting for policy purposes. The steady-state or long-run effects examined in Part II are the changes in endogenous variables to which the actual changes tend asymptotically. Furthermore, the time paths in Chapter 6 are those that one would see if the economy could move to its steady state under the influence of one well-defined disturbance – if no new disturbance deflected it from its path. But we do not enjoy the luxury of watching an economy evolve in this fashion. Disturbances occur continuously. They do not queue up, like aircraft in a holding pattern, waiting for the ones that went before to get out of the way. In brief, statements made about steady-state effects are useful analytically, but we would not give them much weight if we were called upon to offer policy advice.

A second problem in interpretation arises in connection with comparisons between pegged and flexible exchange rates. Having worked through every exercise in Part II under both regimes, we have been able to describe many of their properties. We have seen, for example, that a flexible exchange rate affords partial "insulation" against shifts in demand between export and import goods, changes in foreign prices, and changes in the level of foreign expenditure but not against a change in the foreign interest rate (or other asset-market disturbances coming from abroad). We have seen that the effects of monetary and some fiscal policies wear off eventually with a pegged exchange rate and have shown how asset-market integration influences the effects of those policies. But our findings do not furnish an adequate basis for choosing between exchange-rate regimes. Many other issues must be considered.

At no point in our work, for example, is labor allowed to migrate from one country to another. Yet one of Mundell's major contributions was to show that labor movements can sometimes substitute for exchange-rate movements.[1] We have not allowed for the effects of exchange-rate variability on the demand for money, and these may be decisive for the feasibility of a flexible exchange rate.[2] Most important, the way in which our model is constructed – with stationary expectations, the continuous clearing of all markets, and a well-defined stationary state – precludes consideration of inflation as a process. Prices do move up or down in response to disturbances, but these are once-for-all price changes, even though they are drawn out through time. Therefore, we must set aside many questions raised about exchange-rate flexibility. Do floating rates worsen the trade-off between inflation and unemployment? Do prices and wages respond symmetrically to depreciations and appreciations, or are there "ratchet effects" in price and wage determination that make for asymmetrical responses and, on average, for a faster rate of inflation? Does the character of the exchange-rate regime influence attitudes of governments, firms, and trade unions in ways that affect the rate of inflation?[3]

In our view, moreover, it would not be enough to answer these questions in order to choose wisely between exchange-rate systems. Two additional issues must be faced.

The choice between pegged and flexible exchange rates is not to be made unilaterally. The exchange rate is the price of one country's currency in terms of another, and decisions about the exchange-rate regime should be made collectively, because of their bilateral and systemic implications, not by a single country acting on the basis of narrow national advantages or disadvantages – the degree of insulation or policy autonomy conferred by flexibility.[4] The systemic issue cannot be neglected even

---

[1] R. A. Mundell, "A Theory of Optimum Currency Areas," *American Economic Review*, 51 (December 1961), pp. 657–65.

[2] This is the issue emphasized in R. I. McKinnon, "Optimum Currency Areas: Comment," *American Economic Review*, 53 (September 1963), 44. 717–25.

[3] On these questions, see, e.g., E. M. Claassen, "World Inflation Under Flexible Exchange Rates," and W. M. Corden, "Inflation and the Exchange Rate Regime," *Scandinavian Journal of Economics*, 78, 1976(2), pp. 346–65, 370–83, A. D. Crockett and M. Goldstein, "Inflation Under Fixed and Flexible Exchange Rates," *International Monetary Fund Staff Papers*, 23 (November 1976), pp. 509–44, R. Dornbusch and P. Krugman, "Flexible Exchange Rates in the Short Run," *Brookings Papers on Economic Activity*, 1976(3), pp. 537–75, and M. Goldstein, "Downward Price Inflexibility, Ratchet Effects, and the Inflationary Impact of Import Price Changes: Some Empirical Tests," *International Monetary Fund Staff Papers*, 24 (November 1977), pp. 569–612.

[4] This is, of course, the ultimate reason for having an International Monetary Fund and asking it to exercise "surveillance" over the exchange-rate policies of its members. Elsewhere, however, one of us has complained that Article IV, which gives the Fund this task,

when one of the countries involved is small in some markets. The economy considered in Part II is small in markets for the foreign good and foreign bond but not in its export market. Disturbances affecting its exchange rate, then, may not be unimportant to the outside world.

Finally, the choice between exchange-rate regimes is a problem in political economy and never as simple as the one confronting the small country modeled in Part II. As a practical matter, countries do not choose between a rate pegged immutably and one that floats freely. Countries with pegged rates alter them from time to time. Countries with floating rates intervene to influence the paths or levels of the rates. The problem is to choose a point on the continuum between the two extremes examined in this book. In a world of many countries, moreover, no currency can be pegged to all other currencies if any other exchange rate is floating.

The fundamental issue can be put in different terms. If countries are not willing to behave in ways that would allow them to peg their rates immutably, they must decide on the best way to adjust them. The choice between exchange-rate regimes is in part a choice of means, and it must turn on economic and political judgments additional to those we have already mentioned. What sort of uncertainty about exchange rates is least likely to complicate decisions by private actors, especially investment decisions? Is it easier to plan for the next year or two facing the small probability of a large change in a pegged rate or the large probability of small changes in a floating rate? Which method of changing exchange rates is least likely to consume political capital, at home and in relations among governments? Which method is more likely to prevent exchange-rate policy from rising to the realm of high politics, where it gets in the way of decisions about other issues—economic, diplomatic, and strategic? No model can answer these questions, not even the two-country model in Part IV, which takes account of foreign repercussions and policy interdependence.

The third problem in interpretation has also to do with foreign repercus-

---

obscures brilliantly the fundamental interdependence of exchange-rate regimes. Each member has the right to choose among "(i) the maintenance by a member of a value for its currency in terms of the special drawing right or another denominator, other than gold, selected by the member, or (ii) cooperative arrangements by which members maintain the value of their currencies in relation to the value of the currency or currencies of other members, or (iii) other exchange arrangements of a member's choice." Nowhere is it acknowledged explicitly that each country's choice limits the choices available to others. See P. B. Kenen, "Techniques to Control International Reserves," in R. A. Mundell and J. J. Polak, eds., *The New International Monetary System: Proceedings of the Conference in Memory of J. Marcus Fleming,* Columbia University Press, New York, 1977, pp. 202–22.

sions. The country analyzed in earlier chapters is small in that it has no influence on prices of foreign goods or foreign assets or on the level of foreign expenditure. One must bear this fact in mind when drawing conclusions about the effects of its domestic policies. Taking the example used before, the effects of monetary and some fiscal policies were shown to wear off completely with a pegged exchange rate. This would not be true, however, if the country were not small. If the outflows of reserves that take place in response to an open-market purchase were allowed to influence the money stock in the outside world, there could be a permanent increase in domestic income. The money stock would rise abroad, raising foreign prices and expenditure and reducing the foreign interest rate. These developments would feed back to the domestic economy. Looking at one more example, sales of the foreign bond that take place in response to a budget deficit have not been allowed to influence the foreign interest rate. If they did so, as they will in the two-country model, we would have to take account of "crowding out" in the outside world. Under a flexible exchange rate, moreover, the effects of domestic disturbances might impinge pervasively on prices and expenditure in the outside world, for the reason that insulation does not take place promptly.

To sum up, the conclusions drawn heretofore must be taken either as exact assertions about an economy too small to be very interesting or as approximations valid for larger, more interesting economies. They neglect the influence that medium-sized countries are likely to have on some, if not all, of their neighbors and the repercussions on the country itself.

Omissions and restrictions

These are the important omissions and assumptions that limit the validity of our findings:

1. We have omitted stocks of capital from the production functions, capital formation (investment) from the list of processes that take place on the way to the new steady state, and claims to stocks of capital (equities) from the list of assets included in household wealth.

2. Households do not hold foreign money and do not incur foreign-currency debt, and foreigners do not hold domestic assets.

3. All markets clear continuously, all actors carry out their plans, and portfolios are optimized immediately, not gradually through time.

4. Income does not influence the demand for money. That demand depends only on interest rates and wealth.

5. Expectations are stationary. No one knows the future with perfect certainty, but no one anticipates any change in prices of goods or assets.

6. The government makes lump-sum transfers to foreigners that offset exactly interest earned from foreigners. In the same vein, it imposes lump-sum taxes that regulate exactly the budget deficit and, therefore, the flow supply of bonds.

These six sets of suppositions contribute importantly to mathematical manageability. Some serve to limit the number of equations that must be solved simultaneously. Some serve to limit the number of relationships that must be analyzed when proving stability and studying dynamics.

Consider, for example, the effects of omitting capital goods, capital formation, and equities. If capital goods appeared explicitly in the production functions and were susceptible of reallocation between sectors, it would be harder to subsume "classical" and "Keynesian" labor markets in a single set of goods-market equations. If capital formation took place in the economy, we would have to include stock-flow relationships connecting investment in each sector with the stock of capital in that sector, and we would have to take account of those relationships when dealing with stability and dynamics. Finally, the inclusion of marketable equities would complicate the model in several ways. We would have to add the market for equities and, therefore, another market-clearing equation. We would be unable to partition the model, because changes in goods prices would alter wealth. In the Keynesian case, for instance, an increase in the prices of domestic goods would raise outputs, employment, and nonlabor incomes.[5] There would then be an increase in household wealth (a capital gain on equities) that would stimulate absorption, together with changes in demands for equities, bonds, and money that would affect the interest rate and exchange rate.

The exclusion of foreign-currency debt may be the most serious omission listed at (2), relating to restrictions on holdings of assets. It is unrealistic, because foreign-currency borrowing takes place on a large scale, and is restrictive analytically, because some of our conclusions would be altered if there were such borrowing. Suppose that households were allowed to borrow from foreigners and did so to acquire domestic assets. They could become net debtors in foreign currency, and a depreciation of the home currency would reduce their wealth. Algebraically, V_π would be negative, and a number of conclusions would be affected. An open-market purchase of domestic bonds would cause the home currency to appreciate, and the signs of changes in domestic prices would be ambigu-

[5] See note 12 to Chapter 2.

ous. Most important, the flexible-rate version of the model would be unstable; the argument of Eq. (3.12a) would be positive if V_π were negative. To include foreign-currency borrowing, then, we would have to modify our model in two ways. First, we would have to include a market-clearing equation to determine the relevant interest rate. (It may not be silly to suppose that households can buy foreign bonds at a constant interest rate. It would be silly to suppose that they can issue foreign-currency debt at a constant interest rate.) Second, we would have to change other parts of the model to guarantee against instability, with extensive implications for the workings of the model.[6]

The other omissions listed at (2), relating to holdings of foreign assets, are not too restrictive. We could abandon some of them without affecting partitionability, stability, or our major findings. Households could be allowed to hold foreign currency and foreigners to hold domestic currency. Foreigners could also be allowed to hold the domestic bond (provided their demand was not perfectly elastic). If we were to make these changes, the economy might become a net debtor to the outside world, but it would not become a net debtor in foreign currency. Its liabilities would be in its home currency. The capital-gains term V_π would continue to be positive. There would be additional opportunities for substitution between assets, and additional arguments would appear in the equations for the two domestic assets. Furthermore, there could be shifts between foreign and domestic assets under a flexible exchange rate. But there could be no shift in net claims on the outside world.

By relaxing assumptions listed at (3) and (5), to allow for disequilibria and for expectations of price changes, we would enrich our model in many ways. We could represent explicitly the supposition that asset

---

[6] In Chapter 8, where income is included in the demand function for money, the flexible-rate version need not be unstable when $V_\pi < 0$ (because the determinant, U, does not have to turn negative). It would thus appear that partitionability is the source of instability when $V_\pi < 0$ (when households have foreign-currency debts larger than their foreign-currency claims). When the exchange rate is determined in asset markets and demands for assets do not depend on income, the sign of V_π decides the sign of the change in π; see Eq. (3.3a). When demands for assets do depend on income, the sign of V_π is not decisive; see Eq. (8.9a). To study the effects of foreign-currency indebtedness, we could modify our model along the lines proposed in Chapter 8. The model in that chapter is, in fact, similar to the one employed by Boyer in his recent papers dealing with the currency composition of net wealth, its implications for the effects of a devaluation, and its bearing on the functioning of financial policies under a flexible exchange rate; see R. S. Boyer, "Devaluation and Portfolio Balance," *American Economic Review,* 67 (March 1977), pp. 54–63, and "Financial Policies in an Open Economy," *Economica,* 45 (February 1978), pp. 39–57. The inclusion of stabilizing exchange-rate expectations, as in Chapter 9, can also guarantee stability when $V_\pi < 0$, and partitionability need not be a source of instability.

markets clear faster than goods markets. We could introduce inflation as a process, by making room on the supply side for a short-run Phillips curve, relating the rate of change of wages to unemployment and to expectations of price and exchange-rate changes. To do any of these things, however, would make for many complications. With disequilibria in the labor market, it would be more difficult to draw a clear distinction between the classical and Keynesian cases, at least in the short run. Furthermore, dynamics would have to take account of relationships between expected and actual changes in prices. (We shall, in fact, face this problem in Chapter 9, where we introduce nonstationary expectations, but we shall deal with the problem by adopting strong assumptions regarding the formation of expectations.)

The other assumption listed at (3), that portfolios are optimized continuously, contributes importantly to manageability. Without it, we would have to examine many stock-flow relationships.[7] But this is not the only reason for adopting the approach we took in Part II. It may be the most realistic representation of behavior in national and international markets for government securities and similar financial instruments. The relevant markets are quite large in relation to individual transactions; the typical bond holder does not have to negotiate purchases and sales, being able to obtain firm price quotations from dealers or brokers. Furthermore, the markets are readily accessible, even to bond holders distant geographically from the large financial centers. Finally, securities can be transferred without being shipped from place to place; frequently, indeed, they do not leave the vaults of banks and other institutions that are their

---

[7] The demands for assets would be flow demands, and the corresponding market-clearing equations would have to be written in flows. The demand for money would have to be written as $\dot{L}_1^h = \lambda(*L_1^h - L_1^h)$, and the corresponding market-clearing equation would have to be written as $\dot{L}_1^h - \dot{L}_1 = 0$. The flow supply of money, $\dot{L}_1$, would be the total time derivatives of Eqs. (2.33) and (2.34): $\dot{L}_1 = \dot{B}_1^c + \bar{\pi}\dot{R}$, which implies a respecification of monetary policy. An open-market purchase, $\dot{B}_1^c$, would take place through time, and it would be regulated, much as $\bar{D}$ is regulated, to obtain the requisite cumulative change in the stock B_1^c. This flow formulation has important implications for the time path of the balance of payments. An excess flow demand for money would be mirrored by an excess flow supply of foreign currency, which would show up as an inflow of reserves under a pegged exchange rate: $\dot{L}_1^h - \dot{B}_1^c = \bar{\pi}\dot{R}$. The stock of reserves could not change instantaneously. It is more difficult, however, to prove stability with flow demands for assets, for one must prove that each flow goes to zero. A flow formulation is employed in P. B. Kenen, *Capital Mobility and Financial Integration: A Survey,* Princeton Studies in International Finance 39, Princeton University, Princeton, N.J., 1976. Stock and flow formulations are compared in P. R. Allen and P. B. Kenen, "Portfolio Adjustment in Open Economies: A Comparison of Alternative Specifications," *Weltwirtschaftliches archiv,* 112, 1976 (1), pp. 34–71, where we show that they differ importantly in their short-run implications with a pegged exchange rate. (In both papers, however, the demand for money depends on income, and this is the main cause of the difference in behavior.)

custodians. In brief, transactions costs – the costs of communication, brokerage, and shipment – are relatively small for bonds and similar securities, compared to transactions costs for goods, and it is sensible to assume that wealth holders can alter their portfolios promptly, shifting abruptly from bond to bond or from bonds to money, rather than executing a large number of transactions spread out through time.[8]

The assumption listed at (4), that the demand for money does not depend on income, is needed for partitionability, which is much more than a mathematical convenience. It is used to represent the asset-market view of exchange-rate determination. If the demand for money depended on income, disturbances affecting nominal income would affect demands for money and for bonds and would thus affect at once the interest rate and exchange rate. In terms of the diagrams used in Part II, disturbances affecting income would alter the positions of *MM* and *WW*.

But there are other reasons for adopting our approach, having to do with the theory of money.

Four facts of economic life can be adduced as reasons for holding money, rather than investing all of one's wealth in income-producing assets. First, receipts and payments are not perfectly synchronized. Cash balances are built up when receipts outrun payments; otherwise, they are run down. Imperfect synchronization results from indivisibilities in economic life and from institutional arrangements. We would expect to find it even in a world of perfect certainty, where variations in receipts and payments could be predicted accurately.[9] Second, some receipts and payments are unpredictable. There can be unanticipated fluctuations in incomes and expenditures. There can be unanticipated opportunities to acquire earning assets. Third, transactions costs attach to purchases and sales of earning assets, whether these are made to cover gaps between receipts and payments or to exploit unforeseen investment opportunities. Fourth, the prices of earning assets fluctuate, and these price fluctuations may combine with fluctuations in receipts and payments to generate capital losses when earning assets must be sold to cover shortfalls.

The first two of these four facts are necessary to the existence of a

[8] Instantaneous optimization can be defended in another way. If some investors were restricted to gradual adjustment, as by high transactions costs, others could capture windfall profits. Gradual adjustment, then, is inconsistent with the view that asset markets are efficient in the finance-theory sense, and instantaneous optimization is an analytical approximation to that view.

[9] This point is not always recognized, perhaps because transactions-demand theory uses the variance of net receipts to stand for imperfect synchronization, and the notion of variance is evocative of uncertainty. The point, however, is not new; see W. J. Baumol, "The Transactions Demand for Cash: An Inventory Theoretic Approach," *Quarterly Journal of Economics*, 65 (November 1952), pp. 545–56.

transactions demand for money, but they are not sufficient. If there were no transactions costs and earning assets were not subject to price fluctuations, spending units would not build up cash balances when net receipts were positive. They would invest surplus receipts in income-producing assets and would liquidate the assets when and to the full extent that net receipts were negative. This is indeed what happens when wealth holders can convert surplus cash into earning assets such as saving deposits – assets that can be acquired cheaply and conveniently and can then be converted into cash without cost or loss. The transactions-cum-precautionary demand for money can be explained only by the fact of fluctuations in receipts or payments *and* the existence of nontrivial transactions costs or risks associated with day-to-day investments of surplus receipts.

There is, of course, another motive for holding money that is unrelated to variability in net receipts, to transactions costs, or to the possibility of capital losses attending asset sales. When asset prices are susceptible of permanent change, there is an investment motive for holding money. To hold some part of wealth as money is to reduce the risk that the total return on wealth will be negative because prices of earning assets fall *forever* below those at which one bought them. It is to reduce for all time the variance of the return on wealth, not merely to reduce the likelihood of capital losses that may be incurred when earning assets must be converted into cash. In Tobin's words:[10]

In contrast to transactions balances, the investment balances of an economic unit are those that will survive all the expected seasonal excesses of cumulative expenditures over cumulative receipts during the year ahead. They are balances which will not have to be turned into cash within the year. Consequently, the cost of financial transactions . . . does not operate to encourage the holding of investment balances in cash. If cash is to have any part in the composition of investment balances, it must be because of expectations or fears of loss on other assets.

In our own model, of course, there is little risk of loss on the domestic bond, because both bonds are bills and the domestic bond is issued by the government. The price of the domestic bond is fixed in home currency, and the likelihood of default is minimal. We work with bills for reasons of convenience, however, and our model would not function differently if both bills were long-term bonds. In principle, then, households may be deemed to have an investment motive for holding money – the need to hedge against a permanent loss on the domestic bond.

---

[10] J. Tobin, "Liquidity Preference as Behavior Towards Risk," in D. D. Hester and J. Tobin, eds., *Risk Aversion and Portfolio Choice*, Wiley, New York, 1967, p. 3. The same basic point was made by Keynes, albeit in somewhat different terms; see J. M. Keynes, *The General Theory of Employment, Interest and Money*, Harcourt, Brace, New York, 1936, pp. 201–02.

Demand functions for money usually include variables standing for each of the facts and motives we have just enumerated. Income is a proxy for the variability of net receipts, certain and uncertain. It represents the transactions-cum-precautionary motive for holding money.[11] The interest rate is a proxy for the cost of holding money. It represents the price that wealth holders must pay to guard against the likelihood of capital losses resulting from reductions in asset prices, permanent or temporary. Wealth is a proxy for the size of the portfolio that has to be protected by diversification against the possibility of capital losses. It represents the pure investment motive emphasized by Tobin.

Empirical work on the demand for money has tended to concentrate on income and the interest rate. There is little evidence for including wealth, and the evidence for what we do – using wealth instead of income – is even weaker.[12] It must be borne in mind, however, that the numbers used to stand for wealth are less than satisfactory and that income tends to be collinear with wealth and may therefore preempt its influence. Friedman makes a similar point. When studying behavior by "ultimate" wealth holders, for whom money *is* a form of wealth, rather than by businesses, for which it is a producer's good, the statistical influence of income should be regarded as standing for the influence of wealth. This, he says, is why permanent income should be used in place of measured income, and he goes on to say that: "The emphasis on income as a surrogate for wealth, rather than as a measure of the work to be done by money, is conceptually perhaps the basic difference between more recent work and the earlier versions of the quantity theory."[13] To which we need merely add that

[11] In one strand of analysis developed by Friedman and others, income stands for something more. Drawing an analogy between the service flows supplied by a stock of cash and the flows supplied by stocks of consumer durables, the demand for the services of cash is deemed to depend on income and price, just like the demand for other services. See, e.g., M. Friedman, "The Quantity Theory of Money – A Restatement," in M. Friedman, ed., *Studies in the Quantity Theory of Money*, University of Chicago Press, Chicago, 1956. This view has invited syntheses of Friedman's work on the demand for money and on the permanent-income analysis of consumption. See, e.g., R. E. Peterson, "The Permanent-Income Hypothesis of the Demand for Money," *Review of Economics and Statistics*, 54 (November 1972), pp. 364–73. In recent work we cite later, however, Friedman puts less emphasis on the services of money and more emphasis on money as a form of wealth.

[12] Working with annual data through the late 1950s, Meltzer found that wealth dominated income, but permanent income dominated wealth; see A. H. Meltzer, "The Demand for Money: The Evidence from the Time Series," *Journal of Political Economy*, 71 (June 1963), pp. 219–46. Working with more recent quarterly data, Goldfeld found that income dominates wealth; see S. M. Goldfeld, "The Demand for Money Revisited," *Brookings Papers on Economic Activity*, 1973(3), pp. 577–638.

[13] M. Friedman, "A Theoretical Framework for Monetary Analysis," *Journal of Political Economy*, 78 (March/April 1970), p. 203. Friedman's distinction between classes of hold-

ours is a model in which "ultimate" wealth holders are the only money holders, and that wealth can stand for itself–it needs no surrogate–in work at an abstract level.

Bear another point in mind. There are no transactions costs in our model, and it deals in continuous time, not discrete-time periods. Therefore, all transactions are fully synchronized. There can be unforeseen fluctuations in receipts and payments, but no gaps between them, and households have no reason to hold transactions balances. Commenting on a similar model, Hellwig has written that:[14]

> The discreteness of transactions, which is the essense of the theory of the transactions demand for cash, plays no role in this model. Therefore, there is no presumption in this type of model that the demand for money is increasing with income, if indeed it is possible to justify the existence of a demand for money at all.

Hellwig goes on to show that it is anomalous to put income into the demand function for money in continuous-time models with instantaneous optimization. An increase of income that raises the demand for money reduces the demand for bonds, so that bonds appear to be income-inferior assets.[15]

We hesitate to press this point too far, however, for it can be turned against us. In Hellwig's view, the logical inconsistency inherent in using continuous time, instantaneous optimization, and an income term in the demand function for money should be resolved by retaining the income term and shifting from continuous to period analysis.[16] To do so here, however, would be very difficult.

The assumption listed at (5), about expectations, was exploited heavily in Chapter 2. The model presented there can be consistent and complete only if households and other actors hold strong views about the future. Anticipated rates of change of goods and asset prices must always be zero, but those anticipations cannot be held with certainty.

How would we have to change the model if anticipated rates of change were not zero? First, desired saving would have to depend on real rates of interest, not on r_0 and r_1, as in Eq. (2.13). Second, demands for assets would have to depend on exchange-rate expectations; in Eqs. (2.30)

ers suggests that econometric work on money should disaggregate by holder. This was done by Goldfeld in the paper just cited, but not when comparing the influence of wealth against that of income.

[14] M. Hellwig, "The Demand for Money and Bonds in Continuous-Time Models," *Journal of Economic Theory,* 11 (December 1975), p. 463.

[15] See also Allen and Kenen, "Portfolio Adjustment," and Chapter 8.

[16] Hellwig, "The Demand for Money and Bonds." For a discrete-time analysis of portfolio adjustment, see W. H. Buiter, "Financial Stocks and Flows in the Determination of Short-Run and Long-Run Equilibrium in an Open Economy" (unpublished, 1976).

through (2.32), r_0 would have to be replaced with an interest rate adjusted for the expected rate of change of the exchange rate, so as to allow for anticipations of capital gains or losses on the foreign bond. Finally, a thorough treatment of the problem would require that we alter the demands for goods, Eqs. (2.15) through (2.17), to allow for expectations about changes in goods prices. This cannot be done, however, without also amending the households' balance sheet, Eq. (2.10), to include inventories of the three commodities (or futures contracts in commodities). It is virtually impossible to speculate in goods without adding to one's assets, liabilities, or both.[17]

Taking the opposite tack, let us ask what would happen to the model if stationary expectations were held with certainty. Households would not hold any money and would invest exclusively in one of the two bonds –the one with the higher interest rate. Equations (2.30) through (2.32), defining the demands for money and bonds, are meant to reflect risk-averse behavior. Wealth holders diversify because they are uncertain about the future. They act to reduce the variability of their wealth by accepting a reduction in expected income. If they acted with certainty about the future or disregarded risk, they would not hold foreign and domestic bonds together. In our model, moreover, they would hold no money. We have already seen that uncertainty about bond prices is the only motive for holding money when receipts and payments are fully synchronized.[18]

[17] If inventories were included in wealth, we could not partition our model; the prices of goods would influence wealth and, therefore, the demands for assets. If futures contracts were included, the same problem would arise to the extent that futures prices depended on current prices. In Chapter 9, which deals with nonstationary expectations, we neglect effects on the demands for goods; there are no inventories and no futures markets.

[18] When transactions costs are zero, households have no reason to hold foreign money (and foreigners no reason to hold domestic money). By holding the foreign-currency bond, households can diversify against exchange-rate fluctuations. When expectations are not stationary, moreover, speculation in the foreign bond will dominate speculation in foreign currency. As will be seen in Chapter 9, the expected rate of return on the foreign bond, inclusive of anticipated gains from a depreciation of the home currency, must always exceed the expected rate of return on the foreign currency. The bond bears interest. We do not neglect the possibility of "currency substitution," but handle it by speculation in the foreign bond. There is, of course, one important difference between the effects of speculation in our model and in models that contain home and foreign currencies but no bonds. When households forecast a depreciation of the home currency, they will sell domestic bonds and domestic currency to acquire foreign bonds. The resulting rise in the domestic interest rate will then tend to curb their appetite for foreign bonds. For models that analyze speculation in terms of "currency substitution," see L. Girton and D. Roper, "Some Implications of Currency Substitution for Monetary Control," Board of Governors of the Federal Reserve System, 1976 (mimeograph), and G. Calvo and C. A. Rodriguez, "A Model of Exchange Rate Determination Under Currency Substitution and Rational Expectations," *Journal of Political Economy*, 85 (June 1977), pp. 617–25.

The assumptions listed at (6), about taxes and transfers, are far from realistic and limit the applicability of many results, not only those for fiscal policy itself. But they are vital for our effort to classify disturbances and also for proving dynamic stability. If the government relied on an income tax, instead of a lump-sum tax, it could not balance its budget continuously, and the supply of the domestic bond would become endogenous. Any disturbance affecting income would affect the government's tax revenues and would therefore affect the budget deficit. All of the disturbances examined heretofore would be compound disturbances, as that term was employed in Chapter 5. The bond-market curve WW would move downward with an increase in income, because tax revenues would rise, reducing the supply of bonds. It would move upward with a decrease in income. Under a pegged exchange rate, it would be harder to predict the path of reserves – to locate curve MM at each point in time. Under a flexible exchange rate, the interest rate and wealth would change through time in response to most disturbances, and it would be harder to predict the path of the exchange rate.

Turning to the problem of stability, two complications would arise. Interest payments by the government, $r_1 B_1^h$, would not drop out of the definition of disposable income and would thus affect the level of saving. It would be more difficult to prove that saving goes to zero with the passage of time. More important, this would not be sufficient for stability when government borrowing is endogenous. We would have to prove that the budget deficit goes to zero too – that the supply of bonds comes to be constant. The budget equation would be an endogenous stock-flow relationship. The stock of bonds, B_1, taken together with the interest rate, r_1, would affect the flow supply of bonds, $\dot{B}_1$, and we would have to analyze this stock-flow relationship jointly with the one between the integral of saving, W^{hs}, and the flow of saving, $\dot{W}^{hs}$. To make matters worse, the flow $\dot{B}_1$ would depend positively on $r_1 B_1^h$ in the budget equation, whereas the flow $\dot{W}^{hs}$ depends negatively on W^{hs} in the saving equation. This positive relationship can jeopardize stability, as we shall see in Chapter 10.

Were we to delete transfers to foreigners, we would confront another problem. The number of endogenous dynamic relationships would not be altered (because capital flows must always be zero when saving is zero). But interest earned from foreigners, $\bar{r}_0(\pi B_0^h)$, would appear in two equations from which they are removed by transfers – in the definition of disposable income and in the definition of the current-account balance. The proof of stability would be complicated too, because of effects on saving, and some long-run results would also be affected. We would find, for example, that a flexible exchange rate could not always furnish insulation against an external goods-market disturbance, even in the long run, because the requirements of long-run equilibrium would be altered. Disposable income would have to return eventually to what it was initially, but total nominal income would not. In the absence of transfers (but with lump-sum taxes), the steady-state level of disposable income is defined by

$$Y^d = Y + \bar{r}_0(\pi B_0^h) - \bar{G}_N - \bar{G}_1$$

When Y^d returns to its initial level but the interest-income term is altered, Y cannot return to its initial level. Looking at the problem from another standpoint, the current-account balance must return to zero in the long run, but the trade balance need not do so. In the absence of transfers to foreigners, the current-account balance is zero when

$$(p_1 C_1^f - p_0 C_0) + \bar{r}_0(\pi B_0^h) = 0$$

The trade balance is not zero when $\bar{r}_0(\pi B_0^h)$ is not zero, and it will not return to what it was initially if the interest-income term is affected permanently.

Simplifications

When we build our two-country model, in Chapter 11, we shall require the assumptions listed at (1) through (6). Before doing so, however, we digress to study the effects of relaxing the assumptions listed at (4), (5), and (6), concerning the demand for money, expectations, taxes, and transfers, using a simplified version of the model studied in Part II. It is one in which there are no nontraded goods, "crowding out" does not dominate ($S_W L_{11} > L_{1W} S_1$), and there is "proportionality" in interest-rate responses ($S_1 L_{10} = S_0 L_{11}$, so that $H_0 > 0$).

Using the notation of Chapter 2, the simplified model can be summarized as follows:[19]

$$(7.1) \quad \left[p_1 C_1^f \left(\frac{p_1}{\pi}, \bar{p}_0^f, \bar{C}^f \right) - \pi \bar{p}_0^f C_0(p_1, \pi \bar{p}_0^f, Y^d - {}^*S) + \bar{r}_0(\pi B_0^h) + T^f \right]$$
$$+ D - {}^*S = 0$$

$$(7.2) \quad B_1(\bar{r}_0, r_1, W^h) - (B_1 - \bar{B}_1^c) = 0$$

---

[19] The simplified model is, in effect, the single-good variant discussed in Chapter 4. The solutions can be obtained directly from those shown in Chapter 3, using two conventions: (1) Let $u_{1N} \to \infty$. (2) Let $u'_{1N} = u_{0N} = \sigma_N = m_N = g_N = 0$. Note that Eq. (7.1) is a transforma-

(7.3) $L_1(\bar{r}_0, r_1, W^h) - (\bar{B}_1^c + \pi R - W^c) = 0$

where

(7.4) $Y^d = Y + \bar{r}_0(\pi B_0^h) + r_1(B_1 - \bar{B}_1^c) - T^h$

(7.5) $Y = p_1 Q_1(E)$

(7.6) $w = p_1 Q_{1E}(E)$

(7.7) $E = \bar{E}$ or $w = \bar{w}$

(7.8) $^*S = S(\bar{r}_0, r_1, Y^d, W^h)$

and where

(7.9) $W^h = \pi R + B_1 + \pi B_0^h - W^c$

(7.10) $W^h = L_1(\bar{r}_0, r_1, W^h) + B_1(\bar{r}_0, r_1, W^h) + B_0(\bar{r}_0, r_1, W^h)$

(7.11) $W^h = \int_0^T S\, dt + \int_0^T \pi B_0^h \left(\dfrac{\dot{\pi}}{\pi}\right) dt = W^{hs} + \int_0^T V_\pi\left(\dfrac{\dot{\pi}}{\pi}\right) dt$

(7.12) $^*S = S$

(7.13) $W^c = \int_0^T \pi R \left(\dfrac{\dot{\pi}}{\pi}\right) dt$

(7.14) $B_1 = \int_0^T D\, dt$

(7.15) $D = \bar{G}_1 + r_1(B_1 - \bar{B}_1^c) - T^h - T^f$

Assumptions (6) assert that

(7.16) $D = \bar{D}$

tion of the market-clearing equation for the export good (which is the one domestic good in this instance). From Eq. (2.27a),

$$C_1(p_1, \pi\bar{p}_0^f, Y^d - S) + C_1^f\left(\frac{p_1}{\pi}, \bar{p}_0^f, \bar{C}^f\right) + (\bar{G}_1/p_1) - Q_1(E) = 0$$

without a nontraded good. Multiplying through by p_1 and replacing $p_1 C_1(\ldots)$ by $Y^d - S - \pi p^f C_0(\ldots)$,

$$p_1 C_1^f(\ldots) - \pi\bar{p}_0^f C_0(\ldots) + Y^d - S + \bar{G}_1 - p_1 Q_1(E) = 0$$

Invoking Eqs. (7.4), (7.5), (7.15), (7.16), and (7.17),

$$Y^d + \bar{G}_1 - p_1 Q_1(E) = Y + \bar{r}_0(\pi B_0^h) + r_1(B_1 - \bar{B}_1^c) - T^h + \bar{G}_1 - p_1 Q_1(E)$$
$$= \bar{r}_0(\pi B_0^h) + T^f + D = \bar{D}$$

which gives us Eq. (7.1).

(7.17) $T^f = -\bar{r}_0(\pi B_0^h)$

The choice of exchange-rate regime is defined by

(7.18) $\pi = \bar{\pi}$ or $R = \bar{R}$

The solutions to the model are summarized below and in Tables 7.1 and 7.2.

Impact effects

As Eqs. (7.2) and (7.3) are identical to their counterparts in Chapter 2, the solutions are identical to those in Chapter 3; see Eqs. (3.1a) through (3.3a) for a flexible exchange rate, and Eqs. (3.1b) through (3.3b) for a pegged exchange rate. The goods-market results are different, however, as the system of Eqs. (3.4) reduces to a single equation:

$$
(7.19)\quad (u_t + \sigma_1 N_Y)\left(\frac{\delta p_1}{p_1}\right) - (u_\pi - m_1 S_W V_\pi)\left(\frac{\delta \pi}{\pi}\right)
$$
$$
+ m_1(S_0\,\delta\bar{r}_0 + S_1\,\delta r_1 + S_W\,\delta W^{hs})
$$
$$
- m_1(1 - S_Y)\,\delta\bar{D} - (N_Y)\,\delta\bar{G}_1 - \left[(\delta c_1^f - \delta c_{01}) + u_t\left(\frac{\delta\bar{p}_0^f}{\bar{p}_0^f}\right)\right] = 0
$$

The effects of a shift in demand to the export good ($\delta c_1^f > 0$ or $\delta c_{01} < 0$) are u_t *times* those of an increase in $\bar{p}_0^f$, and the latter are not shown separately below. Furthermore,

$$
(7.20)\quad \delta Y = \sigma_1\left(\frac{\delta p_1}{p_1}\right),\quad \left(\frac{\delta w}{w}\right) = \left(\frac{\delta p_1}{p_1}\right),\quad \text{and}\quad \delta E = [a_1(p_1/w)Q_1]\left(\frac{\delta p_1}{p_1}\right)
$$

so that we can infer the signs of the changes in nominal income and in the wage rate or employment from the signs of the changes in p_1. When income is insulated from a disturbance, the labor market is insulated too, and there is no need to list the changes in p_1, w, or E.[20]

Combining Eqs. (7.19) and (7.20), we obtain the effects of goods-market disturbances:

$$
(7.21)\quad \delta Y = [\sigma_1/(u_t + \sigma_1 N_Y)][m_1(1 - S_Y)\,\delta\bar{D}
$$
$$
+ (N_Y)\,\delta\bar{G}_1 + (\delta c_1^f - \delta c_{01})]
$$

[20] The solutions for $(\delta w/w)$ and δE are obtainable directly from Appendix A. Note in passing that $u_\pi = u_t + p_1 C_1^f$ (because $u_{1N}^f = u_{0N} = 0$). Written in another way, however, it has the same meaning as in Chapter 3. Because $u_t = u_{10} + u_{01}^f = (u_{00} - p_0 C_0) + (u_{11}^f - p_1 C_1^f)$, $u_\pi = u_{00} + u_{11}^f - p_0 C_0$, which is the Marshall-Lerner-Robinson condition.

Table 7.1. *Impact effects in the simplified model*

Disturbance	Effects under flexible rate					Effects under pegged rate					
	$\delta\pi$	δr_1	δY	δY^a	δW^h	$\bar{\pi}\,\delta R$	δr_1	δY	δY^a	δW^h	$\bar{\pi}\,\delta B_0^h$
$\delta\bar{r}_0$	+	?	+	+	+	−	+	−	−	0	+
$\delta\bar{\pi}$	xx	xx	xx	xx	xx	+	−	+	+	+	−
$\delta\bar{B}_1^c$	+	−	+	+	+	−	−	+	+	0	+
$\delta\bar{D}$	0	0	+	+	0	0	0	+	+	0	0
$\delta\bar{G}_1$	0	0	+	−	0	0	0	+	−	0	0
$\delta c_1^f - \delta c_{01}$	0	0	+	+	0	0	0	+	+	0	0
δW^{hs}	−	0	−	−	xx	+	−	+	+	xx	xx
δB_1	+	+	+	+	xx	−	+	−	−	xx	xx

Signs are based on the assumptions that (1) $S_w L_{11} > L_{1w} S_1$, and (2) $S_1 L_{10} = S_0 L_{11}$. Signs of the effects on p_1, w, and E are identical to those for the effects on Y.

Table 7.2. *Steady-state effects in the simplified model*

Disturbance	Effects under flexible rate						Effects under pegged rate					
	$d\pi$	dr_1	dY	dY^a	dW^h	$\pi\,dB_0^h$	$\bar{\pi}\,dR$	dr_1	dY	dY^a	dW^h	$\bar{\pi}\,dB_0^h$
$d\bar{r}_0$	+	?	+	+	+	?	−	?	0	0	+	+
$d\bar{\pi}$	xx	xx	xx	xx	xx	xx	+	−	+	+	+	?
$d\bar{B}_1^c$	+	−	+	+	+	?	−	−	0	0	−	?
$d\bar{B}_1$	+	+	+	+	+	?	−	+	0	0	+	?
$d\bar{G}_1$	+	0	+	0	0	−	−	+	+	−	−	−
$dc_1^f - dc_{01}$	−	0	0	0	0	+	+	−	+	+	+	+

See note to Table 7.1.

Combining Eqs. (7.19) and (7.20) with Eqs. (3.2a) and (3.3a), we obtain the effects of asset-market disturbances with a flexible exchange rate:

$$(7.22a) \quad \delta Y = [\sigma_1/(u_t + \sigma_1 N_Y) H_\pi V_\pi] \{ [m_1 V_\pi (H_0)$$

$$+ u_\pi (B_{10} L_{11} - B_{11} L_{10})] \delta \bar{r}_0$$

$$+ [m_1 V_\pi S_1 (L_{1W} + B_{1W}) - B_{01} (u_\pi - m_1 S_W V_\pi)] \delta \bar{B}_1^c$$

$$+ [m_1 V_\pi (S_W L_{11} - L_{1W} S_1) - u_\pi L_{11}] \delta B_1 - [u_\pi H_\pi] \delta W^{hs} \}$$

Combining Eqs. (7.19) and (7.20) with Eq. (3.2b), we obtain the effects of those same disturbances with a pegged exchange rate:

$$(7.22b) \quad \delta Y = [\sigma_1/(u_t + \sigma_1 N_Y)] \left\{ (m_1/B_{11})[(S_1 B_{10} - S_0 B_{11}) \delta \bar{r}_0 + (S_1) \delta \bar{B}_1^c \right.$$

$$- (S_1) \delta B_1 + (S_1 B_{1W} - S_W B_{11}) \delta W^{hs}]$$

$$\left. + [u_\pi + m_1 (V_\pi / B_{11})(S_1 B_{1W} - S_W B_{11})] \left(\frac{\delta \bar{\pi}}{\pi} \right) \right\}$$

As usual, Y and Y^d move together unless there are changes in $\bar{D}$ and $\bar{G}_1$. In those cases,

$$(7.23) \quad \delta Y^d = [1/(u_t + \sigma_1 N_Y)][(u_t + \sigma_1) \delta \bar{D} - (u_t) \delta \bar{G}_1]$$

Finally, Eqs. (3.10) and (3.11) apply without modification and give the changes in W^h and B_0^h shown in Table 7.1.

Stability and dynamics

There is no major change in the proof of stability. It is again sufficient to demonstrate that $[\delta \dot{W}^{hs}/\delta W^{hs}] < 0$, and this is even easier than in Chapter 3. The counterpart of Eq. (3.12a), for the flexible-rate case, is

$$(7.24a) \quad \frac{\delta \dot{W}^{hs}}{\delta W^{hs}} = -(S_Y/V_\pi)[\sigma_1 u_\pi/(u_t + \sigma_1 N_Y)] < 0$$

The counterpart of Eq. (3.12b), for the pegged-rate case, is

$$(7.24b) \quad \frac{\delta \dot{W}^{hs}}{\delta W^{hs}} = -H_f[(u_t + m_0 \sigma_1)/(u_t + \sigma_1 N_Y) B_{11}] < 0$$

The paths of the balance of payments, $\bar{\pi} \dot{R}$, and of the capital outflow, $\dot{F}$, are given by Eqs. (3.17b) and (3.18b), as before.

Steady-state effects

Under a flexible exchange rate, the steady-state levels of r_1, W^h, and Y^d are determined by Eqs. (7.2), (7.3), and (7.8), given the requirement that saving is zero, and these equations do not differ from the ones in Chapter 3. Accordingly, the signs of the changes in those variables come directly from Eqs. (3.19a), (3.20a), and (3.21a). (The differences between the signs in Table 7.2 and those in Table 3.3A are due to the assumptions adopted here that $S_W L_{11} > L_{1W} S_1$ and that $S_1 L_{10} = S_0 L_{11}$.) In the steady state, moreover, $S = D = 0$, and our assumptions about taxes and transfers combine to say that

(7.25) $dY = dY^d + d\bar{G}_1$

which can be combined with Eq. (7.1) to solve for the steady-state change in the exchange rate:

(7.26a) $\left(\dfrac{d\pi}{\pi}\right) = (1/\sigma_1 u_\pi)[(u_t)\,d\bar{G}_1 - \sigma_1(dc_1^f - dc_{01}) + (u_t + m_0\sigma_1)\,dY^d]$

Under a pegged exchange rate, the steady-state levels of r_1, W^h, and $\bar{\pi}R$ are determined by Eqs. (7.2), (7.3), and (7.8). Accordingly, the signs of the changes in those variables come directly from Eqs. (3.19b), (3.20b), and (3.24b). Equations (7.25) and (7.1) are used to obtain the steady-state change in disposable income:

(7.27b) $dY^d = [1/(u_t + m_0\sigma_1)][(\sigma_1 u_\pi)\left(\dfrac{d\bar{\pi}}{\pi}\right) - (u_t)\,d\bar{G}_1$
$+ \sigma_1(dc_1^f - dc_{01})]$

from which it follows that an increase in government spending raises nominal income.[21] The steady-state changes in holdings of the foreign bond are obtained, as usual, from Eq. (3.25).

In Chapters 8, 9, and 10, we make successive modifications in this model. The principal effects of the modifications can be ascertained by comparing the results obtained in those chapters with those shown by Tables 7.1 and 7.2.

[21] From Eqs. (7.25) and (7.27b), $dY = [m_0\sigma_1/(u_t + m_0\sigma_1)]\,d\bar{G}$.

8

On money, income, and insulation

How would our model behave if the demand for money were made to depend on income, in addition to depending on interest rates and wealth? Although we have argued that this specification is inconsistent logically with other features of our model, especially its setting in continuous time, the question is worth answering. Many other models dealing with our subject – the functioning of pegged and flexible exchange rates and implications of asset-market integration – adopt this specification. It is thus useful to compromise with logical consistency in order to achieve comparability. More generally, we need to know how heavily our own results depend on the specification adopted in Part II and employed again in Parts IV and V.

When income affects the demand for money, asset markets cannot be partitioned from goods markets. It is still possible, of course, to classify disturbances according to the markets in which they originate. It is no longer possible, however, to claim that the exchange rate is determined in the short run by money and bond markets. The demands for assets respond immediately to any disturbance or policy change affecting the level of income. Does this mean, in turn, that a flexible exchange rate can confer continuous insulation? Does it mean that we must modify our conclusions about monetary and fiscal policies? Will it still be true, for example, that the impact effect of a tax cut is unaffected by the exchange-rate regime or by the degree of asset-market integration?

In the first section of this chapter, we show how our model must be modified when the demand for money depends on income and how the solutions differ from those summarized at the end of Chapter 7. In subsequent sections we examine the implications for insulation, for the functioning of monetary and fiscal policies, and for the influence of asset-market integration.

An amended specification

Before we can reply to the questions posed above, there is another to be answered. What measure of income should be used to stand for the transactions demand for cash? Should we use nominal gross domestic product, personal income, or disposable income? A strong case can be made for personal income in the context of this model, because households are the only money holders. Furthermore, it is the most inclusive measure; it is the sum of gross domestic product, Y, and of the interest incomes $\bar{r}_0(\pi B_0^h)$ and $r_1 B_1^h$. For this same reason, however, it is the most cumbersome. We have therefore elected to employ the second-largest measure, nominal gross domestic product,[1] and thus to write the demand for money as

(8.1) $*L_1^h = L_1(\bar{r}_0, r_1, Y, W^h)$

where $L_{10} < 0$, $L_{11} < 0$, and $L_{1W} > 0$, as before, whereas $L_{1Y} > 0$.

Because the demands for money and bonds are constrained by wealth, income will affect demands for bonds, and its effects on the demands for bonds and money must sum to zero:

$$L_{1Y} = -(B_{0Y} + B_{1Y}) > 0$$

where B_{0Y} pertains to the demand for the foreign bond, and B_{1Y} pertains to the demand for the domestic bond. Bonds are "income inferior" assets in that the demands for them, taken together, vary inversely with income. When income rises, households must sell bonds to acquire additional cash. In what follows, however, we go one step further. *Each* bond is assumed to be "income inferior" ($B_{0Y} < 0$ *and* $B_{1Y} < 0$). The reason will be clear presently.

The amended model we must now solve is similar to the one in Chapter 7 but can be written more compactly, using Eqs. (7.15) through (7.17) to dispose of several terms. The market-clearing equation for the export good is

(8.2) $\left[p_1 C_1^f \left(\dfrac{p_1}{\pi}, \bar{p}_0^f, \bar{C}^f \right) - \pi \bar{p}_0^f C_0(p_1, \pi \bar{p}_0^f, Y^d - S) \right] + \bar{D} - S = 0$

The market-clearing equations for domestic bonds and money are

(8.3) $B_1(\bar{r}_0, r_1, Y, W^h) - (B_1 - \bar{B}_1^c) = 0$

(8.4) $L_1(\bar{r}_0, r_1, Y, W^h) - (\bar{B}_1^c + \pi R - W^c) = 0$

[1] In Eq. (8.5), disposable income is shown to be $Y + \bar{D} - \bar{G}_1$, because of our assumptions about fiscal policy. Thus, $Y > Y^d$ unless $\bar{D} > \bar{G}_1$ (in which case the lump-sum tax, T^h, would be too small to cover the government's interest payments plus transfers to foreigners).

The definition of disposable income becomes

(8.5) $Y^d = Y + \bar{D} - \bar{G}_1$

and the model is completed by Eqs. (7.5) through (7.14), defining Y, E, w, S, W^h, W^{hs}, W^c, B_0^h, and B_1, and by Eq. (7.18), defining the exchange-rate regime.

Solving for impact effects

The flexible-rate case. Under a flexible exchange rate, the model generates this system:[2]

$$(8.6a) \quad \begin{bmatrix} -(u_t + \sigma_1 N_Y) & -m_1 S_1 & (u_\pi - m_1 S_W V_\pi) \\ -\sigma_1 B_{1Y} & -B_{11} & -B_{1W} V_\pi \\ -\sigma_1 L_{1Y} & -L_{11} & -L_{1W} V_\pi \end{bmatrix} \begin{bmatrix} \left(\dfrac{\delta p_1}{p_1}\right) \\ \delta r_1 \\ \left(\dfrac{\delta \pi}{\pi}\right) \end{bmatrix}$$

$$= \begin{bmatrix} -N_Y & -(1 - N_Y) & -1 \\ 0 & 0 & 0 \\ 0 & 0 & 0 \end{bmatrix} \begin{bmatrix} \delta \bar{G}_1 \\ \delta \bar{D} \\ (\delta c_1^f - \delta c_{01}) \end{bmatrix}$$

$$+ \begin{bmatrix} m_1 S_0 & 0 & 0 & m_1 S_W \\ B_{10} & 1 & -1 & B_{1W} \\ L_{10} & -1 & 0 & L_{1W} \end{bmatrix} \begin{bmatrix} \delta \bar{r}_0 \\ \delta \bar{B}_1^c \\ \delta B_1 \\ \delta W^{hs} \end{bmatrix}$$

It is not hard to classify disturbances according to the markets in which they originate. A balanced-budget increase in $\bar{G}_1$, for instance, shows up in the market for the export good but not in the asset markets. Yet it is not very useful to classify disturbances in this version of the model, because the system (8.6a) cannot be partitioned. The consequences of a goods-market disturbance are not confined to the good market, even on impact, because it affects r_1 and π, in addition to affecting p_1.

The determinant of the system (8.6a) is denoted by $-U$, where

$$U = V_\pi[(u_t + \sigma_1 N_Y)H_\pi + \sigma_1(m_1 S_1)H_W] + \sigma_1(u_\pi - m_1 S_W V_\pi)H_Y$$

As before, $H_\pi = (L_{1W}B_{11} - L_{11}B_{1W}) > 0$, whereas $H_W = (B_{1W}L_{1Y} - B_{1Y}L_{1W}) > 0$ because $B_{1Y} < 0$, and $H_Y = (B_{11}L_{1Y} - B_{1Y}L_{11}) = (B_{0Y}L_{11} - B_{01}L_{1Y}) > 0$ because $B_{0Y} < 0$. When each of the two bonds is "income inferior," we can be sure that $U > 0$.

[2] We omit the change in $\bar{p}_0^f$, having shown in Chapter 7 that the signs of its effects are the same as those of a change in foreign demand.

Solving for the effects of disturbances and policies on p_1, r_1, and π, and remembering that $\delta Y = \sigma_1(\delta p_1/p_1)$, we have

(8.7a) $\quad \delta Y = (\sigma_1/U)\{(H_\pi V_\pi)[(N_Y)\,\delta\bar{G}_1 + (1 - N_Y)\,\delta\bar{D} + (\delta c_1^f - \delta c_{01})]$
$+ [u_\pi(L_{11}B_{10} - L_{10}B_{11}) + m_1 V_\pi(H_0)]\,\delta\bar{r}_0$
$+ [m_1 S_1 V_\pi(L_{1W} + B_{1W}) - B_{01}(u_\pi - m_1 S_W V_\pi)]\,\delta\bar{B}_1^c$
$+ [m_1 V_\pi(S_W L_{11} - L_{1W}S_1) - u_\pi L_{11}]\,\delta B_1 - (u_\pi H_\pi)\,\delta W^{hs}\}$

(8.8a) $\quad \delta r_1 = (1/U)\{\sigma_1(H_W V_\pi)[(N_Y)\,\delta\bar{G}_1 + (1 - N_Y)\,\delta\bar{D} + (\delta c_1^f - \delta c_{01})]$
$+ [(u_t + \sigma_1 N_Y)V_\pi(B_{1W}L_{10} - B_{10}L_{1W}) - \sigma_1(m_1 S_0 V_\pi)H_W$
$+ \sigma_1(u_\pi - m_1 S_W V_\pi)(B_{1Y}L_{10} - B_{10}L_{1Y})]\,\delta\bar{r}_0$
$- [V_\pi(u_t + \sigma_1 N_Y)(L_{1W} + B_{1W})$
$\quad - \sigma_1(u_\pi - m_1 S_W V_\pi)B_{0Y}]\,\delta\bar{B}_1^c$
$+ [V_\pi(u_t + \sigma_1 N_Y)L_{1W} + \sigma_1(U_\pi - m_1 S_W V_\pi)L_{1Y}]\,\delta B_1$
$- \sigma_1(u_\pi H_W)\,\delta W^{hs}\}$

and

(8.9a) $\quad \left(\dfrac{\delta\pi}{\pi}\right) = (1/U)\{-\sigma_1(H_Y)[(N_Y)\,\delta\bar{G}_1 + (1 - N_Y)\,\delta\bar{D}$
$+ (\delta c_1^f - \delta c_{01})]$
$+ [(u_t + \sigma_1 N_Y)(B_{10}L_{11} - L_{10}B_{11}) + \sigma_1(m_1 S_0)H_Y$
$+ \sigma_1(m_1 S_1)(B_{1Y}L_{10} - B_{10}L_{1Y})]\,\delta\bar{r}_0$
$+ [\sigma_1(m_1 S_1)B_{0Y} - B_{01}(u_t + \sigma_1 N_Y)]\,\delta\bar{B}_1^c$
$+ [\sigma_1(m_1 S_1)L_{1Y} - (u_t + \sigma_1 N_Y)L_{11}]\,\delta B_1$
$- [(u_t + \sigma_1 N_Y)H_\pi + \sigma_1(m_1 S_1)H_W - \sigma_1(m_1 S_W)H_Y]\,\delta W^{hs}\}$

The signs of these results, together with those pertaining to Y^d and W^h, are listed in Table 8.1.[3] Like the signs in Table 7.1, with which we compare them later, they depend in part on the assumptions made throughout Part III (that $S_W L_{11} > L_{1W}S_1$ and $S_0 L_{11} = S_1 L_{10}$) and on the assumption made above that households sell both bonds to augment their cash balances (that $B_{0Y} < 0$, and $B_{1Y} < 0$).

The pegged-rate case. As usual, the pegged-rate case is easier to solve. Writing out the system as a whole,

(8.6b) $\quad \begin{bmatrix} -(u_t + \sigma_1 N_Y) & -m_1 S_1 & 0 \\ -\sigma_1 B_{1Y} & -B_{11} & 0 \\ -\sigma_1 L_{1Y} & -L_{11} & 1 \end{bmatrix} \begin{pmatrix} \dfrac{\delta p_1}{p_1} \\ \delta r_1 \\ \bar{\pi}\,\delta R \end{pmatrix}$

---

[3] Changes in Y^d are obtained directly from Eq. (8.5). Changes in W^h derive from Eq. (7.11), which says that $\delta W^h = \delta W^{hs} + V_\pi(\delta\pi/\pi)$. Because $\delta W^{hs} = 0$, the change in W^h takes the sign of the change in π.

Table 8.1. *Impact effects in the amended model*

Disturbance	Effects under flexible rate					Effects under pegged rate					
	$\delta\pi$	δr_1	δY	δY^a	δW^h	$\bar{\pi}\,\delta R$	δr_1	δY	δY^a	δW^h	$\bar{\pi}\,\delta B_0^h$
$\delta \bar{r}_0$	+	?	+	+	+	−	?	−	−	0	+
$\delta \bar{\pi}$	xx	xx	xx	xx	xx	+	?	+	+	+	−
$\delta \bar{B}_1^c$	?	−	+	+	?	?	−	+	+	0	?
$\delta \bar{D}$	−	+	+	−	−	+	+	+	−	0	−
$\delta \bar{G}_1$	−	+	+	+	−	+	+	+	+	0	−
$\delta c_1^f - \delta c_{01}$	−	+	+	+	−	+	?	+	+	0	−
δW^{hs}	−	−	−	−	xx	+	?	+	+	xx	xx
δB_1	+	+	+	+	xx	−	+	−	−	xx	xx

Signs are based on the assumptions that (1) $S_w L_{11} > L_{1w} S_1$, (2) $S_1 L_{10} = S_0 L_{11}$, and (3) $B_{0Y} < 0$ and $B_{1Y} < 0$. Signs of the effects on p_1, w, and E are identical to those for the effects on Y.

$$= \begin{bmatrix} -(u_\pi - m_1 S_W V_\pi) \\ B_{1W} V_\pi \\ L_{1W} V_\pi \end{bmatrix} \left(\frac{\delta \bar{\pi}}{\bar{\pi}} \right)$$

$$+ \begin{bmatrix} -N_Y & -(1 - N_Y) & -1 \\ 0 & 0 & 0 \\ 0 & 0 & 0 \end{bmatrix} \begin{bmatrix} \delta \bar{G}_1 \\ \delta \bar{D} \\ (\delta c_1^f - \delta c_{01}) \end{bmatrix}$$

$$+ \begin{bmatrix} m_1 S_0 & 0 & 0 & 0 & m_1 S_W \\ B_{10} & 1 & -1 & -1 & B_{1W} \\ L_{10} & -1 & 0 & 0 & L_{1W} \end{bmatrix} \begin{bmatrix} \delta \bar{r}_0 \\ \delta \bar{B}_1^c \\ \delta B_1 \\ \delta W^{hs} \end{bmatrix}$$

Thus p_1 and r_1 are determined jointly, and the solution for reserves can be obtained separately, given the solutions for p_1 and r_1.

The determinant of the system (8.6b) is

$$U_f = (u_t + \sigma_1 N_Y) B_{11} - \sigma_1 (m_1 S_1) B_{1Y} > 0$$

because $B_{1Y} < 0$. The short-run solutions are

(8.7b)
$$\delta Y = (\sigma_1 / U_f) \{ [(u_\pi - m_1 S_W V_\pi) B_{11} + (m_1 S_1 V_\pi) B_{1W}] \left(\frac{\delta \bar{\pi}}{\bar{\pi}} \right)$$
$$+ B_{11} [(N_Y) \delta \bar{G}_1 + (1 - N_Y) \delta \bar{D} + (\delta c_1^f - \delta c_{01})]$$
$$- m_1 (S_0 B_{11} - B_{10} S_1) \delta \bar{r}_0 + (m_1 S_1)(\delta \bar{B}_1^c - \delta B_1)$$
$$+ m_1 (B_{1W} S_1 - S_W B_{11}) \delta W^{hs} \}$$

(8.8b)
$$\delta r_1 = (1 / U_f) \{ - [V_\pi (u_t + \sigma_1 N_Y) B_{1W}$$
$$+ \sigma_1 (u_\pi - m_1 S_W V_\pi) B_{1Y}] \left(\frac{\delta \bar{\pi}}{\bar{\pi}} \right)$$
$$- \sigma_1 B_{1Y} [(N_Y) \delta \bar{G}_1 + (1 - N_Y) \delta \bar{D} + (\delta c_1^f - \delta c_{01})]$$
$$+ [\sigma_1 (m_1 S_0) B_{1Y} - B_{10} (u_t + \sigma_1 N_Y)] \delta \bar{r}_0$$
$$- (u_t + \sigma_1 N_Y)(\delta \bar{B}_1^c - \delta B_1)$$
$$- [(u_t + \sigma_1 N_Y) B_{1W} - \sigma_1 (m_1 S_W) B_{1Y}] \delta W^{hs} \}$$

together with

(8.9b)
$$\bar{\pi} \delta R = (1 / U_f) \{ (U) \left(\frac{\delta \bar{\pi}}{\bar{\pi}} \right) + \sigma_1 (H_Y) [(N_Y) \delta \bar{G}_1 + (1 - N_Y) \delta \bar{D}$$
$$+ (\delta c_1^f - \delta c_{01})]$$
$$- [(u_t + \sigma_1 N_Y)(B_{10} L_{11} - L_{10} B_{11}) + \sigma_1 (m_1 S_0) H_Y$$
$$+ \sigma_1 (m_1 S_1)(B_{1Y} L_{10} - B_{10} L_{1Y})] \delta \bar{r}_0$$
$$- [\sigma_1 (m_1 S_1) B_{0Y} - B_{01} (u_t + \sigma_1 N_Y)] \delta \bar{B}_1^c$$
$$- [\sigma_1 (m_1 S_1) L_{1Y} - (u_t + \sigma_1 N_Y) L_{11}] \delta B_1$$
$$+ [(u_t + \sigma_1 N_Y) H_\pi + \sigma_1 (m_1 S_1) H_W - \sigma_1 (m_1 S_W) H_Y] \delta W^{hs} \}$$

The signs of these solutions, together with those pertaining to Y^d, W^h, and B_0^h, are listed in Table 8.1.[4] They depend in part on the same suppositions cited in connection with the flexible-rate case.

The proof of stability

To prove that this amended model is stable, we must again show that $[\delta \dot{W}^{hs}/\delta W^{hs}] < 0$. In the flexible-rate case,

$$(8.10a) \quad \frac{\delta \dot{W}^{hs}}{\delta W^{hs}} = -\sigma_1 u_\pi (H_k/U) < 0$$

because

$$H_k = S_Y H_\pi + S_1 H_W - S_W H_Y > 0$$

In the pegged-rate case,

$$(8.10b) \quad \frac{\delta \dot{W}^{hs}}{\delta W^{hs}} = -[(u_t + \sigma_1 m_0)/U_f](B_{1W} S_1 - S_W B_{11}) < 0$$

For the sake of brevity, we do not pause to look at time paths. Instead, we move directly to our final task – the derivation of the steady-state solutions.

Solving for steady-state effects

When the budget deficit is policy determined, the steady-state effects of disturbances and policies can be obtained by solving Eqs. (8.2), (8.3), and (8.4), together with usual conditions that $S = \bar{D} = 0$. As in Chapter 3, the method and results are different under flexible and pegged exchange rates.

The flexible-rate case. In this case we must solve simultaneously the equations for the bond and money markets and Eq. (7.8) to obtain the long-run changes in wealth, income, and the interest rate. Thereafter, we can solve the goods-market equation for the change in the exchange rate. These are the results:

$$(8.11a) \quad dY = (1/H_k)_{\text{L}}H_0) \, d\bar{r}_0 + [S_W B_{01} + S_1(L_{1W} + B_{1W})] \, d\bar{B}_1^c$$
$$+ (S_W L_{11} - L_{1W} S_1) \, d\bar{B}_1 + S_Y(H_\pi) \, d\bar{G}_1\}$$

---

[4] As before, changes in Y^d are obtained from Eq. (8.5), and changes in W^h are obtained from Eq. (7.11). Changes in B_0^h are also obtained from Eq. (7.11), which says that $\pi \, \delta B_0^h + \bar{\pi} \, \delta R = 0$, so that the changes in B_0^h are equal absolutely but opposite in sign to the changes in reserves.

(8.12a) $dr_1 = (1/H_k)\{[(S_Y(L_{10}B_{1W} - L_{1W}B_{10}) - S_0(H_W)$
$- S_W(B_{1Y}L_{10} - B_{10}L_{1Y})]d\bar{r}_0$
$- [S_W B_{0Y} + S_Y(L_{1W} + B_{1W})]\, d\bar{B}_1^c + (L_{1W}S_Y - S_W L_{1Y})\, d\bar{B}_1$
$+ S_Y(H_W)\, d\bar{G}_1\}$

(8.13a) $dW^h = (1/H_k)\{[S_Y(B_{10}L_{11} - L_{10}B_{11}) + S_0(H_Y)$
$+ S_1(B_{1Y}L_{10} - B_{10}L_{1Y})]\, d\bar{r}_0$
$+ (S_1 B_{0Y} - B_{01}S_Y)\, d\bar{B}_1^c + (S_1 L_{1Y} - L_{11}S_Y)\, d\bar{B}_1$
$- S_Y(H_Y)\, d\bar{G}_1\}$

so that

(8.14a) $\left(\dfrac{d\pi}{\pi}\right)$ $= -(1/u_\pi)(dc_1^f - dc_{01}) + (1/\sigma_1 u_\pi H_k)(u_t + \sigma_1 m_0)\{(H_0)\, d\bar{r}_0$
$+ [S_W B_{01} + S_1(L_{1W} + B_{1W})]\, d\bar{B}_1^c + (S_W L_{11} - L_{1W}S_1)\, d\bar{B}_1\}$
$-(1/\sigma_1 u_\pi H_k)[\sigma_1 m_0(S_1 H_W - S_W H_Y) - u_t S_Y H_\pi]\, d\bar{G}_1$

The signs of these expressions, together with those for changes in Y^d and B_0^h, are listed in Table 8.2.[5]

The pegged-rate case. In this case we can proceed in three steps. The goods-market equation can be solved for the change in income. The bond-market equation can be solved jointly with Eq. (7.8) for the changes in wealth and the interest rate. Finally, the money-market equation can be solved for the change in reserves. Following this sequence,

(8.11b) $dY = [\sigma_1/(u_t + \sigma_1 m_0)][(u_\pi)\left(\dfrac{d\bar{\pi}}{\bar{\pi}}\right) + (m_0)\, d\bar{G}_1 + (dc_1^f - dc_{01})]$

(8.12b) $dr_1 = (1/H_f)[(S_W B_{10} - S_0 B_{1W})\, d\bar{r}_0 + (S_W)\, d\bar{B}_1^c - (S_W)\, d\bar{B}_1]$
$+ [\sigma_1(B_{1Y}S_W - S_Y B_{1W})/(u_t + \sigma_1 m_0)H_f][u_\pi \left(\dfrac{d\bar{\pi}}{\bar{\pi}}\right)$
$+ (dc_1^f - dc_{01})]$
$+ [1/(u_t + \sigma_1 m_0)H_f][\sigma_1 m_0(B_{1Y}S_W) + u_t(B_{1W}S_Y)]\, d\bar{G}_1$

(8.13b) $dW^h = (1/H_f)[(S_0 B_{11} - B_{10}S_1)\, d\bar{r}_0 - (S_1)\, d\bar{B}_1^c + (S_1)\, d\bar{B}_1]$
$+ [\sigma_1(S_Y B_{11} - B_{1Y}S_1)/(u_t + \sigma_1 m_0)H_f][u_\pi \left(\dfrac{d\bar{\pi}}{\bar{\pi}}\right)$
$+ (dc_1^f - dc_{01})]$
$- [1/(u_t + \sigma_1 m_0)H_f][u_t(S_Y B_{11}) + \sigma_1 m_0(B_{1Y}S_1)]\, d\bar{G}_1$

[5] Here and in the pegged-rate case below, changes in Y^d are obtained as usual from Eq. (8.5), whereas changes in B_0^h are obtained from Eq. (7.11), which says that $\pi\, dB_0^h = dW^h - V_\pi(d\pi/\pi) - \bar{\pi}\, dR - d\bar{B}_1$.

Table 8.2. Steady-state effects in the amended model

Disturbance	Effects under flexible rate						Effects under pegged rate					
	$d\pi$	dr_1	dY	dY^a	dW^h	$\pi\,dB_0^h$	$\bar\pi\,dR$	dr_1	dY	dY^a	dW^h	$\bar\pi\,dB_0^h$
$d\bar{r}_0$	+	?	+	+	+	?	−	?	0	0	+	+
$d\bar{\pi}$	xx	xx	xx	xx	xx	xx	+	?	+	+	+	?
$d\bar{B}_1^e$	+	−	+	+	?	?	−	−	0	0	−	?
$d\bar{B}_1$	+	+	+	−	+	?	−	+	0	0	?	?
$d\bar{G}_1$	?	+	+	−	−	?	?	+	+	−	?	?
$dc_1^f - dc_{01}$	−	0	0	0	0	+	+	?	+	+	+	?

See note to Table 8.1.

so that

(8.14b) $\bar{\pi}\, dR = -(1/H_f)\{(H_0)\, d\bar{r}_0 + [S_W B_{01} + S_1(L_{1W} + B_{1W})]\, d\bar{B}_1^c$

$+ (S_W L_{11} - L_{1W} S_1)\, d\bar{B}_1\}$

$+ [\sigma_1 H_k/(u_t + \sigma_1 m_0)H_f][u_\pi \left(\dfrac{d\bar{\pi}}{\bar{\pi}}\right) + (dc_1^f - dc_{01})]$

$+ [1/(u_t + \sigma_1 m_0)H_f][\sigma_1 m_0(S_1 H_W - S_W H_Y) - u_t S_Y H_\pi]\, d\bar{G}_1$

For the signs of these expressions, see Table 8.2.

Effects of the amendment

It is useful to segregate two sets of results that follow from amending our specification. In Table 7.1, describing impact effects when income did not influence the demand for money, goods-market disturbances did not affect the interest rate, exchange rate, or reserves. In Table 8.1, they do. These are the direct results of the amended specification, reflecting the fact that goods and asset markets cannot be partitioned. But these are not the only differences in outcomes. In Table 7.1, for example, an open-market purchase brought about a prompt depreciation of the home currency or loss of reserves. In Table 8.1, the changes in π and $\bar{\pi}R$ are ambiguous. In Table 7.2, moreover, a balanced-budget increase in government spending had no permanent effect on disposable income (and the balanced-budget multiplier was unity). In Table 8.2, there is a permanent reduction in disposable income (and the balanced-budget multiplier is smaller than unity). These are indirect results of the amendment, reflecting interactions between goods and asset markets that did not take place before and reflecting other, less obvious consequences of inserting income into Eq. (8.1).

We begin to survey differences in outcomes by looking at direct effects of the amendment–the changes in responses to goods-market disturbances. Thereafter, we examine indirect effects by answering four questions: (1) What are the effects, if any, on the degree and speed with which exchange-rate flexibility can confer insulation? (2) What are the effects on the functioning of fiscal policies –of balanced-budget changes in $\bar{G}_1$ and of temporary tax reductions? (3) What are the effects on the functioning of monetary policy? (4) What are the implications for the analysis of devaluation?

Direct effects on outcomes of
goods-market disturbances

When the demand for money depends on income, goods-market disturbances and policy changes that influence income immediately have also to
influence asset-market outcomes. Three examples, all alike, are shown in
Table 8.1. They occur with the shifts in demands, δc_1^f and δc_{01}, and with
the fiscal policies, $\delta \bar{G}_1$ and $\delta \bar{D}$. In each instance, there is an immediate increase in nominal income, as there was in Chapter 7. In the amended ver-
sion of the model, however, there is an increase in the demand for money,
and households seek to sell bonds.

It is, of course, impossible for households to run down their holdings of
the domestic bond; the supply is fixed. Accordingly, the domestic interest
rate must rise to clear the bond market. Under a pegged exchange rate,
however, households can run down their holdings of the foreign bond
(and the increase in r_1 enhances the incentive for them to do so). Thus,
there is an increase in reserves, as households sell foreign bonds for
foreign currency, then sell the foreign currency for home currency. The
central bank must intervene to purchase foreign currency, increasing the
supply of money and satisfying the increase in demand for money.

Before looking at what happens with a flexible exchange rate, we carry
the analysis one step further to note the most important indirect effect of
amending the demand for money. The increase in income brought about
by a goods-market disturbance is smaller in the short run than it was in the
standard version of the model. Denote by δY_b the instantaneous increase
in nominal income given by Eq. (8.7b) for the pegged-rate case. Denote by
δY_0 the corresponding increase given by Eq. (7.21) for both exchange-rate
regimes. Taking the difference between them,

$$\delta Y_b - \delta Y_0 = (B_{1Y}/U_f)\sigma_1 m_1 S_1[\sigma_1/(u_t + \sigma_1 N_Y)][(N_Y)\,\delta\bar{G}_1 + (1 - N_Y)\,\delta\bar{D} + (\delta c_1^f - \delta c_{01})] < 0$$

because $B_{1Y} < 0$. The reason for the smaller increase of income in the
current case is the increase in r_1, which stimulates desired saving and depresses consumption. Goods-market disturbances, regardless of origin,
have smaller short-run effects on aggregate demand, activity, and prices.[6]

Under a flexible exchange rate, the money supply is policy determined.

[6] Note that the long-run changes in Y and Y^d resulting from shifts in demand and
balanced-budget changes in $\bar{G}_1$ are the same as they were in Chapter 7 under a pegged exchange rate.

Money and bond holdings cannot change immediately, because households can sell foreign bonds only to the trivial extent permitted by the instantaneous adjustment of the current-account balance. They cannot convert foreign currency into home currency. As in the standard version of the model, the home currency must appreciate to clear the market for the foreign bond, reducing home-currency holdings of that bond by more than the demand for them. Furthermore, the reduction in wealth resulting from the appreciation helps to clear the money market. The demand for money falls to what it was initially.

There are three separate ways in which changes in r_1 and π limit the size of the increase in income. The increase in the interest rate raises desired saving, just as in the pegged-rate case. The appreciation of the home currency reduces wealth, and this also raises saving. Finally, the appreciation shifts demand away from the export good. For all three reasons, the short-run increase in income is smaller than in Chapter 7, where neither r_1 nor π was affected immediately by goods-market disturbances, and it is also smaller than with a pegged exchange rate. Denote by δY_a the instantaneous increase in income given by Eq. (8.7a) for the flexible-rate case, and calculate the difference between income changes under the amended and standard versions of the model:

$$\delta Y_a - \delta Y_0 = -(\sigma_1/U)[(m_1S_1)H_W V_\pi + (u_\pi - m_1 S_W V_\pi)H_Y]$$
$$\times [\sigma_1/(u_t + \sigma_1 N_Y)][(N_Y)\,\delta \bar{G}_1 + (1 - N_Y)\,\delta \bar{D}$$
$$+ (\delta c_1^f - \delta c_{01})] < 0$$

Calculate the difference between the income changes under flexible and pegged exchange rates:

$$\delta Y_a - \delta Y_b = -(\sigma_1/U)(\sigma_1/U_f)H_Y[(m_1S_1)B_{1W}V_\pi + (u_\pi - m_1 S_W V_\pi)B_{11}]$$
$$\times [(N_Y)\,\delta \bar{G}_1 + (1 - N_Y)\,\delta \bar{D} + (\delta c_1^f - \delta c_{01})] < 0$$

We shall make extensive use of this result when we deal with insulation and with fiscal policies.[7]

Insulation once again

In the standard version of our model, summarized in Chapter 7, the exchange-rate regime had no effect at all on the short-run income changes generated by goods-market disturbances. They were given by Eq. (7.21)

[7] Under a flexible exchange rate, a shift in demand has no effect on steady-state income – which is the result obtained in Chapter 7. As to the effect of an increase in $\bar{G}_1$, denote by dY_a the permanent effect with a flexible exchange rate given by Eq. (8.11a) and denote by

for the two regimes together. By implication, a flexible exchange rate did not afford any insulation in the short run. Insulation did occur through time but was not complete until the economy came to the new steady state.

The proof above that $\delta Y_a < \delta Y_b$ for goods-market disturbances says that partial insulation does take place at once in the amended version of the model. When the demand for money depends on income, the income change brought about by a goods-market disturbance has immediate effects on the exchange rate and the interest rate that influence absorption and the pattern of demand. Any increase in the demand for the domestic good ($\delta c_1^f > 0$, $\delta c_{01} < 0$, $\delta \bar{G}_1 > 0$, or $\delta \bar{D} > 0$) causes the home currency to appreciate. Households want to save more in order to offset capital losses on holdings of the foreign bond (and to capture the rewards of the higher interest rate). In addition, domestic and foreign demands shift from home to foreign goods as the latter become cheaper. The two effects work together to depress demands for domestic output, limiting the increase in income. Nevertheless, insulation does not come to be complete until the economy has settled down into its new steady state.

Turning to effects of asset-market disturbances, there was no insulation whatsoever in the standard version of the model. An increase in the foreign interest rate, $\bar{r}_0$, brought about a permanent increase in income with a flexible exchange rate. That is true here too, although the changes in income are smaller in both the short run and the long run.[8]

Before leaving the question of insulation, we illustrate an important point made in Chapter 4 regarding the conditions that have to be satisfied for instantaneous insulation. Asset markets must respond immediately to events in goods markets, and capital movements must not be affected by a change in the exchange rate. By amending the specification of the demand for money, we satisfy the first condition, allowing us to emphasize the importance of the second. We do so here by showing what would happen if the foreign bond were denominated in home currency, so that an

---

dY_b the permanent effect with a pegged rate given by Eq. (8.11b). Then form the difference, $dY_a - dY_b = [1/(u_t + \sigma_1 m_0) H_k][(S_Y H_\pi) u_t - (S_1 H_W - S_W H_Y) \sigma_1 m_0] d\bar{G}_1$, which is ambiguous.

[8] Using notation analogous to that employed before to denote the short-run changes given by Eqs. (8.7a) and (7.22a) and the long-run changes given by Eqs. (8.11a) and (3.21a),

$$\delta Y_a - \delta Y_0 = -(\sigma_1/U)[\sigma_1/(u_t + \sigma_1 N_Y) H_\pi V_\pi][(m_1 S_1) H_W + \sigma_1(u_\pi - m_1 S_W V_\pi) H_Y]$$
$$\times [u_\pi(L_{11} B_{10} - L_{10} B_{11}) + m_1 V_\pi(H_0)] \delta\bar{r}_0 < 0$$

and

$$dY_a - dY_0 = -(1/S_Y H_\pi H_k)[(S_1 H_W - S_W H_Y) H_0] d\bar{r}_0 < 0$$

exchange-rate change would not give rise to capital gains or losses and would not induce capital flows.

If the foreign bond were denominated in home currency, V_π would be zero in Eqs. (8.7a) through (8.9a), and they would turn out this way:[9]

(8.7a') $\delta Y = (1/H_Y)[(L_{11}B_{10} - L_{10}B_{11}) \delta \bar{r}_0 - (B_{01}) \delta \bar{B}_1^c]$

(8.8a') $\delta r_1 = (1/H_Y)[(B_{1Y}L_{10} - B_{10}L_{1Y}) \delta \bar{r}_0 + (B_{0Y}) \delta \bar{B}_1^c]$

(8.9a') $\left(\dfrac{\delta \pi}{\pi}\right) = -(1/u_\pi)[(N_Y) \delta \bar{G}_1 + (1 - N_Y) \delta \bar{D} + (\delta c_1^f - \delta c_{01})]$

$\qquad\qquad + (1/\sigma_1 u_\pi H_Y)[(\cdots) \delta \bar{r}_0 + (\cdots) \delta \bar{B}_1^c]$

where ellipses denote arguments identical to those in Eq. (8.9a). Goods-market disturbances vanish from the first two equations, which is to say that insulation is complete even in the short run. The instantaneous change in the exchange rate, moreover, comes to be the same as the steady-state change given by Eq. (8.14a). It is the one required to maintain current-account balance. When exchange-rate changes do not affect demands for assets, changes in Y and r_1 are needed to clear asset markets, and the exchange rate must therefore clear the goods market by adjusting the current-account balance.

This last statement is another way of saying that the second condition is satisfied when V_π is zero. Exchange-rate changes do not cause capital movements. To prove the point directly, consider the effects of shifts in the current-account balance and in fiscal policies on $\dot{F}$, the capital outflow, using Eqs. (3.14), (3.15), and (3.16):

(8.15a) $\delta \dot{F} = V_\pi(\sigma_1 H_k/U)(\delta c_1^f - \delta c_{01}) - (1/U)(1 - S_Y)[H_\pi V_\pi(u_t + \sigma_1 m_0)$
$\qquad + H_Y(\sigma_1 u_\pi)] \delta \bar{D} + (1/U)[m_0\sigma_1 V_\pi(S_1 H_W - S_W H_Y)$
$\qquad - S_Y(H_\pi V_\pi u_t + H_Y \sigma_1 U_\pi)] \delta \bar{G}_1$

When the foreign bond is denominated in foreign currency ($V_\pi > 0$), a shift of demand to the export good induces a capital outflow, a budget deficit induces an inflow, and a balanced-budget increase in $\bar{G}_1$ can do one or the other. When the bond is denominated in home currency ($V_\pi = 0$), the shift of demand has no effect on $\dot{F}$, which says that the second condition is satisfied.[10]

---

[9] We neglect effects of changes in B_1 and W^{hs}, as they are not short-run disturbances.

[10] The remaining arguments of Eq. (8.15a) reduce to $\delta \dot{F} = -[(1 - S_Y) \delta \bar{D} + (S_Y) \delta \bar{G}_1]$. The two fiscal policies lead at once to changes in the current-account balance that are equal absolutely but opposite in sign to the changes in domestic demand. By way of explanation, Eq. (8.7a') says that changes in $\bar{D}$ and $\bar{G}_1$ do not affect Y immediately, but they do affect

One final point should be made about the implications of Eq. (8.7a'), dealing with the case in which the foreign bond is denominated in home currency. Although shifts in demand and fiscal policies do not appear in that equation, which says that they do not affect income immediately, their long-term results are different. Insulation against a shift in the current-account balance is instantaneous and permanent. But the neutralization of fiscal policies occurs only in the short run. Income does not change on impact, but disposable income is affected by both fiscal policies, so that there are immediate effects on saving that lead to gradual changes in wealth and in the demands for assets. With a tax cut, moreover, the supply of bonds begins to grow. Thus, the situation is bound to change through time, as it did in Chapter 6. There is no contradiction between the statement made by Eq. (8.7a'), that income does not change at once when V_π is zero, and the statement made by Eq. (8.11a), that there is a permanent change in income regardless of the value of V_π. This point must be borne in mind when we review the functioning of fiscal policies.

To sum up, the conclusions drawn in Chapter 4 regarding insulation are not altered substantially by adding income to Eq. (8.1). When the demand for money depends on income, asset markets respond immediately to goods-market disturbances, but they do not respond sufficiently to confer instantaneous insulation. The denomination of the foreign bond in foreign currency–a basic ingredient of our approach to the theory of exchange-rate determination–continues to stand in the way.

The functioning of fiscal policies

Our work on the direct effects of goods-market disturbances and on insulation has led to a number of results concerning fiscal policies. We now draw those results together and add to them where necessary.

In the standard version of our model, the impact effects of changes in $\bar{D}$ and $\bar{G}_1$ did not depend on the exchange-rate regime or degree of asset-market integration. In the amended version, where markets are not segregated, an increase in $\bar{D}$ or $\bar{G}_1$ causes an immediate increase in the interest rate and an appreciation of the home currency with a flexible exchange rate. The impact effects on income must therefore be smaller than

Y^d. From Eq. (8.5), $\delta Y^d = \delta\bar{D} - \delta\bar{G}_1$, when $\delta Y = 0$. Accordingly, consumption changes by $(1 - S_Y)(\delta\bar{D} - \delta\bar{G}_1)$; a tax cut raises aggregate demand by $(1 - S_Y)\,\delta\bar{D}$, and a balanced-budget increase in $\bar{G}_1$ raises it by $\delta\bar{G}_1 - (1 - S_Y)\,\delta\bar{G}_1$, or $(S_Y)\,\delta\bar{G}_1$. Each such increase in aggregate demand is offset exactly by a deterioration in the current-account balance induced by an appreciation of the home currency–a deterioration equal to the increase in the capital inflow ($\delta\dot{F} < 0$).

in Chapter 7 and, more important in the present context, they are smaller when the exchange rate is flexible than when it is pegged. (The proof is the one above that $\delta Y_a < \delta Y_b < \delta Y_0$ for any goods-market disturbance.)

This last finding echoes the well-known statement by Mundell that exchange-rate flexibility reduces the effectiveness of fiscal policy, because the demand for money rises with income, producing a capital inflow that causes the home currency to appreciate. When there is no capital mobility, he says, fiscal policy is stronger with a flexible exchange rate.[11] When there is perfect mobility, however, it is completely impotent:[12]

Assume an increase in government spending financed by government borrowing. The increased spending creates an excess demand for goods and tends to raise income. But this would increase the demand for money, raise interest rates, attract a capital inflow, and appreciate the exchange rate, which in turn would have a depressing effect on income. In fact, therefore, the negative effect on income of exchange-rate appreciation has to offset exactly the positive multiplier effect on income of the original increase in government spending. Income cannot change unless the money supply or interest rates change, and because the former is constant in the absence of central bank action and the latter is fixed by the world level of interest rates, income remains fixed. . . Fiscal policy thus completely loses its force as a domestic stabilizer when the exchange rate is allowed to fluctuate and the money supply is held constant.

Our own result, however, is different in two ways. First, the effectiveness of fiscal policy does not fall to zero when foreign and domestic bonds are perfect substitutes – the analogue to perfect capital mobility. In Table 8.3, below, we show that it reaches a lower but positive limit. Second, our result holds only in the short run. In the long run, indeed, it is reversed in the standard and amended models alike.

Deferring momentarily the first of these two points, let us examine the permanent effects of a temporary tax cut and an increase in $\bar{G}_1$, taking the two policies one at a time.

In Tables 7.2 and 8.2, a temporary tax cut, leading to an increase in the supply of bonds, is shown to have no permanent effect on income with a pegged exchange rate but to have a permanent positive effect with a flexible rate. Exchange-rate flexibility limits the effectiveness of a temporary tax cut in the short run but sustains it in the long run. In the amended version of the model, moreover, the long-run changes in π and $\bar{\pi}R$ are opposite in sign to the short-run changes. Under a flexible exchange rate, for example, a tax cut causes an immediate appreciation of the home currency. With the passage of time, however, the home currency must depreciate

[11] R. A. Mundell, *International Economics*, Macmillan, New York, 1968, p. 245.
[12] Ibid., p. 254.

Table 8.3. *Influence of capital mobility on the effectiveness of fiscal policy in the amended model*

Case	Result of increase in substitutability	Size of change with perfect substitutability
Pegged exchange rate		
Influence on size of change in income		
Impact effect	$-(B_{1Y}/U_f)(\sigma_1/U_f)\sigma_1 m_1 S_1(1 - N_Y) > 0$	$[\sigma_1/(u_t + \sigma_1 N_Y)](1 - N_Y) > 0$
Steady-state effect	0	0^a
Influence on size of change in reserves		
Impact effect	$-(B_{1Y}/U_f)(\sigma_1/U_f)[\sigma_1 L_{1Y}(m_1 S_1) - L_{11}(u_t + \sigma_1 N_Y)]$ $\times (1 - N_Y) > 0$	$L_{1Y}[\sigma_1/(u_t + \sigma_1 N_Y)](1 - N_Y) > 0$
Steady-state effect	$-(S_W/H_f)[(S_W L_{11} - L_{1W}S_1)/H_f] > 0$	0
Flexible exchange rate		
Influence on size of change in income		
Impact effect	$-\sigma_1(H_W/U)[m_1 V_\pi(S_W L_{11} - L_{1W}S_1) - L_{11}u_\pi](\sigma_1 V_\tau/U)$ $\times (1 - N_Y) < 0$	$L_{1W}(\sigma_1 V_\pi/U^*)(1 - N_Y) > 0^b$
Steady-state effect	$-[(L_{1W}S_Y - S_W L_{1Y})/H_k][(S_W L_{11} - L_{1W}S_1)/H_k] < 0$	0
Influence on size of change in exchange rate		
Impact effect	$-\sigma_1(H_W/U)[\sigma_1 L_{1Y}(m_1 S_1) - L_{11}(u_t + \sigma_1 N_Y)](V_\pi/U)$ $\times (1 - N_Y) < 0$	$-L_{1Y}(\sigma_1/U^*)(1 - N_Y) < 0^b$
Steady-state effect	$-[(L_{1W}S_Y - S_W L_{1Y})/H_k][(S_W L_{11} - L_{1W}S_1)/H_k$ $\times [(u_t + \sigma_1 m_0)/\sigma_1 u_\pi] < 0$	0

[a] Regardless of degree of substitutability.

[b] $U^* = V_\pi(u_t + \sigma_1 N_Y)L_{1W} + \sigma_1(u_\pi - m_1 S_W V_\pi)L_{1Y} > 0.$

compared to what it was initially. It does so in response to the increase in the supply of bonds.

To complicate matters, the long-run effects of an increase in $\bar{G}_1$ are quite different in the standard and amended models. Under a pegged exchange rate, the changes in income and disposable income are identical, and the sign of the change in the interest rate is the same. But the permanent changes in wealth, reserves, and holdings of the foreign bond are listed as uncertain in Table 8.2, and all of them were negative in Table 7.2. Under a flexible exchange rate, moreover, there are permanent reductions in Y^d and W^h in the amended model, and an increase in r_1, but all of them were constant in the standard version. In addition, the long-run change in income is smaller than it was in the standard version (the balanced-budget multiplier is less than unity), and the exchange-rate change is uncertain in Table 8.2, whereas it was positive in Table 7.2.

The main reason for these differences, however, resides in the choice of Y rather than Y^d to represent the transactions demand for money in Eq. (8.1). Under our assumptions about fiscal policy, embodied in Eq. (8.5), a permanent increase in $\bar{G}_1$ widens the gap between Y and Y^d, causing them to move in opposite directions. There are conflicting tendencies at work on the demand for money when it depends on Y rather than Y^d. The increase in income raises the demand for money directly; the decrease in disposable income reduces the demand for money indirectly (by reducing steady-state wealth). It is, in fact, quite easy to demonstrate that the sustitution of Y^d for Y in Eq. (8.1) would cause the signs of the effects of an increase in $\bar{G}_1$ to be the same as those in Table 7.2. Under a flexible exchange rate, indeed, the sizes of the changes would also be the same.

In Chapter 5 we looked at the influence of asset-market integration on the effectiveness of a tax cut. We saw that it had no influence at all on the instantaneous change in income and did not affect the long-run change with a pegged exchange rate. In the standard version of our model, the impact effect is confined to the goods markets, and in both versions of the model, the steady-state effect is nil under a pegged rate. We did find, however, that asset-market integration diminishes the long-run increase in income with a flexible rate and that the increase goes to zero when the two bonds in the model are perfect substitutes.

In the amended version of the model, the impact effects of a tax cut are not confined to the goods markets, and asset-market integration is influential in both the short run and the long run. Its implications are shown in Table 8.3 and can be summarized quite simply.[13]

[13] For the derivation of the terms in Table 8.3, see pp. 119–20.

Under a pegged exchange rate, an increase in substitutability between domestic and foreign bonds enlarges the short-run increase in income resulting from a tax cut. For this reason (and because it limits the increase in r_1), it enlarges the increase in demand for money and, therefore, the addition to reserves. In the long run, of course, income is unaffected, but the permanent loss of reserves is reduced (and falls to zero in the limiting case of perfect substitutability). Under a flexible exchange rate, by contrast, an increase in substitutability diminishes the stimulus to income, on impact and in the steady state. Furthermore, it amplifies the short-run appreciation of the home currency and limits the long-run depreciation. As noted earlier, however, asset-market integration cannot nullify completely the short-run stimulus to income coming from a tax cut; when the foreign bond is denominated in foreign currency, the increase in income is reduced to a lower limit but does not vanish altogether. The change in the exchange rate is smaller than the change defined by Eq. (8.9a'), the one that would occur if the foreign bond were denominated in home currency and would thus keep income constant.

In brief, asset-market integration increases the effectiveness of fiscal policy under a pegged exchange rate, but only in the short run, and decreases its effectiveness under a flexible rate, in the short run and the long run. But the presence in our model of a foreign-currency bond leads us to reject Mundell's conclusion. Even in the case of perfect substitutability, exchange-rate flexibility does not vitiate completely the short-run effect of a tax cut.

Summing up, there are four ways in which the functioning of fiscal policy is modified by the amendment to the demand for money. First, the short-run effects of changes in $\bar{D}$ and $\bar{G}_1$ are reduced by interactions between goods and asset markets; income does not rise as much as in the standard version of the model. Second, the sizes of those short-run effects are affected by the exchange-rate regime. Third, they are affected by the degree of asset-market integration, positively with a pegged exchange rate and negatively with a flexible rate. Fourth, the long-run effects of a balanced-budget increase in government spending are quite sensitive to the form of the amendment to the demand for money. Nevertheless, the signs of the short-run income changes are the same in Table 8.1 as in Table 7.1, and those of the long-run changes are the same in Table 8.2 as in Table 7.2. From a qualitative standpoint, our results are affected more fundamentally by the presence of the foreign-currency bond than by the omission of income from the demand for money in the standard version of the model.

The functioning of monetary policy

When goods and asset markets were segregated, an open-market purchase of the domestic bond had familiar effects on the economy. Under a pegged exchange rate, there was an immediate increase in income and loss of reserves; in the new steady state, income returned to what it was initially, but reserves were lower than they were to start. Under a flexible exchange rate, the immediate increase in income was larger, partly because the home currency depreciated; in the new steady state, income was higher than it was initially and there was likewise a permanent depreciation of the home currency. By implication, monetary policy is more effective with a flexible exchange rate, regardless of the degree of asset-market integration. It was also shown, however, that asset-market integration raises the effectiveness of monetary policy under a flexible rate and reduces it under a pegged rate (and in the limiting case of perfect substitutability, reduces it to zero, even in the short run).[14]

When goods and asset markets interact, as they do when we amend the demand for money, the signs of the income changes are the same, although the sizes are reduced in every instance.[15] But the impact effects on reserves and on the exchange rate are uncertain, and so are the relative sizes of the short-run income changes. For reserves to fall and the exchange rate to depreciate, as in the standard version of our model, it is necessary that

$$\sigma_1(m_1 S_1) B_{0Y} - B_{01}(u_t + \sigma_1 N_Y) > 0$$

The reduction in the domestic interest rate must raise the demand for the foreign bond by more than the increase in income reduces it.[16] The same

[14] On the relative sizes of the short-run effects on income, see p. 113; on the implications of asset-market integration, see pp. 118–24.

[15] Subtracting the relevant argument in Eq. (7.22b) from its counterpart in Eq. (8.7b), we obtain $[(B_{1Y}/B_{11})(\sigma_1 m_1 S_1)^2/(u_t + \sigma_1 N_Y)U_f] \delta\bar{B}_1^c < 0$ for the pegged-rate case. Repeating the exercise with Eqs. (7.22a) and (8.7a), we obtain a similar expression for the flexible-rate case. (The proof for the long-run flexible-rate case resembles the one in note 8.)

[16] Rewriting this condition as $\sigma_1 m_1(S_1 B_{0Y} - S_Y B_{01}) - B_{01}(u_t + \sigma_1 m_0) > 0$, the sufficient condition turns out to be $(S_Y/S_1) > (B_{0Y}/B_{01})$; the income sensitivity of saving must be large relative to its interest sensitivity, compared to the income and interest sensitivities of the demand for the foreign bond. Note, in passing, these additional points: (1) When this same condition is satisfied, the other ambiguities in Table 8.1 are resolved; wealth rises with a depreciation of the home currency resulting from an open-market purchase, and holdings of foreign bonds rise with a decline in the stock of reserves. (2) The changes in π and $\bar{\pi}R$ must always be smaller in the short run and the long run than in the standard version of the model. The home currency cannot depreciate by as much. Reserves cannot fall by as much. (3) Uncertainties about the short-run changes in π or $\bar{\pi}R$ are not resolved by setting $V_\pi = 0$. As a matter of fact, the denomination of the foreign bond is relatively unimportant for the functioning of monetary policy under a flexible exchange rate.

condition must be satisfied for a flexible exchange rate to raise the effectiveness of monetary policy in the short run. Denote by δY_a the short-run change in income given by Eq. (8.7a) for the flexible-rate case. Denote by δY_b the change given by Eq. (8.7b) for the pegged-rate case. Taking the difference between them,

$$\delta Y_a - \delta Y_b = (1/U)(\sigma_1/U_f)[V_\pi(m_1S_1)B_{1W} + (u_\pi - m_1S_WV_\pi)B_{11}]$$
$$\times [\sigma_1(m_1S_1)B_{0Y} - (u_t + \sigma_1N_Y)B_{01}] \delta \bar{B}_1^c$$

so that $\delta Y_a > \delta Y_b$ if and only if the condition is satisfied. For an open-market purchase to have more influence on income under a flexible rate than under a pegged rate, it must cause the home currency to depreciate, raising domestic absorption and switching domestic and foreign demands to domestic output.

This critical condition is more likely to be satisfied when domestic and foreign bonds are close substitutes, and it is certain to be satisfied when they are perfect substitutes. The effects of substitutability are shown in Table 8.4. They are the same as those in Chapter 5. Under a flexible exchange rate, the effects on Y and π are amplified uniformly. Under a pegged exchange rate, the effect on Y is reduced in the short run, and the outflow of reserves rises uniformly. In the limiting case of perfect substitutability, the impact effect on Y is reduced to zero with a pegged exchange rate but rises to an upper limit with a flexible exchange rate.

Summing up, the functioning of monetary policy can be altered significantly when the demand for money depends on income, but only when a critical condition is violated. In this circumstance, the short-run changes in π and $\bar{\pi}R$ will be perverse (opposite in sign to those obtaining in the long run and to those obtaining in the standard version of the model). When those changes are perverse, moreover, exchange-rate flexibility reduces the effectiveness of monetary policy. But when we set aside this possibility, the amendment to the demand for money has no influence at all on the signs of the effects of an open-market operation or on their ordering by size under pegged and flexible exchange rates. Furthermore, that critical condition does not affect the influence of asset-market integration.

The analysis of devaluation

The last of our four questions can be answered briefly. The inclusion of income in Eq. (8.1) is relatively unimportant for the analysis of devaluation. The changes in the interest rate are uncertain in Tables 8.1 and 8.2, because the income-increasing effect of a devaluation reduces the demand

Table 8.4. *Influence of capital mobility on the effectiveness of monetary policy in the amended model*

Case	Result of increase in substitutability	Size of change with perfect substitutability
Pegged exchange rate		
Influence on size of change in income		
Impact effect	$-(1/U_f)m_1S_1(\sigma_1/U_f)(u_t + \sigma_1 N_Y) < 0$	0
Steady-state effect	0	0^a
Influence on size of change in reserves		
Impact effect	$-(1/U_f)[(u_t + \sigma_1 N_Y)/U_f][\sigma_1(m_1S_1L_{1Y} \\ -(u_t + \sigma_1 N_Y)L_{11}] < 0$	-1
Steady-state effect	$(1/H_f)(S_W/H_f)(S_W L_{11} - L_{1W}S_1) < 0$	-1
Flexible exchange rate		
Influence on size of change in income		
Impact effect	$(1/U)(\sigma_1/U)U^{**}[m_1V_\pi(S_W L_{11} - L_{1W}S_1) - L_{11}u_\pi] > 0^b$	$(\sigma_1/U^*)(u_\pi - m_1 S_W V_\pi) > 0^c$
Steady-state effect	$(1/H_k)(S_W L_{11} - L_{1W}S_1)(1/H_k)[S_Y(L_{1W} + B_{1W}) + S_W B_{0Y}] \\ > 0$	$-[S_W/(S_Y L_{1W} - S_W L_{1Y})] > 0$
Influence on size of change in exchange rate		
Impact effect	$(1/U)U^{**}(1/U)[\sigma_1(m_1S_1)L_{1Y} - (u_t + \sigma_1 N_Y)L_{11}] > 0^b$	$[(u_t + \sigma_1 N_Y)/U^*] > 0^c$
Steady-state effect	$(1/H_k)(S_W L_{11} - L_{1W}S_1)(1/H_k)[S_Y(L_{1W} + B_{1W}) + S_W B_{0Y}] \\ \times [(u_t + \sigma_1 m_0)/\sigma_1 u_\pi] > 0$	$-[S_W/(S_Y L_{1W} - S_W L_{1Y})] \\ \times [(u_t + \sigma_1 m_0)/\sigma_1 u_\pi] > 0$

[a] Regardless of degree of substitutability.
[b] $U^{**} = V_\pi(u_t + \sigma_1 N_Y)(L_{1W} + B_{1W}) - \sigma_1(u_\pi - m_1 S_W V_\pi)B_{0Y} > 0$.
[c] See note *b* to Table 8.3.

for the domestic bond, and can do so by more than the wealth-increasing effect of the devaluation raises that demand. All other signs in those tables, however, are the same as those in Tables 7.1 and 7.2, and one important outcome is identical in size. The changes in reserves are larger because the increase in income raises the demand for money, and the increase in income is smaller in the short run. But the steady-state increase in income is the same.

9

Expectations, speculation, and exchange-rate stability

Elsewhere in this book, households have stationary or neutral expectations. Goods prices, interest rates, and the exchange rate prevailing currently are expected to prevail in the future. Under this simple supposition, the nominal interest rates, r_0 and r_1, represent real interest rates, ex ante, because the expected inflation rate is zero. Furthermore, the foreign interest rate, r_0, represents the full rate of return on the foreign bond, because changes in capital values are not anticipated when exchange-rate changes are not anticipated.

This assumption is restrictive. It might indeed be said to violate the spirit of the asset-market approach, which argues that exchange rates are determined in the short run by behavior in bond and money markets based on anticipated rates of return. Expectations about rates of return are affected by forecasts of changes in asset prices, including changes in exchange rates, which alter differentially expected returns on assets denominated in different currencies. It is not enough to say, as we did in Chapter 2, that wealth holders are uncertain about the future and hold foreign-currency assets in their portfolios to hedge against exchange-rate changes. We must introduce nonneutral expectations to replicate exchange-rate behavior realistically.

In the first section of this chapter we show how nonneutral expectations can be introduced into the simplified model summarized in Chapter 7. Next we introduce a convenient way to endogenize those expectations. Households are assumed to have farsighted or *hyperopic* vision, rather than nearsighted or *myopic* vision. They can forecast correctly the long-run effects of a disturbance or policy change, but cannot forecast the disturbance itself or its effects on the path of the economy.[1] Finally, we

[1] The same approach is used in R. Dornbusch, "Expectations and Exchange Rate Dynamics," *Journal of Political Economy,* 84 (December 1976), pp. 1161–76, who shows that it is not inconsistent with perfect foresight. Similar approaches are employed in J. H. Levin, "A Dynamic Model of Monetary and Fiscal Policy Under Floating Exchange Rates with Speculative Capital Flows," 1977 (mimeo), and in D. J. Mathieson, "The Impact of Monetary and Fiscal Policies Under Flexible Exchange Rates and Alternative Expectations Structures," *International Monetary Fund Staff Papers,* 24 (November 1977), pp. 535–68.

show how these specifications, taken together, influence short-run responses to disturbances and policies. (We shall see that they do not affect long-run responses.) Our findings will be organized to answer three questions: (1) How do the short-run responses differ from those shown in Chapter 7, where expectations were neutral? (2) What are the effects of hyperopic forecasting on the path of the economy – on the distance it must travel to reach long-run equilibrium and the speed at which it does so? (3) How sensitive are the results to the degree of asset-market integration?[2]

Forecasts of changes in goods prices will affect the functioning of an economy under a pegged exchange rate. They will impinge on the decision to save, because they will affect estimates of real interest rates. Nevertheless, we deal only with the flexible-rate case, because we seek mainly to identify the implications of nonneutral expectations for the process of exchange-rate determination.

Introducing expectations

In early work on expectations and flexible exchange rates, speculation was added to the foreign-exchange market as a separate, specialized activity conducted by persons or institutions that did nothing else.[3] That need not be done here. The households in our model are potential speculators, in that they hold assets that have uncertain real values. More nar-

See also P. B. Kenen, "Floats, Glides, and Indicators," *Journal of International Economics*, 5 (May 1975), pp. 107–51, where effects of speculation based on hyperopic forecasts are compared with those based on various myopic forecasts.

[2] We do not include this question merely because we have raised it elsewhere. The behavior of the domestic interest rate, and therefore the degree of asset-market integration, would appear to have an important bearing on results obtained in many recent papers analyzing the effects of nonneutral expectations. See the surveys by S. Schadler, "Sources of Exchange Rate Variability: Theory and Empirical Evidence," *International Monetary Fund Staff Papers*, 24 (July 1977), pp. 253–96, and by P. Isard, *Exchange-Rate Determination: A Survey of Popular Views and Recent Models*, Princeton Studies in International Finance 42, Princeton University, Princeton, N.J., 1978, p. 31.

[3] See, e.g., J. E. Meade, *The Balance of Payments*, Oxford University Press, London, 1951, chap. xvii, and M. Friedman, *Essays in Positive Economics*, University of Chicago Press, Chicago, 1953, pp. 157–203 (but attend to the note on p. 175, where Friedman warns against segregating classes of transactions). In work on the theory of forward exchange, deliberate attempts are made to separate speculation from other activities; see, e.g., S. C. Tsiang, "The Theory of Forward Exchange and Effects of Government Intervention on the Forward Exchange Market," *International Monetary Fund Staff Papers*, 7 (April 1959), pp. 75–106, and F. McCormick, "A Multiperiod Theory of Forward Exchange," *Journal of International Economics*, 7 (August 1977), pp. 269–82. For objections to this method, see P. B. Kenen, "Trade, Speculation, and the Forward Exchange Rate," in R. E. Baldwin et al., *Trade, Growth, and the Balance of Payments*, Rand McNally, Chicago, 1965, pp. 143–69.

rowly, they are foreign-exchange speculators, in that they choose between bonds denominated in two currencies, and their choices must reflect their expectations about the evolution of the exchange rate. Speculation can be built directly into our model merely by amending the relevant behavioral equations, rather than attaching it to the model as a separate, specialized activity.

First, we must amend the demands for the three financial assets to reflect nonneutral expectations about the exchange rate. The demand for money, for example, must be written as

$$(9.1) \quad *L_1^h = L_1\left(\bar{r}_0 + \frac{\dot{\pi}^e}{\pi}, r_1, W^h\right)$$

where $(\dot{\pi}^e/\pi)$ is the expected rate of change of the exchange rate, so that $\bar{r}_0 + (\dot{\pi}^e/\pi)$ is the expected rate of return on the foreign bond, including the anticipated capital gain resulting from an increase in the price of foreign currency. Demands for the domestic and foreign bonds must, of course, be amended identically. (If those bonds were long-term securities, instead of bills, we would also have to take account of anticipated changes in nominal interest rates, for they would affect bond prices. We do not have to take account of anticipated changes in goods prices, because they do not affect relative returns on money and the two bonds.)

Second, we must amend the saving function. Decisions to save involve choices between present and future consumption, and desired saving must depend on real rates of return in order for the choice to be free of money illusion. The saving function becomes

$$(9.2) \quad *S = S\left(\bar{r}_0 + \frac{\dot{\pi}^e}{\pi} - \frac{\dot{p}^e}{p}, r_1 - \frac{\dot{p}^e}{p}, Y^d, W^h\right)$$

where $(\dot{p}^e/p)$ is the expected rate of change in the price level, p. The latter is defined by an index of the two goods prices weighted by their shares in domestic consumption:

$$(9.3) \quad p = (\pi \bar{p}_0^f)^{m_0}(p_1)^{m_1}$$

where $m_0 + m_1 = 1$, as usual. Therefore,

$$(9.3') \quad \left(\frac{\dot{p}^e}{p}\right) = m_0\left(\frac{\dot{\pi}^e}{\pi}\right) + m_1\left(\frac{\dot{p}_1^e}{p_1}\right)$$

where $(\dot{p}_1^e/p_1)$ is the expected rate of change in the price of the domestic export good. Because the price $\bar{p}_0^f$ is exogenous, and changes in exogenous variables are unanticipated, the expected rate of change of $\bar{p}_0^f$ is always zero, and it does not appear above. (Note in passing that this is the one place in this book at which we must make use of a price index.)

Writing in full the market-clearing equations for the case of nonneutral expectations and a flexible exchange rate,[4]

$$(9.4) \quad \left[p_1 C_1^f \left(\frac{p_1}{\pi}, \bar{p}_0^f, \bar{C}^f \right) - \pi \bar{p}_0^f C_0(p_1, \pi \bar{p}_0^f, Y^d - *S) \right] + \bar{D} - S = 0$$

$$(9.5) \quad B_1 \left(\bar{r}_0 + \frac{\dot{\pi}^e}{\pi}, r_1, W^h \right) - (B_1 - \bar{B}_1^c) = 0$$

$$(9.6) \quad L_1 \left(\bar{r}_0 + \frac{\dot{\pi}^e}{\pi}, r_1, W^h \right) - (\pi \bar{R} + \bar{B}_1^c - W^c) = 0$$

where Eqs. (9.2) and (9.3′) combine to give

$$(9.2') \quad *S = S \left[\bar{r}_0 + m_1 \left(\frac{\dot{\pi}^e}{\pi} - \frac{\dot{p}_1^e}{p_1} \right), r_1 - m_0 \left(\frac{\dot{\pi}^e}{\pi} \right) - m_1 \left(\frac{\dot{p}_1^e}{p_1} \right), Y^d, W^h \right]$$

and under our fiscal-policy assumptions,

$$(9.7) \quad Y^d = Y + \bar{D} - \bar{G}_1$$

Taken together with Eqs. (7.5) through (7.7) and (7.9) through (7.14), defining Y, E, w, W^h, W^{hs}, W^c, πB_0^h, S, and B_1, these equations can be used to solve the model, *given* expectations about π and p_1. Our first task, however, is to show how hyperopic forecasting generates expectations.

Endogenizing expectations

In most of the early work mentioned above, speculators based their expectations on hindsight or the most myopic foresight. Predictions of the rate of change of the exchange rate depended on the past or current rate of change. Forecasts were regressive, extrapolative, or adaptive. With regressive forecasting, an increase in π generates the expectation of a future decrease; in Hicksian terms, the elasticity of expectations is negative.[5]

---

[4] Equation (9.4) is identical in form to the goods-market equations in Chapters 7 and 8. Goods-market behavior will be different, however, because saving is affected by price expectations, pursuant to Eq. (9.2). If goods could be stored, there would be reason to amend Eq. (9.4) explicitly, to allow for speculation in commodities based on expectations of changes in their prices.

[5] J. R. Hicks, *Value and Capital,* Oxford University Press, London, 1964, p. 205. On the use of the elasticity of expectations to describe behavior in the foreign-exchange market, see V. Argy and M. G. Porter, "The Forward Exchange Market and the Effects of Domestic and External Disturbances Under Alternative Exchange Rate Systems," *International Monetary Fund Staff Papers,* 19 (November 1972), pp. 503–32, and R. Dornbusch, "Ex-

With extrapolative forecasting, an increase in π generates the expectation of a further increase at more or less the same rate; the elasticity of expectations is in the neighborhood of unity. With adaptive forecasting, extrapolations are corrected for earlier mistakes; the elasticity of expectations is adjustable through time, upward if too low before and downward if too high.

Outcomes under these modes of behavior differ with the type of exogenous disturbance in their consequences for the path of the exchange rate, the stability of the economy, and the profitability of speculation. Regressive forecasts of exchange-rate changes, for example, tend to reduce the short-run response to a disturbance. Thus, when the disturbance is transitory or cyclical without trend, they are likely to be stabilizing, in that they combat "overshooting" or narrow the amplitude of exchange-rate fluctuations, and speculation is apt to be profitable. But when the disturbance is one that requires a permanent change in the exchange rate, they may be destabilizing, in that they retard the movement of the rate, and speculation is apt to be unprofitable. By contrast, extrapolative forecasts of rate changes tend to amplify responses to disturbances. They may thus be stabilizing or destabilizing in the short run, depending on the path that the exchange rate would follow in the absence of speculation, but are bound to be destabilizing in the long run. Because extrapolative forecasts tend to be self-validating, speculation feeds upon itself, producing a "run" on the currency and undermining the stability of the economy. Adaptive forecasts of rate changes can have similar results when corrections for mistakes are small or take place slowly, so that adaptive forecasts of exchange-rate changes do not differ much from naive extrapolations.[6]

change Rate Expectations and Monetary Policy," *Journal of International Economics*, 6 (August 1976), pp. 231–44. There appears to be a difference, however, between the definitions used by Dornbusch and Hicks.

[6] For recent work with these three modes of forecasting, see Argy and Porter, "Effects of Domestic and External Disturbances," Dornbusch, "Exchange Rate Expectations and Monetary Policy," and Mathieson, "The Impact of Monetary and Fiscal Policy," cited above; also J. Niehans, "Some Doubts About the Efficacy of Monetary Policy Under Flexible Exchange Rates," *Journal of International Economics*, 5 (August 1975), pp. 275–81, R. Dornbusch, "The Theory of Flexible Exchange Rate Regimes and Macroeconomic Policy," *Scandinavian Journal of Economics*, 78, 1976(2), pp. 255–75, and P. J. K. Kouri, "The Exchange Rate and the Balance of Payments in the Short Run and the Long Run: A Monetary Approach," *Scandinavian Journal of Economics*, 78, 1976(2), pp. 280–304. For an interesting attempt to combine an adaptive process with structural or "rational" expectations, see P. Minford, *Substitution Effects, Speculation and Exchange Rate Stability*, North Holland, Amsterdam, 1978, chap. 5, where speculators act upon their earlier errors to refine their views about the underlying structure of the economy.

In one fundamental sense, however, these three modes of behavior are more similar than different. Economic actors do not know the consequences of disturbances and do not anticipate those disturbances. Speculators can be right about the future, as when they make regressive forecasts and disturbances are transitory, and speculation can stabilize the exchange rate and the economy as a whole. But these things happen accidentally, not because the speculators are well informed. In consequence, other suppositions have come into use in work on expectations and exchange-rate behavior. Economic actors are assumed to know enough about the structure of the economy within which they function to predict the short-run consequences of disturbances as soon as they are able to detect the disturbances. Going further, it is sometimes assumed that they can anticipate the onset of disturbances. The aim is to ascertain if exchange-rate fluctuations can be blamed on gaps in the speculators' knowledge of the underlying economic structure and on the mistakes they make when forecasting disturbances and policy changes.[7]

In some of this recent work, economic actors have *perfect* knowledge of the underlying economic structure, including in that structure the implications of the actions they themselves will take on the basis of their knowledge. In much of this work, moreover, they are assumed to know *all* that can be known about the disturbances – the trends and other nonstochastic parts of movements in exogenous and policy variables and the distributions of the stochastic parts. In brief, their predictions of the relevant endogenous variables, including the exchange rate, are the expected values that would be obtained from a flawless model of the economy, using every bit of information available.[8]

When economic actors have perfect foresight, speculation can be stabi-

---

[7] For examples, see Kouri, "The Exchange Rate and the Balance of Payments," and Minford, *Substitution Effects*, cited above; also S. W. Black, *International Money Markets and Flexible Exchange Rates*, Princeton Studies in International Finance 32, Princeton University, Princeton, N.J., 1973, M. Mussa, "The Exchange Rate, the Balance of Payments, and Monetary and Fiscal Policy Under a Regime of Controlled Floating," *Scandinavian Journal of Economics*, 78, 1976(2), pp. 229–48, J. F. O. Bilson, "Rational Expectations and the Exchange Rate," in J. A. Frenkel and H. G. Johnson, eds., *The Economics of Exchange Rates*, Addison-Wesley, Reading, Mass., 1978, pp. 75–96; and C. A. Rodriguez, "The Role of Trade Flows in Exchange Rate Determination: A Rational Expectations Approach," Columbia University, New York, 1978 (mimeo).

[8] We paraphrase S. J. Turnovsky, "Structural Expectations and the Effectiveness of Government Policy in a Short-Run Macroeconomic Model," *American Economic Review*, 67 (December 1977), p. 851. Expectations of this type are usually called "rational" because they do not waste information. But information is not always free, and a genuinely rational speculator would balance the costs of acquiring more information against the rewards afforded by refining the forecast.

lizing in a strict, strong sense. There will be a smooth path to long-run equilibrium, and expectations will be realized at each point on that path. But it is not the only path that the economy can follow, and none of the others leads to equilibrium. In the monetary model used by Kouri, for example, those paths lead either to hyperinflation or hyperdeflation, even though the stock of money is known to be growing at a steady rate.[9] When the behavior of the economy can be predicted accurately, the initial response of the exchange rate to the onset or anticipation of a disturbance can be shown to be indeterminate, and this initial response determines completely the subsequent path of the economy. There is a large array of outcomes, each of which would satisfy the expectations that brought it into being, and the likelihood of making the "right" choice–the only one that leads to long-run equilibrium–is correspondingly small.[10]

It follows, of course, that behavior based on myopic foresight is almost certain to cause destabilizing speculation. If economic actors do not know where their decisions will lead them eventually, they cannot choose the "right" short-run response. But perfect foresight does not solve the problem, unless it is *defined* to rule out "wrong" choices. Economic actors must know the structure of the economy well enough to forecast its behavior over time, not merely from day to day; they must be able to predict exogenous and policy variables; and they must have two more attributes. First, each actor must possess adequate economic reasons for making "right" choices. Reverting to Kouri's case, each one must believe that hyperinflation and hyperdeflation are "implausible" when the money stock is growing at a constant rate.[11] Second, each actor must have absolute confidence in the ability and willingness of every other actor to make those choices. No one must have reason to protect himself from mistakes by others.[12]

[9] Kouri, "The Exchange Rate and the Balance of Payments," p. 282.

[10] We draw here on Kouri, "The Exchange Rate and the Balance of Payments," pp. 293–4, and W. Ethier, "Expectations and Asset-Market Theories of the Exchange Rate," Discussion Paper 346, Department of Economics, University of Pennsylvania, Philadelphia, 1976 (mimeo), pp. 8–10. See also F. H. Hahn, "On Money and Growth," *Journal of Money, Credit and Banking,* 1 (May 1969), pp. 172–88, where the problem is analyzed in the context of price expectations.

[11] Kouri argues that hyperdeflation will be seen to be implausible in his model because it would terminate abruptly once residents had sold all of their foreign assets. Hyperinflation, he says, may be harder to rule out because there is no comparable limit to the substitution of foreign for domestic assets. "There is no self-evident competitive market mechanism," he concedes, "which rules out society making itself worse off by destroying the value of its money through speculation." (Kouri, "The Exchange Rate and the Balance of Payments," p. 295.)

[12] This condition is much more stringent than the one proposed by Friedman. Speculation, he suggested, will be stabilizing when the activities (and profits) of well-informed profes-

When economic actors have hyperopic foresight and disturbances are unforeseen, no one can know with certainty what will happen next. Expectations cannot be self-fulfilling, as they are when they are "rational," and the short-run response of the exchange rate is not indeterminate. On the one hand, then, we cannot hope for the strict, strong stability that obtains when economic actors have perfect foresight in the extended sense defined above. There can be "overshooting" or "undershooting" in the short run. On the other hand, we need not fear explosive instability. The economy will not set out on a path that carries it away from long-run equilibrium.

The path will not be the one pursued with neutral expectations. Nevertheless, saving will go gradually to zero, and this condition is still sufficient for stability. If hyperopic forecasts are accurate, they are fulfilled eventually, when the economy reaches the steady state. The values of the endogenous variables will be exactly equal to those that were forecast initially, which means that their rates of change must go to zero. Expectations come to be identical to what they were when they were neutral, and they have no further influence on demands for goods or assets.

We do not believe that economic actors have accurate hyperopic foresight–any more than we believe that they have perfect foresight. We use the assumption here because it is convenient for showing how speculation—more or less well informed—can modify the impact effects of disturbances. It is convenient mathematically because we need not solve our model anew to obtain the households' hyperopic forecasts; they can be obtained directly from the standard version of the model summarized in Chapter 7. It is convenient analytically, because we need not rule out arbitrarily the threat of explosive instability or modify in any fundamental way the general structure of the model.

It is, we concede, somewhat artificial to assume that households are fairly well informed about the structure of the economy but cannot anticipate exogenous disturbances. If they know enough to identify correctly the long-run effects of any disturbances, they should perhaps be able to anticipate disturbances, as well as the policy responses to them. Furthermore, our suppositions contain an internal contradiction. We assume that disturbances are unanticipated and their short-run effects unknown. At

sionals dominate the activities (and losses) of poorly informed amateurs. (Friedman, *Essays in Positive Economics,* p. 175.) The mere presence of poorly informed amateurs, however, can cause instability. The extended definition of perfect foresight, which rules out this possibility, is typically implicit in work on "rational" expectations; see, e.g., T. J. Sargent and N. Wallace, "Rational Expectations and the Theory of Economic Policy," *Journal of Monetary Economics,* 2 (April 1976), pp. 169–84, and references given there.

250   **Extending the model**

the same time, we assume that households can detect immediately the
presence and nature of any disturbance; otherwise, they could not make
hyperopic forecasts. In some instances, of course, they may be able to
diagnose disturbances. Open-market purchases, tax reductions, and
changes in exogenous foreign variables are observable, independent of
their effects on the domestic economy. But what of a shift in demand
between goods or assets? These disturbances can be detected only by ob-
serving their effects on prices, interest rates, and other endogenous variables; one can deduce their character only by reasoning backward from
effect to cause. To do this, however, one must know as much about the
economy as one would need to forecast the immediate effects of the disturbances themselves. To have accurate hyperopic foresight, households
cannot know much less than would be needed to display some sort of perfect foresight.

There is one more difficulty. Throughout this book, we have avoided ad
hoc assumptions about speeds of adjustment. They are needed here, however, to represent the households' best subjective estimates of the rates at
which hyperopic forecasts will be realized. The expected rates of change
in π and p_1 are defined by

(9.8) $\quad \left(\dfrac{\dot{\pi}^e}{\pi}\right) = \gamma_\pi \left(\dfrac{\pi^e - \pi}{\pi}\right) \quad \gamma_\pi > 0$

(9.9) $\quad \left(\dfrac{\dot{p}_1^e}{p_1}\right) = \gamma_p \left(\dfrac{p_1^e - p_1}{p_1}\right) \quad \gamma_p > 0$

The π^e and p_1^e are the forecast values of π and p_1, and with accurate hyperopic foresight, they are the (constant) steady-state values to which π
and p_1 will move after a disturbance. The γ_π and γ_p are the households' estimates of the rates at which forecasts will be realized, and they may or
may not be accurate estimates. We assume that γ_π and γ_p are constant
over time and that they do not vary with the type of disturbance.[13]

Solving the model with nonneutral expectations

Although nonneutral expectations introduce additional connections between goods and asset markets, the model outlined above, including

[13] Dornbusch ("Expectations and Exchange Rate Dynamics," p. 1167) has shown how to
calculate the values of γ_π and γ_p that would obtain with perfect foresight and unanticipated
disturbances. The expected rates of change of π and p_1 are equated to the actual rates, and
the equations solved for γ_π and γ_p. In his example, the problem is fairly simple, as there is
only one such equation to be solved (a quadratic in γ_π). The problem is much more complicated here, as two polynomials in γ_π and γ_p must be solved simultaneously, and separate solutions must be obtained for each exogenous disturbance.

Eqs. (9.8) and (9.9), can still be partitioned. This is because the changes in π^e and p_1^e associated with each exogenous disturbance come from the steady-state solutions to the model; they are not determined jointly with the short-run changes in π and p_1. Thus, Eqs. (9.5) and (9.6), for the bond and money markets, can be solved for the immediate effects of disturbances on r_1 and π:[14]

$$
(9.10) \quad
\begin{bmatrix} -B_{11} & -(B_{1W}V_\pi - \gamma_\pi B_{10}) \\ -L_{11} & -(L_{1W}V_\pi - \gamma_\pi L_{10}) \end{bmatrix}
\begin{bmatrix} \delta\hat{r}_1 \\ \left(\dfrac{\delta\hat{\pi}}{\pi}\right) \end{bmatrix}
$$

$$
= \begin{bmatrix} B_{10}(1 + \gamma_\pi\phi_0) & (1 + B_{10}\gamma_\pi\phi_B) \\ L_{10}(1 + \gamma_\pi\phi_0) & -(1 - L_{10}\gamma_\pi\phi_B) \end{bmatrix}
\begin{bmatrix} \delta\bar{r}_0 \\ \delta\bar{B}_1^c \end{bmatrix}
$$

$$
+ \begin{bmatrix} B_{10}\gamma_\pi & 0 \\ 0 & L_{10}\gamma_\pi \end{bmatrix}
\begin{bmatrix} \phi_D & \phi_G & -\phi_C \\ \phi_D & \phi_G & -\phi_C \end{bmatrix}
\begin{bmatrix} \delta\bar{D} \\ \delta\bar{G}_1 \\ (\delta c_1^f - \delta c_{01}) \end{bmatrix}
$$

$$
+ \begin{bmatrix} B_{1W} \\ L_{1W} \end{bmatrix} \delta W^{hs}
$$

Derivatives with a caret, such as $\delta\hat{r}_1$, are impact effects with nonneutral expectations. (The notation is used to distinguish them from their counterparts in Chapter 7, with neutral expectations.) The coefficients ϕ_0, ϕ_B, ϕ_D, ϕ_G, and $-\phi_C$ are the proportionate changes in the expected exchange rate, π^e, brought about by the exogenous disturbances, and are therefore the values of the proportionate changes in the steady-state exchange rate. They are, of course, obtainable from Chapter 7, and their definitions are supplied in full in Table 9.1.[15] It is at once apparent from the system (9.10) that goods-market disturbances affect r_1 and π on impact, by affecting the expected rate of return on the foreign bond.

The determinant of the system (9.10) is

$$
H_e = H_\pi V_\pi + \gamma_\pi(B_{10}L_{11} - L_{10}B_{11}) > 0
$$

and the short-run solutions are

$$
\begin{aligned}
(9.11) \quad \delta\hat{r}_1 = &\ (1/H_e)[(L_{10}B_{1W} - B_{10}L_{1W})V_\pi(1 + \gamma_\pi\phi_0)]\,\delta\bar{r}_0 \\
&- (1/H_e)[V_\pi(L_{1W} + B_{1W}) - \gamma_\pi(B_{10} + L_{10}) \\
&\quad - \gamma_\pi\phi_B(L_{10}B_{1W} - B_{10}L_{1W})V_\pi]\,\delta\bar{B}_1^c \\
&+ (1/H_e)\gamma_\pi(L_{10}B_{1W} - B_{10}L_{1W})V_\pi[(\phi_D)\,\delta\bar{D} + (\phi_G)\,\delta\bar{G}_1 \\
&\quad - (\phi_C)(\delta c_1^f - \delta c_{01})] \\
&+ (1/H_e)\gamma_\pi(L_{10}B_{1W} - B_{10}L_{1W})\,\delta W^{hs}
\end{aligned}
$$

[14] It should be noted that the partial derivatives B_{10} and L_{10} relate to the effects of changes in the total return on the foreign bond shown in Eq. (9.1), not in the nominal interest rate alone. Similarly, the partial derivatives S_0 and S_1, used later, relate to the effects of changes in the real interest rates shown in Eq. (9.2), not in $\bar{r}_0$ and r_1 by themselves.

[15] All of the ϕ_j are positive. The one for the shift in demand, ϕ_C, appears with a minus sign in

Table 9.1. *Proportionate changes in expected values of* π^e *and* p_1^e

Disturbance	Symbol	Definition
Effect on expected exchange rate (π^e)		
$\delta \bar{r}_0$	ϕ_0	$[(u_t + \sigma_1 m_0)/u_\pi \sigma_1 H_\pi S_Y] H_0$
$\delta \bar{B}_1^c$	ϕ_B	$[(u_t + \sigma_1 m_0)/u_\pi \sigma_1 H_\pi S_Y)][S_1(L_{1W} + B_{1W}) + S_W B_{01}]$
$\delta \bar{D}$	ϕ_D	$[(u_t + \sigma_1 m_0)/u_\pi \sigma_1 H_\pi S_Y)](S_W L_{11} - L_{1W} S_1)(\delta B_1^e/\delta \bar{D})$
$\delta \bar{G}_1$	ϕ_G	$(u_t/u_\pi \sigma_1)$
$\delta c_1^f - \delta c_{01}$	$-\phi_C$	$-(1/u_\pi)$
Effect on expected export price (p_1^e)		
$\delta \bar{r}_0$	α_0	$(1/\sigma_1 H_\pi S_Y) H_0$
$\delta \bar{B}_1^c$	α_B	$(1/\sigma_1 H_\pi S_Y)[S_1(L_{1W} + B_{1W}) + S_W B_{01}]$
$\delta \bar{D}$	α_D	$(1/\sigma_1 H_\pi S_Y)(S_W L_{11} - L_{1W} S_1)(\delta B_1^e/\delta \bar{D})$
$\delta \bar{G}_1$	α_G	$(1/\sigma_1)$
$\delta c_1^f - \delta c_{01}$	—	0

Definitions are those of the steady-state changes in the actual values of π and p_1 obtained from the standard version of the model summarized in Chapter 7. The term $(\delta B_1^e/\delta D)$ in the definitions of ϕ_D and α_D are the changes in B_1 that are expected to result from a budget deficit.

and

$$(9.12) \quad \left(\frac{\delta \hat{\pi}}{\pi}\right) = (1/H_e)(B_{10}L_{11} - L_{10}B_{11})(1 + \gamma_\pi \phi_0) \, \delta \bar{r}_0$$
$$+ (1/H_e)[-B_{01} + \gamma_\pi \phi_B(B_{10}L_{11} - L_{10}B_{11})] \, \delta \bar{B}_1^c$$
$$+ (1/H_e)\gamma_\pi(B_{10}L_{11} - L_{10}B_{11})[(\phi_D) \, \delta \bar{D} + (\phi_G) \, \delta \bar{G}_1$$
$$- (\phi_C)(\delta c_1^f - \delta c_{01})]$$
$$- (H_\pi/H_e) \, \delta W^{hs}$$

The signs of these outcomes are shown in Table 9.2, together with those of their counterparts in the standard version of the model, copied from Table 7.1. We have already noted one of the major differences between the two sets of results. The exchange rate responds immediately to goods-market disturbances–to shifts in demand and to the two fiscal policies. In addition, the changes in the domestic interest rate become ambiguous (because $L_{10}B_{1W} \gtrless B_{10}L_{1W}$).

system (9.10) because a shift in demand to the export good reduces the steady-state level of π. The one for a budget deficit, ϕ_D, is defined in Table 9.1 to include the households' forecasts of the change in B_1 resulting in the long run from a budget deficit. It is, of course, assumed that $(\delta B_1^e/\delta \bar{D}) > 0$, and it is necessary for certain purposes that this forecast be accurate.

Table 9.2. *Impact effects with nonneutral and neutral expectations*

Disturbance	Nonneutral expectations			Neutral expectations		
	$\delta\hat{\pi}$	$\delta\hat{r}_1$	$\delta\hat{Y}$	$\delta\pi$	δr_1	δY
$\delta\bar{r}_0$	+	?	?	+	?	+
$\delta\bar{B}_1^c$	+	?	+	+	−	+
$\delta\bar{D}$	+	?	+	0	0	+
$\delta\bar{G}_1$	+	?	+	0	0	+
$\delta c_1^f - \delta c_{01}$	−	?	?	0	0	+

Signs are based on the assumptions that (1) $S_W L_{11} > L_{1W} S_1$, and (2) $S_1 L_{10} = S_0 L_{11}$. Nonneutral expectations are based on hyperopic forecasting. Signs of the effects on p_1, w, and E are identical to those for the effects on Y.

Turning next to Eq. (9.4), we obtain

$$(9.13) \quad N_e \left(\frac{\delta\hat{p}_1}{p_1}\right) - [(u_\pi - m_1 S_W V_\pi) + m_1(m_1 S_0 - S_1 m_0)\gamma_\pi]\left(\frac{\delta\hat{\pi}}{\pi}\right)$$
$$+ (m_1 S_1)\,\delta\hat{r}_1 + (m_1 S_0)\,\delta\bar{r}_0 - m_1(1 - S_Y)\,\delta\bar{D}$$
$$- (N_Y)\,\delta\bar{G}_1 - (\delta c_1^f - \delta c_{01})$$
$$+ m_1(m_1 S_0 - S_1 m_0)\gamma_\pi[(\phi_0)\,\delta\bar{r}_0 + (\phi_B)\,\delta\bar{B}_1^c + (\phi_D)\,\delta\bar{D}$$
$$+ (\phi_G)\,\delta\bar{G}_1 - (\phi_C)(\delta c_1^f - \delta c_{01})]$$
$$- m_1^2(S_0 + S_1)\gamma_p[(\alpha_0)\,\delta\bar{r}_0 + (\alpha_B)\,\delta\bar{B}_1^c + (\alpha_D)\,\delta\bar{D}$$
$$+ (\alpha_G)\,\delta\bar{G}_1]$$
$$+ (m_1 S_W)\,\delta W^{hs} = 0$$

where α_0, α_B, α_D, and α_G are the proportionate changes in the expected price of the export good, p_1^e, brought about by the exogenous disturbances and are defined in full in Table 9.1,[16] and where

$$N_e = (u_t + \sigma_1 N_Y) + \gamma_p[m_1^2(S_0 + S_1)] > 0$$

Combining Eqs. (9.11), (9.12), and (9.13) with the usual relationship between p_1 and Y,

$$(9.14) \quad \delta\hat{Y} = (\sigma_1/N_e H_e)\{[u_\pi(B_{10}L_{11} - L_{10}B_{11}) + m_1 V_\pi(H_0)]$$
$$- m_0 m_1(S_0 + S_1)\gamma_\pi(B_{10}L_{11} - L_{10}B_{11}) + \gamma_\pi(N_{\pi e})\phi_0$$
$$+ \gamma_p[m_1^2(S_0 + S_1)H_e]\alpha_0\}\,\delta\bar{r}_0$$

[16] Because shifts in demand have no permanent effects on p_1, there is no α_C.

$$+ (\sigma_1/N_eH_e)\{[m_1V_\pi S_1(L_{1W} + B_{1W}) - B_{01}(u_\pi - m_1V_\pi S_W)]$$
$$- m_1\gamma_\pi[(m_1S_0 - S_1m_0)B_{01} + S_1(B_{10} + L_{10})]$$
$$+ \gamma_\pi(N_{\pi e})\phi_B + \gamma_p[m_1^2(S_0 + S_1)H_e]\alpha_B\} \, \delta\bar{B}_1^c$$
$$+ (\sigma_1/N_eH_e)\{m_1(1 - S_Y)H_e + \gamma_\pi(N_{\pi e})\phi_D$$
$$+ \gamma_p[m_1^2(S_0 + S_1)H_e]\alpha_D\} \, \delta\bar{D}$$
$$+ (\sigma_1/N_eH_e)\{N_YH_e + \gamma_\pi(N_{\pi e})\phi_G$$
$$+ \gamma_p[m_1^2(S_0 + S_1)H_e]\alpha_G\} \, \delta\bar{G}_1$$
$$+ (\sigma_1/N_eH_e)[H_e - \gamma_\pi(N_{\pi e})\phi_C](\delta c_1^c - \delta c_{01})$$
$$- (\sigma_1/N_eH_e)\{u_\pi(H_\pi) - \gamma_\pi[m_1(H_0)$$
$$+ m_0m_1(S_0 + S_1)H_\pi]\} \, \delta W^{hs}$$

where

$$N_{\pi e} = u_\pi(B_{10}L_{11} - L_{10}B_{11}) + m_1V_\pi[H_0 + m_0(S_0 + S_1)H_\pi] > 0$$

The signs of these results are shown in Table 9.2. For two disturbances, changes in the foreign interest rate and shifts in demand, they become ambiguous with nonneutral expectations. For all others, they are the same as they were in the standard version of the model.[17]

The proof of stability follows directly. Differentiating Eq. (9.2′) with respect to W^{hs} and using Eqs. (9.11), (9.12), and (9.14) to replace terms involving changes in r_1, π, and Y,

$$(9.15) \quad \frac{\delta\dot{W}^{hs}}{\delta W^{hs}} = -(1/N_eH_e)\{u_\pi(H_\pi)[\sigma_1S_Y + \gamma_pm_1(S_0 + S_1)]$$
$$+ \gamma_\pi(u_t + \sigma_1m_0)[H_0 + m_0(S_0 + S_1)H_\pi]\} < 0$$

which is, we said, sufficient for stability when expectations are formed hyperopically. (Note that the coefficients ϕ_j and α_j do not appear in the proof of stability. By implication, saving would go to zero even if households' forecasts were not perfectly accurate. The state to which the economy would converge, however, is one where households would continue to expect changes in π and p_1, and those expectations would not be fulfilled. Eventually, then, households would revise their expectations, and with each such revision, the economy would move closer to the "true" steady state in which expectations are fulfilled.)

Implications of nonneutral expectations

The short-run solutions furnished above allow us to answer the three questions posed at the start of this chapter concerning the effects of ex-

---

[17] To show that an open-market purchase raises income, it must be shown that $-m_1\gamma_\pi[(m_1S_0 - S_1m_0)B_{01} + S_1(B_{10} + L_{10})] > 0$. But this expression can be rewritten as $m_1\gamma_\pi[m_1(S_0 + S_1)(-B_{01}) + S_1(B_{00} + B_{01})]$, and it is positive because $B_{00} > -B_{01} > 0$.

pectations based on hyperopic forecasting, the extent to which they may be stabilizing, and the extent to which asset-market integration affects the functioning of speculation. Rather than answering them one by one, however, or for each disturbance and policy change, we review sequentially the behavior of the principal endogenous variables –the exchange rate, interest rate, price level, and income.

The exchange rate

In all five cases analyzed above, the short-run change in the exchange rate has the same sign as the long-run change. With a shift of demand to the export good, for example, the home currency appreciates at once, which is what it must do eventually in order to restore steady-state equilibrium. In all other cases, it depreciates at once, which is what it must do eventually. The reason for this outcome is obvious. The expectation of an increase in π, based on hyperopic foresight, raises the expected rate of return on the foreign bond, raising the demand for the bond itself, and thus raising the demand for foreign currency to buy the bond. The home currency depreciates at once to clear the foreign-exchange market.

In three of the five cases, the two fiscal policies and the shift in demand, the short-run change in π is unambiguously larger than with neutral expectations, because there was *no* change in π with neutral expectations. In the other cases, an increase in the foreign interest rate and an open-market purchase, the short-run change in π can be either larger or smaller than with neutral expectations.[18] In every instance, however, speculation based on hyperopic foresight can be said to stabilize the exchange rate. It narrows the gap between the immediate change in the rate and the one required in the long run, regardless of the sign of that gap.

To prove this last assertion, we rewrite Eq. (9.12) with the aid of Eq. (3.3a), which defined the short-run change in the exchange rate under neutral expectations:[19]

$$(9.12') \quad \left[\left(\frac{\delta\hat{\pi}}{\pi}\right) - \left(\frac{d\pi}{\pi}\right)\right] = (H_\pi V_\pi/H_e)\left[\left(\frac{\delta\pi}{\pi}\right) - \left(\frac{d\pi}{\pi}\right)\right]$$

[18] With an increase in $\bar{r}_0$, for example, Eqs. (9.12) and (3.3a) say that $[(\delta\hat{\pi}/\pi) - (\delta\pi/\pi)] = [\gamma_\pi(B_{10}L_{11} - L_{10}B_{11})/H_e]\{\phi_0 - [(B_{10}L_{11} - L_{10}B_{11})/H_\pi V_\pi]\}\delta\bar{r}_0$, and $\phi_0 \gtrless [(B_{10}L_{11} - L_{10}B_{11})/H_\pi V_\pi]$. With an open-market purchase, the result is similar.

[19] From Eq. (3.3a), $(\delta\pi/\pi) = (1/H_\pi V_\pi)[(B_{10}L_{11} - L_{10}B_{11})\delta\bar{r}_0 - (B_{01})\delta\bar{B}_1^c]$, so that Eq. (9.12) can be written as $(\delta\hat{\pi}/\pi) = (H_\pi V_\pi/H_e)(\delta\pi/\pi) + [\gamma_\pi(B_{10}L_{11} - L_{10}B_{11})/H_e](d\pi/\pi)$, and $[\gamma_\pi(B_{10}L_{11} - L_{10}B_{11})/H_e] = 1 - (H_\pi V_\pi/H_e)$, from which we obtain Eq. (9.12') directly.

Because $0 < (H_\pi V_\pi / H_e) < 1$ when $\gamma_\pi > 0$, there will be "overshooting" with nonneutral expectations when there was overshooting with neutral expectations, but the former must always be smaller than the latter. Symmetrical results obtain with "undershooting" in the short run. The reason, once again, is obvious. Suppose that a disturbance or policy change causes the home currency to depreciate too much with neutral expectations (that there is overshooting in the short run). When households have hyperopic foresight, they know that the home currency is certain to appreciate eventually, causing them to suffer capital losses on the foreign bond. The expected rate of return is reduced. Households attempt to sell foreign bonds and convert the proceeds into home currency. They raise the demand for the home currency, curtailing the initial depreciation.

Speculation will be more effective in limiting overshooting and undershooting the greater the speed with which the actual exchange rate is expected to approach its long-run level. Define by Δ the ratio $[(\delta\hat{\pi}/\pi) - (d\pi/\pi)]/[(\delta\pi/\pi) - (d\pi/\pi)]$, so that a reduction in Δ testifies to a decline in overshooting or undershooting as the case may be. Equation (9.12') can then be rewritten as

(9.12″) $\Delta = (H_\pi V_\pi / H_e)$

and it can be differentiated with respect to γ_π, the expected speed of adjustment of the exchange rate:

$$(\delta\Delta/\delta\gamma_\pi) = -\Delta(B_{10}L_{11} - L_{10}B_{11})/H_e < 0$$

Speculation is more strongly stabilizing the more rapid the expected speed of adjustment.[20]

An increase in the degree of asset-market integration has the same effect. Assuming, as usual, that $-B_{01}$ and $-B_{10}$ change at the same rates, we can show that the ratio Δ varies inversely with $-B_{01}$ when bonds are gross substitutes (when $B_{11} > -B_{01} > 0$). An increase of substitutability enlarges the reduction in demand for the foreign bond when the home currency depreciates too much, raising the increase in demand for the home currency. Accordingly, speculation limits more effectively the initial depreciation.

Note carefully, however, the form of this last finding. It deals only with the influence of asset-market integration on the difference between out-

[20] If the exchange rate were expected to move instantaneously to its steady-state level, that is what would happen. As $\gamma_\pi \to \infty$, $\Delta \to 0$. This is not to say, however, that the *economy* moves at once to its steady state. Saving or dissaving may be needed to bring the stock of wealth to its steady-state level, and saving can take place only through time.

comes under nonneutral and neutral expectations. It does not deal with the influence of asset-market integration on the *absolute* amounts of over-shooting or undershooting that take place in the short run. The influence on these absolute amounts depends on the way that asset-market integration affects the difference $[(\delta\pi/\pi) - (d\pi/\pi)]$ as well as on the way that it affects the ratio Δ. Consider, for example, the short-run response of the exchange rate to an open-market purchase. In Chapter 5 we saw that there can be either overshooting or undershooting when expectations are neutral. The same possibilities have therefore to exist when expectations are nonneutral; this is the point made by Eq. (9.12′). The influence of asset-market integration, moreover, depends on the nature of the outcome. If there is undershooting in the short run, an increase of substitutability between the two bonds reduces the amount of undershooting absolutely. Speculation is strongly stabilizing. If there is overshooting in the short run, however, an increase of substitutability *raises* the amount of overshooting absolutely.[21] Speculation is still stabilizing; there is less overshooting than with neutral expectations and the same degree of asset-market integration. But an increase of asset-market integration enlarges the task of stabilization by more than it enhances the capacity of speculation to perform that task.

The interest rate

In all five cases analyzed above, the short-run change in the domestic interest rate is ambiguous. The term $(L_{10}B_{1W} - B_{10}L_{1W})$ figures in each argument of Eq. (9.11), and none of the assumptions made about the demands for bonds and money helps us to determine the sign of this expres-

[21] From Eq. (9.12) and Table 9.1,

$$\left[\left(\frac{\delta\hat{\pi}}{\pi}\right) - \left(\frac{d\pi}{\pi}\right)\right] = (1/\sigma_1 u_\pi)(1/H_e)\{(-B_{01})[\sigma_1 u_\pi + V_\pi(S_W/S_Y)(u_t + \sigma_1 m_0)]$$

$$- V_\pi(S_1/S_Y)(L_{1W} + B_{1W})(u_t + \sigma_1 m_0)\} \, \delta\bar{B}_1^c$$

In the initial steady state, however, $V_\pi = B_{0W}W^h = -B_{0W}(S_Y/S_W)Y^d$, so that $[\sigma_1 u_\pi + V_\pi(S_W/S_Y)(u_t + \sigma_1 m_0)] = [\sigma_1 u_\pi - B_{0W}(u_t + \sigma_1 m_0)Y^d]$, which can be shown to be positive using the relationships given in Appendix C to prove that $[\sigma_1 u_\pi - (u_t + \sigma_1 m_0)Y^d] = u_t(a_1 p_1 Q_1 + b_1 G_1) > 0$ and remembering that $B_{0W} < 1$. Thus, the entire expression for $[(\delta\hat{\pi}/\pi) - (d\pi/\pi)]$ is ambiguous (there can be undershooting or overshooting in the short run). Differentiating the argument of that expression with respect to the degree of substitutability, we obtain $(1/\sigma_1 u_\pi)(1/H_e^2)\{V_\pi(S_1/S_Y)(L_{1W} + B_{1W})(u_t + \sigma_1 m_0)[V_\pi(L_{1W}) - \gamma_\pi(L_{11} + L_{10})] - L_{11}[V_\pi(L_{1W} + B_{1W}) + \gamma_\pi(B_{00} + B_{01})][\sigma_1 u_\pi - B_{0W}(u_t + \sigma_1 m_0)Y^d]\}$, which is unambiguously positive because $B_{00} > -B_{01} > 0$. Thus, an increase in substitutability raises $[(\delta\hat{\pi}/\pi) - (d\pi/\pi)]$ for an open-market purchase; it reduces undershooting absolutely but increases overshooting absolutely.

sion. It will be positive if $(B_{10}/L_{10}) > (B_{1W}/L_{1W})$, which is to say that the demand for the domestic bond is relatively sensitive to a change in the foreign interest rate and relatively insensitive to a change in wealth, compared to the demand for money. But we have had no reason to make this supposition heretofore and will have no reason to do so hereafter.

What is the economic meaning of this ambiguity? Suppose that households forecast a depreciation of the home currency (that π^e rises). The reason does not matter. The anticipation of depreciation raises the expected rate of return on the foreign bond, raising the demand for that bond and reducing demands for the domestic bond and money. The reduction in demand for the domestic bond relative to the reduction in demand for money will be proportional to (B_{10}/L_{10}), the ratio of responses of the two demands to an increase in the expected return on the foreign bond. The increase in demand for the foreign bond will cause an immediate depreciation of the home currency, conferring capital gains on holders of the foreign bond, raising wealth, and raising demands for the domestic bond and money. The increase in demand for the domestic bond relative to the increase in demand for money will be proportional to (B_{1W}/L_{1W}), the ratio of responses of the two demands to the wealth-increasing effect of the depreciation. There is thus a special case, where $(B_{10}/L_{10}) = (B_{1W}/L_{1W})$, in which the depreciation will clear the markets for the domestic bond and money without any change in the domestic interest rate. But when, instead, $(B_{10}/L_{10}) < (B_{1W}/L_{1W})$, the depreciation will produce excess demand in the bond market and excess supply in the money market. The domestic interest rate must decline to clear both markets. Conversely, when $(B_{10}/L_{10}) > (B_{1W}/L_{1W})$, there will be excess demand in the money market and excess supply in the bond market. The domestic interest rate must rise.

There is little to be gained by examining further the sizes of the changes in r_1 relative to those with neutral expectations or to those occurring in the long run. It is worth noting, however, what happens with perfect asset-market integration. Under neutral expectations, perfect integration prevents any change in the domestic interest rate unless there is a change in the foreign rate (which causes the domestic rate to change by the same amount). This turns out to be a special case of a general interest-parity condition that holds when expectations are not neutral—a condition used extensively in work on expectations and exchange-rate speculation. Under nonneutral expectations, perfect integration guarantees equality between the change in the expected rate of return on the domestic bond and the change in the expected rate of return on the foreign bond. When

$-B_{01} \to \infty$ and $-B_{01} \to \infty$, Eq. (9.11) reduces to

$$\delta \hat{r}_1 = (1/H_e^*)\{L_{1W}V_\pi(1 + \gamma_\pi \phi_0^*)\, \delta \bar{r}_0 - \gamma_\pi(1 - L_{1W}V_\pi \phi_B^*)\, \delta \bar{B}_1^c$$
$$+ \gamma_\pi L_{1W} V_\pi [(\phi_D^*)\, \delta \bar{D} + (\phi_G^*)\, \delta \bar{G}_1 - (\phi_C^*)(\delta c_1^f - \delta c_{01})]\}$$

where

$$H_e^* = L_{1W}V_\pi - \gamma_\pi(L_{11} + L_{10}) > 0$$

and the ϕ_j^* are the changes in π^e when the foreign and domestic bonds are perfect substitutes. In this same limiting case, however, Eq. (9.12) reduces to

$$\left(\frac{\delta \hat{\pi}}{\pi}\right) = -(1/H_e^*)\{(L_{11} + L_{10})(1 + \gamma_\pi \phi_0^*)\, \delta \bar{r}_0 + [\gamma_\pi(L_{11} + L_{10})\phi_B^* - 1]\, \delta \bar{B}_1^c$$
$$+ \gamma_\pi(L_{11} + L_{10})[(\phi_D^*)\, \delta \bar{D} + (\phi_G^*)\, \delta \bar{G}_1 - (\phi_C^*)(\delta c_1^f - \delta c_{01})]\}$$

And when these two equations are combined,

$$\delta \hat{r}_1 = \delta \bar{r}_0 + \gamma_\pi \left[\phi_j^* - \left(\frac{\delta \hat{\pi}}{\pi}\right)\right] = \delta \bar{r}_0 + \left(\frac{\dot{\pi}^e}{\pi}\right)$$

The change in the domestic interest rate is always equal to the change in the foreign rate *plus* the expected rate of depreciation of the home currency.[22]

Taking the analysis one step further, when expectations are nonneutral and asset markets are perfectly integrated, an increase in $\bar{r}_0$ will cause r_1 to rise, but the short-run increase in r_1 will be smaller than the increase in $\bar{r}_0$. An increase in $\bar{r}_0$ will cause the home currency to depreciate too much (to overshoot its long-run equilibrium level) and will thereby generate expectations of an appreciation.[23] Analogously, it can be shown that r_1 will fall in response to an open-market purchase, despite perfect asset-market integration, because the home currency will depreciate too much. A budget deficit, by contrast, will not affect r_1, whereas an increase in $\bar{G}_1$ will cause r_1 to rise, and a shift in demand to the export good will cause it to fall.

---

[22] If our model contained a forward foreign-exchange market populated by risk-neutral *arbitrageurs*, the forward discount on the domestic currency would equal $(\dot{\pi}^e/\pi)$, and the *covered* interest parity condition would hold too. (But see note 2 to Chapter 2.)

[23] From Table 9.1, $\phi_0^* = [(u_t + \sigma_1 m_0)/u_\pi \sigma_1 L_{1W} S_Y][S_W(L_{11} + L_{10}) - (S_0 + S_1)L_{1W}] > 0$, from which it follows that r_1 rises immediately with an increase in $\bar{r}_0$. Furthermore,

$$\delta \hat{r}_1 - \delta \bar{r}_0 = (\gamma_\pi/\sigma_1 u_\pi S_Y)(1/H_e^*)\{S_Y(L_{11} + L_{10})[\sigma_1 u_\pi - B_{0W}(u_t + \sigma_1 m_0)Y^d]$$
$$- L_{1W}V_\pi(u_t + \sigma_1 m_0)(S_1 + S_0)\}\, \delta \bar{r}_0 < 0$$

because we have already seen that $\sigma_1 u_\pi > B_{0W}(u_t + \sigma_1 m_0)Y^d$ in the initial steady state (see note 21).

The price level and income

Under neutral expectations, all five disturbances raise the price of the export good immediately and serve therefore to raise nominal income. Under nonneutral expectations based on hyperopic foresight, the effects on p_1 and Y are ambiguous in two instances – a change in the foreign interest rate and a shift in demand. The sizes of the other changes, moreover, are hard to compare with those that occur under neutral expectations.

The complications introduced by nonneutral expectations are not due to the influence of price expectations. Looking at the arguments of Eq. (9.14), which give the changes in p_1, as well as those in Y, we see that an increase in p_1^e, the expected price of the export good, always serves to raise the actual price. Its effect is measured in each instance by the term $\gamma_p[m_1^2(S_0 + S_1)/N_e]\alpha_j$, for $j = 0, B, D$, and G,[24] and can be rewritten as $[m_1(S_0 + S_1)/N_e][m_1\gamma_p(\delta p_1^e/p_1)]$. The term $[m_1\gamma_p(\delta p_1^e/p_1)]$ is the positive effect of an increase in p_1^e on the expected inflation rate, and therefore its negative effect on the real interest rates (given the nominal rates). The other term, $[m_1(S_0 + S_1)/N_e]$, measures the increase in the demand for the export good that is the result of the decline in the incentive to save.

The complications that crop up in Eq. (9.14) are due to the effects of exchange-rate expectations. What are these effects and how do they show up? An increase in π^e has its own effects on incentives to save, and these are ambiguous. On the one hand, an increase in π^e raises the expected level of p_0, the home-currency price of the imported good, raising the expected inflation rate, reducing real interest rates, and depressing saving. This effect can be written in a form resembling the expression for the analogous effect of an increase in p_1^e. It is $\gamma_\pi[m_0m_1(S_0 + S_1)/N_e]\phi_j$, for $j = 0, B, D, G$, and C, or $[m_1(S_0 + S_1)/N_e][m_0\gamma_\pi(\delta\pi^e/\pi)]$. On the other hand, an increase in π^e raises the expected rate of return on the foreign bond, which increases the incentive to save. This effect takes the form $-(m_1S_0/N_e) \times [\gamma_\pi(\delta\pi^e/\pi)]$. The sum of these direct effects turns out to be $[m_1(m_0S_1 - m_1S_0)/N_e][\gamma_\pi(\delta\pi^e/\pi)]$, which is ambiguous.[25]

Remember, moreover, that an increase in the expected exchange rate

[24] Recall that $\alpha_C = 0$, which is to say that p_1^e is not affected by a shift in demand to the export good, because the long-run level of p_1 is not affected.

[25] We have no reason to assume that $m_0S_1 = m_1S_0$ (that there is some sort of symmetry or similarity of the type invoked when we assumed that $S_1L_{10} = S_0L_{11}$). The parameters m_0 and m_1 define the effects of changes in consumption on demands for the import and export goods. The parameters S_0 and S_1 define the effects of changes in foreign and domestic interest rates on desired saving. We have assumed that S_0 and S_1 depend on the weights assigned to foreign and domestic bonds in households' portfolios, but there need be no relationship between m_0, the propensity to consume the import good, and the size of holdings of the foreign bond.

raises the actual exchange rate immediately. Hence, it has a number of indirect effects on the demand for the export good and its price, p_1. First, an increase in π has effects on saving that are the same in form but opposite in sign to the direct effects of the increase in π^e. (We have seen, however, that the increase in π will be smaller than the increase in π^e, holding all else constant, so that the net effect on saving via S_0 and S_1 will be same-signed but smaller than the one derived above.) Second, an increase in π has effects on the demand for the domestic good by way of its effect on wealth. By conferring capital gains on holders of the foreign bond, it reduces saving and stimulates absorption. Third, an increase in π has an expenditure-switching effect. It shifts domestic and foreign demands to the export good.

Remember, finally, that an increase in π^e has ambiguous effects on the nominal interest rate, r_1, and this is yet another indirect effect on desired saving, absorption, and the demand for the export good.

With all of these effects occurring at once, it is perhaps surprising that there are few ambiguities in the outcomes shown by Eq. (9.14).

There are, we saw, no doubts about the changes in p_1 resulting from an open-market purchase, a tax cut leading to a budget deficit, and a balanced-budget increase in government spending. Each enlarges the demand for the export good, raising p_1 and Y. In the first two instances, however, we cannot know how nonneutral expectations influence the *sizes* of the changes in p_1, whereas in the third it can be shown that the increase in p_1 is larger than with neutral expectations.

The sign of the change in p_1 is ambiguous when there is an increase in the foreign interest rate, and we can show that the ambiguity is due to exchange-rate speculation. Rewriting the relevant portion of Eq. (9.14),

$$\left(\frac{\delta \hat{p}_1}{p_1}\right) = (1/N_e)\{(1/H_e)[u_\pi(B_{10}L_{11} - L_{10}B_{11})$$

$$+ \, m_1 V_\pi(H_0)](1 + \gamma_\pi \phi_0) + \gamma_p[m_1^2(S_0 + S_1)]\alpha_0\} \, \delta \bar{r}_0$$

$$- \, [m_0 m_1(S_0 + S_1)/N_e]\gamma_\pi \left[\left(\frac{\delta \hat{\pi}}{\pi}\right) - \left(\frac{d\pi}{\pi}\right)\right]$$

Thus, p_1 and Y would rise in the short run if there were no overshooting in the foreign-exchange market [if $(\delta \hat{\pi}/\pi) \leqslant (d\pi/\pi)$]. But this is not the case, so $(\dot{\pi}^e/\pi)$ is negative.[26] Wealth holders come to forecast an appreci-

---

[26] To prove that the exchange rate overshoots in the short run, use Eq. (9.12) and Table 9.1 to form $[(\delta \hat{\pi}/\pi) - (d\pi/\pi)] = (1/H_e)[(B_{10}L_{11} - L_{10}B_{11})(1 + \gamma_\pi \phi_0) - (H_e)\phi_0] \, \delta \bar{r}_0$. Invoking the initial steady-state condition that $V_\pi = -B_{0W}(S_Y/S_W)Y^d$ and the definition of ϕ_0

ation of the home currency, which has the effect of reducing the demand for the export good, by raising real interest rates and thus stimulating saving.

The other ambiguity arises in connection with shifts in domestic and foreign demands to the export good. Under neutral expectations, these shifts raised p_1 and Y immediately but not permanently. There was "insulation" in the new steady state, in that p_1 and Y returned to their initial levels. Under nonneutral expectations based on hyperopic forecasting, insulation is anticipated. There is no expectation of a permanent increase in p_1, but the home currency appreciates at once, because households know that it must do so eventually. Accordingly, three forces come into play: (1) The expected rate of return on the foreign bond is reduced. (2) Holders of that bond suffer capital losses and a reduction in their wealth. (3) Domestic and foreign demands are switched from the export good to the import good. The first effect reduces the incentive to save; the second raises it. The third or expenditure-switching effect, however, can be large enough by itself to swamp the demand-increasing effect of the initial shift in demand. Therefore, the price p_1 will rise by less than with neutral expectations and can even fall. Algebraically,

$$\left[\left(\frac{\delta \hat{p}_1}{p_1}\right) - \left(\frac{\delta p_1}{p_1}\right)\right] = -(1/N_e)\{\gamma_\pi(N_{\pi e}/H_e)\phi_C$$
$$+ \gamma_p[m_1^2(S_0 + S_1)/(u_t + \sigma_1 N_Y)]\}(\delta c_1^f - \delta c_{01}$$

By implication $(\delta p_1/p_1) > (\delta \hat{p}_1/p_1) \gtreqless 0$.

Can we say anything about the effects of hyperopic forecasting on the amounts of overshooting and undershooting in the goods market? In two cases, yes. In the other three, no. We have already seen that an increase in $\bar{G}_1$ causes a larger increase in p_1 with nonneutral expectations than with neutral expectations. We have also seen that a shift in demand to the domestic good causes a smaller increase in p_1 with nonneutral expectations. Therefore, an increase in $\bar{G}_1$ must cause less undershooting with nonneutral expectations (and can even cause overshooting), and a shift in demand to the domestic good must cause less overshooting (and can cause undershooting).

in Table 9.1,

$$\left[\left(\frac{\delta \hat{\pi}}{\pi}\right) - \left(\frac{d\pi}{\pi}\right)\right] = (1/u_\pi \sigma_1 H_e)\{(B_{10}L_{11} - L_{10}B_{11})[\sigma_1 u_\pi - B_{0W}(u_t + \sigma_1 m_0)Y^d]$$
$$+ V_\pi(u_t + \sigma_1 m_0)(L_{1W}/S_Y)(S_0 B_{11} - B_{10}S_1)\} \delta \bar{r}_0$$

so that $(\delta \hat{\pi}/\pi) > (d\pi/\pi)$, because $\sigma_1 u_\pi > B_{0W}(u_t + \sigma_1 m_0) Y^d$ in the initial steady state (see note 21).

To see why we cannot say much about the other cases, let us transform Eq. (9.14), using Eqs. (7.21), (7.22a), and Table 9.1:

$$(9.14') \quad \left[\left(\frac{\delta \hat{p}_1}{p_1}\right) - \left(\frac{dp_1}{p_1}\right)\right] = (1/N_e)\left\{(u_t + \sigma_1 N_Y)\left[\left(\frac{\delta p_1}{p_1}\right) - \left(\frac{dp_1}{p_1}\right)\right]\right.$$
$$\left. - \gamma_\pi (N_{\pi e}/H_e)\left[\left(\frac{\delta \pi}{\pi}\right) - \left(\frac{d\pi}{\pi}\right)\right]\right\}$$

With nonneutral expectations, p_1 overshoots its long-run value if it would have done so with neutral expectations and the exchange rate would *not* have done so. This combination of conditions can occur, however, only in connection with a tax cut, and need not occur even in that case. (Under neutral expectations, a tax cut can cause p_1 to overshoot or undershoot its long-run value. The short-run price change depends on the goods-market effects of the tax cut, the long-run change depends on the asset-market effects of the permanent increase in B_1, and there is no neat relationship between them. But the exchange rate will never overshoot its long-run level, because it does not change at all in the short run and must depreciate in the long run.)

With an increase in $\bar{r}_0$ or an open-market purchase, by contrast, there is a strict relationship between the short-run changes in p_1 and π:

$$\left[\left(\frac{\delta p_1}{p_1}\right) - \left(\frac{dp_1}{p_1}\right)\right] = [u_\pi/(u_t + \sigma_1 N_Y)]\left[\left(\frac{\delta \pi}{\pi}\right) - \left(\frac{d\pi}{\pi}\right)\right]$$

When π overshoots with neutral expectations following an increase in $\bar{r}_0$ or an open-market purchase, p_1 will do so too. Combining this condition with Eq. (9.14'),

$$(9.14'') \quad \left[\left(\frac{\delta \hat{p}_1}{p_1}\right) - \left(\frac{dp_1}{p_1}\right)\right] = (1/N_e H_e)[u_\pi(H_e) - \gamma_\pi(N_{\pi e})]\left[\left(\frac{\delta \pi}{\pi}\right) - \left(\frac{d\pi}{\pi}\right)\right]$$

and $u_\pi(H_e) \gtrless \gamma_\pi(N_{\pi e})$. When expectations are nonneutral, there is no way to forecast the size of the short-run change in p_1 compared to the long-run change, even when we know what would occur with neutral expectations. Households' views about the rate of change of the exchange rate, represented by γ_π, affect the result.[27]

Finally, let us show how the responses of goods markets are affected by the households' views about the rates of change in p_1 and π, using Eq.

---

[27] When there is overshooting in the foreign-exchange market, there will be overshooting in the goods market too if $u_\pi(H_e) > \gamma_\pi(N_{\pi e})$, and this condition will be satisfied if $\gamma_\pi < u_\pi/[m_1(H_0/H_\pi) + m_0 m_1(S_0 + S_1)]$. It is thus the more likely to be satisfied the slower the expected speed of adjustment of the exchange rate.

(9.14′) and denoting by Γ the amount of overshooting in the goods market, $[(\delta\hat{p}_1/p_1) - (dp_1/p_1)]$.[28]

Differentiating with respect to γ_p, the expected speed of adjustment of the price p_1,

$$(\delta\Gamma/\delta\gamma_p) = -[m_1^2(S_0 + S_1)/N_e]\,\Gamma$$

The greater the anticipated speed of adjustment of p_1, the smaller the amount of overshooting or undershooting (whichever is taking place). If households expect p_1 to move rapidly to its long-run level, their behavior will help it to do so. Differentiating with respect to γ_π, the expected speed of adjustment of π, and invoking Eq. (9.12′).

$$(\delta\Gamma/\delta\gamma_\pi) = -(N_{\pi e}/N_e H_e) \left[\left(\frac{\delta\hat{\pi}}{\pi}\right) - \left(\frac{d\pi}{\pi}\right)\right]$$

With overshooting in the foreign-exchange market under nonneutral expectations, p_1 will rise by less, compared to its long-run level, the greater the expected speed of adjustment of the exchange rate. There will thus be less overshooting but more undershooting in the goods market. With undershooting in the foreign-exchange market, by contrast, p_1 will rise by more, compared to its long-run level. There will thus be more overshooting but less undershooting in the goods market.

Conclusions

In what ways do expectations and speculation modify our chief results for the flexible-rate case? When expectations are based on hyperopic foresight, they do not affect our principal findings about the exchange rate itself. Speculation is stabilizing, however, in that it reduces the gaps between impact and steady-state changes in π. But two of our findings about goods markets are called into question. With neutral expectations, an increase in the foreign interest rate causes an immediate increase in income. With nonneutral expectations, this may not happen. The depreciation of the home currency may be smaller than with neutral expectations and may not stimulate demand sufficiently to offset the direct deflationary impact of the increase in $\bar{r}_0$. With neutral expectations, moreover, a shift of demand to the export good causes an immediate increase in income,

---

[28] Although Eq. (9.14′) was developed to explore responses to changes in $\bar{D}$ (and B_1), $\bar{r}_0$, and $\bar{B}_1^c$, it is perfectly general and can thus be used here too. One has only to remember that $(dp_1/p_1) = 0$ for shifts in demands and that $(\delta\pi/\pi) = 0$ for changes in $\bar{D}$ and $\bar{G}_1$, as well as for shifts in demands.

and this may not happen with nonneutral expectations. There will be an immediate appreciation of the home currency, in anticipation of the permanent appreciation that "insulates" goods markets in the long run. The short-run change in income is thus limited and can even be reversed. It should be noted, however, that the effects of fiscal and monetary policies are not altered in any significant way. Finally, it is impossible to forecast the effect of any disturbance on the domestic interest rate, because we cannot know how exchange-rate expectations affect the demands for the domestic bond and money. The ambiguities are resolved only in the limiting case of perfect asset-market integration. When the two bonds in our model are perfect substitutes, the open interest-parity condition holds. The difference between changes in r_1 and $\bar{r}_0$ must equal the expected rate of depreciation of the home currency. This result is not new or exceptional but holds only with perfect asset-market integration.

10

On the specification of fiscal policy

Introduction

In all other chapters of this book, the government's budget deficit is exogenous. The lump-sum tax, T^h, is adjusted continuously to maintain a balanced budget or the deficit selected for policy purposes. Under this specification, the supply of domestic bonds is likewise exogenous. This description of fiscal policy is excessively simple and not the one most frequently employed. It is more common to assume that the government selects a level of expenditure in nominal or real terms together with an income tax (plus, possibly, a lump-sum tax). The budget deficit is made to be endogenous, because income-tax collections are endogenous, and so is the supply of government bonds. For purposes of short-run analysis, at least, this income-tax specification represents reality more closely than the specification adopted in this book.

In this chapter we introduce an income tax into the standard version of our model in order to compare patterns of behavior when the budget deficit is endogenous with those when it is exogenous. We study the responses to fiscal policies – a balanced-budget increase in government expenditure and a tax reduction – and the responses to an open-market purchase. We show that short-run outcomes do not differ markedly under alternative tax specifications but that long-run outcomes differ fundamentally. The differences in long-run outcomes lead us to suggest that the exogenous-deficit specification is preferable for certain purposes to the more familiar endogenous-deficit specification.[1]

When working with an exogenous deficit, we have made it return to zero eventually, because a balanced budget is required for the economy to reach a stationary state. But the budget must be balanced eventually even when the deficit is endogenous. The supply of bonds must come to be con-

[1] The analysis in this chapter condenses one presented in P. R. Allen, "Financing Budget Deficits: The Effects on Income in Closed and Open Economies," *European Economic Review*, 10 (1977), pp. 345–73. It should be noted that we deal here only with the case in which deficits are financed by issuing bonds. The case in which they are financed by issuing money is analyzed briefly in Appendix D.

stant, regardless of the way in which it is determined. When the budget deficit is endogenous, however, two new phenomena take place in the economy. First, the supply of bonds is affected by any disturbance that influences income. Even one that starts out in goods markets impinges directly on asset markets because it affects nominal income, tax receipts, the budget, and the supply of bonds. Second, the budget must move into balance endogenously if the economy is to reach a steady state, and the way in which it does so has important implications for the long-run level of nominal income–a point stressed in several recent papers.

Early analyses of this issue, in the context of a closed economy, defined the budget as the difference between expenditures, G_1, and income-tax collections, τY.[2] Under this definition, steady-state income must equal the ratio of government spending to the tax rate. In a more recent treatment of the problem, Blinder and Solow added interest payments on the government debt, $r_1(B_1 - B_1^c)$, to the budget, and they showed that the behavior of those interest payments is important for stability and for long-run outcomes. Steady-state income is affected by the way in which a budget deficit is financed–whether by issuing bonds or money–as well as by the level of government spending and the tax rate.[3]

Other authors have examined an endogenous deficit in the context of an open economy, and some have come to an intriguing conclusion. A balanced budget may not be required in the stationary state; a continuing budget deficit can be offset by a current-account deficit, and income can be constant.[4] But this conclusion has been challenged by Turnovsky; in an open economy with a pegged exchange rate, income can be constant only in a few special cases.[5] Turnovsky also shows that domestic and

[2] See, for example, C. F. Christ, "A Simple Macroeconomic Model with a Government Budget Restraint," *Journal of Political Economy*, 76 (January/February 1968), pp. 52–67, D. J. Ott and A. Ott, "Budget Balance and Equilibrium Income," *Journal of Finance*, 20 (March 1965), pp. 71–7, and W. L. Silber, "Fiscal Policy in IS-LM Analysis–A Correction," *Journal of Money, Credit and Banking*, 2 (November 1970), pp. 461–72.

[3] A. S. Blinder and R. M. Solow, "Does Fiscal Policy Matter?," *Journal of Public Economics*, 2 (November 1973), pp. 319–38, which anticipates most of the results obtained below for the closed economy (and those in Appendix D).

[4] See, for example, W. E. Oates, "Budget Balance and Equilibrium Income: A Comment on the Efficiency of Fiscal and Monetary Policy in an Open Economy," *Journal of Finance*, 21 (September 1966), pp. 489–98, R. I. McKinnon and W. E. Oates, *The Implications of International Economic Integration for Monetary, Fiscal, and Exchange-Rate Policy*, Princeton Studies in International Finance 16, Princeton University, Princeton, N.J., 1966, and R. I. McKinnon, "Portfolio Balance and International Payments Adjustment," in R. A. Mundell and A. K. Swoboda, eds., *Monetary Problems of the International Economy*, University of Chicago Press, Chicago, 1969, pp. 199–234.

[5] S. J. Turnovsky, "The Dynamics of Fiscal Policy in an Open Economy," *Journal of International Economics*, 6 (May 1976), pp. 115–42.

foreign interest rates influence dynamic stability. Finally, Branson has examined the role of an endogenous deficit in an economy with a flexible exchange rate, but he has dealt only with the case in which it is financed by issuing money rather than bonds and has taken no account of home or foreign interest payments.[6]

It is easiest to compare tax specifications in a closed economy, and the lessons to be learned from that comparison can clarify the processes and complications encountered when we come to an open economy. For this reason, we begin by looking closely at a closed economy. It is based on the model used in Chapter 7, but there is no foreign trade in goods or bonds. Thereafter, we open the economy and compare the tax regimes with flexible and pegged exchange rates. At that point, however, we introduce an extra complication. Heretofore, we have assumed that interest payments from foreigners are offset exactly by transfers to foreigners. By this device, interest payments from foreigners have been deleted from the definitions of the current-account balance and disposable income. When working with the closed economy, however, we show that interest payments on domestic debt appear pervasively in the solutions when the budget deficit is endogenous. Therefore, it makes sense to take account of *all* interest payments when working with the open economy. It is thus an incidental purpose of this chapter to show how our results are modified when interest payments from foreigners are not matched by transfers.

The closed economy

To describe a closed economy, we have merely to collapse the standard model shown in Chapter 7. We eliminate the foreign good (and its price), the foreign demand for the domestic good, and the foreign bond (and its interest rate). The closed economy is described by 15 equations, with (a) and (b) denoting the exogenous-deficit and endogenous-deficit versions, respectively:

(10.1) $D - {}^*S = 0$

(10.2) ${}^*L_1^h - L_1 = 0$

where

(10.3) ${}^*S = S(r_1, Y^d, W^h)$

---

[6] W. H. Branson, "The Dual Roles of the Government Budget and the Balance of Payments in the Movement from Short-Run to Long-Run Equilibrium," *Quarterly Journal of Economics*, 90 (August 1976), pp. 345–68.

(10.4) $*L_1^h = L(r_1, W^h)$

(10.5) $Y^d = Y + r_1 B_1^h - T$

(10.6) $D = \bar{G}_1 + r_1 B_1^h - T$

(10.7) $Y = p_1 Q_1(E)$

(10.8) $w = p_1 Q_{1E}(E)$

(10.9) $E = \bar{E}$ or $w = \bar{w}$

and where

(10.10) $L_1 = \bar{B}_1^c$

(10.11) $W^h = L_1^h + B_1^h$

(10.12) $W^h = *L_1^h + *B_1^h$

(10.13) $*B_1^h = B_1^h$

Finally,

(10.14) $\dot{B}_1 = D$

(10.15a) $T = \bar{G}_1 + r_1 B_1^h - \bar{D}$

or

(10.15b) $T = \bar{T}_0 + \tau(Y + r_1 B_1^h)$

Thus, the closed economy closely resembles the open economy described in Chapter 7. But Eq. (10.1), the goods-market equation, does not contain the current-account balance. And Eq. (10.2), the money-market equation, is the only independent asset-market equation. (Because there is no foreign bond, households hold only money and the domestic bond, and the bond market will clear when the money market clears.) Finally, there is only one dynamic relationship, corresponding in substance but not in form to the one that we have analyzed before. In the closed economy, $W^h = W^{hs}$, and from Eqs. (10.10) and (10.11), $W^h = B_1^h + \bar{B}_1^c = B_1$. Therefore, $\dot{W}^{hs} = \dot{B}_1$, or $*S = D$, which is Eq. (10.1). The level of saving realized through time is always equal to the budget deficit, so that Eq. (10.14), connecting the supply of bonds to the budget deficit, is a useful form in which to state the strategic dynamic relationship.

Equations (10.15a) and (10.15b) are the only ones that differ explicitly between the two specifications of tax policy. But substitutions into Eqs. (10.5), (10.6), and (10.14) yield different formulations for disposable income, the budget deficit, and the growth rate of the government debt.

In the exogenous-deficit version,

(10.5a) $Y^d = Y + D - \bar{G}_1$

(10.6a) $D = \bar{D}$

where $\bar{D}$ is governed by continuous adjustment of the lump-sum tax, T, and $\bar{D} = 0$ at and after time $t = k$. Furthermore,

(10.14a) $\dot{B}_1 = \bar{D}$

so that the stock B_1 is itself exogenous and must come to be constant when the government balances its budget. There is no endogenous bond-supply equation, and the economy can adjust through time only in the policy-determined interval $0 < t < k$, the one in which the government incurs a deficit or surplus deliberately.

In the endogenous-deficit version,

(10.5b) $Y^d = (1 - \tau)(Y + r_1 B_1^h) - \bar{T}_0$

(10.6b) $D = \bar{G}_1 - \bar{T}_0 - \tau Y + (1 - \tau)r_1 B_1^h$

so that the deficit depends on three endogenous variables–income, the interest rate, and the supply of bonds held by the public. Furthermore,

(10.14b) $\dot{B}_1 = \bar{G}_1 - \bar{T}_0 - \tau Y + (1 - \tau)r_1 B_1^h$

so that the stock B_1 is fully endogenous, and we have to prove that the economy is stable by showing that $(\delta\dot{B}_1/\delta B_1) < 0$. In the endogenous-deficit version, moreover, tax collections do not change automatically to offset changes in $\bar{G}_1$, and a tax cut does not necessarily bring about an equal increase in the budget deficit. Therefore, we denote a balanced-budget increase in government expenditure by $\delta(\bar{G}_1, \bar{T}_0)$, indicating that the lump-sum tax $\bar{T}_0$ has been raised by the same amount as $\bar{G}_1$, a device that balances the budget at the initial levels of Y and $r_1 B_1^h$ but does not keep it in continuous balance when those variables change. Similarly, we denote a tax cut by $-\delta\bar{T}_0$ and treat the cut as permanent (because it need not be rescinded to balance the budget).

When solving for the effects of these fiscal policies and those of an open-market purchase, outcomes that pertain exclusively to the endogenous-deficit version are denoted by a caret (e.g., $\delta\hat{Y}$).

Impact effects

Equations (10.1) and (10.2) are solved first for the impact effects of three policies: an open-market purchase of the domestic bond, a balanced-budget increase in government spending, and a cut in lump-sum taxes. (In the endogenous-deficit version, they must also be solved for the impact effects of an increase in B_1, as these are needed to prove stability.)

The instantaneous changes in the interest rate are the same under both specifications. The two fiscal-policy changes are goods-market disturbances that do not affect asset markets immediately. The open-market purchase, by contrast, has effects on asset markets that are transmitted immediately to goods markets and affect the budget, but the instantaneous change in the budget is too small, by definition, to change the stock of bonds. Thus,

(10.16) $\delta r_1 = -(1/B_{11}) \delta \bar{B}_1^c + (L_{1W}/B_{11}) \delta B_1$

As usual, an open-market purchase depresses the interest rate.

The instantaneous changes in income differ between the two specifications—and do so for all three policy changes. When the budget deficit is exogenous,

(10.17a) $\delta Y = (S_1/S_Y B_{11}) \delta \bar{B}_1^c + (1) \delta \bar{G}_1 + [(1 - S_Y)/S_Y] \delta \bar{D}$

The open-market purchase raises income because it reduces the interest rate and depresses desired saving. The two fiscal-policy changes raise income too (and the balanced-budget multiplier is exactly unity).

When the budget deficit is endogenous,

(10.17b) $\delta \hat{Y} = (1/N_n B_{11})\{S_1 - (1 - \tau)(1 - S_Y)V_h[(1/r_1) + (B_{11}/B_1^h)]\} \delta \bar{B}_1^c$
$+ (S_Y/N_n) \delta(\bar{G}_1, \bar{T}_0) + [(1 - S_Y)/N_n](-\delta \bar{T}_0)$
$+ (1/N_n B_{11})\{(S_W L_{11} - L_{1W} S_1)$
$+ (1 - \tau)(1 - S_Y)V_h[(L_{1W}/r_1) + (B_{11}/B_1^h)]\} \delta B_1$

where $N_n = S_Y + \tau(1 - S_Y) > 0$, and $V_h = r_1 B_1^h$, the households' interest income on holdings of domestic bonds. (Any term containing V_h pertains to a change in that interest income.) The effect of an open-market purchase is ambiguous. Desired saving is reduced, just as it was with an exogenous deficit, but not by enough to guarantee an increase in activity. Households' interest incomes fall, because of reductions in r_1 and B_1^h, and disposable income can fall far enough to depress consumption by more than the reduction in desired saving stimulates consumption. (As in other instances studied below, however, the likelihood of this perverse result varies directly with the size of V_h.) The two fiscal policies stimulate activity (but the balanced-budget multiplier is smaller than unity, because the budget does not stay balanced continuously).

Stability

In the exogenous-deficit version of this model, stability is guaranteed by government behavior. By balancing its budget deliberately at time $t = k$, it stabilizes B_1 and thus stabilizes wealth. In the endogenous-deficit version, however, we must prove stability by showing that $(\delta \dot{B}_1 / \delta B_1) < 0$. To this end, we differentiate Eq. (10.14b) with respect to B_1 and obtain

(10.18b) $(\delta \dot{B}_1 / \delta B_1) = -(1/N_n B_{11})N_b$

where

$$N_b = \tau(S_W L_{11} - L_{1W} S_1) - S_Y(1 - \tau)V_h[(L_{1W}/r_1) + (B_{11}/B_1^h)]$$

For stability, then, N_b must be positive. We must therefore assume that crowding out does not dominate, but we go on to make a stronger supposition. When crowding out does not dominate, income rises, raising tax revenues. The increase in revenues, however, must be larger than the increase in the government's interest payments, so as to allow a gradual reduction in the budget deficit and in the flow supply of bonds.[7] The steady-state outcomes shown below are valid, of course, if and only if this condition is fulfilled.

Steady-state effects

When the budget deficit is exogenous, open-market purchases and changes in $\bar{G}_1$ cannot affect the stock of government debt. By implication, the steady-state effects of those two policies are identical to their impact effects – those shown by Eqs. (10.16) and (10.17a). With a temporary tax cut and budget deficit, the steady-state results depend entirely on the increase in the supply of debt:

(10.19a) $dr_1 = (L_{1W}/B_{11}) \, d\bar{B}_1$

(10.20a) $dY = (1/S_Y B_{11})(S_W L_{11} - L_{1W} S_1) \, d\bar{B}_1$

[7] It is worth noting once again that the strength of the crowding-out effect is an empirical matter. In this particular instance, however, there is an additional empirical issue. Even when crowding out does not dominate, the size and sensitivity of the government's interest payments may cause instability. The same problem is emphasized in Blinder and Solow, "Does Fiscal Policy Matter?"

There is a permanent increase in the interest rate and, when crowding out does not dominate, a permanent increase in income too.

When the budget deficit is endogenous, the steady-state effects of the policy changes are obtained by setting Eq. (10.14b) equal to zero and solving it simultaneously with Eqs. (10.1) and (10.2):

(10.21b) $d\hat{r}_1 = (1/N_b)[\tau S_W + S_Y(1 - \tau)V_h(B_{1W}/B_1^h)] \, d\bar{B}_1^c$
$- \tau(S_Y L_{1W}/N_b) \, d(\bar{G}_1, \bar{T}_0) + (S_Y L_{1W}/N_b)(- d\bar{T}_0)$

(10.22b) $d\hat{Y} = (1/N_b)(1 - \tau)V_h[(S_W/r_1) - (H_f/B_1^h)] \, d\bar{B}_1^c$
$- (1/N_b)S_Y(1 - \tau)(V_h/r_1)[L_{1W} + r_1(B_{11}/B_1^h)] \, d(\bar{G}_1, \bar{T}_0)$
$+ (1/N_b)(S_W L_{11} - L_{1W}S_1)(- d\bar{T}_0)$

(10.23b) $d\hat{B}_1 = - (1/N_b)\{\tau S_1 + S_Y(1 - \tau)(V_h/r_1)[1 + r_1(B_{11}/B_1^h)]\} \, d\bar{B}_1^c$
$+ \tau(S_Y L_{11}/N_b) \, d(\bar{G}_1, \bar{T}_0) - (S_Y L_{11}/N_b)(- d\bar{T}_0)$

An open-market purchase can raise or reduce the interest rate, but it causes a permanent *reduction* in income and in the supply of bonds. A balanced-budget increase in government spending, defined in the special sense given above, causes permanent reductions in r_1, Y, and B_1. And a permanent tax cut has the opposite effects, raising r_1, Y, and B_1. (Note that the permanent reductions in income occurring with an open-market purchase and a balanced-budget increase in government spending are due entirely to the inclusion of the interest-income term in the budget equation. If V_h were zero, r_1 and B_1 would fall, but Y would return eventually to its initial level. We revert to this point later.)

The permanent effects on disposable income are obtained by substitution into Eq. (10.5b):

(10.24b) $d\hat{Y}^d = (1/N_b)(1 - \tau)V_h[(S_W/r_1) - (H_f/B_1^h)] \, d\bar{B}_1^c$
$- \tau(1/N_b)(S_W L_{11} - L_{1W}S_1) \, d(\bar{G}_1, \bar{T}_0)$
$+ (1/N_b)(S_W L_{11} - L_{1W}S_1)(- d\bar{T}_0)$

As one would expect, the only difference between the effects on Y and Y^d occurs in the case of an increase in $\bar{G}_1$. Even in that instance, moreover, both effects are negative.

A diagrammatic analysis

The implications of the two tax specifications can be compared graphically by using standard Hicksian *IS* and *LM* curves. In Figure 10.1, the *LM* curve is the locus of combinations of r_1 and Y that clear the money market. It applies to both tax specifications. Because the demand for

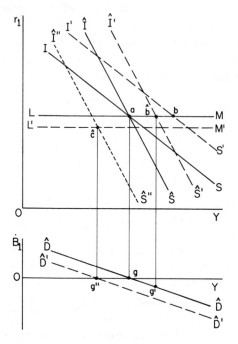

Figure 10.1 Balanced-budget increase in government spending: the closed economy with exogenous and endogenous budget deficits.

money does not depend on income, the *LM* curve is perfectly horizontal. The *IS* curve is the locus of combinations of r_1 and Y that clear the goods market under the exogenous-deficit specification, and the $\hat{I}\hat{S}$ curve is the corresponding locus under the endogenous-deficit specification. The latter is steeper than the former, because some part of any increase in absorption due to a reduction in r_1 will be taxed away under the endogenous-deficit specification, and because a reduction in r_1 depresses income directly by reducing the government's interest payments. In the lower panel of Figure 10.1, the curve $\hat{D}\hat{D}$ depicts the government's budget deficit as a function of income. It is, of course, applicable only to the endogenous-deficit specification.[8]

Figure 10.1 shows the effects of a balanced-budget increase in govern-

---

[8] The equations for the *IS* and $\hat{I}\hat{S}$ curves come from Eq. (10.1). Under the exogenous-deficit specification, it is combined with Eqs. (10.5a) and (10.6a) to give $-(S_Y)\,\delta Y - (S_1)\,\delta r_1 + (1 - S_Y)\,\delta \bar{D} + (S_Y)\,\delta \bar{G}_1 - (S_W)\,\delta B_1 = 0$. Under the endogenous-deficit specification, it is combined with Eqs. (10.5b) and (10.6b) to give

$$-(N_n)\,\delta\hat{Y} - [S_1 - (1 - S_Y)(1 - \tau)(V_h/r_1)]\,\delta\hat{r}_1 + (1 - S_Y)(-\delta\bar{T}_0)$$
$$+ (S_Y)\,\delta(\bar{G}_1,\,\bar{T}_0) + [(1 - S_Y)(1 - \tau)(V_h/B_1^h)](\delta\hat{B}_1 - \delta\bar{B}_1^h) = 0$$

ment spending. When the budget deficit is exogenous, the IS curve moves rightward to $I'S'$, by the full amount of the increase in spending, displacing equilibrium permanently from a to b. The balanced-budget multiplier is unity, on impact and in the steady state. When the budget deficit is endogenous, however, the $\hat{I}\hat{S}$ curve moves rightward to $\hat{I}'\hat{S}'$, by less than the increase in government spending, because of the leakage of personal income into tax payments. The economy moves from a to $\hat{b}$. Furthermore, the additional tax payments produce a budget surplus, shown by the move from g to g' on the $\hat{D}\hat{D}$ curve, and the government begins to retire bonds. Under assumptions sufficient for stability, the government's interest payments start to fall, and the $\hat{D}\hat{D}$ curve begins to move downward. In addition, wealth declines with the contraction in the supply of bonds. Therefore, desired saving rises, shifting $\hat{I}'\hat{S}'$ leftward to $\hat{I}''\hat{S}''$, and the demand for money falls, shifting LM downward to $L'M'$. Eventually, the two curves intersect at an income level that balances the budget on the $\hat{D}'\hat{D}'$ curve. The economy comes to rest at $\hat{c}$ and g'', where the steady-state level of income is lower than it was initially.

In summary, a balanced-budget increase in government spending raises income in the short run, but when tax revenues are endogenous, the budget does not stay in balance. It moves into surplus. Bond holdings and the interest rate start to fall, reducing the government's interest payments. When the stability condition is satisfied, however, income declines through time rapidly enough to reduce tax revenues by more than the reduction in interest payments, and the budget surplus shrinks. In the new steady state, income will be lower than it was initially, because the fall in interest payments has reduced the amount of revenue required to balance the government's budget.

In Figure 10.2, we show the effects of an open-market purchase. The LM curve shifts downward to $L'M'$, because the increase in the money supply calls for a reduction in the interest rate to clear the money market. When the budget deficit is exogenous, the economy moves down the IS curve from a to b and stays there permanently. Income rises and the interest rate falls. When the deficit is endogenous, the open-market purchase reduces absorption, because it reduces the number of bonds held by households, diminishing their interest income. The $\hat{I}\hat{S}$ curve shifts down-

---

where $(\delta \hat{B}_1 - \delta \bar{B}_1^c) = \delta \hat{B}_1^h$. The equation for the LM curve comes from Eq. (10.2): $(L_{11})\, \delta r_1 + (L_{1W})\, \delta B_1 - \delta \bar{B}_1^c = 0$. The equation for the $\hat{D}\hat{D}$ curve comes from Eq. (10.6b): $\delta \hat{D} = -\tau\, \delta \hat{Y} + [(1 - \tau)(V_h/r_1)]\, \delta \hat{r}_1 + (1)(-\delta \bar{T}_0) + [(1 - \tau)(V_h/B_1^h)]\, \delta \hat{B}_1^h$, so that $\hat{D}\hat{D}$ will shift down through time, as assumed in the discussion of Figure 10.1, whenever $[(\delta \hat{r}_1/r_1) + (\delta \hat{B}_1^h/B_1^h)] < 0$ (when there is sure to be a decline in the government's interest payments).

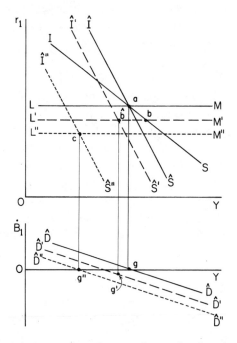

Figure 10.2 An open-market purchase: the closed economy with exogenous and endogenous budget deficits.

ward to $\hat{I}'\hat{S}'$, and the economy moves about a to $\hat{b}$. At this new point, income can be higher or lower than it was initially, depending on the sizes of two effects. It is drawn to be lower in Figure 10.2, which is to assume that the reduction in absorption caused by the decline in interest income dominates the increase in absorption caused by the decline in desired saving. The open-market purchase also causes the $\hat{D}\hat{D}$ curve to shift downward to $\hat{D}'\hat{D}'$ by reducing the government's interest payments. Therefore, it generates a budget surplus at g', despite the reduction in income. The subsequent changes produced by the budget surplus and reduction in the supply of bonds move the economy gradually from $\hat{b}$ to $\hat{c}$ (and thus from g' to g''). The dynamics are identical to those shown for the balanced-budget increase in expenditure, and there is a permanent reduction in income.

With an endogenous deficit, then, an open-market purchase may either raise or lower income on impact, but it will always be less expansionary than with an exogenous deficit. Furthermore, it will always produce a

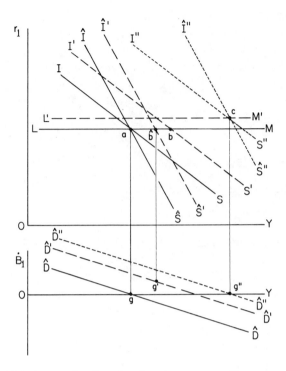

Figure 10.3 A tax reduction: the closed economy with exogenous and endogenous budget deficits (tax reduction temporary with an exogenous deficit but permanent with an endogenous deficit).

budget surplus and will thus be deflationary through time. The steady-state level of income will be lower than it was initially.

The impact effects of a tax cut are much like those of a balanced-budget increase in spending. In Figure 10.3, the IS curve shifts rightward to $I'S'$ with an exogenous budget deficit, moving the economy from a to b and raising income. (If $S_Y > \frac{1}{2}$, the multiplier will exceed unity and income will rise by more than the amount of the tax cut.) With an endogenous deficit, the $\hat{I}\hat{S}$ curve shifts to $\hat{I}'\hat{S}'$, moving the economy from a to $\hat{b}$ and raising income but by less. The tax cut also raises the $\hat{D}\hat{D}$ curve by enough to generate a budget deficit despite the increase in income. As bonds are issued to finance that deficit, income rises through time, moving the economy from $\hat{b}$ to c (and from g' to g''). The dynamics are opposite to those of the previous policy changes, because a tax cut causes deficits rather than surpluses. With an endogenous deficit, then, the steady-state level of income is higher than it was before the tax cut.

When the budget deficit is exogenous, the tax cut must be temporary, and the increase in the supply of bonds is policy determined by the time at which the tax cut is rescinded. When the deficit is endogenous, the tax cut is permanent, and the increase in the supply of bonds is self-limiting when the economy is stable. To compare the steady-state effects of the two specifications, let us assume that the same number of bonds is issued in each instance. Because $B_{11} + L_{11} = 0$ when there are no foreign bonds, we obtain from Eq. (10.23b)

$$d\bar{B}_1 = d\hat{B}_1 = (S_Y B_{11}/N_b)(-d\bar{T}_0)$$

Replacing $d\bar{B}_1$ in Eq. (10.20a), we find that

(10.25) $dY = (1/N_b)(S_W L_{11} - L_{1W} S_1)(-d\bar{T}_0) = d\hat{Y}$

The changes in steady-state income are identical. Returning to Figure 10.3, the shift in the LM curve is the same for both tax specifications, because the same number of bonds is issued. But the shift from $I'S'$ to $I''S''$ is smaller than the corresponding shift from $\hat{I}'\hat{S}'$ to $\hat{I}''\hat{S}''$, so that long-run equilibrium is established at the same point c under both specifications.

This method of standardization has a more general application. With an endogenous budget deficit, the steady-state effect of any disturbance can be divided into two parts, and each part is itself one of the steady-state effects obtained with an exogenous deficit. The first is the effect that the disturbance would have if the budget were balanced continuously. The second is the effect of the change in B_1 induced by the surplus or deficit that develops with an income tax. With an open-market purchase, for example,

(10.26) $(d\hat{Y}/d\bar{B}_1^c) = (dY/d\bar{B}_1^c) + (dY/d\bar{B}_1)(d\hat{B}_1/d\bar{B}_1^c)$

Thus, an open-market purchase and a balanced-budget increase in spending–policies designed to stimulate the economy–are deflationary in the long run when revenues are raised by an income tax. By generating budget surpluses and reducing the supply of bonds, they cause income to decline. In brief, it is impossible to know the long-run effects of any disturbance or policy change without knowing how the government finances the budgetary consequences of the disturbance.

At the start of this chapter, we said that the specification used elsewhere in this book–one that makes the deficit exogenous–may be more realistic for purposes of long-run analysis. The reason is the one that we have just adduced. Under the alternative specification–one that makes the deficit endogenous–monetary and fiscal policies can have perverse effects on the steady-state level of income. Governments may be prepared to tolerate the smaller income changes that take place in the short run with an income-tax regime. It is harder to believe, however, that they will remain passive indefinitely, as perverse effects develop. Sooner or later, they are apt to change the tax rate, τ, or the lump-sum tax term, $\bar{T}_0$, to ward off those effects. The long-run results of these responses, moreover, do not differ much from the long-run effects of the budget-balancing strategy posited elsewhere in this book.

The open economy without transfers to foreigners

Before we introduce an income tax into the open economy and face the complications it will pose, let us see what happens to the open economy when the interest income earned on foreign bonds is no longer offset automatically by transfers to foreigners. By taking up this issue first, we can sort out the complications introduced by endogenous variations in the interest-income term from those introduced by endogenous variations in the budget deficit.

To make this modification in our standard model, we replace Eq. (7.17) with

$$(10.27) \quad T^f = 0$$

But modifications have then to be made at three other points. The market-clearing equation for the domestic good comes to be

$$(10.28) \quad \left[p_1 C_1^f \left(\frac{p_1}{\pi}, \bar{p}_0^f, \bar{C}^f \right) - \pi \bar{p}_0^f C_0(p_1, \pi \bar{p}_0^f, Y^d - {}^*S) + \bar{r}_0(\pi B_0^h) \right]$$
$$+ D - {}^*S = 0$$

The budget equation comes to be

$$(10.29) \quad D = \bar{G}_1 + r_1(B_1 - \bar{B}_1^c) - T$$

And the interest-income term, $\bar{r}_0(\pi B_0^h)$, does not drop out of disposable income. Substituting Eq. (10.29) into Eq. (7.4),

$$(10.30) \quad Y^d = Y + \bar{r}_0(\pi B_0^h) + D - \bar{G}_1$$

At this juncture, however, the budget deficit is still exogenous, so D can be replaced by $\bar{D}$ in Eqs. (10.28), (10.29), and (10.30).

Impact effects

Under pegged and flexible exchange rates alike, goods-market disturbances do not impinge immediately on asset markets. There can thus be no change in the interest-income term, and the short-run effects of goods-market disturbances are not altered by setting $\bar{T}^f = 0$. They are given, as before, by Eq. (7.20). Under a pegged exchange rate, however, an asset-market disturbance does affect the interest-income term by producing an immediate change in holdings of the foreign bond. And under a flexible rate, any such disturbance will affect the interest-income term by producing an immediate change in the exchange rate itself. (Under both regimes, moreover, a change in $\bar{r}_0$ will affect that term directly.)

Consider the effects of an open-market purchase. Because households will buy foreign bonds when the exchange rate is pegged and the home currency will depreciate when the rate is flexible, an open-market purchase will raise the interest-income term under both regimes. Therefore, it will raise disposable income and stimulate the demand for goods. Under a flexible exchange rate,

$$(10.31) \quad \delta Y = [\sigma_1/(u_t + \sigma_1 N_Y)H_\pi V_\pi][m_1 V_\pi S_1(L_{1W} + B_{1W})$$
$$- B_{01}(u_\pi - m_1 S_W V_\pi) - m_1(1 - S_Y)V_f B_{01}] \, \delta\bar{B}_1^c$$

and under a pegged rate,

$$(10.32) \quad \delta Y = [\sigma_1/(u_t + \sigma_1 N_Y)B_{11}]m_1[S_1 - (1 - S_Y)V_f(B_{01}/\pi B_0^h)] \, \delta\bar{B}_1^c$$

where $V_f = \bar{r}_0(\pi B_0^h)$, the foreign interest-income term. (Any term containing V_f pertains to a change in that term.) Under both exchange-rate regimes, the impact effect on income is reinforced by the increase in the interest-income term. Compare the arguments of Eqs. (10.31) and (10.32) with their counterparts in Eqs. (7.22a) and (7.22b).

Stability

The inclusion of the foreign interest-income term has no effect on the stability or dynamic behavior of the economy when the exchange rate is flexible. As in other versions of this model, the rate of change of the exchange rate always offsets the rate of change in holdings of the foreign bond, so that the home-currency value of those holdings does not change through time, and interest payments on those holdings do not change either.

This is not the case, however, when the exchange rate is pegged. As saving adds to wealth through time, households buy more foreign bonds.

The interest-income term is raised, and so is disposable income. The growth of disposable income, however, enlarges the flow of saving and thus the rate of growth of wealth. With a pegged exchange rate, then, interest payments from foreigners can impair stability when they can affect disposable income. Formally,

$$(10.33) \quad \frac{\delta \dot{W}^{hs}}{\delta W^{hs}} = -[1/(u_t + \sigma_1 N_Y)B_{11}]N_r$$

where

$$N_r = H_f(u_t + m_0\sigma_1) - S_Y(V_f/\pi B_0^h)(B_{11}B_{0W} - B_{01}B_{1W})(u_t + \sigma_1)$$

For stability, then, it is necessary and sufficient that $N_r > 0$, which says that the first term in N_r must dominate the second. (The first term appeared in the proof of stability for the standard version of this model. It says that saving will decline in response to the changes in income, the interest rate, and wealth that take place when the interest-income term is not allowed to influence disposable income. The second term describes the positive response of saving to the income, interest-rate, and wealth effects of the increase in the interest-income term. Because this response is positive, it serves at least to slow the movement to the steady state, and if it is sufficiently large, it can prevent that movement, undermining stability.)

Steady-state effects

Under a flexible exchange rate, the steady-state values of disposable income, the interest rate, and wealth are determined by the requirements of asset-market equilibrium and by the requirement that saving be zero. They are thus unaffected by the assumption that $T^f = 0$. But the steady-state level of income (and of p_1) is determined by the relationship between Y and Y^d, and the steady-state exchange rate is determined by the requirement that the current-account balance be zero (the requirement that clears the goods market). Therefore, those variables *are* affected by foreign interest payments. The current-account requirement is

$$(10.34) \quad p_1 C_1^f \left(\frac{p_1}{\pi}, \bar{p}_0^f, \bar{C}^f\right) - \pi \bar{p}_0^f C_0(p_1, \pi \bar{p}_0^f, Y^d) + \bar{r}_0(\pi B_0^h) = 0$$

where

$$Y^d = Y + \bar{r}_0(\pi B_0^h) - \bar{G}_1$$

With a flexible exchange rate and no budget deficit, however, the only changes in the interest-income term are those that occur on impact, because subsequent changes in B_0^h are exactly offset by changes in π. By implication, goods-market disturbances (other than a tax reduction) have no effect whatsoever on income earned from foreigners, and the steady-state changes in Y and π are unaffected by assuming that $T^f = 0$. An open-market purchase, by contrast, affects the interest-income term immediately and thus does so permanently too. Therefore, the steady-state change in income equals the change in disposable income given by Eq. (3.21a) *less* the increase in the interest-income term. Furthermore, the steady-state change in the exchange rate must accommodate the increase in the interest-income term when balancing the current account, which means that the home currency will depreciate by less than when interest-income changes are offset by transfers. Finally, the increase in supply of domestic bonds resulting from a temporary tax cut affects the interest-income term over time, even though it does not do so immediately. The steady-state change in that term is

$$(10.35)\quad \bar{r}_0\, d(\pi B_0^h) = \bar{r}_0\left[\left(\frac{dW^h}{d\bar{B}_1}\right) - \left(\frac{dB_1^h}{d\bar{B}_1}\right)\right] d\bar{B}_1$$

$$= \bar{r}_0(1/H_\pi)(L_{1W}B_{01} - L_{11}B_{0W})\, d\bar{B}_1$$

and is therefore ambiguous. (It is the more likely to be negative, however, the greater the degree of substitutability between the foreign and domestic bonds.) As a result, the long-run effects on Y and π are also ambiguous.

The steady-state changes in income and the flexible exchange rate produced by the three policy changes are given by

$$(10.36)\quad dY = (1)\, d\bar{G}_1 + (1/H_\pi S_Y)[S_1(L_{1W} + B_{1W}) + S_W B_{01}$$
$$+ S_Y V_f(B_{01}/\pi B_0^h)]\, d\bar{B}_1^c$$
$$+ (1/H_\pi S_Y)\{(S_W L_{11} - L_{1W}S_1) - S_Y V_f[(L_{1W}B_{01}$$
$$- L_{11}B_{0W})/\pi B_0^h]\}\, d\bar{B}_1$$

$$(10.37)\quad \left(\frac{d\pi}{\pi}\right) = (u_t/\sigma_1 u_\pi)\, d\bar{G}_1$$
$$+ (1/H_\pi S_Y \sigma_1 u_\pi)\{[S_1(L_{1W} + B_{1W}) + S_W B_{01}](u_t + m_0\sigma_1)$$
$$+ V_f(B_{01}/\pi B_0^h)(u_t + \sigma_1)\}\, d\bar{B}_1^c$$
$$+ (1/H_\pi S_Y \sigma_1 u_\pi)\{(S_W L_{11} - L_{1W}S_1)(u_t + m_0\sigma_1)$$
$$- S_Y V_f[(L_{1W}B_{01} - L_{11}B_{0W})/\pi B_0^h](u_t + \sigma_1)\}\, d\bar{B}_1$$

An open-market purchase raises the foreign interest-income term, causing Y and π to rise by smaller amounts than when interest income was offset by transfers. An increase in the supply of domestic bonds has an ambigu-

Table 10.1. *Effects on selected outcomes when changes in interest income from foreigners are not offset by transfers* ($T^f = 0$)

Effect	Policy change		
	Balanced-budget increase in $\bar{G}_1$	Temporary tax reduction	Open-market purchase
On impact with flex-ible or pegged rate			
Income	None	None	Larger increase
Exchange rate or reserves	None	None	None
Interest income	None	None	Positive
In steady state with flexible rate			
Income	None	Uncertain[a]	Smaller increase[b]
Exchange rate	None	Uncertain[a]	Smaller increase[b]
Interest income	None	Uncertain	Positive
In steady state with pegged rate			
Income	Smaller increase[b]	Uncertain[c]	Uncertain[c]
Reserves	Larger loss	Uncertain[d]	Uncertain[d]
Interest income	Negative	Uncertain	Uncertain

Effects on income, exchange rate, and reserves refer to *alterations* in the changes (i.e., comparisons with outcomes in the standard model summarized by Tables 7.1 and 7.2); effects on interest income refer to the changes themselves (i.e., the increase or decrease in interest income on the foreign bond). Results for pegged-rate case assume stability ($N_r > 0$).
[a] Can cause larger or smaller increase than the one when $T^f \neq 0$ (and can transform increase into decrease).
[b] Can transform increase into decrease when V_f is large.
[c] Income change is zero when $T^f \neq 0$ (so that income can rise or fall when $T^f = 0$).
[d] Can cause larger or smaller loss than the one when $T^f \neq 0$ (and can transform loss into gain).

ous effect on the interest-income term, so that the effects on Y and π are likewise ambiguous when the interest-income term is large. These results are recapitulated in Table 10.1.

The effects of changes in the foreign interest-income term are more pervasive with a pegged exchange rate. We can no longer obtain the long-run change in income by solving the goods-market equation by itself; that equation must be solved simultaneously with the others that define steady-state equilibrium–the market-clearing equations for the domestic

bond and money, the statement that saving is zero, and the equation relating Y and Y^d.[9] The solutions are as follows:

(10.38) $dY = (\sigma_1/N_r)\{m_0(S_1B_{1W} - S_WB_{11})$
$- S_YV_f[(B_{11}B_{0W} - B_{01}B_{1W})/\pi B_0^h]\}\,d\bar{G}_1$
$+ (\sigma_1/N_r)m_1V_f[(S_WB_{01} - S_1B_{0W})/\pi B_0^h](d\bar{B}_1^c - d\bar{B}_1)$

(10.39) $dY^d = -(u_t/N_r)(S_1B_{1W} - S_WB_{11})\,d\bar{G}_1$
$+ (1/N_r)(u_t + \sigma_1)V_f[(S_WB_{01} - S_1B_{0W})/\pi B_0^h](d\bar{B}_1^c - d\bar{B}_1)$

(10.40) $dr_1 = (u_t/N_r)(S_YB_{1W})\,d\bar{G}_1 + (1/N_r)[S_W(u_t + m_0\sigma_1)$
$+ S_YV_f(B_{0W}/\pi B_0^h)(u_t + \sigma_1)](d\bar{B}_1^c - d\bar{B}_1)$

(10.41) $dW^h = -(u_t/N_r)(S_YB_{11})\,d\bar{G}_1 - (1/N_r)[S_1(u_t + m_0\sigma_1)$
$+ S_YV_f(B_{01}/\pi B_0^h)(u_t + \sigma_1)](d\bar{B}_1^c - d\bar{B}_1)$

(10.42) $\bar{\pi}\,dR = -(u_t/N_r)(S_YH_\pi)\,d\bar{G}_1$
$- (1/N_r)\{[S_1(L_{1W} + B_{1W}) + S_WB_{01}](u_t + m_0\sigma_1)$
$+ S_YV_f(B_{01}/\pi B_0^h)(u_t + \sigma_1)\}\,d\bar{B}_1^c$
$- (1/N_r)\{(S_WL_{11} - L_{1W}S_1)(u_t + m_0\sigma_1)$
$+ S_YV_f[(L_{11}B_{0W} - L_{1W}B_{01})/\pi B_0^h]\}\,d\bar{B}_1$

and

(10.43) $\bar{r}_0\,d(\pi B_0^h) = -(u_t/N_r)(V_f/\pi B_0^h)S_Y(B_{11}B_{0W} - B_{01}B_{1W})\,d\bar{G}_1$
$+ (1/N_r)(V_f/\pi B_0^h)(S_WB_{01} - S_1B_{0W})$
$\times (u_t + m_0\sigma_1)(d\bar{B}_1^c - d\bar{B}_1)$

where $N_r > 0$ if and only if the model is stable. The principal implications
for income and reserves are shown in Table 10.1.

Changes in the foreign interest-income term affect the steady-state values of all variables. If interest income rises, disposable income is raised,
stimulating the demand for goods. Therefore, the value of output is
raised, adding further to the increase in Y^d (compared to what Y^d would
be without any change in interest income). The increase in disposable income, moreover, means that the interest rate must be lower and wealth
must be higher (compared to what they would be), in order for saving to be
zero. If interest income falls, of course, disposable income will be lower,
the interest rate higher, and wealth lower.

[9] The relevant equations are (10.28), (10.30), (2.11a), (2.42a), and (2.43a). The change in the
foreign interest-income term shown later by Eq. (10.43) is obtained from the change in
πB_0^h: $\bar{r}_0(d\pi B_0^h) = (V_f/\pi B_0^h)[(B_{01})\,dr_1 + (B_{0W})\,dW^h]$, into which we substitute the appropriate
values of dr_1 and dW^h for each disturbance or policy change given by Eqs. (10.40) and
(10.41).

When the interest-income term was offset by transfers, a balanced-budget increase in government spending raised the steady-state interest rate and reduced the stock of wealth, depressing the demand for foreign bonds. When there are no transfers, the reduction in demand for foreign bonds amplifies the decline in disposable income and thus the decline in desired saving. To offset this effect and bring saving to zero, the interest rate must rise further and wealth must fall further. These adjustments reinforce the reductions in demand for the foreign bond and in the demand for money, so that there is a larger loss of reserves.

An open-market purchase and an increase in B_1 affect the interest-income term to the same extent but in opposite directions. The sign of their influence, however, is uncertain unless the two bonds in our model are close substitutes. Therefore, the implications for other variables are uncertain too. The changes in income and disposable income take their signs entirely from the change in the interest-income term; they would not change at all if interest payments were offset by transfers. The changes in the interest rate, wealth, and reserves are also affected, but the alteration is different in each instance (and in the case of $\bar{\pi}R$ is different for an open-market purchase than for an increase in B_1). When changes in the interest-income term were offset by transfers, an open-market purchase led to permanent reductions in r_1, W^h, and $\bar{\pi}R$. When those changes are not offset and V_f is large enough, the movements in r_1, W^h, and $\bar{\pi}R$ can be reversed.[10]

The open economy with an endogenous budget deficit

To introduce an income tax into our standard model, we retain Eqs. (10.27), (10.28), and (10.29), so that the interest-income term, $\bar{r}_0(\pi B_0^h)$, is not offset by transfers, but we replace Eq. (7.16) of the standard model with an appropriate definition of tax revenues:

(10.44b) $T^h = \bar{T}_0 + \tau[Y + r_1 B_1^h + \bar{r}_0(\pi B_0^h)]$

---

[10] Thus, an open-market purchase leads to a permanent loss of reserves only if $[S_1(L_{1W} + B_{1W}) + S_W B_{01}](u_t + m_0\sigma_1) > -S_Y V_f(B_{01}/\pi B_0^h)(u_t + \sigma_1)$, and this condition is more likely to be violated the larger the interest-income term V_f. An increase in B_1 leads to a permanent loss of reserves only if $(S_W L_{11} - L_{1W} S_1)(u_t + m_0\sigma_1) > -S_Y V_f[(L_{11}B_{0W} - L_{1W}B_{01})/\pi B_0^h]$, but the sign of the right-hand side of this inequality is itself ambiguous, because $L_{11}B_{0W} \gtrless L_{1W}B_{01}$. Thus, the change in the interest-income term can add to or substract from the loss of reserves that takes place in the standard version of our model (and can be strong enough to raise reserves).

Substituting into Eq. (7.4), the definition of disposable income,

(10.30b) $Y^d = (1 - \tau)[Y + r_1 B_1^h + \bar{r}_0(\pi B_0^h)] - \bar{T}_0$

Substituting into Eq. (10.29), the budget equation,

(10.45b) $D = \bar{G}_1 - \bar{T}_0 - \tau[Y + \bar{r}_0(\pi B_0^h)] + (1 - \tau)r_1 B_1^h$

Because $\dot{B}_1 = D$, as usual, dynamic analysis of this economy is quite complicated. The economy is propelled through time by *two* endogenous stock-flow relationships – one that links the stock B_1 with the budget deficit, and one that links the stock W^{hs} with household saving.

Impact effects

As in previous analyses, the impact effects of goods-market disturbances are the same with flexible and pegged exchange rates, such that

(10.46) $\delta \hat{Y} = (\sigma_1/N_d)[(N_Y) \, \delta(\bar{G}_1, \bar{T}_0) + m_1(1 - S_Y)(-\delta \bar{T}_0)]$

where

$$N_d = u_t + \sigma_1[N_Y + \tau m_1(1 - S_Y)] > 0$$

But the impact effects of an open-market purchase are different with flexible and pegged exchange rates. The changes in the asset-market variables, r_1 and π or $\bar{\pi}R$, do not differ from those with a lump-sum tax; see Eqs. (3.2a) and (3.3a) for a flexible rate and Eqs. (3.2b) and (3.3b) for a pegged rate. The changes in income, however, are influenced by the endogeneity of the budget deficit. With a flexible exchange rate,

(10.47b) $\delta \hat{Y} = (\sigma_1/N_d H_\pi)\{[m_1 S_1(L_{1W} + B_{1W}) - (B_{01}/V_\pi)(u_\pi - m_1 S_W V_\pi)]$
$\qquad - m_1(1 - S_Y)(1 - \tau)(V_h/r_1)[(L_{11} + B_{1W}) + r_1(H_\pi/B_1^h)]$
$\qquad - m_1(1 - S_Y)(1 - \tau)V_f(B_{01}/\pi B_0^h)\} \, \delta \bar{B}_1^c$

With a pegged exchange rate,

(10.48b) $\delta \hat{Y} = (\sigma_1/N_d B_{11})m_1\{S_1 - (1 - S_Y)(1 - \tau)(V_h/r_1)[1 + r_1(B_{11}/B_1^h)]$
$\qquad - (1 - S_Y)(1 - \tau)V_f(B_{01}/\pi B_0^h)\} \, \delta \bar{B}_1^c$

Under both regimes, the change in foreign interest income, reflected by the arguments containing V_f, tends to enlarge the increase in income resulting from the open-market purchase. But the change in domestic interest income, reflected by the arguments containing V_h, tends to reduce the increase in income.

To compare the tax specifications more closely, imagine that τ and V_h were zero. The income changes would then be identical to those with an exogenous budget deficit. As in the case of the closed economy, the use of an income tax reduces the income multiplier (because N_d contains the tax rate τ), diminishing the short-run effect of any macroeconomic policy change. In addition, the use of an income tax reduces the effectiveness of an open-market purchase by reducing $r_1 B_1^h$ and thereby reducing disposable income. As a matter of fact, an open-market purchase can be deflationary when V_h is very large.

Note finally one important characteristic of the flexible-rate case. If there were no capital mobility and no holdings of the foreign bond initially, the impact effects on income would be proportional to those that occur in a closed economy (proportional rather than identical because the income multiplier is reduced by the leakage into imports). To see that this is true for an open-market purchase, remember that $L_{1W} + B_{1W} = 1$ when $B_{0W} = 0$ and that $B_{11} + L_{11} = 0$ when $B_{01} = 0$. Therefore, the change in income given by Eq. (10.47b) for the flexible-rate case reduces to a fraction, m_1, of the change in income given by Eq. (10.17b) for the closed economy. Repeating a point we made before, an open economy with a flexible exchange rate is similar in many ways to a closed economy, because the supply of money is policy determined in both situations.

Stability

To investigate stability under an income-tax specification, we must form and analyze this matrix of derivatives:

$$
\begin{bmatrix}
\left(\dfrac{\delta \dot{W}^{hs}}{\delta W^{hs}}\right) & \left(\dfrac{\delta \dot{W}^{hs}}{\delta B_1}\right) \\[2ex]
\left(\dfrac{\delta \dot{B}_1}{\delta W^{hs}}\right) & \left(\dfrac{\delta \dot{B}_1}{\delta B_1}\right)
\end{bmatrix}
$$

Stability requires that its trace be negative and its determinant positive.[11]

---

[11] To derive the requisite expressions for the four derivatives, thereby to obtain the trace and determinant, we need the partial derivatives of Y, r_1, W^h, and π or πR with respect to W^{hs} and B_1. All of these are found in Chapter 3, except the ones for Y, which are different with an income-tax specification. Under a flexible exchange rate,

$$
\begin{aligned}
\delta \hat{Y} = &- (\sigma_1 u_\pi / N_d V_\pi)\, \delta W^{hs} + (\sigma_1 / N_d H_\pi)\{m_1 (S_W L_{11} - L_{1W} S_1) - u_\pi (L_{11}/V_\pi) \\
&+ m_1(1 - S_Y)(1 - \tau)(V_h/r_1)[L_{1W} + r_1(H_\pi/B_1^h)] \\
&- m_1(1 - S_Y)(1 - \tau)V_f[(B_{0W}L_{11} - B_{01}L_{1W})/\pi B_0^h]\}\, \delta B_1
\end{aligned}
$$

Under a flexible exchange rate, the trace can be written as

$$-(1/N_dH_\pi)[\sigma_1\{\tau m_1(S_WL_{11} - L_{1W}S_1) + (u_\pi/V_\pi)[S_Y(1 - \tau)H_\pi - \tau L_{11}]\}$$
$$-(1 - \tau)\,V_h[(L_{1W}/r_1) + (H_\pi/B_1^h)](u_t + \sigma_1 N_Y)$$
$$- \tau V_f[(L_{11}B_{0W} - B_{01}L_{1W})/\pi B_0^h](u_t + \sigma_1)]$$

and the determinant can be written as $(\sigma_1 u_\pi/N_dH_\pi V_\pi)N_c$, where

$$N_c = \tau(S_WL_{11} - L_{1W}S_1) - S_Y(1 - \tau)V_h[(L_{1W}/r_1) + (H_\pi/B_1^h)]$$

The trace and determinant are both ambiguous, even when crowding out does not dominate, and there is thus the possibility of instability.

The sources of the problem can most readily be isolated by looking at the special case examined above. If there were no capital mobility and no holdings of the foreign bond initially, the conditions sufficient for a positive determinant would be the same as those for a closed economy (H_π would reduce to B_{11}, so that N_c would become N_b). In a closed economy, stability required that the revenue-raising effect of the term $\tau(S_WL_{11} - L_{1W}S_1)$ be large enough to cover any increase in the government's interest payments and leave something over to reduce its deficit. Otherwise, the economy could not converge to a steady state. (The requirement that the trace be negative has additional implications for the size of that term, and they may be either more or less stringent than those needed for a positive determinant.) When we allow for capital mobility, we add a second source of instability. It can indeed be shown that the model is unstable when foreign and domestic bonds are perfect substitutes.[12]

Why does asset-market integration have this effect? For our model to be stable, an increase in B_1 must raise tax revenues (by raising income) faster than it raises the government's interest payments. If foreign and domestic bonds are close substitutes, however, the increase in revenues is reduced relative to interest payments. As new bonds are issued to finance a budget deficit, the domestic interest rate must rise. Households must be

Under a pegged exchange rate,
$$\delta\hat{Y} = (\sigma_1/N_dB_{11})m_1\{H_f - (1 - S_Y)(1 - \tau)V_h(B_{1W}/r_1)$$
$$+ (1 - S_Y)(1 - \tau)V_f[(B_{11}B_{0W} - B_{1W}B_{01})/\pi B_0^h]\} \,\delta W^{hs}$$
$$- (\sigma_1/N_dB_{11})m_1\{S_1 - (1 - S_Y)(1 - \tau)(V_h/r_1)[1 + r_1(B_{11}/B_1^h)]$$
$$- (1 - S_Y)(1 - \tau)V_f(B_{01}/\pi B_0^h)\} \,\delta B_1$$

[12] With perfect substitutability, $H_\pi \to \infty$, and the determinant becomes $-(\sigma_1 u_\pi/N_dV_\pi)$ $\times S_Y(1 - \tau)(V_h/B_1^h)$, which is unambiguously negative. In Blinder and Solow, "Does Fiscal Policy Matter?," a similar model for a closed economy is shown to be stable when the government finances its deficits by issuing money rather than bonds. In Appendix D, we show that this is also true for an open economy with a flexible exchange rate.

made to buy the new bonds. They are induced to do so in two ways. First, they are persuaded to save more and thus to raise their flow demands for all assets, including the domestic bond. Second, they are pursuaded to substitute domestic for foreign bonds. But with a flexible exchange rate, sales of the foreign bond cause the home currency to appreciate (or to depreciate by less), depressing income and tax revenues, and the strength of this effect varies directly with the degree of asset-market integration. There is, of course, less increase in the domestic interest rate when the two bonds are close substitutes and, therefore, less increase in the government's interest payments. But the revenue-depressing effect of the change in the exchange rate is larger than the reduction in interest payments, making it harder to balance the budget. When the two bonds are perfect substitutes, the appreciation of the home currency is large enough to keep income from rising, and there is *no* increase in tax revenues. There is no increase in the interest rate either, but interest payments rise with the increase in B_1, and the government cannot possibly balance its budget. In fact, its deficit grows through time, adding to the increase in B_1.

Under a pegged exchange rate, the trace can be written as

$$-(1/N_d B_{11})[\{H_f[u_t + \sigma_1(m_0 + \tau m_1)] - \sigma_1(\tau m_1 S_1)\}$$
$$+ (1 - \tau)(V_h/r_1)\{S_Y B_{1W}(u_t + \sigma_1)$$
$$- [u_t + \sigma_1(m_0 + m_1 S_Y)][1 + r_1(B_{11}/B_1^h)]\}$$
$$- (u_t + \sigma_1)V_f\{S_Y(1 - \tau)[(B_{11}B_{0W} - B_{01}B_{1W})/\pi B_0^h] - \tau(B_{01}/\pi B_0^h)\}]$$

which is thoroughly ambiguous.[13] Furthermore, the determinant is

$$(1/N_d^2 B_{11})[(1 - \tau)(V_h/r_1)[r_1(H_f/B_1^h) - S_W]\{(u_t + \sigma_1)\sigma_1(\tau m_1 S_Y)$$
$$- [(u_t + \sigma_1) - m_1(1 - \tau)\sigma_1][(u_t + \sigma_1) - m_1(1 - S_Y)\sigma_1]\}$$
$$+ \tau V_f(u_t + \sigma_1)N_d[(S_1 B_{0W} - S_W B_{01})/\pi B_0^h]$$
$$+ (1 - \tau)S_Y(V_f/\pi B_0^h)(V_h/r_1)(u_t + \sigma_1)N_d$$
$$\times \{B_{0W} + r_1[(B_{11}B_{0W} - B_{01}B_{1W})/B_1^h]\}]$$

which is the sum of one term in V_h, one in V_f, and one in the product of the two. The first term is negative, the second is ambiguous, and the third is positive. Therefore, the determinant is ambiguous.[14] It is, of course,

---

[13] The first major part is itself ambiguous, because $H_f[u_t + \sigma_1(m_0 + \tau m_1)] - \sigma_1(\tau m_1 S_1) = H_f(u_t + \sigma_1 m_0) - \sigma_1 \tau m_1[S_1(1 - B_{1W}) + S_W B_{11}]$, and $S_1(1 - B_{1W}) + S_W B_{11}$ is itself ambiguous. The term prefixed by V_h is likewise ambiguous. The term prefixed by V_f is positive.

[14] To show that the first term is negative, rewrite the expression within braces as

$$-(u_t + \sigma_1)[u_t + \sigma_1\{1 - m_1[1 - (1 - \tau)(1 - S_Y)]\}] - (m_1\sigma_1)^2[(1 - \tau)(1 - S_Y)]$$

Because $1 > (1 - \tau)(1 - S_Y)$, the entire expression is necessarily negative.

possible to choose combinations of parameters that cause the determinant to be positive, but these also cause the trace to be positive. We have indeed found no single set of parameters that can guarantee simultaneously a negative trace and positive determinant, and we come thus to conclude that the economy is unstable with a pegged exchange rate.

To understand the economic issues involved, suppose that there were no capital mobility and pick a point in time when the budget deficit is exactly equal to the current-account deficit (one when there is no saving and, therefore, no change in wealth). As bonds are issued to finance the budget deficit, the domestic interest rate will rise, and when r_1 and B_1 are rising simultaneously, the government's interest payments will be rising too. When r_1 is rising, moreover, desired saving rises, depressing the demand for goods, reducing income, and diminishing tax revenues. The budget deficit is bound to grow, raising the rate of increase of B_1. Furthermore, the current-account deficit must be financed by an outflow of reserves in the absence of capital mobility, an outflow that reduces the money supply. Thus, the pegging of what is, in effect, an overvalued currency deprives the economy of a vital stabilizing force. With a flexible exchange rate, by contrast, the domestic currency would depreciate in the absence of capital mobility, raising the demand for goods, the level of income, and the government's revenues, and helping to balance the budget over time.

When we introduce capital mobility, matters are improved in the pegged-rate case. The domestic interest rate cannot rise as rapidly in response to the increase in B_1. Interest payments grow more slowly, and tax revenues decline more slowly (because the incentive to save is weakened). But even when the foreign and domestic bonds are perfect substitutes, the economy is unstable with a pegged exchange rate.[15]

---

[15] With perfect substitutability, the first (V_h) term of the determinant remains negative; the second (V_f) term becomes unambiguously negative; and the third (multiplicative) term continues to be positive. The determinant as a whole remains ambiguous. When the two bonds are perfect substitutes, a budget deficit equal to the current-account deficit can be financed by foreign borrowing. Households will buy the new domestic bonds and sell foreign bonds to make room for them. In the process, of course, they will finance the current-account deficit; there will be no loss of reserves. The budget deficit will grow through time (at $r_1\dot{B}_1$) and the current-account deficit will grow at the same rate if $r_1 = \bar{r}_0$. In Turnovsky, "The Dynamics of Fiscal Policy," this state of affairs is described as an equilibrium, because there is no change in any market-clearing variable. In Chapter 6, we chose to call it a quasi-equilibrium, not because the budget deficit would go on growing with the increase in $r_1 B_1$, but because the situation it is not sustainable. Households will run out of foreign bonds eventually and will not be able to sell any more of them to make room for additional domestic bonds.

Steady-state effects

Steady-state solutions for a model are meaningful only when the model is stable. In the present instance, then, we limit attention to the flexible-rate case and assume that the relevant determinant is positive (that $N_c > 0$). This is to assume that crowding out does not dominate and that the two bonds in the model are less than perfect substitutes, so that the revenue-raising effect of growth in B_1 is large enough to offset the corresponding growth in the government's interest payments.[16]

To obtain the steady-state changes in r_1, Y, W^h, and B_1, we set saving and the budget deficit equal to zero and solve Eqs. (7.8), (10.45b), (7.2), and (7.3) simultaneously. Thereafter, we solve Eqs. (10.30b) and (10.34) for Y and π, using the first set of solutions. Omitting the solutions for π, because the outcomes are thoroughly ambiguous,

(10.49b)
$$d\hat{r}_1 = (1/N_c)[\tau S_W + S_Y(1 - \tau)V_h(B_{1W}/B_1^h)] \, d\bar{B}_1^c$$
$$- \tau(S_Y L_{1W}/N_c) \, d(\bar{G}_1, \bar{T}_0) + (S_Y L_{1W}/N_c)(-d\bar{T}_0)$$

(10.50b)
$$d\hat{Y} = (1/N_c)[(1 - \tau)V_h[(S_W/r_1) - (H_f/B_1^h)]$$
$$- \tau V_f[(S_W B_{01} - S_1 B_{0W})/\pi B_0^h]$$
$$+ S_Y(1 - \tau)(V_f/\pi B_0^h)(V_h/r_1)$$
$$\times \{B_{0W} + r_1[(B_{11}B_{0W} - B_{01}B_{1W})/B_1^h]\}] \, d\bar{B}_1^c$$
$$- (S_Y/N_c)\{(1 - \tau)(V_h/r_1)[L_{1W} + r_1(H_\pi/B_1^h)]$$
$$- \tau V_f[(L_{11}B_{0W} - B_{01}L_{1W})/\pi B_0^h]\} \, d(\bar{G}_1, \bar{T}_0)$$
$$+ (1/N_c)\{(S_W L_{11} - L_{1W}S_1)$$
$$+ S_Y V_f[(L_{11}B_{0W} - B_{01}L_{1W})/\pi B_0^h]\}(-d\bar{T}_0)$$

(10.51b)
$$d\hat{Y}^d = (1/N_c)\{(1 - \tau)V_h[(S_W/r_1) - (H_f/B_1^h)]\} \, d\bar{B}_1^c$$
$$- \tau(1/N_c)(S_W L_{11} - L_{1W}S_1) \, d(\bar{G}_1, \bar{T}_0)$$
$$+ (1/N_c)(S_W L_{11} - L_{1W}S_1)(-d\bar{T}_0)$$

(10.52b)
$$d\hat{W}^h = -(1/N_c)\{\tau S_1 + S_Y(1 - \tau)(V_h/r_1)[1 + r_1(B_{11}/B_1^h)]\} \, d\bar{B}_1^c$$
$$+ \tau(S_Y L_{11}/N_c) \, d(\bar{G}_1, \bar{T}_0) - (S_Y L_{11}/N_c)(-d\bar{T}_0)$$

[16] Although there are more sources of instability in the open economy, the condition that $N_c > 0$ is less stringent than the condition for the closed economy. Because $N_c = N_b + S_Y(1 - \tau)V_h[(B_{11}B_{0W} - B_{01}B_{1W})/B_1^h]$, we can be sure that $N_c > 0$ when $N_b > 0$. For the trace to be negative, however, it is also necessary that

$$\sigma_1 m_1(N_c) + (\sigma_1 u_\pi/V_\pi)[S_Y(1 - \tau)H_\pi - \tau L_{11}]$$
$$> (1 - \tau)V_h[(L_{1W}/r_1) + (H_\pi/B_1^h)][u_t + m_0(1 - S_Y)\sigma_1]$$
$$+ \dot{\tau}V_f[(L_{11}B_{0W} - B_{01}L_{1W})/\pi B_0^h](u_t + \sigma_1)$$

and this condition is more likely to be satisfied the larger N_c but is not automatically satisfied when $N_c > 0$.

(10.53b) $d\hat{B}_1 = -(1/N_c)\{\tau[S_1(L_{1W} + B_{1W}) + S_W B_{01}] + S_Y(1 - \tau)(V_h/r_1)$
$\times [(L_{1W} + B_{1W}) + r_1(H_\pi/B_1^h)]\} d\bar{B}_1^c$
$- \tau(S_Y H_\pi/N_c) d(\bar{G}_1, \bar{T}_0) + (S_Y H_\pi/N_c)(-d\bar{T}_0)$

When we compare these results to those for the closed economy, in Eqs. (10.21b) through (10.24b), we find that the changes in r_1, Y^d, and W^h are smaller but strictly proportional. (In the closed economy, the change in wealth is the change in B_1.) In each of these three instances, the numerator is the same for the open and closed economies, but the denominator is larger for the open economy ($N_c > N_b$). In an open economy, where households can substitute foreign for domestic bonds, changes in B_1 lead to smaller changes in r_1. Hence, saving can be brought to zero by smaller changes in Y^d and W^h.[17] In the open economy, however, the changes in income can differ in sign, because they are affected by endogenous changes in the foreign interest-income term, $\bar{r}_0(\pi B_0^h)$. In fact, each income change shown by Eq. (10.50b) is ambiguous, because the terms containing V_f are ambiguous. (In the case of an open-market purchase, moreover, the first and third terms have opposite signs.)

Conclusions

This chapter has compared two versions of our model–one used elsewhere in this book, where taxes are adjusted continuously to regulate the government's budget, and one where an income tax is used to raise revenue, causing the budget to become endogenous. The income-tax specification is more realistic for purposes of short-run analysis but does not make much difference for the impact effects of the disturbances and policies studied in this book. The short-run income multiplier is reduced by the leakage into taxes, and an open-market purchase can be deflationary. But these are the only qualitative differences in short-run outcomes. For purposes of long-run analysis, moreover, it makes much more sense to assume that the budget deficit is exogenous. An income-tax specification can cause instability, particularly in an open economy. It is virtually certain to do so when the exchange rate is pegged or when the rate is flexible and there is a high degree of capital mobility. Furthermore, policies can have perverse long-run results under an income-tax specification, even when the economy is stable dynamically. Governments do rely heavily on income taxes, but our analysis suggests that they are not likely to do so

[17] Reverting to the algebra of the previous note, $B_{01} = B_{0W} = 0$ without capital mobility, so that $N_c = N_b$.

mechanically. If income begins to decline because a budget surplus emerges in the wake of an open-market purchase or balanced-budget increase in government spending, a government is apt to cut the tax rate or take other measures to combat the surplus. Over the long run, the budget and supply of debt have to be regarded as policy instruments.

The specification used elsewhere in this book has a number of advantages. It helps us to classify disturbances. It removes ambiguities resulting from changes in interest-income terms. It does these things because it allows us to impound the budgetary side-effects of various disturbances and their implications for the stock of debt. In this chapter, however, we have shown that it has another virtue. It is one way to represent the need for the government deliberately to manage the behavior of the budget. Continuous management may be impractical. Long-run management is imperative.

PART IV

Analyzing interdependence

11

A two-country model

Openness and interdependence

Previous parts of this book have dealt with the implications of economic openness for the behavior of a single economy and the conduct of its national policies. This part and the next deal with the implications of economic interdependence. The distinction can be introduced by asking how openness and interdependence each affect the answer to this question: Can those who make policies for a single country ignore the consequences of their decisions for the policies of other countries? The fact of openness does not give an answer. The fact of interdependence gives a negative answer.[1]

Clearly, the notion of interdependence has to do with economic size. The small-country assumption exploited heavily heretofore precludes interdependence. Those who make policies for a small country must respond to changes in other countries' policies. This is an implication of openness. But they do not have to ask if changes in *their* policies will engender changes in other countries' policies.

Openness affects the small economy in two ways. First, the effects of domestic disturbances and changes in domestic policies are different from what they would be in a closed economy. The managers of monetary and fiscal policies have to allow for leakages through goods and asset markets that modify pervasively the way that the economy responds to disturbances and policy changes. Openness can even nullify certain policies. Under a pegged exchange rate, monetary policy can have no permanent influence on domestic activity (and when domestic and foreign securities are perfect substitutes, it cannot affect activity even temporarily).[2] Sec-

---

[1] The distinction drawn here and the discussion that follows reflect the treatment of these issues in R. C. Bryant, *Money and Monetary Policy in Interdependent Nations,* The Brookings Institution, Washington, D.C., 1980, chaps. 10–12.

[2] Under our version of the small-country assumption, moreover, the managers of policies must also take account of certain foreign repercussions. Because the economy is not a price taker in all international markets, the effects of domestic disturbances and policy changes are modified by their effects on foreign behavior (but not on foreign policies);

ond, disturbances originating in the outside world, including those reflecting the effects of other countries' policies, impinge on the markets in which the small country participates. Its managers must therefore respond to additional disturbances if they are to regulate domestic activity.

The small country, however, is too small to influence other countries' policies. Its policy decisions must take account of decisions made elsewhere but are not *inter*dependent with them. This was true for the small country studied in Parts II and III even though it was not a price taker in all markets. Its policies affected the foreign-currency price of its export good, p_1^f, but changes in that price were not allowed to influence the prices of foreign goods, foreign output, or foreign expenditure, and nothing that happened in that economy was allowed to influence foreign wealth. No one responsible for policies abroad had cause to react to the small country's policies.[3]

It would be important to study the interdependence of policies even if we sought merely to synthesize recent contributions to exchange-rate theory. The approach we have adopted, stressing portfolio optimization and asset-market integration, is most directly relevant to conditions in advanced economies, where private portfolios are large and financial markets are well developed, and few advanced economies are so small that they have no influence on their neighbors' policies. Furthermore, a country small enough to disregard policy interdependence may be unable to exploit its apparent autonomy. It may not be a feasible currency area and is likely to become a monetary satellite of a larger neighbor.[4] In brief, the theory developed here is most readily susceptible of application to countries and policy problems for which one must acknowledge policy interdependence and work out its implications.

terms like u_{10}^f appear in the solutions for domestic effects of domestic policies, reflecting changes in foreign behavior induced by endogenous changes in the foreign-currency price of the export good. If the economy were a price taker in all markets, u_{10}^f would appear only in solutions for the effects of exogenous changes in foreign prices. Furthermore, certain foreign disturbances would differ in form; shifts in levels or patterns of foreign spending, for example, would appear as exogenous changes in foreign prices.

[3] They might have cause to react to changes in the foreign-currency price of the small country's export good (due to changes in its home-currency price or in the exchange rate), as these would affect any index of foreign prices that included import prices, and the stabilization of that index might be a policy target.

[4] For more on this matter, see R. I. McKinnon, "Optimum Currency Areas: Comment," *American Economic Review*, 53 (September 1963), pp. 717–25, W. M. Corden, *Monetary Integration*, Essays in International Finance 93, Princeton University, Princeton, N.J., 1972, and E. Tower and T. D. Willett, *The Theory of Optimum Currency Areas and Exchange-Rate Flexibility: A More General Framework*, Special Papers in International Economics 11, Princeton University, Princeton, N.J., 1976, chap. 2.

There is another reason for introducing interdependence at this juncture. Much of this book is concerned with market integration, but the last part will examine problems involved in coordinating national policies and the quintessential form of coordination–policy unification. The costs and benefits of unification, however, can be fully appraised only in models that allow for policy interdependence.

When countries coordinate or unify policies, they give up formal autonomy–the right to make decisions unilaterally. But the sacrifice of real autonomy depends on the degree of market integration and the degree of policy interdependence. The relevance of market integration should be obvious by now. Recall the point just made about monetary policy. A country with a pegged exchange rate may not sacrifice any real autonomy by joining a monetary union; if its asset markets are closely integrated with those of other members of the union, the preservation of formal autonomy would not preserve much real autonomy. The relevance of policy interdependence is equally easy to demonstrate. A country with the formal autonomy to conduct an independent monetary policy may not have the opportunity to do so. Its autonomy may be circumscribed ex post by the responses of its neighbors and circumscribed ex ante by its own expectations concerning those responses.

To study policy unification, we must first examine these possibilities. We must ascertain how much autonomy a country can exercise in situations of policy interdependence and how the degree of interdependence is itself affected by the degree of market integration and the exchange-rate regime. It is thus time to drop the small-country assumption and to model interactions between national economies.

Unhappily, it does not suit our purpose merely to convert the model we have used before into a conventional two-country model. A world containing only two countries is not the one in which to study policy unification. A monetary union between the two countries would be a global union. There would be no way to study its responses to an external disturbance; all disturbances would be internalized. There would be no way to study the choice between a flexible and pegged exchange rate for the union as a whole and the implications for its members; the union would not have an external exchange rate. At a different analytical level, a conventional two-country model constrains the range of national responses to an exogenous disturbance. Events in one country are necessarily and mechanically reflected by the other in several important respects. In particular, there is little scope for independent changes in national wealth holdings. In a world without real capital formation, saving in one country must always be matched by dissaving in the other.

To meet our special needs and also to break new ground analytically, we borrow the technique employed in customs-union theory. We build a model containing two countries but cause them to function in a global setting. Each country exchanges goods and bonds with the other but also deals with the outside world. We present the model in this chapter, imitating deliberately the presentation of the small-country model in Chapter 2.

It is convenient, however, to impose restrictions on demand conditions, incomes, and wealth in the two countries, so as to limit the number of differences between their economies and the scope for differences between their reactions to disturbances and policy changes. These restrictions are described in Chapter 12, following the presentation of the model, so that the need for them and their severity are fully apparent. Finally, we solve the model in Chapter 13 and comment on some of the results. We show, for example, that asset-market integration cannot guarantee that the two economies will react identically to a disturbance, not even to a pure asset-market disturbance or one that has identical effects on impact. We are then ready for our final task–the analysis of policy unification.

An overview of the model

The basic framework of Chapter 2 is easily enlarged to include a second country. It was indeed designed with that in mind. The two countries, North and South, will trade with each other and the outside world. Each one is small, moreover, in the same sense as before. It can buy all it wants from the outside world at a constant world price but cannot export its own output at a constant price–not to the other country or to the outside world. By implication, neither country can import from the other without affecting the other's price. Each country is also small in that it can buy any quantity of bonds from the outside world at a constant world interest rate, and outsiders do not hold any of its bonds. Each country's households, however, hold bonds issued by the other country, and each central bank is likewise allowed to do so.

The two countries taken together thus bear a *joint* relationship to the outside world similar to that of the small country studied in previous chapters. But there are connections between North and South that had no counterparts in Chapter 2 and make the present model somewhat less symmetrical. The North, for example, is not a price taker in all markets where it is a buyer. It is a price taker in the markets for the world export good and the world bond. But it is not a price taker in the markets for the Southern good and Southern bond. (Turning the point around, the South faces a downward-sloping demand curve for its export good that is the sum of the Northern and world demand curves. It faces an upward-sloping supply curve for its imports from the North that is the difference between the Northern supply curve and the world demand curve. It faces a perfectly elastic supply curve, by contrast, for its imports from the outside world.)

To emphasize the similarities and differences between this model and the one in Chapter 2, we cast some of our results in terms of joint outcomes; we look at sums or averages of changes in Northern and Southern incomes, interest rates, and reserves. This approach is helpful even when the North and South do not have joint policy targets or unified policy instruments. It is especially helpful in Part V, where we study policy integration and attach normative significance to the joint outcomes. (In that context, the terms "joint" and "aggregate" come to be synonymous with the term "union" but are used in preference to that more familiar term unless we intend to imply that the North and South have agreed to treat sums or averages of national variables as policy targets. For the same reason, we describe the North and South as "neighbors" rather than "partners" unless they have established some sort of formal union. Finally, we use "world" and "foreign" interchangeably, to describe variables, functions, and events external to the North and South, and we do not describe anything Southern as being "foreign" when viewed from a Northern standpoint.)

The model constructed in this chapter features five financial assets – Northern, Southern, and world bonds, and Northern and Southern currencies. It likewise features three traded goods – Northern, Southern, and world exports. There are, then, at least six markets to be cleared by Northern and Southern variables (goods prices, interest rates, and exchange rates or reserves, depending on the choice of exchange-rate regime).[5] Were we to introduce nontraded goods, as in Chapter 2, there would be eight markets to be cleared in this fashion, making the mathematics much more difficult. We have already shown, however, that the inclusion of nontraded goods is important mainly for studying reactions to

[5] There are six markets, not eight, to be cleared by Northern and Southern variables, because the markets for the world bond and world export are cleared by instantaneous adjustments in quantities supplied; the world interest rate and world export price are exogenous. There is, of course, a set of foreign-exchange markets, but they clear automatically when other asset markets clear. There is also a labor market in each country, but it can be analyzed separately, as in Appendix A. It poses no special problems on the suppositions adopted heretofore (the extreme classical assumption that the supply of labor is fixed and the money wage flexible, and the corresponding Keynesian assumption that the money wage is fixed and the supply of labor perfectly elastic). We do not allow labor migration between North and South (i.e., labor-market integration).

goods-market disturbances that call for changes in resource allocation. Nontraded goods are not essential for understanding how incomes, interest rates, and exchange rates (or reserves) respond to changes in monetary and fiscal policies. We therefore exclude them, as we did in Part III. This makes our task easier than it would be if we were to transplant our small-country model to its new environment without trying to prune it in every way possible.

We *do* carry over to the new environment all of our assumptions concerning portfolio optimization, stationary expectations, and the ways that markets respond to disturbances. All markets are perfectly competitive and clear continuously. There are no transactions costs and no lags in households' responses to changes in prices, interest rates, and exchange rates.

There are two ways to present the new model–country by country or sector by sector. We adopt the second, using the same rubrics employed in Chapter 2 and analogous notational conventions. Variables prefixed by an asterisk are quantities desired (demanded), and variables carrying a bar are exogenous or policy determined. Bonds and money are denominated in the currency of the country in which they are issued. With two countries in the model, however, additional conventions are required. Prices expressed in foreign (world) currency are denoted by the superscript f, prices in Northern currency by unprimed variables, and prices in Southern currency by primed variables. The same devices are employed to denote sources of supply, demand, or ownership for goods and assets. In addition, goods and bonds originating in the outside world are denoted by the subscript 0, those in the North by 1, and those in the South by 2. Thus, p_0^f, p_0, and p_0' are the prices of the world export in foreign, Northern, and Southern currencies, respectively, the subscript indicating origin and the superscripts indicating currency. Similarly, $*B_1^{h'}$ is the demand by Southern households for the Northern bond, the asterisk indicating a quantity demanded, the subscript indicating the bond's origin and currency of denomination, and the superscripts indicating the source of the demand. (The variables used in this and other chapters dealing with the two-country model are listed with brief definitions in Section II of the Glossary.)

Production and the labor market

One good is produced in each country, the Northern export good 1 and the Southern export good 2. The output of each good depends on the amount of labor used, which equals the total demand for labor, and production is subject to diminishing returns:

(11.1) $Q_1 = Q_1(*E)$ $Q_{1E} > 0, Q_{1EE} < 0$

(11.2) $Q_2' = Q_2(*E')$ $Q_{2E} > 0, Q_{2EE} < 0$

where Q_1 and Q_2' are physical outputs, and $*E$ and $*E'$ are the total demands for labor in the North and South, respectively. In the present context, moreover, the two countries' nominal incomes (gross domestic products) are

(11.3) $Y = p_1 Q_1$

(11.4) $Y' = p_2' Q_2'$

where p_1 and p_2' are the prices of the goods in their own home currencies.

Because firms maximize profits at all times, their demands for labor are those that equate marginal value products to money wage rates:

(11.5) $w = p_1 Q_{1E}(*E)$

(11.6) $w' = p_2' Q_{2E}(*E')$

and the market-clearing equations for labor are

(11.7) $*E - E = 0$

(11.8) $*E' - E' = 0$

In the classical variant of the model, supplies of labor are perfectly inelastic:

(11.9a) $E = \bar{E}$

(11.10a) $E' = \bar{E}'$

and the market-clearing equations determine wage rates. In the Keynesian variant, supplies of labor are perfectly elastic at fixed money wage rates:

(11.9b) $w = \bar{w}$

(11.10b) $w' = \bar{w}'$

and the market-clearing equations determine levels of employment.

Wealth, saving, and the households' demands for goods

Households in each country hold all three bonds, but no household holds any currency other than the one issued domestically. Thus, there are four assets in households' portfolios.

The Northern households' balance sheet is

(11.11) $W^h = L_1^h + B_1^h + (\pi/\pi')B_2^h + \pi B_0^h$

where W^h is Northern household wealth denominated in Northern currency, where L_1^h is the households' stock of Northern money, B_1^h is their stock of Northern bonds, B_2^h is their stock of Southern bonds, and B_0^h is their stock of world bonds, and where π and π' are the prices of world currency in units of Northern and Southern currency, respectively (the spot exchange rates). The three bonds are bills, as in Chapter 2, and each is a promise to pay one unit of the currency in which it is issued. That is why Northern holdings of the Southern bond, B_2^h, must be converted from Southern to Northern currency (by way of world currency), and Northern holdings of the world bond must be converted from world to Northern currency.

The Southern households' balance sheet is

(11.12) $W^{h\prime} = L_2^{h\prime} + (\pi'/\pi)B_1^{h\prime} + B_2^{h\prime} + \pi'B_0^{h\prime}$

where $W^{h\prime}$ is Southern household wealth denominated in Southern currency, $L_2^{h\prime}$ is the households' stock of Southern money, and $B_1^{h\prime}$, $B_2^{h\prime}$, and $B_0^{h\prime}$ are Southern households' stocks of Northern, Southern, and world bonds, respectively.

It is again important to distinguish carefully between two ways in which nominal wealth can be altered–by current saving, S in the North and S' in the South, and by capital gains or losses resulting from exchange-rate changes. Defining the amounts of wealth accumulated through time T in consequence of saving,

(11.13) $W^{hs} = \int_0^T S\, dt$

(11.14) $W^{hs\prime} = \int_0^T S'\, dt$

we can write W^h and $W^{h\prime}$ as the sums of the histories of saving and of changes in exchange rates:

$$(11.15) \quad W^h = W^{hs} + \int_0^T \left[(\pi/\pi')B_2^h \left(\frac{\dot{\pi}}{\pi} - \frac{\dot{\pi}'}{\pi'} \right) + (\pi B_0^h) \frac{\dot{\pi}}{\pi} \right] dt$$

$$(11.16) \quad W^{h'} = W^{hs'} + \int_0^T \left[(\pi'/\pi)B_1^{h'} \left(\frac{\dot{\pi}'}{\pi'} - \frac{\dot{\pi}}{\pi} \right) + (\pi' B_0^{h'}) \frac{\dot{\pi}'}{\pi'} \right] dt$$

Desired saving depends positively on interest rates and disposable income, and negatively on actual wealth:

$$(11.17) \quad {}^*S = S(r_0, r_1, r_2, Y^d, W^h)$$

with $S_i > 0$ $(i = 0, 1, 2)$, $0 < S_Y < 1$, $S_W < 0$, and

$$(11.18) \quad {}^*S' = S'(r_0, r_1, r_2, Y^{d'}, W^{h'})$$

with $S_i' > 0$ $(i = 0, 1, 2)$, $0 < S_Y' < 1$, $S_W' < 0$, where $r_0, r_1,$ and r_2 are the nominal interest rates on world, Northern, and Southern bonds, and where Y^d and $Y^{d'}$ are disposable incomes. The saving functions are assumed to be homogeneous of first degree in disposable income and wealth. (In Chapter 12, we assume that the two functions are identical in certain ways and symmetrical in others.)

As in the one-country case, disposable income is the sum of gross domestic product and interest income *less* lump-sum tax payments by each country's households to their government, T^h and $T^{h'}$. Here, however, there are three types of interest income. Therefore:

$$(11.19) \quad Y^d = Y + r_0(\pi B_0^h) + r_1(B_1^h) + r_2(\pi/\pi')B_2^h - T^h$$

$$(11.20) \quad Y^{d'} = Y' + r_0(\pi' B_0^{h'}) + r_1(\pi'/\pi)B_1^{h'} + r_2(B_2^{h'}) - T^{h'}$$

Northern households consume all three traded goods, and their demands are defined, as usual, in physical terms:

$$(11.21) \quad {}^*C_0 = C_0(p_0, p_1, p_2, {}^*C)$$

$$(11.22) \quad {}^*C_1 = C_1(p_0, p_1, p_2, {}^*C)$$

$$(11.23) \quad {}^*C_2 = C_2(p_0, p_1, p_2, {}^*C)$$

subject to

$$(11.23a) \quad {}^*C = p_0 {}^*C_0 + p_1 {}^*C_1 + p_2 {}^*C_2$$

Desired consumption, ${}^*C$, is defined by

$$(11.24) \quad {}^*C = Y^d - {}^*S$$

Similarly, for Southern households,

(11.25) $*C_0' = C_0'(p_0', p_1', p_2', *C')$

(11.26) $*C_1' = C_1'(p_0', p_1', p_2', *C')$

(11.27) $*C_2' = C_2'(p_0', p_1', p_2', *C')$

subject to

(11.27a) $*C' = p_0'*C_0' + p_1'*C_1' + p_2'*C_2'$

where

(11.28) $*C' = Y^{d'} - *S'$

The six demand functions (11.21) through (11.23) and (11.25) through (11.27) are assumed to have properties identical to those of their counterparts in Chapter 2. They are homogeneous of degree zero in all prices and nominal consumption; they satisfy the requirements of gross substitutability; and they display unitary elasticities with respect to nominal consumption. Thus, the price elasticities of Northern demand obey these relationships:

$$e_{ij} > 0, \qquad e_{ij} = 1 + \sum_j e_{ij}, \qquad p_i*C_i e_{ij} = p_j*C_j e_{ji}$$

for $i, j = 0, 1, 2$ ($i \neq j$), and we have the usual relationship among the marginal propensities to spend:

$$\sum_i m_i = 1$$

where $m_i = p_i C_{ic}$, $i = 0, 1, 2$. Analogous relationships hold for Southern elasticities and propensities.

Government and foreign consumption

Each government consumes Northern and Southern output, and its spending decisions are policy determined in nominal terms. Formally:

(11.29) $*G_1 = \bar{G}_1$

(11.30) $*G_2 = \bar{G}_2$

(11.31) $*G_1' = \bar{G}_1'$

(11.32) $*G_2' = \bar{G}_2'$

where $*G_1$ and $*G_2$ are Northern government expenditures on Northern and Southern goods, respectively, and are denominated in Northern currency, whereas $*G_1'$ and $*G_2'$ are Southern government expenditures and are denominated in Southern currency.

The foreign demand for each country's export good is defined in physical terms and assumed to depend in the usual way on prices and nominal foreign consumption:

(11.33) $*C_1^f = C_1^f(p_0^f, p_1^f, p_2^f, *C^f)$

(11.34) $*C_2^f = C_2^f(p_0^f, p_1^f, p_2^f, *C^f)$

These functions have the same properties as their Northern and Southern counterparts, but foreign consumption, $*C^f$, is exogenous:

(11.35) $*C^f = \bar{C}^f$

Finally, goods-market arbitrage is assumed to align the three prices for each traded good:

(11.36) $p_0 = \pi p_0^f$

(11.37) $p_0' = \pi' p_0^f$

(11.38) $p_1 = \pi p_1^f$

(11.39) $p_1' = \pi' p_1^f$

(11.40) $p_2 = \pi p_2^f$

(11.41) $p_2' = \pi' p_2^f$

The goods markets

The supply of foreign (world) exports is perfectly elastic at a fixed foreign-currency price:

(11.42) $p_0^f = \bar{p}_0^f$

Quantities supplied adjust instantaneously to satisfy Northern and Southern demands, $*C_0$ and $*C_0'$, clearing the market continuously. The markets for Northern and Southern goods are cleared by instantaneous price adjustments, and the market-clearing equations are

(11.43) $*C_1 + *C_1' + *C_1^f + (*G_1/p_1) + (*G_1'/p_1') - Q_1 = 0$

(11.44) $*C_2 + *C_2' + *C_2^f + (*G_2/p_2) + (*G_2'/p_2') - Q_2' = 0$

And because we assume that each sector in each country is able always to obtain the quantities that it demands, there can be no unintended saving in either country:

(11.45) $S = {}^*S$

(11.46) $S' = {}^*S'$

Households' demands for money and bonds

Households' demands for money and bonds are expressed in the relevant domestic currency. They depend on interest rates and nominal wealth. Therefore, in the North,

(11.47) ${}^*L_1^h = L_1(r_0, r_1, r_2, W^h)$

(11.48) $\pi^*B_0^h = B_0(r_0, r_1, r_2, W^h)$

(11.49) ${}^*B_1^h = B_1(r_0, r_1, r_2, W^h)$

(11.50) $(\pi/\pi')^*B_2^h = B_2(r_0, r_1, r_2, W^h)$

The demand for money varies inversely with each interest rate ($L_{1i} < 0$, for $i = 0, 1, 2$). The bonds are gross substitutes; the demand for any bond increases with its interest rate and decreases with each of the other interest rates ($B_{ii} > 0$, and $B_{ij} < 0$, for $i \neq j$). All four demands increase with wealth; they are indeed assumed to be homogeneous of first degree in nominal wealth.[6] Finally, the demands are constrained by

(11.50a) $W^h = {}^*L_1^h + {}^*B_1^h + (\pi/\pi')^*B_2^h + \pi^*B_0^h$

implying that

$$L_{1j} + \sum_i B_{ij} = 0 \quad \text{and} \quad L_{1W} + \sum_i B_{iW} = 1$$

for $i, j = 0, 1, 2$.

Similarly, in the South,

(11.51) ${}^*L_2^{h'} = L_2'(r_0, r_1, r_2, W^{h'})$

(11.52) $\pi'^*B_0^{h'} = B_0'(r_0, r_1, r_2, W^{h'})$

(11.53) $(\pi'/\pi)^*B_1^{h'} = B_1'(r_0, r_1, r_2, W^{h'})$

---

[6] Recall that this is tantamount to writing the demand for any asset, ${}^*A_j$, as ${}^*A_j = A_j(r_0, r_1, r_2)W^h$. We use this formulation when we describe similarities between demands for assets in the North and South.

(11.54) $*B_2^{h\prime} = B_2^{\prime}(r_0, r_1, r_2, W^{h\prime})$

where

(11.54a) $W^{h\prime} = *L_2^{h\prime} + (\pi^{\prime}/\pi)*B_1^{h\prime} + *B_2^{h\prime} + \pi^{\prime}*B_0^{h\prime}$

and these demands display analogous properties.

The central banks and monetary policies

Northern money, L_1, is issued by the Northern central bank and Southern money, $L_2^{\prime}$, by the Southern central bank. There are no commercial banks. Each central bank, in turn, holds Northern bonds, Southern bonds, and foreign-exchange reserves denominated in world currency. Thus, the balance sheet of the Northern bank is

(11.55) $L_1 + W^c = B_1^c + (\pi/\pi^{\prime})B_2^c + \pi R$

where

(11.56) $W^c = \int_0^T \left[(\pi/\pi^{\prime})B_2^c \left(\frac{\dot{\pi}}{\pi} - \frac{\dot{\pi}^{\prime}}{\pi^{\prime}} \right) + (\pi R) \frac{\dot{\pi}}{\pi} \right] dt$

being the history of capital gains and losses due to the effects of exchange-rate changes on the home-currency values of the bank's external assets. The balance sheet of the Southern bank is

(11.57) $L_2^{\prime} + W^{c\prime} = (\pi^{\prime}/\pi)B_1^{c\prime} + B_2^{c\prime} + \pi^{\prime}R^{\prime}$

where

(11.58) $W^{c\prime} = \int_0^T \left[(\pi^{\prime}/\pi)B_1^{c\prime} \left(\frac{\dot{\pi}^{\prime}}{\pi^{\prime}} - \frac{\dot{\pi}}{\pi} \right) + (\pi^{\prime}R^{\prime}) \frac{\dot{\pi}^{\prime}}{\pi^{\prime}} \right] dt$

being the history of that bank's capital gains and losses.

Each central bank's demand for bonds is determined in accordance with its policy objectives:

(11.59) $*B_1^c = \bar{B}_1^c$

(11.60) $*B_2^c = \bar{B}_2^c$

(11.61) $*B_1^{c\prime} = \bar{B}_1^{c\prime}$

(11.62) $*B_2^{c\prime} = \bar{B}_2^{c\prime}$

The banks' demands for foreign-exchange reserves will necessarily reflect their exchange-rate policies, and these call for careful specification.

Intervention, exchange rates, and reserve settlements

A world with two independent exchange rates, π and π', admits of four distinct exchange-rate regimes. Before we can describe them algebraically, however, we must say more about the definition of reserves.

If the assets measured by R and R' are *held* in world currency, not merely expressed in that currency, the central banks' balance sheets must be read to say that neither bank holds the other's currency; no term in Eq. (11.55) represents Northern holdings of Southern currency, and no term in Eq. (11.57) represents Southern holdings of Northern currency.[7] How, then, can we model the effects of intervention in the foreign-exchange market by one of the two central banks to influence the bilateral (North–South) exchange rate? We can do so by assuming that the two central banks have concluded a reciprocal agreement concerning redemptions of currency balances. Alternatively, we can reinterpret R and R' to include (with appropriate signs) the net claims of one bank on the other.

If the Northern central bank abstains from accumulating Southern currency, it must be able to convert into world currency all of the Southern currency it may acquire when it intervenes in the foreign-exchange market to influence the bilateral exchange rate. The Southern central bank must agree to redeem the Southern currency presented by the Northern bank (to purchase it with world currency at the current exchange rate π'), and the Northern bank must make a reciprocal commitment. Each central bank must honor its commitment even when it does not buy its domestic currency from private holders. The Southern bank, for example, must purchase Southern currency presented by the Northern bank even when it does not intervene to peg π' in the foreign-exchange market. To use language made familiar by debates about intervention and convertibility under floating rates, central banks wishing to avoid reciprocal currency accumulations must agree to "mandatory asset settlement." Failing to do so, each may see its currency become a reserve asset as the incidental consequence of intervention by the other central bank.[8]

---

[7] Each central bank holds the other country's bonds, but these holdings do not function as foreign-currency reserves. They do not vary endogenously to settle imbalances between North and South when there is a pegged exchange rate between those countries' currencies. They function instead as policy variables. A change in B_S^g, for example, is an open-market operation by the Northern bank in the Southern bond.

[8] For more on these issues, see P. B. Kenen, "Techniques to Control International Reserves," in R. A. Mundell and J. J. Polak, eds., *The New International Monetary System: Proceedings of the Conference in Memory of J. Marcus Fleming*, Columbia University Press, New York, 1977, pp. 202–22.

With mandatory settlement in world currency, a Northern purchase of Southern currency in the foreign-exchange market causes an increase of Northern reserves and an equal decrease of Southern reserves, both measured in world currency. In the absence of offsetting open-market operations, the two countries' money stocks will change by equal but opposite amounts. The same things would happen automatically, however, if the central banks agreed to accumulate claims on each other. It is easy to accommodate this possibility. We have only to reinterpret R and R' as the *net* claims of the two central banks *expressed* in world currency, including but not exclusively the claims that are *held* in world currency. Let R be Northern bank holdings of world *and* Southern currencies taken together *less* liabilities to the Southern bank. Similarly, let R' be Southern bank holdings of world *and* Northern currencies *less* liabilities to the Northern bank. On these interpretations, a Northern purchase of Southern currency is by definition an addition to Northern reserves and a subtraction from Southern reserves, and it has the same effects on money supplies as when the Southern currency is converted into world currency.[9]

The chief point to note here is that the absence of mandatory asset settlement elevates each currency to reserve-currency status but does so without insulating either country from the money-supply effects of its own or its neighbor's interventions in the foreign-exchange market. The international monetary system has been accused of conferring an "exorbitant" privilege on the principal reserve-currency country, partly because that country is insulated automatically from the money-supply effects of movements in its net reserves. The truth of that charge, insofar as it pertains to automatic insulation, derives from the fact that official holdings of the reserve currency have been invested in government securities and similar money-market instruments. Changes in those holdings affect the net reserve position of the reserve-currency country but do not affect its money supply, because they do not affect the size or composition of the liabilities of its central bank.

[9] We can make these points formally with the aid of three new variables: Let L_2^c be Northern bank holdings of Southern currency (measured in Southern currency); let $L_1^{c'}$ be Southern bank holdings of Northern currency (measured in Northern currency); and let R^f be Northern holdings of world currency (measured in that currency). Rewriting Eq. (11.55), $L_1 + L_1^{c'} + W^c = B_1^c + (\pi/\pi')B_2^c + \pi R^f + (\pi/\pi')L_2^c$, where L_1 must now be interpreted as the Northern money stock held by Northerners. Rearranging this equation, we get $L_1 + W^c = B_1^c + (\pi/\pi')B_2^c + \pi R^n$, where $R^n = R^f + (L_2^c/\pi') - (L_1^{c'}/\pi)$, which is the world-currency value of Northern *net* reserves. The new balance-sheet equation for the Northern bank is fully equivalent to Eq. (11.55). R^n has replaced R. (To use the new equation, however, we would have to redefine W^c, because the history of capital gains and losses caused by exchange-rate changes would have now to include the effects of changes in π' on the Northern-currency value of L_2^c.)

To catalogue exchange-rate arrangements succinctly, it is useful to employ two new variables. The first is the bilateral exchange rate between the Northern and Southern currencies:

(11.63) $z = (\pi/\pi')$

defined here as the Northern-currency price of the Southern currency. The second is the sum of Northern and Southern reserves:

(11.64) $R^t = R + R'$

denominated in world currency. (In Part V, R^t will measure the external assets of a reserve pool, payments union, or full-fledged monetary union between North and South. Its use here, however, has no specific institutional connotation.)

Under two of the four exchange-rate regimes, the bilateral exchange rate, z, will be pegged by unilateral intervention conducted by one central bank; under the others, it will be flexible (endogenous). The four regimes can then be cross-classified according to their implications for R^t. The four regimes, however, can be put into effect by no fewer than 10 methods, without even counting those that involve joint action by the two central banks or by the monetary union studied in Part V. Eight of the 10 methods are listed in Table 11.1.[10] Here are the four regimes to which they give rise:

A. *The joint float.* In case 1 of Table 11.1, the Southern central bank refrains from intervention in the foreign-exchange market. But the Northern bank operates to stabilize the bilateral rate, z, by purchasing or selling Southern currency against Northern currency. Under these arrangements π and π' are endogenous, and z is exogenous. Furthermore, changes in R and R' offset each other, and R^t cannot change. (Reserves will behave this way whether there is mandatory asset settlement or because the definitions of reserves include bilateral currency claims.) Formally,

(11.65a) $\pi = \bar{z}\pi'$

(11.66a) $R^t = \bar{R}^t$

---

[10] The two strategies omitted from the table are those involving intervention in both currencies by one central bank and no intervention by the other bank. The Southern central bank could intervene in world *and* Northern currencies, and the Northern bank would do nothing; in this instance, as in case 3 of Table 11.1, π' and z would be pegged directly, and π would be pegged by private arbitrage. Alternatively, the Northern central bank could intervene in world *and* Southern currencies, and the Southern bank would do nothing; in this instance, as in case 4 of the table, π and z would be pegged directly, and π' would be pegged by arbitrage.

Table 11.1. *Intervention policies and exchange-rate regimes*

Case	Currency of Southern intervention	Currency of Northern intervention	Exchange-rate behavior			Reserve behavior		
			π	π'	z	R	R'	R^t
1	None	Southern	Flexible	Flexible	Pegged	Variable	Variable	Constant[a]
2	Northern	None	Flexible	Flexible	Pegged	Variable	Variable	Constant[a]
3	World	Southern	Pegged[b]	Pegged	Pegged	Variable	Variable	Variable
4	Northern	World	Pegged	Pegged[b]	Pegged	Variable	Variable	Variable
5	World	World	Pegged	Pegged	Pegged[b]	Variable	Variable	Variable
6	None	World	Pegged	Flexible	Flexible	Variable	Constant	Variable[c]
7	World	None	Flexible	Pegged	Flexible	Constant	Variable	Variable[c]
8	None	None	Flexible	Flexible	Flexible	Constant	Constant	Constant

[a] Variations in R and R' equal with opposite signs.
[b] By private arbitrage.
[c] Variations in R^t equal to those of R or R'.

Case 2 is symmetrical. It differs only by assigning to the Southern bank all of the responsibility for intervention. The two cases, then, can be analyzed together, which is what we do in Chapter 13.

We call this first regime a common or joint float, because π and π' move together (unless the central bank assigned to intervene shifts its support point for z). It is equivalent analytically to a full-fledged monetary union with a floating exchange rate vis-à-vis the outside world. When we describe it hereafter, we usually refer to the particulars of case 1. This is because we examine disturbances and policies from the Northern viewpoint, and it is convenient to do so by assuming that the South has adopted a particular exchange-rate policy (nonintervention in this instance), leaving the North to choose the policy best suited to its aims and circumstances.

B. *The joint peg.* In case 3 of Table 11.1, the Southern central bank intervenes to peg its currency in terms of world currency. The Northern bank, in turn, intervenes to peg its currency in terms of Southern currency. Under these arrangements, π is endogenous, but because π' and z are exogenous, π will be pegged by private arbitrage. Here, moreover, R and R' are endogenous, so that R^t is endogenous as well. As before,

(11.65b) $\pi = \bar{z}\pi'$

but the second condition is replaced by

(11.66b) $\pi' = \bar{\pi}'$

Cases 4 and 5 are virtually symmetrical with case 3, and we study the three cases together.[11]

[11] There are small formal differences among the three cases. In case 4, for example, Eq. (11.66b) must be replaced by $\pi = \bar{\pi}$, and π' is pegged by arbitrage; in case 5, the *two* exchange-rate equations must be replaced by $\pi = \bar{\pi}$ and $\pi' = \bar{\pi}'$, and z is pegged by arbitrage. In case 3, moreover, changes in R, reflecting Northern intervention in the Southern currency, will cause opposite changes in R', but R' will change independently too, whenever the Southern central bank intervenes in world currency to stabilize π'. Similarly, in case 4, changes in R', reflecting Southern intervention in the Northern currency, will cause opposite changes in R, but R will change independently as well. Finally, in case 5, changes in R and R' will be completely independent of each other. Nevertheless, the changes in R, R', and R^t caused by a particular disturbance will be the same in cases 3 through 5. The three cases would be slightly different if central banks allowed exchange rates to fluctuate within fixed limits (between intervention points). Suppose that they adopt k percent margins on both sides of each pegged rate, leaving the margins for the third rate to be determined by arbitrage. In case 5, the spreads for π and π' will total $2k$ percent, and those for z will total roughly $4k$ percent. In cases 3 and 4, the margins for π and π', respectively, are the ones that will be doubled. It is, of course, possible to narrow the margins for the third exchange rate by narrowing those for one of the other two. This is what was done by participants in the so-called snake confining bilateral exchange rates

We call this regime a common or joint peg, because no exchange rate can move (unless one central bank shifts its support point). It is equivalent analytically to a monetary union with a pegged exchange rate vis-à-vis the outside world. We usually describe it in terms of case 3, which is the operational analogue of case 1.

C. *The mixed regime.* In case 6 of Table 11.1, the Southern central bank abstains from intervention. But the Northern bank pegs the rate between its own currency and the world currency. Under these arrangements, π' and z are endogenous, and π is exogenous. Here, moreover, R' cannot change, not even as a consequence of Northern intervention to peg π, and changes in R^t can occur only with changes in R. Algebraically,

(11.65c) $\bar{\pi} = z\pi'$

(11.66c) $R' = \bar{R}'$

In case 7, strategies, conditions, and outcomes are reversed, but there is no fundamental analytical asymmetry.

We do not study these mixed cases, however, because they are not likely to prevail in the economic and political circumstances on which we concentrate hereafter. It is our chief concern to investigate the implications of financial integration, and a flexible bilateral exchange rate is apt to interfere with both market integration and policy integration.[12]

D. *No intervention.* In case 8 of Table 11.1, there is no intervention whatsoever. All three exchange rates are endogenous, and there can be no changes in R, R', or R^t. Algebraically,

(11.65d) $R = \bar{R}$

between European currencies to margins narrower than those set by the International Monetary Fund. On these and other operational problems, see H. W. Mayer, *The Anatomy of Official Exchange-Rate Intervention Schemes,* Essays in International Finance 104, Princeton University, Princeton, N.J., 1974.

[12] It would be anomalous, moreover, to analyze this regime (or the fourth regime below) on the assumptions we adopt in Chapter 12, where we impose symmetrical asset preferences on Northern and Southern households. Northerners view Southern bonds in the same way that Southerners view Northern bonds, and both take the same view of foreign bonds. This assumption is not plausible when π' is pegged and π is not. The price of the foreign bond is fixed in Southern currency (barring a once-for-all change in the pegged Southern exchange rate), but it is variable in Northern currency. In consequence, Southerners may hold more foreign than Northern bonds, as they may regard foreign bonds to be closer substitutes for Southern bonds and currency. But Northerners have no analogous reason for holding more foreign than Southern bonds, because the prices of both bonds are variable in terms of Northern currency. (The same objection can be made against any attempt to analyze a change in the bilateral exchange rate, z, under a joint float or peg. If households in either country foresee the possibility of changes in the bilateral rate, they may not display the symmetrical asset preferences on which our analysis is based.)

(11.66d) $R' = \bar{R}'$

But this regime will not occupy us further, for the same reason that we set aside the mixed regime.

The governments' budgets and fiscal policies

Turning from monetary to fiscal policies, we revert to the assumptions adopted in Chapter 2. Each government uses lump-sum taxes and transfers to exercise control over receipts from households and foreigners. The taxes and transfers are T^h and T^f in the North, $T^{h\prime}$ and $T^{f\prime}$ in the South.

Each government's receipts include taxes from households, transfers from nonresidents, and interest income earned by the central bank. Its outlays include the government's spending on Northern and Southern goods and its interest payments. In the North, then, the budget deficit is

(11.67) $D = \bar{G}_1 + \bar{G}_2 + r_1 B_1 - T^h - T^f - [r_1 B_1^c + r_2(\pi/\pi')B_2^c]$

where D is the deficit, B_1 is the public debt, and both are denominated in Northern currency. Similarly, in the South,

(11.68) $D' = \bar{G}_1' + \bar{G}_2' + r_2 B_2' - T^{h\prime} - T^{f\prime} - [r_1(\pi'/\pi)B_1^{c\prime} + r_2 B_2^{c\prime}]$

where D' and B_2' are denominated in Southern currency.

Government deficits are financed by issuing bonds, so that

(11.69) $B_1 = \displaystyle\int_0^T D \, dt$

(11.70) $B_2' = \displaystyle\int_0^T D' \, dt$

and nominal deficits are policy determined, so that

(11.71) $D = \bar{D}$

(11.72) $D' = \bar{D}'$

As in Chapter 2, moreover, deficits are produced by tax reductions and have finite lives. Eventually, each government balances its budget by raising taxes, and these decisions terminate the cumulative changes in B_1 and B_2'.

Transfers from nonresidents play the same roles they did in the one-country model. They offset interest income on the current account of each country's balance of payments and, in conjunction with the lump-sum taxes, cancel interest earnings from disposable incomes.[13] The transfers are defined by

(11.73) $T^f = r_1(B_1^{h'} + B_1^{c'}) - [r_0(\pi B_0^h) + r_2(\pi/\pi')(B_2^h + B_2^c)]$

(11.74) $T^{f'} = r_2(B_2^h + B_2^c) - [r_0(\pi' B_0^{h'}) + r_1(\pi'/\pi)(B_1^{h'} + B_1^{c'})]$

When these conditions hold and deficit spending is policy determined, the two countries' taxes, T^h and $T^{h'}$, have by implication to be adjusted continuously in order to realize the desired deficits.[14]

The asset markets

The supply of foreign bonds is perfectly elastic at a constant world interest rate:

(11.75) $r_0 = \bar{r}_0$

The market for that bond is cleared continuously by instantaneous variations in the quantity supplied. The markets for other financial assets are cleared by variations in r_1 and r_2 and in the exchange rates π and π' (or the stocks of central-bank reserves).

The market-clearing equations for Northern and Southern bonds are

(11.76) $*B_1^h + *B_1^{h'} + *B_1^c + *B_1^{c'} - B_1 = 0$

(11.77) $*B_2^h + *B_2^{h'} + *B_2^c + *B_2^{c'} - B_2' = 0$

The market-clearing equations for the two currencies are

(11.78) $*L_1^h - L_1 = 0$

(11.79) $*L_2^{h'} - L_2' = 0$

---

[13] In Chapter 12, we show that the bilateral balance of payments between North and South plays no significant role in our work. In consequence, we need not identify separately transfers between North and South and transfers from the outside world. The point is similar to one made by Meade. To balance the external accounts of a monetary union, it is sufficient for each member to balance its own accounts on a global basis; it is neither necessary nor appropriate for each member to seek bilateral balance with every other member and, separately, with the outside world. See J. E. Meade, "The Balance of Payments Problem of a Free Trade Area," *Economic Journal*, 67 (September 1957), pp. 379–96.

[14] In the North, for example, Eqs. (11.67), (11.71), and (11.73) together imply that

$$T^h = \bar{G}_1 + \bar{G}_2 + r_0\pi B_0^h + r_2(\pi/\pi')B_2^h + r_1(B_1 - B_1^c - B_2^c - B_1^{h'}) - \bar{D}$$
$$= \bar{G}_1 + \bar{G}_2 + r_0\pi B_0^h + r_2(\pi/\pi')B_2^h + r_1 B_1^h - \bar{D}$$

which gives us the relationship required later to rewrite the definition of disposable income.

Finally, we assume that each sector in each country is able to carry out its plans, obtaining the desired quantities of assets:

(11.80) $*B_1^c = B_1^c$

(11.81) $*B_2^c = B_2^c$

(11.82) $*B_1^h = B_1^h$

(11.83) $*B_2^h = B_2^h$

(11.84) $*B_1^{c\prime} = B_1^{c\prime}$

(11.85) $*B_2^{c\prime} = B_2^{c\prime}$

(11.86) $*B_1^{h\prime} = B_1^{h\prime}$

(11.87) $*B_2^{h\prime} = B_2^{h\prime}$

(11.88) $*L_1^h = L_1^h$

(11.89) $*L_2^{h\prime} = L_2^{h\prime}$

Taken together with Eqs. (11.11), (11.12), (11.50a), and (11.54a), these statements also say that $*B_0^h = B_0^h$, and $*B_0^{h\prime} = B_0^{h\prime}$.

Summary

The 89 equations presented above determine the endogenous variables in this model (the variables listed in Section II of the Glossary). We can write the model more compactly, however, by focusing on the market-clearing equations for Northern and Southern goods, bonds, and currencies.

The goods-market equations can be rewritten as

$$(11.43a) \quad C_1(z\pi'\bar{p}_0^f, p_1, zp_2', Y^d - *S) + C_1'\left(\pi'\bar{p}_0^f, \frac{p_1}{z}, p_2', Y^{d\prime} - *S'\right)$$

$$+ C_1^f\left(\bar{p}_0^f, \frac{p_1}{z\pi'}, \frac{p_2'}{\pi'}, \bar{C}^f\right) + (\bar{G}_1/p_1) + (z\bar{G}_1'/p_1) - \theta_1(p_1) = 0$$

$$(11.44a) \quad C_2(z\pi'\bar{p}_0^f, p_1, zp_2', Y^d - *S) + C_2'\left(\pi'\bar{p}_0^f, \frac{p_1}{z}, p_2', Y^{d\prime} - *S'\right)$$

$$+ C_2^f\left(\bar{p}_0^f, \frac{p_1}{z\pi'}, \frac{p_2'}{\pi'}, \bar{C}^f\right) + (\bar{G}_2/zp_2') + (\bar{G}_2'/p_2') - \theta_2(p_2') = 0$$

where the functions $\theta_1(p_1)$ and $\theta_2(p_2')$ stand for the outputs Q_1 and Q_2', reflecting the fact that the labor-market equations of the model allow us to express each output as a function of its own price.[15]

The bond-market equations can be rewritten as

(11.76a) $B_1(\bar{r}_0, r_1, r_2, W^h) + zB_1'(\bar{r}_0, r_1, r_2, W^{h\prime}) + \bar{B}_1^c + \bar{B}_1^{c\prime} - B_1 = 0$

(11.77a) $B_2(\bar{r}_0, r_1, r_2, W^h) + zB_2'(\bar{r}_0, r_1, r_2, W^{h\prime}) + z\bar{B}_2^c + z\bar{B}_2^{c\prime} - zB_2' = 0$

The money-market equations can be rewritten as

(11.78a) $L_1(\bar{r}_0, r_1, r_2, W^h) - [\bar{B}_1^c + z\bar{B}_2^c + z\pi'R - W^c] = 0$

(11.79a) $zL_2'(\bar{r}_0, r_1, r_2, W^{h\prime}) - [\bar{B}_1^{c\prime} + z\bar{B}_2^{c\prime} + z\pi'R' - zW^{c\prime}] = 0$

As in Chapter 2, however, W^h and $W^{h\prime}$ can be replaced wherever they appear, using the histories of saving and capital gains given by Eqs. (11.15) and (11.16), whereas W^c and $W^{c\prime}$ can be replaced, using the histories of capital gains given by Eqs. (11.56) and (11.58). Furthermore, the two countries' histories of saving, W^{hs} and $W^{hs\prime}$, and their public debts, B_1 and B_2', are state variables. They cannot change instantaneously. Changes in those variables are described by the dynamic equations:

(11.13a) $\dot{W}^{hs} = {}^*S = S(\bar{r}_0, r_1, r_2, Y^d, W^h)$

(11.14a) $\dot{W}^{hs\prime} = {}^*S' = S'(\bar{r}_0, r_1, r_2, Y^{d\prime}, W^{h\prime})$

(11.69a) $\dot{B}_1 = \bar{D}$

(11.70a) $\dot{B}_2' = \bar{D}'$

where $\bar{D}$ and $\bar{D}'$ go to zero at the policy-determined time $t = k$, so that the proof of stability involves only the first two dynamic equations.

For purposes of analyzing impact effects, the six market-clearing equations can be deemed to contain 10 endogenous variables; the prices p_1 and p_2, the interest rates r_1 and r_2, the exchange rates π' and z (or stocks of reserves, R and R'), the disposable incomes Y^d and $Y^{d\prime}$, and the levels of desired saving, ${}^*S$ and ${}^*S'$. These last two variables, moreover, are functions of interest rates, disposable incomes, and stocks of household wealth (and the latter, we said, can be replaced by the histories of saving

---

[15] The procedure is no different in principle from the one in Appendix A and is slightly simpler, because each country produces only one commodity. (By implication, each supply is perfectly inelastic in the classical case, where total employment is fixed.) Note that π has been replaced by $z\pi'$ wherever it appeared. This substitution anticipates our treatment of the two exchange-rate regimes A and B in subsequent chapters.

and capital gains). Furthermore, disposable incomes depend on outputs, budget deficits, and government expenditures:[16]

(11.19a) $Y^d = Y + \bar{D} - \bar{G}_1 - \bar{G}_2$

(11.20a) $Y^{d\prime} = Y' + \bar{D}' - \bar{G}_1' - \bar{G}_2'$

where

(11.3a) $Y = p_1 \theta_1(p_1)$

(11.4a) $Y' = p_2' \theta_2(p_2')$

We have enough equations to determine the impact effects of disturbances and policies on p_1, p_2', r_1, r_2, π', and z (or R and R'), the six market-clearing variables.

Turning to the steady-state effects, we proceed just as we did in Chapter 2. Once we have proven stability, we set $*S = *S' = 0$. We then solve Eqs. (11.13a) and (11.14a) simultaneously with the six market-clearing equations to obtain the steady-state changes in each country's wealth and in goods prices, interest rates, and exchange rates (or reserves).

Before we perform these tasks, however, we introduce a series of restrictions on the dissimilarities between North and South. These are meant to simplify the algebra and, more important, to highlight the subset of differences between the two countries that may be most germane to financial integration and policy interdependence.

---

[16] These statements derive from Eqs. (11.19) and (11.20), together with the statements about T^h and $T^{h\prime}$ illustrated in note 14.

12

Similarities and symmetries in goods and asset markets

The market-clearing equations and the balance-of-payments accounts

The model presented in Chapter 11 was simplified in several ways in order to facilitate solution and interpretation. Because we omitted nontraded goods, only two goods-market equations have to be solved simultaneously, and nominal income in each country depends exclusively on that country's export price. Because demands for money depend on wealth but not on income and there are no real capital stocks, the model is partitionable, and we can depict the roles of asset markets in the instantaneous determination of exchange rates. Finally, because taxes and transfers are adjusted continuously, interest-income terms drop out of disposable incomes and current-account balances, changes in stocks of debt become exogenous, and we can work with only two dynamic equations when we come to prove stability.

Nevertheless, the model contains six market-clearing equations, and each one includes a number of arguments. The equation for the Northern bond, for example, includes demands by Northern and Southern households, each demand depending on three interest rates and on two exchange rates (affecting stocks of wealth). It also includes demands by central banks, along with the supply of bonds from the Northern government. Were we to solve the six market-clearing equations as they stand, the outcomes would contain large numbers of parameters, reflecting Northern, Southern, and foreign responses to changes in goods prices, exchange rates, and interest rates.

In this chapter, then, we impose additional simplifications aimed at reducing the number of parameters and at resolving a number of ambiguities. These make it easier to solve the model and, more important, to interpret the results. By way of introduction, we set out the balance-of-payments accounts for the North and South and extract a number of assertions about trade flows, transfers, and reserve flows. Thereafter, we impose restrictions on behavior in goods markets, on behavior in bond

321

and money markets, and on desired saving in North and South. Finally, we impose a series of restrictions analogous to those adopted in Part III. These serve to preclude "crowding out" and to guarantee "proportionality" between interest-rate effects on saving and on demands for money.

To derive a balance-of-payments equation for the North, we must first rearrange the market-clearing equation for Northern output:[1]

(12.1) $[(p_1C_1^f + p_1C_1' + z\bar{G}_1') - (p_0C_0 + p_2C_2 + \bar{G}_2)] + [T^f + r_0(\pi B_0^h)$
$+ r_2(zB_2^h + z\bar{B}_2^c) - r_1(B_1^{h'} + \bar{B}_1^{c'})] + \bar{D} - S = 0$

The first term in brackets is the Northern trade balance; it is the sum of merchandise exports to foreigners and Southerners (including exports to the Southern government) *less* the sum of merchandise imports from foreigners and Southerners (including imports by the Northern government). The second term in brackets is the net inflow on account of transfers and interest; it is the sum of transfers from foreigners and interest income earned on foreign and Southern bonds (including Southern bonds held by the Northern central bank) *less* interest income paid on Northern bonds (including Northern bonds held by the Southern central bank). The two terms together are the current-account balance, and Eq. (12.1) is therefore the familiar national-income identity. With no investment in the model, a current-account surplus must be matched by the sum of public and private saving.

Next, we take the total time derivatives of household and central-bank balance sheets and of the market-clearing equations for Northern bonds and money to obtain this statement:[2]

(12.2) $S - \bar{D} = \pi \dot{R} + \pi \dot{B}_0^h + z\dot{B}_2^h - \dot{B}_1^{h'}$

---

[1] Proceeding sequentially, we rewrite Eq. (11.43) in terms of Northern currency and invoke Eq. (11.3):

$$p_1(^*C_1 + {}^*C_1' + {}^*C_1^f) + (\bar{G}_1 + z\bar{G}_1') - Y = 0$$

Using Eqs. (11.23a) and (11.24) to replace $p_1{}^*C_1$ by $[(Y^d - {}^*S) - p_0{}^*C_0 - p_2{}^*C_2]$ and rearranging terms,

$$(p_1{}^*C_1' + p_1{}^*C_1^f + z\bar{G}_1') - (p_0{}^*C_0 + p_2{}^*C_2) + \bar{G}_1 - (Y - Y^d) - {}^*S = 0$$

But the difference between Y and Y^d can be replaced using Eqs. (11.19) and (11.67):

$$Y - Y^d = T^h - r_0(\pi B_0^h) - r_1(B_1^h) - r_2(zB_2^h)$$
$$= (\bar{G}_1 + \bar{G}_2) - \bar{D} - T^f + r_1(B_1^{h'} + \bar{B}_1^{c'}) - r_0(\pi B_0^h) - r_2(zB_2^h + z\bar{B}_2^c)$$

Substituting into the new version of Eq. (11.43) and replacing desired with actual quantities (because they are always equal), we obtain Eq. (12.1).

[2] From the time derivatives of Eqs. (11.11) and (11.15), $\dot{W}^{hs} = \dot{L}_1^h + \dot{B}_1^h + z\dot{B}_2^h + \pi\dot{B}_0^h$. But from Eqs. (11.55), (11.56), and (11.76), $\dot{L}_1 = \dot{B}_1^c + z\dot{B}_2^c + \pi\dot{R}$, and $\dot{B}_1^h = \dot{B}_1 - \dot{B}_1^c -$

Substituting into Eq. (12.1),

$$(12.3) \quad [(p_1C_1^f + p_1C_1' + z\bar{G}_1') - (p_0C_0 + p_2C_2 + \bar{G}_2)]$$
$$+ [T^f + r_0(\pi B_0^h) + r_2(zB_2^h + z\bar{B}_2^c) - r_1(B_1^{h'} + \bar{B}_1^{c'})]$$
$$+ [\dot{B}_1^{h'} - \pi\dot{B}_0^h - z\dot{B}_2^h] - \pi\dot{R} = 0$$

This *is* the Northern balance-of-payments equation. The current-account balance, the net capital inflow, and the reserve flow must sum to zero.

The same statement is reproduced as the final column of Table 12.1, which also shows the Northern balance of payments with the South and with the outside world. In the regional columns, T^b denotes a bilateral transfer from South to North (denominated in Southern currency), and $\dot{R}^b$ denotes a bilateral reserve flow from South to North (denominated in world currency). Table 12.2 shows the corresponding balance-of-payments equation for the South.[3]

Several propositions used in this and later chapters can be obtained by inspecting the balance-of-payments equations and tables:

1. Because saving and government deficits go to zero in the steady state, Eq. (12.1) and its Southern counterpart demonstrate directly that each country's current-account balance must also be zero in the steady state.

2. The cancellation of interest-income flows by the transfers T^f and $T^{f'}$ does not require that those transfers be distributed by region to offset bilateral interest-income flows. When we aggregate the regional accounts in Tables 12.1 or 12.2, the bilateral transfer T^b drops out completely; its size is irrelevant to the global outcome.

3. The regional pattern of transfer payments is likewise irrelevant to the state of the two countries' balance with the outside world. Their joint balance is obtained by summing the global balances of the North and South or by summing their regional balances with the outside world. In both cases, T^b drops out. Following the second procedure, we convert to Northern currency the Southern balance with the outside world and add it

---

$\dot{B}_1^{c'} - \dot{B}_1^{h'}$. Furthermore, $\dot{L}_1 = \dot{L}_1^h$, and $\dot{B}_1^c = \dot{B}_1^{c'} = \dot{B}_2^c = 0$, because open-market operations are conducted instantaneously. Therefore, $\dot{W}^{hs} = \pi\dot{R} + \dot{B}_1 - \dot{B}_1^{h'} + z\dot{B}_2^h + \pi\dot{B}_0^h$. But $W^{hs} = S$, and $\dot{B}_1 = \bar{D}$ giving Eq. (12.2).

[3] In Tables 12.1 and 12.2, the Northern exchange rate π is replaced by its equivalent $z\pi'$, to facilitate comparisons between tables. In both tables, moreover, transfers are shown to offset interest-income flows, pursuant to Eqs. (11.73) and (11.74). Note in passing that the balance-of-payments equations and tables deal entirely in flows; they omit the instantaneous shifts between assets already encountered in our work with the one-country model and encountered again in Chapter 13 below. These shifts, however, appear only in the capital accounts. The propositions in the text would not be affected substantially if the equations and tables were amended to include those shifts.

Table 12.1. *The Northern balance of payments (in Northern currency)*

Item	Regional		Global
	South	Rest of world	
Merchandise trade:			
Exports	$p_1 C_1' + z G_1'$	$p_1 C_1^f$	$p_1 C_1' + z G_1' + p_1 C_1^f$
Imports	$p_2 C_2 + G_2$	$p_0 C_0$	$p_2 C_2 + G_2 + p_0 C_0$
Interest and transfers, net	$z T^b + r_2(z B_2^h + z B_2^c) - r_1(B_1^{h'} + B_1^{c'})$	$(T^f - z T^b) + r_0 \pi B_0^h$	0
Capital inflow (+), net	$\dot{B}_1^{h'} - z \dot{B}_2^h$	$-\pi \dot{B}_0^h$	$\dot{B}_1^{h'} - z \dot{B}_2^h - \pi \dot{B}_0^h$
Overall (monetary) surplus (−)	$-\pi \dot{R}^b$	$-\pi(\dot{R} - \dot{R}^b)$	$-\pi \dot{R}$

Table 12.2. *The Southern balance of payments (in Southern currency)*

Item	Regional		Global
	North	Rest of world	
Merchandise trade:			
Exports	$p_2' C_2 + (1/z) G_2$	$p_2' C_2^f$	$p_2' C_2 + (1/z) G_2 + p_2' C_2^f$
Imports	$p_1' C_1 + G_1'$	$p_0' C_0$	$p_1' C_1 + G_1' + p_0' C_0$
Interest and transfers, net	$-T^b - r_2(B_2^h + B_2^c) + r_1(1/z)(B_1^{h'} + B_1^{c'})$	$(T^{f'} + T^b) + r_0 \pi' B_0^h$	0
Capital inflow (+), net	$-(1/z)\dot{B}_1^{h'} + \dot{B}_2^h$	$-\pi' \dot{B}_0^{h'}$	$-(1/z)\dot{B}_1^{h'} + \dot{B}_2^h - \pi' \dot{B}_0^{h'}$
Overall (monetary) surplus (−)	$\pi' \dot{R}^b$	$-\pi'(\dot{R}' + \dot{R}^b)$	$-\pi' \dot{R}'$

to the corresponding Northern balance:

$$[(p_1C_1^f + p_2C_2^f) - (p_0C_0 + p_0C_0')] - \pi[\dot{B}_0^h + \dot{B}_0^{h'}] - \pi\dot{R}^t = 0$$

where

$$\dot{R}^t = \dot{R} + \dot{R}'$$

There is no place in this equation for the bilateral transfer T^b or the bilateral reserve flow $\dot{R}^b$.

4. The absence of $\dot{R}^b$ from that same joint balance has an additional implication. The joint change in reserves, R^t, can be zero even when the North and South are not in bilateral balance. It is sufficient that one country's surplus with the outside world offset the other's deficit.

5. Bilateral balancing is not needed even for each country to achieve global balance by itself–a special instance of joint balance. One country can achieve a surplus with the other country to offset a deficit with the outside world. (This is what happens in the steady state, when $\dot{R} = \dot{R}' = 0$.)

6. There is no reason to *expect* bilateral balancing of current accounts, not even in the steady state, when all financial flows go to zero. The Northern balance of payments becomes

$$[(p_1C_1' + z\bar{G}_1') - (p_2C_2 + \bar{G}_2)] + [p_1C_1^f - p_0C_0] = 0$$

and the joint balance becomes

$$(p_1C_1^f - p_0C_0) + (p_2C_2^f - p_0C_0') = 0$$

Bilateral balancing would satisfy these conditions, but it is not the only way to do so.

We return to the matter of bilateral balancing after we have introduced additional restrictions on incomes and demand conditions in the North and South. We show that those restrictions do not modify the statements made above, especially statement 6.

Similarities and symmetries in goods markets

It is common in trade theory to assume that demand conditions are the same in all countries and invariant with respect to country size. All consumers are assumed to have identical tastes and homothetic indifference maps. Under these assumptions, each country's demands for goods are unaffected by the distribution of domestic income given by factor supplies and factor prices; all demands display unitary elasticities with respect to aggregate expenditure; and demand functions for a single good are not different across countries.[4]

Some of these same strict assumptions are required here, if only to preclude shifts in demands for goods resulting from changes in factor prices. We have not mentioned any factor price other than the money wage rate, but the assumption of diminishing returns to labor imposed on Eqs. (11.1) and (11.2) may be taken to imply that there is at least one other factor of production. Changes in the money wage rate may therefore involve changes in the income distribution, and these could shift demands for goods within the North or South if all households in each country did not have identical tastes and homothetic indifference maps. (The same distributional effects were cited in Chapter 2 as one reason for neglecting stocks of real capital in the definition of household wealth. If changes in commodity and factor prices can influence the incomes of industry-specific capital stocks, they can change the market values of those stocks, affecting stocks of wealth and interfering with partitionability.) But we do *not* assume that tastes are identical in the North, the South, and the outside world.

At one stage in our work, we adopted that assumption. Households in the North and South were made to display identical marginal propensities to spend on each country's good; we set $m_i = m_i'$, for $i = 1, 2$. This assumption, however, is inappropriate to the class of problems studied in Part V. When tastes are identical across countries and there are no non-traded goods, an open-market purchase of the Northern bond does not have more influence on Northern income than an open-market purchase of the Southern bond, even when Northern and Southern bonds are not perfect substitutes.

An open-market purchase of the Northern bond reduces the Northern interest rate by more than the Southern rate, and under the assumptions made below concerning the behavior of Northern saving, spending by Northerners rises more than spending by Southerners. When tastes are identical in both countries, however, the marginal propensity to spend on the Northern good can be smaller in both countries than the marginal propensity to spend on the Southern good. In this event, the increase in demand for the Northern good will be smaller than the increase in demand

[4] See, e.g., P. A. Samuelson, "Social Indifference Curves," *Quarterly Journal of Economics*, 70 (February 1956), pp. 1–22, P. B. Kenen, "On the Geometry of Welfare Economics," *Quarterly Journal of Economics*, 71 (August 1957), pp. 426–47, and P. B. Kenen, "Distribution, Demand and Equilibrium in International Trade," *Kyklos*, 12 (1959), pp. 629–36.

for the Southern good, and there will then be a smaller increase in Northern income. The relative effects of an open-market purchase will not depend on the nationality of the bank or bond involved in the purchase. This is an inappropriate starting point for studying effects of asset-market integration and monetary unification.[5]

We must therefore adopt a different strategy–one that has been used before in open-economy models. Tastes are identical across households in each country but differ symmetrically between the two countries. Formally, $m_1 = m_2'$ and $m_2 = m_1'$, which says, of course, that $m_0 = m_0'$, and we use this statement too. Furthermore, household demands are biased toward home goods. Each country's marginal propensity to consume its home good is larger than its marginal propensity to consume the other country's good. In the North, $m_1 > m_2$, which implies that $m_2' > m_1'$ in the South, because tastes are symmetrical.[6]

From time to time in Part V, we impose additional restrictions on conditions in goods markets, to give what we call *full-scale goods-market symmetry* and eliminate certain ambiguities. We assume that price elasticities are fully symmetrical and that government and foreign demands are likewise symmetrical in the initial steady state. We assume that the production functions are the same in the two countries and that levels of employment are the same in the initial steady state.[7] We impose full-scale goods-market symmetry when we want to illustrate as clearly as possible the consequences of economic interdependence and reactions by one country to the other country's policies. We do not impose it from the start, however, because we would rule out a wide range of differences between the ways in which the North and South are affected by disturbances and policies. Differences in the effects of monetary, fiscal, and exchange-rate policies are narrowed but not ruled out completely by the restrictions we have placed on the m_i (and by those that we place later on desired saving).

[5] Were we to restore nontraded goods to this model, we could solve the problem by assuming that $m_N + m_1 > m_2$ in the North and that $m_N' + m_2' > m_1'$ in the South, where m_N and m_N' are the marginal propensities to spend on nontraded goods. (These suppositions would not be inconsistent with assuming that $m_i = m_1'$, $i = N, 0, 1, 2$.)

[6] These assumptions could be taken to imply that price elasticities are also symmetrical–that $u_{10} = u_{20}'$ and $u_{20} = u_{10}'$, in the notation of Chapter 13. But we do not impose this additional requirement (and even if we did, it would not affect our findings significantly, unless we were to make the additional assumption that $u_{10}' = u_{20}'$).

[7] Putting these assumptions algebraically, $Q_1(*E) = Q_2(*E')$, $e_{i0} = e_{j0}'$, and $e_{10}' = e_{20}'$, for i, $j = 1, 2$. In the initial steady state, moreover, $\bar{G}_1 = z\bar{G}_2'$ and $\bar{G}_2 = z\bar{G}_1'$, $*E = *E'$, and $p_1*C_1' = p_2*C_2'$. Combining these assumptions with those made later about asset-market symmetry and using the notation of Chapter 13, we obtain $\sigma_1 = \sigma_2'$, and $u_{10}' = u_{20}'$. These are the equalities that we invoke when we impose full-scale goods-market symmetry.

Similarities and symmetries in asset markets

As we were tempted to suppose that demands for goods are the same in North and South, we were also tempted to suppose that demands for assets are the same. But here again it is more useful to suppose that they are symmetrical rather than identical. The case for symmetry, moreover, is stronger logically on the asset-market side than on the goods-market side.

Although it is convenient to assume symmetrical demands for goods, it is not easy to reconcile that assumption with the microeconomic underpinnings of our model. Consider the reasons given by Meade for assuming symmetrical demands for goods in his model:[8]

Quite apart from import duties or other artificial restrictions on imports, the facts that transport costs will be less in the purchase of [domestic] products and that the purchasers in each country have greater familiarity with the qualities, conditions of sale, supplies, etc., of their own country's products will cause purchasers in each country to have some natural preference for the purchase of home products. Indeed, many products, including bulky commodities like houses and perishable services like haircuts, cannot be transported and must be purchased from home production.

But there are no transport costs in our model, and we assume throughout that households are perfectly familiar with all goods and with conditions in all markets. Furthermore, we have deleted nontraded goods–Meade's houses and perishable services–and there are no inventories or capital goods. All outputs are consumed when they are produced. Accordingly, uncertainties about the time paths of goods prices, including the path of the exchange rate, are irrelevant to the specification of the demands for goods.[9] Hence, there is no fundamental justification for assuming that Northern and Southern households have different demands for goods merely because of the goods' geographic origins. Northern goods should not bulk larger in Northern consumption than in Southern consumption merely because they are produced in the North.

To assume symmetrical demands for assets, however, is not just convenient. It is logical. Money and bonds are long-lived, and wealth holders'

[8] J. E. Meade, *The Balance of Payments,* Oxford University Press, London, 1951, p. 67.
[9] Expectations about time paths of goods prices are *not* irrelevant to the determination of desired saving, which is concerned with the allocation of consumption over time. This was one of the chief complications encountered in Chapter 9. But the way in which we specify the demands for goods precludes any indirect effect on patterns of demand in the North and South; saving affects demands for goods by affecting aggregate consumption, and the marginal propensities to spend on individual commodities are invariant with respect to aggregate consumption.

views about the future have therefore to influence current demands. Furthermore, the nationalities of bonds and money say something about their characteristics as seen from North and South. Northern bonds and money are denominated in Northern currency, Southern bonds and money in Southern currency. Northern bonds are apt to be closer substitutes for Northern money than Southern (or foreign) bonds, and Southern bonds are apt to be closer substitutes for Southern money. By the same token, Northern bonds and money, taken together, may be closer substitutes for Southern and for foreign bonds, viewed from a Northern standpoint. This would be the case if Northerners believe that the North-South exchange rate will be more stable than the rate between the Northern and world currencies. In other words, a monetary union may increase the degree of market integration, and the *modus operandi* of the union itself may thus depend in part on the extent to which Northerners and Southerners are persuaded that the union will be permanent – that the North-South exchange rate will be fixed forever.

Other facts impinge upon wealth holders' attitudes in ways that cause them to be more secure about investments in domestic assets. We repeat what one of us has written elsewhere:[10]

A wealth holder's *willingness* to hold claims on foreigners can be affected by a number of circumstances. Some of these derive from the exercise of sovereignty – from the governments' powers to tax, to coin money, and to legislate the terms on which private individuals and institutions enter and uphold contractual obligations. Some of them derive from the costs of buying knowledge and from the risks of acting with incomplete knowledge. . . .

A wealth holder's willingness to hold any asset depends directly on the costs he must incur to obtain information concerning its quality. Borrowers and the instruments they issue are not homogeneous, and the differences between them are one major reason for limitations on the domain of any asset and on the substitutability of one asset for another. . . .

When one turns from the domestic to the world scene, the heterogeneity of borrowers and instruments is amplified. The domains of nonfinancial activity are more remote, and lenders are not as familiar with borrowers, even with institutions whose size and financial situation compare favorably with those of domestic institutions. . . .

Compounding these effects of distance and environment, there are large international differences in the amounts of information that borrowers are required to disclose. Most borrowers, including governments, are creatures of law, not natural persons, and laws differ significantly from country to country. There are, in fact, three distinct juridical dimensions to the distinction between domestic and foreign investment, bearing upon the costs of gathering information and of redeeming one's mistakes. First, there are differences in the rights and duties that laws confer on artificial persons. . . . Second, debt instruments are defined, is-

[10] P. B. Kenen, *Capital Mobility and Financial Integration: A Survey*, Princeton Studies in International Finance 39, Princeton University, Princeton, N.J., 1976, pp. 24–31.

sued, and traded under the specific provisions of national statutes that regulate accounting practices, the disclosure of financial information, the rights of claimants in instances of default, and the organization of securities markets. Third, the administration of the law is itself an attribute of national sovereignty, and one's standing before the law can depend precariously on one's nationality.

The last points are the ones that pertain directly to our model. The bonds with which we deal here are short-term bills. The only reason for uncertainty about their prices, apart from changes in exchange rates, is.the possibility of default. That possibility may not be judged to be the same–or viewed with the same concern–by wealth holders in different countries. Northerners may attach less risk to default on the Northern bond than they do to default on the Southern or foreign bond, even though the three bonds are issued by governments, and they may be more confident of recourse in domestic courts. Southerners may feel the same way about the risks and costs of default on the Southern bond relative to those on the Northern or foreign bond.

Whatever the reasons for national or local biases in wealth holders' preferences, the biases can be embodied in our model by placing three sets of restrictions on the demands for assets. Working first with Northern demands, Eqs. (11.47) through (11.50), we impose these conditions:

1. Northern bonds are not perfect substitutes for Southern or foreign bonds, so that $0 < -B_{1j} < \infty$, and $0 < -B_{j1} < \infty$, for $j = 0, 2$.[11]

2. Northern money is a closer substitute for Northern bonds than for Southern or foreign bonds, so that $0 < -L_{1j} < -L_{11} < \infty$, for $j = 0, 2$.

3. Northerners hold more Northern bonds and add more to their holdings with an increase in their wealth, so that $B_1^h > zB_2^h$, and $B_1^h > \pi B_0^h$ for all sets of interest rates, and $B_{1W} > B_{jW}$, for $j = 0, 2$.[12]

---

[11] We place no restrictions on the relative sizes of the partial derivatives B_{10} and B_{01}, measuring substitutability between Northern and foreign bonds, or on those of B_{12} and B_{21} relative to B_{10} and B_{01}, measuring substitutability between Northern and Southern bonds on the one hand and Northern and foreign bonds on the other. The suggestion above, that a monetary union will increase the substitutability between Northern and Southern bonds, may be taken to assert that B_{12} and B_{21} will be larger absolutely than B_{10} and B_{01}, but this is not the only important possibility. To take a practical example, dollar-denominated bonds may be closer substitutes for domestic bonds in European portfolios than for bonds issued in other European countries. In such instances, of course, the integration of European asset markets takes place indirectly, by way of external markets. See P. R. Allen, *Organization and Administration of a Monetary Union,* Princeton Studies in International Finance 38, Princeton University, Princeton, N.J., 1976, pp. 21–2.

[12] Because demands for bonds are homogeneous of first degree in nominal wealth, one set of inequalities is redundant; because $B_{1W} = (B_1^h/W^h)$, $B_{2W} = (zB_2^h/W^h)$, and $B_{0W} = (\pi B_0^h/W^h)$, one set of inequalities implies the other. We return to these matters later.

The first condition is antecedent to the others. If Northern bonds were perfect substitutes for Southern or foreign bonds, there could be no national biases in Northern asset preferences. (Mathematically, the second and third conditions disappear from the results in Chapter 13 when $-B_{1j}$ and $-B_{j1}$ become infinitely large.)

To install qualitative symmetry between Northern and Southern preferences, we impose analogous restrictions on Southern demands for assets. First, $0 < -B'_{2j} < \infty$, and $0 < -B'_{j2} < \infty$; second, $0 < -L'_{2j} < -L'_{22} < \infty$; and third, $B_2^{h'} > (1/z)B_1^{h'}$, $B_2^{h'} > \pi'B_0^{h'}$, and $B'_{2W} > B'_{jW}$. (In all instances, $j = 0, 1$.)

Qualitative symmetry, however, does not simplify sufficiently the work that lies ahead. We require quantitative symmetry, and it is achieved by imposing restrictions on initial exchange rates, on initial interest rates, and on the forms of the demand functions for bonds and money:

A. In the initial steady state, the exchange rates π and π' are assumed to imply a North-South exchange rate, z, that equalizes stocks of wealth in the North and South (i.e., $W^h = zW^{h'}$). Furthermore, interest rates are equal initially in the North and South (i.e., $r_1 = r_2$) but not necessarily equal to the foreign rate.

B. The two demands for money, Eqs. (11.47) and (11.51), are assumed to be symmetrical in one respect and identical in others. They are symmetrical in that the roles of r_1 and r_2 are reversed. They are identical in that the roles of r_0 and wealth are identical. The same restrictions are imposed on the demands for foreign bonds, Eqs. (11.48) and (11.52).[13]

C. The two demands for Northern bonds and those for Southern bonds are assumed to be symmetrical in *two* respects and identical in others. They are symmetrical in that the roles of r_1 and r_2 are reversed, just as in the demands for money and for foreign bonds. They are also symmetrical in that the Northern demand for Northern bonds, Eq. (11.49), is assumed to be identical in all other ways to the Southern demand for Southern bonds, Eq. (11.54), whereas the Northern demand for Southern bonds, Eq. (11.50), is assumed to be identical in all other ways to the Southern demand for Northern bonds, Eq. (11.53).

Taken together with the three sets of restrictions on the Northern demand functions (or their Southern counterparts), these assumptions generate two series of equalities.

First, they produce pairwise equalities in money and bond holdings. In

---

[13] These restrictions are not independent of those in A and C, because one demand equation is redundant in each country.

the initial steady state,

$$L_1^h = zL_2^{h\prime}, \quad B_1^h = zB_2^{h\prime}, \quad zB_2^h = B_1^{h\prime}$$

By implication, of course, $B_0^h = B_0^{h\prime}$.

Second, they produce pairwise equalities between the partial derivatives of the various demand functions. In the neighborhood of the initial steady state,

$$
\begin{array}{llll}
L_{1W} = L_{2W}', & L_{11} = zL_{22}', & L_{12} = zL_{21}', & L_{10} = zL_{20}' \\
B_{1W} = B_{2W}', & B_{11} = zB_{22}', & B_{12} = zB_{21}', & B_{10} = zB_{20}' \\
B_{2W} = B_{1W}', & B_{22} = zB_{11}', & B_{21} = zB_{12}', & B_{20} = zB_{10}'
\end{array}
$$

from which there follows a similar set of equalities with respect to demands for the foreign bond.[14]

Similarities, symmetries, and saving

Because saving translates income into wealth, it is the link between goods and asset markets. This fact is reflected in the way we treat the saving functions, Eqs. (11.17) and (11.18). They are made to be similar in some respects and symmetrical in others.

The saving functions are assumed to be identical in the roles assigned to income and wealth. Formally,

$$S_Y = S_Y' \quad \text{and} \quad S_W = S_W'$$

In the initial steady state, then, disposable incomes will be equal in the

---

[14] To show how the restrictions A through C produce these inequalities, we revert to the notation suggested in note 6 of Chapter 11 and write each country's demand function for its own domestic bond as $*B_1^h = b_1(r_0, r_1, r_2)W^h$ and $*B_2^h = b_2'(r_0, r_1, r_2)W^{h\prime}$. Our assumption in A about exchange rates says that $W^h = zW^{h\prime}$ initially. Our first statement about symmetry in C says that the roles of r_1 and r_2 are reversed in the second equation, and we can represent this supposition by reversing the order in which they appear. Therefore, $*B_2^h = b_2'(r_0, r_2, r_1)(1/z)W^h$. Our second statement about symmetry in C asserts that the functions $b_1(r_0, r_1, r_2)$ and $b_2'(r_0, r_2, r_1)$ are identical, but actual demands obtained from those functions will not be equal initially unless r_1 and r_2 are equal initially, as assumed in A. In proof, suppose that r_1 were larger than r_2. Then $b_1(.\ .\ .)$ would be larger than $b_2'(.\ .\ .)$, because the higher rate, r_1, enters positively into $b_1(.\ .\ .)$ and negatively into $b_2'(.\ .\ .)$, whereas the lower rate, r_2, enters negatively into $b_1(.\ .\ .)$ and positively into $b_2'(.\ .\ .)$. When actual demands are equal, however, we obtain directly the first set of equalities given in the text, as $b_1 = B_{1W}$ and $b_2' = B_{2W}'$. To derive the remaining equalities, we differentiate the two equations with respect to the ith interest rate, obtaining $B_{1i} = b_{1i}(r_0, r_1, r_2)W^h$ and $zB_{2i} = b_{2i}'(r_0, r_2, r_1)W^h$. But our statements about symmetry assert that $b_{11}(.\ .\ .) = b_{22}'(.\ .\ .)$, that $b_{12}(.\ .\ .) = b_{21}'(.\ .\ .)$, and that $b_{10}(.\ .\ .) = b_{20}'(.\ .\ .)$ when $r_1 = r_2$, which yield the remaining equalities.

North and South. As saving is zero and the saving functions are homogeneous of first degree in disposable income and wealth, $^-Y^d = -(S_W/S_Y)W^h$ in the North, and $zY^{d\prime} = -(S'_W/S'_Y)zW^{h\prime}$ in the South, so that $Y^d = zY^{d\prime}$ because we have assumed that $W^h = zW^{h\prime}$.

The two functions are assumed to be symmetrical in the roles assigned to interest rates. In the neighborhood of the initial steady state, where $r_1 = r_2$ and $W^h = zW^{h\prime}$,

$$S_1 = zS'_2, \qquad S_2 = zS'_1, \qquad S_0 = zS'_0$$

These restrictions are consistent with our suppositions about asset preferences. When r_1 and r_2 play symmetrical roles in determining demands for bonds and money, they should also play symmetrical roles in determining desired saving, for saving is the way that households accumulate the wealth they invest in bonds and money.

Bilateral balancing once again

The similarities and symmetries adopted in this chapter eliminate large numbers of coefficients from the solutions to our model. Their roles will not be obvious, however, because we use them from the start to substitute one term for another, rather than invoking them later on to simplify expressions that have already been displayed in their full complexity. For this reason, however, care must be taken in interpreting the m_i, S_i, B_{ij}, and other terms. Because $m_1 = m'_2$, for example, m_1 stands for the Northern marginal propensity to spend on the Northern good *and* for the Southern marginal propensity to spend on the Southern good; in other words, it is the marginal propensity to spend on the home good in each country, not on the Northern good per se. Similarly, m_2 is the marginal propensity to spend on the neighbor's good, not on the Southern good per se. Analogous interpretations must be attached to S_1, S_2, etc.

But two things must be done before we can solve the model. First, we must ask if the assumptions introduced in this chapter have restrictive implications for trade patterns. Second, we must impose additional restrictions to preclude crowding out and those needed to obtain proportionality in interest-rate responses, just as we did throughout Part III.

When stocks of wealth are equal initially in the North and South, disposable incomes are also equal. And under the assumptions adopted above that $m_1 = m'_2$ and $m_2 = m'_1$, Northern consumption of the Southern good will equal Southern consumption of the Northern good (i.e.,

$p_2 C_2 = p_1 C_1'$). But these equalities do not imply bilateral balancing. The trade balance between North and South is given in Table 12.1 by

$$(p_1 C_1' + z G_1') - (p_2 C_2 + G_2)$$

and this expression will not be zero unless *government* demands are symmetrical too–unless Northern government spending on the Southern good is equal to Southern government spending on the Northern good. (By implication, there is bilateral balancing at those points in the argument of Part V where we impose full-scale goods-market symmetry to simplify the exposition. Even at those points, however, bilateral balancing obtains only with respect to the initial steady state. Government demands are symmetrical initially, but changes in one country's fiscal policies may introduce asymmetries.)

Crowding out and proportionality

The possibility of crowding out arises when private expenditure (absorption) is relatively sensitive to changes in interest rates and the demand for money is relatively sensitive to changes in wealth. In this model, however, the responses of absorption mirror those of household saving. There is no investment. To preclude the possibility that crowding out will dominate, we have therefore to assume that desired saving is relatively sensitive to changes in wealth whereas the demand for money is relatively sensitive to changes in interest rates. As in Part III, then,

$$(S_W/S_i) < (L_{1W}/L_{1i}) \qquad i = 0, 1, 2$$

Under the assumptions made above concerning the saving functions and demands for money, this supposition holds automatically in the North and South.

Ambiguities in the effects of changes in r_0, the foreign interest rate, cropped up in Part II partly from the possibility of crowding out and partly from the ways in which the demand for money and desired saving can respond collectively to changes in interest rates. The same ambiguities appeared pervasively in Chapter 9, where expectations of exchange-rate changes were perforce reflected in expectations about p_0, the home-currency price of the foreign good, affecting real interest rates and desired saving. By that time, however, we had taken steps to resolve the problem. We assumed proportionality in interest-rate effects and make the same assumption now:

$$(S_0/L_{10}) = (S_1/L_{11}) = (S_2/L_{12})$$

Again, the assumption of asset-market symmetry extends these equalities automatically, causing them to hold in the North and South alike.[15]

[15] As in Chapter 5, proportionality combines with the assumption that $(S_W/L_{1W}) < (S_1/L_{11})$ to preclude crowding out with respect to other interest rates.

13

Comparative statics in the two-country model

Solving for impact effects

We turn now to the solution of the two-country model presented in Chapter 11, using the assumptions introduced in Chapter 12. We proceed much as we did in Chapter 3, from impact to dynamic to steady-state effects, but pause to comment briefly on important outcomes as we go along, rather than waiting until later chapters.

As in the one-country case, impact effects of disturbances and policies are obtained by solving the market-clearing equations for changes in interest rates, goods prices, and exchange rates (or reserves), given the integrals of saving, W^{hs} and $W^{hs\prime}$, and stocks of government bonds, B_1 and B_2'.[1] At this juncture, moreover, we are able again to partition the model – to solve the equations for the bond and money markets to obtain effects on interest rates and exchange rates (or reserves), then to solve the two goods-market equations for effects on prices, incomes, and employment (or money wage rates).

Impact effects in asset markets

Differentiating totally Eqs. (11.76a), (11.77a), (11.78a), and (11.79a), we obtain four equations relating changes in r_1, r_2, π', z, R, and R' to changes in $\bar{r}_0$, $\bar{B}_1^c$, $\bar{B}_1^{c\prime}$, $\bar{B}_2^c$, and $\bar{B}_2^{c\prime}$, and in the stocks W^{hs}, $W^{hs\prime}$, B_1, and B_2'. In this and all subsequent chapters, however, the bilateral exchange rate is pegged irrevocably (i.e., z is unity and δz is zero). We are thus concerned with changes in π', which comes to represent the joint external exchange rate. We never have to solve simultaneously any more than three asset-market equations. They are the total derivatives of Eqs. (11.76a) and (11.77a) and the *sum* of the total derivatives of Eqs. (11.78a) and (11.79a). These give the changes in r_1, r_2, and π' or R^t resulting from open-market operations by the two central banks, from an exogenous change in the foreign interest rate, and from exogenous changes in various stocks.

---

[1] As in Chapter 3, however, we include in our solutions the effects of changes in those stocks, which are needed to obtain dynamic effects.

336

A flexible external rate. When the Southern central bank permits its exchange rate π' to float freely, and the Northern bank pegs the bilateral exchange rate, there can be no change in R^t, the sum of Northern and Southern reserves. Therefore:[2]

$$(13.1a) \quad \begin{bmatrix} -B_{11}^t & -B_{12}^t & -B_{1W}^t \\ -B_{12}^t & -B_{11}^t & -B_{1W}^t \\ -L_{11}^t & -L_{11}^t & -2L_{1W} \end{bmatrix} \begin{bmatrix} \delta r_1 \\ \delta r_2 \\ V_\pi\left(\dfrac{\delta\hat\pi'}{\pi'}\right) \end{bmatrix}$$

$$= \begin{bmatrix} B_{10}^t \\ B_{10}^t \\ 2L_{10} \end{bmatrix} [\delta\bar r_0] + \begin{bmatrix} 1 & 1 & 0 & 0 \\ 0 & 0 & 1 & 1 \\ -1 & -1 & -1 & -1 \end{bmatrix} \begin{bmatrix} \delta\bar B_1^c \\ \delta\bar B_1^{c'} \\ \delta\bar B_2^c \\ \delta\bar B_2^{c'} \end{bmatrix}$$

$$+ \begin{bmatrix} B_{1W} & B_{2W} & -1 & 0 \\ B_{2W} & B_{1W} & 0 & -1 \\ L_{1W} & L_{1W} & 0 & 0 \end{bmatrix} \begin{bmatrix} \delta W^{hs} \\ \delta W^{hs'} \\ \delta B_1 \\ \delta B_2' \end{bmatrix}$$

where, with symmetrical asset preferences,

$$B_{10}^t = B_{10} + B_{20} < 0 \qquad B_{11}^t = B_{11} + B_{22} > 0$$
$$B_{12}^t = B_{12} + B_{21} < 0 \qquad L_{11}^t = L_{11} + L_{12} < 0$$

and

$$B_{1W}^t = B_{1W} + B_{2W} > 0 \qquad V_\pi = \pi B_0^h = \pi' B_0^{h'} > 0$$

It follows, of course, that

$$B_{11}^t + B_{12}^t + B_{01}^t + L_{11}^t = 0$$

where

$$B_{01}^t = B_{01} + B_{01} < 0$$

and that

$$B_{1W}^t + B_{0W} + L_{1W} = 1$$

and we make extensive use of these relationships later.[3] Finally, we denote the change in π', the Southern exchange rate vis-à-vis the outside

[2] Here and in subsequent sections of this chapter, equations numbered a and b relate to flexible and pegged external rates, respectively, whereas those without suffixes relate equally to both regimes.

[3] The terms B_{10}^t, B_{11}^t, B_{12}^t, and L_{11}^t reflect the effects of interest-rate changes on the sum of Northern and Southern demands for a single asset. Thus, B_{11}^t appears in the Northern bond equation as $B_{11} + B_{11}'$ and in the Southern bond equation as $B_{22} + B_{22}'$; symmetrical preferences, however, render each of these two terms equal to $B_{11} + B_{22}$. (The term L_{11}^t reflects

world, by $\delta\hat{\pi}'$, in order to remind us that it is a change in *both* countries' rate. It is, in effect, an endogenous change in a jointly floating rate, because the bilateral rate is pegged.

The determinant of this system is $-2(B^t_{11} - B^t_{12})J_\pi$, and it is negative because

$$J_\pi = [L_{1W}(B^t_{11} + B^t_{12}) - B^t_{1W}(L^t_{11})] = -[(1 - B_{0W})L^t_{11} + L_{1W}B^t_{01}] > 0$$

The impact effects on the two countries' interest rates are

$$
\begin{aligned}
(13.2\text{a}) \quad \delta r_1 = {}& (1/J_\pi)[B^t_{1W}L_{10} - L_{1W}B^t_{10}]\,\delta\bar{r}_0 \\
& - [2(B^t_{11} - B^t_{12})J_\pi]^{-1}[B^t_{1W}(B^t_{11} - B^t_{12}) \\
& \quad + (2L_{1W}B^t_{11} - B^t_{1W}L^t_{11})](\delta\bar{B}^c_1 + \delta\bar{B}^{c'}_1) \\
& + [2(B^t_{11} - B^t_{12})J_\pi]^{-1}[2(1 - B_{0W})B^t_{12} + B^t_{1W}B^t_{01}](\delta\bar{B}^c_2 + \delta\bar{B}^{c'}_2) \\
& - [2(B^t_{11} - B^t_{12})]^{-1}[B_{1W} - B_{2W}](\delta W^{hs} - \delta W^{hs'}) \\
& + [2(B^t_{11} - B^t_{12})J_\pi]^{-1}[2L_{1W}B^t_{11} - B^t_{1W}L^t_{11}]\,\delta B_1 \\
& - [2(B^t_{11} - B^t_{12})J_\pi]^{-1}[2L_{1W}B^t_{12} - B^t_{1W}L^t_{11}]\,\delta B'_2
\end{aligned}
$$

$$
\begin{aligned}
(13.3\text{a}) \quad \delta r_2 = {}& (1/J_\pi)[B^t_{1W}L_{10} - L_{1W}B^t_{10}]\,\delta\bar{r}_0 \\
& + [2(B^t_{11} - B^t_{12})J_\pi]^{-1}[2(1 - B_{0W})B^t_{12} + B^t_{1W}B^t_{01}](\delta\bar{B}^c_1 + \delta\bar{B}^{c'}_1) \\
& - [2(B^t_{11} - B^t_{12})J_\pi]^{-1}[B^t_{1W}(B^t_{11} - B^t_{12}) \\
& \quad + (2L_{1W}B^t_{11} - B^t_{1W}L^t_{11})](\delta\bar{B}^c_2 + \delta\bar{B}^{c'}_2) \\
& + [2(B^t_{11} - B^t_{12})]^{-1}[B_{1W} - B_{2W}](\delta W^{hs} - \delta W^{hs'}) \\
& - [2(B^t_{11} - B^t_{12})J_\pi]^{-1}[2L_{1W}B^t_{12} - B^t_{1W}L^t_{11}]\,\delta B_1 \\
& + [2(B^t_{11} - B^t_{12})J_\pi]^{-1}[2L_{1W}B^t_{11} - B^t_{1W}L^t_{11}]\,\delta B'_2
\end{aligned}
$$

The impact effects on the Southern exchange rate are

$$
\begin{aligned}
(13.4\text{a}) \quad \left(\frac{\delta\hat{\pi}'}{\pi'}\right) = {}& -(1/V_\pi J_\pi)[L_{10}(B^t_{11} + B^t_{12}) - L^t_{11}B^t_{10}]\,\delta\bar{r}_0 \\
& - (1/2V_\pi J_\pi)(B^t_{01})(\delta\bar{B}^c_1 + \delta\bar{B}^{c'}_1 + \delta\bar{B}^c_2 + \delta\bar{B}^{c'}_2) \\
& - (1/2V_\pi)(\delta W^{hs} + \delta W^{hs'}) - (1/2V_\pi J_\pi)(L^t_{11})(\delta B_1 + \delta B'_2)
\end{aligned}
$$

which is, we said, the same as the change in the Northern rate, because the bilateral rate is pegged.

The signs of these effects and of certain other outcomes are shown in Table 13.1A. Those pertaining to goods prices and nominal incomes are

the effects of interest-rate changes on the demands for money taken together; it appears in the third equation because we have summed up those demands.) The term B^t_{1W} is slightly different. It appears in the Northern bond equation as $B_{1W} + B'_{1W}$ and in the Southern bond equation as $B_{2W} + B'_{2W}$. The former seems to resemble the term $B_{11} + B'_{11}$, but it stands for something different. The sum $B_{11} + B'_{11}$ denotes the effect of a change in r_1 on Northern and Southern demands for the Northern bond. The sum $B_{1W} + B'_{1W}$ denotes the effects of changes in *two* variables, W^h and $W^{h'}$, on the two demands. The wealth effects appear as a sum only because they have a common cause–the effect of a change in π' on the home-currency values of B^h_0 and $B^{h'}_0$ (the two countries' holdings of foreign bonds).

Table 13.1A. *Selected impact effects under a flexible external exchange rate*

Disturbance	δπ̂'	π δRᵃ	δr₁	δr₂	δrᵗ	δp₁ᵇ	δp₂ᵇ	δYᵃᶜ	δYᵃ'ᶜ	δYᵗ	δYᵃᵗ
δr̄₀	+	0	?	?	?	+	+	+	+	+	+
δB̄₁ᶜ	+	−	−	−	−	+	+	+	+	+	+
δB̄₁ᶜ'	+	+	−	−	−	+	+	+	+	+	+
δB̄₂ᶜ	+	−	−	−	−	+	+	+	+	+	+
δB̄₂ᶜ'	+	+	−	−	−	+	+	+	+	+	+
δD̄	0	0	0	0	0	+	+	+	+	+	+
δD̄'	0	0	0	0	0	+	+	+	+	+	+
δḠ₁	0	0	0	0	0	+	?	−	?	?	−
δḠ₁'	0	0	0	0	0	+	?	+	−	?	?
δḠ₂	0	0	0	0	0	?	+	−	+	?	?
δḠ₂'	0	0	0	0	0	?	+	?	−	?	?
δc₀₁ᵗ	0	0	0	0	0	−	−	−	−	−	−
δc₀₂ᵗ	0	0	0	0	0	−	−	−	−	−	−

(Effect)

Some signs shown here are different in certain limiting cases considered in subsequent chapters.

ᵃ Because $\delta R^t = 0$ with a flexible external rate, changes in Southern reserves are equal with opposite signs to changes in Northern reserves.

ᵇ Because each country produces a single good, the changes in incomes (δY and $\delta Y'$) and in money wage rates (δw and $\delta w'$) or levels of employment (δE and $\delta E'$) have the same signs as the price changes.

ᶜ Changes in Northern disposable income, δY^d, equal the changes in Northern gross national product, δY, except when the disturbances are δD, δG_1, and δG_2, which affect Northern taxes; similarly, changes in Southern disposable income, $\delta Y^{d\prime}$, equal the changes in Southern gross national product, $\delta Y'$, except when the disturbances are $\delta D'$, $\delta G_1'$, and $\delta G_2'$, which affect Southern taxes.

derived when we study the goods markets; we discuss them in that context. Those pertaining to Northern reserves are derived in Appendix E. And those pertaining to the *average* interest rate, r^t, come from Eqs. (13.2a) and (13.3a):[4]

(13.5a) $\delta r^t = (1/2)(\delta r_1 + \delta r_2)$

$$= - (1/J_\pi)(B^t_{1W}L_{10} - L_{1W}B^t_{10})\,\delta\bar{r}_0$$
$$- (1/2J_\pi)(1 - B_{0W})(\delta\bar{B}^c_1 + \delta\bar{B}^{c\prime}_1 + \delta\bar{B}^c_2 + \delta\bar{B}^{c\prime}_2)$$

Two brief comments are in order:

1. The impact effects on $\hat{\pi}'$ and r^t of a change in $\bar{r}_0$ and of all four open-market operations are the same in sign and nature as the effects on the exchange rate and domestic interest rate of the single small economy studied in Part II. That this should be true for the response of r^t to a change in $\bar{r}_0$ is not at all surprising; although r_1 and r_2 react ambiguously, they nevertheless react identically when asset preferences are symmetrical. That it should be true for the response of r^t to any open-market operation is perhaps more surprising, as r_1 and r_2 react quite differently to purchases of Northern and Southern bonds. But it is not hard to prove equivalence between the change in r^t and in the domestic interest rate of the small economy or to prove equivalence between the exchange-rate changes. We encounter additional analogues when we come to pegged exchange rates.[5] It is indeed possible to draw a comprehensive generalization about the short-run effects of asset-market disturbances. *When wealth holders have symmetrical preferences, the joint responses of the two economies are equal in aggregate or on average to those of a single small economy.*

2. The effects of an open-market operation on $\hat{\pi}'$ and r^t are, we said, identical for all such operations, whether they are undertaken by the Northern or Southern bank, and regardless of the bond bought or sold. The effects on individual interest rates, however, depend on the choice of bond but not on the choice of bank, whereas the effects on Northern and Southern reserves depend on the bank *and* the bond. Any open-market purchase reduces the two interest rates, but a purchase of the Northern

---

[4] Because the effects of δW^{hs}, $\delta W^{hs\prime}$, δB_1, and $\delta B'_2$ are used only to obtain dynamic outcomes, we do not show them for r^t or for other composite variables defined later in this chapter. (For this same reason, we omit them from Tables 13.1A and 13.1B.)

[5] The proof for a jointly flexible exchange rate requires only that we drop the superscripts t from all terms in Eqs. (13.4a) and (13.5a), delete B^t_{12} wherever it appears (because there is no second domestic bond in the small-country case), and standardize the sizes of the open-market operations. The term J_π becomes identical to H_π in Chapter 3, and the expressions for the changes in $\hat{\pi}'$ and r^t in Eqs. (13.4a) and (13.5a) become identical to the corresponding expressions in Eqs. (3.3a) and (3.2a).

bond depresses r_1 relative to r_2, and a purchase of the Southern bond has the opposite effect.[6] Turning to reserves, any open-market purchase by the Northern bank shifts reserves from North to South, but the shift is larger when the bank buys the Southern bond. Similarly, any open-market purchase by the Southern bank shifts reserves from South to North, but the shift is larger when the bank buys the Northern bond.

A pegged external rate. When the Southern central bank pegs its external exchange rate, π' becomes exogenous and R^t endogenous. Therefore:

$$(13.1b) \quad \begin{bmatrix} -B^t_{11} & -B^t_{12} & 0 \\ -B^t_{12} & -B^t_{11} & 0 \\ L^t_{11} & L^t_{11} & -1 \end{bmatrix} \begin{bmatrix} \delta r_1 \\ \delta r_2 \\ \bar{\pi}\,\delta R^t \end{bmatrix} = \begin{bmatrix} B^t_{1W} \\ B^t_{1W} \\ -2L_{1W} \end{bmatrix} \left[V_\pi \left(\frac{\delta \bar{\pi}'}{\bar{\pi}'} \right) \right]$$

$$+ \begin{bmatrix} B^t_{10} \\ B^t_{10} \\ -2L_{10} \end{bmatrix} [\delta \bar{r}_0] + \begin{bmatrix} 1 & 1 & 0 & 0 \\ 0 & 0 & 1 & 1 \\ 1 & 1 & 1 & 1 \end{bmatrix} \begin{bmatrix} \delta \bar{B}^c_1 \\ \delta \bar{B}^{c'}_1 \\ \delta \bar{B}^c_2 \\ \delta \bar{B}^{c'}_2 \end{bmatrix}$$

$$+ \begin{bmatrix} B_{1W} & B_{2W} & -1 & 0 \\ B_{2W} & B_{1W} & 0 & -1 \\ -L_{1W} & -L_{1W} & 0 & 0 \end{bmatrix} \begin{bmatrix} \delta W^{hs} \\ \delta W^{hs'} \\ \delta B_1 \\ \delta B'_2 \end{bmatrix}$$

The determinant of this system is $-J$, and it is negative because

$$J = (B^t_{11} - B^t_{12})(B^t_{11} + B^t_{12}) = -(B^t_{11} - B^t_{12})(L^t_{11} + B^t_{01}) > 0$$

The impact effects on the two countries' interest rates are

$$(13.2b) \quad \delta r_1 = -(1/J)B^t_{1W}(B^t_{11} - B^t_{12})V_\pi \left(\frac{\delta \bar{\pi}'}{\bar{\pi}'} \right) - (1/J)[B^t_{10}(B^t_{11} - B^t_{12})]\,\delta \bar{r}_0$$

$$- (1/J)[B^t_{11}(\delta \bar{B}^c_1 + \delta \bar{B}^{c'}_1) - B^t_{12}(\delta \bar{B}^c_2 + \delta \bar{B}^{c'}_2)]$$
$$- (1/J)[(B_{1W}B^t_{11} - B_{2W}B^t_{12})\,\delta W^{hs}$$
$$+ (B_{2W}B^t_{11} - B_{1W}B^t_{12})\,\delta W^{hs'}]$$
$$+ (1/J)[(B^t_{11})\,\delta B_1 - (B^t_{12})\,\delta B'_2]$$

$$(13.3b) \quad \delta r_2 = -(1/J)B^t_{1W}(B^t_{11} - B^t_{12})V_\pi \left(\frac{\delta \bar{\pi}'}{\bar{\pi}'} \right) - (1/J)[B^t_{10}(B^t_{11} - B^t_{12})]\,\delta \bar{r}_0$$

$$+ (1/J)[B^t_{12}(\delta \bar{B}^c_1 + \delta \bar{B}^{c'}_1) - B^t_{11}(\delta \bar{B}^c_2 + \delta \bar{B}^{c'}_2)]$$
$$- (1/J)[(B_{2W}B^t_{11} - B_{1W}B^t_{12})\,\delta W^{hs}$$
$$+ (B_{1W}B^t_{11} - B_{2W}B^t_{12})\,\delta W^{hs'}]$$
$$- (1/J)[(B^t_{12})\,\delta B_1 - (B^t_{11})\,\delta B'_2]$$

[6] From Eqs. (13.2a) and (13.3a), $\delta r_1 - \delta r_2 = -[1/(B^t_{11} - B^t_{12})][(\delta \bar{B}^c_1 + \delta \bar{B}^{c'}_1) - (\delta \bar{B}^c_2 + \delta \bar{B}^{c'})]$.

The impact effects on the sum of reserves are

$$(13.4b) \quad \bar{\pi}\, \delta R^t = (1/J_S)J_\pi\, 2V_\pi\!\left(\frac{\delta\bar{\pi}'}{\bar{\pi}'}\right)$$

$$+ (1/J_S)2[L_{10}(B^t_{11} + B^t_{12}) - L^t_{11}B^t_{10}]\, \delta\bar{r}_0$$
$$+ (1/J_S)(B^t_{01})(\delta\bar{B}^c_1 + \delta\bar{B}^{c\prime}_1 + \delta\bar{B}^c_2 + \delta\bar{B}^{c\prime}_2)$$
$$+ (1/J_S)(J_\pi)(\delta W^{hs} + \delta W^{hs\prime}) + (1/J_S)(L^t_{11})(\delta B_1 + \delta B'_2)$$

where

$$J_S = (B^t_{11} + B^t_{12}) = -(L^t_{11} + B^t_{10}) > 0$$

And the changes in the average interest rate are

$$(13.5b) \quad \delta r^t = -(1/J_S)B^t_{1W}V_\pi\!\left(\frac{\delta\bar{\pi}'}{\bar{\pi}'}\right) - (1/J_S)(B^t_{10})\, \delta\bar{r}_0$$

$$- (1/2J_S)(\delta\bar{B}^c_1 + \delta\bar{B}^{c\prime}_1 + \delta\bar{B}^c_2 + \delta\bar{B}^{c\prime}_2)$$

The signs of these and other outcomes pertaining to a pegged external rate are shown in Table 13.1B. There are, again, strong similarities between the joint outcomes here and those for the small country in Chapter 3, thanks to the influence of asset-market symmetry:

1. The impact effects of a joint devaluation (an increase of $\bar{\pi}'$) illustrate that influence with special clarity. The changes in r^t and R^t resemble the interest-rate and reserve changes in Chapter 3.[7] Furthermore, Northern and Southern reserves increase by the same amounts, and the two countries' interest rates fall by the same amounts.

2. The impact effects of an increase in $\bar{r}_0$ on r^t and R^t are likewise analogous to the ones obtained for the small economy. As in Chapter 3, moreover, the changes in the interest rates are different from those that take place with a flexible exchange rate. The responses of r_1 and r_2 are identical, as they were with a flexible rate, but are not ambiguous. Both rates rise on impact – an outcome associated with the fact that there are reductions in both countries' reserves.

3. The effects of open-market purchases have features similar to those in the flexible-rate case. Each country's interest rate declines, reducing r^t, and there is a reduction in R^t (corresponding to the depreciation of the flexible external rate shown in Table 13.1A). The fall in the average interest rate, moreover, and joint loss of reserves are the same for all four

[7] Deleting the superscripts t and the term B^t_{12} and standardizing the sizes of reserves and open-market operations, J_S becomes B_{11} (its counterpart in Chapter 3), and the expressions pertaining to $\delta\pi'$, $\delta\bar{r}_0$, and open-market operations in Eqs. (13.4b) and (13.5b) become identical to the corresponding expressions in Eqs. (3.3b) and (3.2b).

Table 13.1B. Selected impact effects under a pegged external exchange rate

Disturbance	Effect										
	$\bar{\pi}\,\delta R^t$	$\bar{\pi}\,\delta R^{a}$	δr_1	δr_2	δr^t	$\delta p_1^{\,b}$	$\delta p_2'^{\,b}$	$\delta Y^{a\,c}$	$\delta Y^{a'\,c}$	δY^t	δY^{at}
$\delta\bar{\pi}'$	+	$+^{d}$	−	−	−	+	+	+	+	+	+
$\delta\bar{r}_0$	−	$-^{d}$	+	+	+	−	−	−	−	−	−
$\delta\bar{B}_1^{c}$	−	−	−	−	−	+	+	+	+	+	+
$\delta\bar{B}_1^{c'}$	−	+	−	−	−	+	+	+	+	+	+
$\delta\bar{B}_2^{c}$	−	−	−	−	−	+	+	+	+	+	+
$\delta\bar{B}_2^{c'}$	−	+	−	−	−	+	+	+	+	+	+
$\delta\bar{D}$	0	0	0	0	0	+	+	+	+	+	+
$\delta\bar{D}'$	0	0	0	0	0	+	+	+	+	+	+
$\delta\bar{G}_1$	0	0	0	0	0	+	?	−	?	?	−
$\delta\bar{G}_1'$	0	0	0	0	0	?	?	+	−	?	?
$\delta\bar{G}_2$	0	0	0	0	0	?	?	−	+	?	?
$\delta\bar{G}_2'$	0	0	0	0	0	+	+	+	−	?	−
δc_{01}^{t}	0	0	0	0	0	−	−	−	−	−	−
δc_{02}^{t}	0	0	0	0	0	−	−	−	−	−	−

Some signs shown here are different in certain limiting cases considered in subsequent chapters.

^{a} Because $\delta R^t \neq 0$ with a pegged external rate, the changes in Southern reserves are *not* equal with opposite signs to the changes in Northern reserves.

^{b} See corresponding note to Table 13.1A.

^{c} See corresponding note to Table 13.1A.

^{d} Equal algebraically to one-half the change in R^t.

open-market operations, with the sizes of the changes in r_1 and r_2 depending on the choice of bond but not on the bank. An open-market purchase of the Northern bond reduces r_1 relative to r_2, and vice versa. Finally, the reserve effects depend once again on the choice of bond *and* bank. Any purchase by the Northern bank causes it to lose reserves, the loss being larger if it buys the Southern bond. With a pegged external rate, however, reserves are lost to the outside world as well as to the South. The drop in the average interest rate leads households in both countries to buy foreign bonds, and both countries lose reserves to the outside world, enlarging the loss of Northern reserves and reducing the gain of Southern reserves. (It can be shown, however, that an open-market purchase by the Northern bank cannot cause the South to *lose* reserves, even when the Northern bank buys the Southern bond. The proof is given in Appendix E, where we show that the North cannot lose reserves when the Southern central bank makes an open-market purchase, and the proof is symmetrical.)

Impact effects in goods markets

We turn now to the impact effects of disturbances on the two goods prices, p_1 and p_2', and on the related variables–incomes, wage rates, and employment. Differentiating totally Eqs. (11.43a) and (11.44a) and imposing the goods-market assumptions discussed in Chapter 12,

$$(13.6) \quad \begin{bmatrix} -\{u_{10}^t + u_{12}^t + [1 - m_1(1 - S_Y)]\sigma_1\} & [u_{12}^t + m_2(1 - S_Y)\sigma_2'] \\ [u_{12}^t + m_2(1 - S_Y)\sigma_1] & -\{u_{20}^t + u_{12}^t + [1 - m_1(1 - S_Y)]\sigma_2'\} \end{bmatrix} \begin{bmatrix} \left(\dfrac{\delta p_1}{p_1}\right) \\ \left(\dfrac{\delta p_2'}{p_2'}\right) \end{bmatrix}$$

$$= \begin{bmatrix} (m_1 + m_2)S_W V_\pi - (u_{10}^t + p_1 C_1^t) \\ (m_1 + m_2)S_W V_\pi - (u_{20}^t + p_2 C_2^t) \end{bmatrix} \left[\left(\dfrac{\delta \pi'}{\pi'}\right) \right]$$

$$+ \begin{bmatrix} (m_1 + m_2)S_0 \\ (m_1 + m_2)S_0 \end{bmatrix} [\delta \bar{r}_0]$$

$$+ \begin{bmatrix} (m_1 S_1 + m_2 S_2) & (m_1 S_2 + m_2 S_1) \\ (m_1 S_2 + m_2 S_1) & (m_1 S_1 + m_2 S_2) \end{bmatrix} \begin{bmatrix} \delta r_1 \\ \delta r_2 \end{bmatrix}$$

$$+ \begin{bmatrix} -[1 - m_1(1 - S_Y)] & m_1(1 - S_Y) \\ m_2(1 - S_Y) & -[1 - m_2(1 - S_Y)] \end{bmatrix} \begin{bmatrix} \delta \bar{G}_1 \\ \delta \bar{G}_2 \end{bmatrix}$$

$$+ \begin{bmatrix} -[1 - m_2(1 - S_Y)] & m_2(1 - S_Y) \\ m_1(1 - S_Y) & -[1 - m_1(1 - S_Y)] \end{bmatrix} \begin{bmatrix} \delta \bar{G}_1' \\ \delta \bar{G}_2' \end{bmatrix}$$

$$- \begin{bmatrix} m_1(1 - S_Y) & m_2(1 - S_Y) \\ m_2(1 - S_Y) & m_1(1 - S_Y) \end{bmatrix} \begin{bmatrix} \delta \bar{D} \\ \delta \bar{D}' \end{bmatrix}$$

$$+ \begin{bmatrix} 1 & 0 \\ 0 & 1 \end{bmatrix} \begin{bmatrix} \delta c_{01}^t \\ \delta c_{02}^t \end{bmatrix} + \begin{bmatrix} m_1 S_W & m_2 S_W \\ m_2 S_W & m_1 S_W \end{bmatrix} \begin{bmatrix} \delta W^{hs} \\ \delta W^{hs'} \end{bmatrix}$$

The terms and expressions in this system resemble those in Chapter 3. Thus, the u_{ij}^t are sums of Northern, Southern, and foreign demand elasticities weighted by expenditures:

$$u_{ij}^t = u_{ij} + u_{ij}' + \pi' u_{ij}^f$$

where $u_{ij} = p_i C_i e_{ij}$, $u_{ij}' = p_i' C_i' e_{ij}'$, and $u_{ij}^f = p_i^f C_i^f e_{ij}^f$. Under our assumptions, all such sums are positive. Similarly,

$$\sigma_1 = p_1 Q_1 (1 + a_1) \quad \text{and} \quad \sigma_2' = p_2' Q_2' (1 + a_2)$$

describing supply responses in the North and South.[8]

There are two new disturbances in this system, the sums of shifts in spending in the North, the South, and the outside world:

$$\delta c_{01}^t = \delta c_{01} + \delta c_{01}' + \pi' \, \delta c_{01}^f$$
$$\delta c_{02}^t = \delta c_{02} + \delta c_{02}' + \pi' \, \delta c_{02}^f$$

where δc_{01}^t is a shift of consumption from Northern to foreign goods, and δc_{02}^t is a shift of consumption from Southern to foreign goods. (By implication, a shift of demand from Northern to Southern goods can be represented by setting $\delta c_{01}^t = -\delta c_{02}^t > 0$). The shifts of Northern and Southern demands, δc_{01}, δc_{02}, $\delta c_{01}'$, and $\delta c_{02}'$, play the same role together that δc_{01} played by itself in the small-country model. The shifts of foreign demands, δc_{01}^f and δc_{02}^f, play the same role together that $-\delta c_1^f$ played there. There is, of course, no counterpart to δc_{N1}, the shift from nontraded to traded goods in Chapter 3, and we have no need to analyze separately the disturbance $\delta \bar{p}_0^f$ studied in that chapter (one can always represent $\delta \bar{p}_0^f$ by a weighted sum of δc_{01}^t and δc_{02}^t).

The determinant of the goods-market system is denoted by

$$M_s = M_g + [1 - m_1(1 - S_Y)][\sigma_2' u_{10}^t + \sigma_1 u_{20}^t]$$
$$+ M_Y \{ u_{12}^t (\sigma_1 + \sigma_2') + \sigma_1 \sigma_2' [1 - (m_1 - m_2)(1 - S_Y)] \}$$

where

$$M_g = u_{10}^t u_{20}^t + u_{12}^t (u_{10}^t + u_{20}^t)$$
$$M_Y = S_Y + m_0 (1 - S_Y)$$

---

[8] In the classical case, the a_i may be treated as though they were zero; in the Keynesian case, they are deemed to be positive. For details, see Appendix A.

Thus M_s is positive, because $1 > (m_1 - m_2) > 0$.[9] It is also useful to write M_s in these ways:

$$M_s = M_{11}M_{22} + M_{11}M_{21} + M_{22}M_{12}$$

or

$$M_s = M_k + S_Y\{m_1(\sigma_2'M_{11} + \sigma_1M_{22}) + (1 - m_0)[\sigma_2'M_{12} + \sigma_1M_{21} - S_Y(m_1 - m_2)\sigma_1\sigma_2']\}$$

where

$$M_{11} = u_{10}^t + M_Y\sigma_1 \qquad\qquad M_{22} = u_{20}^t + M_Y\sigma_2'$$
$$M_{12} = u_{12}^t + m_2(1 - S_Y)\sigma_1 \qquad M_{21} = u_{12}^t + m_2(1 - S_Y)\sigma_2'$$

and

$$M_k = M_g + (1 - m_1)(\sigma_2'u_{10}^t + \sigma_1u_{20}^t) + m_0\{u_{12}^t(\sigma_1 + \sigma_2') + (\sigma_1\sigma_2')[1 - (m_1 - m_2)]\}$$

so that M_k is also positive.

As in Chapter 3, the solutions for δp_1 and $\delta p_2'$ are presented in two parts. The first are the effects of goods-market disturbances–those having no immediate effects on asset markets and thus no effects on r_1, r_2, or π'. The second are effects of asset-market disturbances and must, as usual, be derived separately for flexible and pegged exchange rates.

Effects of goods-market disturbances. Solving for the instantaneous effects of the fiscal and other goods-market disturbances contained in system (13.6),

$$(13.7) \quad \left(\frac{\delta p_1}{p_1}\right) = [(1 - S_Y)/M_s][m_1M_{22} + (1 - m_0)M_{21}] \, \delta\bar{D}$$
$$+ [(1 - S_Y)/M_s][m_2M_{22} + (1 - m_0)M_{21}] \, \delta\bar{D}'$$
$$+ (1/M_s)\{u_{20}^t[1 - m_1(1 - S_Y)] + M_Yu_{12}^t + M_Y[1 - (m_1 - m_2)(1 - S_Y)]\sigma_2'\} \, \delta\bar{G}_1$$
$$+ (1/M_s)\{u_{20}^t[1 - m_2(1 - S_Y)] + M_Y(u_{12}^t + \sigma_2')\} \, \delta\bar{G}_1'$$
$$+ (1/M_s)[M_YM_{21} - m_1(1 - S_Y)M_{22}] \, \delta\bar{G}_2$$
$$+ (1/M_s)[M_Yu_{12}^t - m_2(1 - S_Y)u_{20}^t] \, \delta\bar{G}_2'$$
$$- (1/M_s)\{(u_{20}^t + u_{12}^t) + [1 - m_1(1 - S_Y)]\sigma_2'\} \, \delta c_{01}^t$$
$$- (M_{21}/M_s) \, \delta c_{02}^t$$

[9] The term M_Y is mathematically identical to N_Y in Chapter 3, and can be interpreted similarly; N_Y was the sum of the small country's marginal propensities to save and import (the leakages from the domestic income stream), and M_Y is the sum of either country's marginal propensities to save and import from the outside world (the leakages from the joint income stream). Note that M_Y does *not* include each country's marginal propensity to import from the other.

$$
\text{(13.8)} \quad \left(\frac{\delta p_2'}{p_2'} \right) = [(1 - S_Y)/M_s][m_2 M_{11} + (1 - m_0)M_{12}] \, \delta\bar{D}
$$
$$
+ [(1 - S_Y)/M_s][m_1 M_{11} + (1 - m_0)M_{12}] \, \delta\bar{D}'
$$
$$
+ (1/M_s)[M_Y u_{12}^t - m_2(1 - S_Y)u_{10}^t] \, \delta\bar{G}_1
$$
$$
+ (1/M_s)[M_Y M_{12} - m_1(1 - S_Y)M_{11}] \, \delta\bar{G}_1'
$$
$$
+ (1/M_s)\{u_{10}^t[1 - m_2(1 - S_Y)] + M_Y(u_{12}^t + \sigma_1)\} \, \delta\bar{G}_2
$$
$$
+ (1/M_s)\{u_{10}^t[1 - m_1(1 - S_Y)] + M_Y u_{12}^t
$$
$$
+ M_Y[1 - (m_1 - m_2)(1 - S_Y)]\sigma_1\} \, \delta\bar{G}_2'
$$
$$
- (M_{12}/M_s) \, \delta c_{01}^t
$$
$$
- (1/M_s)\{(u_{10}^t + u_{12}^t) + [1 - m_1(1 - S_Y)]\sigma_1\} \, \delta c_{02}^t
$$

The signs of these effects are shown in Table 13.1A (and are repeated in Table 13.1B because they hold for both exchange-rate regimes). They are not unlike the signs of the price effects shown in Table 3.1A for the small-country model.

A tax cut by one country, increasing its budget deficit, raises the prices of both products. A balanced-budget increase in government spending raises the price of the product purchased, regardless of the country making the purchase. Its effect on the other price is ambiguous. Finally, a shift of demand to the foreign good depresses prices in both countries. As one would expect, however, the reduction in p_1 is larger absolutely and compared to the reduction in p_2' when the shift is from the Northern to the foreign good than when the shift is from the Southern to the foreign good.

The signs of the changes in nominal incomes resulting from these and other disturbances are given by the signs of the price changes. This is because each country produces just one good, so that

$$
\delta Y = \sigma_1 \left(\frac{\delta p_1}{p_1} \right) \quad \text{and} \quad \delta Y' = \sigma_2' \left(\frac{\delta p_2'}{p_2'} \right)
$$

The signs of the changes in Northern and Southern employment (or, in the classical case, of the changes in money wage rates) can likewise be inferred from the signs of the price changes.[10] There is no need to list them in our tables.

A disturbance that does not involve a change in tax policy has the same effects on disposable incomes, Y^d and $Y^{d'}$, as it has on the two countries' nominal incomes, Y and Y'. But each one of the six fiscal-policy changes in system (13.6) implies a change in Northern or Southern taxes, and the corresponding changes in disposable incomes may not have the same signs as the changes in Y and Y'. Reductions of Northern taxes and

---

[10] The changes in employment levels are $\delta E = [a_1(p_1/w)Q_1](\delta p_1/p_1)$ and $\delta E' = [a_2'(p_2'/w')Q_2'](\delta p_2'/p_2')$. The changes in money wage rates are proportional to the corresponding changes in goods prices.

balanced-budget changes in Northern spending have these effects on Northern disposable income:

$$(13.9) \quad \delta Y^d = \{1 + \sigma_1[(1 - S_Y)/M_s][m_1M_{22} + (1 - m_0)M_{21}]\} \,\delta\bar{D}$$
$$- (1/M_s)[M_g + M_Y(u_{10}^t + u_{12}^t)\sigma_2' + u_{10}^t m_2(1 - S_Y)\sigma_2'] \,\delta\bar{G}_1$$
$$- (1/M_s)[M_g + M_Y(u_{10}^t + u_{12}^t)\sigma_2' + u_{10}^t m_2(1 - S_Y)\sigma_2'$$
$$+ \sigma_1 M_{22}] \,\delta\bar{G}_2$$

The corresponding changes in Southern policies have these effects on Southern disposable income:

$$(13.10) \quad \delta Y^{d\prime} = \{1 + \sigma_2'[(1 - S_Y)/M_s][m_1M_{11} + (1 - m_0)M_{12}]\} \,\delta\bar{D}'$$
$$- (1/M_s)[M_g + M_Y(u_{20}^t + u_{12}^t)\sigma_1 + u_{20}^t m_2(1 - S_Y)\sigma_1$$
$$+ \sigma_2' M_{11}] \,\delta\bar{G}_1'$$
$$- (1/M_s)[M_g + M_Y(u_{20}^t + u_{12}^t)\sigma_1 + u_{20}^t m_2(1 - S_Y)\sigma_1] \,\delta\bar{G}_2'$$

The signs of the expressions in these two equations are shown separately in Table 13.1A (and Table 13.1B). They are, as always, unambiguous. Tax reductions, leading to budget deficits, increase disposable incomes; balanced-budget increases in government spending reduce disposable income locally, regardless of the product purchased.

Finally, our tables show the signs of sums of changes in nominal incomes and in disposable incomes. The sums of the income changes, δY^t, are unambiguous whenever p_1 and p_2' move together, and this is what happens with changes in $\bar{D}$ and $\bar{D}'$ and with the two shifts in demand to the foreign good. In those instances, then,

$$(13.11) \quad \delta Y^t = \delta Y + \delta Y'$$
$$= [(1 - S_Y)/M_s][\sigma_2' m_2 M_{11} + \sigma_1 m_1 M_{22}$$
$$+ (1 - m_0)(\sigma_2' M_{12} + \sigma_1 M_{21})] \,\delta\bar{D}$$
$$+ [(1 - S_Y)/M_s][\sigma_2' m_1 M_{11} + \sigma_1 m_2 M_{22}$$
$$+ (1 - m_0)(\sigma_2' M_{12} + \sigma_1 M_{21})] \,\delta\bar{D}'$$
$$- (1/M_s)[\sigma_1 M_{22} + (\sigma_2' M_{12} + \sigma_1 M_{21})] \,\delta c_{01}^t$$
$$- (1/M_s)[\sigma_2' M_{11} + (\sigma_2' M_{12} + \sigma_1 M_{21})] \,\delta c_{02}^t$$

But with balanced-budget changes in government expenditure, prices may not move together. Therefore,

$$(13.12) \quad \delta Y^t = (M_Y/M_s)\{u_{12}^t(\sigma_1 + \sigma_2') + [1 - (m_1 - m_2)(1 - S_Y)]\sigma_1\sigma_2'\}$$
$$\times (\delta\bar{G}_1 + \delta\bar{G}_1' + \delta\bar{G}_2 + \delta\bar{G}_2')$$
$$+ (1/M_s)[M_Y\sigma_1 u_{20}^t + m_2(1 - S_Y)(\sigma_1 u_{20}^t - \sigma_2' u_{10}^t)] \,\delta\bar{G}_1$$
$$+ (1/M_s)[M_Y\sigma_1 u_{20}^t + m_1(1 - S_Y)(\sigma_1 u_{20}^t - \sigma_2' u_{10}^t)] \,\delta\bar{G}_1'$$

$$+ (1/M_s)[M_Y\sigma_2' u_{10}^t - m_1(1 - S_Y)(\sigma_1 u_{20}^t - \sigma_2' u_{10}^t)] \,\delta\bar{G}_2$$
$$+ (1/M_s)[M_Y\sigma_2' u_{10}^t - m_2(1 - S_Y)(\sigma_1 u_{20}^t - \sigma_2' u_{10}^t)] \,\delta\bar{G}_2'$$

Each of these results is ambiguous, and the ambiguities cannot be resolved without restricting the dissimilarities between North and South– without imposing full-scale goods-market symmetry, defined but set aside in Chapter 12.

Some of the ambiguities in Eq. (13.12) are reflected in δY^{dt}, the sum of the changes in disposable incomes:

$$(13.13) \quad \delta Y^{dt} = \delta Y^d + \delta Y^{d\prime}$$
$$= -(1/M_s)\{M_g + u_{10}^t[1 - (m_1 - m_2)(1 - S_Y)]\sigma_2'\} \,\delta\bar{G}_1$$
$$- (1/M_s)[M_g + \sigma_2' u_{10}^t - (m_1 - m_2)(1 - S_Y)\sigma_1 u_{20}^t] \,\delta\bar{G}_1'$$
$$- (1/M_s)[M_g + \sigma_1 u_{20}^t - (m_1 - m_2)(1 - S_Y)\sigma_2' u_{10}^t] \,\delta\bar{G}_2$$
$$- (1/M_s)\{M_g + u_{20}^t[1 - (m_1 - m_2)(1 - S_Y)]\sigma_1\} \,\delta\bar{G}_2'$$

A balanced-budget increase of Northern spending on the Northern good reduces the sum of disposable incomes; so does a balanced-budget increase of Southern spending on the Southern good. But the effect of Northern spending on the Southern good is ambiguous, and so is the effect of Southern spending on the Northern good. It is not easy to explain these ambiguities completely; note the presence in Eq. (13.13) of the elasticities u_{10}^t and u_{20}^t, reflecting the response of consumers to the price effects of the fiscal policies. But the underlying reason is quite simple. When the Northern government buys more of the Southern good, it increases Southern income, and Southern disposable income rises by the same amount (because there is no change in Southern taxes). There is, we know, an increase in Northern taxes and, therefore, a decline in Southern sales to Northern households, but this decline must always be smaller than the increase in demand by the Northern government. As the increase in Southern disposable income can be larger than the decrease in Northern disposable income defined by Eq. (13.9), the sum of disposable incomes can rise. Analogous effects occur, of course, when the Southern government buys more of the Northern good, raising Northern disposable income.

Effects of financial disturbances under a flexible external rate. With a pegged (exogenous) bilateral exchange rate and a flexible (endogenous) external rate, the short-run effects of financial disturbances are obtained by solving system (13.6) for the effects of $\delta\hat{\pi}'$, $\delta\bar{r}_0$, δr_1, δr_2, δW^{hs}, and $\delta W^{hs\prime}$ on the two goods prices, then replacing $\delta\hat{\pi}'$, δr_1, and δr_2 with Eqs.

(13.4a), (13.2a), and (13.3a), respectively. These operations yield

$$
\begin{aligned}
(13.14a) \quad \left(\frac{\delta p_1}{p_1}\right) &= (1/M_sJ_\pi)[(M_{1\pi}/V_\pi)(B^t_{10}L^t_{11} - J_SL_{10}) + M_{1U}J_0]\,\delta\bar{r}_0 \\
&+ (1/2M_sJ_\pi)\{2(1 - B_{0W})[(m_1S_2 + m_2S_1)M_{22} + S^t_1(1 - m_0) \\
&+ [(m_1 - m_2)(S_1 - S_2)M_{22}](B^t_{11} - B^t_{12})^{-1} \\
&\times [B^t_{1W}(B^t_{11} - B^t_{12}) + 2L_{1W}B^t_{11} - B^t_{1W}L^t_{11}] \\
&- B^t_{01}[(M_{1\pi}/V_\pi) - S_WM_{1U}]\}(\delta\bar{B}^c_1 + \delta\bar{B}^{c\prime}_1) \\
&+ (1/2M_sJ_\pi)\{2(1 - B_{0W})[(m_1S_2 + m_2S_1)M_{22} + S^t_1((1 - m_0 \\
&- [(m_1 - m_2)(S_1 - S_2)M_{22}](B^t_{11} - B^t_{12})^{-1} \\
&\times [2(1 - B_{0W})B^t_{12} + B^t_{1W}B^t_{01}] \\
&- B^t_{01}[(M_{1\pi}/V_\pi) - S_WM_{1U}]\}(\delta\bar{B}^c_2 + \delta\bar{B}^{c\prime}_2) \\
&- (1/2M_s)[(M_{1\pi}/V_\pi) - (m_1 - m_2)M_{22}(B^t_{11} - B^t_{12})^{-1}J_W]\,\delta W \\
&- [(1/2M_s)(M_{1\pi}/V_\pi) + (m_1 - m_2M_{22})(B^t_{11} - B^t_{12})^{-1}J_W]\,\delta W \\
&- (1/2M_sJ_\pi)\{2L_{1W}[(m_1S_2 + m_2S_1)M_{22} + S^t_1(1 - m_0)M_{21}] \\
&+ [(m_1 - m_2)(S_1 - S_2)M_{22}](B^t_{11} - B^t_{12})^{-1}[2L_{1W}B^t_{11} \\
&- B^t_{1W}L^t_{11}] + L^t_{11}[(M_{1\pi}/V_\pi) - S_WM_{1U}]\}\,\delta B_1 \\
&- (1/2M_sJ_\pi)\{2L_{1W}[(m_1S_2 + m_2S_1)M_{22} + S^t_1(1 - m_0)M_{21}] \\
&- [(m_1 - m_2)(S_1 - S_2)M_{22}](B^t_{11} - B^t_{12})^{-1}[2L_{1W}B^t_{12} \\
&- B^t_{1W}L^t_{11}] + L^t_{11}[(M_{1\pi}/V_\pi) - S_WM_{1U}]\}\,\delta B_2'
\end{aligned}
$$

$$
\begin{aligned}
(13.15a) \quad \left(\frac{\delta p_2'}{p_2'}\right) &= (1/M_sJ_\pi)[(M_{2\pi}/V_\pi)(B^t_{10}L^t_{11} - J_SL_{10}) + M_{2U}J_0]\,\delta\bar{r}_0 \\
&+ (1/2M_sJ_\pi)\{2(1 - B_{0W})[(m_1S_2 + m_2S_1)M_{11} + S^t_1(1 - m_0) \\
&- [(m_1 - m_2)(S_1 - S_2)M_{11}](B^t_{11} - B^t_{12})^{-1} \\
&\times [2(1 - B_{0W})B^t_{12} + B^t_{1W}B^t_{01}] \\
&- B^t_{01}[(M_{2\pi}/V_\pi) - S_WM_{2U}]\}(\delta\bar{B}^c_1 + \delta\bar{B}^{c\prime}_1) \\
&+ (1/2M_sJ_\pi)\{2(1 - B_{0W})[(m_1S_2 + m_2S_1)M_{11} + S^t_1(1 - m_0) \\
&+ [(m_1 - m_2)(S_1 - S_2)M_{11}](B^t_{11} - B^t_{12})^{-1}[B^t_{1W}(B^t_{11} - B^t \\
&+ 2L_{1W}B^t_{11} - B^t_{1W}L^t_{11}] \\
&- B^t_{01}[(M_{2\pi}/V_\pi) - S_WM_{2U}]\}(\delta\bar{B}^c_2 + \delta\bar{B}^{c\prime}_2) \\
&- (1/2M_s)[(M_{2\pi}/V_\pi) + (m_1 - m_2)M_{11}(B^t_{11} - B^t_{12})^{-1}J_W]\,\delta W \\
&- (1/2M_s)[(M_{2\pi}/V_\pi) - (m_1 - m_2)M_{11}(B^t_{11} - B^t_{12})^{-1}J_W]\,\delta W \\
&- (1/2M_sJ_\pi)\{2L_{1W}[(m_1S_2 + m_2S_1)M_{11} + S^t_1(1 - m_0)M_{12}] \\
&- [(m_1 - m_2)(S_1 - S_2)M_{11}](B^t_{11} - B^t_{12})^{-1}[2L_{1W}B^t_{12} \\
&- B^t_{1W}L^t_{11}] + L^t_{11}[(M_{2\pi}/V_\pi) - S_WM_{2U}]\}\,\delta B_1 \\
&- (1/2M_sJ_\pi)\{2L_{1W}[(m_1S_2 + m_2S_1)M_{11} + S^t_1(1 - m_0)M_{12}] \\
&+ [(m_1 - m_2)(S_1 - S_2)M_{11}](B^t_{11} - B^t_{12})^{-1}[2L_{1W}B^t_{11} \\
&- B^t_{1W}L^t_{11}] + L^t_{11}[(M_{2\pi}/V_\pi) - S_WM_{2U}]\}\,\delta B_2'
\end{aligned}
$$

where

$$S_1^t = S_1 + S_2 = S_1' + S_2'$$
$$M_{1U} = (1 - m_0)(M_{22} + 2M_{21})$$
$$= (1 - m_0)\{u_{20}^t + 2u_{12}^t + [1 - (m_1 - m_2)(1 - S_Y)]\sigma_2'\}$$
$$M_{2U} = (1 - m_0)(M_{11} + 2M_{12})$$
$$= (1 - m_0)\{u_{10}^t + 2u_{12}^t + [1 - (m_1 - m_2)(1 - S_Y)]\sigma_1\}$$
$$M_{1\pi} = M_{22}(u_{10}^t + p_1 C_1^f) + M_{21}[(u_{10}^t + p_1 C_1^f) + (u_{20}^t + p_2 C_2^f)]$$
$$M_{2\pi} = M_{11}(u_{20}^t + p_2 C_2^f) + M_{12}[(u_{10}^t + p_1 C_1^f) + (u_{20}^t + p_2 C_2^f)]$$
$$J_W = (S_1 - S_2)(B_{1W} - B_{2W}) - S_W(B_{11}^t - B_{12}^t)$$

and

$$J_0 = B_{1W}^t(L_{11}^t S_0 - L_{10} S_1^t) + J_S(S_W L_{10} - L_{1W} S_0) - B_{10}^t(S_W L_{11}^t - L_{1W} S_1^t)$$

Because M_{11}, M_{12}, M_{21}, and M_{22} are positive, we can be sure that M_{1U} and M_{2U} are positive. So are $M_{1\pi}$ and $M_{2\pi}$. Furthermore, J_W is positive (because $S_1 > S_2$ and $B_{1W} > B_{2W}$, whereas $S_W < 0$), and J_0 is positive, because we have assumed proportionality and that crowding out does not dominate. (Under the assumption of proportionality, $L_{11} S_0 = L_{10} S_1$, and $L_{12} S_0 = L_{10} S_2$, so that $L_{11}^t S_0 = L_{10} S_1^t$. Under the assumption that crowding out does not dominate, each of the remaining terms in J_0 is positive.)

The signs of the price effects, their implications for disposable incomes, and their implications for the sums of incomes are shown in Table 13.1A. Because J_0 is positive, an increase of the foreign interest rate is certain to raise prices in North and South, even though it has uncertain effects on the countries' interest rates. An open-market purchase also raises prices, with the sizes of the price changes depending on the bond bought but not on the bank buying it. The increase in the Northern price caused by a purchase of the Northern bond will be larger than the one caused by a purchase of the Southern bond, no matter which bank makes the purchase. Similarly, the increase in the Southern price caused by a purchase of the Southern bond will be larger than the one caused by a purchase of the Northern bond. (It is not possible to say, however, that the increase in the Northern price caused by a purchase of the Northern bond will be larger than the increase in the Southern price. To compare price changes between countries, we would have to impose additional restrictions on the goods-market differences between North and South.)

Effects of financial disturbances under a pegged external rate. With a pegged (exogenous) external exchange rate, the short-run effects of financial disturbances are obtained by solving system (13.6) for the effects of $\delta\bar{\pi}'$, $\delta\bar{r}_0$, δr_1, δr_2, δW^{hs}, and $\delta W^{hs\prime}$ on goods prices, then replacing δr_1 and δr_2 with Eqs. (13.2b) and (13.3b), respectively. Here, we obtain

$$(13.14b) \quad \left(\frac{\delta p_1}{p_1}\right) = (1/M_s)[M_{1\pi} + V_\pi(J_K/J_S)M_{1U}]\left(\frac{\delta\bar{\pi}'}{\bar{\pi}'}\right)$$

$$- (M_{1U}/M_s J_S)[S_0(B_{11}^t + B_{12}^t) - S_1^t B_{10}^t]\,\delta\bar{r}_0$$
$$+ (1/M_s J_S)\{[(m_1 S_2 + m_2 S_1)M_{22} + S_1^t(1 - m_0)M_{21}]$$
$$+ B_{11}^t[(m_1 - m_2)(S_1 - S_2)M_{22}](B_{11}^t - B_{12}^t)^{-1}\}(\delta\bar{B}_1^c + \delta\bar{B}_1^c)$$
$$+ (1/M_s J_S)\{[(m_1 S_2 + m_2 S_1)M_{22} + S_1^t(1 - m_0)M_{21}]$$
$$- B_{12}^t[(m_1 - m_2)(S_1 - S_2)M_{22}](B_{11}^t - B_{12}^t)^{-1}\}(\delta\bar{B}_2^c + \delta\bar{B}_2^c)$$
$$+ (1/M_s J_S)\{M_{22}[B_{1W}^t(m_1 S_2 + m_2 S_1) - m_1 S_W(B_{11}^t + B_{12}^t)$$
$$+ (m_1 - m_2)(S_1 - S_2)(B_{1W}B_{11}^t - B_{2W}B_{12}^t)(B_{11}^t - B_{12}^t)^{-1}]$$
$$+ J_K(1 - m_0)M_{21}\}\,\delta W^{hs}$$
$$+ (1/M_s J_S)\{M_{22}[B_{1W}^t(m_1 S_2 + m_2 S_1) - m_2 S_W(B_{11}^t + B_{12}^t)$$
$$+ (m_1 - m_2)(S_1 - S_2)(B_{2W}B_{11}^t - B_{1W}B_{12}^t)(B_{11}^t - B_{12}^t)^{-1}]$$
$$+ J_K(1 - m_0)M_{21}\}\,\delta W^{hs\prime}$$
$$- (1/M_s J_S)\{[(m_1 S_2 + m_2 S_1)M_{22} + S_1^t(1 - m_0)M_{21}]$$
$$+ B_{11}^t[(m_1 - m_2)(S_1 - S_2)M_{22}](B_{11}^t - B_{12}^t)^{-1}\}\,\delta B_1$$
$$- (1/M_s J_S)\{[(m_1 S_2 + m_2 S_1)M_{22} + S_1^t(1 - m_0)M_{21}]$$
$$- B_{12}^t[(m_1 - m_2)(S_1 - S_2)M_{22}](B_{11}^t - B_{12}^t)^{-1}\}\,\delta B_2'$$

$$(13.15b) \quad \left(\frac{\delta p_2'}{p_2'}\right) = (1/M_s)[M_{2\pi} + V_\pi(J_K/J_S)M_{2U}]\left(\frac{\delta\bar{\pi}'}{\bar{\pi}'}\right)$$

$$- (M_{2U}/M_s J_S)[S_0(B_{11}^t + B_{12}^t) - S_1^t B_{10}^t]\,\delta\bar{r}_0$$
$$+ (1/M_s J_S)\{[(m_1 S_2 + m_2 S_1)M_{11} + S_1^t(1 - m_0)M_{12}]$$
$$- B_{12}^t[(m_1 - m_2)(S_1 - S_2)M_{11}](B_{11}^t - B_{12}^t)^{-1}\}(\delta\bar{B}_1^c + \delta\bar{B}_1^c)$$
$$+ (1/M_s J_S)\{[(m_1 S_2 + m_2 S_1)M_{11} + S_1^t(1 - m_0)M_{12}]$$
$$+ B_{11}^t[(m_1 - m_2)(S_1 - S_2)M_{11}](B_{11}^t - B_{12}^t)^{-1}\}(\delta\bar{B}_2^c + \delta\bar{B}_2^c)$$
$$+ (1/M_s J_S)\{M_{11}[B_{1W}^t(m_1 S_2 + m_2 S_1) - m_2 S_W(B_{11}^t + B_{12}^t)$$
$$+ (m_1 - m_2)(S_1 - S_2)(B_{2W}B_{11}^t - B_{1W}B_{12}^t)(B_{11}^t - B_{12}^t)^{-1}]$$
$$+ J_K(1 - m_0)M_{12}\}\,\delta W^{hs}$$
$$+ (1/M_s J_S)\{M_{11}[B_{1W}^t(m_1 S_2 + m_2 S_1) - m_1 S_W(B_{11}^t + B_{12}^t)$$
$$+ (m_1 - m_2)(S_1 - S_2)(B_{1W}B_{11}^t - B_{2W}B_{12}^t)(B_{11}^t - B_{12}^t)^{-1}]$$
$$+ J_K(1 - m_0)M_{12}\}\,\delta W^{hs\prime}$$
$$- (1/M_s J_S)\{[(m_1 S_2 + m_2 S_1)M_{11} + S_1^t(1 - m_0)M_{12}]$$
$$- B_{12}^t[(m_1 - m_2)(S_1 - S_2)M_{11}](B_{11}^t - B_{12}^t)^{-1}\}\,\delta B_1$$
$$- (1/M_s J_S)\{[(m_1 S_2 + m_2 S_1)M_{11} + S_1^t(1 - m_0)M_{12}]$$
$$+ B_{11}^t[(m_1 - m_2)(S_1 - S_2)M_{11}](B_{11}^t - B_{12}^t)^{-1}\}\,\delta B_2'$$

where

$$J_K = B^t_{1W} S^t_1 - S_W(B^t_{11} + B^t_{12})$$

Because J_K is positive, a devaluation of the joint external rate raises prices in both countries. With a pegged external rate, moreover, an increase in the foreign interest rate reduces prices in both countries; it is not necessary to assume proportionality or that crowding out does not dominate. Furthermore, the price changes are opposite in sign to those with a flexible external rate. Finally, the external exchange-rate regime does not alter the direction of the price effects of open-market operations. On our suppositions about asset-market symmetry, all open-market purchases raise both countries' prices, with the size of the increase in each price depending on the bond bought but not on the bank buying it. Thus, a purchase of the Northern bond will raise prices in the North by more than a purchase of the Southern bond (but Northern prices need not rise by more than Southern prices). The signs of these outcomes and of the corresponding income changes are shown in Table 13.1B.

The proof of stability

Because this model has two endogenous stocks, W^{hs} and $W^{hs'}$, the proof of stability is more complicated than the one in Chapter 3. The necessary and sufficient conditions for local stability pertain to the derivatives in this matrix:

$$\begin{bmatrix} \left(\dfrac{\delta \dot{W}^{hs}}{\delta W^{hs}} \right) & \left(\dfrac{\delta \dot{W}^{hs}}{\delta W^{hs'}} \right) \\ \left(\dfrac{\delta \dot{W}^{hs'}}{\delta W^{hs}} \right) & \left(\dfrac{\delta \dot{W}^{hs'}}{\delta W^{hs'}} \right) \end{bmatrix}$$

The trace must be negative. The determinant must be positive. Let us show that these conditions are satisfied under the two exchange-rate regimes considered in this chapter.

With a flexible external rate, the elements of the matrix can be written as

$$\frac{\delta W^{hs}}{\delta W^{hs}} = -(1/2M_s)\{S_Y(\sigma_1 M_{1\pi}/V_\pi)$$

$$+ J_W(B^t_{11} - B^t_{12})^{-1}[M_s - S_Y(m_1 - m_2)\sigma_1 M_{22}]\}$$

$$\frac{\delta \dot{W}^{hs\prime}}{\delta W^{hs\prime}} = -(1/2M_s)\{S_Y(\sigma_2' M_{2\pi}/V_\pi)$$
$$+ J_W(B_{11}^t + B_{12}^t)^{-1}[M_s - S_Y(m_1 - m_2)\sigma_2' M_{11}]\}$$

$$\frac{\delta \dot{W}^{hs}}{\delta W^{hs\prime}} = \frac{\delta \dot{W}^{hs}}{\delta W^{hs}} + (1/M_s)J_W(B_{11}^t - B_{12}^t)^{-1}[M_s - S_Y(m_1 - m_2)\sigma_1 M_{22}]$$

$$\frac{\delta \dot{W}^{hs\prime}}{\delta W^{hs}} = \frac{\delta \dot{W}^{hs\prime}}{\delta W^{hs\prime}} + (1/M_s)J_W(B_{11}^t - B_{12}^t)^{-1}[M_s - S_Y(m_1 - m_2)\sigma_2' M_{11}]$$

Therefore, the trace is

$$-(1/2M_s)\{S_Y(M_\pi/V_\pi) + J_W(B_{11}^t - B_{12}^t)^{-1}[2M_s - S_Y(m_1 - m_2)$$
$$\times (\sigma_1 M_{22} + \sigma_2' M_{11})]\}$$

where

$$M_\pi = \sigma_1 M_{1\pi} + \sigma_2' M_{2\pi} > 0$$

It can be shown, however, that

$$2M_s - S_Y(m_1 - m_2)(\sigma_1 M_{22} + \sigma_2' M_{11})$$
$$= 2M_k + (1 - m_0)S_Y[(\sigma_2' u_{10}^t + \sigma_1 u_{20}^t) + 2M_0]$$

where

$$M_0 = u_{12}^t(\sigma_1 + \sigma_2') + \sigma_1\sigma_2'[1 - (m_1 - m_2)] > 0$$

Thus, the trace is negative. Turning next to the determinant, it can be written as

$$(S_Y/2M_s)(J_W/M_s)(B_{11}^t - B_{12}^t)^{-1}\{(\sigma_1 M_{1\pi}/V_\pi)[M_s - S_Y(m_1 - m_2)\sigma_2' M_{11}]$$
$$+ (\sigma_2' M_{2\pi}/V_\pi)[M_s - S_Y(m_1 - m_2)\sigma_1 M_{22}]\}$$

and rewritten as

$$(S_Y/2M_s)(J_W/M_s)(B_{11}^t - B_{12}^t)^{-1}\{(M_\pi/V_\pi)[M_k + S_Y(1 - m_0)M_0]$$
$$+ S_Y[\sigma_1(M_{1\pi}/V_\pi)(m_2\sigma_2' u_{10}^t + m_1\sigma_1 u_{20}^t)$$
$$+ \sigma_2'(M_{2\pi}/V_\pi)(m_1\sigma_2' u_{10}^t + m_2\sigma_1 u_{20}^t)]\}$$

Thus, the determinant is positive. The model is stable with a flexible external rate.[11]

[11] Four assumptions play strategic roles in this and the next proof: (1) All goods are gross substitutes, so that u_{10}^t, u_{20}^t, and u_{12}^t are positive. (2) Households in the North and South spend more on domestic goods than on the other country's goods, so that $m_1 > m_2$. (3) Households in each country devote a larger fraction of an increase in wealth to purchasing the domestic bond than purchasing the other country's bond, so that $B_{1W} > B_{2W}$. (4) National biases in asset preferences are reflected in the sensitivities of saving to changes in the interest rates r_1 and r_2, so that $S_1 > S_2$ when $B_{1W} > B_{2W}$. Assumptions 3 and 4 function together to guarantee that $J_W > 0$.

With a pegged external rate, the elements of the matrix can be written as

$$\frac{\delta \dot{W}^{hs}}{\delta W^{hs}} = -(1/M_s J_S)\{M_s J_K - S_Y J_K \sigma_1[m_1 M_{22} + (1 - m_0)M_{21}]$$
$$- (B_{11}^t - B_{12}^t)^{-1} J_F[M_s - S_Y(m_1 - m_2)\sigma_1 M_{22}]\}$$

$$\frac{\delta \dot{W}^{hs\prime}}{\delta W^{hs\prime}} = -(1/M_s J_S)\{M_s J_K - S_Y J_K \sigma_2'[m_1 M_{11} + (1 - m_0)M_{12}]$$
$$- (B_{11}^t - B_{12}^t)^{-1} J_F[M_s - S_Y(m_1 - m_2)\sigma_2' M_{11}]\}$$

$$\frac{\delta \dot{W}^{hs}}{\delta W^{hs\prime}} = (1/M_s J_S)\{S_Y J_K \sigma_1[m_2 M_{22} + (1 - m_0)M_{21}]$$
$$- (B_{11}^t - B_{12}^t)^{-1} J_F[M_s - S_Y(m_1 - m_2)\sigma_1 M_{22}]\}$$

$$\frac{\delta \dot{W}^{hs\prime}}{\delta W^{hs}} = (1/M_s J_S)\{S_Y J_K \sigma_2'[m_2 M_{11} + (1 - m_0)M_{12}]$$
$$- (B_{11}^t - B_{12}^t)^{-1} J_F[M_s - S_Y(m_1 - m_2)\sigma_2' M_{11}]\}$$

where

$$J_F = S_1(B_{2W}B_{11}^t - B_{1W}B_{12}^t) + S_2(B_{1W}B_{11}^t - B_{2W}B_{12}^t)$$

Therefore, the trace is

$$- (1/M_s J)\{J_K(B_{11}^t - B_{12}^t)[M_k + M_s - S_Y(m_1 - m_2)(1 - m_0)S_Y \sigma_1 \sigma_2']$$
$$- J_F[2M_s - S_Y(m_1 - m_2)(\sigma_1 M_{22} + \sigma_2' M_{11})]\}$$

which is, in turn, susceptible of rearrangement as[12]

$$- (1/M_s J)\{J_K(B_{11}^t - B_{12}^t)[M_k + S_Y(m_1 - m_2)m_0\sigma_1\sigma_2']$$
$$+ J_W(B_{11}^t + B_{12}^t)[M_s - S_Y(m_1 - m_2)M_Y\sigma_1\sigma_2']$$
$$+ J_F S_Y(m_1 - m_2)(\sigma_2' u_{10}^t + \sigma_1 u_{20}^t)\}$$

and $M_s > S_Y(m_1 - m_2)M_Y\sigma_1\sigma_2'$, so that the trace is negative. Turning finally to the determinant, it can be written as $(J_K/J)(M_k/M_s)J_W$ and is therefore positive. The model is stable with a pegged external rate.

The time paths of the market-clearing variables

At this point in our work on the single small economy, we paused to study the time paths of endogenous variables. But the results obtained in

[12] Two steps are strategic here. First, replace $(1 - m_0)S_Y$ with $(M_Y - m_0)$. Second, invoke the fact that $J_K(B_{11}^t - B_{12}^t) - 2J_F = J_W(B_{11}^t + B_{12}^t)$, which follows from the definitions of J_K, J_F, and J_W, thereby regrouping the remaining terms. (The same relationship among these terms is invoked later, together with the fact that $M_s = M_{11}M_{22} + M_{11}M_{21} + M_{22}M_{12}$, in order to collect terms in the determinant.)

Chapter 3 suggest that many outcomes would be uncertain, especially with a flexible external rate. Furthermore, the task would be far more formidable in the context of a two-country model. At any point in time, the endogenous variables depend on *four* stocks – the accumulations of household saving, W^{hs} and $W^{hs\prime}$, and the accumulations of government debt, B_1 and B_2'. Therefore, the corresponding rates of change depend simultaneously on Northern and Southern saving and on the two countries' budget deficits. Using the notation employed in Chapter 3, the analogue to Eq. (3.14) would be

$$(13.16) \quad \delta\dot{x} = \left(\frac{\delta x}{\delta W^{hs}}\right)\left(\frac{\delta\dot{W}^{hs}}{\delta z_j}\right)\delta z_j + \left(\frac{\delta x}{\delta W^{hs\prime}}\right)\left(\frac{\delta\dot{W}^{hs\prime}}{\delta z_j}\right)\delta z_j$$
$$+ \left(\frac{\delta x}{\delta B_1}\right)\delta\bar{D} + \left(\frac{\delta x}{\delta B_2'}\right)\delta\bar{D}'$$

There is thus room for ambiguity whenever $(\delta x/\delta W^{hs})$ and $(\delta x/\delta W^{hs\prime})$ have opposite signs, or when a disturbance, δz_j, has opposite effects on the two countries' saving.[13]

But one such path deserves attention. It is $\bar{\pi}\dot{R}^t$, the time path of the joint balance of payments under a pegged external rate. Using Eqs. (13.16) and (13.4b), its total derivative can be written as

$$(13.17) \quad \bar{\pi}\,\delta\dot{R}^t = (1/J_S)[J_\pi(\delta\dot{W}^{hs} + \delta\dot{W}^{hs\prime}) + L_{11}^t(\delta\bar{D} + \delta\bar{D}')]$$

where

$$(13.18) \quad \delta\dot{W}^{hs} + \delta\dot{W}^{hs\prime} = S_Y\,\delta Y^{dt} + 2S_0\,\delta\bar{r}_0 + 2S_1^t\,\delta r^t + S_W 2V_\pi\left(\frac{\delta\bar{\pi}'}{\bar{\pi}'}\right)$$

With goods-market disturbances (for which $\delta r^t = 0$), Eq. (13.18) simplifies substantially; the sum of Northern and Southern saving takes its sign from the sign of δY^{dt} for each disturbance in Table 13.1B. Thus, shifts in demand to the foreign good worsen the two countries' joint balance of payments ($\bar{\pi}\,\delta\dot{R}^t < 0$); so does a balanced-budget increase of Northern spending on the Northern good or a balanced-budget increase of Southern spending on the Southern good. The outcomes are ambiguous, however, for a balanced-budget increase of one country's spending on the other country's good or for an increase in a budget deficit. With an increase in the Northern deficit, we have

$$\bar{\pi}\,\delta\dot{R}^t = (1/M_s J_S)\{(B_{0W}L_{11}^t - L_{1W}B_{01}^t)S_Y[M_k + S_Y(m_1 - m_2)\sigma_2'(u_{10}^t + m_0\sigma_1)$$
$$+ (m_1\sigma_1 M_{22} + m_2\sigma_2' M_{11}) + (1 - m_0)(\sigma_1 M_{21} + \sigma_2' M_{12})]$$
$$+ L_{11}^t(1 - S_Y)[M_k + S_Y(m_1 - m_2)\sigma_2'(u_{10}^t + m_0\sigma_1)]\}\,\delta\bar{D}$$

---

[13] We examine one such case in Appendix E, involving the effects of selected disturbances on the bilateral balance of payments under a flexible external rate.

and is ambiguous because $B_{0W}L_{11}^t \gtreqless L_{1W}B_{01}^t$. The corresponding expression for $\delta\bar{D}'$ differs only in detail.

With financial disturbances, the algebra is more complicated, but there is only one ambiguous outcome, pertaining to a change in the pegged external rate,

$$\bar{\pi}\,\delta\dot{R}^t = (J_\pi/M_sJ_S)\{S_YM_\pi - V_\pi(J_K/J_S)[2M_k + S_Y(m_1 - m_2)(\sigma_2'u_{10}^t$$
$$+\ \sigma_1u_{20}^t + 2m_0\sigma_1\sigma_2')]\}\left(\frac{\delta\bar{\pi}'}{\bar{\pi}'}\right)$$

This expression is ambiguous because the first term within brackets is multiplied by S_Y, the second is multiplied by V_π, and the two terms cannot be combined. This ambiguity is, of course, the counterpart of the one encountered in the small-country case. Although a joint devaluation raises R^t instantaneously, it can lead thereafter to a surplus or a deficit vis-à-vis the outside world.

An increase in the foreign interest rate improves the two countries' joint balance of payments:

$$\bar{\pi}\,\delta\dot{R}^t = \lfloor(J_\pi/M_sJ_S)[S_0 - B_{10}^t(S_1^t/J_S)][2M_k + S_Y(m_1 - m_2)(\sigma_2'u_{10}^t + \sigma_1u_{20}^t$$
$$+\ 2m_0\sigma_1\sigma_2')]\,\delta\bar{r}_0$$

There is an inflow of reserves that works through time to offset the immediate loss defined by Eq. (13.4b).

An open-market purchase worsens the joint balance of payments, regardless of the bond or central bank involved. But the *size* of the change in the joint balance differs with the bond. With an open-market purchase of the Northern bond,

$$\bar{\pi}\,\delta\dot{R}^t = -(J_\pi/M_sJ_S)(1/J)\{S_1^t[M_k + S_Y(m_1 - m_2)m_0\sigma_1\sigma_2'](B_{11}^t - B_{12}^t)$$
$$+\ S_Y(m_1 - m_2)[\sigma_1u_{20}^t(S_2B_{11}^t - S_1B_{12}^t)$$
$$+\ \sigma_2'u_{10}^t(S_1B_{11}^t - S_2B_{12}^t)]\}(\delta\bar{B}_1^c + \delta\bar{B}_1^{c'})$$

With an open-market purchase of the Southern bond, $\sigma_1u_{20}^t$ and $\sigma_2'u_{10}^t$ change places. In all cases, however, there is an outflow of reserves that compounds the immediate loss of reserves defined by Eq. (13.4b).[14]

[14] We would therefore predict that the loss of reserves will be larger in the long run than it was on impact, and this is what we find. Subtracting the impact change, $\bar{\pi}\,\delta R^t$, given by Eq. (13.4b) from the steady-state change, $\bar{\pi}\,dR^t$, given by Eq. (13.22b), we get $-(S_1^t/J_SJ_K)[L_{1W}(B_{11}^t + B_{12}^t) - B_{1W}^tL_{11}^t] < 0$, which holds for any open-market purchase. Incidentally, Eq. (13.22b) reaffirms a lesson learned in Chapter 6. A joint devaluation raises reserves no matter what happens to the balance of payments during the transition to the steady state. There is, we saw, an increase of reserves on impact; there can be a surplus or deficit through time; but steady-state reserves must always be higher than they were initially. Notice, finally, one more analogy. An increase in a budget deficit, being a

Solving for steady-state effects

With the proof of stability behind us, we take the last step in the solution
of the model, asking how disturbances and policy changes affect the economies in the long run. To do so, we must solve anew the equations for the
goods, bond, and money markets. Our task is simplified by obtaining
directly the long-run changes in disposable incomes and stocks of household wealth, using the fact that saving is zero in the steady state. It is also
simplified by exploiting the fact emphasized earlier that the sums of
changes in disposable incomes, the averages of changes in interest rates,
and the changes in the common external exchange rate behave much like
their analogues in Chapter 3.

Steady-state effects under a flexible external rate

Here, it is convenient to write the model in a form resembling that employed in Chapter 3. Starting with the bond and money markets (and re-
calling that $z = 1$),

(11.76a) $B_1(\bar{r}_0, r_1, r_2, W^h) + B_1'(\bar{r}_0, r_1, r_2, W^{h\prime}) + \bar{B}_1^c + \bar{B}_1^{c\prime} - \bar{B}_1 = 0$

(11.77a) $B_2(\bar{r}_0, r_1, r_2, W^h) + B_2'(\bar{r}_0, r_1, r_2, W^{h\prime}) + \bar{B}_2^c + \bar{B}_2^{c\prime} - \bar{B}_2' = 0$

(11.78a) $L_1(\bar{r}_0, r_1, r_2, W^h) - [\bar{B}_1^c + \bar{B}_2^c + \pi'R - W^c] = 0$

(11.79a) $L_2'(\bar{r}_0, r_1, r_2, W^{h\prime}) - [\bar{B}_1^{c\prime} + \bar{B}_2^{c\prime} + \pi'(\bar{R}^t - R) - W^{c\prime}] = 0$

We have replaced R' by $(R^t - R)$ and designated R^t, B_1, and B_2' as exogenous variables (the last two being counterparts of $\bar{D}$ and $\bar{D}'$, which
must go to zero at time $t = k$, before the economies can go to a steady
state). When saving is zero, moreover, we have two more equations:

(11.13a) $S(\bar{r}_0, r_1, r_2, Y^d, W^h) = 0$

(11.14a) $S'(\bar{r}_0, r_1, r_2, Y^{d\prime}, W^{h\prime}) = 0$

Finally, the goods-market equations become

(11.43a) $C_1(\pi' \bar{p}_0^f, p_1, p_2', Y^d) + C_1'(\pi' \bar{p}_0^f, p_1, p_2', Y^{d\prime})$

$$+ C_1^f\left(\bar{p}_0^f, \frac{p_1}{\pi'}, \frac{p_2'}{\pi'}, \bar{C}^f\right) + (\bar{G}_1/p_1) + (\bar{G}_1'/p_1) - \theta_1(p_1) = 0$$

goods-market disturbance, cannot affect reserves on impact. We have just shown, moreover, that it has ambiguous flow effects. According to Eq. (13.22b), however, the cumulative increase in the supply of bonds corresponding to a temporary deficit has an unambiguous negative effect on the steady-state level of R^t (assuming as we do that crowding
out does not dominate).

(11.44a) $\quad C_2(\pi' \bar{p}_0^f, p_1, p_2', Y^d) + C_2'(\pi' \bar{p}_0^f, p_1, p_2', Y^{d'})$

$$+ C_2^f\left(\bar{p}_0^f, \frac{p_1}{\pi'}, \frac{p_2'}{\pi'}, \bar{C}^f\right) + (\bar{G}_2/p_2') + (\bar{G}_2'/p_2') - \theta_2(p_2') = 0$$

where

(11.19b) $\quad Y^d + \bar{G}_1 + \bar{G}_2 - p_1\theta_1(p_1) = 0$

(11.20b) $\quad Y^{d'} + \bar{G}_1' + \bar{G}_2' - p_2'\theta_2(p_2') = 0$

The goods-market equations differ from what they were before only in that $*S$ and $*S'$ vanish; the definitions of disposable incomes differ only in that $\bar{D}$ and $\bar{D}'$ vanish.

At this point in Chapter 3, we were able to partition our model, using the equations for bonds and money to solve for the domestic interest rate and stock of wealth, the statement about saving to solve for disposable income (given the solutions for the interest rate and wealth), and the remaining equations to solve for goods prices and the flexible exchange rate.

We cannot adopt that strategy here. The first four equations listed above involve *five* endogenous variables–two domestic interest rates, two stocks of wealth, and the stock of Northern (or Southern) reserves. But what we have already learned about sums and averages suggests another strategy: (1) We can solve the *sum* of Eqs. (11.76a) and (11.77a) and the *sum* of Eqs. (11.78a) and (11.79a) for the sums of changes in the stocks of wealth and for changes in r^t, the average interest rate. (2) Using those solutions, we can solve the *sum* of Eqs. (11.13a) and (11.14a) for the sums of changes in disposable incomes. (3) We can then solve Eqs. (11.43a) and (11.44a), together with the *sum* of Eqs. (11.19b) and (11.20b) for the changes in p_1, p_2', and π', given the solution obtained in step 2 for the sums of changes in disposable incomes. (4) We can obtain the changes in each country's income from the changes in p_1 and p_2', then obtain the changes in disposable incomes from Eqs. (11.19b) and (11.20b). (5) The solutions for Y^d and $Y^{d'}$ can be combined with the bond and saving equations to obtain simultaneously the changes in r_1 and r_2, together with the changes in each country's wealth. (6) We can then employ Eq. (11.78a) to obtain the changes in Northern reserves, given the solutions for r_1, r_2, and Northern wealth.[15]

---

[15] Step 6 is relegated to Appendix E, but the signs of the results are listed in Tables 13.2A and 13.2B. We do not show the changes in W^h and $W^{h'}$, jointly or separately.

Proceeding in this fashion, steps 1 and 2 yield

(13.19a) $dr^t = (1/J_\pi)(L_{10}B^t_{1W} - L_{1W}B^t_{10})\, d\bar{r}_0$
$- (1/2J_\pi)(1 - B_{0W})(d\bar{B}^c_1 + d\bar{B}^{c'}_1 + d\bar{B}^c_2 + d\bar{B}^{c'}_2)$
$+ (1/2J_\pi)L_{1W}(d\bar{B}_1 + d\bar{B}'_2)$

(13.20a) $dY^{dt} = (2/S_Y J_\pi)J_0\, d\bar{r}_0$
$+ (1/S_Y J_\pi)[(1 - B_{0W})S^t_1 + S_W B^t_{01}](d\bar{B}^c_1 + d\bar{B}^{c'}_1$
$+ d\bar{B}^c_2 + d\bar{B}^{c'}_2)$
$+ (1/S_Y J_\pi)J_B(d\bar{B}_1 + d\bar{B}'_2)$

where

$$J_B = S_W L^t_{11} - L_{1W}S^t_1 > 0$$

which is to say that crowding out does not dominate.

These equations are the counterparts of Eqs. (3.19a) and (3.21a), describing the changes in r_1 and Y^d for the single small economy, and they have analogous implications. Under a flexible external exchange rate, permanent changes in the average interest rate and in the sum of disposable incomes take place only in response to asset-market disturbances – changes in the foreign interest rate, open-market operations, and changes in stocks of government debt reflecting budget deficits. Goods-market disturbances do not appear in these equations, which says that a flexible external rate serves in this longest of long runs to insulate the two economies together from the effects of goods-market disturbances.

The two countries' total incomes taken together behave in the same ways as disposable incomes unless, of course, there is a balanced-budget change in Northern or Southern government spending. From Eqs. (11.19b) and (11.20b),

(13.21a) $dY^t = dY^{dt} + (d\bar{G}_1 + d\bar{G}'_1 + d\bar{G}_2 + d\bar{G}'_2)$

The "balanced-budget multiplier" is unity when defined with respect to the sum of changes in the countries' incomes.

Because a flexible external rate does serve to insulate the sum of the countries' incomes from goods-market disturbances, all of those disturbances appear in the solution for the flexible exchange rate. It must also respond, however, to changes in Y^{dt} reflecting the effects of financial disturbances. Proceeding to step 3 of our analysis,

(13.22a) $\left(\dfrac{d\hat{\pi}'}{\pi'}\right) = (1/M_w)\{M_g + \sigma'_2 u^t_{10}[1 - (m_1 - m_2)]\}\, d\bar{G}_1$
$+ (1/M_w)[M_g + \sigma'_2 u^t_{10} - (m_1 - m_2)\sigma_1 u^t_{20}]\, d\bar{G}'_1$
$+ (1/M_w)[M_g + \sigma_1 u^t_{20} - (m_1 - m_2)\sigma'_2 u^t_{10}]\, d\bar{G}_2$

$$+ (1/M_w)\{M_g + \sigma_1 u_{20}^t[1 - (m_1 - m_2)]\} \, d\bar{G}_2'$$
$$+ (1/M_w)[M_0 + \sigma_1 u_{20}^t] \, dc_{01}^t + (1/M_w)[M_0 + \sigma_2' u_{10}^t] \, dc_{02}^t$$
$$+ (M_k/M_w) \, dY^{dt}$$

where

$$M_w = (u_{10}^t + p_1 C_1^f)(\sigma_1 u_{20}^t + M_0) + (u_{20}^t + p_2 C_2^f)(\sigma_2' u_{10}^t + M_0)$$

Thus, the determination of the flexible exchange rate has passed from asset to goods markets, as it did in Chapter 3. The flexible external rate is responsive to financial disturbances only insofar as they affect disposable incomes, impinging on goods markets. In the two-country case, however, it is the *sum* of changes in disposable incomes that appears in the final term of the exchange-rate equation.

This last fact, moreover, has an important corollary for which there is no clear-cut antecedent in the single-country case. *If any disturbance has different effects on the Northern and Southern economies and the bilateral exchange rate is pegged, a flexible external exchange rate is unable to insulate each of the economies even when it insulates them jointly.* Accordingly, we can expect to find differences in the responses of p_1 and p_2' to various goods-market disturbances and, therefore, in the responses of the countries' incomes. Furthermore, we can expect the causes of those differences to be represented by the terms that testify to differences between their goods markets – by σ_1 and σ_2', the price elasticities of output values, by u_{10}^t and u_{20}^t, the cross-price elasticities of demand, and by $p_1 C_1^f$ and $p_2 C_2^f$, the levels of Northern and Southern exports to the outside world.[16]

The price and income responses to which we refer emerge at steps 3 and 4. The changes in incomes are

$$dY = \sigma_1 \left(\frac{dp_1}{p_1}\right) \quad \text{and} \quad dY' = \sigma_2' \left(\frac{dp_2'}{p_2'}\right)$$

The price changes are

$$(13.23a) \quad \left(\frac{dp_1}{p_1}\right) = (1/M_w)\{u_{20}^t(u_{10}^t + p_1 C_1^f) + u_{12}^t U_\pi$$
$$+ \sigma_2' U_\pi[1 - (m_1 - m_2)]\} \, d\bar{G}_1$$

---

[16] There is a crude analogy in the small-country case. If we were to calculate the incomes (product values) of the two *industries* in the small economy, the incomes of producers of traded and nontraded goods, we would find that they respond quite differently to goods-market disturbances, even in the Keynesian version of the model when both outputs move together. Changes in a flexible exchange rate vis-à-vis the outside world offset the effects of goods-market disturbances on aggregate disposable income but do not offset their effects on the incomes of each sector.

$$+ (1/M_w)[u_{20}^t(u_{10}^t + p_1 C_1^t) + u_{12}^t U_\pi + \sigma_2' U_\pi] \, d\bar{G}_1'$$
$$+ (1/M_w)[u_{20}^t(u_{10}^t + p_1 C_1^t) + u_{12}^t U_\pi$$
$$\quad - \sigma_2' U_\pi(m_1 - m_2)] \, d\bar{G}_2$$
$$+ (1/M_w)[u_{20}^t(u_{10}^t + p_1 C_1^t) + u_{12}^t U_\pi] \, d\bar{G}_2'$$
$$- (1/M_w)[\sigma_2'(u_{20}^t + p_2 C_2^t)] \, dc_{01}^t$$
$$+ (1/M_w)[\sigma_2'(u_{10}^t + p_1 C_1^t)] \, dc_{02}^t + (U_{1\pi}/M_w) \, dY^{dt}$$

(13.24a) $\left(\dfrac{dp_2'}{p_2'}\right) = (1/M_w)[u_{10}^t(u_{20}^t + p_2 C_2^t) + u_{12}^t U_\pi] \, d\bar{G}_1$
$$+ (1/M_w)[u_{10}^t(u_{20}^t + p_2 C_2^t) + u_{12}^t U_\pi$$
$$\quad - \sigma_1 U_\pi(m_1 - m_2)] \, d\bar{G}_1'$$
$$+ (1/M_w)[u_{10}^t(u_{20}^t + p_2 C_2^t) + u_{12}^t U_\pi + \sigma_1 U_\pi] \, d\bar{G}_2$$
$$+ (1/M_w)\{u_{10}^t(u_{20}^t + p_2 C_2^t) + u_{12}^t U_\pi$$
$$\quad + \sigma_1 U_\pi[1 - (m_1 - m_2)]\} \, dG_2'$$
$$+ (1/M_w)[\sigma_1(u_{20}^t + p_2 C_2^t)] \, dc_{01}^t$$
$$- (1/M_w)[\sigma_1(u_{10}^t + p_1 C_1^t)] \, dc_{02}^t + (U_{2\pi}/M_w) \, dY^{dt}$$

where

$$U_\pi = (u_{10}^t + p_1 C_1^t) + (u_{20}^t + p_2 C_2^t)$$
$$U_{1\pi} = (u_{10}^t + p_1 C_1^t)[u_{20}^t + u_{12}^t + (1 - m_1)\sigma_2']$$
$$\quad + (u_{20}^t + p_2 C_2^t)(u_{12}^t + m_2 \sigma_2')$$
$$U_{2\pi} = (u_{20}^t + p_2 C_2^t)[u_{10}^t + u_{12}^t + (1 - m_1)\sigma_1]$$
$$\quad + (u_{10}^t + p_1 C_1^t)(u_{12}^t + m_2 \sigma_1)$$

so that

$$M_w = (\sigma_1 U_{1\pi} + \sigma_2' U_{2\pi})$$
$$= M_0 U_\pi + \sigma_1 u_{20}^t(u_{10}^t + p_1 C_1^t) + \sigma_2' u_{10}^t(u_{20}^t + p_2 C_2^t)$$

We shall not discuss each of these results. Their signs are shown in Table 13.2A. One result, however, needs brief comment here.

When studying the impact effects of open-market operations, we saw that a purchase of the Northern bond had more effect on p_1 and, therefore, on Northern income than did a purchase of the Southern bond. Similarly, a purchase of the Southern bond had more effect on p_2' and, therefore, on Southern income. These differences obtained because a purchase of the Northern bond had more effect on r_1 than r_2, because a change in r_1 had more effect on Northern saving and, therefore, on Northern consumption, and because a change in Northern consumption had more effect on the demand for the Northern good than on the demand for the Southern good. In Eqs. (13.23a) and (13.24a), however, we see that these distinctions vanish eventually. Open-market operations affect p_1 and p_2'

Table 13.2A. Selected steady-state effects under a flexible external exchange rate

Disturbance	Effect										
	$d\hat{\pi}'$	$\pi\,dR^a$	dr_1	dr_2	dr^t	dp_1^b	$dp_2'^b$	dY^{ac}	$dY^{a'c}$	dY^t	dY^{at}
$d\bar{r}_0$	+	?	?	?	?	+	+	+	+	+	+
$d\bar{B}_1^c$	+	?	?	?	−	+	+	+	+	+	+
$d\bar{B}_1^{c'}$	+	?	?	?	−	+	+	+	+	+	+
$d\bar{B}_2^c$	+	?	?	?	−	+	+	+	+	+	+
$d\bar{B}_2^{c'}$	+	?	?	?	−	+	+	+	+	+	+
$d\bar{B}_1$	+	?	?	?	+	+	+	+	+	+	+
$d\bar{B}_2$	+	?	?	?	+	+	+	+	+	+	+
$d\bar{G}_1$	?	−	+	−	0	+	+	−	+	1	0
$d\bar{G}_1'$	?	+	−	+	0	+	?	+	−	1	0
$d\bar{G}_2$	?	−	+	−	0	?	+	−	+	1	0
$d\bar{G}_2'$	+	+	−	+	0	−	+	+	−	1	0
dc_{01}^t	+	−	+	−	0	+	+	−	+	0	0
dc_{02}^t	+	+	−	+	0	+	−	+	−	0	0

Some signs shown here are different in certain limiting cases considered in subsequent chapters.

[a] Because $dR^t = 0$ with a flexible external rate, changes in Southern reserves are equal with opposite signs to changes in Northern reserves.

[b] Because each country produces a single good, the changes in incomes (dY and dY') and in money wage rates (dw and dw') or levels of employment (dE and dE') have the same signs as the price changes.

[c] Changes in Northern disposable income, dY^a, equal the changes in Northern gross national product, dY, except when the disturbances are $d\bar{G}_1$ and $d\bar{G}_2$, which affect Northern taxes; similarly, changes in Southern disposable income, $dY^{a'}$, equal the changes in Southern gross national product, dY', except when the disturbances are $d\bar{G}_1'$ and $d\bar{G}_2'$.

only by affecting the *sum* of disposable incomes, and the size of the change in Y^{dt} does not depend on the bond bought or on the bank buying it.

Before we can turn to the next step in this analysis, we need to extract more information about the long-run changes in disposable incomes, taken individually. Equation (13.20a) told us that Y^{dt} is unaffected in the long run by goods-market disturbances, and this assertion is reflected in Eqs. (13.23a) and (13.24a). The price changes given for dc^t_{01} and dc^t_{02} generate equal but opposite changes in Northern and Southern incomes (which are in these instances the same as the changes in the corresponding disposable incomes). For the four fiscal policies, moreover, the price changes yield

$$(13.25a) \quad dY^d = -(\sigma'_2/M_w)[u^t_{10}(u^t_{20} + p_2C^t_2) + u^t_{12}U_\pi]\, d\bar{G}_1$$
$$- (\sigma'_2/M_w)[u^t_{10}(u^t_{20} + p_2C^t_2) + (u^t_{12} + \sigma_1)U_\pi]\, d\bar{G}_2$$

$$(13.26a) \quad dY^{d\prime} = -(\sigma_1/M_w)[u^t_{20}(u^t_{10} + p_1C^t_1) + (u^t_{12} + \sigma'_2)U_\pi]\, d\bar{G}'_1$$
$$- (\sigma_1/M_w)[u^t_{20}(u^t_{10} + p_1C^t_1) + u^t_{12}U_\pi]\, d\bar{G}'_2$$

Therefore, $dY^d = -dY^{d\prime}$ for *all* goods-market disturbances. For each such disturbance then,

$$dY^d - dY^{d\prime} = 2\, dY^d$$

a fact that we shall use below to ascertain the changes in national interest rates.

With asset-market disturbances, of course, the sums of changes in disposable incomes are not zero, and this point is likewise made by Eqs. (13.23a) and (13.24a). In these instances, moreover,

$$dY^d - dY^{d\prime} = (1/M_w)(\sigma_1 U_{1\pi} - \sigma'_2 U_{2\pi})\, dY^{dt}$$

and we shall use this fact as well.[17]

Finally, we come to the steady-state changes in each country's interest rate. These, we said, can be obtained, together with the changes in each country's wealth, by solving Eqs. (11.76a), (11.77a), (11.13a), and (11.14a) now that we know the changes in disposable incomes. With goods-market disturbances, the interest-rate changes are equal absolutely

[17] Note that the difference $(\sigma_1 U_{1\pi} - \sigma'_2 U_{2\pi})$ can be rewritten to feature three distinct goods-market differences between North and South. It can be written as

$$[M_g + u^t_{12}(p_1C^t_1 + p_2C^t_2)][\sigma_1 - \sigma'_2] + m_0\sigma_1\sigma'_2[(u^t_{10} - u^t_{20}) + (p_1C^t_1 - p_2C^t_2)]$$
$$+ [\sigma_1 u^t_{20}(p_1C^t_1) - \sigma'_2 u^t_{10}(p_2C^t_2)]$$

but have opposite signs, a result foreshadowed by our finding that $dr^t = 0$ for all such disturbances. With asset-market disturbances (other than $d\bar{r}_0$), the changes in the interest rates differ absolutely but do so symmetrically:[18]

$$
\begin{aligned}
(13.27a) \quad dr_1 = &-(1/2J_W)[S_Y(B_{1W} - B_{2W})](dY^d - dY^{d'}) \\
&+ (1/J_\pi)[L_{10}B_{1W}^t - L_{1W}B_{10}^t]\,d\bar{r}_0 \\
&- (1/2J_\pi J_W)[(1 - B_{0W})J_W - S_W J_\pi](d\bar{B}_1^c + d\bar{B}_1^{c'}) \\
&- (1/2J_\pi J_W)\{(1 - B_{0W})(S_1 - S_2)(B_{1W} - B_{2W}) \\
&\quad + S_W[2B_{12}^t(1 - B_{0W}) + B_{1W}^t B_{01}^t]\}(d\bar{B}_2^c + d\bar{B}_2^{c'}) \\
&+ (1/2J_\pi J_W)[L_{1W}(S_1 - S_2)(B_{1W} - B_{2W}) \\
&\quad - S_W(2L_{1W}B_{11}^t - B_{1W}^t L_{11}^t)]\,d\bar{B}_1 \\
&+ (1/2J_\pi J_W)[L_{1W}(S_1 - S_2)(B_{1W} - B_{2W}) \\
&\quad + S_W(2L_{1W}B_{12}^t - B_{1W}^t L_{11}^t)]\,d\bar{B}_2'
\end{aligned}
$$

$$
\begin{aligned}
(13.28a) \quad dr_2 = &(1/2J_W)[S_Y(B_{1W} - B_{2W})](dY^d - dY^{d'}) \\
&+ (1/J_\pi)[L_{10}B_{1W}^t - L_{1W}B_{10}^t]\,d\bar{r}_0 \\
&- (1/2J_\pi J_W)\{(1 - B_{0W})(S_1 - S_2)(B_{1W} - B_{2W}) \\
&\quad + S_W[2B_{12}^t(1 - B_{0W}) + B_{1W}^t B_{01}^t]\}(d\bar{B}_1^c + d\bar{B}_1^{c'}) \\
&- (1/2J_\pi J_W)[(1 - B_{0W})J_W - S_W J_\pi](d\bar{B}_2^c + d\bar{B}_2^{c'}) \\
&+ (1/2J_\pi J_W)[L_{1W}(S_1 - S_2)(B_{1W} - B_{2W}) \\
&\quad + S_W(2L_{1W}B_{12}^t - B_{1W}^t L_{11}^t)]\,d\bar{B}_1 \\
&+ (1/2J_\pi J_W)[L_{1W}(S_1 - S_2)(B_{1W} - B_{2W}) \\
&\quad - S_W(2L_{1W}B_{11}^t - B_{1W}^t L_{11}^t)]\,d\bar{B}_2'
\end{aligned}
$$

The signs of the changes in r_1 and r_2, shown in Table 13.2A, are usually dominated by the signs of the differences between dY^d and $dY^{d'}$, featured in the first term of each equation.[19] The signs of those differences, in turn, are given by expressions in the text above. The differences between dY^d and $dY^{d'}$ dominate even in respect of financial disturbances–those that appear explicitly in Eqs. (13.27a) and (13.28a); the ambiguities introduced

[18] Because every asset-market disturbance affects disposable income, the influence of any such disturbance on r_1 is the sum of the effect shown explicitly in Eq. (13.27a) and the effect on r_1 of the corresponding change in the difference between disposable incomes. Note that $dr_1 = dr_2 = d\bar{r}_0$ with perfect substitutability between Northern and foreign bonds (or Southern and foreign bonds); this is true on impact, as well as in the steady state. It can be demonstrated in Eqs. (13.27a) and (13.28a) by showing that $J_W \to \infty$ and $J_\pi \to \infty$ when $-B_{01}^t \to \infty$.

[19] There are two exceptions to this generalization: (1) With full-scale goods-market symmetry, $\sigma_1 = \sigma_2'$, $u_{10}^t = u_{20}^t$, and $p_1 C_1^t = p_2 C_2^t$, so that $dY^d = dY^{d'}$ for financial disturbances. (2) With perfect substitutability between Northern and Southern bonds, $J_W \to \infty$, so that $dr_1 = dr_2 = dr^t$, and the steady-state changes in interest rates are given by Eq. (13.19a).

by the disposable-income terms cannot be removed by combining those terms with the asset-market disturbance terms.[20]

Thus, we come to a striking conclusion about the effects of open-market operations (and long-run changes in supplies of bonds). Although the impact effects are always unambiguous, even with regard to the relative changes in r_1 and r_2, their steady-state effects are not. An open-market purchase causes a permanent decline in the average interest rate; Eq. (13.19a) asserts that $dr^t < 0$ for each such purchase, regardless of the bank or bond involved. But we cannot know which interest rate will fall further. We cannot even rule out an increase in one rate when there are significant goods-market differences between North and South. It is not inconceivable, no matter how implausible, that an open-market purchase of the Northern bond will cause the Northern interest rate to increase in the long run.

There is just one thing we can say with perfect certainty, having to do with the size of the change in a *single* interest rate. An open-market purchase of the Northern bond will cause a larger decrease in r_1 (or a smaller increase if there is one) than an open-market purchase of the Southern bond. Conversely, an open-market purchase of the Southern bond will cause a larger decrease (or smaller increase) in r_2. We can compare effects on a single interest rate because the comparison does not involve the goods-market terms in the interest-rate equations; the difference between changes in Y^d and $Y^{d\prime}$ is the same for any open-market operation standardized for size (and for any change in B_1 or B_2').

We return to these matters in Chapters 15 and 16, when we examine the effects of goods-market differences between North and South on the conduct of the countries' monetary policies, the costs and benefits of asset-market integration, and the operations of a monetary union.

Steady-state effects under a pegged external rate

Once again, it is convenient to list the steady-state equations in a slightly different order:

(11.43a) $C_1(\bar{\pi}'\bar{p}_0^f, p_1, p_2', Y^d) + C_1'(\bar{\pi}'\bar{p}_0^f, p_1, p_2', Y^{d\prime})$

$$+ C_1^f\left(\bar{p}_0^f, \frac{p_1}{\bar{\pi}'}, \frac{p_2'}{\bar{\pi}'}, \bar{C}^f\right) + (\bar{G}_1/p_1) + (\bar{G}_1'/p_1) - \theta_1(p_1) = 0$$

---

[20] To illustrate, consider the effects on r_1 of an open-market operation in the Northern bond. Writing out in full the relevant terms from Eq. (13.27a):

$$dr_1 = -(1/2J_\pi J_w M_w)\{[(1 - B_{0w})J_w - S_w J_\pi](\sigma_1 U_{1\pi} + \sigma_2' U_{2\pi})$$
$$+ (B_{1w} - B_{2w})[(1 - B_{0w})S_1^f + S_w B_{01}^f](\sigma_1 U_{1\pi} - \sigma_2' U_{2\pi})\}(d\bar{B}_1^c + d\bar{B}_1^{c\prime})$$

(11.44a) $C_2(\bar{\pi}'p_0^f, p_1, p_2', Y^d) + C_2'(\bar{\pi}'\bar{p}_0^f, p_1, p_2', Y^{d'})$

$$+ C_2^f\left(\bar{p}_0^f, \frac{p_1}{\bar{\pi}'}, \frac{p_2'}{\bar{\pi}'}, \bar{C}^f\right) + (\bar{G}_2/p_2') + (\bar{G}_2'/p_2') - \theta_2(p_2') = 0$$

(11.19b) $Y^d + \bar{G}_1 + \bar{G}_2 - p_1\theta_1(p_1) = 0$

(11.20b) $Y^{d'} + \bar{G}_1' + \bar{G}_2' - p_2'\theta_2(p_2') = 0$

(11.13a) $S(\bar{r}_0, r_1, r_2, Y^d, W^h) = 0$

(11.14a) $S'(\bar{r}_0, r_1, r_2, Y^{d'}, W^{h'}) = 0$

(11.76a) $B_1(\bar{r}_0, r_1, r_2, W^h) + B_1'(\bar{r}_0, r_1, r_2, W^{h'}) + \bar{B}_1^c + \bar{B}_1^{c'} - \bar{B}_1 = 0$

(11.77a) $B_2(\bar{r}_0, r_1, r_2, W^h) + B_2'(\bar{r}_0, r_1, r_2, W^{h'}) + \bar{B}_2^c + \bar{B}_2^{c'} - \bar{B}_2 = 0$

(11.78a) $L_1(\bar{r}_0, r_1, r_2, W^h) - [\bar{B}_1^c + \bar{B}_2^c + \bar{\pi}'R - W^c] = 0$

(11.79a) $L_2'(\bar{r}_0, r_1, r_2, W^{h'}) - [\bar{B}_1^{c'} + \bar{B}_2^{c'} + \bar{\pi}'(R^t - R) - W^{c'}] = 0$

These equations are the same as those for the flexible external exchange rate, except for the designation of R^t as endogenous and π' as exogenous, but they are arranged to show how they can be solved and to stress the economic consequences of a pegged external rate.

This system of equations can be partitioned without additional modification. Because π' is exogenous, we can solve the first four equation for changes in p_1, p_2', Y^d and $Y^{d'}$ and can use the solutions to obtain the changes in Y and Y' (together with the usual sums of changes). Thereafter, we can solve the next four equations for the changes in r_1, r_2, W^h, and $W^{h'}$, given the changes in Y^d and $Y^{d'}$, and can solve the last two for the changes in R^t and R, given the solutions for the changes in interest rates and in stocks of wealth.[21]

In economic terms, steady-state prices and incomes are determined entirely in goods markets and are thus affected only by disturbances originating in those markets. Interest rates and stocks of wealth are determined in bond markets and by the requirement that saving be zero, given disposable incomes in the North and South. Finally, each country's money

Collecting terms involving S_1 and S_2 (those in J_W and S_1'), we have

$$2(1 - B_{0W})(B_{1W} - B_{2W})[(\sigma_1 U_{1\pi})S_1 - (\sigma_2' U_{2\pi})S_2] \gtrless 0$$

[21] Alternatively, the sums of Eqs. (11.13a) and (11.14a) and of Eqs. (11.76a) and (11.77a) could be solved for the sums of changes in interest rates and wealth, as in the flexible-rate case, and the sum of Eqs. (11.78a) and (11.79a) could be solved for the changes in R^t. We adopt this last suggestion here, relegating to Appendix E the solution of Eq. (11.78a) for the changes in Northern reserves.

supply is adjusted endogenously to the demand for money by cumulative changes in reserves held by the country's central bank.

Solving the goods-market and income equations,

(13.23b) $\left(\dfrac{dp_1}{p_1}\right) = (U_{1\pi}/M_k)\left(\dfrac{d\bar{\pi}'}{\bar{\pi}'}\right)$

$\qquad + (1/M_k)\{(1 - m_1)u^t_{20} + m_0 u^t_{12}$
$\qquad\qquad + m_0[1 - (m_1 - m_2)]\sigma'_2\}\, d\bar{G}_1$
$\qquad + (1/M_k)[(1 - m_2)u^t_{20} + m_0(u^t_{12} + \sigma'_2)]\, d\bar{G}'_1$
$\qquad + (1/M_k)[m_0 u^t_{12} - m_1 u^t_{20} - m_0(m_1 - m_2)\sigma'_2]\, d\bar{G}_2$
$\qquad + (1/M_k)[m_0 u^t_{12} - m_2 u^t_{20}]\, d\bar{G}'_2$
$\qquad - (1/M_k)[u^t_{20} + u^t_{12} + (1 - m_1)\sigma'_2]\, dc^t_{01}$
$\qquad - (1/M_k)[u^t_{12} + m_2\sigma'_2]\, dc^t_{02}$

(13.24b) $\left(\dfrac{dp'_2}{p'_2}\right) = (U_{2\pi}/M_k)\left(\dfrac{d\bar{\pi}'}{\bar{\pi}'}\right)$

$\qquad + (1/M_k)[m_0 u^t_{12} - m_2 u^t_{10}]\, d\bar{G}_1$
$\qquad +. (1/M_k)[m_0 u^t_{12} - m_1 u^t_{10} - m_0(m_1 - m_2)\sigma_1]\, d\bar{G}'_1$
$\qquad + (1/M_k)[(1 - m_2)u^t_{10} + m_0(u^t_{12} + \sigma_1)]\, d\bar{G}_2$
$\qquad + (1/M_k)\{(1 - m_1)u^t_{10} + m_0 u^t_{12}$
$\qquad\qquad + m_0[1 - (m_1 - m_2)]\sigma_1\}\, d\bar{G}'_2$
$\qquad - (1/M_k)[u^t_{12} + m_2\sigma_1]\, dc^t_{01}$
$\qquad - (1/M_k)[u^t_{10} + u^t_{12} + (1 - m_1)\sigma_1]\, dc^t_{02}$

The signs of these outcomes are shown in Table 13.2B, and they convey the signs of the income changes that go with each disturbance. The signs of the sums of the changes in income are, of course, clear cut when the two countries' incomes rise or fall together, but this is not the case for balanced-budget changes in government spending, and there are ambiguities in those instances:

(13.21b) $dY^t = (1/M_k)[m_0 M_0 + m_0\sigma_1 u^t_{20} + m_2(\sigma_1 u^t_{20} - \sigma'_2 u^t_{10})]\, d\bar{G}_1$
$\qquad + (1/M_k)[m_0 M_0 + m_0\sigma_1 u^t_{20} + m_1(\sigma_1 u^t_{20} - \sigma'_2 u^t_{10})]\, d\bar{G}'_1$
$\qquad + (1/M_k)[m_0 M_0 + m_0\sigma'_2 u^t_{10} - m_1(\sigma_1 u^t_{20} - \sigma'_2 u^t_{10})]\, d\bar{G}_2$
$\qquad + (1/M_k)[m_0 M_0 + m_0\sigma'_2 u^t_{10} - m_2(\sigma_1 u^t_{20} - \sigma'_2 u^t_{10})]\, d\bar{G}'_2$

As always, disposable incomes can move differently from total incomes only on account of balanced-budget changes in government spending (and only in the country whose government alters its spending). Thus,

(13.25b) $dY^d = -(1/M_k)\{M_g + [(1 - m_1)u^t_{10} + m_0(u^t_{12})]\sigma'_2\}\, d\bar{G}_1$
$\qquad \div (1/M_k)\{M_g + [(1 - m_1)u^t_{10} + m_0(u^t_{12})]\sigma'_2$
$\qquad\qquad + (u^t_{20} + m_0\sigma'_2)\sigma_1\}\, d\bar{G}_2$

Table 13.2B. *Selected steady-state effects under a pegged external exchange rate*

Disturbance	Effect										
	$\bar{\pi}\,dR^t$	$\bar{\pi}\,dR^{a}$	dr_1	dr_2	dr^t	$dp_1{}^b$	$dp_2'{}^b$	$dY^{a\,c}$	$dY^{a'\,c}$	dY^t	dY^{at}
$d\bar{\pi}'$	+	+	?	?	−	+	+	+	+	+	+
$d\bar{r}_0$	−	−	?	?	?	0	0	0	0	0	0
$d\bar{B}_1^c$	−	−	−	?	−	0	0	0	0	0	0
$d\bar{B}_1^{c\prime}$	−	?	−	?	−	0	0	0	0	0	0
$d\bar{B}_2^c$	−	?	?	−	−	0	0	0	0	0	0
$d\bar{B}_2^{c\prime}$	−	?	?	−	−	0	0	0	0	0	0
$d\bar{B}_1$	−	?	+	?	+	0	0	0	0	0	0
$d\bar{B}_2$	−	?	?	+	+	0	0	0	0	0	0
$d\bar{G}_1$	?	−	+	?	+	+	?	−	?	?	?
$d\bar{G}_1'$	?	?	?	?	?	+	?	+	−	?	?
$d\bar{G}_2$	?	?	?	?	?	?	+	−	+	?	?
$d\bar{G}_2'$	−	?	?	+	+	?	+	?	−	?	−
dc_{10}^t	−	−	?	?	+	−	−	−	−	−	−
dc_{20}^t	−	−	?	?	+	−	−	−	−	−	−

Some signs shown here are different in certain limiting cases considered in subsequent chapters.

[a] Because $dR^t \neq 0$ with a pegged external rate, the changes in Southern reserves are *not* equal with opposite signs to the changes in Northern reserves.

[b] See corresponding note to Table 13.2A.

[c] See corresponding note to Table 13.2A.

(13.26b) $dY^{d\prime} = -(1/M_k)\{M_g + [(1 - m_1)u_{20}^t + m_0(u_{12}^t)]\sigma_1$
$+ (u_{10}^t + m_0\sigma_1)\sigma_2'\} \, d\bar{G}_1'$
$- (1/M_k)\{M_g + [(1 - m_1)u_{20}^t + m_0(u_{12}^t)]\sigma_1\} \, d\bar{G}_2'$

Therefore,

(13.20b) $dY^{dt} = -(1/M_k)\{M_g + u_{10}^t[1 - (m_1 - m_2)]\sigma_2'\} \, d\bar{G}_1$
$- (1/M_k)[M_g + \sigma_2'u_{10}^t - (m_1 - m_2)\sigma_1 u_{20}^t] \, d\bar{G}_1'$
$- (1/M_k)[M_g + \sigma_1 u_{20}^t - (m_1 - m_2)\sigma_2'u_{10}^t] \, d\bar{G}_2$
$- (1/M_k)\{M_g + u_{20}^t[1 - (m_1 - m_2)]\sigma_1\} \, d\bar{G}_2'$

With a handful of exceptions noted later, the price and income effects of goods-market disturbances are unambiguous with a pegged external rate. But there are more ambiguities in the sums of income changes than there were in Table 13.2A, for a flexible external rate, because there are more differences between the signs of income changes in the North and South. The explanation harks back to the point we made earlier concerning the role of a flexible external rate and long-run responses to changes in that rate.

Under a flexible external rate, goods-market disturbances cannot have permanent effects on the sum of disposable incomes ($dY^{dt} = 0$ for all such disturbances in Table 13.2A). But that sum is stabilized by driving Northern and Southern incomes in opposite directions; see in particular the responses to the shifts in demand, dc_{01}^t and dc_{02}^t.

Under a pegged external rate, the sum of disposable incomes is not constrained ($dY^{dt} \neq 0$ for every goods-market disturbance in Table 13.2B). In this case, then, a goods-market disturbances can drive the two countries' incomes in the same direction, and differences between the goods-market characteristics of the two economies can affect the *signs* of sums of income changes, not merely the distribution of those changes.

When the external rate is flexible, moreover, there is just one type of goods-market disturbance that has uncertain consequences for long-run income levels. A balanced-budget increase in Northern spending on the Southern good has an uncertain influence on Northern income, and an increase in Southern spending on the Northern good has an uncertain influence on Southern income. When the external exchange rate is pegged, this is not the only type that has uncertain consequences. In Table 13.2B, we find that a balanced-budget increase in one country's spending on its *own* good, an increase of $\bar{G}_1$ or $\bar{G}_2'$, has an uncertain influence on the *other* country's income.

We shall not pause to trace the reasons for this difference in results; they are examined at length in Chapters 17 and 18, where we look more closely at fiscal policies. It is worth noting, however, that the ambiguities in Table 13.2B are not new. They appeared in Tables 13.1A and 13.1B, pertaining to impact effects with flexible and pegged exchange rates. The *new* result occurs in Table 13.2A, where two ambiguities are resolved. Over the long run, a flexible external rate is able to respond to goods-market disturbances, and the depreciation of that rate noted in Table 13.2A sustains the demand for the other country's good when there is an increase of $\bar{G}_1$ or $\bar{G}_2'$.

Although asset-market disturbances do not affect steady-state prices and incomes when the external exchange rate is pegged, goods-market disturbances do affect asset-market variables. Because those disturbances can cause changes in disposable incomes, they lead to permanent changes in wealth, and interest rates must therefore adjust to clear the bond markets.[22] And because the changes in Y^d and $Y^{d'}$ do not sum to zero with a pegged external rate, the changes in the interest rates do not do so either. There are changes in r^t, the average interest rate.

The steady-state changes in national interest rates are

$$
\begin{aligned}
(13.27\text{b}) \quad dr_1 = \; & -(S_Y/J_WJ_K)[B_{1W}^t S_1(B_{1W} - B_{2W}) \\
& - S_W(B_{1W}B_{11}^t - B_{2W}B_{12}^t)] \, dY^d \\
& + (S_Y/J_WJ_K)[B_{1W}^t S_2(B_{1W} - B_{2W}) \\
& + S_W(B_{2W}B_{11}^t - B_{1W}B_{12}^t)] \, dY^{d'} \\
& + (1/J_K)(S_W B_{10}^t - S_0 B_{1W}^t) \, d\bar{r}_0 \\
& + (S_W/J_WJ_K)[S_1 B_{1W} + S_2 B_{2W} \\
& - S_W B_{11}^t][(d\bar{B}_1^c + d\bar{B}_1^{c'}) - d\bar{B}_1] \\
& - (S_W/J_WJ_K)[S_1 B_{2W} + S_2 B_{1W} \\
& - S_W B_{12}^t][(d\bar{B}_2^c + d\bar{B}_2^{c'}) - d\bar{B}_2']
\end{aligned}
$$

$$
\begin{aligned}
(13.28\text{b}) \quad dr_2 = \; & (S_Y/J_WJ_K)[B_{1W}^t S_2(B_{1W} - B_{2W}) \\
& + S_W(B_{2W}B_{11}^t - B_{1W}B_{12}^t)] \, dY^d \\
& - (S_Y/J_WJ_K)[B_{1W}^t S_1(B_{1W} - B_{2W}) \\
& - S_W(B_{1W}B_{11}^t - B_{2W}B_{12}^t)] \, dY^{d'} \\
& + (1/J_K)(S_W B_{10}^t - S_0 B_{1W}^t) \, d\bar{r}_0 \\
& - (S_W/J_WJ_K)[S_1 B_{2W} + S_2 B_{1W} \\
& - S_W B_{12}^t][(d\bar{B}_1^c + d\bar{B}_1^{c'}) - d\bar{B}_1] \\
& + (S_W/J_WJ_K)[S_1 B_{1W} + S_2 B_{2W} \\
& - S_W B_{11}^t][(d\bar{B}_2^c + d\bar{B}_2^{c'}) - d\bar{B}_2']
\end{aligned}
$$

---

[22] The money markets must clear too, but this function is performed by changes in reserves. This is the economic counterpart of the fact that the steady-state changes in W^h, $W^{h'}$, r_1, and r_2 come from Eqs. (11.13a), (11.14a), (11.76a), and (11.77a), the saving and bond-market equations, whereas the corresponding changes in R^t come from the sum of Eqs. (11.78a) and (11.79a).

Because asset preferences are symmetrical, these results are thoroughly symmetrical; the response of the Northern interest rate to an increase of Northern disposable income is the same as the response of the Southern rate to an increase of Southern disposable income. But most of the responses to goods-market disturbances, via disposable incomes, are uncertain. This is one more consequence of refusing to assume full-scale goods-market symmetry.

To see that this is true for shifts in demand (dc_{01}^t and dc_{02}^t) and also for a change in the pegged external rate, we rearrange the income terms of Eq. (13.27b):

$$dr_1 = -(S_Y/J_W J_K)\{B_{1W}^t(B_{1W} - B_{2W})[S_1(dY^d) - S_2(dY^{d\prime})]$$
$$- S_W[(B_{1W}B_{11}^t - B_{2W}B_{12}^t) dY^d + (B_{2W}B_{11}^t - B_{1W}B_{12}^t) dY^{d\prime}]\}$$

It is then a simple matter to prove conclusively that the difference $[S_1(dY^d) - S_2(dY^{d\prime})]$ is ambiguous for shifts in demand and for exchange-rate changes; we need merely replace dY^d and $dY^{d\prime}$ with the relevant portions of Eqs. (13.23b) and (13.24b). And the same method can be used, with the same result, for the other interest rate.

Turning to balanced-budget changes in spending, we find only one clear-cut result. When there is more spending on the domestic good, the domestic interest rate must rise. (When the Northern government raises $\bar{G}_1$, the steady-state level of r_1 rises too; when the Southern government raises $\bar{G}_2'$, the steady-state level of r_2 rises too.) In all other instances, the outcomes are uncertain.

Asset-market disturbances have clear-cut effects where one would expect them. An open-market purchase of the Northern bond depresses the Northern interest rate permanently. An increase in supply of the Northern bond, reflecting an interval of budget deficits, raises that rate permanently. The same things can be said about a purchase of the Southern bond, an increase in supply of the Southern bond, and the Southern interest rate. But we do not know how an open-market operation in one country's bond will affect the interest rate on the other bond; we do not know the cross effects of changes in supplies of bonds; and we do not know how r_1 and r_2 will respond to an increase in $\bar{r}_0$ (unless, of course, the foreign bond is a perfect substitute for the Northern or the Southern bond, in which case the relevant domestic rate will move with the foreign rate and will not move without a movement in the foreign rate).

Few of these ambiguities, however, are reflected by the long-run outcomes for the average interest rate. These are given by

$$(13.19b) \quad dr^t = -(S_Y/2J_K)(B^t_{1W})\, dY^{dt} + (1/J_K)(S_W B^t_{10} - S_0 B^t_{1W})\, d\bar{r}_0$$
$$+ (S_W/2J_K)[(d\bar{B}^c_1 + d\bar{B}^{c\prime}_1 + d\bar{B}^c_2 + d\bar{B}^{c\prime}_2) - (d\bar{B}_1 + d\bar{B}'_2)]$$

and there are only two uncertainties here–regarding the effects of an increase in $\bar{r}_0$ (whose effects are always uncertain without perfect substitutability between foreign and domestic bonds) and regarding the effects of balanced-budget changes in one country's spending on the other country's good (whose effects on dY^{dt} are uncertain).

Consider, finally, the effects of various disturbances on the sum of reserves:

$$(13.22b) \quad \bar{\pi}\, dR^t = (S_Y/J_K)(J_\pi)\, dY^{dt} - (2J_0/J_K)\, d\bar{r}_0$$
$$- (1/J_K)[S_W B^t_{01} + S^t_1(1 - B_{0W})](d\bar{B}^c_1 + d\bar{B}^{c\prime}_1$$
$$+ d\bar{B}^c_2 + d\bar{B}^{c\prime}_2)$$
$$- (1/J_K)(J_B)(d\bar{B}_1 + d\bar{B}'_2)$$

Because the joint change in reserves must satisfy the joint change in the demand for money resulting from a change in r^t and the sum of changes in disposable incomes, our outcomes for $\bar{\pi}R^t$ are unambiguous in all but one instance–the now-familiar case of a balanced-budget increase in one country's spending on the other country's good. (The outcome for an increase in $\bar{r}_0$ is unambiguous despite ambiguities in the responses of r_1, r_2, and r^t; the demand for money falls in the North and South together, whatever happens to domestic interest rates, and the two economies expel reserves.) Furthermore, the cumulative changes in reserves have the expected signs. A devaluation of the pegged external rate raises the sum of disposable incomes, increasing the demand for money and raising reserves; shifts of demand to the foreign good reduce the sum of disposable incomes, reducing reserves, and so do balanced-budget changes in a country's spending on its domestic good. On the financial side, every disturbance or policy change described above leads to a loss of reserves, no matter what it does to any other variable.

The distribution of the changes in reserves is not so clear. There are, indeed, few cases in which one can be sure that the change in $\bar{\pi}R^t$ is *shared* between the North and South. In other words, we cannot always rule out movements of reserves between North and South that swamp the corresponding movements vis-à-vis the outside world.[23] This matter will come up again in subsequent discussions of monetary policy, reserve pooling, and monetary unification.

[23] The signs of the changes in $\bar{\pi}R$ come from Appendix E. There we also show to what extent the ambiguities result from uncertainties about the signs and sizes of the steady-state changes in r_1 and r_2.

PART V

The theory of financial integration

14

Dimensions of integration

Markets, targets, and instruments

When markets connecting national economies are closely integrated, governments lose much of their control over their domestic economies. Cooper has described the situation in these terms.[1]

In a highly integrated economic area which surpasses in size the jurisdiction, of governments, each group of policymakers is subject to such strong interactions with the surrounding area that the constraints on its actions become very severe. Indeed, in the hypothetically limiting case, these constraints determine entirely the course of action each jurisdiction must take. The region, or the nation, in a highly integrated economy becomes analogous to the perfect competitor – or at best the oligopolist – in a market economy. The range of choice it has, consistent with economic survival, is very small; for the most part it simply adapts its behavior to stimuli from outside.

Cooper would appear to have in mind the very small open economy. We deal here with the less extreme case modeled in Part IV. Markets are closely integrated but not to the extent that governments lose all control over their economies or have only negligible influence on their neighbors' economies. The case that we study more nearly resembles oligopoly than perfect competition in its description of relations among governments.

It is our aim to show as precisely as possible how market integration limits autonomy in monetary and fiscal policies, to show how one government may be required to react to decisions by another, and to assess the gains that may accrue from the coordination or harmonization of national policies and from outright policy unification.

The two economies analyzed in Part IV were *integrated structurally*, insofar as there was unobstructed trade between them in both goods and assets. The extent of structural or market integration was measured by the substitutability between the goods they produced and the assets they issued. But they were also *interdependent structurally*, because each was large enough in the markets of the other to influence its prices, income, interest rate, and wealth. By contrast, the two countries were said to be

[1] R. N. Cooper, *The Economics of Interdependence*, McGraw-Hill, New York, 1968, p. 170.

377

dependent in their relations with the outside world. Because they were small in world markets, other than their export markets, they were influenced by changes in world prices and world interest rates but did not have any influence on them.[2]

It is the combination of structural or market integration with structural interdependence that makes for *policy interdependence*. When one country's policies spill into another country's economy, the other is compelled to alter its own policies in order to achieve its domestic goals. Doing so, however, it is bound to provoke additional changes in the first country's policies. With structural dependence, rather than interdependence, this process is short circuited.

Once we understand the relationships among market integration, structural interdependence, and policy interdependence, we shall be able to explore the case for *policy integration*.[3] At that point, however, we shall have to draw additional distinctions. First, it will be useful to distinguish between policy coordination or harmonization on the one hand and outright policy unification on the other. Second, it will be necessary to distinguish between the *targets* and *instruments* of economic policy. By integrating targets, governments relinquish independent national objectives in favor of jointly agreed objectives (harmonization) or a single multinational objective (unification). By integrating instruments, governments agree on the way that each will use a particular device (harmonization) or pass control of that device to a central body (unification).

The mention of targets and instruments brings to mind Tinbergen's rule that the number of independent instruments must be no smaller than the number of independent targets.[4] It is applicable here. When policy instruments are integrated, reducing the number of independent instruments, the number of targets has to be reduced. Furthermore, we shall find that

[2] The terminology used in this discussion draws on R. C. Bryant, *Money and Monetary Policy in Interdependent Nations,* The Brookings Institution, Washington, D.C., 1980, chap. 10.

[3] For an early analysis of the links between asset-market integration and policy integration, see R. N. Cooper, "Macroeconomic Policy Adjustment in Interdependent Economies," *Quarterly Journal of Economics,* 83 (February 1969), pp. 1–26. Cooper's own conclusion, however, is based mainly on his finding that high capital mobility raises the likelihood that the economies in his model will overshoot their equilibria, not directly on the loss of policy autonomy.

[4] J. Tinbergen, *On the Theory of Economic Policy,* North-Holland, Amsterdam, 1955, chap. iv. Johnson has pointed out that most post-Keynesian analyses of balance-of-payments policy, including the important contributions by Meade, Fleming, and Mundell, are applications of Tinbergen's rule; see H. G. Johnson, "The Monetary Approach to the Balance of Payments: A Nontechnical Guide," *Journal of International Economics,* 7 (August 1977), p. 257.

structural or market integration can impair the feasibility of using particular policy instruments independently. They have to be harmonized or unified de jure because they have been harmonized or unified de facto, and targets must be integrated when instruments are integrated, in order to restore equality between the number of instruments and number of targets.[5]

Consider the use of monetary policies for domestic stabilization. When asset markets are perfectly integrated, countries with pegged exchange rates will find that open-market operations have the same effects on incomes, even in the short run, regardless of the bond bought or central bank buying it. There is thus only one monetary instrument, and if there is no other instrument available to influence each country's income independently, the governments involved must forego the pursuit of independent income targets. Otherwise, they will become embroiled in fruitless attempts to manipulate their monetary instruments, with harmful side effects on other targets, especially balance-of-payments targets.[6]

In other cases, the degree of market integration may not preclude completely the pursuit of independent policy targets but can raise the costs of achieving them. It may be necessary to make larger changes in instruments, and governments may bump against political constraints. They may then find it beneficial, economically and politically, to integrate their separate national targets into a single multinational target. By integrating targets, moreover, governments may acquire the freedom to pursue *additional* targets. In terms of Tinbergen's rule, they may define a larger set of feasible targets given the number of available instruments. But whether or not they will choose to integrate targets can be predicted only when we know how they will answer many questions. How much autonomy is

[5] On the way in which market integration can reduce the number of instruments, see S. W. Arndt, "Joint Balance: Capital Mobility and the Monetary System of a Currency Area," in H. G. Johnson and A. K. Swoboda, eds., *The Economics of Common Currencies,* Harvard University Press, Cambridge, Mass., 1973, pp. 196–209. Arndt argues mistakenly, however, that two countries trading with each other and the outside world will have three separate balance-of-payments targets – a bilateral target and a target for each country vis-à-vis the outside world. When currencies are convertible, this is false; each country needs to be concerned only with its overall balance of payments. See Chapter 12, and J. E. Meade, "The Balance of Payments Problem of a Free Trade Area," *Economic Journal,* 67 (September 1957), pp. 379–96.

[6] On the possibility of policy conflicts between countries having too few independent instruments, see A. K. Swoboda, "Policy Conflict, Inconsistent Goals, and the Co-ordination of Economic Policies," in Johnson and Swoboda, eds., *The Economics of Common Currencies,* pp. 133–42. Swoboda anticipates a number of the points made in this chapter. He also notes that conflicts can be resolved either by the harmonization of targets or by the creation of additional instruments.

actually sacrificed by integrating policy targets or instruments when markets are already integrated closely? How strongly do the governments subscribe to common political aims like those that have animated European integration? How much influence can governments expect to have on the processes that formulate integrated targets and on the multinational institutions to which they confer control of integrated instruments?

The two types of policy integration–of targets and instruments– normally must go together. When targets are unified, there must be agreement on the tasks to be performed by each of the relevant national instruments–on the harmonization if not unification of instruments. When instruments are unified to face the fact of market integration, in order to reach targets more efficiently or control the side effects of independent use, there must be at least limited agreement on the use of each unified instrument. The integration of policy instruments must necessarily involve a redistribution of costs and benefits among the participating countries, and these may be perceived to be quite large even when they are in fact fairly small.

The countries of the European Community (EC), confronting close policy interdependence and subscribing in principle to the aim of monetary integration, have tried to integrate their policy targets. They have agreed on the need to narrow disparities in growth rates and inflation rates and have at times agreed to raise or lower aims together. They have not yet begun to integrate the principal instruments of macroeconomic policy. Balassa and Resnick have examined this experiment in target integration, using multicountry simulations of goods markets. They have found strong structural interdependence, measured by the sizes of dynamic income multipliers, but conclude that policy targets have been inconsistent, among and within EC countries.[7] Balassa has gone on to suggest that coordinated targets have been implemented only when coordination has not called for any significant compromise with national priorities.[8] In this same vein, Swoboda has stressed the importance of agreeing on consistent goals and devising simultaneously the ways to achieve them. The coordination of policy targets is no panacea.[9] We would put the point more strongly. The integration of targets may be more harmful than

[7] B. Balassa and S. Resnick, "Monetary Integration and the Consistency of Policy Objectives in the European Common Market," *Weltwirtschaftliches archiv*, 110 (December 1974), pp. 564–79. (The model itself is discussed more fully in S. A. Resnick, "A Macro Model for Western Europe," and "Dynamic Properties of the European Macro Model," in B. Balassa, ed., *European Economic Integration*, North-Holland, Amsterdam, 1975, pp. 121–74.)

[8] B. Balassa, "Monetary Integration in the European Common Market," in Balassa, ed., *European Economic Integration*, pp. 175–224.

[9] Swoboda, "Policy Conflict," p. 141.

helpful unless it is accompanied by an appropriate integration of instruments. Otherwise, expectations cannot be fulfilled, credibility is impaired, and recriminations follow.

The case for full-fledged monetary union, as compared to the mere pegging of exchange rates, can be made in these same terms. When governments form a monetary union, relinquishing the right to pursue autonomous monetary policies, adjustments in national money supplies take place automatically, in response to balance-of-payments flows between members of the union. The members of a monetary union, however, must still decide how to conduct its monetary policy and must agree on the exchange-rate regime to govern its relations with the outside world. This last choice may be crucial for survival of the union. Even when countries are interdependent structurally, they may differ significantly in their exposure to external disturbances. Their endogenous responses, moreover, will affect the other members of the union. There will be direct effects, stemming from structural interdependence; there will be indirect effects, stemming from balance-of-payments flows or exchange-rate changes between the union as a whole and the outside world. Thus, asymmetries in vulnerability and in domestic responses to external disturbances pose problems for the members of a union and for its managers. Our refusal to impose goods-market symmetry on the model in Part IV was intended to make room for the study of these problems, and they crop up frequently in subsequent chapters. Before we start to use that model, however, let us survey briefly the relevant literature. Much of it focuses on monetary issues, and we begin with them.

Monetary integration

One sizable body of literature deals with the optimum currency area, a concept introduced by Mundell. It seeks to identify the economic attributes which characterize areas that should be linked by pegged exchange rates and surrounded by flexible exchange rates. It relates to our concerns because it calls attention to the costs of exchange-rate unification and monetary integration. Individual authors have emphasized different attributes, but most of them agree at least implicitly that optimality itself pertains to the minimization of the costs of balance-of-payments adjustment.

In his initial contribution to the subject, Mundell identified factor mobility as the strategic attribute of an optimum currency area.[10] When factors move freely within an area, adjustments to real disturbances can take

[10] R. A. Mundell, "A Theory of Optimum Currency Areas," *American Economic Review*, 51 (December 1961), pp. 657–65.

place without large price and income changes. Subsequent contributors have acknowledged that mobility can reduce the costs of balance-of-payments adjustment but have said that it is not decisive. Several other attributes have been proposed as substitutes or supplements.

Reviewing the large literature on this subject, Tower and Willett conclude that, other things being equal, the gains from exchange-rate unification increase with the degree of openness inside an area.[11] They measure openness by the ratio of exports or imports to full-employment gross national product. Tower and Willett concede that other aspects of openness facilitate balance-of-payments adjustment, such as high price elasticities of demand for foreign exchange and the strength of the effects of changes in the terms of trade on the price level and absorption, but claim that these are apt to be associated with openness as they define it.

Others also emphasize openness but try to define it broadly – to include in the concept itself some of its implications. McKinnon, for example, measures openness by the ratio of tradeable to nontradeable output, because this definition stresses the extent to which the prices of domestic outputs must remain in line with foreign prices. He argues that open economies, defined by this device, are good candidates for membership in an exchange-rate union.[12] Corden makes a similar point. When tradeable goods bulk large in domestic consumption, it may be difficult to alter real wage rates by changing exchange rates, and economies that are small in this sense may have to join larger currency areas, whether or not optimal in any other way, because they cannot stand alone as feasible currency areas.[13] Whitman's definition of openness is even broader, hinging on the size and relative frequency of external disturbances and on the sensitivity of the economy to those disturbances.[14]

We emphasize the degree of market integration, rather than the concept of openness. In the small-country model of Part II, the responsiveness of domestic prices was shown to depend not only on the size of the tradeable goods sector but also on quantities actually traded, on own and cross-price elasticities of demand for tradeable and nontradeable goods, and on the degree of substitutability between domestic and foreign financial

[11] E. Tower and T. D. Willett, *The Theory of Optimum Currency Areas and Exchange-Rate Flexibility: A More General Framework*, Special Papers in International Economics 11, Princeton University, Princeton, N.J., 1976, pp. 40–6 and 69–80.

[12] R. I. McKinnon, "Optimum Currency Areas: Comment," *American Economic Review*, 53 (September 1963), pp. 717–25.

[13] W. M. Corden, *Monetary Integration*, Essays in International Finance 93, Princeton University, Princeton, N.J., 1972.

[14] M. v. N. Whitman, *International and Interregional Payments Adjustment: A Synthetic View*, Princeton Studies in International Finance 19, Princeton University, Princeton, N.J., 1967.

assets. In the two-country model of Part IV, all goods and assets were tradeable, yet the solutions to that model shown in Chapter 13 can be used to demonstrate that the character and speed of balance-of-payments adjustment depend on quantities actually traded and price elasticities, as well as on the degree of asset-market integration. (We have in fact expressed responses to price changes in terms of value-weighted price elasticities, the u_{ij}, which combine quantities traded with price elasticities.)

Others also emphasize the importance of asset-market integration for successful exchange-rate unification, especially Ingram.[15] When payments imbalances are financed automatically by well-integrated short-term financial markets, balance-of-payments adjustment can take place without changes in exchange rates. Automatic financing cannot postpone forever the need to deal with permanent disturbances, but current-account balances can be altered gradually, by wage and price changes and by factor movements, reducing the costs of adjustment. It may indeed be possible to deal with real disturbances by regulating relative rates of growth in real incomes, instead of reducing real incomes absolutely.

The optimality of a currency area depends not only on the ease with which its members adapt to disturbances, but also on the frequency and sizes of disturbances–a point stressed by Whitman's definition of openness, mentioned earlier. Accordingly, one of us has suggested that large, diversified economies may be the best candidates for membership in currency unions.[16] Real disturbances are apt to average out and will be small in any case relative to total domestic output, so that large economies may find it comparatively easy to maintain pegged exchange rates. Others, such as Giersch, come to the same conclusion, but for a different reason; large economies are least likely to import big cyclical disturbances from the outside world.[17] Tower and Willett cite these arguments as the principal qualifications to their emphasis on openness in judging the optimality of a currency union.[18] (But they also suggest, in answer to

[15] J. C. Ingram, *The Case for European Monetary Integration,* Essays in International Finance 98, Princeton University, Princeton, N.J., 1973.

[16] P. B. Kenen, "The Theory of Optimum Currency Areas: An Eclectic View," in R. A. Mundell and A. K. Swoboda, eds., *Monetary Problems of the International Economy,* University of Chicago Press, Chicago, 1969, pp. 41–60. A similar point is made by Vaubel, who argues that an optimum currency area is one within which *real* exchange rates need not be altered; see R. Vaubel, "Real Exchange-Rate Changes in the European Community," *Journal of International Economics,* 8 (May 1978), pp. 319–39.

[17] H. Giersch, "Entrepreneurial Risk Under Flexible Exchange Rates," in G. Halm, ed., *Approaches to Greater Flexibility of Exchange Rates: The Burgenstock Papers,* Princeton University Press, Princeton, N.J., 1970, pp. 145–50, and "On the Desirable Degree of Flexibility of Exchange Rates," *Weltwirtschaftliches archiv,* 109, 1973(2), pp. 191–213.

[18] Tower and Willett, *The Theory of Optimum Currency Areas.*

Giersch, that asset-market openness or integration may interfere with the ability of a flexible exchange rate to insulate economies against external disturbances – an answer endorsed by our own findings in Chapters 4 and 8.)

The notion of an optimum currency area may be too abstract. It pays no attention to the fact of nationality and the corresponding quest for autonomy. Furthermore, no single country is likely to possess all of the attributes required to make it an ideal member of a currency union. It may thus be more useful to weigh pragmatically the costs and benefits of currency unification or monetary integration from the viewpoint of the members individually and from that of the group collectively.[19]

This type of analysis has been stimulated by European efforts to move toward monetary union. Proposals aimed at this objective, including the ill-fated Werner plan of 1970, have typically envisaged a step-by-step process, beginning with exchange-rate unification and going on gradually to the federation or unification of the members' central banks and the instruments of monetary policy.[20] Academic and political debates about European monetary unification have therefore concentrated on the costs and benefits of currency unification, rather than the abstract criteria proposed by the theory of optimum currency areas. Furthermore, debates about European plans and prospects have had to take account of sovereignty and its implications – of national problems, interests, and institutions.

The long list of claims made for monetary union usually begins with the assertion that the use of a single European currency would enhance economic efficiency. It would remove uncertainty about exchange rates, as

---

[19] In Y. Ishiyama, "The Theory of Optimum Currency Areas: A Survey," *International Monetary Fund Staff Papers*, 22 (July 1975), pp. 344–83, the search for a single attribute is described as the "traditional" approach and is severely criticized. Ishiyama argues for the need to weigh benefits and costs comprehensively, and favors a pragmatic approach.

[20] For the Werner plan, see European Communities, *Economic and Monetary Union in the Community*, Bulletin of the European Communities, Supplement 11, Brussels, 1970. For a post mortem, see European Communities, *Report of the Study Group, "Economic and Monetary Union 1980,"* Brussels, 1975 (the Marjolin Report). The most recent plan, adopted in December 1978 and initiated in March 1979, likewise starts with exchange-rate unification. But it differs from earlier plans in three respects. First, it lays down no firm schedule for unifying monetary policies. Second, it allows for periodic realignments of exchange rates. Third, it provides for the establishment of a large European Monetary Fund (EMF) to supplement the members' own reserves, so that they will find it easier to honor their commitments to the pegging of European exchange rates. If drawings on the EMF are to be conditional on modifications of members' monetary policies, it may serve as a partial if not permanent substitute for the coordination or unification of monetary policies.

well as the transactions costs of converting one national currency into an other.[21] It is also asserted that monetary union would promote the integration of financial markets and of goods markets too (the latter less directly and partly in response to the integration of financial markets). An increase of market integration, in turn, would aid in the efficient allocation of resources, open up economies of scale, and foster economic growth.[22] But no one knows how large these gains would be, and some have even wondered whether there should be more market integration. Oppenheimer, for example, has suggested that more market integration would make exchange-rate changes ineffective in dealing with real disturbances but would not obviate the need for such changes.[23]

Some of the strongest claims for monetary union are, of course, political and institutional. Thus, Lamfalussy has argued that monetary unification would give Europe more influence in negotiations and arrangements with other countries,[24] and Williamson has seen it as a way of driving European governments toward fiscal and political integration–objectives that he treats as ends in themselves.[25] It has also been suggested that a European central bank might make better policies than those followed by certain of its national predecessors.[26]

The disadvantages of a monetary union include, of course, the costs of

[21] See R. Z. Aliber, "Uncertainty, Currency Areas and the Exchange Rate System," *Economica,* 39 (November 1972), pp. 432–41.

[22] All of these claims are, of course, the claims made for international money; see C. P. Kindleberger, "The Benefits of International Money," *Journal of International Economics,* 2 (September 1972), pp. 425–42. (But Kindleberger does not say that they are sufficient arguments for European monetary union.)

[23] P. M. Oppenheimer, "Monetary Union: A Survey of the Main Issues," *De Economist,* 122 (November 1974), pp. 32–48.

[24] A. Lamfalussy, "Monetary and Fiscal Integration," in F. Machlup, ed., *Economic Integration: Worldwide, Regional, Sectoral,* Macmillan, London, 1976, pp. 218–28. Considerations of this sort may have inspired the surprising French endorsement of monetary union in 1969. Similarly, the need to "coordinate" exchange-market intervention vis-à-vis the dollar was given as one reason for the Franco-German proposals that led to the 1978 agreement mentioned in note 20.

[25] J. H. Williamson, "Comments on Dr. Lamfalussy's Paper," in Machlup, ed., *Economic Integration,* pp. 233–6. The same point has been made by others (but criticized by those who fear that obstacles to fiscal and political integration may have the opposite effect of undermining monetary unification).

[26] See J. M. Fleming, "On Exchange Rate Unification," *Economic Journal,* 81 (September 1971), pp. 467–88. But Fleming is guarded in his endorsement of European monetary unification, as are Corden and Lamfalussy in the papers cited previously. For stronger endorsements, see Ingram, *The Case for European Monetary Unification;* G. Magnifico, *European Monetary Unification,* Macmillan, London, 1973; and M. Parkin, "Monetary Union and Stabilization Policy in the European Community," Banca Nazionale del Lavoro, *Quarterly Review,* 118 (September 1976), pp. 222–40.

balance-of-payments adjustment when exchange rates are fixed among countries that are far from being an optimum currency area. A number of writers remind us, however, that these costs would not be the same for a complete monetary union, with irrevocably fixed exchange rates, a unified monetary policy, and a pooling of external reserves, as for a simple exchange-rate union, comprising only the commitment to peg exchange rates within narrow margins.[27] It is by now commonly understood that an exchange-rate union cannot survive indefinitely without consistent monetary policies. Within a full-fledged monetary union, inconsistencies cannot arise, even temporarily, and there can be no need to correct for them.

But the differences go deeper. In a full-fledged union, adjustment may take place more gradually. There will still be money flows between the members of the union, but the flows are likely to be smaller than between the members of a simple exchange-rate union. On the one hand, imbalances will not be amplified by exchange-rate speculation, because exchange rates *cannot* change within a full-fledged union. On the other hand, the integration of financial markets and financial institutions that is induced by monetary unification will foster the financing of imbalances by automatic capital flows. Finally, no member of a full-fledged union will have to defend its external reserves by deliberately reducing its own money supply (by open-market sales of securities), because reserve constraints apply only to the union as a whole, and intra-union settlements do not alter the union's reserves. For purposes of intra-union settlements, a member's means of payments is coextensive with its money supply.[28]

Some of the critics of monetary unification have emphasized the costs of unifying policy targets, rather than the costs of balance-of-payments adjustment. Because countries with a common currency cannot maintain different inflation rates, they may be compelled to sacrifice or compromise employment or growth targets. This risk was stressed by Corden, who worried about differences between countries' Phillips curves, as well as differences between policy preferences, and it was also cited by Tower

[27] The latter is what Corden calls a pseudo-exchange-rate union (*Monetary Integration*, p. 3).

[28] Meade's classic article emphasized these differences between a monetary union and a simple exchange-rate union, and they are basic to Ingram's case for European monetary unification; see Meade, "The Balance of Payments Problem of a Free Trade Area," and Ingram, *The Case for European Monetary Integration*. They have also been discussed in B. J. Cohen, "The Euro-dollar, the Common Market, and Currency Unification," *Journal of Finance*, 18 (December 1963), pp. 605–21, and P. R. Allen, *Organization and Administration of a Monetary Union*, Studies in International Finance 38, Princeton University, Princeton, N.J., 1976.

and Willett as the major cost of an exchange-rate union.[29] These concerns derive from the belief that there is indeed a Phillips curve – that governments confront a stable trade-off between inflation and unemployment. And those who continue in this belief are more fearful now than they were a few years ago. The increase in inflation rates and widening of differences between inflation rates among European countries have led them to warn that exchange-rate unification may be too costly, if it is achievable at all. The same increase in inflation rates, however, coexisting as it has with high unemployment rates, has led many to conclude that there is no stable trade-off. Even those who do not yet believe in a unique "natural" rate of unemployment have come to doubt that governments can gain very much by choosing high inflation rates.

There has thus emerged a "monetarist" argument for exchange-rate unification, and it reverses old concerns. Far from interfering with the achievement of full employment or rapid growth, exchange-rate unification can help governments to attain them. It promises to discipline governments that have been unwilling or unable to fight inflation effectively and have avoided the need to do so by allowing their currencies to depreciate. In other words, exchange-rate unification can help to dissipate inflationary expectations and can thus help to foster full employment and more rapid growth. This argument echoes the traditional assertion that fixed exchange rates are needed for monetary discipline, but it goes much further. The new point is the claim that a commitment to exchange-rate unification would enhance the credibility of promises to fight inflation, and a full-fledged monetary union would do so more strongly, in that the control of monetary policy would be transferred to a new central body pledged explicitly to that objective.[30]

Another "monetarist" argument has gained favor recently. Worldwide inflation, it is said, has routed money illusion, and exchange-rate changes are less effective than before in adjusting real wage rates. Changes in nominal exchange rates have no lasting effects on real exchange rates, and the autonomy conferred by monetary sovereignty is illusory. Countries may be able to create more money than they could with fixed exchange

[29] See Corden, *Monetary Integration,* and Tower and Willett, *The Theory of Optimum Currency Areas,* pp. 35–8; also M. v. N. Whitman, "Place Prosperity and People Prosperity: The Delineation of Optimal Social Areas," in M. Perlman et al., eds., *Spacial, Regional and Population Economics,* Gordon & Breach, New York, 1972, pp. 359–93.

[30] This supposition is the basis for the strong support of monetary unification in Parkin, "Monetary Union and Stabilization Policy," and in G. Basevi et al., *Optica Report '75: Towards Economic Equilibrium and Monetary Unification in Europe,* Commission of the European Communities, Brussels, 1976; see also M. Fratianni and T. Peeters, eds., *One Money for Europe,* Macmillan, London, 1978.

rates but gain no freedom to pursue independent aims with respect to employment or growth. On this view, moreover, exchange-rate flexibility is inefficient in dealing with real disturbances, which call for changes in real exchange rates, and there is thus *nothing* to be gained in the long run from monetary sovereignty and exchange-rate flexibility.[31] (The same issue arises, of course, when a monetary union decides what to do with its common external exchange rate.)

There are fears that monetary integration may exacerbate differences in growth rates between member countries and also between regions of those countries. It might even impose absolute losses on the laggards. These fears reflect the belief that monetary integration may diminish flexibility in real wages and may cause an exodus of capital from the lagging regions. It may lead indirectly to alliances or federations of trade unions and thus to multinational collective bargaining that would limit the scope for relative reductions in money wages in regions with slowly growing productivity. Those areas would then experience increases in unemployment.[32] Emigration from the slowly growing regions would be one solution, but would be resisted. The regions and countries to which labor would migrate are likely to object to the increase of congestion and the costs of investments they would have to make in housing, urban transport, and other social services. The regions and countries from which labor would migrate are likely to object for other reasons. They are apt to lose young, productive workers, and the costs of supplying social services would not be reduced proportionately, because of indivisibilities, and would have to be borne by those who stayed behind.

Monetary unification might also encourage an exodus of long-term capital from slowly growing regions, which are likely to be those with chronic current-account deficits, to regions of rapid growth, which are likely to be those with current-account surpluses. Balance-of-payments problems would be magnified within the union. Furthermore, capital movements between regions would not necessarily tend to equalize social rates of return, even when they tended to equalize private rates of return. Social and

[31] See Vaubel, "Real Exchange Rate Changes," Basevi et al., *The Optica Report '75*, and N. Thygesen, "Inflation and Exchange Rates: Evidence and Policy Guidelines for the European Community," *Journal of International Economics*, 8 (May 1978), pp. 301–17.
[32] For a recent restatement of these issues, see P. De Grauwe, "Conditions for Monetary Integration–A Geometric Interpretation," *Weltwirtschaftliches Archiv*, 111, 1975(4), pp. 634–46, where it is argued that the viability of a monetary union would be threatened not only by differences in inflation rates but also by differences in rates of growth of productivity, as these would make for differences in rates of growth of real wages. The resulting differences in rates of growth of real incomes would have to be offset by continuing transfers from high-growth to low-growth regions.

private returns can differ systematically for the reasons already mentioned, that capital movements, like labor movements, can create new needs for social services, and because of other externalities.[33]

Fiscal integration

Turning to the literature on fiscal integration, it is useful to distinguish between work done on the microeconomic aspects of taxation, transfers, and public expenditures and work on the macroeconomic aspects. Much has been written on the microeconomic aspects, and some progress has been made in Europe, impelled by the concern to remove distortions and fiscal barriers to trade and factor movements.[34] The shift from sales to value-added taxes and the related standardization of border-tax adjustments are well-known examples. Much less has been written and far less done on the harmonization or unification of fiscal systems in the large, for purposes of redistribution and the joint pursuit of stabilization targets.

Fiscal unification of this larger variety involves a substantial transfer of authority over decisions affecting the levels and types of public expenditure. By inference, it involves transfers of sovereignty in matters that are guarded jealously by governments, including matters affecting defense and foreign policy. Corden has reminded us, moreover, that transfers of authority over expenditures call also for transfers of revenue-raising authority.[35] A union-wide agency having the power to spend requires in addition the power to tax. It need not be authorized to tax individuals and firms. It could tax its member governments instead. But if it is to use tax policy for macroeconomic purposes, it must be able to require that changes in the taxes it levies on governments are passed on as changes in national taxes on individuals and firms. More important, it must have the power to borrow. To conduct an effective stabilization policy, it must be free to run budget deficits and surpluses.[36]

These considerations help to explain why there has been much less said and done about large forms of fiscal integration, compared with compara-

---

[33] See, e.g., A. Cairncross et al., *Economic Policy for the European Community*, Macmillan, London, 1974, and B. Balassa, "Structural Policies for the European Common Market," in Balassa, ed., *European Economic Integration*, pp. 225–74.

[34] See, e.g., Balassa, "Structural Policies," and the references there; also C. S. Shoup, ed., *Fiscal Harmonization in Common Markets*, Columbia University Press, New York, 1967, vols. I and II.

[35] Corden, *Economic Integration*.

[36] This is emphasized in Cairncross et al., *Economic Policy for the European Community*.

ble steps toward monetary integration. But there are other reasons too. There is the belief, for example, that market integration does not create as strong a need for fiscal integration as for monetary integration. Once countries fix their exchange rates, money supplies become interdependent, and so do monetary policies, drawing attention to the benefits and costs of monetary union. Structural integration is not without importance for fiscal policies, as we show in later chapters, but the degree of policy interdependence is not as conspicuous.[37] In addition, there would appear to be widespread agreement that significant fiscal unification can take place only after monetary unification, because it would be hard to manage a single, multinational budget covering a number of currency areas.[38] Finally, there is less agreement on the degree of fiscal integration that has to accompany monetary integration, even in the long run, together with the view that governments will want to retain fiscal autonomy to compensate for sacrificing monetary autonomy.[39]

[37] Nevertheless, a recent EC study on public finance in European integration indicates increasing interest in the possibilities for fiscal integration; see European Communities, *Report of the Study Group on the Role of Public Finance in European Integration,* Brussels, 1977. Furthermore, the "new Cambridge view" would appear to argue for the primacy of fiscal integration. That view stresses the direct link between budget deficits and current-account deficits, on the implicit assumption that the private sector spends whatever it earns. Accordingly, it argues that fiscal policies should be geared to balance-of-payments targets and exchange-rate policies geared to domestic employment targets. See J. Spraos, "New Cambridge Macroeconomics, Assignment Rules and Interdependence," in R. Z. Aliber, ed., *The Political Economy of Monetary Reform,* Allanheld, Osman, and Co., Montclair, N.J., 1977, pp. 97–105. We find it difficult, however, to accept the underlying assumption about private behavior.

[38] This point was made in Kenen, "The Theory of Optimum Currency Areas," and has been widely accepted. See, however, Corden, *Monetary Integration,* where it is suggested that exchange-rate changes can be made within a single fiscal area. More recently, analyses of European integration have suggested that there may be need for fiscal unification *before* monetary unification, but the emphasis has been on regional transfers, not on demand-management aspects of fiscal policy. See Cairncross et al., *Economic Policy for the European Community,* Lamfalussy, "Monetary and Fiscal Integration," and R. S. Masera, "A 'Stylized' Model of a Highly Open Economy Under a System of Fixed Exchange Rates and Its Implications for the Establishment of Currency Areas," *Oxford Bulletin of Economics and Statistics,* 37 (August 1975), pp. 211–26.

[39] Thus, the Werner plan, which proposed monetary union in the EC by 1981, envisaged "a Community budget whose economic significance will be weak compared with that of the national budgets, the harmonized management of which will be an essential feature of cohesion in the union" (European Communities, *Economic and Monetary Union,* p. 11). Some said, moreover, that the Werner plan went too far even in its limited emphasis on budgetary harmonization. See H. G. Johnson, "Problems of European Monetary Union," *Journal of World Trade Law,* 5 (July/August 1971), pp. 377–87, and F. A. Lutz, "Foreign Exchange Rate Policy and European Economic Integration," in F. Machlup et al., *International Monetary Problems,* American Enterprise Institute, Washington, D.C., 1972, pp. 107–23. In the discussion following Lutz's paper, Robert Triffin agreed, but Eric Lundberg and Tibor Scitovsky stressed the importance of budgetary harmonization.

As the aims and instruments of fiscal policies are more numerous than those of monetary policies, so are the varieties of fiscal integration. The arguments for some varieties stem from the intrinsic consequences of structural or market integration. They have little to do with the macroeconomic issues raised in debates about monetary integration. The arguments for other varieties, however, stem from the commonality of monetary and fiscal targets and from the ways in which the two types of policies impinge on each other. We begin with arguments for fiscal integration that have the least to do with monetary integration, then consider those that are more closely related.

First, the market-distorting effects of differences in national fiscal policies, especially tax rates and subsidies, become more serious the greater the degree of market integration. Fiscal neutrality among integrated economies is important for efficient resource allocation and for the functioning of integrated capital markets. Concern about the influence of these distortions was, we said, one reason for European efforts to standardize systems of indirect taxation.

Second, the fiscal function of redistributing income, by way of taxation, transfers, and the provision of public goods, is seen to require some degree of fiscal unification across regions among which there is significant factor mobility. Otherwise, differences in fiscal systems will induce migrations of labor and capital to maximize net benefits.[40]

Third, the gains from market integration may be distributed unevenly, as was noted before, and some regions may suffer absolute losses of income and wealth. These disparities, moreover, may not occur uniformly among countries; some may have more than their share of afflicted regions. Therefore, unified regional policies may be needed to transfer income from countries that are net beneficiaries to those that are net losers, owing to the distribution of regional effects between and within the countries involved.

Finally, close integration of goods markets reduces the national income multiplier. Stabilization policies have weaker effects on the domestic economy and larger spillover effects on neighboring economies. It is more difficult for any single government to execute an effective stabilization policy.[41] Concomitantly, cyclical disturbances are transmitted strongly

[40] This point is emphasized in R. A. Musgrave and P. A. Musgrave, *Public Finance in Theory and Practice*, McGraw-Hill, New York, 1973, p. 606.

[41] On these issues, see Balassa and Resnick, "Monetary Integration and the Consistency of Policy Objectives," and R. I. McKinnon and W. E. Oates, *The Implications of International Economic Integration for Monetary, Fiscal, and Exchange-Rate Policy*, Studies in International Finance 16, Princeton University, Princeton, N.J., 1966.

and rapidly across integrated areas, calling for synchronized stabilization policies.[42] In brief, market integration results in a redistribution of authority in fiscal matters. The real issue has been put concisely by Magnifico. Should policy-making powers be allowed to migrate de facto into the hands of one or two dominant countries, or should they be shared more evenly by the deliberate integration of fiscal targets and instruments?[43]

When asset markets are closely integrated across countries, the financing of budget deficits involves more foreign borrowing, directly or indirectly, than when markets are more isolated. The ability to borrow easily abroad has certain advantages. It can strengthen stabilization policy by holding down domestic interest rates and thus diminish the likelihood that a budget deficit will "crowd out" private spending.[44] Furthermore, it can reduce total debt-service costs. Extensive external financing, however, has its disadvantages. Firstly, the burden of financing government expenditures varies with the source of that financing. Taxation puts a burden on the current generation to the extent that it reduces current consumption. Internal borrowing can do so too.[45] But external borrowing shifts the burden to the next generation, which is the one required to repay the debt. Furthermore, when borrowing is employed to avoid the need for reducing consumption, the burden placed on the next generation may exceed the benefit conferred on the current generation. Finally, continuous external borrowing, especially if used to finance consumption, can reduce a country's ability to borrow in the future, by raising its external liabilities. For this reason, Oates and Engerman have each suggested that the expected level of deficit financing by local governments, forced as they are to borrow externally, will probably be smaller than optimal.[46] And that possibility is made stronger when one's neighbors' fiscal policies have large spillover effects; a government may be tempted to ride free on its neighbors' policies so as to avoid the costs of issuing its own debt.

[42] W. E. Oates, "Fiscal Federalism in Theory and Practice: Applications to the European Community," in European Communities, Report of the Study Group on the Role of Public Finance, vol. II, pp. 279–320.
[43] Magnifico, European Monetary Unification, p. 19.
[44] See Chapters 5 and 6, where we showed that when crowding out does not dominate, asset-market integration raises the effectiveness of fiscal policy under a pegged exchange rate.
[45] See, e.g., Musgrave and Musgrave, Public Finance, pp. 585–91.
[46] W. E. Oates, Fiscal Federalism, Harcourt Brace Jovanovich, New York, 1972, pp. 28–9, and S. Engerman, "Regional Aspects of Stabilization Policy," in R. A. Musgrave, ed., Essays in Fiscal Federalism, The Brookings Institution, Washington, D.C., 1965, pp. 53–6.

The analysis of fiscal integration cannot be completely separated from the analysis of monetary integration.[47] The entire theory of fiscal federalism, which seeks to identify the levels at which various fiscal functions should be performed, assumes that there is a single central government and a unified currency area. Oates warns us to distinguish that familiar framework from the one confronted internationally, with several separate national governments and national currencies, even when the markets of the countries under study are closely integrated.[48]

It can be argued, moreover, that fiscal and monetary unification must go hand in hand, because an effective stabilization policy calls for the coordinated use of monetary and fiscal instruments, coinciding in domain and managed at the same level of government.[49] Turning the same point around, the integration of one policy instrument may be required to protect the integration of another. Reserve pooling in a monetary union may be unacceptable to governments if fiscal policies are not unified. When governments are free to carry out independent fiscal policies, they can generate balance-of-payments problems for the monetary union, draining the pool of reserves.[50] There is also the relationship, mentioned earlier, between structural integration and policy integration. National policies are less effective in economies with closely integrated markets, and the integration of one policy instrument may have the effect of intensifying market integration, making other instruments less effective when used independently. Ingram points out, for example, that the existence of a single national market for federal government securities has intensified significantly the integration of all securities markets in the United States, with important implications for the uses of many policy instruments at various levels of government.[51]

Relevant in this regard is the evidence concerning the relationship between interregional balance-of-payments behavior and fiscal policies in

---

[47] For a longer discussion of relationships between the two, including a more thorough treatment of issues mentioned in previous paragraphs, see Allen, *Organization and Administration of a Monetary Union,* pp. 56–72.

[48] Oates, "Fiscal Federalism in Theory and Practice."

[49] This point was stressed in Meade, "The Balance of Payments Problem of a Free Trade Area," and in T. Scitovsky, *Economic Theory and Western European Integration,* Stanford University Press, Stanford, Calif., 1958. For a recent restatement of the case, see European Communities, *Report of the Study Group on the Role of Public Finance.*

[50] For another view, see Johnson, "Problems of European Monetary Union," where it is argued that national fiscal policies cannot get out of control when governments lack automatic access to central-bank credit–access they would not enjoy in a full-fledged monetary union.

[51] Ingram, *The Case for European Monetary Integration.*

countries where both fiscal and monetary policies are integrated. Have flows of public funds, reflecting fiscal policies, financed or exacerbated payments imbalances between the regions of those countries? Hartland found that flows of public funds were accommodating, in that they financed interregional imbalances in the United States during the 1920s and 1930s.[52] Whitman has raised doubts, suggesting that flows of public funds were perhaps perverse at times and that private short-term flows financed the imbalances.[53] But recent work on the EC has revived the suggestion that interregional flows of public funds have been accommodating. They have not been directed intentionally to deficit regions, but they have been dispersed on the basis of criteria, such as income levels, that favor deficit regions.[54]

Integrated regional policies are needed when market integration or exchange-rate unification threatens to amplify regional disparities. No one would appear to dissent from this assertion. Yet a larger variety of regional policies may be needed. Existing policies emphasize transfers to low-income individuals or communities. But transfers of this type are ameliorative rather than corrective. They do not usually eliminate basic disparities in levels of earnings. They must be accompanied by regional policies to stimulate structural change—by investment incentives, employment incentives, and spending on infrastructure. These programs, moreover, have to be unified, partly because regions cross national boundaries, but also because national policies tend to have "beggar-thy-neighbor" effects. Balassa has stressed these issues, and Magnifico has stressed the additional need for stabilization policies aimed at the ills of particular regions.[55] Clearly, this last task must be done by fiscal policy, not monetary policy, especially when asset markets are closely integrated.

In our own analysis of fiscal integration, we focus on the stabilization and distribution of income at national rather than regional levels. We do so on the basis of the two-country model presented in Part IV, which lends itself to this particular objective. We examine the effects of market integration on the conduct of national and unified policies aimed at demand management, including the problems of financing budget deficits in integrated asset markets, and at the additional problems that arise when there is a full-fledged monetary union. We also look at the costs and ben-

---

[52] P. C. Hartland, "Interregional Payments Compared with International Payments," *Quarterly Journal of Economics*, 63 (August 1949), pp. 393–407.

[53] Whitman, *International and Interregional Payments Adjustment*.

[54] European Communities, *Report of the Study Group on the Role of Public Finance*.

[55] Balassa, "Structural Policies," and Magnifico, *European Monetary Unification*.

efits of integrating fiscal policies, including tax policies and government borrowing.

What lies ahead

In Chapter 15 we investigate the implications of market integration for the short-run independence of monetary policies, dealing with two countries that peg their exchange rates, bilaterally and vis-à-vis the outside world. We ask how independence is restricted by market integration and look at the manifestations of policy interdependence. In Chapter 16 we go on to ask if market integration makes it advantageous for countries to unify their monetary policies–to set common targets and to transfer control of the monetary instruments to a single central bank. We examine in addition the costs and benefits of pegging the common external exchange rate and of allowing it to float.

In Chapter 17 we return temporarily to the case in which countries pursue independent monetary policies and ask how market integration affects fiscal policies. We deal only with the case of pegged exchange rates, but we look at the problem of internal policy coordination–the analogue of the assignment problem studied by Mundell and others.[56] Thereafter, in Chapter 18, we study the uses of fiscal policies in a monetary union, looking at both pegged and flexible external rates. We ask how monetary unification affects the degree to which members of the union are able to pursue independent fiscal policies, how fiscal policies impinge on the operations of the monetary union, and how much fiscal integration is required of countries that have formed a monetary union.

We are not able to deal directly with one of the interesting issues raised from time to time in the course of this chapter. Policy unification can have effects on the degree of market integration, by influencing tastes and judgments about risks, but processes like these have no place in our model. We have to get at them indirectly by asking how policies are affected by degrees and types of market integration. In other words, we can draw conditional conclusions about the implications of policy integration; we can say how policies would be affected if policy integration were in fact to foster market integration.

Another limitation needs to be noted. We are not able to discuss the problems posed by the transition to market or policy integration, although these may be paramount, economically and politically, for the outcome of

[56] See, e.g., R. A. Mundell, *International Economics,* Macmillan, New York, 1968, chap. 16.

the process. Our model is not fashioned to deal with these problems. Its dynamics are not specified in adequate detail, and we have not endogenized the processes by which private and public behavior might change. For these same reasons, among others, we make no attempt to forecast the timing of countries' responses to structural changes or to new opportunities for policy unification.[57]

[57] See K. Hamada, "On the Political Economy of Monetary Integration: A Public Economics Approach," in Aliber, ed., *The Political Economy of Monetary Reform*, pp. 13–31. Hamada suggests that the time paths of the costs and benefits of monetary integration may differ sufficiently to make monetary integration difficult, even if it is seen to be worthwhile in the long run, unless it is accompanied by political integration.

15

Market integration, interdependence, and monetary policy under pegged exchange rates

In Part II we looked at the effects of monetary policy in a single small economy facing the outside world, tracing the responses to open-market operations in the domestic bond. We showed why pegged and flexible exchange rates affect those responses and why asset-market integration is important for the functioning of monetary policy. We now need to examine the effects of monetary policy in interdependent economies, using the model developed in Part IV. We begin with the case in which the two countries maintain pegged exchange rates, bilaterally and vis-à-vis the outside world.[1] We are particularly interested in showing how market integration affects the degree of monetary interdependence and thus the ability of one country to conduct an autonomous monetary policy in the short run.

Impact effects of open-market operations

When working with two countries, we must deal with four types of open-market purchases. Each central bank can buy the domestic bond ($\delta \bar{B}_1^c > 0$ in the North and $\delta \bar{B}_2^{c\prime} > 0$ in the South); each bank can also buy the other country's bond ($\delta \bar{B}_2^c > 0$ in the North and $\delta \bar{B}_1^{c\prime} > 0$ in the South). We must study the effects of these transactions, moreover, on aggregates or averages for the two economies (Y^t, $\bar{\pi}R^t$, W^{ht}, and r^t) and on each economy separately. The aggregates assume particular importance in Chapter 16, where we analyze the workings of a monetary union. Even at this stage, however, they furnish a convenient point of departure. Our

---

[1] Girton and Henderson have studied the effects of open-market operations on countries with pegged rates. But theirs is a partial-equilibrium analysis, in that it does not deal with effects on goods markets and is limited to the short run. See L. Girton and D. Henderson, "Central Bank Operations in Foreign and Domestic Assets Under Fixed and Flexible Exchange Rates," in P. Clark et al., eds., *The Effects of Exchange Rate Adjustments*, U.S. Treasury, Washington, D.C., 1974, pp. 151–78, and "Financial Capital Movements and Central Bank Behavior in a Two-Country, Short-Run Portfolio Balance," *Journal of Monetary Economics*, 2 (January 1976), pp. 33–61.

findings for the aggregates can be compared directly with our findings for the single small economy.

In Table 13.1B we showed the signs of the short-run responses to each of the four open-market purchases listed above. The results are unambiguous. Prices, incomes, and disposable incomes rise in every instance, and interest rates and aggregate reserves fall. A country's own reserves, however, fall only with a purchase by its own central bank ($\bar{\pi}\ \delta R < 0$ when $\delta\bar{B}_1^c > 0$ or $\delta\bar{B}_2^c > 0$) and rise with a purchase by the other central bank ($\bar{\pi}\ \delta R > 0$ when $\delta\bar{B}_1^{c\prime} > 0$ or $\delta\bar{B}_2^{c\prime} > 0$). Clearly, the effects of open-market purchases are transmitted from country to country, but we need to know much more about the sizes of the spillovers and the reasons for them.

Effects in asset markets

The direct effects of open-market purchases take place in asset markets, and they are independent of the indirect effects induced in the goods markets. Therefore, the responses of asset-market variables can be described by a diagram similar to one used extensively in Part II.

Figure 15.1A depicts combinations of the average interest rate, r^t, and of aggregate wealth, W^{ht}, at which there is no excess demand or supply in the *sum* of the Northern and Southern bond markets, no excess demand or supply in the *sum* of their money markets, and no net saving in the North and South taken together. Points on W^tW^t are those at which the sum of bond markets clears (but do not guarantee that each bond market will clear by itself). Similarly, points on M^tM^t are those at which the sum of money markets clears (but do not guarantee that each money market will clear by itself). And points on S^tS^t are those at which there is no net saving (although there can be saving in one country offset by dissaving in the other). The equations for these curves and for others used below are listed in the tables at the end of this chapter.

The explanations for the slopes of these curves are the same as those we gave for their single-country counterparts in Figure 4.4A, and so are their responses to open-market operations. Any open-market purchase, of either bond by either bank, raises the aggregate demand for bonds, and the average interest rate must fall to eliminate excess demand. The bond-market curve shifts down to $W^{t\prime}W^{t\prime}$. Furthermore, an open-market purchase adds to the aggregate supply of money, and the average interest rate must fall to eliminate excess supply. The money-market curve shifts down to $M^{t\prime}M^{t\prime}$. Under pegged exchange rates, moreover, wealth cannot change immediately, so that asset-market equilibrium must be displaced

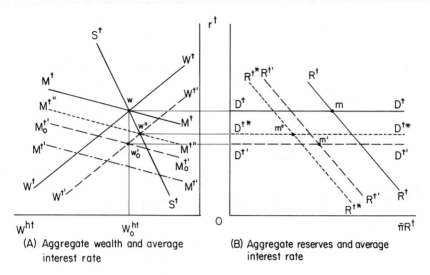

(A) Aggregate wealth and average
interest rate

(B) Aggregate reserves and average
interest rate

Figure 15.1 Open-market purchase of the Northern or Southern bond by either central bank: impact and steady-state effects on aggregate asset markets under pegged exchange rates.

from w to w'_0, where the sum of bond markets is cleared at the initial level of aggregate wealth, W_0^{ht}. By implication, the sum of money markets must be cleared by an instantaneous reduction of reserves ($\bar{\pi}\ \delta R^t < 0$), and the money-market curve shifts back to $M_0^{t\prime}M_0^{t\prime}$.

Figure 15.1B depicts explicitly the movement of reserves implied by the short-run solution in Figure 15.1A. Curve $D^t D^t$ shows the combinations of r^t and $\bar{\pi}R^t$ that clear the two bond markets jointly; curve $R^t R^t$ shows the combinations that clear the two money markets jointly. The downward shift of the bond-market curve to $D^{t\prime}D^{t\prime}$ denotes the reduction in r^t required to clear the bond markets. The leftward shift of the money-market curve to $R^{t\prime}R^{t\prime}$ measures the open-market purchase (the increase in the sum of money stocks). Measured vertically, however, the downward shift of the money-market curve is larger than the downward shift of the bond-market curve, so that their intersection at m' lies to the left of m, and aggregate reserves must fall.

Two points should be emphasized here. First, the aggregate or average responses of the North and South are the same qualitatively as those of the single small economy studied in Chapter 5. Second, it makes no difference for these aggregate responses which of the two bonds is purchased or by which central bank. The solutions shown in Figure 15.1 apply to all open-market purchases of Northern and Southern bonds.

Wealth cannot change on impact when exchange rates are pegged, and

(B) Northern interest rate and reserves   (A) Northern and Southern interest rate

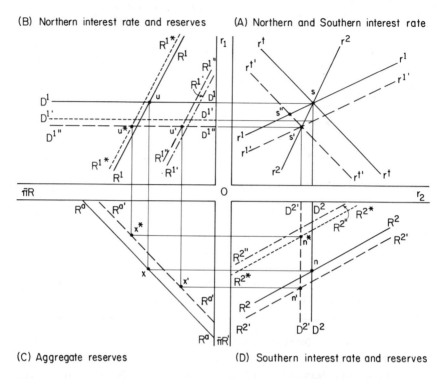

(C) Aggregate reserves   (D) Southern interest rate and reserves

Figure 15.2 Open-market purchase of the Northern bond by the Northern and Southern central banks: impact effects on national asset markets under pegged exchange rates.

this is true for the individual countries as well as for the two together. Yet r^t and $\bar{\pi}R^t$ fall on impact, and we must therefore ask what these reductions mean for each of the two countries' interest rates and holdings of reserves. Figure 15.2 is constructed for this purpose.

Beginning with Figure 15.2A, curve $r^t r^t$ traces combinations of national interest rates, r_1 and r_2, that are consistent with a given average interest rate, r^t, whereas curves $r^1 r^1$ and $r^2 r^2$ show the combinations of r_1 and r_2 that clear the Northern and Southern bond markets, respectively. Each of these bond-market curves is positively sloped, but $r^1 r^1$ is flatter than $r^2 r^2$. An increase in the Southern interest rate diminishes the demand for the Northern bond, requiring an increase in the Northern rate to eliminate excess supply. The demand for the Northern bond, however, is assumed to respond more strongly to a change in r_1 than to a change in r_2, so that the slope of $r^1 r^1$ is smaller than unity. For matching reasons, the slope of $r^2 r^2$ is positive and larger than unity. With asset-market symmetry, as defined in Chapter 12, r^1r^1 and r^2r^2 must in fact be symmetrical around a 45° line.

An open-market purchase of either bond shifts $r^t r^t$ downward to $r^{t'} r^{t'}$, reflecting the move from w to w'_0 in Figure 15.1A. The choice of the bond to be purchased, however, determines the point on $r^{t'} r^{t'}$ to which the economies move. With an open-market purchase of the Northern bond by either central bank, r^1r^1 shifts down, r^2r^2 remains in place, and asset-market equilibrium is established at s', where the new Northern curve intersects $r^{t'} r^{t'}$ at its intersection with r^2r^2. Both interest rates fall, but the Northern rate falls farther. (Had the Southern bond been purchased instead of the Northern bond, r^2r^2 would have shifted, asset-market equilibrium would have been established at s'', and the Southern rate would have fallen farther than the Northern rate.)

In Figure 15.2C, schedule $R^a R^a$ measures the level of aggregate reserves as the sum of Northern reserves (on the horizontal axis) and Southern reserves (on the vertical axis). The immediate reduction of aggregate reserves resulting from any open-market purchase is shown by the inward shift from $R^a R^a$ to $R^{a'} R^{a'}$. The new distribution of reserves, however, cannot be determined without knowing the bond that is purchased and the central bank that makes the purchase. Figures 15.2B and 15.2D depict the changes in Northern and Southern reserves, respectively, resulting from an open-market purchase of the Northern bond. We use them first to study the effects of a purchase by the Northern central bank ($\delta \bar{B}_1^c > 0$).

In Figure 15.2B, curve $D^1 D^1$ shows the combinations of the Northern interest rate and Northern reserves that clear the Northern bond market, and curve $R^1 R^1$ shows those combinations that clear the Northern money market. The relationships depicted by these curves are analogous to the relationships depicted by the aggregate curves in Figure 15.1B. An open-market purchase of the Northern bond by either central bank shifts the Northern bond-market curve to $D^{1'} D^{1'}$. The size of the shift measures the reduction in r_1 that would clear the market for the Northern bond if r_2 remained unchanged. But r_2 also falls, as was shown at s' in Figure 15.2A, and this necessitates a further fall in r_1, causing the bond-market curve to shift all the way to $D^{1''} D^{1''}$. The responses of the money-market curves differ with the central bank that buys the Northern bond. A purchase by the Northern bank raises the Northern money supply, and the Northern interest rate must fall to clear the Northern money market. This effect is shown in Figure 15.2B by the shift of the Northern money-market curve from $R^1 R^1$ to $R^{1'} R^{1'}$. But the demand for money in the North is raised by the reduction of the Southern interest rate, reversing in part the shift in the curve. This effect is shown by the shift from $R^{1\prime}R^{1\prime}$ to $R^{1\prime\prime}R^{1\prime\prime}$, and it is necessarily larger than the sum of the downward shifts of the Northern bond-market curve, from D^1D^1 to $D^{1\prime\prime}D^{1\prime\prime}$. Accordingly, the movement from u to u' involves a reduction in Northern reserves.

Events in Southern asset markets are pictured in Figure 15.2D. Curve D^2D^2 shows the combinations of the Southern interest rate and Southern reserves that clear the Southern bond market, and curve R^2R^2 shows those that clear the Southern money market. An open-market purchase of the Northern bond by the Northern central bank does not affect Southern markets directly, but they are affected indirectly by the fall in the Northern interest rate. It raises the demand for the Southern bond, requiring a fall in the Southern interest rate. The Southern bond-market curve shifts to the left, from D^2D^2 to $D^{2\prime}D^{2\prime}$, by a distance consistent with the movement from s to s' in Figure 15.2A. The fall in the Northern interest rate also raises the Southern demand for money, shifting the Southern money-market curve to the right, from R^2R^2 to $R^{2\prime}R^{2\prime}$. Asset-market equilibrium is displaced from n to n', and there is an increase in Southern reserves. The increase in the Southern demand for money, caused by the reductions in r_1 and r_2, is satisfied by transferring money (reserves) from North to South.

The loss of reserves by the North, described by the move from u to u' in Figure 15.2B, exceeds the gain of reserves by the South, described by the move from n to n' in Figure 15.2D. The difference between the loss and the gain measures the aggregate loss of reserves to the outside world, shown by the move from x to x' in Figure 15.2C.

If the Northern bond is purchased by the Southern central bank ($\delta \bar{B}_1^{c\prime} > 0$), the change in aggregate reserves is the same, but the redistribution is reversed. The responses of the bond-market curves, D^1D^1 and D^2D^2, are not altered, but the shifts in the money-market curves are quite different. When the Southern central bank makes the open-market purchase, it is the Southern money supply that rises. In Figure 15.2D, the Southern money-market curve shifts from R^2R^2 to $R^{2\prime\prime}R^{2\prime\prime}$, then back to $R^{2*}R^{2*}$, because of the fall in the Northern interest rate. The leftward shift of the money-market curve, moreover, is larger than the shift of the bond-market curve, displacing equilibrium from n to n^*. The South loses reserves. In Figure 15.2B, the Northern money-market curve shifts from R^1R^1 to $R^{1*}R^{1*}$, because of the fall in the Southern interest rate, and equilibrium is established at u^*. The increase in the Northern demand for money is satisfied by transferring money (reserves) from South to North.

But the fall in Southern reserves exceeds the gain in Northern reserves, and there is again a loss to the outside world, shown by the move from x to x^* in Figure 15.2C.

Let us summarize the short-run asset-market effects of an open-market purchase:

1. A purchase of either bond by either central bank depresses the average interest rate and causes a loss of reserves to the outside world.

2. The interest rate on the bond that is purchased falls farther than the interest rate on the other bond.

3. The country whose central bank makes the purchase loses reserves to the outside world and to the other country, and the loss to the other country will be larger when that country's bond is purchased instead of the domestic bond. With asset-market symmetry, however, the choice of the bond does not affect the size of the aggregate loss to the outside world.

Effects in goods markets with goods-market symmetry

To study the effects of open-market purchases on aggregate and national incomes, we turn now to the markets for the two countries' goods. Heretofore, we have imposed only two types of restrictions on those markets, pertaining to the marginal propensities to spend and the saving functions. Households have identical marginal propensities to spend on their respective domestic goods and on imported goods ($m_1 = m_2'$, $m_2 = m_1'$, and $m_0 = m_0'$), and consumption in each country is biased in favor of the domestic good ($m_1 > m_2$). The saving functions have identical income and wealth effects ($S_Y = S_Y'$ and $S_W = S_W'$) and symmetrical interest-rate effects ($S_1 = S_2'$ and $S_2 = S_1'$). We have not imposed restrictions on price elasticities of demand or supply, because we were concerned to show how differences in price elasticities can affect the sizes and sometimes the signs of price and income changes.

At this particular point, however, it is convenient to simplify the exposition by adopting temporarily assumptions that give us what we have described as full-scale goods-market symmetry.[2] Under those assumptions, we can construct a simple relationship between the *sum* of gross domestic products and the common external exchange rate – a relationship comparable to the one depicted in Figure 4.2 for the single-country case. In Figure 15.3A, curve Z^tZ^t shows the steady-state relationship between

[2] See p. 327.

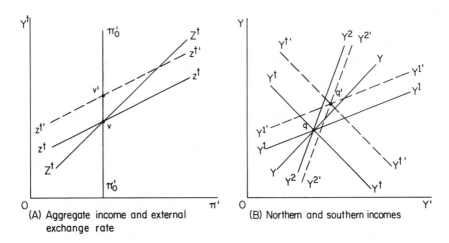

(A) Aggregate income and external
    exchange rate

(B) Northern and southern incomes

Figure 15.3 Open-market purchase of the Northern bond by either central bank: impact effects on aggregate and national goods markets under pegged exchange rates.

aggregate income, Y^t, and the external exchange rate, π'. At any point on that curve, the sum of national goods markets is cleared, and no net saving takes place in the North and South together. (This does not guarantee that the goods markets clear individually and does not preclude saving in one country offset by dissaving in the other.) Curve $z^t z^t$ shows the short-run relationship between Y^t and π'. At each point on that curve, the sum of the goods markets clears, but there can be net saving or dissaving. As in the single-country case, $Z^t Z^t$ is steeper than $z^t z^t$, because there is no leakage into saving in the steady state.

As an open-market purchase reduces r_1 and r_2, it fosters dissaving in each country and thus stimulates aggregate absorption. Curve $z^t z^t$ shifts upward to $z^{t'} z^{t'}$. Because the external exchange rate is pegged, the economies move directly from v to v', a move comparable to the one in Figure 5.2 for the single-country case. Open-market purchases do not affect goods markets in any other way, and the position of $Z^t Z^t$ is not altered. Under full-scale goods-market symmetry, moreover, the increase in aggregate income is the same for any open-market purchase.

The change in each country's income is shown in Figure 15.3B. There, curve $Y^1 Y^1$ shows the combinations of Y and Y' that clear the market for the Northern good, and $Y^2 Y^2$ shows those combinations that clear the market for the Southern good. Changes in Northern and Southern incomes are due directly to changes in Northern and Southern prices, p_1

and p_2', because each country's nominal income depends uniquely on the price of that country's product.

Any increase in Southern income (and the price of the Southern good) raises the Southern demand for the Northern good, by way of income and substitution effects, requiring an increase in Northern income (and the price of the Northern good) to clear the Northern goods market. The demand for the Northern good, however, responds more strongly to a change in Northern income than to a change in Southern income. Accordingly, the slope of Y^1Y^1 is positive but smaller than unity. For matching reasons, the slope of Y^2Y^2 is positive but larger than unity. With full-scale goods-market symmetry, moreover, the two curves are symmetrical around the 45° line YY. Finally, Y^tY^t shows the combinations of national incomes that add up to a constant aggregate income.

The increase of aggregate income shown in Figure 15.3A is recorded in Figure 15.3B by the shift from Y^tY^t to $Y^{t\prime}Y^{t\prime}$ and by shifts in Y^1Y^1 and Y^2Y^2 that cause them to intersect at a point on $Y^{t\prime}Y^{t\prime}$. Because an open-market purchase raises demands for both goods, Y^1Y^1 must shift upward and Y^2Y^2 rightward. The sizes of these shifts and, therefore, the change in relative incomes depend on the bond involved in the open-market purchase. If it is the Northern bond, the Northern interest rate falls farther than the Southern rate, as shown in Figure 15.2A, raising Northern consumption by more than Southern consumption. Northern consumption, moreover, is biased toward the Northern good ($m_1 > m_2$), so that the demand for the Northern good rises by more than the demand for the Southern good. In Figure 15.3B, an open-market purchase of the Northern bond causes Y^1Y^1 to shift upward by more than Y^2Y^2 shifts rightward. Goods-market equilibrium is displaced from q to q', and the increase in Northern income exceeds the increase in Southern income. (Had the Southern bond been purchased instead, Y^2Y^2 would have shifted by more than Y^1Y^1, and goods-market equilibrium would have been displaced to a point on $Y^{t\prime}Y^{t\prime}$ as far to the southeast of YY as q' is to the northwest.)

To sum up, the sizes of the changes in the two countries' incomes resulting from an open-market purchase depend on the bond involved but not on the bank. If central banks confine their operations to their own bond markets, each is bound to influence its own country's income by more than its neighbor's income. If they operate instead in the other country's market, the spillover effects will dominate, reversing the result. This conclusion must be qualified, however, when asset or goods markets are perfectly integrated and when we forego goods-market symmetry.

Steady-state effects of open-market operations

We have had several occasions to show that open-market operations cannot have permanent effects on goods-market outcomes when exchange rates are pegged. In Figure 15.3A, the steady-state curve Z^tZ^t does not shift, and the two-country economy must return to v, bringing aggregate income back to its initial level. Each country's income, moreover, must also return to its initial level. The shifts in Y^1Y^1 and Y^2Y^2 shown in Figure 15.3B were due solely to changes in saving (absorption), and they are reversed with the passage of time. As each economy moves to its steady state, the movement of its income curve must be proportional to the size of the shift that took place on impact. In consequence, Y^1Y^1 and Y^2Y^2 can come to intersect Y^tY^t only at q, where Northern and Southern incomes are what they were initially.[3]

Looking next at long-run outcomes in the asset markets and returning to Figure 15.1A, we invoke a familiar result. If aggregate income returns to its initial level, there can be no shift in S^tS^t. Long-run equilibrium must be established at w'', the intersection of $W^{t'}W^{t'}$ with S^tS^t, and the money-market curve must move upward to $M^{t'''}M^{t'''}$ so as to join this intersection. By implication, reserves decline through time, and aggregate wealth is reduced by dissaving. In Figure 15.1B, the reduction in wealth causes the bond-market curve to shift upward from $D^{t'}D^{t'}$ to $D^{t*}D^{t*}$ and the money-market curve to shift leftward from $R^{t'}R^{t'}$ to $R^{t*}R^{t*}$. Asset-market equilibrium is established at m''. In the new steady state, the average interest rate, aggregate wealth, and aggregate reserves are lower than they were originally, and the sizes of the changes are the same for all open-market purchases.

The long-run changes in individual interest rates, by contrast, depend on the bond bought. In Figure 15.4 we depict one set of possibilities for an open-market purchase of the Northern bond. The shifts of r^tr^t to $r^{t'}r^{t'}$ and of r^1r^1 to $r^{1'}r^{1'}$ reproduce the impact effects shown in Figure 15.2A, moving asset-market equilibrium from s to s'. The passage thereafter to

[3] The North and South cannot achieve permanent changes in income by open-market operations because there are leakages to the outside world. One of us has analyzed open-market operations in a closed two-country model–with no outside world. See P. R. Allen, "A Portfolio Approach to International Capital Flows," *Journal of International Economics,* 3 (May 1973), pp. 135–60. In that particular model, open-market purchases had no permanent effects on incomes, but only because the model made no allowance for wealth effects on the demands for goods. In the model studied here, the outcome would be different. If the North and South were cut off from the outside world, open-market operations would produce permanent changes in aggregate income, even with a pegged bilateral exchange rate, just as in a single closed economy.

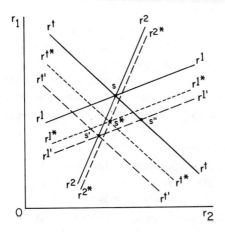

Figure 15.4 Open-market purchase of the Northern bond: impact and steady-state effects on national asset markets under pegged exchange rates.

the new steady state was shown in Figure 15.1 to involve a partial reversal of the short-run reduction in the average interest rate (the movement from w_0' to w'') and a decline in aggregate wealth. The same change in the average interest rate is described in Figure 15.4 by the shift from $r^{t'}r^{t'}$ to $r^{t*}r^{t*}$, and long-run equilibrium must lie on that new curve. As each country's wealth declines through time, so does its demand for bonds, shifting the bond-market curves. The Northern curve shifts upward from $r^{1'}r^{1'}$ to $r^{1*}r^{1*}$, and the Southern curve shifts rightward from r^2r^2 to $r^{2*}r^{2*}$. The two curves intersect at s^*, lying on $r^{t*}r^{t*}$, where each country's interest rate is lower than it was before the open-market purchase.

But this is only one of many possibilities. Long-run equilibrium must always lie on $r^{t*}r^{t*}$, somewhere between $r^{1'}r^{1'}$ and r^2r^2. Furthermore, the upward shift of the Northern curve must always be larger than the rightward shift of the Southern curve. Accordingly, the Northern interest rate is always lower in the new stationary state following a purchase of the Northern bond. But the Southern rate can be higher or lower than it was initially.[4]

---

[4] We can prove that an open-market purchase of the Northern bond produces permanent reductions in the Northern interest rate and Northern wealth. The permanent reductions in r^t and W^{ht} require that there be reductions in at least one interest rate and one country's wealth. We know, moreover, that there are no permanent income changes and that saving goes to zero in each country, so that Eqs. (11.13a) and (11.14a) can be used to write $dW^h = (S_1\,dr_1 + S_2\,dr_2)/(-S_W)$ and $dW^{h'} = (S_1'\,dr_1 + S_2'\,dr_2)/(-S_W')$. But $S_1' = S_2$, $S_2' = S_1$, and $S_W' = S_W$, so that $(dW^h - dW^{h'}) = [(S_1 - S_2)(dr_1 - dr_2)]/(-S_W)$. Therefore, W^h will fall by more than $W^{h'}$ when r_1 falls by more than r_2, because $S_1 > S_2$. Using this result,

Similar ambiguities arise in connection with the steady-state changes in reserves. Although aggregate reserves fall by the same amount with any open-market purchase, many redistributions can take place between North and South, and it is possible to make only one strong statement. When a country's central bank purchases the domestic bond, its reserves are bound to fall in the short run and the long run. There is little to be gained, then, by a graphical analysis of the long-run changes in national reserves.

As open-market operations have no permanent effects on incomes under pegged exchange rates, the remainder of this chapter is confined to the further analysis of impact effects. It deals first with the implications of market integration, then with the problems of policy interdependence. Finally, it relaxes the assumption of goods-market symmetry imposed above, so as to explore the consequences of goods-market differences for short-run responses to open-market operations.

Implications of market integration

In this two-country model, asset-market integration can refer to substitutability between the bonds of the two countries and those of the outside world or to substitutability between Northern and Southern bonds. The implications are quite different.

we can show that r_1 must fall farther than r_2. Differentiating Eqs. (11.76a) and (11.77a) for the case of an open-market purchase of the Northern bond,

$$B_{11}^t \, dr_1 + B_{12}^t \, dr_2 + B_{1W} \, dW^h + B_{2W} \, dW^{h\prime} + d\bar{B}_1^c + d\bar{B}_1^{c\prime} = 0$$
$$B_{12}^t \, dr_1 + B_{11}^t \, dr_2 + B_{2W} \, dW^h + B_{1W} \, dW^{h\prime} = 0$$

Subtracting the second equation from the first and rearranging terms, we obtain $(B_{11}^t - B_{12}^t)(dr_1 - dr_2) + (B_{1W} - B_{2W})(dW^h - dW^{h\prime}) = -(d\bar{B}_1^c + d\bar{B}_1^{c\prime}) < 0$. As the ordering of changes in interest rates must be the same as the ordering of changes in stocks of wealth, it follows directly that r_1 must fall by more than r_2 and W^h must fall by more than $W^{h\prime}$. Looking at Figure 15.4, the shift of the Northern bond-market curve from $r^{1\prime}r^{1\prime}$ to $r^{1*}r^{1*}$ is $dr_1|_{\bar{r}_2} = -(B_{1W} \, dW^h + B_{2W} \, dW^{h\prime})/B_{11}^t = -[(B_{1W} - B_{2W}) \, dW^h + B_{2W} \, dW^{ht}]/B_{11}^t$, which is an upward shift when, as here, $dW^h < dW^{ht} < 0$. The shift of the Southern curve from r^2r^2 to $r^{2*}r^{2*}$ is $dr_2|_{\bar{r}_1} = -(B_{1W} dW^{h\prime} + B_{2W} dW^h)/B_{11}^t = -[(B_{1W} - B_{2W}) \, dW^{h\prime} + B_{2W} \, dW^{h\prime}]/B_{11}^t$, which is unequivocally smaller than the shift in the Northern curve, because $dW^h < dW^{h\prime}$. (It might indeed appear that the Southern curve could shift to the left, not to the right as shown in Figure 15.4, because $dW^{h\prime}$ can be positive. But a leftward shift would yield a permanent decline in r_2, along with the decline in r_1, and we saw above that $W^{h\prime}$ cannot rise when both interest rates fall. Thus, the Southern bond-market curve must shift to the right, and the steady-state equilibrium point s^* must lie within the triangle $ss's''$.)

Integration with the external bond market

Substitutability between one or both of the two countries' bonds and those of the outside world diminishes the influence of monetary policy. It reduces the changes in interest rates and incomes, just as it did in the single-country case. The greater the degree of integration with the external bond market, the flatter the bond-market curve W^tW^t in Figure 15.1A, and the smaller the downward shift of the curve in response to an open-market purchase. (In Figure 15.1B, the downward shift of D^tD^t becomes smaller too.) In the extreme case of perfect substitutability $(-B_{01}^t \rightarrow \infty)$, W^tW^t becomes perfectly horizontal and does not respond at all to an open-market purchase. The slope of the money-market curve M^tM^t is not affected by the degree of integration with the external bond market, and the size of the initial shift, from M^tM^t to $M^{t\prime}M^{t\prime}$, is not affected either. But the shift from $M^{t\prime}M^{t\prime}$ to $M_0^{t\prime}M_0^{t\prime}$ becomes bigger, enlarging the loss of reserves. With perfect integration, indeed, the initial shift from M^tM^t to $M^{t\prime}M^{t\prime}$ is reversed completely, the loss of reserves is equal in size to the open-market purchase, and the average interest rate and aggregate wealth are not affected at all.

These conclusions also hold for interest rates and stocks of wealth in each country separately. In Figure 15.2A, closer integration with the external bond market makes r^1r^1 flatter and r^2r^2 steeper, and it reduces the shifts of the curves. An open-market purchase has less effect on each national interest rate.[5] In the limiting case of perfect integration, the two bond-market curves become perpendicular to their respective axes, and they cannot shift at all. The only effect of an open-market purchase is a loss of reserves to the outside world by the central bank making the open-market purchase. The reserves of the other country do not change.

---

[5] Stating the point algebraically, the equation for r^1r^1 given at the end of this chapter says that $\delta r_1 = -(B_{12}^t/B_{11}^t)\,\delta r_2$. Thus, an increase in substitutability between the domestic bonds and the external bond has the effect of reducing the change in r_1 resulting from a change in r_2 (because it raises B_{11}^t by raising $-B_{01}^t$). It weakens the connections between the two interest rates. With asset-market symmetry, moreover, $B_{01} = B_{02}'$, $B_{02} = B_{01}'$, $B_{10} = B_{20}'$, and $B_{20} = B_{10}'$. Thus, an increase in the degree of integration between one domestic market and the external market necessarily implies an identical increase between the other domestic market and the external market. An increase of integration with the external market reduces the responses of *both* domestic interest rates to open-market operations and other domestic disturbances and cannot affect their *relative* responses. Asset-market symmetry eliminates the possibility that one country's interest rate will be closely tied to the world rate while the other country's rate responds freely to monetary stimuli from one country or the other.

Some discussions of asset-market integration have suggested that close integration with external markets can have consequences similar to those of direct bilateral integration. For institutional and other reasons, the assets issued by European countries are not deemed to be close substitutes for each other; nevertheless, the asset markets of those countries are integrated indirectly because each one is integrated with the Euro-dollar market.[6] It would not be hard to introduce this possibility into our two-country model; we could endogenize the interest rate $\bar{r}_0$ by causing the supply of the external bond to be less than perfectly elastic. In its present form, however, the model does not permit indirect integration. As an open-market purchase of the Northern bond cannot affect $\bar{r}_0$, its influence is dissipated by close integration, not transmitted to the South via the external market.

Integration between Northern and Southern bond markets

More interesting for our purposes are the implications of direct, bilateral integration between Northern and Southern bond markets. An increase of substitutability between the two countries' bonds (of $-B_{12}^t$) has no influence on aggregate or average variables, so that Figure 15.1 is unaffected. Neither is there any influence on the size of the change in aggregate income, under our provisional assumption of goods-market symmetry, so that Figure 15.3A is likewise unaffected. But the *relative* responses of the two economies *are* affected systematically.

Figure 15.5 is drawn to show the interest-rate responses that correspond to various degrees of bilateral integration. An open-market purchase of either bond by either bank reduces the average interest rate and shifts $r^t r^t$ to $r^{t'} r^{t'}$, regardless of the degree of substitutability between the two bonds. When the Northern bond is purchased, however, $r^1 r^1$ shifts downward to meet the intersection of $r^2 r^2$ and $r^{t'} r^{t'}$, and the location of this point depends on the slopes of the national bond-market curves, which depend in turn on the degree of substitutability between the Northern and Southern bonds.

With asset-market symmetry, the national bond-market curves are always symmetrical with respect to the 45° line rr. The size of the wedge between them, however, varies with the degree of substitutability. At one

[6] See C. P. Kindleberger, "Economic Integration via External Markets and Factors," in W. Sellekaerts, ed., *International Trade and Finance: Essays in Honour of Jan Tinbergen*, Macmillan, London, 1974, pp. 103–16; also B. J. Cohen, "The Euro-dollar, the Common Market, and Currency Unification," *Journal of Finance*, 18 (December 1963), pp. 605–21.

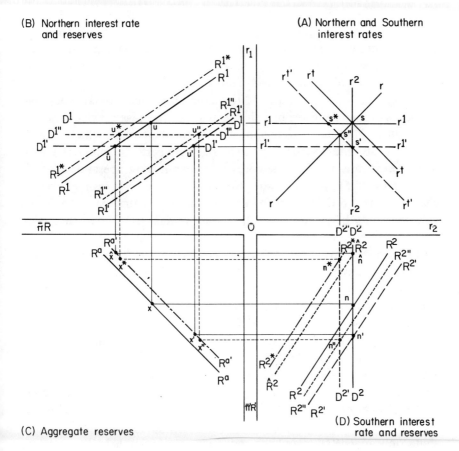

(B) Northern interest rate and reserves

(A) Northern and Southern interest rates

(C) Aggregate reserves

(D) Southern interest rate and reserves

Figure 15.5 Open-market purchase of the Northern bond with zero and perfect asset-market integration: impact effects on national asset markets under pegged exchange rates.

extreme, with no substitutability $(-B_{12}^t = 0)$, the curves are perpendicular to their respective axes, as shown by r^1r^1 and r^2r^2 in Figure 15.5A. Therefore, an open-market purchase of the Northern bond displaces asset-market equilibrium from s to s' as the Northern curve shifts downward from r^1r^1 to $r^{1\prime}r^{1\prime}$. The Southern interest rate remains unchanged, and the reduction in the average rate is due entirely to the reduction in the Northern rate. With some substitutability between the bonds, the wedge between the national bond-market curves is narrower, as it was in Figure 15.2A. An open-market purchase of the Northern bond reduces each national interest rate, with r_1 falling farther than r_2 but by less than the distance ss' in Figure 15.5A. Finally, at the opposite extreme, with perfect substitutability ($-B_{12}^t \to \infty$), the two bond-market curves coincide completely with the 45° line rr, and the wedge between them vanishes. An open-market purchase of the Northern bond reduces each national interest rate by the same amount (by the decline in the average interest rate) as asset-market equilibrium is displaced from s to s''.

The effects of a purchase of the Southern bond are symmetrical. Responses range from the one shown at $s*$ for the case in which there is no substitutability to the one shown at s'' for the case in which there is perfect substitutability. When bond markets are perfectly integrated, relative interest rates are not altered by any open-market operation.

In Figure 15.5B we show how Northern reserves can respond to purchases of the Northern bond by each of the two central banks. With no substitutability between the bonds, the movement from s to s' in Figure 15.5A is matched in Figure 15.5B by a shift of the Northern bond-market curve from D^1D^1 to $D^{1'}D^{1'}$. As there is no change in r_2, the behavior of the Northern money-market curve depends entirely on the change in the money supply produced by the open-market purchase. When it is the Northern bank that makes the purchase, the Northern money supply is raised, and the curve is shifted from R^1R^1 to $R^{1'}R^{1'}$. When it is the Southern bank that makes the purchase, the Northern money supply is not affected directly, and the curve remains in place at R^1R^1. Accordingly, a purchase by the Northern central bank causes a movement from u to u', and the North loses reserves, whereas a purchase by the Southern bank causes a movement from u to $\hat{u}$, and the North gains reserves. With perfect substitutability between the bonds, the Northern bond-market curve shifts only to $D^{1''}D^{1''}$, and the reduction in the Southern interest rate raises the Northern demand for money and affects the position of the money-market curve. With a purchase by the Northern bank, the reduction in r_2 shifts the curve from $R^{1'}R^{1'}$ to $R^{1''}R^{1''}$. With a purchase by the Southern bank, the reduction in r_2 shifts the curve from R^1R^1 to $R^{1*}R^{1*}$. Thus, a Northern open-market purchase of the Northern bond produces a movement from u to u'', and a Southern purchase produces a movement from u to $u*$. Once again, the North loses reserves with a Northern purchase and gains them with a Southern purchase. But the effect of asset-market integration is reserve reducing for the North, in that an open-market purchase of the Northern bond causes a larger loss of reserves when the Northern bank buys the bond and a smaller gain when the Southern bank buys it.

In Figure 15.5D, we tell the corresponding story for Southern reserves. When there is no substitutability between the two bonds, the Southern bond-market curve does not shift, because there is no change in the Southern interest rate. It remains at D^2D^2. But the money-market curve does not stay put. The reduction in the Northern interest rate raises the Southern demand for money, inducing a rightward shift, whereas the increase in the Southern money supply that takes place when the Southern bank makes the open-market purchase causes a leftward shift.[7] Therefore, a purchase by the Northern bank causes the curve to shift from R^2R^2 to $R^{2\prime}R^{2\prime}$, displacing equilibrium from n to n'. But a purchase by the Southern bank causes the curve to shift from R^2R^2 to $\hat{R}^2\hat{R}^2$, as the rightward shift resulting from the fall in r_1 is swamped by the leftward shift resulting from the increase in the money supply, and equilibrium is displaced from n to $\hat{n}$. With perfect asset-market integration, the Southern bond-market curve shifts too, from D^2D^2 to $D^{2\prime}D^{2\prime}$, because of the reduction in the Southern interest rate. Furthermore, the reduction in the Northern rate is smaller, putting less rightward pressure on the money-market curve. When it is the Northern bank that makes the purchase, then, the money-market curve shifts only to $R^{2\prime\prime}R^{2\prime\prime}$, displacing equilibrium to n'', and when it is the Southern bank that makes the purchase, the curve shifts farther to $R^{2*}R^{2*}$, displacing equilibrium to n^*. The effect of asset-market integration is reserve increasing for the South, in that an open-market purchase of the Northern bond causes a larger increase in Southern reserves when the Northern bank buys the bond and a smaller decrease in Southern reserves when the Southern bank buys it.

The range of changes in reserves is summarized by Figure 15.5C. The shift from R^aR^a to $R^{a\prime}R^{a\prime}$ describes the reduction in aggregate reserves. It is not affected by the bond or bank involved or by the degree of asset-market integration. When the Northern central bank buys the Northern bond, the two countries move from x to x' if there is no integration and from x to x'' if there is perfect integration. When the Southern bank buys the Northern bond, the countries move from x to $\hat{x}$ if there is no integration and from x to x^* if there is perfect integration. Restating our earlier conclusion, asset-market integration tends to shift reserves from North to

---

[7] The shift of the Southern money-market curve due to the reduction in r_1 says that Southerners hold Northern bonds even when there is no substitutability between the two countries' bonds. If they did not hold them, their demand for money would not be affected by a change in the Northern interest rate. There is, of course, a logical difficulty here, but it does not reside in the assumption that Southerners hold Northern bonds. They may hold them for reasons of currency diversification, even when the North–South exchange rate is pegged. When they do so, however, they are quite likely to regard Northern and Southern bonds as partial substitutes. Thus, the logical difficulty resides in our use of the limiting case in which $-B_{12}^t \to 0$. We use it, however, only for purposes of exposition.

South when the Northern bond is purchased and from South to North when the Southern bond is purchased. With asset-market symmetry, moreover, the strength of this redistributional effect does not depend on the bond that is bought or on the bank that buys it.[8]

As bilateral asset-market integration makes for more similar changes in interest rates, it makes for more similar changes in incomes. This is not surprising, because incomes are affected only indirectly by an open-market purchase. They respond to the changes in absorption induced by the changes in interest rates. In Figure 15.3B, the degree of substitutability between the bonds determines the relative sizes of the shifts in the two income curves. In all instances, of course, they intersect at a point on $Y''Y''$. But with less than perfect integration, an open-market purchase of the Northern bond causes an upward shift of Y^1Y^1 larger than the rightward shift of Y^2Y^2, and Northern income rises by more than Southern income. This difference is maximized when there is no integration. The greater the degree of asset-market integration, however, the smaller the difference between the shifts in Y^1Y^1 and Y^2Y^2 and the smaller the difference between the income changes. With perfect integration, an open-market purchase of the Northern bond causes the two curves to shift by identical distances, so that they intersect where $Y''Y''$ intersects the 45° line YY, and the income changes are equalized completely.

In brief, bilateral asset-market integration reduces the difference between short-run income changes in the North and South, and perfect integration eliminates the difference. With perfect integration, then, a purchase of the Southern bond has the same effects on incomes as a purchase of the Northern bond. This conclusion must be qualified, however, when we abandon goods-market symmetry.

Integration between Northern and Southern goods markets

Spillovers from national monetary policies are increased by goods-market integration, as well as by asset-market integration. With full-scale goods-market symmetry, the size of the change in aggregate income is unaffected by the degree of integration between Northern and Southern

[8] The relevant changes in reserves are given by Eq. (E.2b) in Appendix E. Under the assumption of asset-market symmetry, that equation applies to all of the relevant cases. It can be shown that $(\bar\pi'\ \delta R'/\delta\bar B_1^c) = (\bar\pi\ \delta R/\delta\bar B_2^{c'})$ and $(\bar\pi'\ \delta R'/\delta\bar B_1^{c'}) = (\bar\pi\ \delta R/\delta\bar B_2^c)$. Therefore,

$$\delta(\bar\pi\ \delta R/\delta\bar B_1^c)/\delta(-B_{12}^t) = -\delta(\bar\pi'\ \delta R'/\delta\bar B_1^c)/\delta(-B_{12}^t) = -\delta(\bar\pi\ \delta R/\delta\bar B_1^{c'})/\delta(-B_{12}^t)$$
$$= -\delta(\bar\pi'\ \delta R'/\delta\bar B_1^{c'})/\delta(-B_{12}^t) = (L_{11}-L_{12})(B_{11}^t-B_{12}^t)^2$$

which is unambiguously negative, because $L_{11} < L_{12} < 0$.

goods markets. But the degree of integration does affect its distribution. An increase in substitutability between Northern and Southern goods (in u_{12}^t) reduces the difference between the changes in goods prices and, therefore, the difference between changes in nominal incomes. Goods-market integration, like asset-market integration, diminishes the scope for use of monetary policies in pursuit of independent income targets.[9]

In Figure 15.3B, an increase in substitutability between Northern and Southern goods narrows the wedge between the income curves, bringing their slopes closer to unity. It also reduces the shifts in the curves resulting from an open-market purchase, and the curves intersect on $Y^{t'}Y^{t'}$ at a point that is closer to YY, the 45° line. In the limiting case of perfect goods-market integration ($u_{12}^t \to \infty$), the curves coincide completely with YY and are not shifted by an open-market purchase. Each country's income moves to the level denoted by the intersection of $Y^{t'}Y^{t'}$ and YY. The changes in incomes are equalized, and they are the same for any open-market purchase.

Summary

Integration between a country's bond market and any other market reduces the impact of domestic monetary policy. But bilateral bond-market integration, even when perfect, cannot prevent monetary policy from affecting domestic income in the short run, whereas perfect integration with the world market eliminates its influence. Perfect bilateral integration does not undermine the effectiveness of monetary policy, because each country can affect its neighbor's interest rate. The countries in our model have no such influence on the world interest rate.

The higher the degree of integration between the countries' asset markets, the smaller the effect of an open-market purchase of one country's bond on that country's interest rate and, therefore, its influence on that country's income. Concomitantly, the effect on the other country's interest rate is larger, and so is the change in its income. By implication, an increase of asset-market integration means that a country wishing to achieve a given change in its own income must make a bigger change in its monetary policy; its central bank must buy or sell a larger quantity of bonds.

The same statement can be made concerning the effects of goods-

[9] For more on the role of goods-market integration in spreading the effects of monetary policy from one country to another, see P. R. Allen, *Organization and Administration of a Monetary Union,* Princeton Studies in International Finance 38, Princeton University, Princeton, N.J., 1976, pp. 32–7.

market integration. A high degree of integration between North and South does not eliminate the short-run influence of monetary policy but does reduce the change in domestic income resulting from an open-market operation. In other words, it also works to raise the size of the policy change needed to achieve a given effect on domestic income.

Policy interdependence

Thus far, our analysis has dealt only with exogenous policy changes–with open-market operations by one central bank. We have made no allowance for responses by the other. When asset and goods markets are closely integrated, however, spillover effects are bound to be large, and the other country's central bank has to react if it wants to stabilize its own economy or to achieve some other national target. We have therefore to turn to the problem of policy interdependence. We must measure the extent to which *both* central banks can conduct independent monetary policies simultaneously so as to control short-run changes in their own countries' incomes. (We have seen that open economies with pegged exchange rates cannot make permanent changes in incomes, regardless of the degree of market integration.)

For this purpose, we turn our analysis on end. We ask what combinations of open-market operations are consistent with desired short-run changes in incomes. Each country is deemed to set its own income target. In order to achieve its target, however, it must take into consideration the other country's policy and the corresponding leakages and spillovers.

Figure 15.6 depicts combinations of Northern and Southern monetary policies that will yield the desired short-run changes in incomes. The vertical axis is used to measure open-market operations in the Northern bond, δB_1^{ct}, and the horizontal axis to measure open-market operations in the Southern bond, δB_2^{ct}. Because income changes do not depend on the central bank that conducts the open-market operations, Figure 15.6 does not identify the bank involved. Its axes measure the *sums* of the two banks' operations in the relevant bond.

Curve I–I is the policy reaction curve for the North, showing the combinations of open-market operations in Northern and Southern bonds that will keep Northern income constant ($\delta \bar{Y} = 0$). As an open-market purchase of the Southern bond has positive spillover effects on Northern income, any such purchase must be offset by an open-market sale of the Northern bond to hold Northern income constant. A purchase of the Northern bond, however, has a stronger effect on Northern income than a

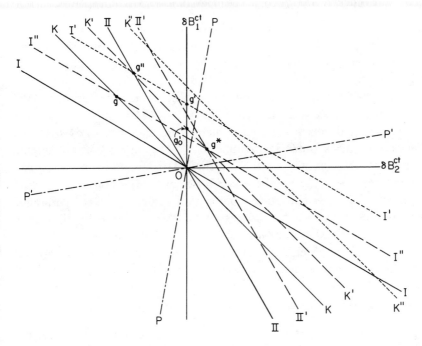

Figure 15.6 Policy interdependence: policy reaction curves for open-market operations required to achieve short-run income targets under pegged exchange rates.

purchase of the Southern bond, so that a purchase of the Southern bond can be offset by a somewhat smaller purchase of the Northern bond. Therefore, the Northern policy reaction curve is negatively sloped, but its slope is smaller absolutely than that of the $-45°$ line $K-K$.[10]

[10] The equations for the policy reaction curves in Figure 15.6 are given at the end of this chapter. They are obtained by solving for the open-market operations required by the countries' income targets, $\delta \bar{Y}$ and $\delta \bar{Y}'$. Rearranging Eqs. (13.14b) and (13.15b),

$$\delta B_1^{ct} = M_s J[\sigma_1 \sigma_2'(M_{1d}M_{2d} - M_{1e}M_{2e})]^{-1}[(\sigma_2'M_{2d})\,\delta \bar{Y} - (\sigma_1 M_{1e})\,\delta \bar{Y}']$$
$$\delta B_2^{ct} = M_s J[\sigma_1 \sigma_2'(M_{1d}M_{2d} - M_{1e}M_{2e})]^{-1}[(\sigma_1 M_{1d})\,\delta \bar{Y}' - (\sigma_2'M_{2e})\,\delta \bar{Y}]$$

where

$$M_{1d} = (B_{11}^t - B_{12}^t)[(m_1 S_2 + m_2 S_1)M_{22} + S_1^t(1 - m_0)M_{21}] + B_{11}^t(m_1 - m_2)(S_1 - S_2)M_{22}$$
$$M_{2d} = (B_{11}^t - B_{12}^t)[(m_1 S_2 + m_2 S_1)M_{11} + S_1^t(1 - m_0)M_{12}] + B_{11}^t(m_1 - m_2)(S_1 - S_2)M_{11}$$
$$M_{1e} = (B_{11}^t - B_{12}^t)[(m_1 S_2 + m_2 S_1)M_{22} + S_1^t(1 - m_0)M_{21}] + B_{12}^t(m_1 - m_2)(S_1 - S_2)M_{22}$$
$$M_{2e} = (B_{11}^t - B_{12}^t)[(m_1 S_2 + m_2 S_1)M_{11} + S_1^t(1 - m_0)M_{12}] + B_{12}^t(m_1 - m_2)(S_1 - S_2)M_{11}$$

In this and subsequent chapters, policy reaction curves are used to solve for the combinations of policy instruments required by the countries' own policy targets. As their names imply, however, they can be used to study the duopolistic processes involved in achieving the appropriate combinations–the response by the South to a change in Northern policy,

Curve II–II is the policy reaction curve for the South, showing the combinations of open-market operations that will keep Southern income constant ($\delta \bar{Y}' = 0$). For reasons corresponding to those given above, the Southern reaction curve is negatively sloped, but its slope is larger absolutely than that of $K-K$.

Curve $K-K$ itself depicts combinations of open-market operations that will keep aggregate income constant ($\delta \bar{Y} + \delta \bar{Y}' = \delta Y^t = 0$). Under asset-market and goods-market symmetry, the national policy reaction curves are always symmetrical around $K-K$. At g on $K-K$, for example, an open-market purchase of the Northern bond is offset by an equal open-market sale of the Southern bond. Because g lies above I–I and to the left of II–II, this particular combination of open-market operations raises Northern income but depresses Southern income by the same amount. By implication, the only combination of open-market operations that has no effect on either country's income is the one at the origin, where there are no net purchases or sales of either bond.

Expansion in the North and stabilization in the South

Consider first a Northern policy aimed at increasing Northern income by an amount $\delta \bar{Y} > 0$, combined with a Southern policy aimed at insulating Southern income from the effects of the new Northern policy. The desired increase in Northern income shifts the Northern policy reaction curve upward from I–I to I′–I′ in Figure 15.6. The size of the vertical shift, $0g'$, measures the Northern purchase of the Northern bond that would achieve the new Northern target in the absence of any Southern reaction. Because g' is to the right of II–II, this particular purchase would raise Southern income.

The Southern central bank can prevent an increase in Southern income by an open-market sale of the Northern or Southern bond if it holds both bonds in its portfolio. It can sell a quantity of Northern bonds equal to the quantity purchased by the Northern bank (so that $\delta B_1^{ct} = 0$). In this case, however, the two economies remain at the origin, and the North does not

the reaction by the North to the Southern response, and so on. In the present instance, this sequential process will be stable, converging on the proper combination, if the Northern central bank operates exclusively in the Northern bond and the Southern bank operates exclusively in the Southern bond. In general, sequential adjustments will be stable in this sense if each policy-making agency uses the policy instrument that has the larger impact on its own target variable than on the other agency's target variable. The reader may prove this proposition easily by working with the curves in Figure 15.6 and those for fiscal policies in Figure 17.5. (The proposition is, of course, an adaptation of the "principle of effective market classification" set forth in R. A. Mundell, *International Economics,* Macmillan, New York, 1968, p. 163.)

achieve its income target. Generalizing, there is no combination of Northern and Southern operations in the *same* bond that can allow the two countries to achieve independent income targets.

Fortunately, the Southern central bank has another option. It can sell the Southern bond to offset the undesired effect of the Northern purchase of the Northern bond. This is the response shown at g'' in Figure 15.6, where I'–I' and II–II intersect. As each country's income responds more strongly to an open-market operation in its own domestic bond than in the other country's bond, the size of the sale of the Southern bond required to stabilize Southern income is smaller than the sale of the Northern bond that would be needed for that purpose. Consequently, the Southern response does not prevent the North from achieving its income target, although it does compel the Northern bank to buy a larger quantity of Northern bonds (g'' lies to the northwest of g'). In this particular case, of course, the change in aggregate income equals the change in Northern income. This fact is indicated by the shift from $K–K$ to $K'–K'$ in Figure 15.6, a shift that causes $K'–K'$ to intersect the policy reaction curves at g''.

The second option is the one that the South should follow. It has to sell fewer bonds than would have been necessary if it sold the Northern bond. More important, it is the neighborly option, in that the North is able to achieve its new income target. Yet the side effects on interest rates and reserves have to be considered. If the South seeks to stabilize Southern income by selling Northern bonds, there will be no change in either country's interest rate or in aggregate reserves, but the South will gain reserves from the North (in an amount equal to the Southern sale of the Northern bond). If the South sells Southern bonds instead, the Southern interest rate will rise, the Northern rate will fall, and the average interest rate will also fall. Furthermore, there will be a reduction in aggregate reserves, along with a shift from North to South (and the Northern loss will be larger at g'' than when the South responds by selling Northern bonds or does not respond at all). These effects on interest rates and reserves are summarized by the first two rows of Table 15.1.[11]

---

[11] The interest-rate effects of a Southern attempt to stabilize Southern income can be found by substituting the sizes of the requisite open-market purchases into equations (13.2b) and (13.3b). If the South responds by operating in the Northern bond, $\delta B_1^{c'} = -\delta B_1^c$ and $\delta r_1 = \delta r_2 = 0$. If the South responds by operating in the Southern bond, the values of δB_1^c and $\delta B_2^{c'}$ are obtained from the equations in note 10, after setting $\delta \bar{Y} > 0$ (the Northern target) and $\delta \bar{Y}' = 0$ (the Southern target). The corresponding interest-rate responses are

$$\delta r_1 = -M_s J[\sigma_1(M_{1d}M_{2d} - M_{1e}M_{2e})]^{-1}[(m_1 S_1 + m_2 S_2)M_{11} + S_1^t(1 - m_0)M_{12}] \, \delta \bar{Y}$$
$$\delta r_2 = M_s J[\sigma_2'(M_{1d}M_{2d} - M_{1e}M_{2e})]^{-1}[(m_1 S_2 + m_2 S_1)M_{11} + S_1^t(1 - m_0)M_{12}] \, \delta \bar{Y}$$

Table 15.1. *Side effects of policies aimed at independent income targets: Southern response to a Northern purchase of the Northern bond*

Target	Southern response	δr_1	δr_2	$\bar{\pi}\,\delta R^t$	$\bar{\pi}\,\delta R$	$\bar{\pi}'\,\delta R'$
				Side effects		
$\delta\bar{Y} > 0,\ \delta\bar{Y}' = 0$ [a]	In Northern bond market $(\delta B_1^{c\prime} < 0)$ [c]	0	0	0	−	+
	In Southern bond market $(\delta B_2^{c\prime} < 0)$	−	+	−	−	+
$\delta\bar{Y} = \delta\bar{Y}' > 0$ [b]	In Southern bond market $(\delta B_2^{c\prime} > 0)$	−	−	−	−	−

[a] Possible only in the case of imperfect integration with external asset and goods markets and only with imperfect integration between the two countries' bond and goods markets.

[b] With perfect integration between the countries' bond or goods markets, this is only one of many possible policies. Other policies would have different effects on reserves (without affecting the size of the loss of aggregate reserves), and with perfect integration of goods markets, they would have different effects on interest rates (without affecting the size of the decline in the average interest rate).

[c] Both countries' targets cannot be achieved simultaneously in the face of a Southern response in the Northern bond market. With this response, $\delta B_2^{c\prime} = -\delta B_1^c$, so that $\delta\bar{Y} = \delta\bar{Y}' = 0$, and the North fails to attain its income target.

Expansion in both countries

We turn next to a case in which policy targets are harmonized. The countries agree to raise their incomes by equal amounts $(\delta\bar{Y} = \delta\bar{Y}' > 0)$. In Figure 15.6, the upward shift in the Northern policy reaction curve from I–I to I″–I″ is matched by a rightward shift in the Southern curve from II–II to II′–II′. The intersection at g^* defines the requisite policy combination–equal open-market purchases of both countries' bonds. The corresponding increase in aggregate income is indicated by the shift from

so that $\delta r_1 < 0$ and $\delta r_2 > 0$. The effects on reserves can be found by substituting the appropriate values of the open-market operations into Eq. (E.2b) of Appendix E. When the South sells the Northern bond, so that $\delta B_1^{c\prime} = -\delta B_1^c$, it is easily shown that $\bar{\pi}'\,\delta R' = -\bar{\pi}\,\delta R = \delta B_1^c$. When it sells the Southern bond,

$$\bar{\pi}\,\delta R = -M_s J[\sigma_1(M_{1d}M_{2d} - M_{1e}M_{2e})]^{-1}\{[(B_{11}^t - B_{12}^t) + (L_{11} - L_{12})]$$
$$\times [(m_1 S_2 + m_2 S_1)M_{11} + S_1^t(1 - m_0)M_{12}]$$
$$+ (B_{11}^t + L_{11})(m_1 - m_2)(S_1 - S_2)M_{11}\}\,\delta\bar{Y} < 0$$

$$\bar{\pi}'\,\delta R' = M_s J[\sigma_1(M_{1d}M_{2d} - M_{1e}M_{2e})]^{-1}\{[(B_{11}^t - B_{12}^t) + (L_{11} - L_{12})]$$
$$\times [(m_1 S_2 + m_2 S_1)M_{11} + S_1^t(1 - m_0)M_{12}]$$
$$- (B_{12}^t + L_{12})(m_1 - m_2)(S_1 - S_2)M_{11}\}\,\delta\bar{Y} > 0$$

$K–K$ to $K'–K'$, which shares the intersection at g^*.[12] If each bank operates in its own domestic bond but both operate simultaneously, each bank's open-market purchase will be smaller than the one required if the bank had acted alone in pursuit of its national target, without the active collaboration of the other bank.

The side effects on interest rates and reserves are unambiguous and identical for each country. Both interest rates fall (by an amount equal to the drop in the average interest rate), and both countries experience a loss of reserves (by an amount equal to half of the reduction in aggregate reserves). There is no redistribution of reserves between North and South. The signs of these effects are summarized by the third row of Table 15.1.[13]

Market integration and monetary independence

In the two examples offered above, it was assumed implicitly that asset and goods markets are not perfectly integrated. Both types of market integration are important in determining if countries can achieve independent income targets.[14]

The degrees of asset-market and goods-market integration between North and South determine the slopes of the policy reaction curves in Figure 15.6. Those curves are always negatively sloped, because each country has a positive marginal propensity to consume the other country's good. Even if there were no substitutability between their bonds or goods ($-B_{12}^t = 0$ and $u_{12}^t = 0$), open-market operations would have spillover effects akin to the Keynesian income multipliers. But the wedge between the curves would be at its maximum. As substitutability increases, whether between bonds or goods, the slopes of the policy reaction curves become more alike, narrowing the wedge. In the limiting case

[12] To simplify the diagram, it is assumed that each country seeks to raise its income by half as much as the North sought to raise its income in the previous example. That is why $K'–K'$ describes the increase in aggregate income in both examples.

[13] Equal open-market purchases are needed because we have assumed goods-market symmetry, as well as asset-market symmetry. With full-scale goods-market symmetry, $\sigma_1 = \sigma_2'$; furthermore, $M_{1d} = M_{2d}$ and $M_{1e} = M_{2e}$. When $\delta\bar{Y} = \delta\bar{Y}'$, then, the equations in note 10 give $\delta B_1^{ct} = \delta B_2^{ct} = [1/\sigma_1(M_{1d} + M_{1e})](M_s J)\,\delta\bar{Y} > 0$, and Eqs. (13.2b) and (13.3b) give $\delta r_1 = \delta r_2 = -[1/\sigma_1(M_{1d} + M_{1e})]M_s(B_{11}^t - B_{12}^t)\,\delta\bar{Y} < 0$. The effects on reserves come from Eq. (E.2b). Assuming that each central bank buys its own domestic bond, $\bar{\pi}\,\delta R = \bar{\pi}'\,\delta R' = -[1/\sigma_1(M_{1d} + M_{1e})]M_s(-B_{01}^t)(B_{11}^t - B_{12}^t)\,\delta\bar{Y} < 0$.

[14] Integration between domestic and world bond markets has been seen to make monetary policy less effective. For any set of income targets ($\delta\bar{Y} \neq 0$, $\delta\bar{Y}' \neq 0$, or both), substitutability between domestic and world bonds enlarges the requisite shifts in the policy reaction curves. With perfect integration ($-B_{01}^t \to \infty$), the shifts become infinitely large, saying that it is impossible for either country to influence its income even in the short run.

of perfect substitutability between bonds $(-B_{12}^t \to \infty)$ or between goods $(u_{12}^t \to \infty)$, each curve comes to have a slope of $-45°$, and the two curves coincide or are parallel.[15] In other words, curve $K-K$ in Figure 15.6, which describes the policy combinations that keep aggregate income constant, serves also to depict the policy reaction curve for a country that does not want to alter its own income, whereas curve $K'-K'$, which describes the policy combinations that raise aggregate income, serves also to depict the policy reaction curve for a country that wants to raise its own income.

Consider the effects of asset-market integration on the combination of monetary policies that is needed when the North and South have identical income targets (on the location of g^* in Figure 15.6). As Northern and Southern bonds become closer substitutes, the wedge between $I''-I''$ and $II'-II'$ narrows, as each policy reaction curve comes to be more like $K'-K'$. But the intersection point remains the same. An increase in asset-market integration has no effect on the required policy combination when income targets are identical. With perfect asset-market integration, however, many combinations of policies are possible. When the policy reaction curves coincide completely with $K'-K'$, the combination at g^* continues to be feasible and effective. But *any* combination of open-market operations lying on $K'-K'$ will allow the countries to achieve their targets. The *sum* of open-market purchases must equal $0g_0'$, but it does not matter which country's bond is purchased. When asset markets are perfectly integrated, there is in effect a single composite bond.

Similar results obtain with an increase in goods-market integration, but the sizes of the requisite open-market purchases need not remain constant. Equal open-market purchases are needed, but the amounts that must be bought may either rise or fall. As Northern and Southern goods become closer substitutes, the slopes of the policy reaction curves become more alike, but the process is more complicated.

With an increase in asset-market integration, the policy reaction curves pivot around a common point that lies on a 45° line from the origin in Figure 15.6, and g^* is one such point, so that the required policy combination

---

[15] The slopes of the policy reaction curves appear in the equations at the end of this chapter. The effects of asset-market integration on those slopes are found by taking their derivatives with respect to $-B_{12}^t$:

$$\delta(\delta B_1^{ct}/\delta B_2^{ct})_I/\delta(-B_{12}^t) = -[(M_{1d} - M_{1e})/(M_{1d})^2]S_1^i(1 - m_0)(M_{22} + 2M_{21}) < 0$$
$$\delta(\delta B_1^{ct}/\delta B_2^{ct})_{II}/\delta(-B_{12}^t) = [(M_{2d} - M_{2e})/(M_{2e})^2]S_1^i(1 - m_0)(M_{11} + 2M_{12}) > 0$$

In the limiting case of perfect asset-market integration or perfect goods-market integration, $(\delta B_1^{ct}/\delta B_2^{ct})_I \to -1$ and $(\delta B_1^{ct}/\delta B_2^{ct})_{II} \to -1$, as $-B_{12}^t \to \infty$ or $u_{12}^t \to \infty$

is unaffected. With an increase in goods-market integration, the two curves need not pivot around a common point. The pivot points are located symmetrically around the 45° line but may lie on either side of it. In Figure 15.6, for example, the locus of pivot points for the Northern reaction curve can be PP, and the locus of pivot points for the Southern reaction curve can be $P'P'$. With an increase in goods-market integration, then, the Northern curve $I''-I''$ will rotate around its intersection with PP, becoming flatter, and the Southern curve $II'-II'$ will rotate around its intersection with $P'P'$, becoming steeper. The two countries' policy reaction curves will converge on a common curve parallel to $K'-K'$ but southwest of it. Point g^* will shift to the southwest, and the sizes of the open-market purchases will fall with an increase in goods-market integration. But the roles of PP and $P'P'$ are reversible. The Northern reaction curve can rotate around its intersection with $P'P'$, and the Southern curve can rotate around its intersection with PP. In this case, the two countries' policy reaction curves will converge on a common curve parallel to $K'-K'$ but northwest of it, and the sizes of the open-market purchases will rise.[16]

When goods and asset markets are not perfectly integrated, equal

---

[16] At a pivot point for a policy reaction curve, the combination of δB_1^{ct} and δB_2^{ct} is unaffected by a change in the slope of the curve. We can find the locus of pivot points for a country's policy reaction curves (the curves corresponding to different income targets for the country) as they respond to a change in a particular type of market integration. To do so, we define $\delta B_2^{ct} = a_i \, \delta B_1^{ct}$, for the case of an increase in substitutability between bonds, and $\delta B_2^{ct} = b_i \, \delta B_1^{ct}$, for the case of an increase in substitutability between goods, where $i = 1$ when we are working with the Northern reaction curve and $i = 2$ when we are working with the Southern curve. Next, we use these expressions to replace δB_2^{ct} in both of the policy reaction curves. Finally, we take the derivatives of the equation for each reaction curve with respect to $-B_{12}^t$ or u_{12}^t, as appropriate, set the derivatives equal to zero, and solve for the a_i or b_i. The solutions for the a_i and b_i are the slopes of the loci of pivot points. For the case of an increase in asset-market integration, the results are $a_1 = (\delta B_1^{ct}/\delta B_2^{ct}) = 1$ for the locus of pivot points of the Northern curve, and $(1/a_2) = (\delta B_2^{ct}/\delta B_1^{ct}) = 1$ for the locus of pivot points of the Southern curve. The pivot points for changes in the degree of asset-market integration lie on a 45° line from the origin, for the Northern and Southern curves alike. For the case of an increase in goods-market integration, the results are $b_1 = (\delta B_1^{ct}/\delta B_2^{ct}) = 1 + \beta_1$ for the locus of pivot points of the Northern curve, and $(1/b_2) = (\delta B_2^{ct}/\delta B_1^{ct}) = 1 + \beta_2$ for the locus of pivot points of the Southern curve, where

$$\beta_1 = \frac{(B_{11}^t - B_{12}^t)(m_1 - m_2)(S_1 - S_2)M_{ii}}{M_{je}[u_{10}^t + u_{20}^t + M_Y(\sigma_1 + \sigma_2')] - M_s S_1^t(1 - m_0)(B_{11}^t - B_{12}^t)} \gtreqless 0$$

for $i, j = 1, 2$. With full-scale goods-market symmetry, however, $M_{11} = M_{22}$ and $M_{1e} = M_{2e}$, so that $\beta_1 = \beta_2$ and $b_1 = (1/b_2)$. The loci of pivot points for the Northern and Southern curves are symmetrical about a 45° line. But their slopes can still be positive or negative, and the Northern locus can be steeper or flatter than the Southern locus.

open-market operations in Northern and Southern bonds are always needed to raise Northern and Southern incomes by the same amounts. When goods markets are perfectly integrated, however, the range of policy combinations is enlarged, much as it was with perfect asset-market integration. It is necessary only that the *sum* of open-market purchases be sufficiently large. The composition does not matter. When Northern and Southern goods are perfect substitutes, the effects of *any* open-market operation are spread evenly across the two countries' goods markets, even if they are not spread evenly across the asset markets. (With perfect asset-market integration, the combination of open-market purchases affects the distribution of reserves, but r_1 and r_2 fall by the same amounts. With perfect goods-market integration but less than perfect asset-market integration, the combination of open-market operations affects not only the distribution of reserves but also the relative changes in interest rates. In both cases, however, the reductions in the average interest rate and aggregate reserves are unaffected, as they do not depend on the degree of market integration or the composition of the open-market purchase.)

To summarize a complicated set of findings, perfect goods-market integration may be viewed as a partial substitute for perfect asset-market integration. When asset markets are perfectly integrated, the interest-rate effects of open-market operations are identical, regardless of the bond bought, so that the effects on absorption are identical. Northern and Southern goods markets are affected equally because bond markets are affected equally. When goods markets are perfectly integrated, the interest-rate effects are not identical, which means that the changes in absorption are not identical. But the difference between changes in absorption cannot have any influence on relative demands for the two countries' goods. They are in effect a single, composite good.

Perfect market integration of either variety raises the possibility of conflict between countries even when their income targets are identical. Precisely because the combination of open-market purchases makes no difference for the sizes of the income changes, one country may abstain from any policy change, in the hope that the other may do what is needed.

Suppose that the South declines to make any open-market purchase, leaving the task entirely to the North. If the Northern central bank buys the Northern bonds required to achieve the Northern income target, the policy outcome will be at g_0' in Figure 15.6. Both countries will achieve their income targets. But the North will lose reserves to the South and the outside world. The South will enjoy a free ride, and will gain reserves in the bargain. With close market integration, each country has an incentive to refrain from costly policy actions – to take advantage of the spillover effects of its neighbor's actions when the countries' income targets are consistent.

When the income targets differ, it will be hard to achieve them if asset and goods markets are closely integrated. Let us return to our first example, in which the North sought to raise Northern income ($\delta \bar{Y} > 0$) and the South sought to stabilize Southern income ($\delta \bar{Y}' = 0$). In the case of imperfect market integration, the requisite policy combination was given at g'' in Figure 15.6. As the degree of asset-market integration rises, however, the Northern reaction curve, $I'-I'$, rotates clockwise toward $K''-K''$, and the Southern curve, $II-II$, rotates counterclockwise toward $K-K$. The curves continue to intersect at a point on $K'-K'$ (denoting the change in aggregate income, $\delta Y^t = \delta \bar{Y} > 0$), but that point moves to the northwest. More Northern bonds must be purchased and more Southern bonds sold. At the limit, with perfect asset-market integration, the Northern curve comes to coincide with $K''-K''$, the Southern curve comes to coincide with $K-K$, and the two curves are parallel. No combination of open-market operations can satisfy both countries' income targets when, as here, those targets are not identical.[17]

For two countries to achieve independent income targets, there must be limitations on market integration. Even with imperfect but close integration, it may be hard for them to do so. Very large open-market operations are required when the income targets differ, and these may be unacceptable, because of their effects on the bond markets themselves, or because they involve large shifts in reserves between the two countries.[18]

Implications of asymmetries in goods markets

The perfect symmetry of income changes and the concomitant symmetry of policy prescriptions obtained heretofore stem from the assumption of

---

[17] The effect of goods-market integration is essentially the same. Although the Northern reaction curve may rotate toward a curve parallel to $K''-K''$, rather than coinciding with it, and the intersections of the two reaction curves do not always lie on $K'-K'$, the intersections do move to the northwest with an increase of goods-market integration. With perfect goods-market integration, moreover, the reaction curves are parallel, and there is again no policy combination that can satisfy both countries' targets.

[18] DeGrauwe has examined the reserve flows between European countries that would result from the sterilization of reserve flows. In our terms, he has examined the effects of pursuing constant money-supply targets rather than constant income targets. In his work, systematic sterilization by two or more countries led to explosive reserve flows and negligible monetary independence. See P. DeGrauwe, "The Interaction of Monetary Policies in a Group of European Countries," *Journal of International Economics*, 5 (August 1975), pp. 207–28.

goods-market symmetry adopted to simplify the exposition. We now must abandon that assumption and ask how our conclusions are modified by differences between price elasticities (when $u_{10}^t \neq u_{20}^t$, and $\sigma_1 \neq \sigma_2'$). Asymmetries between these price elasticities have no bearing on asset-market responses. They do not affect the short-run changes in interest rates or stocks of reserves that take place with open-market operations. Only the changes in incomes are affected.

Income effects of open-market operations

In Figure 15.3B, the income curves Y^1Y^1 and Y^2Y^2 were symmetrical about the 45° line YY, and the shifts in the curves were symmetrical too. When we allow for differences between price elasticities, many possibilities open up. In all cases, the income curves are positively sloped or, in the extreme, perpendicular to their respective axes, and the Southern curve is always at least as steep as the Northern curve. Any open-market purchase, moreover, shifts Y^1Y^1 upward and Y^2Y^2 rightward, if it shifts them at all. Thus, neither country's income can be *reduced* by an open-market purchase. Nevertheless, many changes in relative incomes can take place. Let us delineate the range of possibilities by looking at two special cases. In each case, the price of one country's good is prevented from changing because the good is a perfect substitute for the foreign (world) good.

In Figure 15.7A, the Northern good is a perfect substitute for the foreign good ($u_{10}^t \rightarrow \infty$), and an open-market operation cannot affect p_1 under pegged exchange rates. Because Northern income depends exclusively on p_1, Northern income cannot change, and the Northern income curve, Y^1Y^1, becomes horizontal and immovable. The Southern income curve, Y^2Y^2, is positively sloped, as usual, and shifts rightward in response to any open-market purchase (provided $B_{12}^t \neq 0$). One shift shown in Figure 15.7A, from Y^2Y^2 to $Y^{2\prime}Y^{2\prime}$, occurs in response to an open-market purchase of the Northern bond, and goods-market equilibrium is displaced from q to q'. The other shift, from Y^2Y^2 to $Y^{2\prime\prime}Y^{2\prime\prime}$, occurs in response to an open-market purchase of the Southern bond, which has a larger effect on Southern absorption, and equilibrium is displaced from q to q''. Southern income rises in each instance and rises farther when the Southern bond is purchased. But there is no change in Northern income. Accordingly, the increase in aggregate income is equal to the increase in Southern income and comes thus to depend on the bond

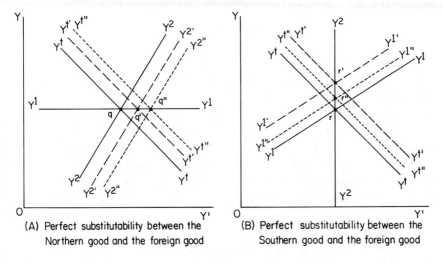

(A) Perfect substitutability between the Northern good and the foreign good

(B) Perfect substitutability between the Southern good and the foreign good

Figure 15.7 Open-market purchases without goods-market symmetry: impact effects on national goods markets under pegged exchange rates.

that is purchased. The increase in aggregate income resulting from the purchase of the Northern bond is denoted by the shift from Y^tY^t to $Y^{t\prime}Y^{t\prime}$, and the one resulting from the purchase of the Southern bond is denoted by the larger shift to $Y^{t\prime\prime}Y^{t\prime\prime}$. In the absence of goods-market symmetry, we can no longer say that the change in aggregate income is independent of the bond that is purchased.

In Figure 15.7B, the Southern good is a perfect substitute for the foreign good ($u_{20}^t \to \infty$), so that the Southern income curve is vertical and cannot be shifted by an open-market operation. The Northern curve is positively sloped and shifts upward in response to any open-market purchase. Thus, a purchase of the Northern bond shifts it from Y^1Y^1 to $Y^{1\prime}Y^{1\prime}$, displacing equilibrium from r to r', whereas a purchase of the Southern bond shifts it to $Y^{1\prime\prime}Y^{1\prime\prime}$, displacing equilibrium to r''. In this case, the purchase of the Northern bond has the larger effect on aggregate income; the shift to $Y^{t\prime}Y^{t\prime}$ is bigger than the shift to $Y^{t\prime\prime}Y^{t\prime\prime}$.

In the absence of goods-market symmetry, a country's income will still respond more strongly to an open-market purchase of its own domestic bond than to a purchase of its neighbor's bond–if it responds at all. But we can no longer say that an open-market purchase of one country's bond will necessarily raise that country's income by more than it raises the other country's income. In Figure 15.7A, an open-market purchase of the Northern bond has a larger effect on Southern than Northern income; in

Figure 15.7B, an open-market purchase of the Southern bond has a larger effect on Northern than Southern income.

We can express this same conclusion in a slightly different way. When demands for assets and desired saving respond symmetrically to interest-rate changes, a country's absorption will always respond more strongly to an open-market purchase of its own domestic bond than to a purchase of its neighbor's bond (except in the limiting case of perfect asset-market integration). Furthermore, an increase of absorption will always raise a country's demand for its domestic good by more than the demand for its neighbor's good (except in the limiting case of perfect goods-market integration). Nevertheless, the country's income may not rise by more than its neighbor's income. Differences in supply responses and in other goods-market characteristics can get in the way. Here is the strongest statement we can make: If a country's income is more responsive than that of its neighbor to an open-market purchase of the neighbor's bond, it must be more responsive and by a greater margin to an open-market purchase of its own domestic bond.

Interdependent monetary policies

These examples and generalizations have important implications for the policy responses required to achieve predetermined income targets. Those responses will not be symmetrical when countries' goods markets are not symmetrical in their reactions to changes in demands. If Northern income is the more responsive to a change in demand, the open-market purchase of the domestic bond needed to raise Northern income will be smaller than the purchase needed to raise Southern income by the same amount. This is the case described by Figure 15.8, where the Northern good is less readily substitutable for the foreign good ($u_{10}^t < u_{20}^t$) and the value of Northern output is more price responsive ($\sigma_1 > \sigma_2'$). Both differences make Northern income more sensitive than Southern income to changes in absorption, wherever they originate. There is a wider wedge between the Northern policy reaction curve, I–I, and a $-45°$ line (not drawn) than between that line and the Southern curve, II–II. As before, the reaction curves are drawn for the case in which each country seeks to stabilize its income, assuming less than perfect integration in both asset and goods markets, and $K-K$ is the locus of open-market operations that cause no change in aggregate income.[19]

---

[19] The slope of $K-K$ is greater or less than $-45°$ as $\sigma_1 u_{20}^t > \sigma_2' u_{10}^t$. Because $u_{20}^t > u_{10}^t$ and $\sigma_1 > \sigma_2'$ in this example, $K-K$ is flatter than it was in Figure 15.6.

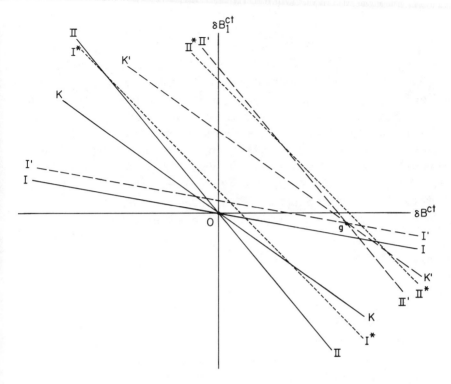

Figure 15.8 Policy interdependence without goods-market symmetry: policy reaction curves for open-market operations required to achieve short-run income targets under pegged exchange rates.

Curve $K'-K'$ is the locus of policy combinations that yield an increase of aggregate income ($\delta Y^t > 0$). If each country seeks to raise its own national income by half of that amount, both countries' targets will be achieved at some point on $K'-K'$. It is shown by the shift of the Northern reaction curve from I–I to I'–I' and the shift of the Southern curve from II–II to II'–II'. Because Northern income is more sensitive to changes in absorption, a smaller open-market purchase is required to achieve the Northern goal; the upward shift of the Northern curve to I'–I' is smaller than the rightward shift of the Southern curve to II'–II'. The two curves intersect at g, which lies on $K'-K'$, and the corresponding policy combination involves an open-market purchase of the Southern bond and an open-market sale of the Northern bond. Northern income has been made so much more sensitive to changes in absorption that the spillover effects from the purchase of the Southern bond stimulate Northern income excessively and must be offset in part by a sale of the Northern bond.

The side effects on interest rates and reserves are asymmetrical when, as here, unequal policy changes are required to achieve equal income targets. With the large open-market purchase of the Southern bond and small open-market sale of the Northern bond shown at g, the Southern interest rate declines unambiguously, and the direction of change in the Northern rate is ambiguous (it depends on the relative sizes of the open-market operations).[20] The average interest rate declines, however, whenever aggregate income rises. Furthermore, aggregate reserves decline, but the way in which reserves are redistributed depends, as usual, on the distribution of transactions between central banks. If each central bank confines itself to its own bond market, the policy combination at g shifts reserves from South to North, because the Southern bank buys Southern bonds and the Northern bank sells Northern bonds.

Market integration once again

With an increase in bilateral asset-market integration, the policy reaction curves in Figure 15.8 rotate around their respective intersections with a 45° line, just as they did with goods-market symmetry. In this instance, however, the pivot points of the policy reaction curves are *not* the intersection point g. Thus, as asset-market integration increases, point g moves to the southeast, and the two central banks must engage in increasingly large offsetting open-market operations. (Concomitantly, $K'-K'$ changes position and slope, with the slope approaching $-45°$.) In the limiting case of perfect asset-market integration, the Northern policy reaction curve will be I^*-I^*, the Southern curve will be II^*-II^*, and the two will be parallel. When goods-market responses are asymmetrical and bond markets are perfectly integrated, there is *no* combination of monetary policies that allows the North and South to alter their incomes by equal amounts. The two countries' interest rates move together, and any combination of open-market purchases adding up to the same sum has the same effects on aggregate demands in the North and South. When goods markets respond asymmetrically, however, identical changes in aggregate demands have different effects on the two countries' incomes. Generalizing from this example, two countries can achieve their income targets simultaneously only if the ratio of desired income changes is consistent with the ratio of actual income changes resulting from changes in ag-

[20] Algebraically, $\delta r_1 \gtrless 0$ as $\delta B_1^{ct} \gtrless (B_{12}^t/B_{11}^t) \delta B_2^{ct}$, and $\delta r_2 \gtrless 0$ as $\delta B_1^{ct} \gtrless (B_{11}^t/B_{12}^t) \delta B_2^{ct}$. In our example, with $\delta B_2^{ct} > 0$, $\delta B_1^{ct} < 0$, and $\delta B_2^{ct} > -\delta B_1^{ct}$, it is clear that $\delta r_2 < 0$, but $\delta r_1 \gtrless 0$.

gregate demands. No other set of income targets can be achieved with perfect asset-market integration.[21]

A similar story can be told about the effects of bilateral goods-market integration. With an increase of goods-market integration, larger open-market operations are required to raise the two countries' incomes by the same amounts. Furthermore, in the limiting case of perfect goods-market integration, p_1 and p'_2 will move together, and the ratio of income changes will come to depend entirely on the ratio of supply responses. For any combination of open-market operations, $(\delta \bar{Y}/\delta \bar{Y}') = (\sigma_1/\sigma'_2)$. The general conclusion for goods-market integration is the same as for asset-market integration. When goods markets are perfectly integrated, countries cannot pursue independent income targets by the use of monetary policies. There is one and only one feasible ratio of income changes.

Summing up, close integration of asset or goods markets interferes with the pursuit of independent income targets, and perfect integration of either type prohibits it. When two countries' goods markets respond symmetrically to an increase in aggregate demand and there is perfect integration of one type or the other, the two countries' incomes rise by the same amounts in response to any open-market purchase. When the countries' goods markets respond asymmetrically, the income effects are different, but the ratio of changes in incomes cannot be affected by adjusting the mix of open-market purchases.

[21] To find the feasible combination of income targets, we rewrite the equations for the policy reaction curves for the limiting case in which $-B^t_{12} \to \infty$, and solve for the ratio of income changes that causes the curves to coincide. We find that $(\delta \bar{Y}/\delta \bar{Y}') = (\sigma_1/\sigma'_2)[(M_{22} + 2M_{21})/(M_{11} + 2M_{12})]$. Thus $(\delta \bar{Y}/\delta \bar{Y}') = 1$ when $u^t_{10} = u^t_{20}$ and $\sigma_1 = \sigma'_2$.

Equations for the policy reaction curves

Desired change in Northern income: combinations of open-market operations (I–I) (Eq. 13.14b)

$$\delta B^{ct}_1 = (M_s J/\sigma_1 M_{1d})\, \delta \bar{Y} - (M_{1e}/M_{1d})\, \delta B^{ct}_2$$

Desired change in Southern income: combinations of open-market operations (II–II) (Eq. 13.15b)

$$\delta B^{ct}_2 = (M_s J/\sigma'_2 M_{2d})\, \delta \bar{Y}' - (M_{2e}/M_{2d})\, \delta B^{ct}_1$$

Given change in aggregate income: combinations of open-market operations (K–K) (Eqs. 13.14b and 13.15b)

$$\delta B^{ct}_1 = [1/(\sigma_1 M_{1d} + \sigma'_2 M_{2e})][(M_s J)\, \delta \bar{Y}^t - (\sigma_1 M_{1e} + \sigma'_2 M_{2d})\, \delta B^{ct}_2]$$

Equations for the income curves

Aggregate gross domestic product in income and exchange-rate space (Eq. 13.6)
Impact version ($z^t z^t$):

$$\delta Y^t = (M_\pi/M_s)\left(\frac{\delta\pi'}{\pi'}\right)$$

$$- (1/M_s)\{(m_1 S_1 + m_2 S_2)[(M_{22} + M_{21})\sigma_1 + M_{12}\sigma_2^t] + (m_1 S_2 + m_2 S_1)[(M_{11} + M_{12})\sigma_2' + M_{21}\sigma_1]\}\ \delta r_1$$

$$- (1/M_s)\{(m_1 S_1 + m_2 S_2)[(M_{11} + M_{12})\sigma_2' + M_{21}\sigma_1] + (m_1 S_2 + m_2 S_1)[(M_{22} + M_{21})\sigma_1 + M_{12}\sigma_2']\}\ \delta r_2$$

$$- (1/M_s)(1 - m_0)S_0[(M_{11} + 2M_{12})\sigma_2' + (M_{22} + 2M_{21})\sigma_1]\ \delta\bar{r}_0^t$$

$$+ (1/M_s)\{(-m_1 S_W)[(M_{22} + M_{21})\sigma_1 + M_{12}\sigma_2'] - m_2 S_W[(M_{11} + M_{12})\sigma_2' + M_{21}\sigma_1]\}\ \delta W^h$$

$$+ (1/M_s)\{(-m_1 S_W)[(M_{11} + M_{12})\sigma_2' + M_{21}\sigma_1] - m_2 S_W[(M_{22} + M_{21})\sigma_1 + M_{12}\sigma_2']\}\ \delta W^{h'}$$

$$- (1/M_s)[\sigma_1(M_{22} + M_{21}) + \sigma_2'(M_{11} + M_{12}) + \sigma_1(M_{21})]\ \delta c_{01}^t - (1/M_s)[\sigma_2'(M_{11} + M_{12}) + \sigma_1(M_{21})]\ \delta c_{02}^t$$

$$+ (1/M_s)\{[1 - m_1(1 - S_Y)]M_{22}\sigma_1 - m_2(1 - S_Y)]M_{11}\sigma_2' + M_Y(M_{21}\sigma_1 + M_{12}\sigma_2')\}\ \delta\bar{G}_1$$

$$+ (1/M_s)\{[1 - m_2(1 - S_Y)]M_{11}\sigma_2' - m_1(1 - S_Y)]M_{22}\sigma_1 + M_Y(M_{21}\sigma_1 + M_{12}\sigma_2')\}\ \delta\bar{G}_2$$

$$+ (1/M_s)\{[1 - m_2(1 - S_Y)]M_{22}\sigma_1 - m_1(1 - S_Y)]M_{11}\sigma_2' + M_Y(M_{21}\sigma_1 + M_{12}\sigma_2')\}\ \delta\bar{G}_1'$$

$$+ (1/M_s)\{[1 - m_1(1 - S_Y)]M_{22}\sigma_1 - m_2(1 - S_Y)]M_{11}\sigma_2' + M_Y(M_{21}\sigma_1 + M_{12}\sigma_2')\}\ \delta\bar{G}_2'$$

$$+ (1/M_s)(1 - S_Y)[m_1 M_{22}\sigma_1 + m_2 M_{11}\sigma_2' + (1 - m_0)(M_{21}\sigma_1 + M_{12}\sigma_2')]\ \delta\bar{D}$$

$$+ (1/M_s)(1 - S_Y)[m_2 M_{22}\sigma_1 + m_1 M_{11}\sigma_2' + (1 - m_0)(M_{21}\sigma_1 + M_{12}\sigma_2')]\ \delta\bar{D}'$$

Steady-state version ($Z^t Z^t$):

$$dY^t = (M_w/M_k)\left(\frac{d\pi'}{\pi'}\right) - (1/M_k)(M_0 + \sigma_1 u_{20}^t)\ dc_{01}^t - (1/M_k)(M_0 + \sigma_2' u_{10}^t)\ dc_{02}^t$$

$$+ (1/M_k)[(1 - m_1)u_{20}^t\sigma_1 - m_2 u_{10}^t\sigma_2' + m_0 M_0]\ d\bar{G}_1 + (1/M_k)[(1 - m_2)u_{10}^t\sigma_2' - m_1 u_{20}^t\sigma_1 + m_0 M_0]\ d\bar{G}_2$$

$$+ (1/M_k)[(1 - m_2)u_{20}^t\sigma_1 - m_1 u_{10}^t\sigma_2' + m_0 M_0]\ d\bar{G}_1' + (1/M_k)[(1 - m_1)u_{10}^t\sigma_2' - m_2 u_{20}^t\sigma_1 + m_0 M_0]\ d\bar{G}_2'$$

The market for the Northern good in income space on impact (Y^1Y^1) (Eq. 11.43a)

$$\delta Y = [\sigma_1/(M_{11} + M_{12})]\{[(u^t_{12}/\sigma'_2) + m_2(1 - S_Y)]\ \delta Y' + (u^t_{10} + p_1 C^t_1)\left(\frac{\delta\pi}{\pi'}\right)$$

$$- (m_1 S_1 + m_2 S_2)\ \delta r_1 - (m_1 S_2 + m_2 S_1)\ \delta r_2 - S_0(1 - m_0)\ \delta\bar{r}_0 + (-m_1 S_W)\ \delta W^h + (-m_2 S_W)\ \delta W^{h'} - \delta c^t_{01}$$

$$+ [1 - m_1(1 - S_Y)]\ \delta\bar{G}_1 - m_1(1 - S_Y)\ \delta\bar{G}_2 + [1 - m_2(1 - S_Y)]\ \delta\bar{G}'_1 - m_2(1 - S_Y)\ \delta\bar{G}'_2 + m_1(1 - S_Y)\ \delta\bar{D} + m_2(1 - S_Y)\ \delta\bar{D}'\}$$

The market for the Southern good in income space on impact (Y^2Y^2) (Eq. 11.44a)

$$\delta Y' = [\sigma'_2/(M_{22} + M_{21})]\{[(u^t_{12}/\sigma_1) + m_2(1 - S_Y)]\ \delta Y + (u^t_{20} + p_2 C^t_2)\left(\frac{\delta\pi'}{\pi'}\right)$$

$$- (m_1 S_2 + m_2 S_2)\ \delta r_1 - (m_1 S_1 + m_2 S_2)\ \delta r_2 - S_0(1 - m_0)\ \delta\bar{r}_0 + (-m_2 S_W)\ \delta W^h + (-m_1 S_W)\ \delta W^{h'} - \delta c^t_{02}$$

$$- m_2(1 - S_Y)\ \delta\bar{G}_1 + [1 - m_2(1 - S_Y)]\ \delta\bar{G}_2 - m_1(1 - S_Y)\ \delta\bar{G}'_1 + [1 - m_1(1 - S_Y)]\ \delta\bar{G}'_2 + m_2(1 - S_Y)\ \delta\bar{D} + m_1(1 - S_Y)\ \delta\bar{D}'\}$$

Constant aggregate gross domestic product in income space (Y^tY^t) (Eqs. 11.3a, 11.3b, and 13.12)

Impact version:

$$\delta Y = -\delta Y' + \delta Y^t$$

where δY^t is the change in aggregate income given by the equation for the curve $z^t z^t$

Steady-state version:

$$dY = -dY' + dY^t$$

where dY^t is the change in aggregate income given by the equation for the curve $Z^t Z^t$

The sign of each slope and shift coefficient is given by the sign (+ or −) preceding the coefficient unless otherwise indicated.

Equations for the asset-market curves

The steady-state requirement (S^tS^t) (Eqs. 11.13a plus 11.14a for $S + S' = 0$)

$$dr^t = (-S_W/2S_1^t)\, dW^{ht} - (S_Y/2S_1^t)\, dY^{at} - (S_0/S_1^t)\, d\bar{r}_0$$

The sum of the markets for domestic bonds (Eqs. 11.76a plus 11.77a)
In average interest-rate and aggregate wealth space (W^tW^t):

$$dr^t = -(B_{1W}^t/2J_S)\, dW^{ht} - (1/2J_S)(dB_1^{ct} + dB_2^{ct}) + (-B_{10}^t/J_S)\, d\bar{r}_0 + (1/2J_S)(dB_1 + dB_2')$$

In average interest-rate and aggregate reserve space (D^tD^t):

$$dr^t = (0)\bar{\pi}\, dR^t - (B_{1W}^t/J_S)V_\pi\left(\frac{d\pi}{\pi'}\right) - (1/2J_S)(dB_1^{ct} + dB_2^{ct}) + (-B_{10}^t/J_S)\, d\bar{r}_0 + (1/2J_S)(dB_1 + dB_2) - (B_{1W}^t/2J_S)\, dW^{hst}$$

The sum of the markets for domestic currencies (Eqs. 11.78a plus 11.79a)
In average interest-rate and aggregate wealth space (M^tM^t):

$$dr^t = [L_{1W}/(-2L_{11}^t)]\, dW^{ht} - [1/(-2L_{11}^t)]\bar{\pi}\, dR^t - [1/(-2L_{11}^t)](dB_1^{ct} + dB_2^{ct}) - (L_{10}/L_{11}^t)\, d\bar{r}_0$$

In average interest-rate and aggregate reserve space (R^tR^t):

$$dr^t = [L_{1W}/(-2L_{11}^t)]\bar{\pi}\, dR^t + [L_{1W}/(-L_{11}^t)]V_\pi\left(\frac{d\pi}{\pi'}\right) - [1/(-2L_{11}^t)]V_\pi\left(\frac{\delta\pi}{\pi'}\right) - [1/(-2L_{11}^t)](dB_1^{ct} + dB_2^{ct}) - (L_{10}/L_{11}^t)\, d\bar{r}_0 + [L_{1W}/(-2L_{11}^t)]\, dW^{hst}$$

The market for the Northern bond in interest-rate space (r^1r^1) or in Northern interest-rate and Northern reserve space (D^1D^1) (Eq. 11.76a)

$$\delta r_1 = (1/B_{11}^t)[(-B_{12}^t)\, \delta r_2 + (0)\bar{\pi}\, \delta R - B_{1W}^t V_\pi\left(\frac{\delta\pi}{\pi'}\right) - \delta \bar{B}_1^{ct} + (-B_{10}^t)\, \delta\bar{r}_0 - (B_{1W})\, \delta W^{hs} - (B_{2W})\, \delta W^{hst} + \delta B_1']$$

434

The market for the Southern bond in interest-rate space (r^2r^2) or in Southern reserve space (D^2D^2) (Eq. 11.77a)

$$\delta r_2 = (1/B_{11}^t)[(-B_{12}^t)\,\delta r_1 + (0)\bar{\pi}'\,\delta R' - B_{1W}^t V_\pi\left(\frac{\delta\pi'}{\pi'}\right) - \delta\bar{B}_2^{ct} + (-B_{10}^t)\,\delta\bar{r}_0 - (B_{2W})\,\delta W^{hs} + (B_{1W})\,\delta W^{hs'} + \delta B_2']$$

The market for Northern money in Northern interest-rate and Northern reserve space (R^1R^1) (Eq. 11.78a)

$$\delta r_1 = (-1/L_{11})[-\bar{\pi}\,\delta R - (-L_{12})\,\delta r_2 + L_{1W}V_\pi\left(\frac{\delta\pi'}{\pi'}\right) - (d\bar{B}_1^c + \delta\bar{B}_2^c) + (L_{1W})\,\delta W^{hs} - (-L_{10})\,\delta\bar{r}_0]$$

The market for Southern money in Southern interest-rate and Southern reserve space (R^2R^2) (Eq. 11.79a)

$$\delta r_2 = (-1/L_{11})[-\bar{\pi}'\,\delta R' - (-L_{12})\,\delta r_1 + L_{1W}V_\pi\left(\frac{\delta\pi'}{\pi'}\right) - (\delta\bar{B}_1^{c'} + \sigma\bar{B}_2^{c'}) + (L_{1W})\,\delta W^{hs'} - (-L_{10})\,\delta\bar{r}_0]$$

Constant average interest rate in interest-rate space (r^tr^t) (equation for the curve W^tW^t)

$$\delta r_1 = -\delta r_2 - (B_{1W}^t/J_S)\,\delta W^{ht} - (1/J_S)(\delta\bar{B}_2^{ct} + \delta\bar{B}_2^{ct}) + (-2B_{10}^t)/J_S)\,\delta\bar{r}_0 + (1/J_S)(\delta B_1 + \delta B_2')$$

Constant aggregate reserves in reserve space (R^aR^a) (equation for the curve M^tM^t)

$$\bar{\pi}\,\delta R = -\bar{\pi}'\,\delta R' - (-2L_{11}^t)\,\delta r^t + (L_{1W})\,\delta W^{ht} - (\delta\bar{B}_1^{ct} + \delta\bar{B}_2^{ct}) - (-2L_{10})\,\delta\bar{r}_0$$

The equations shown here for the sums of the markets for bonds and of markets for currencies are the steady-state versions. The equations for the impact versions of W^tW^t, D^tD^t, M^tM^t, and R^tR^t differ only in that they omit terms relating to dB_1, dB_2', and dW^{hst}.

16

The analytics of a monetary union

Monetary unification and
the balance-of-payments constraint

In the previous chapter we showed that the scope for independent national monetary policies is severely limited when countries adopt pegged exchange rates and their economies are structurally integrated. The decision by two countries to peg exchange rates, bilaterally and vis-à-vis the outside world, becomes in the long run an assignment of each country's monetary instrument to an exchange-rate target. Even in the short run, moreover, the countries in our model can aim their monetary instruments at separate income targets only if the countries' markets are not closely integrated, and a country's freedom to pursue its own income target is still constrained by the size of its reserves. When two countries' goods or asset markets are perfectly integrated, they have no freedom whatsoever to pursue independent income targets. Their monetary instruments are unified de facto into a single instrument that can be used in the short run to influence the sum of the two countries' incomes, or aggregate income, but not the *distribution* of aggregate income. When markets are perfectly integrated, the distribution of aggregate income is determined by goods-market responses – the nature and extent of goods-market asymmetries. It cannot be affected by the manipulation of the countries' single monetary instrument.

When two countries' monetary instruments are unified de facto, or very nearly so, it is essential to coordinate the use of those instruments, and a strong case can be made for full-fledged monetary unification. At the very least, the two countries must agree on their short-run income targets, within the constraints imposed by goods-market responses, if they propose to use monetary policies to pursue those targets. Even when markets are not perfectly integrated, so that income targets can be differentiated, each country needs to take account of spillovers from the other. Furthermore, with closely integrated markets, offsetting open-market operations are required to achieve differentiated income targets, and these opera-

436

tions may be unacceptable, because they have large effects on the distribution of reserves. It may be necessary to limit the independent use of
monetary instruments in order to prevent large shifts of reserves from one
country to the other, and limitations on the uses of the instruments call in
turn for limitations on the differentiation of income targets.

Coming at this last point from the opposite direction, suppose that two
countries are able to harmonize their short-run income targets, whether
by choosing a single target for aggregate income or by aligning their separate national targets to guarantee feasibility. They still must coordinate
the uses of their monetary instruments. There must be an agreed division
of responsibilities between the central banks. This may not be possible if
each country must protect its own reserve position. Inconsistencies and
conflicts can arise in any arrangement under which countries harmonize
their income and exchange-rate targets and then try to use their monetary
instruments to achieve the income targets. Each country is left with the
need to protect its own reserve position but has given up the requisite
flexibility in the use of its monetary instrument.[1] Reverting to the language of Chapter 14, the number of independent instruments is smaller
than the number of policy targets (but partly because we have yet to allow
for the use of fiscal policies to pursue the countries' income or balance-
of-payments targets).

There are three ways out of this difficulty. (1) Each country can give up
its exchange-rate target, letting its currency float. This option was one
studied in Part II, for the single small economy. (2) The two countries can
abandon the pursuit of income targets by monetary policies, leaving each
to use its monetary instrument to achieve its reserve target and to pursue
its income target by another means. We return to this option in Chapter
17, where we ask to what extent countries can use fiscal policies to pursue
their income targets when goods and asset markets are closely integrated.
(3) The two countries can abandon the pursuit of independent reserve
targets, which is to say that they must pool their reserves and thus form a
full-fledged monetary union. This is the option studied here.

---

[1] In the United States, the Federal Reserve System resolves this problem by centralizing
responsibility for the conduct of open-market operations and apportioning securities
bought or sold among the 12 Federal Reserve Banks to protect the Banks' reserve positions. Settlements among the Banks, reflecting surpluses and deficits in interregional payments, are made in "external" reserves (Gold Certificates), but any Bank that runs short of
reserves can replenish them by transferring government securities to other Banks. There
can be no balance-of-payments crisis within the System. See D. B. McCalmont, "Gold-
Reserve Sharing Among Federal Reserve Banks," *Review of Economics and Statistics*, 45
(May 1963), pp. 211–15.

Why is it necessary to pool reserves? Would it not be possible for countries to agree to settle their bilateral imbalances in another way–by using bookkeeping credits to offset the shifts of reserves resulting from the joint use of their monetary instruments? The answer is obvious and negative.

If countries agreed to settle bilateral imbalances by bookkeeping credits rather than transfers of reserves, there would be no reason for conflict concerning the division of responsibilities between central banks. If the credits were unlimited in size, moreover, and did not have to be repaid, the arrangement might never break down. But it could distort real resource allocation. Suppose that the North tended normally to run a balance-of-payments surplus with the South and a deficit of similar absolute size with the outside world. If the North had agreed to accept bookkeeping credits from the South, rather than reserves, it could not finance its deficit with the outside world and might be driven to employ discriminatory restrictions or incentives to shift the pattern of trade and payments.[2] There is even the danger of predatory behavior. The South might seek to run a larger deficit with the North, using bookkeeping credits to lay claim to Northern resources.

If the credits were limited or had to be repaid, these difficulties would be minimized. But others would take their place. If credits were limited in size, the South would exhaust them eventually because of its ongoing deficit with the North (and might exhaust them more rapidly because of the role assigned to the Southern central bank in the conduct of an integrated monetary policy). It would then have to start using its reserves. If credits had to be repaid, they would serve merely to postpone the day of reckoning; the South might not be able to repay them, given the size of its surplus with the outside world (or its role in the integrated monetary policy). Credits that are limited or have to be repaid do not fully relieve a country of the need to protect its reserves.

Credit arrangements can play an important part in monetary unification, especially in the transition to a full-fledged monetary union, while the members are working to harmonize policy targets and instruments.[3] In the end, however, countries that agree to integrate their monetary instruments must also agree to give up the pursuit of independent reserve targets, which is tantamount to saying that they must agree to pool their reserves in one way or another. They must form a full-fledged monetary union.

This line of argument should not be read to say that countries must

[2] Difficulties of this type arose in the European Payments Union. See R. Triffin, *Europe and the Money Muddle,* Yale University Press, New Haven, Conn., 1957, pp. 203–4.
[3] Thus, credit arrangements are given an important role in the plan for exchange-rate unification adopted by members of the European Community in December 1978.

agree to join a monetary union whenever they peg their exchange rates. The optimal degree of monetary unification depends in large measure on the degree of market integration and thus on the degree to which monetary unification has taken place de facto. It also depends on issues and considerations that lie outside the scope of our formal model. Furthermore, countries that might be good candidates for membership in a monetary union may underestimate the actual extent of monetary integration and, therefore, overestimate the independence they enjoy under pegged exchange rates. They will then overestimate the extent to which monetary unification requires a sacrifice or compromise of national objectives. Above all, political difficulties, internal to each country and in their relations with each other, stand in the way of monetary unification and are hard to overcome.[4]

Finally, our argument is incomplete. Countries that agree to harmonize their income targets, unify their monetary instruments, and pool their reserves must take one more step. They must agree on a common reserve target or balance-of-payments policy and take account of it when they choose an income target. Alternatively, they can agree to let their common external exchange rate float, so as to free their common monetary policy not only to pursue a short-run income target but also to make permanent income changes.

We begin our formal analysis by looking at this last possibility, with a view to answering a number of questions. What are the effects of open-market operations under a flexible external exchange rate? How do they influence aggregate income? How do they influence the members' incomes taken separately? How do aggregate and national incomes respond to external disturbances under a flexible external rate, as compared with a pegged rate, and how are these responses affected by goods-market asymmetries?

Open-market operations under a flexible external rate

When two countries form a monetary union and pool their reserves, the two stocks of reserves, R and R', are replaced by their sum, R^t. Accordingly, the analysis of open-market operations in Chapter 15, although cast in terms of autonomous decisions by national central banks, applies fully to the conduct of monetary policy by a single union-wide central bank

---

[4] For a formal attempt to deal with some of the issues that fall outside our model, see K. Hamada, "A Strategic Analysis of Monetary Interdependence," *Journal of Political Economy*, 84 (August 1976), pp. 677–700. Using a two-country, pegged-rate model, he finds that the Cournot (noncooperative) solution is not Pareto optimal, except under very special conditions.

when the union pegs its external exchange rate. The effects of open-market operations on aggregate and average variables, such as W^{ht}, Y^t, R^t, and r^t, do not depend on the bond bought or sold or on the bank involved; their effects on national variables, apart from holdings of reserves, depend on the nationality of the bond but not that of the bank. (The nationality of the bond ceases to have any importance in the limiting case of perfect asset-market integration, and it is unimportant for the distribution of income changes in the case of perfect goods-market integration.)

When a union opts for a flexible external rate, the union-wide effects of open-market operations continue to be independent of the bond bought or sold. Like the effects obtaining with a pegged external rate, they correspond completely to the effects of open-market operations in the domestic bond of the single small economy studied in Part II. The effects on the national economies, however, continue to depend on the nationality of the bond, and they are somewhat different with a flexible external rate than they were in Chapter 15, with a pegged external rate. We look first at the union-wide effects, then at the effects on the national economies.

Effects on union aggregates

When the union's central bank purchases the Northern or Southern bond, raising the demand for bonds within the union, it reduces the average interest rate, r^t. As a result, households want to increase their holdings of the foreign (world) bond. Under a pegged external rate, the demand for the foreign bond is satisfied by an instantaneous exchange of money for bonds; there is an immediate loss of reserves (a fall in R^t). Under a flexible external rate, the demand is satisfied by a joint depreciation of the countries' currencies, as in Chapter 5. Furthermore, the capital gains conferred by the depreciation add to the demands for domestic bonds by raising wealth, so that the average interest rate falls farther than it does with a pegged external rate.

These instantaneous effects on asset markets are shown in Figure 16.1, the counterpart of Figure 5.3 for the single small economy. The equations for the curves in Figure 16.1A were given in the tables at the end of Chapter 15; those for the curves in Figure 16.1B are given in the table at the end of this chapter.[5] In Figure 16.1A, asset-market equilibrium moves from w to w^*, where the increase in aggregate wealth, W^{ht}, reflects the capital gain conferred by the joint depreciation of the countries' cur-

---

[5] Equations for the curves W^1W^1, W^2W^2, M^1M^1, M^2M^2, S^1S^1, S^2S^2, and $W^{ht}W^{ht}$, used in Figure 16.3, also appear at the end of this chapter, whereas those for other curves used in this chapter appear at the end of Chapter 15.

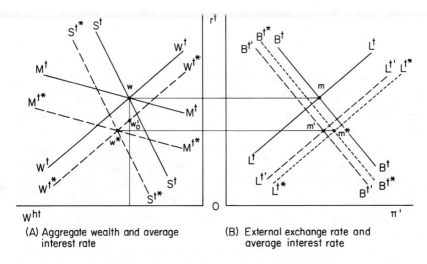

(A) Aggregate wealth and average
interest rate

(B) External exchange rate and
average interest rate

Figure 16.1 Open-market purchase of the Northern or Southern bond by the union central bank: impact and steady-state effects on aggregate asset markets under a flexible external rate.

rencies. If the external rate were pegged, as in Chapter 15, asset-market equilibrium would have moved to w'_0, as wealth could not change instantaneously, and the decline in the average interest rate would have been smaller. In Figure 16.1B, asset-market equilibrium is displaced from m to m', reducing r^t and raising π'.

The increase in aggregate wealth and decline in the average interest rate reduce aggregate saving within the monetary union, raising aggregate absorption. In addition, the joint depreciation of the countries' currencies switches demands, as usual. Northerners, Southerners, and foreigners buy more Northern and Southern goods and fewer foreign goods. The increase of absorption and switch in demands cause an immediate increase in aggregate income. Thus, in Figure 16.2A, the short-run income curve shifts from z^tz^t to $z^{t'}z^{t'}$, reflecting the increase of absorption, and there is a movement along the curve, reflecting the switch in demands. (The size of the latter depends, of course, on the size of the depreciation. It is denoted by the shift from $\pi'_0\pi'_0$ to $\pi'_1\pi'_1$ and is determined in the short run by the asset markets.) Goods-market equilibrium is displaced from v to v'. With a pegged external rate, by contrast, goods-market equilibrium would have been displaced to a point below v'_0, and the increase in aggregate income would have been smaller.[6]

[6] The point would lie *below* v'_0 because the shift of the short-run income curve would be smaller with a pegged external rate; aggregate wealth would not increase, and the average interest rate would fall by less.

In Chapter 5 we showed that an open-market purchase could give rise to a current-account deficit or surplus, depending on the size of the increase in absorption compared to the size of the switch in demands. That is true here too. In Figure 16.2A, the North and South together are shown to run a current-account deficit (which is, of course, a deficit vis-à-vis the outside world), because there is dissaving at v'. If the short-run income curve had shifted less, however, v' could have been below the long-run income curve, $Z^t Z^t$, given the size of the exchange-rate change and the slope of the short-run income curve, which determine the switch in demands. There would have been saving, not dissaving, and a current-account surplus rather than a deficit. (The same thing would have happened, given the size of the shift in $z^t z^t$, if the exchange-rate change had been large enough to locate v' to the right of v^* and, therefore, below the long-run curve.)

If a current-account deficit emerges on impact, dissaving and the capital inflow that goes with it cause a gradual depreciation of the countries' currencies, additional to the depreciation shown by the shift to $\pi'_1 \pi'_1$ in Figure 16.2A. This depreciation eliminates the current-account deficit, causing an additional increase in aggregate income that serves, in turn, to eliminate dissaving. The passage to long-run equilibrium is depicted in Figure 16.2A by the move from v' to v^*.[7] The permanent level of the external exchange rate is determined by the requirement of steady-state equilibrium in Northern and Southern goods markets taken together. Furthermore, the capital inflow that takes place through time is such as to guarantee that aggregate wealth and the average interest rate remain unchanged during the transition to the new steady state. Reverting to Figure 16.1A, asset-market equilibrium stays at w^*, and the steady-state (zero-saving) curve shifts from $S^t S^t$ to $S^{t*} S^{t*}$, which is to say that Y^t rises permanently. In Figure 16.1B, asset-market equilibrium moves gradually from m' to m^* under the influence of dissaving, causing the bond-market curve to move from $B^{t'} B^{t'}$ to $B^{t*} B^{t*}$ and the money-market curve to move from $L^{t'} L^{t'}$ to $L^{t*} L^{t*}$.

There are thus two ways in which a flexible external rate enhances the effectiveness of a unified monetary policy. First, it enlarges the short-run increase in aggregate income resulting from an open-market purchase. It does so more potently, moreover, the higher the degree of substitutability between the partners' bonds and those of the outside world. (With a

[7] If a current-account surplus emerges on impact, the countries' currencies appreciate jointly through time, and aggregate income falls. There is "overshooting" in the short run, as was shown in Chapter 5 for the single small economy.

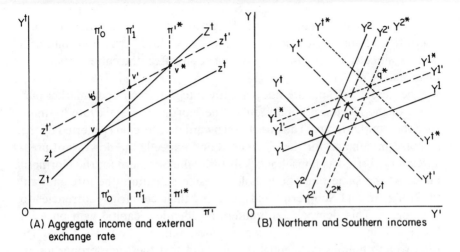

(A) Aggregate income and external exchange rate

(B) Northern and Southern incomes

Figure 16.2 Open-market purchase of the Northern or Southern bond by the union central bank: impact and steady-state effects on aggregate and national goods markets under a flexible external rate.

pegged external rate, by contrast, the effectiveness of monetary policy varies inversely with substitutability, and it falls to zero even in the short run when the partners' bonds are perfect substitutes for the foreign bond.)[8] Second, and more fundamental, a flexible external rate confers on a monetary union the capacity to influence permanently the sum of its members' incomes, Y^t, just as it gives a single country the capacity to influence permanently its national income. As is always the case in this book, however, a permanent increase in income can be a pure price change or a combination of price and output changes, depending on conditions in the labor markets.

Effects on the members' economies

When the external exchange rate is pegged, the responses of the Northern and Southern economies, taken individually, depend on the bond involved in an open-market operation. If goods-market responses are symmetrical, for example, and goods and asset markets are not perfectly integrated, an open-market purchase of the Northern bond causes an immediate increase in each country's income but a larger increase in Northern income. When the external exchange rate is flexible, the same

[8] See the discussion in Chapter 5, especially pp. 120–2.

things happen, but Northern and Southern incomes are affected permanently. We must therefore look at long-run outcomes, not merely at impact effects, and must also show how a flexible external rate interacts with asymmetrical goods-market responses to affect the pattern of income changes.

When asset markets are not perfectly integrated, an open-market purchase of the Northern bond reduces the Northern interest rate by more than the Southern rate. The direct downward pressure on r_1 exerted by the increase in demand for the Northern bond exceeds the downward pressure on r_2 exerted as households substitute the Southern for the Northern bond. At the same time, households seek to substitute the foreign bond for Northern and Southern bonds, causing their countries' currencies to depreciate. This depreciation confers an identical capital gain on each household in each country, given our assumptions about asset holdings (that wealth holdings are equal initially and that the same proportion of each household's wealth is invested in the foreign bond). By raising wealth, these capital gains raise the demands for Northern and Southern bonds, putting additional downward pressure on the Northern and Southern interest rates. The consequences are shown in Figure 16.3A, where the Northern bond-market curve shifts from r^1r^1 to $r^{1'}r^{1'}$, the Southern curve shifts from r^2r^2 to $r^{2'}r^{2'}$, and asset-market equilibrium is displaced from s to s'. The increase in aggregate wealth is shown in Figure 16.3C by the shift from $W^{ht}W^{ht}$ to $W^{ht*}W^{ht*}$, and the equal increase in each country's wealth is shown by the movement from x to x'.

If goods-market responses are symmetrical, the purchase of the Northern bond will raise Northern income by more than Southern income. When r_1 falls farther than r_2, the reduction in Northern saving is larger than in Southern saving, and there is thus a larger increase in the demand for the Northern good. (There is a larger increase in Northern absorption, and each country's marginal propensity to consume its own domestic good is larger than its marginal propensity to consume its partner's good.) The result is shown in Figure 16.2B, where the Northern income curve shifts upward by more than the Southern curve shifts rightward, and goods-market equilibrium is displaced from q to q'. (An equivalent purchase of the Southern bond would have caused r_2 to fall by more than r_1 and Y' to rise by more than Y, although the effects on r^t and Y^t would have been the same.)

Thus, the introduction of a flexible external rate does not modify the short-run result obtained in Chapter 15. When markets are imperfectly integrated and goods-market responses are symmetrical, a centralized mon-

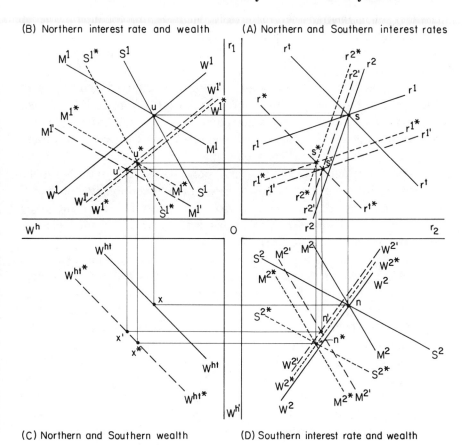

(B) Northern interest rate and wealth

(A) Northern and Southern interest rates

(C) Northern and Southern wealth

(D) Southern interest rate and wealth

Figure 16.3 Open-market purchase of the Northern bond by the union central bank: impact and steady-state effects on national asset markets under a flexible external rate.

etary policy can control the distribution of short-run income changes. The central bank merely has to choose the appropriate national securities when making open-market purchases and sales.

But an important qualification has also to be carried over from Chapter 15. As asset markets become more closely integrated, it is increasingly difficult to control the distribution of income changes. The links between interest rates grow stronger, making it harder to manipulate interest-rate differences and thus harder to control the distribution of changes in saving (absorption). As goods markets become more closely integrated, moreover, the relevance of differences in interest rates diminishes. The links between prices grow stronger, making it harder to manipulate price differences, even when the central bank is able to control the distribution of changes in saving. In general, then, market integration reduces the extent to which a monetary union can control the incidence of short-run income changes.

How do the Northern and Southern economies adapt through time to an open-market purchase of the Northern bond? When goods markets respond symmetrically, the initial depreciation of the countries' currencies has the same demand-switching effects on each country's trade balance. When asset markets are not perfectly integrated, however, an open-market purchase of the Northern bond was seen to raise Northern absorption by more than Southern absorption. Accordingly, the North must experience a larger deterioration or smaller improvement in its current-account balance, which means that Northerners must dissave more or save less than Southerners.

Taken by itself, this finding tells us that Northern wealth must fall more or rise less than Southern wealth as the countries travel to their new steady state. But taken together with another fact – that aggregate wealth remains unchanged after the initial increase – it tells us that there must be a gradual redistribution from North to South. Northern wealth must fall and Southern wealth must rise, each by the same absolute amount. When North and South together run a current-account deficit, the North will run the larger deficit, and dissaving in the North will more than offset the wealth-increasing effect of the gradual additional depreciation of the countries' currencies. Northern wealth will fall. When North and South together run a current-account surplus, the North will run the smaller surplus, and saving in the North will not completely offset the wealth-decreasing effect of the gradual appreciation.[9] The redistribution of wealth through time is shown in Figure 16.3C by the movement from x' to x^*.

As Northern wealth falls and Southern wealth rises, demand for the Northern bond will fall and demand for the Southern bond will rise; Northern demands for all assets will fall, Southern demands for all assets

---

[9] The change through time in aggregate wealth must equal the inflow of assets (the capital outflow) *plus* the net capital gain on holdings of the foreign bond:

$$\dot{W}^{ht} = \pi'(\dot{B}_0^h + \dot{B}_0^{h\prime}) + \pi'(B_0^h + B_0^{h\prime})\left(\frac{\dot{\pi}'}{\pi'}\right) = (\dot{W}^{hs} + \dot{W}^{hs\prime}) + 2V_\pi\left(\frac{\dot{\pi}'}{\pi'}\right)$$

But $\dot{W}^{ht} = 0$, so that $(\dot{\pi}'/\pi') = -[(\dot{W}^{hs} + \dot{W}^{hs\prime})/2V_\pi]$. Thus, $\dot{W}^h = \dot{W}^{hs} + V_\pi(\dot{\pi}'/\pi') = [(\dot{W}^{hs} - \dot{W}^{hs\prime})/2]$ and $\dot{W}^{h\prime} = \dot{W}^{hs\prime} + V_\pi(\dot{\pi}'/\pi') = -[(\dot{W}^{hs} - \dot{W}^{hs\prime})/2]$. When the North has the smaller current-account surplus (or larger current-account deficit), so that $\dot{W}^{hs} < \dot{W}^{hs\prime}$, Northern wealth falls and Southern wealth rises.

will rise, but the fall in the Northern demand for the Northern bond will exceed the rise in the Southern demand. The Northern interest rate will rise through time, and the Southern rate will fall, narrowing the difference between the changes in interest rates.

When an open-market purchase causes the monetary union as a whole to run a current-account deficit, aggregate income will rise through time; the two countries' currencies will continue to depreciate. But Northern income cannot rise as rapidly as Southern income, even with full-scale goods-market symmetry. As wealth is redistributed from North to South, while r_1 rises and r_2 falls, Southern absorption must rise relative to Northern absorption. Eventually, Southern income will catch up with Northern income, and when the steady state is reached, the income changes will be equal in the North and South, regardless of the bond bought by the central bank. Each national goods market must clear at the long-run equilibrium exchange rate given by v^* in Figure 16.2A, and when goods markets respond symmetrically to price and exchange-rate changes, this happens only at q^* in Figure 16.2B, where income changes are the same in the North and South.

Each country's interest rate is lower in the new steady state, but the reduction in the Northern rate is the larger of the two when the Northern bond is purchased – despite the convergence of interest rates that takes place through time. In Figure 16.3A, the increase in r_1 and the decrease in r_2 that occur with the movement from s' to s^* are not big enough to offset the change in relative interest rates that occurred on impact, with the movement from s to s'. Finally, Southern wealth is sure to rise, as is shown by the movement from n' to n^* in Figure 16.3D, for this movement is additional to the one from n to n'. But the long-run change in Northern wealth is ambiguous. It is shown to rise in Figure 16.3B, where the decline that takes place with the movement from u' to u^* is smaller than the increase that took place with the movement from u to u'. But the gradual decline in Northern wealth on the way to the steady state may or may not be sufficiently large to swamp the capital gain that was realized on impact.

In summary, the changes in steady-state incomes are the same in North and South under full-scale goods-market symmetry. They are thus independent of the bond that is purchased and cannot be controlled by monetary policy. By allowing its common external exchange rate to float, a monetary union can achieve long-lasting control over the level of aggregate income, but it cannot achieve control over the distribution of aggregate income. Nevertheless, the union's central bank should not be indifferent to the long-run effects of buying one bond or the other. When asset markets are not perfectly integrated, a purchase of the Northern bond will cause a larger decrease in the Northern interest rate and a smaller increase (even a decrease) in Northern wealth.

Extending the analysis

There are two ways of extending this analysis. First, we can allow for goods-market asymmetries, just as we did in the previous chapter. Second, we can reinterpret our results to ask what would happen if two countries were to form a simple exchange-rate union or joint float but were also to conduct autonomous monetary policies.[10]

How heavily do the results obtained above depend on the assumption of goods-market symmetry? If goods markets do *not* respond symmetrically to price and exchange-rate changes, it is impossible to know which country's income will rise farther in the short run, even when we know which bond is bought by the union's central bank. When the value of Southern output is more price responsive than the value of Northern output (when $\sigma_2' > \sigma_1$), and in other circumstances too, Southern income may be more responsive to an increase of absorption, whatever its origin. An open-market purchase of the Northern bond is then capable of raising Southern income by more than Northern income. (In this case, however, we can draw one conclusion. Southern income would rise even farther, absolutely and by comparison to Northern income, in response to a purchase of the Southern bond.)

This is, of course, the same agnostic conclusion that we drew in Chapter 15 when we allowed for goods-market asymmetries. The introduction of a flexible external exchange rate does not alter it. Putting the point in general terms, a unified monetary policy is able in principle to control the distribution of short-term income changes when goods and asset markets are not perfectly integrated, but goods-market asymmetries make the task more complicated. The central bank must know the direction and degree of asymmetry in order to choose the appropriate mix of Northern and Southern securities. It cannot count on raising Northern income relative to Southern income merely by purchasing the Northern bond.[11]

---

[10] This is, of course, the analogue of the question asked in Chapter 15, where the North and South pursued autonomous monetary policies but pegged their exchange rates completely. It is not a hypothetical question; the members of the European "snake" have operated in this fashion.

[11] With a flexible external rate, moreover, the task is especially complicated. If the external exchange rate is pegged, Eqs. (13.14b) and (13.15b) can be made to yield simple sufficient

When goods markets respond asymmetrically, moreover, no simple statements can be made concerning the responses of current-account balances, the direction in which wealth is redistributed, or the changes through time in national interest rates. It is therefore impossible to make any simple statement about the paths of Northern and Southern incomes, even when we know the path of aggregate income. By implication, it is harder to know where each country's income will come to rest. With symmetrical goods markets, the changes in steady-state incomes are identical. With asymmetrical markets, they need not be the same, and the relationship between them will not necessarily correspond to the relationship between the short-run changes.[12] These findings, however, serve merely to reinforce the basic point made above. The configuration of changes in national incomes is determined in the long run by the responses of goods markets to changes in the flexible external exchange rate and thus by the particular characteristics of Northern and Southern goods markets. That configuration cannot be controlled by monetary policy.

We have had no occasion heretofore to mention movements of reserves between North and South. We have been dealing with a full-fledged monetary union, in which monetary targets and instruments are unified and reserves are pooled. It is not difficult, however, to deal with the case in which two countries form a simple exchange-rate union and opt for a joint float but continue to pursue autonomous monetary policies. We do so briefly here, by showing what happens when the Northern central bank tries to stimulate the Northern economy by purchasing the Northern bond.

In Figure 16.3B, the Northern bond-market curve shifts downward from W^1W^1 to $W^{1'}W^{1'}$, on account of the increase in the central bank's demand for the Northern bond and the influence of the reduction in the Southern interest rate induced by substitution of the Southern for the Northern bond. In Figure 16.3D, the Southern bond-market curve shifts leftward from W^2W^2 to $W^{2'}W^{2'}$, on account of the reduction in the Northern interest rate. (This shift is smaller than the shift in the Northern

conditions under which an open-market purchase of the Northern bond will raise Northern income relative to Southern income. This "normal" outcome will occur whenever $\sigma_1 \geq \sigma_0'$ and $u_{20}^t \geq u_{10}^t$. If the external rate is flexible, Eqs. (13.14a) and (13.15a) apply, and one can show that these conditions are far from sufficient. Nevertheless, the equations and tables in Chapter 13 convey one important fact. No open-market purchase can reduce a country's income – not in the short run or the long run.

[12] The relationship between the short-run changes depends in part on asset-market responses; see Eqs. (13.14a) and (13.15a). The relationship between the long-run changes depends exclusively on goods-market responses. From Eqs. (13.23a) and (13.24a), $(dY/dY') = (\sigma_1 U_{1\pi}/\sigma_2' U_{2\pi})$, which is always nonnegative and is equal to unity when $\sigma_1 = \sigma_2'$, $u_{10}^t = u_{20}^t$, and $p_1 C_1^t = p_2 C_2^t$ (the conditions that obtain with goods-market symmetry).

curve, which includes the direct effect of the open-market purchase.) In Figure 16.3A, moreover, the Northern bond-market curve shifts from r^1r^1 to $r^{1'}r^{1'}$ and the Southern curve shifts from r^2r^2 to $r^{2'}r^{2'}$, displacing bond-market equilibrium from s to s'.[13] In the North, then, asset-market equilibrium is displaced from u to u', the point on $W^{1'}W^{1'}$ consistent with the new Northern interest rate, and the Northern money-market curve must shift from M^1M^1 to $M^{1'}M^{1'}$. In the South, asset-market equilibrium is displaced from n to n', and the Southern money-market curve must shift from M^2M^2 to $M^{2'}M^{2'}$.

This last shift is especially important. It denotes an increase in the Southern money supply and, by inference, a transfer of reserves from North to South. (If the Southern money supply were constant, M^2M^2 would have shifted in the opposite direction; an increase in r_2 would have been needed to clear the Southern money market in the face of the decrease in r_1. An increase in the Southern money supply implies a transfer of reserves, because the Southern central bank has taken no initiative.) At the initial interest rates given by s in Figure 16.3A, the open-market purchase by the Northern central bank produces an excess supply of money in the North and, thus, an excess demand for Northern, Southern, and foreign bonds. The excess demand for Southern bonds shows up in the foreign-exchange market as an increase in demand for Southern currency, and the central banks must intervene to keep it from appreciating in terms of Northern currency. It is this intervention that transfers reserves from North to South.[14] Intervention does not alter the sum of the supplies of money in the North and South, as it does when the external exchange rate is pegged. Instead, it transforms Northern money into Southern money, so that each country's money market can be cleared.

When goods markets are symmetrical, the movement from impact to steady state involves, as we have seen, a gradual redistribution of wealth from North to South, a rise in the Northern interest rate, and a decline in the Southern rate. The redistribution of wealth is reflected in Figure 16.3A by the upward shift of the Northern bond-market curve from $r^{1'}r^{1'}$ to $r^{1*}r^{1*}$ and the leftward shift of the Southern curve from $r^{2'}r^{2'}$ to $r^{2*}r^{2*}$,

[13] The shift of r^1r^1 is just large enough to hold r_2 constant in the face of the changes in r_1 and W^h and the change induced in $W^{h'}$. The shift of W^2W^2, by contrast, is just large enough to hold $W^{h'}$ constant in the face of the changes in r_1 and W^h and the change induced in r_2.

[14] On the modes of intervention that can give this result, see Chapter 11, especially pp. 312–14. If the Northern bank had bought the Southern bond, the Northern interest rate would have fallen by less than the Southern rate. With asset-market symmetry, however, Northern reserves would have fallen. They would in fact have fallen farther, because the Northern central bank would have had to purchase Southern currency in order to buy the Southern bond. See Eq. (E.2a) in Appendix E.

displacing asset market equilibrium from s' to s^*. In Figure 16.3B, moreover, the decrease in the Southern interest rate causes a downward shift of the Northern bond-market curve from $W^{1'}W^{1'}$ to $W^{1*}W^{1*}$, and in Figure 16.3D, the increase in the Northern rate causes a rightward shift of the Southern curve from $W^{2'}W^{2'}$ to $W^{2*}W^{2*}$. Steady-state equilibria are established at u^* and n^* in the North and South, respectively (at the points on $W^{1*}W^{1*}$ and $W^{2*}W^{2*}$ that go with the interest rates prevailing at s^*). In the North, then, the steady-state zero-saving curve is displaced from S^1S^1 to $S^{1*}S^{1*}$, and the money-market curve is displaced from $M^{1'}M^{1'}$ to $M^{1*}M^{1*}$, and analogous shifts occur in the South.[15]

The shifts in the money-market curves do not tell us what we want to know about reserves. The shift in the Northern curve, for example, would seem to say that the North has lost reserves, but some such shift would occur, even if there were no loss, to reflect the effect of the decline in the Southern interest rate. When goods markets are symmetrical, however, it can be shown that the North continues to lose reserves on the way to the steady state.[16] A movement of reserves from North to South is, in fact, implied by the transfer of wealth from North to South, shown by the shift from x' to x^* in Figure 16.3C.

When goods markets are not symmetrical, long-run outcomes can be different. Reserves can flow from South to North over the long run. These possibilities, however, do not weaken the general conclusions to be drawn from Figure 16.3.

First, it is clear that the Northern central bank can raise Northern income in the short run, and when the external exchange rate is flexible, can raise it permanently too. In the process, however, it will raise Southern income in the short run and the long run, and the Southern central bank may undertake offsetting measures. By participating in a joint float, each central bank acquires the power to influence domestic income permanently, something it does not have with a pegged external rate. By rais-

---

[15] Although the changes in incomes (and disposable incomes) are the same in the two countries with goods-market symmetry, the shift from S^1S^1 to $S^{1*}S^{1*}$ in Figure 16.3B is larger than the shift from S^2S^2 to $S^{2*}S^{2*}$ in Figure 15.3D. This is because r_1 declines farther than r_2. The increase in Northern disposable income shifts S^1S^1 downward, but the decline in r_2 limits the size of this shift. Similarly, the increase in Southern disposable income shifts S^2S^2 leftward, but the decline in r_1 limits the size of this shift. As the changes in Y^d and $Y^{d'}$ are identical, the shifts in the two curves would be identical if they were not limited by interest-rate effects. But the actual shift in S^2S^2 is smaller, because the larger decrease in r_1 limits it more sharply.

[16] From Eqs. (E.2a) and (E.9a), and with goods-market symmetry, $\bar{\pi}(dR - \delta R) = [(L_{11} - L_{12})/2(B^t_{11} - B^t_{12})] d\bar{B}^c_1$, so that $dR < \delta R$. The long-run loss is larger, implying an outflow of reserves on the way to the steady state.

ing the aggregate money supply, each bank can bring about a joint depreciation of the two countries' currencies, and this will raise the income of each participant. But a joint float does not diminish the interdependence of national monetary policies. On the contrary, it may make for closer interdependence, in that the policies of one participant have permanent effects on the others' incomes.

Second, the degree of substitutability between Northern and Southern bonds affects the extent of monetary interdependence in the short run but not in the long run. The higher the degree of substitutability, the larger the reduction in the Southern interest rate resulting from an open-market purchase of the Northern bond, the larger the increase in Southern absorption, and the larger the short-run increase in Southern income. But the configuration of permanent income changes does not depend on the degree of substitutability between the countries' bonds. It does not even depend on the nationality of the bond that is bought. It depends exclusively on conditions in goods markets – on the responses to the permanent joint depreciation of the countries' currencies.[17]

Third, and most important, the degree to which a single central bank can pursue an independent monetary policy depends not only on the nature of the other banks' responses – on the extent of structural interdependence and, therefore, the extent of policy interdependence – but also on the size of the bank's reserves. If the North is unwilling to lose reserves,

[17] Putting the point in different terms, the exchange-rate regime has no importance whatsoever for the effects of internal asset-market integration on the distribution of income changes. In the long run, the income changes are zero under a pegged external rate, and they are determined solely by goods-market conditions under a flexible rate. In the short run, the influence of internal asset-market integration is not negligible but is not affected by the exchange-rate regime. Using Eqs. (13.14a) and (13.14b), for flexible and pegged rates, respectively, it can be shown that the partial derivative of $(\delta Y/\delta \bar{B}_1^{ct})$ with respect to $-B_{12}^t$ is $-(\sigma_1 M_{22}/M_s)(m_1 - m_2)(S_1 - S_2)[(B_{11}^t - B_{12}^t)^{-2}] < 0$ under both regimes, whereas the partial derivative of $(\delta Y/\delta \bar{B}_2^{ct})$ is the same but with opposite sign. An increase of internal asset-market integration reduces the increase in Northern income resulting from an open-market purchase of the Northern bond and raises the increase resulting from a purchase of the Southern bond. But the sizes of the changes are the same under pegged and flexible external rates. Using Eqs. (13.15a) and (13.15b), moreover, it can be shown that the partial derivatives of the changes in Southern income are $-(\sigma_2' M_{11}/\sigma_1 M_{22})$ times those of Northern income. With goods-market symmetry, however, $\sigma_2' M_{11} = \sigma_1 M_{22}$, which says that an increase of internal asset-market integration reduces the effect of δB_1^{ct} on Northern income but raises the effect on Southern income by the same amount. The change in aggregate income is not altered. With goods-market asymmetries, of course, $\sigma_2 M_{11} \gtrless \sigma_1 M_{22}$, and an increase of internal asset-market integration may affect the response of Northern income by more or less than it affects the response of Southern income. The change in aggregate income can thus be affected. Even in this instance, however, the influence of asset-market integration does not depend on the exchange-rate regime.

its central bank cannot make open-market purchases, for they are certain to produce reserve losses in the short run. The losses will be smaller with a flexible external rate than with a pegged external rate, as long as there is any substitutability between the partners' bonds and the foreign bond, but they are not negligible. With asset-market symmetry, they can be up to half as large as the open-market purchase.[18]

In brief, the decision to float or peg a common external exchange rate is best made from the standpoint of the countries as a group, rather than the standpoint of a single participant. Under a joint float, a single central bank is not likely to enjoy much independence. It can be independent only if the other banks have no income targets of their own and if *all* banks look with equanimity on large short-run changes in reserves. The advantage of a joint float derives from the additional influence that it confers on an *integrated* monetary policy. The participating countries, acting together or through a unified central bank, can have more influence on aggregate income in the short run, especially when asset markets are closely integrated with those of the outside world, and can control it in the long run too.

Goods-market disturbances, insulation, and the external exchange-rate regime

In Chapters 4 and 5, where we studied the responses of a single, small economy to various disturbances and policy changes, we showed that the choice between exchange-rate regimes was important for a number of outcomes, not only for the functioning of monetary policies. A flexible exchange rate, for example, could not provide instantaneous insulation from goods-market disturbances and could not prevent permanent changes in relative prices or real outputs when the disturbance involved a shift of demand from one good to another. Nevertheless, it could prevent a permanent change in nominal disposable income. Furthermore, an increase in the foreign interest rate was deflationary under a pegged exchange rate, because it reduced domestic absorption, but was inflationary under a flexible rate, because the domestic currency depreciated under the influence

---

[18] Defining by δR_p the short-run loss that takes place with a pegged external rate, and defining by δR_f the one that takes place with a flexible rate, we can use Eqs. (E.2a) and (E.2b) to show that $\bar{\pi}(\delta R_p - \delta R_f) = [B_{01}^t/2(B_{11}^t + B_{12}^t)]\delta \bar{B}_1^c$, so that $\delta R_p < \delta R_f$. The loss is larger with a pegged external rate, because households can substitute foreign bonds for domestic money. Under a flexible external rate, Eq. (E.2a) says that $\bar{\pi} \, \delta R = -\frac{1}{2}[1 + (L_{11} - L_{12})(B_{11}^t - B_{12}^t)] \, \delta \bar{B}_1^c$, so that $\bar{\pi} \, \delta R > -\frac{1}{2} \, \delta \bar{B}_1^c$. But it approaches $-\frac{1}{2}$ as $B_{12}^t \to \infty$ or $-B_{01}^t \to \infty$ (with perfect internal or external asset-market integration).

of the increase in demand for the foreign bond, and the several effects of the depreciation swamped the direct effect on absorption. Finally, the choice between exchange-rate regimes was important for the long-run effects of fiscal policies. Under a pegged exchange rate, the increase in the stock of domestic debt induced by a temporary tax reduction had no permanent effect on income; under a flexible rate, it caused a permanent increase in income when "crowding out" did not dominate.

The members of a monetary union or simple exchange-rate union cannot decide to peg or float their common external exchange rate without looking at the analogues of these results. We have already seen that a flexible external rate enhances the influence of a unified monetary policy on the participants' aggregate income. But the governments involved will want to know what price they must pay for this additional influence. What will happen to aggregate income and to the participants' national incomes, taken individually, when there are exogenous shifts of demand between pairs of goods? What will happen when there is a change in the foreign interest rate? How will fiscal policies be affected?

Algebraic answers to these questions were supplied in Chapter 13 and summarized by tables of signs. We need not repeat all of them here. In the balance of this chapter, however, we look at responses to shifts in demand, and in the next two chapters we study the influence of the exchange-rate regime on responses to various fiscal policies.

External and internal disturbances

In Chapter 13 we defined two types of shifts in demand–shifts between the foreign good and the Northern or Southern good (δc_{01}^t and δc_{02}^t) and shifts between the Northern and Southern goods (δc_{12}^t). We showed that these shifts are not neutral; the Northern and Southern economies are affected differently in each case. We also showed that their effects are independent of origin; a shift of demand from the Southern to the Northern good has the same effects on the Northern and Southern economies whether it originates in the North, South, or outside world.[19]

[19] If a shift of demand from the Southern to the Northern good originates in the North, it will be seen by Northerners as a switch from an import good to the domestic good and by Southerners as a decrease of demand for their export good. If it originates in the South, it will be seen by Northerners as an increase of demand for their export good and by Southerners as a shift of demand from the domestic good to an import good. If it originates in the outside world, it will be seen as an increase of demand for the Northern export good and a decrease of demand for the Southern export good. The effects on the Northern and Southern economies, however, will be the same in all three instances.

It is useful, nonetheless, to treat the first type of shift as an external disturbance and the second as an internal disturbance. Taken by itself, before it has any time to affect the Northern and Southern economies, a shift of demand from the foreign to the Northern good ($\delta c_{01}^t < 0$) improves the Northern trade balance with the outside world and, therefore, the joint trade balance of the North and South together. Thus it must affect directly the foreign demand for the two countries' currencies, taken together, and their aggregate reserves or common external exchange rate. By contrast, a shift of demand from the Southern to the Northern good ($\delta c_{12}^t < 0$) taken by itself alters the bilateral trade balance between the North and South but does not affect their joint trade balance with the outside world. It can therefore affect the demand for the two countries' currencies only indirectly, by way of its influence on their economies. Let us see how far this distinction takes us.

Effects of an external disturbance

Let there be a shift of Northern, Southern, or foreign demand from the foreign to the Northern good. What are its effects on the Northern and Southern economies, taken together? What are its effects on the two economies individually?

As was the case with an open-market operation, the sum of the responses of the two economies corresponds to the response of a single, small economy. On impact, the increase of demand for the Northern good raises aggregate income, and the size of the increase in Y^t does not depend on the exchange-rate regime, because asset markets do not respond instantaneously to any goods-market disturbance. The increase in aggregate income is shown in Figure 16.4A by the shift of the short-run income curve from $z^t z^t$ to $z^{t\prime} z^{t\prime}$ and the displacement of equilibrium from v to v'. This disturbance, however, must also raise the long-run curve, from $Z^t Z^t$ to $Z^{t\prime} Z^{t\prime}$, and v' must lie below $Z^{t\prime} Z^{t\prime}$. Aggregate saving is positive, and the two countries together begin to run a current-account surplus vis-à-vis the outside world. (Figure 16.4A is, of course, comparable to Figure 4.2, which dealt with the effects on the single small economy of a shift in demand from the foreign to the export good.)

Under a pegged external rate, the gradual increase in aggregate wealth resulting from the joint current-account surplus and the concomitant decline in the average interest rate cause saving to decline, raising aggregate absorption and eliminating the current-account surplus. In Figure 16.4A, the short-run income curve shifts eventually from $z^{t\prime} z^{t\prime}$ to $z^{t\prime\prime} z^{t\prime\prime}$, and

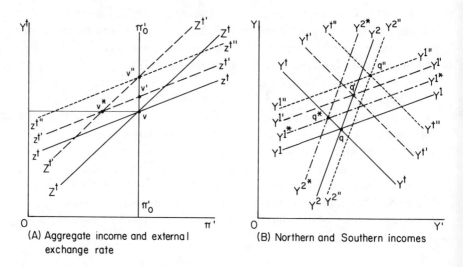

Figure 16.4   Shift of demand from the foreign good to the Northern good: impact and steady-state effects on aggregate and national goods markets.

goods-market equilibrium is displaced from v' to v''. There is a further increase in aggregate income. The effects on asset markets are depicted in Figure 16.5. A gradual increase in reserves causes the money-market curve to move from M^tM^t to $M^{t*}M^{t*}$, until it intersects the bond-market curve at w^*. The position of that point, of course, depends on the size of the shift in the steady-state zero-saving curve from S^tS^t to $S^{t*}S^{t*}$ resulting from the permanent increase in aggregate disposable income.

Under a flexible external rate, the joint current-account surplus causes a gradual appreciation of that rate—one that is just large enough to generate a capital outflow that matches the current-account surplus, while maintaining asset-market equilibrium at w in Figure 16.5. Aggregate wealth and the average interest rate remain unchanged. By implication, net saving can be reduced to zero only by bringing Y^{dt} back to its initial level. This task is accomplished by the demand-switching effects of the appreciation. The demands for Northern and Southern goods are reduced through time, and aggregate income falls. In Figure 16.4A, long-run goods-market equilibrium is established at v^*, where aggregate income has returned to what it was initially.

It is thus the function of a flexible exchange rate to insulate the long-run level of aggregate income from an external goods-market disturbance—which is what it did for the single small economy. But we still have to examine the effects on the individual economies involved. Are Northern

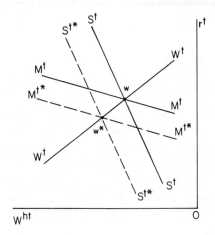

Figure 16.5 Shift of demand from the foreign good to the Northern good: impact and steady-state effects on aggregate asset markets.

and Southern incomes insulated individually? If not, what can we say about the changes in national incomes under pegged and flexible external rates?

We have already shown that goods-market asymmetries can make for a wide range of outcomes in the North and South, because one economy can be more sensitive than the other to price and exchange-rate changes and to changes in absorption, wherever they occur. The range of possibilities is not open ended, but it is nearly true to say that anything can happen. Let us therefore narrow the set of possibilities by imposing full-scale goods-market symmetry.

In this special case, the shift in demand will raise Northern income by more than Southern income. In Figure 16.4B, the Northern income curve shifts from Y^1Y^1 to $Y^{1'}Y^{1'}$ on account of the increase in demand for the Northern good, and the Southern curve does not shift at all. Accordingly, goods-market equilibrium is displaced at once from q to q', where the increase in Northern income is larger. (The shift of the aggregate income curve from Y^tY^t to $Y^{t'}Y^{t'}$ reflects the corresponding movement from v to v' in Figure 16.4A.)

In this instance, moreover, the North is sure to run a current-account surplus, because the increase of Northern absorption is too small to swamp the direct export-increasing effect of the shift in demand. The South, however, can run a deficit or surplus. The North buys more from the South, on account of the increase in Northern income, but the South buys more from the North and from the outside world, on account of the increase in Southern income. The net effect on the Southern current account can be positive or negative.[20]

The subsequent responses of the two economies depend on the external exchange-rate regime. Consider first the case of a pegged external rate.

Because the North will run a current-account surplus, Northern households will save and will thus seek to add to their holdings of all assets. Accordingly, the North will finance its current-account surplus by acquiring foreign bonds, Southern bonds, and reserves.[21] As households try to buy the Northern bond, however, they will drive down the Northern interest rate. Furthermore, Northern saving will raise Northern wealth. Therefore, the desire to save will diminish through time, raising Northern absorption and income. The paths of the Southern interest rate and Southern wealth are, of course, uncertain when the sign of the current-account balance is uncertain, and we cannot know how Southern income will behave on the way to the new steady state. To complicate matters, the current-account balances can turn around in time, rather than moving monotonically to zero. If the South begins in deficit, for example, the gradual decline in income that goes along with a deficit will reduce Southern imports, while the gradual increase in Northern income that goes along with the Northern surplus will raise Southern exports. The Southern deficit can give way to a surplus.[22]

When the two countries reach a steady state, however, the outcomes are clear, if incomes are compared to what they were before the distur-

[20] The change in the Southern current-account balance is $m_2 \, \delta Y - (m_2' + m_0') \; \delta Y' = m_2(\delta Y - \delta Y') - m_0 \, \delta Y'$. The first term in the second expression is the change in the current-account balance with the North and is unambiguously positive (because $\delta Y > \delta Y'$). The remaining term is the change in the current-account balance with the outside world and is unambiguously negative, but it can be larger or smaller absolutely than the change in the balance with the North.

[21] In a full-fledged monetary union, the North will not hold reserves. But union (aggregate) reserves will rise, because the two countries, taken together, will run an overall balance-of-payments surplus with the outside world. Here and hereafter, we speak of changes in Northern and Southern reserves so that our analysis can be applied to a simple exchange-rate union, as well as to a monetary union. When they take place between North and South, however, and the countries belong to a monetary union, they do not involve reserves per se. The union's currency will be transferred between Northern and Southern households. (Transfers of this type occur in the pegged-rate case, together with transfers of reserves to or from the outside world, but they are the only transfers that occur in the flexible-rate case, as there are no transfers to or from the outside world.)

[22] The single small economy studied in Part II had to move monotonically to its steady state, because its behavior was governed by a single dynamic equation. The two economies studied here may do so in an oscillatory way, because their behavior is governed by two dynamic equations.

banoo and to what they were immediately afterward. The Northern income curve must move from $Y^{1'}Y^{1'}$ to $Y^{1''}Y^{1''}$ in Figure 16.4B, under the influence of the increase in Northern wealth and decline in the Northern interest rate that takes place through time.[23] The Southern curve can move as shown, from Y^2Y^2 to $Y^{2''}Y^{2''}$, or in the opposite direction. With full-scale goods-market symmetry, however, long-run equilibrium must be established at some such point as q'', to the northeast of q', where each country's income is higher than it was at q or q', and the permanent increase in Northern income is larger than the permanent increase in Southern income.[24] In this same special case, moreover, there will be a permanent decline in the Northern interest rate, a permanent increase in Northern wealth, and a permanent increase in Northern reserves. (The Southern interest rate can increase, however, when the South runs a current-account deficit on impact, and there can then be reductions in Southern wealth and Southern reserves. But the decrease in Southern reserves can never be as large as the increase in Northern reserves. Aggregate reserves must rise.)

To sum up, each country's income will be raised, immediately and permanently, when the external exchange rate is pegged. With goods-market symmetry, moreover, the changes in incomes will be larger in the long run than the short run, and Northern income will rise farther than Southern income when, as here, the external disturbance involves an increase in demand for the Northern good.

Under a flexible external exchange rate, a shift of demand from the foreign good to the Northern or Southern good causes the countries' cur-

---

[23] In Table 13.2B, the change in r_1 is said to be ambiguous, but this is because it depends on the difference between changes in Y^d and $Y^{d'}$ and the sign of this difference is ambiguous when goods markets are not symmetrical. When those markets *are* symmetrical, the increase in Y^d will be large enough, compared to the increase in $Y^{d'}$, to guarantee a decrease in r_1 (and an increase in W^h). It will not be large enough, however, to guarantee an increase in r_2 (and a decrease in $W^{h'}$).

[24] The Northern income curve shifts upward and the Southern shifts outward with an increase in either country's wealth or a decrease in an interest rate. Hence the size of the upward shift of the Northern curve would be limited if there were a decrease in $W^{h'}$ and an increase in r_2. With goods-market symmetry, however, the effects of the increase in W^h and decrease in r_1 dominate, causing the Northern curve to shift upward. But changes in $W^{h'}$ and r_2 have strong effects on the Southern income curve, relative to the effects of changes in W^h and r_1, so that a decrease in $W^{h'}$ and an increase in r_2 could cause the Southern curve to shift leftward rather than rightward. To prove that each country's income must rise more in the long run than the short run (that q'' lies to the northeast of q' in Figure 16.4B), it is necessary merely to compare the sizes of the changes in p_1 given by Eqs. (13.7) and (13.23b) and the sizes of the changes in p_2 given by Eqs. (13.8) and (13.24b) after imposing goods-market symmetry (so that $\sigma_1 = \sigma_2'$ and $u_{10}^t = u_{20}^t$).

rencies to appreciate gradually, as was shown in Figure 16.4A. With asset-market symmetry, moreover, this appreciation generates an identical capital outflow from each country to the outside world, as households in the North and South respond to identical reductions in the home-currency values of their holdings of the foreign bond. The North, however, has the larger current-account surplus (the South can even have a deficit). Therefore, the identical capital outflows that offset exactly the joint current-account surplus will leave the North in overall balance-of-payments surplus and the South in deficit by the same amount. (Capital will also flow from North to South, but this flow will not cover all of the imbalance between the two countries, so that reserves must bridge the gap.) The North must gain reserves and the South must lose them. Furthermore, Northern wealth must rise through time, and the Northern interest rate must fall, while Southern wealth and the Southern interest rate must move in the opposite directions and by the same amounts. No other outcome is possible, because aggregate wealth and the average interest rate do not change through time.

The joint appreciation of the countries' currencies will cause aggregate wealth to fall, until it returns to its initial level. But the redistribution of wealth from South to North and the corresponding change in relative interest rates will cause Southern income to decline by more than Northern income. In the new steady state, then, Northern income will be lower than it was immediately after the disturbance but higher than it was initially, whereas Southern income will be lower than it was initially. There will, in fact, be equal but opposite changes in the two countries' incomes, compared to their initial levels, as aggregate income must return to its initial level. In Figure 16.4B, the Northern income curve moves to $Y^{1*}Y^{1*}$, the Southern curve moves to $Y^{2*}Y^{2*}$, and long-run equilibrium is established at q^*. This strong relationship between the long-run income changes holds even when goods markets are not symmetrical. By implication, the long-run changes in the countries' interest rates, stocks of wealth, and holdings of reserves have also to be mirror images of each other (because there are no changes in the average interest rate, aggregate wealth, or aggregate reserves).

In brief, a flexible external exchange rate insulates aggregate income in the long run, but by driving the two countries' incomes in opposite directions, rather than by insulating each of them separately. The permanent increase in Northern income that takes place with an increase in demand for the Northern good must be matched by a permanent decrease in Southern income, even in the absence of goods-market symmetry.

Before drawing general conclusions from this case, let us ask how our results are affected by goods-market integration, taking the three types of integration one at a time.

When Northern and Southern goods markets are perfectly integrated (when $u^t_{12} \to \infty$), the two countries' goods prices must move together. Under a pegged external rate, then, the difference between income changes must take its sign from the difference between σ_1 and σ'_2 (and the income changes must therefore be equal with goods-market symmetry, because $\sigma_1 = \sigma'_2$). Under a flexible external rate, by contrast, each country's income must return eventually to its initial level in response to an increase in demand for either country's good. Incomes cannot move in opposite directions when p_1 and p_2 move together, and incomes cannot move together when aggregate income does not change. When the North and South produce a single composite good, a flexible external rate insulates *each* country's income from an external disturbance.

When the Northern goods market is perfectly integrated with the foreign market (when $u^t_{10} \to \infty$), an increase of demand for the Northern good cannot have any immediate effect on Northern income, and if there is no change in Northern income, there can be none in Southern income. In this case, moreover, there can be no saving in the North or South, which means that there can be no changes in interest rates or stocks of wealth and no change in a flexible external rate.[25] By implication, there can be no changes in incomes in the long run either. The disturbance is inconsequential.

When the Southern goods market is perfectly integrated with the foreign market (when $u^t_{20} \to \infty$), the results are much like those obtained in the general case, above. Under a pegged external rate, however, the entire increase in aggregate income will accrue to the North; there can be no change in p_2 unless there is a change in p^f_0, and the latter cannot change unless there is a change in the exchange rate. Under a flexible external rate, by contrast, Southern income will fall in the long run, because p^f_0 will fall with an appreciation of a flexible exchange rate, and Northern income will rise by the same amount.[26]

[25] When Northerners look upon Northern and foreign goods as perfect substitutes, an increase of foreign or Southern demand for the Northern good, reducing the supply available to Northerners, will be offset by an increase in Northern purchases of the foreign good, and the Northern current-account balance will not change. When Southerners look upon the two goods as perfect substitutes, an increase of foreign or Northern demand for the Northern good will be offset by an increase in Southern purchases of the foreign good, and there will be no change in any current-account balance. Trade patterns will change in these and other cases, and bilateral imbalances may arise, but there will be no global imbalances.
[26] The changes in incomes will be $dY' = \sigma'_2(dp_2/p_2) = \sigma'_2(d\pi'/\pi') = -dY$. As $(d\pi'/\pi') < 0$, it follows that $dY > 0$ and $dY' < 0$.

Returning to the general goods-market case analyzed above, what can we say about the merits of a flexible external rate, compared to a pegged rate, looking at the problem from the standpoint of the North or South rather than the union's standpoint?

When goods-market asymmetries are large, it is hard to make exact comparisons between the two regimes. Under a flexible external rate, goods-market asymmetries can affect the sizes of the income changes but not their distribution; the permanent change in Southern income must always be the mirror image of the change in Northern income. Under a pegged external rate, however, asymmetries can have large effects on the distribution of the income changes. There can be no reduction in either country's income on account of an increase in demand for the Northern good, but the increase in Southern income need not be smaller than the increase in Northern income.[27]

When goods-market asymmetries are small, however, two features of a flexible external rate should commend it to the members of a monetary union.

First, it can be shown that a flexible rate will reduce the variability of each country's income when the distributions of external disturbances are themselves symmetrical. The proof is in four steps: (1) A change in demand for the Northern good will have smaller effects on Northern income when the external exchange rate is flexible than when the rate is pegged. In Figure 16.4B, q'' must always be northeast of q^*. (2) A change in demand for the Northern good can have larger or smaller effects on Southern income. The increase in Southern income that takes place with the movement from q to q'' can be bigger or smaller absolutely than the decrease that takes place with the movement from q to q^*. Correspondingly, a change in demand for the Southern good can have larger or smaller effects on Northern income. (3) But the reduction in the amplitude

[27] To take an extreme example, let there be no substitutability between Southern and foreign goods ($u_{20}^t = 0$). Under a pegged external exchange rate, $dY = (1/M_k^t)\sigma_1[u_{12}^t + (m_2 + m_0)\sigma_2'](-dc_{10}^t)$ and $dY' = (1/M_k^t)\sigma_2'[u_{12}^t + (m_2)\sigma_1](-dc_{01}^t)$, where $M_k^t = u_{10}^t[u_{12}^t + (m_2 + m_0)\sigma_2'] + m_0 M_0$. If, in addition, the Southern supply response is larger than the Northern ($\sigma_2' > \sigma_1$), and the marginal propensity to import, m_0, is smaller than $(1/\sigma_1\sigma_2')(\sigma_2' - \sigma_1)u_{12}^t$, Southern income will rise by more than Northern income. (In this case, the spread between the income changes, defined below, could be reduced by pegging the external exchange rate. This would be true, however, only for the spread produced by an external disturbance affecting the demand for the Northern good. The spread produced by a disturbance affecting the demand for the Southern good could be widened. By implication, goods-market asymmetries do not weaken the second argument, below, in favor of a flexible external rate unless one knows the nature of the asymmetries and of the disturbances with which they interact.)

of changes in Northern income resulting from shifts in the demand for the Northern good must exceed any increase in the amplitude of changes resulting from shifts in the demand for the Southern good. (4) If the distributions of external disturbances are symmetrical, in that the probability of an increase in demand for the Northern good is the same as the probability of an equal increase in demand for the Southern good, the overall variability of Northern income consequent upon external disturbances must therefore be reduced by a flexible external rate.[28]

Second, it can be shown that a flexible external rate will allow the members of a monetary union to offset at least some of the unwanted effects of an external disturbance, even though the spread induced between the countries' incomes is unaffected by the exchange-rate regime. The proof is simple. When goods markets are symmetrical, the spread between the long-run income changes is given by

$$dY - dY' = (1/M_k)[\sigma_1(u_{10}^t + m_0\,\sigma_1)](-dc_{01}^t)$$

whether the external rate is pegged or flexible.[29] Therefore, a monetary union can offset the decline in Southern income resulting from an increase in demand for the Northern good and can do so without raising Northern

[28] Using the notation defined in note 18, together with Eqs. (13.23a) and (13.23b), we can ascertain the difference between the long-run changes in Northern income produced by each external disturbance. Working with absolute values and goods-market symmetry (so that $\sigma_1 = \sigma_2'$, $u_{10}^t = u_{20}^t$, and $p_1C_1' = p_2C_2'$),

$$|(dY_f/dc_{01}^t)| - |(dY_p/dc_{01}^t)| = -(\sigma_1/2M_k)\{u_{10}^t + 2u_{12}^t + [1 - (m_1 - m_2)]\} < 0$$

and

$$|(dY_f/dc_{02}^t)| - |(dY_p/dc_{02}^t)| = (\sigma_1 2M_k)[u_{10}^t - 2u_{12}^t + (m_0 - 2m_2)\sigma_1] \gtreqless 0$$

Thus, a flexible external rate reduces the variability of Northern income resulting from disturbances affecting the demand for the Northern good and has ambiguous effects on the variability resulting from disturbances affecting the demand for the Southern good. Nevertheless,

$$[|(dY_f/dc_{01}^t)| - |(dY_p/dc_{01}^t)|] - [|(dY_f/dc_{02}^t)| - |(dY_p/dc_{02}^t)|] = -(\sigma_1/M_k)(u_{10}^t + m_0\sigma_1) < 0$$

The reduction of variability due to disturbances affecting the demand for the Northern good swamps any increase of variability due to disturbances affecting the demand for the Southern good. An analogous proof can be constructed for the change in the variability of Southern income. It must be emphasized, however, that these proofs and the corresponding statements in the text hold only in respect of external goods-market disturbances. In Chapter 18 we show that a flexible external rate will increase the spread between income changes resulting from certain internal disturbances, such as an increase of $\bar{G}_1$.

[29] This result can be obtained from Eqs. (13.23a) and (13.24a), for a flexible external rate, and from Eqs. (13.23b) and (13.24b), for a pegged external rate. It holds under the assumptions of goods-market symmetry listed in the previous note.

income by as much as it would rise with a pegged external rate. An appropriate open-market purchase by the union's central bank will stabilize Southern income rather than allowing it to fall on account of the joint appreciation of the two countries' currencies. That purchase will produce an increase of aggregate income, all of which must accrue to the North when Southern income does not change. But the sum of the stimuli to Northern income that come from the disturbance and the open-market purchase will not be as large as the stimulus that comes from the disturbance alone when the external exchange rate is pegged. It will equal the spread defined above (because $dY' = 0$), whereas the increase that takes place with a pegged exchange rate is larger by the increase in Southern income that occurs with the movement from q to q'' in Figure 16.4B.

Effects of an internal disturbance

As one might expect, the responses to an internal disturbance have less bearing on the choice between exchange-rate regimes. We look here at a shift in internal demand, postponing to Chapters 17 and 18 the analysis of changes in levels of demand.

Let there be a shift of demand from the Southern to the Northern good. What are its effects on aggregate income and on national incomes? Does the external exchange-rate regime influence the outcomes?

When goods-market responses are symmetrical, this shift in demand does not have any effect on aggregate or external variables. There is an immediate increase of Northern income and decrease of Southern income, but the sizes of the changes are equal absolutely, and aggregate income is thus unaffected. The North starts to run a current-account surplus, but the South starts to run an identical deficit, so that there is no change in the sum of current-account balances with the outside world and no change in aggregate saving.[30]

---

[30] If the disturbance originates in the North or South, the Northern trade surplus with the South will equal $\delta c_{12}^t - m_2 \, \delta Y + m_1 \, \delta Y' = \delta c_{12}^t - 2m_2 \, \delta Y$, because $\delta Y' = -\delta Y$. The change in Northern imports from the outside world will be $m_0 \, \delta Y$, and the change in Southern imports will be $m_0' \, \delta Y' = -m_0 \, \delta Y$. There will be no change in the countries' joint trade balance with the outside world. The North will run a global trade surplus equal to $\delta c_{12}^t - (2m_2 + m_0) \, \delta Y$, but the South will run a deficit of equal size. If the disturbance originates in the outside world, the Northern trade surplus with the outside world will equal $\delta c_{12}^t - m_0 \, \delta Y$, and the Southern trade deficit will equal $-\delta c_{12}^t - m_0' \, \delta Y' = -(\delta c_{12}^t - m_0 \, \delta Y)$ and will thus equal the Northern trade surplus. In this case, however, the North will run a bilateral trade deficit with the South equal to $2m \, \delta Y$, rather than running a surplus. (The North will run the same global surplus as it did in the previous instance, but its geographic distribution will be different.)

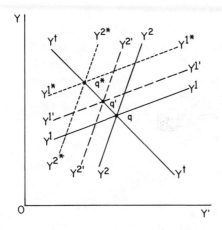

Figure 16.6 Shift of demand from the Southern good to the Northern good with goods-market symmetry: impact and steady-state effects on national goods markets.

Northerners will start to save and seek to accumulate bonds and money. Events will take the opposite course in the South. Accordingly, wealth will be redistributed gradually from South to North. With asset-market symmetry, moreover, Northerners will add to their holdings of the foreign bond and to their holdings of money (reserves) at the same rates that Southerners will reduce their holdings. But Northerners will want to buy more Northern bonds and fewer Southern bonds than Southerners will want to sell. The Northern interest rate will rise and the Southern rate will fall. With the passage of time, then, Northerners will have less incentive to save and Southerners less incentive to dissave, and each country's current-account balance will move gradually to zero.

In the new steady state, income, wealth, and reserves will be higher in the North than they were initially, and the Northern interest rate will be lower, but opposite changes will take place in the South. There will be no change in aggregate income, aggregate wealth, or the average interest rate. There will be no change in aggregate reserves when the external exchange rate is pegged and no change in the rate itself when it is flexible. The choice of exchange-rate regime is irrelevant.

The changes in Northern and Southern incomes are shown in Figure 16.6. There is at first a movement from q to q', followed by a gradual movement to q^*. But these three points (and all intervening points) fall on the same aggregate income curve.

When goods-market symmetry does not obtain, these last statements are not true. The changes in the Northern and Southern economies need not mirror one another, so that Y^t, W^{ht}, and r^t need not be constant. By implication, aggregate reserves will change when the external exchange rate is pegged and the rate itself will change when it is flexible. The signs and sizes of these changes, however, will depend on the nature and degree of the goods-market asymmetries.

Under a pegged external rate, the changes in steady-state national incomes are given by[31]

$$dY = (1/M_k)\sigma_1(u_{20}^t + m_0\sigma_2') \, dc_{12}^t$$
$$dY' = -(1/M_k)\sigma_2'(u_{10}^t + m_0\sigma_1) \, dc_{12}^t$$

so that

$$dY^t = (1/M_k)(\sigma_1 u_{20}^t - \sigma_2' u_{10}^t) \, dc_{12}^t$$

The net effect on aggregate income will depend on the sign of the difference between (u_{20}^t/σ_2') and (u_{10}^t/σ_1). Northern reserves will rise, as they did with goods-market symmetry, and Southern reserves will fall. But the changes in reserves need not offset each other:

$$\bar{\pi}' \, dR^t = (S_Y/M_k)(J_\pi/J_K)(\sigma_1 u_{20}^t - \sigma_2' u_{10}^t) \, dc_{12}^t$$

To illustrate the implications of these statements, suppose that Southern and foreign goods are deemed to be closer substitutes than Northern and foreign goods (that $u_{20}^t > u_{10}^t$) but that there are no other goods-market asymmetries. A shift of demand from the Southern to the Northern good, causing an increase in p_1 and a decrease in p_2, will cause households to substitute the Southern for the foreign good by more than they substitute the foreign for the Northern good. There will be a smaller deterioration in the Southern trade balance, so that the two countries, taken together, will run a current-account surplus vis-à-vis the outside world, and aggregate reserves will rise through time. In the new steady state, moveover, the decrease of Southern income will be smaller than it was when goods markets were symmetrical, and there will be an increase of aggregate income. The same changes in outcomes can be shown to obtain when the Northern supply response is larger than the Southern response (when $\sigma_1 > \sigma_2'$).

Under a flexible external rate, the changes in steady-state national in-

---

[31] These results are obtained by defining $dc_{12}^t = -dc_{01}^t = dc_{02}^t > 0$ and combining the appropriate arguments in Eqs. (13.23b) and (13.24b). The equation for the change in R^t shown below comes from Eq. (13.22b) and from the fact that $dY^{dt} = dY^t$ in the present instance. The equations for the flexible-rate case shown later in the text come from Eq. (13.23a), (13.24a), and (13.22a).

comes are given by

$$dY = (\sigma_1 \sigma_2' U_\pi / M_w)\, dc_{12}^t$$
$$dY' = -(\sigma_1 \sigma_2' U_\pi / M_w)\, dc_{12}^t$$

The changes in national incomes continue to be mirror images of one another, which means that there will be no change in aggregate income, even when goods-market asymmetries are large. But there can be a change in the external exchange rate:

$$d\hat{\pi}' = (1/M_w)(\sigma_2' u_{10}^t - \sigma_1 u_{20}^t)\, dc_{12}^t$$

If aggregate reserves would rise with a pegged external rate, the two countries' currencies will appreciate with a flexible external rate.

Returning to the illustration offered earlier, with $u_{20}^t > u_{10}^t$, the changes in national incomes will be different than they were with symmetrical goods markets (and different than they were with a pegged exchange rate), but there is no change in the relationship between them. The permanent increase of Northern income will be matched by the permanent decrease of Southern income. When $u_{20}^t > u_{10}^t$, however, there will be a permanent appreciation of the countries' currencies.

What does this analysis have to say about the choice between exchange-rate regimes? Answering the question from the standpoint of the North and South together, exchange-rate flexibility is advantageous because it can stabilize aggregate income in the long run, just as it did in the face of an external disturbance. Looking at the question from the standpoint of a single country, there is no simple answer. When goods-market responses are symmetrical, a shift of demand from one country to the other leads to the same change in Northern income whether the exchange rate is pegged or flexible. When those responses are not symmetrical, the size of the Northern income change does depend on the exchange-rate regime, but we cannot say that it will be bigger or smaller under a flexible external rate without knowing how and why goods-market responses differ.

Equations for the asset-market curves

The sum of the markets for domestic bonds (Eqs. 11.76a plus 11.77a).
In average interest-rate and external exchange-rate space (B^tB^t):

$$dr^t = -(B^t_{1W}/J_S)V_\pi\left(\frac{d\pi'}{\pi'}\right) - (1/2J_S)(d\overline{B}^{ct}_1 + d\overline{B}^{ct}_2) + (-B^t_{10}/J_S)\,d\overline{r}_0 + (1/2J_S)(dB_1 + dB'_2) - (B^t_{1W}/2J_S)\,dW^{hst}$$ (Eq. 11.76a)

The sum of the markets for domestic currencies (Eqs. 11.78a plus 11.79a)
In average interest-rate and external exchange-rate space (L^tL^t):

$$dr^t = [L_{1W}/(-L^t_{11})]V_\pi\left(\frac{d\pi'}{\pi'}\right) - [1/(-2L^t_{11})](d\overline{B}^{ct}_1 + d\overline{B}^{ct}_2) - (L_{10}/L^t_{11})\,d\overline{r}_0 + [L_{1W}/(-2L^t_{11})]\,dW^{hst}$$ (Eq. 11.77a)

The market for the Northern bond in Northern interest-rate and Northern wealth space (W^1W^1) (Eq. 11.76a)

$$\delta r_1 = (1/B^t_{11})[(-B_{1W})\,\delta W^h + (-B^t_{12})\,\delta r_2 - (B_{2W})\,\delta W^{h'} - \delta B^{ct}_1 + (-B^t_{10})\,\delta\overline{r}_0 + \delta B_1]$$

The market for the Southern bond in Southern interest-rate and Southern wealth space (W^2W^2) (Eq. 11.77a)

$$\delta r_2 = (1/B^t_{11})[(-B_{1W})\,\delta W^{h'} + (-B^t_{12})\,\delta r_1 - (B_{2W})\,\delta W^h - \delta B^{ct}_2 + (-B^t_{10})\,\delta\overline{r}_0 + \delta B^t_2]$$

The market for Northern money in Northern interest-rate and Northern wealth space (M^1M^1) (Eq. 11.78a)

$$\delta r_1 = (-1/L_{11})[(L_{1W})\,\delta W^h - (-L_{12})\,\delta r_2 - (\delta\overline{B}^{ct}_1 + \delta\overline{B}^{ct}_2) - \pi\,\delta R - (-L_{10})\,\delta\overline{r}_0]$$

The market for Southern money in Southern interest-rate and Southern wealth space (M^2M^2) (Eq. 11.79a)

$$\delta r_2 = (-1/L_{11})[(L_{1W})\,\delta W^{h'} - (-L_{12})\,\delta r_1 - (\delta\overline{B}^{ct}_1 + \delta\overline{B}^{ct}_2) - \pi'\,\delta R' - (-L_{10})\,\delta\overline{r}_0]$$

The Northern steady-state requirement (S^1S^1) (Eq. 11.13a for $S = 0$)

$$dr_1 = (-S_W/S_1)\,dW^h - (S_2/S_1)\,dr_2 - (S_Y/S_1)\,dY^d - (S_0/S_1)\,d\overline{r}_0$$

The Southern steady-state requirement (S^2S^2) (Eq. 11.14a for $S' = 0$)

$$dr_2 = (-S_W/S_1)\,dW^{h'} - (S_2/S_1)\,dr_1 - (S_Y/S_1)\,dY^{d'} - (S_0/S_1)\,d\overline{r}_0$$

Constant aggregate wealth in wealth space ($W^{ht}W^{ht}$) (equations for the curves B^tB^t and L^tL^t)

$$\delta W^h = -\delta W^{h'} - (1/J_\pi)\{B^t_{01}(\delta\overline{B}^{ct}_1 + \delta\overline{B}^{ct}_2) + L^t_{11}(\delta B_1 + \delta B_2) + 2[L_{10}(B^t_{11} + \delta B_2) + L^t_{11}(B^t_{12} + B^t_{12}) - L^t_{11}B^t_{10}]\,\delta\overline{r}_0\}]$$

The equations for the sums of the markets for bonds and of markets for currencies are steady-state versions.

17

Market integration, interdependence, and fiscal policy under pegged exchange rates

In Chapter 15 we examined the implications of market integration and structural interdependence for the monetary policies of two countries having pegged exchange rates with the outside world. Here we undertake a similar investigation for fiscal policies. What are the implications of structural interdependence for fiscal policies, and what are the effects on national autonomy under pegged exchange rates?

In the context of our model, monetary policies are ineffective in the long run; they have no permanent effects on income when exchange rates are pegged. Accordingly, fiscal policies must be used to regulate long-run income levels. Recall our findings in Part II. In a single small economy, the government can engineer a permanent increase in nominal income by a balanced-budget increase in its spending on domestic goods (unless those goods are perfect substitutes for the import good). We found the same thing to be true in the larger model of Part IV, but saw also that an increase in one country's income would spill over to the other.

We must now look closely at the causes and results of these spillover effects, in the short run and the long run. Which aspects of structural interdependence are most important in determining their size? How do they affect the strength of fiscal policies? Can one country adopt a defensive fiscal policy to neutralize the spillover effects of its neighbor's policies? If so, will it nullify the efforts of the other to influence its own domestic economy? Or is it possible, instead, for the two countries to achieve independent income targets simultaneously, and what will be the side effects on their reserves? Finally, we ask whether and to what extent each country can combine its fiscal and monetary policies to attain internal and external targets. We reconsider the "assignment problem" in the context of structural interdependence and a model different from those used to study it before.[1]

[1] Most of the early work on the "assignment problem" was done for a single country; see, e.g., R. A. Mundell, *International Economics,* Macmillan, New York, 1968, chap. 16, J. M. Fleming, *Essays in International Economics,* Harvard University Press, Cambridge, Mass., 1971, chap. 9, and the survey in M. v. N. Whitman, *Policies for Internal and Ex-*

The instruments of fiscal policy

In earlier chapters of this book we studied the uses of two fiscal instruments – a balanced-budget increase in government spending on domestic goods and a temporary cut in lump-sum taxes. The tax cut was temporary because it had to be rescinded to halt the increase in the supply of bonds – to let the economy converge on a stationary state. Each policy appeared at first as a pure goods-market disturbance; it had no instantaneous effects on asset markets. Each policy, moreover, produced an immediate increase in income. Their long-run effects, however, were quite different. When a tax cut was rescinded, demands for goods declined, and nominal income returned to its initial level, even though the tax cut gave rise to a permanent increase in the supply of bonds. Under pegged exchange rates, changes in supplies of assets can have no effect on the steady-state level of income, and the long-run effects of a temporary tax cut were seen exclusively in asset-market variables, including the level of reserves. A balanced-budget increase in spending, by contrast, had permanent effects on demands for goods and raised the steady-state level of income. And though it did not alter the supply of bonds, it had indirect effects on asset-market variables.

In this chapter, we examine an additional fiscal instrument – an interval of deficit spending on domestic goods.[2] It has to be temporary in our model, for the same reason that a tax cut must be temporary. But there are two ways of ending it – by rescinding the increase of spending or by raising taxes. In either case, of course, deficit spending will appear at first as a goods-market disturbance (but will be more powerful than other fiscal

ternal Balance, Special Papers in International Economics 9, Princeton University, Princeton, N.J., 1970. There has been some work with two-country models; see, e.g., J. Patrick, "The Optimum Policy Mix: Convergence and Consistency," in P. B. Kenen, ed., *The Open Economy,* Columbia University Press, New York, 1968, pp. 263–88, and M. Aoki, "On Decentralized Stabilization Policies and Dynamic Assignment Problems," *Journal of International Economics,* 6 (May 1976), pp. 143–72. In most of this literature, however, targets and instruments have been defined as flows. The external target has been a balance-of-payments surplus or deficit (a flow of reserves), and the fiscal instrument has been a budget deficit or surplus (a flow of new bond issues or redemptions). Here we work with stock demands for assets and a system that must move to a stationary state. The external target must be defined as a change in the stock of reserves, and the fiscal instrument must not produce an unending change in the supply of bonds.

[2] The effects of deficit spending can be obtained from the equations in Chapter 13. They are the combined effects of a balanced-budget increase in government spending and an equivalent tax cut. We denote deficit spending by the North as $\delta(\bar{G}_1, \bar{D})$ or $\delta(\bar{G}_2, \bar{D})$, depending on the good purchased by the government, and deficit spending by the South as $\delta(\bar{G}'_1, \bar{D}')$ or $\delta(\bar{G}'_2, \bar{D}')$. Thus, the impact effect on Northern income of Northern deficit spending on the Northern good is given by $[\delta Y/\delta(\bar{G}_1, \bar{D})] = (\delta Y/\delta\bar{G}_1) + (\delta Y/\delta\bar{D})$, for $\delta\bar{G}_1 = \delta\bar{D}$.

instruments). Its long-run effects, however, depend on the way that it is ended. When terminated by a cut in expenditure, it will cease to influence demands for goods and will thus resemble a temporary tax cut; it will have no permanent effect on income. When terminated by an increase in taxes, it will continue to affect demands for goods and, viewed retrospectively, will resemble a balanced-budget increase in expenditure; it will raise the steady-state level of income. In both cases, of course, it will leave as its legacy an increase in the supply of bonds that affects reserves and other asset-market variables.

To study fiscal policies under pegged exchange rates, we must therefore examine three sets of effects: (1) impact effects in goods markets, where all three fiscal policies make their first appearance; (2) steady-state effects in goods markets, where a balanced-budget increase in government spending will still be felt, whether the budget is balanced from the start or after an interval of deficit spending; and (3) steady-state effects in asset markets, where we have again to look at all three policies, especially to study their effects on reserves.

Impact effects of fiscal policies

When working with a single small economy, in Parts II and III, we did not discuss deficit spending. There was little cause to do so in that context, because the responses would have been quite similar to those we traced at length for a temporary tax cut. We have to do so here, however, because the spillover effects from country to country differ significantly (and differ in turn from the spillover effects of a balanced-budget increase in one country's spending). Let us begin with deficit spending.

Suppose that the Northern government steps up its spending on the Northern good, raising the price of the good and thus raising Northern income. Substitution and income effects, acting together, will raise imports from the South and from the outside world. The price of the Southern good must rise, raising Southern income, and increasing Southern imports from the North and outside world. Northern income will rise further. But these feedbacks cannot continue indefinitely, as some part of the increase in each country's income will be saved and some part will be lost to the outside world. The full effects on Northern and Southern incomes are shown in Figure 17.1, for the case of full-scale goods-market symmetry. Northern deficit spending on the Northern good shifts the Northern income curve upward, from Y^1Y^1 to $Y^{1'}Y^{1'}$, displacing goods-market equilibrium from q to q', along the Southern income curve Y^2Y^2. There is an

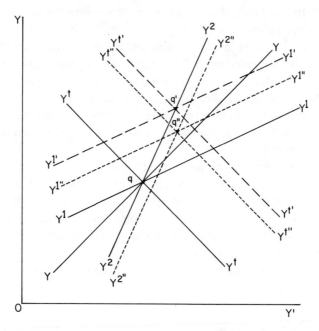

Figure 17.1 Deficit spending on the Northern good and a tax cut by the North: impact effects on national goods markets under pegged exchange rates.

instantaneous increase in Northern income and a smaller increase in Southern income. The increase in aggregate income, Y^t, is shown by the shift of Y^tY^t, passing through q, to $Y^{t'}Y^{t'}$ passing through q'.[3]

When we studied the effects of monetary policies, we found that the degree of asset-market integration affected the sizes of the spillover effects and thus the distribution of the increase in aggregate income resulting on impact from an open-market purchase. Here, by contrast, the degree of goods-market integration (the size of u^t_{12}) is strategic for the outcome. The greater the degree of integration between Northern and Southern goods markets, the smaller the difference between the slopes of the income curves and the smaller the upward shift of the Northern curve. The increase in aggregate income is unaffected, but the increase in Northern income is reduced and the increase in Southern income is enlarged. (Goods-market equilibrium still lies on $Y^{t'}Y^{t'}$, but to the southeast of q'.)

[3] Equations for the curves in Figure 17.1 and for most of the other curves used in this chapter are given in the tables at the end of Chapters 15 and 16. They have been used before. Equations for the Northern income curves, z^1z^1 and Z^1Z^1, used in Figure 17.4, for the fiscal-policy reaction curves, and for the new relationships used in the analysis of external and internal balance are found in tables at the end of this chapter.

In the limiting case of perfect goods-market integration ($u_{12}^t \to \infty$), each country's income curve comes to coincide with the 45° line, YY, the Northern curve does not shift, and each country's income rises by the same amount. (Goods-market equilibrium lies at the intersection of YY with $Y^{t'}Y^{t'}$.) In brief, goods-market integration between North and South strengthens structural interdependence, which means that it will strengthen policy interdependence. The higher the degree of goods-market integration, the harder it will be for each country to use fiscal policy in pursuit of an independent income target.[4]

In Chapter 12 we imposed two types of restrictions on demand conditions. Tastes differ symmetrically between North and South ($m_1 = m_2'$ and $m_2 = m_1'$), and they are also biased toward home goods ($m_1 > m_2$). The degree of bias turns out to be important for the strength of structural interdependence. As that bias is reduced, the slopes of the income curves in Figure 17.1 come to be more nearly equal, and deficit spending by the North causes a smaller upward shift in the Northern curve. As with an increase in goods-market integration, the behavior of aggregate income is unaffected (Y^tY^t shifts to $Y^{t'}Y^{t'}$), but the increase in Y^t is divided more evenly between North and South. Absent *any* bias, however, the increase in Y^t is not evenly divided, as it is with perfect goods-market integration. When $m_1 = m_2$, the two income curves do not come to coincide with YY, and there is still a shift in the Northern curve. The increase in Northern income continues to exceed the increase in Southern income. (Goods-market equilibrium lies between q' and the intersection of YY with $Y^{t'}Y^{t'}$.)[5]

[4] An increase of integration with the foreign goods market reduces the increase in aggregate income and likewise reduces the increase in each country's income. With full-scale goods-market symmetry, $u_{10}^t = u_{20}^t$, and an increase of one elasticity implies an equal increase of the other, limiting the impact of deficit spending on prices and incomes in the North and South. In the limiting case of perfect integration with the outside world (u_{10}^t, $u_{20}^t \to \infty$), deficit spending is ineffectual. The Northern income curve becomes vertical, the Southern curve becomes horizontal, and neither curve can shift in response to deficit spending. The same statements hold for temporary tax cuts and balanced-budget increases in government spending.

[5] An increase of m_2 or m_0 at the expense of m_1 is an increase in a marginal propensity to import and reduces the increase of demand for the domestic good created by deficit spending. In a simple Keynesian model, with fixed prices and interest rates, a larger leakage into imports reduces the expenditure multiplier. That is true here too, but the presence of price effects in our outcomes makes it hard to isolate the change in the multiplier. For treatments of the problem in a Keynesian context, see R. I. McKinnon and W. E. Oates, *The Implications of International Economic Integration for Monetary, Fiscal, and Exchange-Rate Policy,* Studies in International Finance 16, Princeton University, Princeton, N.J., 1966, and G. K. Shaw, "European Economic Integration and Stabilization Policy," in C. S. Shoup, ed., *Fiscal Harmonization in Common Markets,* Vol. II, Columbia University Press, New York, 1967, pp. 344–439.

As the Northern government aims at raising Northern income, one would expect it to devote its deficit spending to the Northern good. The reason can be seen in Figure 17.1. If the Northern government bought more of the Southern good, the income changes would be reversed. The Southern income curve would shift rightward, and the increase in Southern income would be larger than the increase in Northern income. The stimulus to Northern income would come entirely from spillover effects and would always be smaller than the stimulus produced by the same amount of deficit spending on the Northern good. With full-scale goods-market symmetry, indeed, the changes in Northern and Southern incomes would be the mirror images of those in Figure 17.1. By implication, the impact effects of deficit spending depend on its commodity composition, not on the government that undertakes it.

A reduction in the Northern lump-sum tax, T^h, also serves to raise incomes in both countries. But a tax cut that generates a deficit, $\bar{D}$, equal to the one produced by deficit spending has less impact on aggregate income, Y^t, and its influence is distributed more evenly between North and South. The first effect of deficit spending is the increase in government demand, which is reflected fully in the relevant goods market. The first effect of a tax cut is an increase in disposable income, which is not reflected fully in any single market. A portion will be saved, and the rest will be divided among Northern, Southern, and foreign goods. In Figure 17.1, the Northern income curve will shift upward from $Y^1 Y^1$ to $Y^{1''} Y^{1''}$, and the Southern curve will shift rightward from $Y^2 Y^2$ to $Y^{2''} Y^{2''}$. The sum of the vertical shift to $Y^{1''} Y^{1''}$ and the horizontal shift to $Y^{2''} Y^{2''}$ is smaller than the shift from $Y^1 Y^1$ to $Y^{1'} Y^{1'}$ that was the first effect of deficit spending on the Northern good.[6] Goods-market equilibrium is displaced from q to q'', and the increase of aggregate income is shown by the shift from $Y^t Y^t$ to $Y^{t''} Y^{t''}$, a shift smaller than the one to $Y^{t'} Y^{t'}$ that took place in response to deficit spending.

As demands are biased toward domestic goods, Northern income will rise farther than Southern income. The shift in the Northern income curve will be larger than the shift in the Southern curve. In other words, the distribution of the stimulus afforded by a tax cut depends on the country in

[6] With goods-market symmetry, the upward shift of $Y^1 Y^1$ to $Y^{1''} Y^{1''}$ is $\alpha m_1 (1 - S_Y)$, and the rightward shift of $Y^2 Y^2$ to $Y^{2''} Y^{2''}$ is $\alpha m_2 (1 - S_Y)$, where $\alpha = [\sigma_1 / (M_{11} + M_{12})] \delta\bar{D} = [\sigma_2' / (M_{21} + M_{22})] \delta\bar{D} = [\sigma_1 / (M_{11} + M_{12})] \delta(\bar{G}_1, \bar{D})$, assuming that $\delta\bar{D} = \delta(\bar{G}_1, \bar{D})$. These two distances together are smaller than the vertical distance from $Y^1 Y^1$ to $Y^{1''} Y^{1''}$, which equals α by itself. The difference between the sum of the two shifts and the shift from $Y^1 Y^1$ to $Y^{1'} Y^{1'}$ is αM_Y, where $M_Y = [S_Y + m_0 (1 - S_Y)]$ and measures the leakages into saving and imports from the outside world.

which the cut is made an inference different from the one we drew above concerning the effects of deficit spending. But the increase in Northern income will be smaller than the one produced by deficit spending, whereas the increase in Southern income can be larger or smaller. It is drawn to be larger in Figure 17.1, where q'' lies to the southeast of q', but it would be smaller if there were a smaller shift in the Southern income curve.

How do goods-market integration and the bias toward domestic goods influence responses to a Northern tax cut? The effects of integration are the same as they were in the case of Northern deficit spending. The greater the degree of goods-market integration, the smaller the difference between price changes and, therefore, the difference between income changes. With perfect integration, p_1 and p_2 must rise by the same amounts, and with full-scale goods-market symmetry, incomes must likewise rise by the same amounts. The effects of a reduction in the bias toward domestic goods are slightly different than they were with deficit spending. The shifts in the income curves come to be more nearly equal, reducing the difference between the income changes. Without any bias, moreover, the shifts become identical, making the income changes identical. In brief, structural interdependence is strengthened by goods-market integration and by a decrease in bias toward the domestic good. With perfect integration or the absence of bias, the distribution of the stimulus afforded by a tax cut does *not* depend on the country in which the cut is made.

Figure 17.2 illustrates the impact effects of a balanced-budget increase in one country's spending. Suppose that the Northern government spends more on the Northern good and finances its spending by raising Northern taxes. The increase in the government's demand for the Northern good necessarily exceeds the reduction in private demand caused by the increase in taxes. Therefore, the Northern income curve must shift upward from $Y^1 Y^1$ to $Y^{1'} Y^{1'}$. But there is no increase in the government's demand for the Southern good, and there is a decrease in private demand. Therefore, the Southern curve must shift leftward from $Y^2 Y^2$ to $Y^{2'} Y^{2'}$.[7] Goods-market equilibrium is displaced from q to q', and aggregate income rises ($Y^t Y^t$ shifts to $Y^{t'} Y^{t'}$). There is, of course, an increase in Northern income, but there can be a decrease in Southern income. It is shown to

---

[7] With goods-market symmetry, the upward shift of $Y^1 Y^1$ in Figure 17.2 is $\alpha[1 - m_1(1 - S_Y)]$, and the leftward shift of $Y^2 Y^2$ to $Y^{2'} Y^{2'}$ is $\alpha m_2(1 - S_Y)$, where $\alpha = [\sigma_1/(M_{11} + M_{12})] \delta \bar{G}_1 = [\sigma_2'/(M_{21} + M_{22})] \delta \bar{G}_1$. When $\delta \bar{G}_1 = \delta \bar{D} = \delta(\bar{G}_1, \bar{D})$, the shift to $Y^{1'} Y^{1'}$ in Figure 17.2 has as its counterpart in Figure 17.1 the shift to $Y^{1'} Y^{1'}$ *less* the shift to $Y^{1''} Y^{1''}$, whereas the shift to $Y^{2'} Y^{2'}$ in Figure 17.2 has as its counterpart in Figure 17.1 the negative of the shift to $Y^{2''} Y^{2''}$.

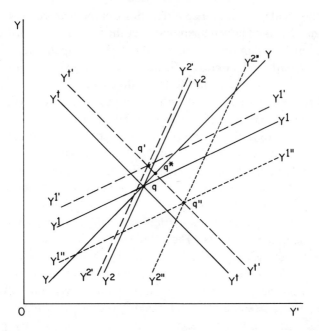

Figure 17.2 Balanced-budget increase in Northern spending on the Northern good and Southern good: impact effects on national goods markets under pegged exchange rates.

rise slightly in Figure 17.2 (q' is northeast of q), but this result is not inevitable. Southern income will rise only when spillover effects from the North, consisting of both income and substitution effects, are large enough to offset the initial leftward shift of the Southern income curve.

It would, of course, be possible for the Northern government to undertake a balanced-budget increase in spending on the Southern good, but this is quite likely to reduce Northern income. There is, in fact, more danger of a drop in Northern income than when the Northern government undertakes deficit spending on the Southern good, because the requisite increase in Northern taxes reduces the private demand for the Northern good. In Figure 17.2, the Southern income curve shifts rightward from $Y^2 Y^2$ to $Y^{2\prime\prime} Y^{2\prime\prime}$, the Northern curve shifts downward from $Y^1 Y^1$ to $Y^{1\prime\prime} Y^{1\prime\prime}$, and goods-market equilibrium is displaced from q to q''.[8] The in-

[8] The rightward shift of Y^2Y^2 to $Y^{2\prime\prime}Y^{2\prime\prime}$ in Figure 17.2 is $\alpha[1 - m_2(1 - S_Y)]$, where α is defined as it was in notes 6 and 7. It is thus equal to the shift to $Y^{1\prime}Y^{1\prime}$ in Figure 17.1 *less* the shift to $Y^{2\prime\prime}Y^{2\prime\prime}$. It measures the effect on the demand for the Southern good of the increase in government spending *plus* the negative effect of the reduction in Northern disposable income caused by the increase in Northern taxes. The downward shift of Y^1Y^1 to $Y^{1\prime\prime}Y^{1\prime\prime}$ in Figure 17.2 is $\alpha m_1(1 - S_Y)$ and is thus the negative of the shift to $Y^{1\prime}Y^{1\prime}$ in Fig-

crease in aggregate income is the same as when the Northern government
spends more on the Northern good, but Southern income rises and
Northern income can fall. When demands are biased toward the domestic
good, moreover, Northern spending on the Southern good raises
Southern income by more than the increase in Northern income that takes
place with Northern spending on the Northern good. As the increase in
aggregate income is the same in each instance, the increase in Northern
income has to be smaller (and may give way to a decrease).

To examine the implications of goods-market integration and the size of
the bias toward the domestic good, we consider once again a balanced-
budget increase of Northern spending on the Northern good. Clearly, an
increase of goods-market integration reduces the likelihood of a decline in
Southern income, and perfect integration precludes it completely. When
Northern and Southern goods are perfect substitutes, incomes cannot
move in opposite directions, and with goods-market symmetry, they must
rise by the same amounts. The income curves in Figure 17.2 come to coincide with YY, and goods-market equilibrium is displaced from q to q^* for
any balanced-budget increase in spending – on either good by either government. As usual, goods-market integration strengthens structural interdependence. This is not necessarily the case, however, with a reduction
in the bias toward the domestic good. As in other instances, it narrows the
gap between the two countries' income curves. With a balanced-budget
increase in Northern spending on the Northern good, however, a reduction in bias amplifies the upward shift of the Northern curve and the leftward shift of the Southern curve. In consequence, it *widens* the difference between the income changes and raises the likelihood of a decline
in Southern income; goods-market equilibrium lies to the northwest of q'
in Figure 17.2. (With a balanced-budget increase in Northern spending on
the Southern good, by contrast, a reduction in bias diminishes the difference between the income changes.)[9]

In the absence of full-scale goods-market symmetry, each of the three

---

ure 17.1. It measures the effect on the demand for the Northern good of the reduction in
Northern disposable income caused by the increase in Northern taxes.

[9] Using Eqs. (13.7) and (13.8) and invoking full-scale goods-market symmetry, the difference
between income changes can be written as

$$\delta Y' = (\sigma_1/M_s)(u_{10}^t + \sigma_1 M_Y)\{[1 - (m_1 - m_2)(1 - S_Y)]\, \delta\bar{G}_1$$
$$- [1 + (m_1 - m_2)(1 - S_Y)]\, \delta\bar{G}_2'\}$$

Differentiating this expression with respect to m_2 (and assuming that $\delta m_2 = -\delta m_1$), it can be
shown that a reduction in the bias toward the domestic good increases the difference
between income changes when there is an increase in $\bar{G}_1$ and decreases the difference when
there is an increase in $\bar{G}_2'$.

fiscal policies examined above can cause a wide range of outcomes. Differences between supply-side responses (σ_1 and σ_2') and between price elasticities (u_{10}^t and u_{20}^t) can reverse the ordering of income changes. Thus, deficit spending on the Northern good and a Northern tax cut can raise Southern income by more than Northern income; they can do so when the value of Southern output is the more responsive to price changes (when $\sigma_2 > \sigma_1$) or when the Northern goods market is more closely integrated with the foreign market (when $u_{10}^t > u_{20}^t$) so that changes in p_1 are restricted more narrowly than changes in p_2. (When, in fact, the Northern good is a perfect substitute for the foreign good, p_1 cannot change, and deficit spending on the Northern good can have no effect on Northern or Southern income. A tax cut in the North, however, will still raise Southern income; by raising Northern disposable income, it raises the Northern demand for the Southern good and thus raises p_2.)

Asymmetries like these, however, cannot change the *signs* of the short-run income changes when they would be definite with goods-market symmetry. If Northern income rises with full-scale symmetry, it must also rise in the absence of symmetry. (At worst, the increase in one country's income will be held to zero, because that country's good is a perfect substitute for the foreign good.) Even with asymmetries, moreover, two strong statements can be made about the relationship between income changes. (1) Deficit spending on one country's good will always raise that country's income by at least as much as an equal amount of deficit spending on its neighbor's good, regardless of the government involved. (2) A tax cut by one country will always raise that country's income by at least as much as an identical tax cut by the other country. These generalizations hold in the long run too and hold also with a flexible external exchange rate. Accordingly, we continue to invoke full-scale goods-market symmetry in this chapter and the next. It is not too restrictive for our purposes.

Short-run reactions by the South

Can the South protect itself against the effects of Northern fiscal policies? The answer depends on the degree of structural interdependence, just as it did in Chapter 15. With fiscal policies, however, goods markets, not asset markets, are the ones that matter in the short run and long run alike.

When goods markets are not perfectly interdependent, deficit spending on one country's good and a tax cut by that country have larger short-run effects on that country's income than deficit spending on its neighbor's

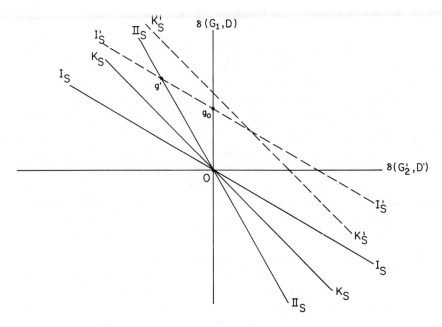

Figure 17.3 Policy interdependence: policy reaction curves for levels of deficit spending required to achieve short-run income targets under pegged exchange rates.

good or a tax cut by its neighbor. Therefore, each government can use its fiscal policies to achieve its income target and can thus offset the spillover effects of its neighbor's policies.

In Figure 17.3 we draw fiscal-policy reaction curves for deficit spending by the North on the Northern good and deficit spending by the South on the Southern good. Curve I_S–I_S is the Northern curve; it shows how much deficit spending must be undertaken by the North to keep Northern income constant, given the policy followed by the South. Curve II_S–II_S is the Southern curve; it shows how much deficit spending must be undertaken by the South to keep Southern income constant, given the policy followed by the North. When both countries seek to keep their incomes constant, and there are no exogenous disturbances at work, the two curves intersect at the origin. There is no need for deficit spending by either country.

Suppose, now, that the North decides to raise Northern income ($\delta\bar{Y} > 0$). The Northern policy reaction curve shifts upward from I_S–I_S to I'_S–I'_S. In the absence of a change in Southern policy, the North would achieve its new target by undertaking $0g_0$ of deficit spending. But Southern income will rise too, and if the Southern government does not want this to happen, it must cut its spending. Its response, moreover, has negative spillover effects, so that the North must raise its spending further. The fiscal-policy combination that satisfies each country's income target is given at g', where $I_S'-I_S'$ intersects II_S-I_S.[10]

An increase of structural interdependence, resulting from a reduction in the bias toward the domestic good or an increase of goods-market integration, reduces the difference between the slopes of the policy reaction curves. By implication, each government must make larger policy changes to offset spillover effects. With perfect goods-market integration and thus complete structural interdependence, the curves come to coincide when the countries' income targets are the same and come to be parallel when the targets differ. Initially, then, they come to coincide with K_S-K_S in Figure 17.3; their slopes are equal to $-45°$ with goods-market symmetry. When the North seeks to raise Northern income, however, its curve shifts to $K_S'-K_S'$ and can no longer intersect the Southern curve, K_S-K_S. No set of fiscal policies can satisfy both countries.[11] When structural interdependence is complete, policy interdependence is likewise complete; neither country can pursue an independent income target.

Much the same analysis can be conducted for tax policies and balanced-budget changes in expenditures. Given the degree of structural interdependence, the reaction curves for tax reductions would resemble the curves drawn in Figure 17.3, but the spread between them would be narrower, because a tax cut is less potent than an equal amount of deficit spending and has larger spillover effects. Therefore, a change in one

[10] To find the policy combinations that satisfy on impact both countries' income targets, we sum the price responses to δG_1 and δD and to $\delta G_2'$ and $\delta D'$, using Eqs. (13.7) and (13.8), and multiply the sums by σ_1 and σ_2', respectively, to convert price changes into income changes. Inverting our results, we solve for $\delta(G_1, D)$ and $\delta(G_2', D')$ in terms of the income targets, $\delta \bar{Y}$ and $\delta \bar{Y}'$:

$$\delta(G_1, D) = (1/\sigma_1\sigma_2')[\sigma_2'\{u_{10}^t + u_{12}^t + [M_Y + m_2(1 - S_Y)]\sigma_1\} \delta\bar{Y}$$
$$- \sigma_1[u_{12}^t + m_2(1 - S_Y)\sigma_2'] \delta\bar{Y}']$$
$$\delta(G_2', D') = (1/\sigma_1\sigma_2')[\sigma_1\{u_{20}^t + u_{12}^t + [M_Y + m_2(1 - S_Y)]\sigma_2'\} \delta\bar{Y}'$$
$$- \sigma_2'[u_{12}^t + m_2(1 - S_Y)\sigma_1] \delta\bar{Y}]$$

With perfect goods-market integration, then, the policy changes become infinitely large: as $u_{12}^t \to \infty$, then $\delta(G_1, D)$, $\delta(G_2', D') \to \infty$.

[11] When goods-market symmetry does not prevail, the reaction curves are not necessarily symmetrical around K_S-K_S. With perfect goods-market integration, however, the slopes of the two curves have still to be identical, even though they do not coincide with K_S-K_S (or $K_S'-K_S'$). The countries cannot follow independent policies. (With perfect goods-market integration, the countries' income targets are consistent only if $\sigma_2' \delta\bar{Y} = \sigma_1 \delta\bar{Y}'$, which means that the targets must be equal when there is full-scale goods-market symmetry.)

country's income target will lead to larger changes in both countries' taxes. With balanced-budget changes in expenditures, the policy reaction curves can be quite different from the ones in Figure 17.3. Because the spillover effects can be positive or negative, the slopes of the relevant reaction curves can be positive or negative. We look at curves like these later in this chapter, when we study long-run outcomes. Here, it is enough to note that the implications of structural interdependence are the same for all three fiscal policies. An increase of structural interdependence raises policy interdependence, and complete structural interdependence produces complete policy interdependence; the North and South cannot pursue independent income targets, even in the short run.[12]

Steady-state effects of fiscal policies

Because budgets must be balanced in the long run, deficit spending must be brought to an end and tax cuts have to be rescinded. Furthermore, the changes in supplies of bonds brought about by temporary budget deficits have no permanent effects on incomes under pegged exchange rates. Hence, the steady-state effects of fiscal policies can be described completely by answering two questions. What are the long-run effects on nominal incomes of a balanced-budget increase in expenditure – whether it is balanced from the start or terminates an interval of deficit spending? What are the long-run effects of the three fiscal policies on holdings of reserves and other asset-market variables?

Effects in goods markets

To simplify the treatment of goods-market effects, let us look at the results of an increase of Northern spending on the Northern good balanced from the start by an increase of Northern taxes. When we describe the passage to the stationary state, we shall not have to make allowance for the flow supply of bonds generated by a budget deficit.

---

[12] There is one difference, however, between the implications for tax changes on the one hand and for expenditure changes on the other. Elimination of the bias toward the domestic good leads to perfect policy interdependence when taxes are involved; the changes in the countries' incomes are the same, regardless of the country in which taxes are altered. But elimination of that bias does not lead to perfect policy interdependence when expenditures are involved; the changes in the countries' incomes are not the same with deficit spending and are apt to be opposite in sign with balanced-budget changes in government spending. Perfect policy interdependence, however, is always produced by perfect goods-market integration (when $u_{12}^t \to \infty$).

With full-scale goods-market symmetry and incomplete structural inter-dependence, the immediate increase of Northern income exceeds the increase of Southern income. (The latter, indeed, can decrease rather than increase.) Northern households will start to dissave because of the reduction in disposable income brought on by the increase in Northern taxes. The North will move into current-account deficit, bilaterally with the South and also with the outside world, and its global deficit will be larger than the Southern deficit. (The South can have a surplus rather than a deficit if the increase in its income is sufficiently small or there is a decrease in Southern income.)

The Northern deficit will be financed in part by capital inflows from the South and the outside world; its households will sell Northern and Southern bonds to households in the South and will sell foreign bonds to the outside world. The rest of its deficit will be financed by an outflow of reserves. Northern wealth will fall through time, and the Northern interest rate will rise. Dissaving will diminish in the North, reducing absorption and the demand for the Northern good. Northern income will decline, but not by enough to offset completely the increase of income that took place on impact. (There will, of course, be feedback effects from the South, but these may be of either sign and can never dominate domestic events in the North.)

In Figure 17.4A, Northern income is drawn as a function of the external exchange rate. With a balanced-budget increase in Northern spending on the Northern good, the short-run income curve shifts upward from z^1z^1 to $z^{1\prime}z^{1\prime}$, displacing equilibrium from v to v' at the pegged exchange rate denoted by $\pi_0'\pi_0'$. The long-run income curve shifts upward too, from Z^1Z^1 to $Z^{1\prime}Z^{1\prime}$, but by less than the short-run curve. The gap between the two new curves, the distance v^*v', indicates the current-account deficit that opens up on impact (and dissaving in the North). With the passage of time, the short-run curve travels downward, responding to the gradual decline in Northern wealth and increase in the Northern interest rate. It comes to rest at $z^{1*}z^{1*}$, when it intersects $Z^{1\prime}Z^{1\prime}$ at v^*.

In Figure 17.4B we show the relationships between the two countries' incomes. The shifts from Y^1Y^1 to $Y^{1\prime}Y^{1\prime}$ and from Y^2Y^2 to $Y^{2\prime}Y^{2\prime}$, displacing equilibrium from q to q', replicate the impact effects shown in Figure 17.2. The subsequent decrease in Northern wealth and increase in r_1 (reinforced or dampened, as the case may be, by changes in Southern wealth and in r_2) cause the Northern income curve to move down gradually, from $Y^{1\prime}Y^{1\prime}$ to $Y^{1*}Y^{1*}$. The corresponding movement of the Southern curve can go either way, depending on the signs and sizes of the

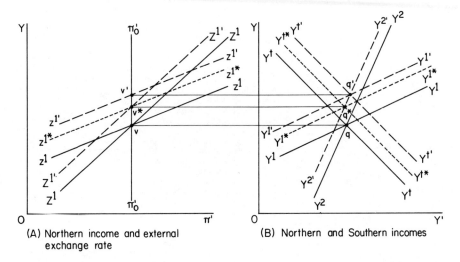

Figure 17.4 Balanced-budget increase in Northern spending on the Northern good: impact and steady-state effects on national goods markets under pegged exchange rates.

changes in $W^{h'}$ and r_2, combined with the changes in W^h and r_1. Figure 17.4B is drawn for the special case in which these balance out; the Southern curve remains at $Y^{2'}Y^{2'}$. Goods-market equilibrium moves gradually from q' to q^*, reflecting the same change in Northern income as the movement from v' to v^* in Figure 17.4A. In the new steady state, Northern income is higher than it was before the change in Northern policy, and the change in Southern income is ambiguous. The permanent increase in Northern income, however, is smaller than the increase that took place on impact and also smaller than the increase in government spending (which means that there must be a permanent reduction in Northern disposable income).

To sum up, the North can control its income in the long run if the Northern government is able to adjust its purchases and taxes and the South does not seek to neutralize the effects on Southern income. Is it possible, however, for both countries to control their incomes simultaneously – to achieve independent income targets in the long run? The answer is much the same as for the short run. If goods markets are not perfectly integrated, structural interdependence is incomplete, and policy interdependence is likewise incomplete. Each country can achieve its own income target.

As a balanced-budget increase in government spending has ambiguous

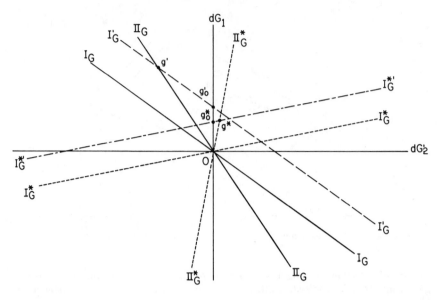

Figure 17.5 Policy interdependence: policy reaction curves for balanced-budget changes in spending required to achieve long-run income targets under pegged exchange rates.

effects on income in the other country, the analysis of policy reactions is somewhat more complicated than the one conducted for deficit spending. In Figure 17.5 we draw two pairs of reaction curves to illustrate the two types of policy combinations that may be required in this instance. The curves I_G^*–I_G^* and II_G^*–II_G^* pertain to the case in which a balanced-budget increase in one country's spending has negative effects on its neighbor's income, because goods markets are not closely integrated. (With a balanced-budget increase in Northern spending on the Northern good, the negative income effects of the reduction in Northern disposable income resulting from the increase in Northern taxes dominate the positive substitution effects resulting from the increase in the price of the Northern good, and the demand for the Southern good declines.) The policy reaction curves have positive slopes, because the South must stimulate Southern income whenever the North stimulates Northern income. The curves I_G–I_G and II_G–II_G pertain to the case in which a balanced-budget increase in one country's spending has positive effects on its neighbor's income, because goods markets are closely integrated. (The positive substitution effects dominate the negative income effects.) The policy reaction curves have negative slopes, because the South must restrain

Southern income whenever the North stimulates Northern income. In general, the policy reaction curves have positive slopes when goods-market integration is low and negative slopes when it is high. With perfect goods-market integration, moreover, the slopes must be identical as well as negative (and must equal $-45°$ when, in addition, the countries' goods markets are fully symmetrical).[13]

An increase in the Northern income target ($d\bar{Y} > 0$) causes an upward shift in the relevant Northern reaction curve. If the South seeks to keep its income constant, the Southern curve remains in place. With negative spillover effects, I_G^*–I_G^* and II_G^*–II_G^* are applicable, the Northern curve shifts upward to $I_G^{*'}$–$I_G^{*'}$, and the appropriate policy combination is shown at g^*. As Southern income would fall if the Southern government did nothing, a balanced-budget increase in Southern expenditure is required to keep Southern income constant. With positive spillover effects, I_G–I_G and II_G–II_G are applicable, the Northern curve shifts upward to I_G'–I_G', and the appropriate policy combination is shown at g'. As Southern income would rise if the Southern government did nothing, a balanced-budget decrease in Southern expenditure is required.

Carrying the argument one step further, let us compare the sizes of the policy changes evoked by the two types of spillover effects. With negative effects and no Southern reaction, the North would have to raise its spending by $0g_0^*$ to achieve its target. When the South responds, the North must raise spending further (g^* is northeast of g_0^*), but not by much. With positive effects and no Southern reaction, the North would have to raise its spending by $0g_0'$, which is larger than $0g_0^*$, because some part of the stimulus to Northern income is lost to the South. When the South responds, moreover, the North must raise its spending very much further (g' is northwest of g_0', and the vertical distance between g' and g_0' exceeds the one between g^* and g_0^*). With positive spillover effects, the South must make a large deflationary change in its budget. This change tends to depress Northern income, and the North must react strongly to achieve its target.[14]

The closer the integration of goods markets, the larger are the fiscal-

---

[13] Without structural interdependence (when $u_{12}^i = 0$ and $m_2 = m_1' = 0$), the Northern reaction curve would be vertical and Southern curve horizontal. A change in one country's policy would not evoke a change in its neighbor's policy, and the size of the change in a country's fiscal policy required to achieve a predetermined income target would be smaller than it is with interdependence.

[14] To find the combinations of balanced-budget policies that satisfy both countries' income targets in the long run, we use Eqs. (13.23b) and (13.24b). The price responses to dG_1 and dG_2' are multiplied by σ_1 and σ_2', respectively, and are then inverted to solve for dG_1 and

policy adjustments required to achieve independent income targets in the
North and South. At some point short of perfect integration, moreover,
the adjustments can become impractical, because of limitations on the
size of the budget. Government spending cannot be negative, and this sets
a lower limit to the budget. Taxes cannot exceed personal income and
have to be much smaller as a practical matter, and this sets an upper limit
to the budget. When economies are highly interdependent, governments
may be unable to achieve independent income targets in the long run.
They may be unable to balance their budgets at the requisite levels.

Effects in asset markets

Although incomes are apt to be the principal targets of national fiscal policies, governments must be concerned about the effects on their reserves
and other asset-market variables. In the model we use here, these effects
do not occur at once; fiscal policies start out as goods-market disturbances. But they become important with the passage of time, as budget
deficits affect supplies of assets and current-account deficits affect
wealth. We begin with the legacy of a budget deficit–the increase in
supply of the Northern bond that takes place gradually when the North
engages in deficit spending or cuts taxes temporarily. There are, of
course, no permanent effects on incomes in the North and South. (They
cannot occur unless deficit spending is terminated by raising Northern
taxes, producing a permanent balanced-budget increase in spending.)
Therefore, we can concentrate on effects in asset markets.

In Figure 17.6A we draw the familiar asset-market curves for the North
and show the steady-state effects of an increase in B_1 resulting from a
Northern budget deficit. The Northern bond-market curve shifts upward
from W^1W^1 to $W^{1*}W^{1*}$, and asset-market equilibrium is displaced from w
to w^*, where $W^{1*}W^{1*}$ intersects S^1S^1.[15] The money-market curve must
therefore shift from M^1M^1 to $M^{1*}M^{1*}$ in order to join this intersection, and

dG_2' in terms of the income targets, $d\bar{Y}$ and $d\bar{Y}'$:

$$dG_1 = (1/m_0\sigma_1\sigma_2')[1 - (m_1 - m_2)]^{-1}[\sigma_2'((1 - m_1)u_{10}^t + m_0u_{12}^t + m_0[1 - (m_1 - m_2)]\sigma_1\}d\bar{Y} - \sigma_1(m_0u_{12}^t - m_2u_{20}^t)\,d\bar{Y}']$$

$$dG_2' = (1/m_0\sigma_1\sigma_2')[1 - (m_1 - m_2)]^{-1}[\sigma_1((1 - m_1)u_{20}^t + m_0u_{12}^t + m_0[1 - (m_1 - m_2)]\sigma_2'\}\,d\bar{Y}' - \sigma_2'(m_0u_{12}^t - m_2u_{10}^t)\,d\bar{Y}]$$

When $u_{12}^t \to \infty$, then, $dG_1, dG_2' \to \infty$.

[15] Figure 17.6 is drawn for the special case in which r_2 does not change, so that S^1S^1 does not
shift. (If r_2 were to rise, S^1S^1 would shift downward; if it were to fall, S^1S^1 would shift upward.) The shift in the bond-market curve, moreover, must be deemed to include the effects of changes in r_2 and Southern wealth. These feedback effects, however, are never
large enough to reverse the principal conclusions in the text.

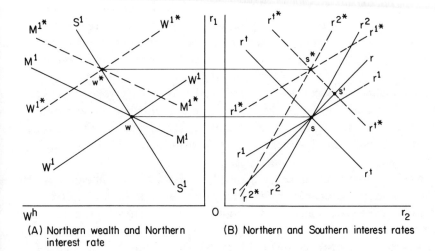

(A) Northern wealth and Northern
interest rate

(B) Northern and Southern interest rates

Figure 17.6 Increase in the supply of the Northern bond resulting from a Northern budget deficit: steady-state effects on national asset markets under pegged exchange rates.

the direction of this shift says that the North has lost reserves during the transition to the new steady state.

In Figure 17.6B we show the relationship between the countries' interest rates. Given the supplies of bonds, stocks of wealth, and the world interest rate, $\bar{r}_0$, the market for the Northern bond is cleared by combinations of r_1 and r_2 lying on r^1r^1, and the market for the Southern bond is cleared by combinations lying on r^2r^2. The level of the average interest rate, r^t, is shown by r^tr^t. The upward shift of the Northern curve from r^1r^1 to $r^{1*}r^{1*}$ reflects the increase in supply of the Northern bond, net of the increase in demand resulting from the growth of Northern wealth shown in Figure 17.6A. It has also to reflect the influence of the change in demand resulting from the change in Southern wealth, but that change is ambiguous and relatively small. The leftward shift of the Southern curve from r^2r^2 to $r^{2*}r^{2*}$ reflects the increase in demand resulting from the growth in Northern wealth and the change in demand resulting from the change in Southern wealth.[16] Asset-market equilibrium is displaced from s to s^*, and there is an increase in the average interest rate, denoted by the shift

[16] The leftward shift of r^2r^2 is given by

$$dr_2|_{\bar{r}_1} = -(1/B_{11}^t)[B_{2W}(dW^h/dB_1) + B_{1W}(dW^{h\prime}/dB_1)]\,dB_1$$

But $(dW^{h\prime}/dB_1) = (dW^h/dB_2^t)$ under our assumptions, and expressions for (dW^h/dB_2^t) and (dW^h/dB_1) are given by Eq. (E.7b). Substituting into the equation above,

$$dr_2|_{\bar{r}_1} = (S_W/B_{11}^t J_W J_K)[(B_{11}^t - B_{12}^t)S_1^t B_{2W} + (B_{1W} - B_{2W})(S_2 B_{11}^t - S_1 B_{12}^t)]\,dB_1 < 0$$

from $r^t r^t$ to $r^{t*} r^{t*}$. As Figure 17.6B is drawn, the increase in r^t is due entirely to the increase in the Northern rate. The Southern rate does not change. But this is a special case; the Southern rate can move either way, depending on the degree of substitutability between the two countries' bonds.

In summary, a budget deficit in the North leaves in its wake an increase in B_1 that raises the Northern interest rate and Northern wealth but reduces Northern reserves. The effects on the Southern interest rate, Southern wealth, and Southern reserves are smaller absolutely but ambiguous in sign.

How are these outcomes influenced by asset-market integration? It does not affect the change in the average interest rate but does affect the spread between the changes in the countries' rates. Therefore, it does not affect the size of the change in aggregate wealth or loss of reserves but does affect their distributions between North and South. The higher the degree of substitutability between the two countries' bonds, the smaller the spread between the changes in the interest rates; the increase in r_1 is reduced, and r_2 is more likely to rise than fall. The growth of Northern wealth is smaller, and so is the loss of reserves. Accordingly, Southern wealth is more likely to rise, and the South is more likely to lose reserves. With perfect substitutability, the countries' interest rates must rise by the same amounts; asset-market equilibrium must be displaced to s' in Figure 17.6B, where $r^{t*} r^{t*}$ intersects rr. In this limiting case, then, each country must experience the same increase in wealth and same loss of reserves.

Consider next an increase in Northern spending on the Northern good, and assume that is balanced from the start by an increase in Northern taxes (so that there is no increase in B_1). As the Northern current account shifts into deficit, the Northern interest rate will rise through time, Northern wealth will fall, and the North will lose reserves. In the new steady state, Northern income will be higher than it was initially but lower than it was on impact. Northern disposable income, however, will be lower than it was initially. (This is why Northern wealth must fall and the Northern interest rate must rise; otherwise, Northerners would want to dissave.)

These assertions are illustrated in Figure 17.7A. The reduction in Northern disposable income shifts $S^1 S^1$ to $S^{1*} S^{1*}$. The Northern bond-market curve, $W^1 W^1$, can shift up or down through time, depending on the ways in which changes in r_2 and Southern wealth affect the Southern demand for the Northern bond. As before, however, those changes are ambiguous, and we have canceled their effects to simplify the diagram;

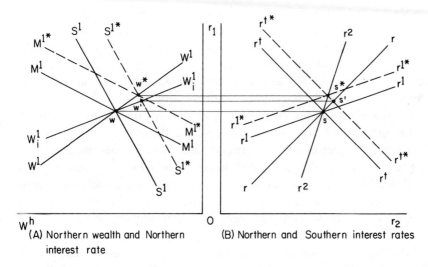

(A) Northern wealth and Northern interest rate

(B) Northern and Southern interest rates

Figure 17.7 Balanced-budget increase in Northern spending on the Northern good with different degrees of asset-market integration: steady-state effects on national asset markets under pegged exchange rates.

the bond-market curve remains in place. Asset-market equilibrium is displaced from w to w^*, where $S^{1*}S^{1*}$ intersects W^1W^1. The North loses reserves, as the Northern money-market curve moves from M^1M^1 to $M^{1*}M^{1*}$ to join the intersection at w^*. The movement from w to w^* is gradual, occurring in response to dissaving in the North and the corresponding current-account deficit. Part of that deficit is offset by a capital inflow; the rest is financed by the loss of reserves.

The effects on Southern asset markets are ambiguous. As Southern income can rise or fall, so can disposable income. The signs of the results are also affected by the degree of asset-market integration. When Northern and Southern bonds are close substitutes, the Southern interest rate is apt to rise, following the Northern rate, and the South is likely to lose reserves. The relationships between r_1 and r_2 are shown in Figure 17.7B. The Northern bond-market curve shifts upward gradually from r^1r^1 to $r^{1*}r^{1*}$ as a result of the decline in Northern wealth. (The shift would be reinforced by a decrease in Southern wealth and moderated by an increase, but the direction of the shift would not be affected.) The Southern bond-market curve can shift up or down, depending on the change in Southern wealth and the strength of the effect of the decline in Northern wealth, but is drawn to remain in place. Therefore, asset-market equilibrium is displaced from s to s^*. The Northern interest rate rises, as was shown in Figure 17.7A, and the average interest rate rises too, as is shown by the shift from $r^t r^t$ to $r^{t*} r^{t*}$ in Figure 17.7B. In this particular example, the Southern rate rises, but a large increase in Southern wealth, raising the demand for the Southern bond despite the reduction in Northern wealth, could cause the Southern bond-market curve to shift leftward by enough to reduce the Southern rate.

The sum of disposable incomes, Y^{dt}, determines the steady-state levels of aggregate wealth, aggregate reserves, and the average interest rate.[17] The degree of asset-market integration determines the distribution of the long-run changes in W^{ht}, R^t, and r^t. Repeating what we said above, r_1 and r_2 will tend to move together when asset markets are closely integrated, and both countries are apt to lose reserves. But close integration will enlarge the spread between the changes in wealth. With perfect integration, of course, r_1 and r_2 must rise by the same amounts. In Figure 17.7B, $r^1 r^1$ and $r^2 r^2$ come to coincide with rr, and equilibrium is displaced to s'. In Figure 17.7A, the Northern bond-market curve is represented by $W_i^1 W_i^1$, and equilibrium is displaced to w', where $S^{1*} S^{1*}$ intersects $W_i^1 W_i^1$. The increase in the Northern interest rate is smaller and the decrease in wealth is larger. Furthermore, the money-market curve has less distance to travel in order to join the new intersection, so that the loss of reserves is reduced.[18] Outcomes change conversely in the South. The decrease in wealth is minimized (the increase maximized), and the loss of reserves is maximized (the gain minimized).

To sum up, a Northern fiscal policy aimed at raising Northern income must always raise the Northern interest rate in the long run and must reduce Northern reserves. It will have these side effects whether it involves a budget deficit and an increase in B_1 or a balanced-budget increase in Northern spending. (The distinction is important only for the sign of the change in Northern wealth.) The effects on the Southern interest rate and Southern reserves are typically ambiguous, but the greater the degree of asset-market integration, the more likely they are to resemble the effects in the North. With perfect integration, the two countries' interest rates

[17] When we examined open-market operations in Chapter 15, we saw in Figure 15.1 that the steady-state levels of aggregate wealth, aggregate reserves, and the average interest rate depend on Y^{dt}, B_1^{ct}, B_2^{ct}, B_1, and B_2, and that the responses of W^{ht}, R^t, and r^t to changes in those variables were unaffected by the degree of substitutability between the two countries' bonds (by B_{12}^t). Because an increase in $\bar{G}_1$ causes a permanent reduction in Y^{dt}, we know that W^{ht} and R^t have to fall, and r^t has to rise.

[18] The shift in the money-market curve is not shown in the diagram but must be smaller than the shift from $M^1 M^1$ to $M^{1*} M^{1*}$ because w' lies below $M^{1*} M^{1*}$. Note in passing that $W_i^1 W_i^1$ is flatter than $W^1 W^1$ but not perfectly horizontal. It would be horizontal only if the Northern bond were a perfect substitute for the foreign bond.

must move together, and the changes in reserves are made to be most similar. When, indeed, Northern fiscal policy involves an increase in B_1 and no permanent change in Northern taxes, the changes in Northern and Southern reserves become identical. When it involves a balanced-budget increase in Northern spending, initially or sequentially, the loss of reserves is larger in the North (there can still be an increase in Southern reserves), but the dissimilarity is minimized.

Fiscal and monetary policies for internal and external balance

Thus far we have been concerned with the ways in which fiscal and monetary policies can be used, one by one, to pursue independent income targets. We must now consider a more complicated question. Can fiscal and monetary policies be used simultaneously to achieve independent internal (income) targets and independent external (reserve) targets when the countries involved are structurally interdependent? If so, what is the appropriate policy combination in each country, and will it be the same in the long run as in the short run?

Conclusions reached in this and earlier chapters suggest that fiscal policies should be employed to pursue internal targets and monetary policies to pursue external targets. Fiscal policies do not affect reserves on impact, and monetary policies do not affect incomes permanently. The fiscal policies, however, must involve permanent changes in expenditures and taxes if they are to have permanent effects on incomes; they must be balanced-budget changes in expenditure, initially or sequentially. To illustrate and analyze this policy assignment, we examine a single, simple case, with targets chosen arbitrarily. The North seeks to raise its income immediately and permanently ($\delta \bar{Y} = d\bar{Y} > 0$) and also to raise its reserves ($\delta \bar{R} = d\bar{R} > 0$). The South seeks to avoid any change in Southern income or reserves ($\delta \bar{Y}' = d\bar{Y}' = 0$, and $\delta \bar{R}' = d\bar{R}' = 0$).

As fiscal policies do not affect reserves immediately but monetary policies have immediate effects on incomes, countries must first choose the monetary policies that will achieve their reserve targets, then choose the fiscal policies that will achieve their income targets, given the effects of their monetary policies. To do so accurately, of course, each government must be able to forecast precisely the consequences of its own policies, the policy reactions of the other government, and the feedback effects of those reactions. This supposition is utterly unrealistic, but we adopt it nonetheless, to simplify the exposition. In this example, moreover, we as-

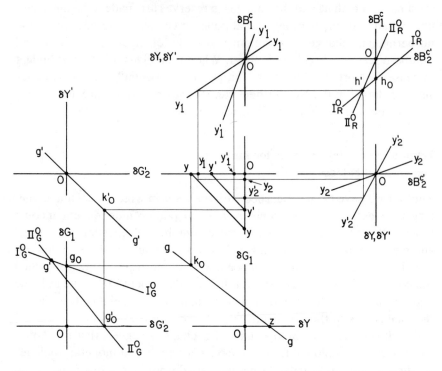

Figure 17.8 Monetary and fiscal policies for external and internal balance: short-run solutions.

sume that budgets are balanced from the start, so as to suppress the complications introduced by changes in supplies of bonds.

The sequence of decisions described above is traced in Figure 17.8. It is drawn to assert that goods and asset markets are not perfectly integrated, so that policy interdependence is incomplete, but that goods-market integration is close enough to guarantee that balanced-budget changes in government spending have positive spillover effects.

In the upper right-hand corner of Figure 17.8, we draw reaction curves for the open-market operations required to achieve the countries' short-run reserve targets. The curve II_R^0–II_R^0 is the Southern curve; as the South wants to stabilize its reserves, the curve passes through the origin. The curve I_R^0–I_R^0 is the Northern curve; as the North wants to raise its reserves, the curve intersects the vertical axis at h_0, below the origin. In the absence of any Southern reaction, the Northern central bank would achieve its reserve target by selling $0h_0$ of Northern bonds. The intersection at h' gives the combination of open-market operations that permits each country to achieve its reserve target. Both central banks must make open-market sales, but the Northern bank must make the larger sale (which must be bigger than $0h_0$ to offset the spillover effect of the Southern sale).

To the left of these reaction curves, we show the effects of Northern monetary policy on Northern and Southern incomes. Curve y_1y_1 shows the response of Northern income; curve $y_1'y_1'$ shows the response of Southern income. With an open-market sale by the Northern bank, both countries' incomes fall. Beneath the reaction curves, we show the effects of Southern monetary policy. Curve y_2y_2 shows the response of Northern income; curve $y_2'y_2'$ shows the response of Southern income. With an open-market sale by the Southern bank, both countries' incomes fall. In the middle of the diagram, we add up the income changes in each country. Looking first at Northern income, the Northern open-market sale reduces it by $0y_1$, and the Southern sale reduces it by $0y_2$. The sum of the reductions is $0y$, whether measured vertically or horizontally. Looking next at Southern income, the Northern sale reduces it by $0y_1'$, the Southern sale reduces it by $0y_2'$, and the sum of the reductions is $0y'$.[19]

As the South wants to stabilize its income, it must use its fiscal policy to offset the reduction $0y'$. Curve $g'g'$ shows what it would do if it made no allowance for a change in Northern fiscal policy; it shows the response of

[19] General solutions for these income changes can be obtained from results presented in Chapter 13 and Appendix E. First, define the income changes as $\delta\hat{Y} = (\delta Y/\delta B_1^c)\,\delta B_1^c + (\delta Y/\delta B_2^c)\,\delta B_2^c$ and $\delta\hat{Y}' = (\delta Y'/\delta B_1^c)\,\delta B_1^c + (\delta Y'/\delta B_2^c)\,\delta B_2^c$. Next, invoke the fact that $\bar{\pi}'(\delta R'/\delta B_2^c) = \bar{\pi}'(\delta R/\delta B_1^c)$ and $\bar{\pi}'(\delta R/\delta B_2^c) = \bar{\pi}'(\delta R/\delta B_2^c)'$ with asset-market symmetry, so that we can extract from Eq. (E.2b) expressions for the changes in each country's reserves resulting from changes in B_1^c and B_2^c. Inverting those expressions, we can define the open-market operations required to achieve reserve targets:

$$\delta B_1^c = (J_S/J_R)[(J_S L_{12} - B_{12}^t L_{11}^t)\bar{\pi}'(\delta\bar{R} + \delta\bar{R}') + B_{01}^t(B_{11}^t - B_{12}^t)\bar{\pi}'\,\delta\bar{R}]$$
$$\delta B_2^{c\prime} = (J_S/J_R)[(J_S L_{12} - B_{12}^t L_{11}^t)\bar{\pi}'(\delta\bar{R} + \delta\bar{R}') + B_{01}^t(B_{11}^t - B_{12}^t)\bar{\pi}'\,\delta\bar{R}']$$

where $J_R = B_{01}^t[2(J_S L_{12} - B_{12}^t L_{11}^t) + B_{01}^t(B_{11}^t - B_{12}^t)] > 0$. Thus, $\delta B_1^c < 0$ and $\delta B_2^{c\prime} < 0$ when, as in the text, $\delta\bar{R} > 0$ and $\delta\bar{R}' = 0$. Substituting these expressions into the equations for the income changes, and using Eqs. (13.14b) and (13.15b) to replace the income coefficients $(\delta Y/\delta B_1^c)$, etc.,

$$\delta\hat{Y} = -(\sigma_1/M_s J_S J_R)\{(M_{1p})\bar{\pi}'(\delta\bar{R} + \delta\bar{R}') + M_{1q}[(B_{11}^t)\bar{\pi}'\delta\bar{R} - (B_{12}^t)\bar{\pi}'\delta\bar{R}']\}$$
$$\delta\hat{Y}' = -(\sigma_2'/M_s J_S J_R)\{(M_{2p})\bar{\pi}'(\delta\bar{R} + \delta\bar{R}') + M_{2q}[(B_{11}^t)\bar{\pi}'\delta\bar{R}' - (B_{12}^t)\bar{\pi}'\delta\bar{R}]\}$$

where

$$M_{1p} = -2J_S[B_{01}^t B_{11}^t + J_S(B_{12}^t + L_{12})][(m_1 S_2 + m_2 S_1)M_{22} + S_1^t(1 - m_0)M_{21}] > 0$$
$$M_{2p} = -2J_S[B_{01}^t B_{11}^t + J_S(B_{12}^t + L_{12})][(m_1 S_2 + m_2 S_1)M_{11} + S_1^t(1 - m_0)M_{12}] > 0$$
$$M_{1q} = -B_{01}^t(m_1 - m_2)(S_1 - S_2)J_S M_{22} > 0$$
$$M_{2q} = -B_{01}^t(m_1 - m_2)(S_1 - S_2)J_S M_{11} > 0$$

Thus, $\delta Y < 0$ and $\delta\hat{Y}' < 0$ when $\delta\bar{R} > 0$ and $\delta\bar{R}' = 0$.

Southern income (with sign reversed) to a balanced-budget change in Southern spending on the Southern good. The South would have to increase its spending by the amount defined at k'_0 (the amount $0g'_0$ on the horizontal axis in the lower left-hand corner of the diagram). As the North wants to raise its income, it must use its fiscal policy to offset the reduction $0y$ and also to achieve its new income target. Curve gg shows what it would do if it made no allowance for a change in Southern fiscal policy; it is the Northern counterpart of $g'g'$ but intersects the horizontal axis at z, not the origin, because the North seeks to raise its income ($\delta \bar{Y} = 0z$). The North would have to increase its spending by the amount defined at k_0 (the amount $0g_0$ on the vertical axis in the lower left-hand corner of the diagram).

Each country's fiscal policy, however, has spillover effects on its neighbor's income, and each government thus has to adjust its fiscal policy to neutralize them. The requisite adjustments are defined by the policy reaction curves in the lower left-hand corner. The Northern curve, $I^0_G - I^0_G$, intersects the vertical axis at g_0. The Southern curve, $II^0_G - II^0_G$, intersects the horizontal axis at g'_0. The intersection of the policy reaction curves at g' shows the combination of budgetary changes that will allow each country to achieve its income target. In this particular example, the North must increase its spending, and the South must decrease its spending.[20] The peculiar combination is required because $0g_0$ of extra Northern spend-

---

[20] General solutions for these budgetary changes can be obtained from the results supplied in Chapter 13 and in the previous note. Equations (13.7) and (13.8) are multiplied by σ_1 and σ'_2, respectively, producing expressions for the responses of Y and Y' to changes in G_1 and G'_2, and these expressions are inverted to solve for the budgetary changes required to achieve predetermined income changes. But the relevant income changes are $\delta Y = \delta \bar{Y} - \delta \hat{Y}$, and $\delta Y' = \delta \bar{Y}' - \delta \hat{Y}'$. Replacing $\delta \hat{Y}$ and $\delta \hat{Y}'$ with the values obtained in the previous note, the requisite budgetary changes can be written as functions of the income targets, $\delta \bar{Y}$ and $\delta \bar{Y}'$, and the reserve targets, $\delta \bar{R}$ and $\delta \bar{R}'$:

$$\delta G_1 = [1/(M_{1g}M_{2g} - M_{1h}M_{2h})]\{M_s[(M_{2g})\,\delta \bar{Y} - (M_{1h})\,\delta \bar{Y}']$$
$$+ (1/J_S J_R)[\sigma_1(M_{2g}M_{1p}) - \sigma'_2(M_{1h}M_{2p})]\bar{\pi}'(\delta \bar{R} + \delta \bar{R}')$$
$$+ (1/J_S J_R)[\sigma_1(M_{2g}M_{1q})B^t_{11} + \sigma'_2(M_{1h}M_{2q})B^t_{12}]\bar{\pi}'\,\delta \bar{R}$$
$$- (1/J_S J_R)[\sigma'_2(M_{1h}M_{2q})B^t_{11} + \sigma_1(M_{2g}M_{1q})B^t_{12}]\bar{\pi}'\,\delta \bar{R}'\}$$

$$\delta G'_2 = [1/(M_{1g}M_{2g} - M_{1h}M_{2h})]\{M_s[(M_{1g})\,\delta \bar{Y}' - (M_{2h})\,\delta \bar{Y}]$$
$$+ (1/J_S J_R)[\sigma'_2(M_{1g}M_{2p}) - \sigma_1(M_{2h}M_{1p})]\bar{\pi}'(\delta \bar{R} + \delta \bar{R}')$$
$$+ (1/J_S J_R)[\sigma'_2(M_{1g}M_{2q})B^t_{11} + \sigma_1(M_{2h}M_{1q})B^t_{12})]\bar{\pi}'\,\delta \bar{R}'$$
$$- (1/J_S J_R)[\sigma_1(M_{2h}M_{1q})B^t_{11} + \sigma'_2(M_{1g}M_{2q})B^t_{12}]\pi'\,\delta \bar{R}\}$$

where M_{1p}, M_{2p}, M_{1q}, and M_{2q} are what they were in the previous note, and

$$M_{1g} = \sigma_1 u^t_{20}[1 - m_1(1 - S_Y)] + M_Y(\sigma_1 u^t_{12}) + M_Y[1 - (m_1 - m_2)(1 - S_Y)]\sigma_1\sigma'_2 > 0$$
$$M_{2g} = \sigma'_2 u^t_{10}[1 - m_1(1 - S_Y)] + M_Y(\sigma'_2 u^t_{12}) + M_Y[1 - (m_1 - m_2)(1 - S_Y)]\sigma_1\sigma'_2 > 0$$
$$M_{1h} = \sigma_1[M_Y(u^t_{12}) - m_2(1 - S_Y)u^t_{20}] \gtrless 0$$
$$M_{2h} = \sigma'_2[M_Y(u^t_{12}) - m_2(1 - S_Y)u^t_{10}] \gtrless 0$$

ing has spillover effects that more than offset the reduction $\delta y'$ in Southern income, and the South has to offset the excess effects. An outcome of this type is the more likely, the larger the Northern income target, $0z$, and the higher the degree of goods-market integration.

If the two countries' asset markets were more closely integrated, the slopes of $I_R^0 - I_R^0$ and $II_R^0 - II_R^0$ would have been more nearly equal to $45°$, and the curves would be more nearly parallel. The size of the sum of the open-market operations would not be affected, but the operations would be differently distributed. In this particular example, where both countries are obliged to make open-market sales, the sizes of their sales would be more alike. Even in the case of perfect integration, however, the slopes of the two curves would differ; a change in B_1^c would affect Northern reserves more strongly than Southern reserves, and the converse would be true for a change in B_2^c. Asset-market integration does not preclude the use of monetary policies to achieve independent reserve targets.

But asset-market integration affects incomes as well. The greater the degree of integration, the smaller the difference between the income changes resulting from a set of open-market operations. (With perfect integration and goods-market symmetry, the income changes are identical.) Accordingly, the tasks of fiscal policy are modified. In Figure 17.8, the distance $0y$ is reduced by closer asset-market integration, causing k_0 to travel down gg and shifting $I_G^0 - I_G^0$ downward. The distance $0y'$ is enlarged, causing k_0' to travel down $g'g'$ and shifting $II_G^0 - II_G^0$ rightward. The policy reaction curves are made to intersect at a point to the southeast of g', reducing absolutely the budgetary changes. But asset-market integration cannot invalidate the policy assignments illustrated by Figure 17.8. Each country can achieve its targets independently.

If goods markets were more closely integrated, there would be no change in the position of h', defining the monetary policies required to achieve the reserve targets. Here too, however, the income changes would be made more alike ($0y$ would be reduced and $0y'$ enlarged). Furthermore, an increase of goods-market integration would reduce the difference between the slopes of gg and $g'g'$ and would thereby reduce the difference between $0g_0$ and $0g_0'$. (With perfect goods-market integration and goods-market symmetry, those distances would differ only when there was a difference between income targets and would thus be equal if

---

With goods-market symmetry, however, it can be shown that $M_{1g}M_{2g} > M_{1h}M_{2h}$, that $\sigma_1(M_{2g}M_{1p}) > \sigma_2'(M_{1h}M_{2p})$, and that $\sigma_1(M_{2g}M_{1q})B_{11}^t > -\sigma_2'(M_{1h}M_{2q})B_{12}^t$, so that $\delta G_1 > 0$ when $\delta\bar{R} > 0$, $\delta\bar{Y} > 0$, and $\delta\bar{R}' = \delta\bar{Y}' = 0$. Nevertheless, $\delta G_2'$ is ambiguous, because M_{2h} is ambiguous (spillover effects can be positive or negative).

0z were zero.) Most important, the slopes of $I_G^0-I_G^0$ and $II_G^0-II_G^0$ are made more alike by goods-market integration (and become identical with perfect integration). Each country must make larger budgetary changes. With close goods-market integration, then, it may be quite difficult, if not impossible, for countries to achieve independent income targets, even when they can achieve independent reserve targets.

When exchange rates are pegged, as they are here, the income changes caused by open-market operations are not permanent; they wear off through time. Furthermore, fiscal policies lose some of their strength. A balanced-budget increase in government spending raises income in the short run more than in the long run. Therefore, fiscal policies must be adjusted over time in order to maintain internal balance. The signs of the adjustments are uncertain, however, as the tendencies just mentioned have conflicting implications. Because the effects of monetary policies wear off gradually, fiscal policies have less work to do. Because the effects of fiscal policies are weakened gradually, they must be reinforced to do the same amount of work. On balance, then, it may be necessary to relax or to intensify the fiscal policies defined at g' in Figure 17.8.

Although it is impossible to compare precisely the fiscal policies required in the short run and the long run, it is easy enough to illustrate the policy combination that must be adopted to achieve the long-run targets—increases of Northern income and reserves with no changes in Southern income and reserves. The policy assignment is the same as in the short run. Fiscal policies must be employed to achieve the countries' income targets; monetary policies must be employed to achieve their reserve targets. When looking at the steady-state assignments, however, we have to invert the policy-making sequence. Fiscal policies affect incomes and reserves; monetary policies affect reserves but do not affect incomes. We have therefore to start by choosing the fiscal policies required to achieve the countries' income targets, then to choose the monetary policies required to achieve their reserve targets, given the effects of their fiscal policies.

This strategy is followed in Figure 17.9. In the upper right-hand corner of that diagram, we draw the fiscal-policy reaction curves pertaining to the income targets. These curves are the counterparts of those we drew in Figure 17.5 (the Southern curve is the same in both diagrams, and the Northern curve in Figure 17.9 corresponds to $I_G'-I_G'$ in Figure 17.5). In other words, the fiscal-policy solution at g^* in Figure 17.9 is the same as the solution at g' in Figure 17.5. The North must increase its spending to

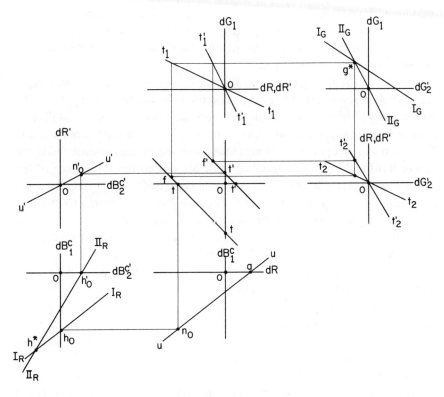

Figure 17.9 Monetary and fiscal policies for external and internal balance: long-run solutions.

raise Northern income. The South must decrease its spending to stabilize Southern income.

To the left of these reaction curves, we draw the relationships between changes in G_1 and changes in the steady-state levels of reserves. Curve t_1t_1 traces the relationship for Northern reserves; curve $t'_1t'_1$ illustrates one possibility for Southern reserves (as they may rise, not fall, with an increase in G_1). Beneath the reaction curves, we draw the relationships between changes in G'_2 and changes in reserves. Curve $t'_2t'_2$ traces the relationship for Southern reserves; curve t_2t_2 illustrates one possibility for Northern reserves. In this example, the permanent increase in G_1 required to raise Northern income causes a reduction in Northern reserves and a smaller reduction in Southern reserves. Analogously, the decrease in G'_2 required to stabilize Southern income causes an increase in Northern reserves and a larger increase in Southern reserves. In the middle of the diagram, we add up the changes in each country's reserves, using the device adopted in Figure 17.8. Northern reserves are shown to fall by $0t$, whether measured vertically or horizontally, and Southern reserves are shown to rise by $0t'$.[21]

Moving to the left again, curve $u'u'$ shows what the South would do to achieve its reserve target if it did not take account of Northern policy. The curve passes through the origin, because the South wants to stabilize its reserves, and the location of n_0' says that the Southern central bank would have to make an open-market purchase (denoted by the distance $0h_0'$ in the lower left-hand corner of the diagram). Moving to the lower part of the diagram, curve uu is the Northern counterpart of $u'u'$. It intersects the horizontal axis at a, not the origin, because the North wants to increase its reserves ($0a = d\bar{R}$), and the location of n_0 says that the Northern central bank would have to make an open-market sale (denoted by the distance $0h_0$ in the lower left-hand corner).

Finally, the reaction curves I_R–I_R and II_R–II_R show what the central banks will do when each one takes account of the other's policy. They pass through h_0 and h_0', respectively, indicating what each bank would do in the absence of policy interdependence; they are positively sloped, on the assumption that spillover effects are positive (that the South gains reserves when the North expels them by an open-market purchase of the Northern bond).[22] The long-run combination of monetary policies is given at h^*. Both central banks must make open-market sales, but the Northern bank must make the larger sale. It would lose reserves if it did nothing and

---

[21] General solutions for these budgetary changes can be derived from Eqs. (13.23b) and (13.24b). Multiplying those equations by σ_1 and σ_2', respectively, we obtain expressions for the changes in Y and Y' resulting from changes in G_1 and G_2. Inverting those expressions, the budgetary changes can be written as functions of the income targets:

$$dG_1 = (1/m_0\sigma_1\sigma_2')[1 - (m_1 - m_2)]^{-1}[\sigma_2'\{(1 - m_1)u_{10}^t + m_0u_{12}^t + m_0[1 - (m_1 - m_2)]\sigma_1\} \, d\bar{Y} - \sigma_1(m_0u_{12}^t - m_2u_{20}^t) \, d\bar{Y}']$$

$$dG_2' = (1/m_0\sigma_1\sigma_2')[1 - (m_1 - m_2)]^{-1}[\sigma_1\{(1 - m_1)u_{20}^t + m_0u_{12}^t + m_0[1 - (m_1 - m_2)]\sigma_2'\} \, d\bar{Y}' - \sigma_2'(m_0u_{12}^t - m_2u_{10}^t) \, d\bar{Y}]$$

When $d\bar{Y} > 0$ and $d\bar{Y}' = 0$, then, $dG_1 > 0$ and $dG_2' \gtrless 0$. The corresponding changes in reserves, shown at the center of Figure 17.9 and denoted elsewhere by $d\hat{R}$ and $d\hat{R}'$, are obtained in two steps: (1) substitute the expressions for dG_1 and dG_2' into Eqs. (13.23b), (13.24b), (13.25b), and (13.26b), to obtain the changes in disposable incomes, remembering that $dY^{d'} = dY'$ for changes in G_1 and $dY^d = dY$ for changes in G_2'; (2) using the changes in Y^d and $Y^{d'}$ and remembering that $(dR'/dY^{d'}) = (dR/dY^d)$ and $(dR/dY^d) = (dR'/dY^{d'})$, from Eq. (E.8b), extract expressions for the changes in reserves as functions of the income targets. (We do not display the expressions here, as they are very long.)

[22] It was not necessary to make this assumption in order to draw the short-run curves I_R^0–I_R^0 and II_R^0–II_R^0, as the signs of the relevant spillover effects are always positive on impact. See Table 13.1B.

wants in fact to augment its reserves, whereas the Southern bank seeks merely to stabilize its holdings.[23]

The spillover effects of changes in G_1 and G_2' are, of course, ambiguous; an increase in G_1 can reduce Southern income and thus evoke an increase in G_2'. (See Figure 17.5, where $I_G^*-I_G^*$ and $II_G^*-II_G^*$ illustrate this possibility.) Furthermore, an increase in one country's spending can cause the other country to gain reserves. (Curves $t_1't_1'$ and t_2t_2 can be positively sloped.) Finally, an open-market purchase by one central bank can reduce the other bank's reserves in the long run. (Curves I_R-I_R and II_R-II_R can be negatively sloped.) Thus, Figures 17.8 and 17.9 serve merely to describe one of many possibilities. Nevertheless, we can draw two general conclusions from our work on this one case: (1) When countries' goods markets are not too closely integrated, bilaterally or with the markets of the outside world, those countries can use fiscal and monetary policies to achieve internal and external targets, simultaneously and independently. (2) In the context of our model, where fiscal policies do not affect reserves on impact and monetary policies do not affect incomes in the long run, fiscal policies should be assigned to the internal (income) targets and monetary policies to the external (reserve) targets. Both conclusions hold for the short run and the long run.

In practice, of course, no government can know enough about its own economy to choose its policies precisely, even in the absence of structural interdependence. And when it faces structural interdependence, its problems are compounded, for it must know the nature of that interdependence and the policy targets of other governments. The policy problem is difficult indeed when spillover effects can be positive or negative. It is hard to know the signs, let alone the sizes, of the changes in fiscal and monetary policies needed to achieve a country's targets or to offset the effects of other countries' policies.

To make matters worse, policies may be constrained in several ways.

[23] General solutions for these open-market operations can be obtained by substituting expressions for the changes in reserves into Eq. (E.9b), remembering that $(dR'/dB_2^c{}') = (dR/dB_1^c)$ and $(dR'/dB_1^c) = (dR/dB_2^c{}')$. The relevant changes in reserves are $dR = d\bar{R} - d\hat{R}$, and $dR' = d\bar{R}' - d\hat{R}'$, where $d\hat{R}$ and $d\hat{R}'$ are the changes in reserves discussed in note 21. The expressions obtained from Eq. (E.9b) can then be inverted to produce the changes in B_1^c and $B_2^c{}'$ required by the income and reserve targets. (We do not write out the equations for those changes, as they depend on the expressions for $d\hat{R}$ and $d\hat{R}'$ and are therefore very long.) It should be noted that the sales shown at h^* are not *additional* to the sales shown at h' in Figure 17.8. They are the permanent reductions in the central banks' bond holdings required to achieve the countries' long-run reserve targets in the face of the effects of the permanent changes in G_1 and G_2' shown at g^*, and they bear no simple algebraic relationship to the size of the initial sales shown at h'.

500   The theory of financial integration

Limits on the levels of expenditures and taxes can constrain adjustments in fiscal policies. We made this point early on, when we looked at fiscal policies in isolation. It came up again when we looked at the effects of goods-market integration on the policy assignments in Figure 17.8. Even when goods markets are not perfectly integrated, it may not be feasible to achieve internal targets by balanced-budget changes in government expenditures; the requisite changes may be much too large. Policies can also be constrained by concerns about their side effects on interest rates and wealth. Fiscal policies designed to stimulate activity tend always to raise interest rates, even when they do not add to supplies of bonds. Monetary policies designed to raise reserves have this same effect. The two in combination may drive domestic interest rates to very high levels.

Although it would be wrong to claim that the findings in this section can be made to yield practical advice, it would likewise be wrong to denigrate their implications—that policy interdependence does not invalidate the conventional policy assignments, that those assignments hold for long-run targets as well as short-run targets, and that the degree of goods-market integration, rather than asset-market integration, is decisive for their feasibility.

Miscellaneous equations used in the analysis of external and internal balance

Impact effect on Northern income of open-market operations in the Northern bond (y_1y_1) (Eq. 13.14b)

$$\delta Y = (\sigma_1/M_s J)(M_{1d})\, \delta B_1^c$$

Impact effect on Southern income of open-market operations in the Northern bond ($y_1'y_1'$) (Eq. 13.15b)

$$\delta Y' = (\sigma_2'/M_s J)(M_{2e})\, \delta B_1^c$$

Impact effect on Northern income of open-market operations in the Southern bond (y_2y_2) (Eq. 13.14b)

$$\delta Y = (\sigma_1/M_s J)(M_{1e})\, \delta B_2^{c'}$$

Impact effect on Southern income of open-market operations in the Southern bond ($y_2'y_2'$) (Eq. 13.15b)

$$\delta Y' = (\sigma_2'/M_s J)(M_{2d})\, \delta B_2^{c'}$$

Balanced-budget changes in Northern spending required to achieve Northern income target given open-market operations to achieve short-run reserve targets (gg) (Eq. 13.7)

$$\delta G_1 = (M_s/M_{1g})(\delta \bar{Y} - \delta \hat{Y})$$

where $\delta \hat{Y}$ is the value given in note 19 (and the definition of M_{1g} is supplied in note 20)

Miscellaneous equations used in the analysis of external and internal balance (cont.)

Balanced-budget changes in Southern spending required to achieve Southern income target given open-market operations to achieve short-run reserve targets $(g'g')$ (Eq. 13.8)

$$\delta G_2' = (M_s/M_{2g})(\delta \bar{Y}' - \delta \hat{Y})$$

where $\delta \hat{Y}'$ is the value given in note 19 (and the definition of M_{2g} is supplied in note 20)

Long-run effects on Northern reserves of balanced-budget changes in Northern spending $(t_1 t_1)$ (Eqs. E.8b, 13.24b, and 13.25b and note 21)

$$dR = [(dR/dY^d)(dY^d/dG_1) + (dR/dY^{d'})(dY^{d'}/dG_1)]\, dG_1$$

Long-run effects on Southern reserves of balanced-budget changes in Northern spending $(t_1' t_1')$ (Eqs. E.8b, 13.24b, and 13.25b and note 21)

$$dR' = [(dR/dY^{d'})(dY^d/dG_1) + (dR/dY^d)(dY^{d'}/dG_1)]\, dG_1$$

Long-run effects on Northern reserves of balanced-budget changes in Southern spending $(t_2 t_2)$ (Eqs. E.8b, 13.23b, and 13.26b and note 21)

$$dR = [(dR/dY^d)(dY^d/dG_2') + (dR/dY^{d'})(dY^{d'}/dG_2')]\, dG_2'$$

Long-run effects on Southern reserves of balanced-budget changes in Southern spending $(t_2' t_2')$ (Eqs. E.8b, 13.23b, and 13.26b and note 21)

$$dR' = [(dR/dY^{d'})(dY^d/dG_2') + (dR/dY^d)(dY^{d'}/dG_2')]\, dG_2'$$

Northern open-market operations required to achieve Northern reserve target given balanced-budget changes in spending to achieve long-run income targets (uu) (Eq. E.9b)

$$dB_1^c = (J_W J_K/J_{N1})(d\bar{R} - d\hat{R})$$

where $d\hat{R}$ is the value defined in note 21 and J_{N1} is the coefficient of dB_1^c in (Eq. E.9b)

Southern open-market operations required to achieve Southern reserve target given balanced-budget changes in spending to achieve long-run income targets $(u'u')$ (Eq. E.9b)

$$dB_2^{c'} = (J_W J_K/J_{N2})(d\bar{R}' - d\hat{R}')$$

where $d\hat{R}'$ is the value defined in note 21 and J_{N2} is the coefficient of $dB_2^{c'}$ in (Eq. E.9b)

The equations in this table are written for the case in which the exchange rates equal unity initially. The same assumption is made in drawing the corresponding diagrams.

Equations for the policy reaction curves

Desired short-run change in Northern income: combinations of changes in deficit spending (I_S-I_S) (Eq. 13.7)

$$\delta(G_1, D) = (1/M_{1S})\{(M_s)\,\delta\bar{Y} - [u_{1i}^t \tau_1 + m_2(1 - S_Y)\sigma_1\sigma_2']\,\delta(G_2', D')\}$$

where $M_{1S} = \sigma_1(u_{20}^t + u_{12}^t) + [1 - m_1(1 - S_Y)]\sigma_1\sigma_2'$.

Desired short-run change in Southern income: combinations of changes in deficit spending (II_S-II_S) (Eq. 13.8)

$$\delta(G_2', D') = (1/M_{2S})\{(M_s)\,\delta\bar{Y} - [u_{12}^t\sigma_2' + m_2(1 - S_Y)\sigma_1\sigma_2']\,\delta(G_1, D)\}$$

where $M_{2S} = \sigma_2'(u_{10}^t + u_{12}^t) + [1 - m_1(1 - S_Y)]\sigma_1\sigma_2'$.

Given short-run change in aggregate income: combinations of changes in deficit spending (K_S-K_S) (Eqs. 13.7 and 13.8)

$$\delta(G_1, D) = (1/M_{TS})\,[(M_s)\,\delta\bar{Y} - \{\sigma_2'u_{10}^t + u_{12}^t(\sigma_1 + \sigma_2') + [1 - m_1 - m_2](1 - S_Y)]\sigma_1\sigma_2'\}\,\delta(G_2', D')]$$

where $M_{TS} = \sigma_1u_{20}^t + u_{12}^t(\sigma_1 + \sigma_2') + [1 + (m_1 - m_2)(1 - S_Y)]\sigma_1\sigma_2'$.

Desired long-run change in Northern income: combinations of balanced-budget changes in spending (I_G-I_G) (Eq. 13.23b)

$$dG_1 = (1/M_{1K})[(M_k)\,d\bar{Y} - \sigma_1(m_0u_{12}^t - m_2u_{20}^t)\,dG_2']$$

where $M_{1K} = \sigma_1(1 - m_1)u_{20}^t + m_0(\sigma_1u_{12}^t) + m_0[1 - (m_1 - m_2)]\sigma_1\sigma_2'$.

Desired long-run change in Southern income: combinations of balanced-budget changes in spending (II_G-II_G) (Eq. 13.24b)

$$dG_2' = (1/M_{2K})[(M_k)\,d\bar{Y}' - \sigma_2'(m_0u_{12}^t - m_2u_{10}^t)\,dG_1]$$

where $M_{2K} = \sigma_2'(1 - m_1)u_{10}^t + m_0(\sigma_2'u_{12}^t) + m_0[1 - (m_1 - m_2)]\sigma_1\sigma_2'$.

Desired short-run change in Northern reserves: combinations of open-market operations $(I_R^0-I_R^0)$ (Eq. E.2b)

$$\delta B_1^c = (1/J_T)[(-J)\,\delta R + (B_{12}'L_{11} - B_{11}'L_{12})\,\delta B_2^c]$$

Desired short-run change in Southern reserves: combinations of open-market operations $(II_R^0 - II_R^0)$ (Eq. 2b)

$$\delta B_2' = (1/J_T)[(-J)\,\delta \bar{R}' + (B_{12}^t L_{11} - B_{11}^t L_{11})\,\delta B_1^c]$$

Desired short-run change in Northern income given open-market operations to achieve short-run reserve targe's: combinations of balanced-budget changes in spending $(I_G^0 - II_G^0)$ (Eq. 13.7)

$$\delta G_1 = (1/M_{1g})[M_s(\delta \bar{Y} - \delta \bar{Y}') - (M_{1h})\,\delta G_2'^*]$$

where $\delta G_2'^*$ is the value given in note 20 (which also supplies definitions of M_{1g} and M_{1h})

Desired short-run change in Southern income given open-market operations to achieve short-run reserve targets: combinations of balanced-budget changes in spending $(II_G^0 - II_G^0)$ (Eq. 13.8)

$$\delta G_2' = (1/M_{2g})[M_s(\delta \bar{Y}' - \delta \bar{Y}) - (M_{2h})\delta G_1^*]$$

where δG_1^* is the value given in note 20 (which also supplies definitions of M_{2g} and M_{2h})

Desired long-run change in Northern reserves given balanced-budget changes in spending to achieve long-run income targets: combinations of open-market operations $(I_R - I_R)$ (Eq. E.9b)

$$dB_1^c = (1/J_{N1})[(J_W J_K)(d\bar{R} - d\bar{R}) - (J_{N2})\,dB_2']$$

where J_{N1} and J_{N2} are the coefficients of dB_1^c and dB_2', respectively, in Eq. (E.9b) and $d\bar{R}$ is the change in Northern reserves resulting from the changes in G_1 and G_2' required to achieve long-run income targets (see note 21)

Desired long-run change in Southern reserves given balanced-budget changes in spending to achieve long-run income targets: combinations of open-market operations $(II_R - II_R)$ (Eq. E.9b)

$$dB_2' = (1/J_{N2})[(J_W J_K)(d\bar{R}' - d\bar{R}') - (J_{N1})\,dB_1^c]$$

where $d\hat{R}'$ is the change in Southern reserves resulting from the changes in G_1 and G_2' required to achieve long-run income targets (see note 21)

The equations in this table are written for the case in which the exchange rates equal unity initially. The same assumption is made in drawing the corresponding diagrams.

503

Equations for the Northern income curves

Northern gross domestic product in Northern income and external exchange-rate space
Impact version (z^1z^1):

$$\delta Y = (\sigma_1/v_n)\{(u_{10}^t + p_1 C_1^t)\left(\frac{\delta\pi'}{\pi'}\right) + [(u_{12}^t/\sigma_2) + m_2(1 - S_Y)]\,\delta Y' - (m_1 S_1 + m_2 S_2)\,\delta r_1 - (m_1 S_2 + m_2 S_1)\,\delta r_2$$

$$- S_0(1 - m_0)\,\delta\bar{r}_0 - (m_1 S_W)\,\delta W^h - (m_2 S_W)\,\delta W^{h'} + [1 - m_1(1 - S_Y)]\,\delta\bar{G}_1 - m_1(1 - S_Y)\,\delta\bar{G}_2$$

$$+ [1 - m_2(1 - S_Y)]\,\delta\bar{G}_1' - m_2(1 - S_Y)\,\delta\bar{G}_2' + m_1(1 - S_Y)\,\delta\bar{D} + m_2(1 - S_Y)\,\delta\bar{D}' - \delta c_{01}^t - \delta c_{02}^t\}$$

where $v_n = u_{10}^t + u_{12}^t + [1 - m_1(1 - S_Y)]\sigma_1$

Steady-state version (Z^1Z^1):

$$dY = (\sigma_1/v_n^*)\{(u_{10}^t + p_1 C_1^t)\left(\frac{d\pi'}{\pi'}\right) + [(u_{12}^t/\sigma_2) + m_2]\,dY' + (1 - m_1)\,d\bar{G}_1 - (m_1)\,d\bar{G}_2 + (1 - m_2)\,d\bar{G}_1'$$

$$- (m_2)\,d\bar{G}_2' - dc_{01}^t - dc_{02}^t\}$$

where $v_n^* = u_{10}^t + u_{12}^t + (1 - m_1)\sigma_1$

18

Fiscal policy in a monetary union

The issues

When we analyzed the operations of a monetary union in Chapter 16, we were able to deal expeditiously with the pegged-rate case. We drew directly on results obtained in Chapter 15, where we studied national monetary policies under pegged exchange rates. When we came to the flexible-rate case, however, we had to begin with an analysis of national monetary policies in an exchange-rate union with a flexible external rate before we could study the effects of a unified monetary policy.

We follow a similar strategy here. First, we use results obtained in Chapter 17 to show how members of a monetary union with a pegged external rate can use fiscal policies to influence their incomes and analyze the interplay between those policies and the union's monetary policy. Thereafter, we digress to study fiscal policies in an exchange-rate union with a flexible external rate, showing its members can use fiscal policies and analyzing the interplay between the members' policies and the union's monetary policy.

But we come across one new complication. When the members of a monetary union execute independent fiscal policies, there is the possibility of policy conflict. The aims of the union and those of its members may be inconsistent. The members' incomes, Y and Y' in the North and South, must add up to the union's income, Y^t. This is always true ex post, but it must also be true ex ante if there is to be no conflict between the members' targets and the union's target.

Conflict is least likely to arise directly when the union has a pegged external rate and its monetary policy is aimed at external balance – at the regulation of aggregate reserves, R^t, rather than aggregate income, Y^t. The members' fiscal policies will determine Y^t, one way or another. Outcomes in this case differ only in detail from those in Chapter 17, where the North and South, acting on their own, used monetary policies for external balance and fiscal policies for internal balance. Conflict is more likely when the union tries to influence Y^t and the members try to influence their own countries' incomes. It is thus very likely in the flexible-rate case, as the union has no need to seek external balance and monetary policy has permanent effects on aggregate income.

We must therefore answer several questions in this chapter. How does the existence of a monetary union and the choice between exchange-rate regimes affect the functioning of members' fiscal policies? How do the union's policies interact with its members' policies? What are the possibilities of conflict, how do they show up, and how are they to be resolved? Is it sufficient to coordinate the members' fiscal policies, or would it be better from one standpoint or another to unify those policies–to form a full-fledged fiscal union?

These questions must be answered, moreover, for each fiscal policy examined heretofore–for intervals of deficit spending and temporary tax cuts, which alter supplies of bonds, and for balanced-budget changes in government spending. We do not deal with all three at each point in our work. This would be laborious, and it is unnecessary. Balanced-budget changes in government spending can be used to illustrate the main points we want to make. But we shall have to look at the other policies when it is important to examine the effects of changes in supplies of bonds, especially to ask if they affect the conduct of the union's monetary policy.

National fiscal policies with a pegged external rate

In Chapter 17 we showed that governments can use certain fiscal instruments to influence their countries' incomes and that the effects do not wear off through time, even when the countries maintain pegged exchange rates. A balanced-budget increase of Northern spending on the Northern good raises Northern income in the short run and the long run. Structural interdependence, creating policy interdependence, does not necessarily interfere. If the North seeks to increase Northern income and the South does not want Southern income to change, the South can adjust its fiscal policy to offset the spillover effects of Northern policy. The North must make a bigger budgetary change when spillover effects are positive and the South acts to offset them, but it can still achieve its income target. By implication, fiscal policies can be used not only to influence aggregate income but also to influence *relative* incomes, and they can do so in the short run and the long run, whatever the degree of asset-market integration. Monetary policies, by contrast, can influence relative incomes only in the short run, even with a flexible external exchange rate, and cannot even do that much in the face of perfect asset-market integration.

The effects of fiscal policies, however, depend on the degree to which consumption is biased in favor of domestic goods and on the degree of goods-market integration. When one country's good is a close substitute for the foreign good, that country's fiscal policies will not exert much influence on domestic income. And when one country's good is a close substitute for its neighbor's good, it may not be able to pursue an independent income target. A balanced-budget increase in one country's spending will raise incomes in both countries, and it may be impractical, if not actually impossible, for the other country to offset the spillover effects.

We went on to make another point. When goods markets are not too closely integrated, two countries can pursue external and internal targets, simultaneously and independently. Recall the example in Chapter 17. The Northern central bank can make an open-market sale to raise Northern reserves; the Northern government can then raise its spending to offset the deflationary side effects on Northern income, or even to stimulate Northern income if that is its aim. Responding to these policies, the Southern central bank can make an open-market sale to ward off a reduction in Southern reserves, and the Southern government can adjust its spending to stabilize Southern income.

When countries enter into a monetary union, establishing a single central bank to hold their reserves, to control the quantity of money by open-market operations, and to peg the external exchange rate, some of these conclusions hold but others must be modified. Once monetary policies are unified, no single government can use them to complement or reinforce its fiscal policies. The converse is also true and much more important. The decision to create a monetary union is not, by itself, a commitment by the members to coordinate their fiscal policies with the monetary policies of the union. There is, indeed, an extra danger. Once governments have transferred their reserves to a central pool and do not need them to make settlements among themselves because they have a common currency, they may feel free to adopt domestic targets that come into conflict with those of the union.

We must therefore ask if the members of a monetary union can continue to conduct autonomous fiscal policies. The answer, we shall see, depends in part on the aims adopted by the union. If it seeks to influence its members' incomes, Y and Y', or the sum of incomes, Y^t, conflict is quite

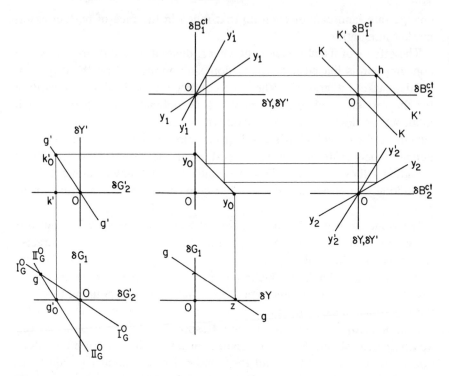

Figure 18.1 Monetary and fiscal policies to influence incomes in a monetary union with a pegged external rate: short-run solutions.

likely, and limitations on autonomy are essential. The union and its members must harmonize their targets. If instead the union is concerned exclusively to manage the pool of reserves, R^t, harmonization may not be required. But serious practical problems can still arise. If governments pursue fiscal policies that cause the union to lose reserves, the responses of the union may frustrate the members' aims.

Consider first the case in which conflict is most likely. Suppose that the union seeks to raise aggregate income (that $\delta \bar{Y}^t > 0$) and makes open-market purchases of its members' bonds. In the upper right-hand corner of Figure 18.1, schedule K–K shows how the union's central bank might alter its holdings of Northern and Southern bonds, B_1^{ct} and B_2^{ct}, respectively, without affecting aggregate income.[1] Schedule K'–K' shows how

[1] The equation for K–K is given in the table at the end of Chapter 15, and those for the other curves in Figure 18.1 are given in the tables at the end of Chapter 17. Equations for the curves that make their first appearance in Chapter 18 are shown in the table at the end of this chapter.

the bank might alter its bond holdings to reach its income target. Assume that it moves to h, by purchasing equal amounts of the two countries' bonds. The effects on Northern income are shown by the curves y_1y_1 and y_2y_2, as in Figure 17.8; the effects on Southern income are shown by $y_1'y_1'$ and $y_2'y_2'$. With full-scale goods-market symmetry, the countries' incomes rise on impact by the same amounts, as shown by the common curve y_0y_0 in the middle of the diagram. The increase in each country's income is the distance $0y_0$, measured either vertically or horizontally. The increase in aggregate income is, of course, *twice* the distance $0y_0$ (i.e., $\delta Y^t = \delta \bar{Y}^t > 0$).

Suppose next that the Northern government acquiesces in the increase of Northern income that comes about in consequence of the union's policy and the way it is executed, but the Southern government wants no change whatsoever in Southern income. The attitude of the Northern government is reflected by the way we draw curve gg, which shows how Northern policy would change if the North could disregard reactions by the South. The distance $0z$ is the increase in Northern income acceptable to the Northern government. As $0z$ is exactly equal to $0y_0$, the North will not change its fiscal policy unless there is a change in Southern policy, and the policy reaction curve for the North, I_G^0–I_G^0, is drawn through the origin in the lower left-hand corner of the diagram. The attitude of the Southern government is reflected by the way we draw curve $g'g'$. Because the Southern government objects to any change in Southern income, $g'g'$ passes through the origin, and the increase in Southern income, $0y_0$, requires a modification of Southern policy. If it could disregard reactions by the North, the Southern government would decrease its spending by $0k'$, and the policy reaction curve for the South, II_G^0–II_G^0, is thus drawn through g_0', vertically below k'. When each country takes account of the other's policy, they will wind up at g in the lower left-hand panel. The South will make a balanced-budget decrease in spending (larger than the decrease $0k'$); the North will make a balanced-budget increase in spending (to offset the spillover effects of Southern policy).

At this point, of course, both governments are satisfied. Income in the North has risen by $0y_0$, and income in the South has not changed. But the central bank cannot be satisfied, because aggregate income has not risen sufficiently. There is a clear conflict between policy targets, and it can be resolved only by altering one of the targets. In all likelihood, of course, the governments are apt to prevail, for political and economic reasons alike. The political reason is obvious. The South can threaten to withdraw from the monetary union or demand a change in management. The eco-

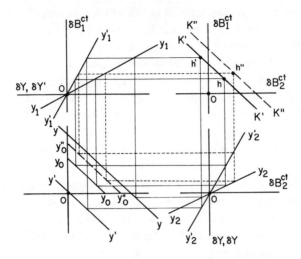

Figure 18.2 Central-bank responses to a policy conflict in a monetary union with a pegged external rate: impact effects on members' incomes.

nomic reasons are no less compelling. When the monetary union has a pegged external rate, the domestic effects of monetary policy wear off eventually, and the governments' fiscal policies will come to prevail. Even in the short run, moreover, the powers of the central bank are limited. In Figure 18.2, adapted from the upper part of Figure 18.1, we show what it might do and the problems it would face.

1. If asset markets are not too closely integrated, the bank could reduce the impact on Southern income by adjusting the *composition* of its open-market purchase. Rather than purchasing both bonds, as at h on $K'-K'$, it could buy the Northern bond and sell the Southern bond, moving to h'. The larger purchase of the Northern bond raises Southern income, but the sale of the Southern bond reduces it, and the net effect is shown by curve $y'y'$ in the lower left-hand corner of the diagram. As $y'y'$ passes through the origin, Southern income does not change, and the Southern government has no reason to react. The net effect on Northern income is shown by yy; as this curve lies above y_0y_0, the increase in Northern income is larger than the one in Figure 18.1 and is thus unacceptable to the Northern government. Northern fiscal policy will be tightened, preventing the increase in aggregate income sought by the central bank.

2. The central bank could combat Southern fiscal policy by adjusting the *size* of its open-market purchase. It could move to some such point as h'' on the new open-market curve $K''-K''$, and each country would con-

front an increase in its income equal to $0y_0'$ and therefore larger than $0y_0$. In this instance, however, both governments have reasons to react. The South will offset the whole increase in its income, just as it did before; the North will offset the excess over $0y_0$ (the distance y_0y_0'). The central bank will fail to achieve its target.

There is, of course, one circumstance in which the central bank can dominate temporarily. When goods markets are closely integrated, governments must make large budgetary changes to influence their countries' incomes independently, and changes of the sizes needed to offset a large open-market purchase may not be feasible. In this same circumstance, moreover, the countries' incomes move together in response to any fiscal-policy change. Therefore, no single country may be able to neutralize the monetary policies of the central bank or the fiscal policies of the other government. But there are likewise limits to the sizes of the purchases by the central bank, as it has to protect the union's reserves. A move to h'' in Figure 18.2 may be imprudent, if not impossible, because it would reduce R^t by more than the move to h. There is thus no way to forecast with certainty the short-run outcome of a policy conflict like the one described by Figure 18.1.

When open-market operations are employed exclusively to regulate reserves and fiscal policies to regulate income levels, the targets of the member governments cannot be inconsistent with the target of the union. But difficulties can arise when political or economic circumstances limit the ability of member governments to adjust their budgets or the freedom of the central bank to conduct large open-market operations.

Suppose that the union seeks to raise reserves (that $\delta \bar{R}^t = d\bar{R}^t > 0$), that the Northern government wants to raise its country's income (that $\delta \bar{Y} = d\bar{Y} > 0$), and that the Southern government wants to keep its country's income constant (that $\delta \bar{Y}' = d\bar{Y}' = 0$). The short-run solution is the one described by Figure 17.8, with a slight change in the interpretation of the point h' in the upper right-hand corner. When monetary policy is conducted by a single central bank, h' is not defined by policy reaction curves. It is chosen by the central bank to achieve its reserve target. From Eq. (13.4b),

$$\delta B_1^{ct} = (J_S/B_{01}^t)\bar{\pi}'\delta\bar{R}^t - \delta B_2^{ct}$$

and h' is any point that satisfies this equation.[2] When the central bank

---

[2] When, as here, $\delta\bar{R}^t > 0$, the schedule defined by this equation intersects the vertical axis below the origin (because $B_{01}^t < 0$), and its slope must always equal $-45°$. (By contrast, curve $K-K$ in Figure 18.1, defining the set of open-market operations that leave Y^t unchanged, has that slope only with goods-market symmetry.) Unless the central bank has

sells both bonds, as at h', both countries' incomes fall. The impact effect on Northern income is the reduction $0y$, in the middle of Figure 17.8, and the effect on Southern income is the reduction $0y'$. As the North seeks to raise Northern income by $0z$, and the South seeks to keep Southern income constant, the requisite changes in fiscal policies are given at g', in the lower left-hand corner. The North must make a balanced-budget increase in spending; the South must make a balanced-budget cut.

Because fiscal policies do not affect reserves immediately, the budgetary changes shown at g' do not interfere with the achievement of the central bank's objective, and no policy conflict arises at this stage. Governments may find it difficult, of course, to adjust their budgets by the amounts required to achieve their income targets. But the central bank can help them if its initial holdings of Northern and Southern bonds give it the freedom to choose the composition of its open-market sale. If the North cannot raise its spending by enough to reach its income target, the central bank can sell Southern bonds rather than Northern bonds, to place less burden on Northern fiscal policy. (It can even swap Southern for Northern bonds, as illustrated at h' in Figure 18.2.)

The long-run solution to this policy problem can be described by reinterpreting Figure 17.9, but it is more useful to show it anew. As monetary policies have no permanent effects on incomes when the external exchange rate is pegged, national fiscal policies can be geared to the pursuit of income targets without taking account of union monetary policy. The appropriate combination of fiscal policies is shown in the upper right-hand corner of Figure 18.3. The North must make a balanced-budget increase in spending to raise Northern income, and the South must make a balanced-budget decrease in spending to offset the spillover effects of Northern policy (assuming, as before, that those effects are positive). This part of the solution is the same as the one in Figure 17.9.

Fiscal policies, however, influence steady-state reserves, in the manner shown by two new curves, T_1T_1 and T_2T_2, to the left of and below the fiscal-policy solution. (The former is the horizontal sum of the curves t_1t_1 and $t_1't_1'$ in Figure 17.9, showing the effect on R^t, the sum of R and R', of a change in G_1. The latter is the vertical sum of the curves t_2t_2 and $t_2't_2'$, showing the effect on R^t of a change in G_2'.) The two countries' fiscal poli-

some reason to be interested in the distribution of reserves between its Northern and Southern branches or in the distribution of the income changes resulting from its open-market purchase, it is free to choose any point on the schedule that passes through h'. There is, of course, no good economic reason for interest in the distribution of reserves. There may be reason for concern about the distribution of the income changes. We return to them later.

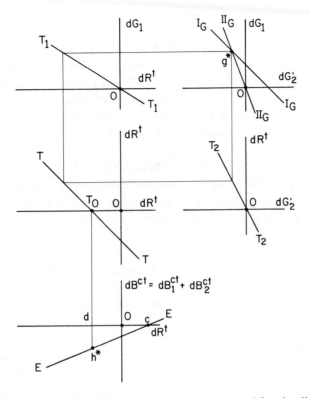

Figure 18.3 Monetary policies to influence reserves and fiscal policies to influence incomes in a monetary union with a pegged external rate: long-run solutions.

cies, taken together, reduce the union's reserves by $0T_0$, and the task of the central bank is shown at $h*$ in the lower part of the diagram. Because it wants to raise R^t, curve EE, defining the long-run relationship between changes in reserves and open-market operations, intersects the horizontal axis at c $(d\bar{R}^t = 0c > 0)$. The central bank could not be passive even if fiscal policies did not reduce reserves, and with the reduction by $0T_0$, it has to respond more vigorously. It must sell some combination of the two countries' bonds amounting to $dh*$.[3]

As the three targets can be achieved independently, there is, again, no possibility of conflict. The governments, however, may have problems

---

[3] The central bank would have to reduce bond holdings by more than $dh*$ if there were an increase in the supply of bonds on the way to the new steady state. If the North, for example, had begun with deficit spending, rather than a balanced-budget increase in spending, and had balanced its budget thereafter by raising lump-sum taxes, B_1 would be larger in the new steady state, and the long-run reduction in R^t would be larger too. See Eq. (13.22b).

making the requisite budgetary changes, and the central bank may have a problem too. If the increase in G_1 is large enough, relative to the decrease in G_2', the reduction in reserves, $0T_0$, may be too large to offset. The central bank may not have enough bonds to sell. The same thing could happen to a single country having its own income target and managing its own reserves, but the risk is larger in the present context, where responsibilities are lodged at different levels. Governments pursue their own income targets and leave the union's central bank to safeguard their reserves.

Our diagrams gloss over one more difficulty. On impact, fiscal policies do not affect reserves. In the steady state, monetary policy does not affect incomes. Between these extremes, however, there are important interactions that can cause problems for the union and its member governments. On the way to the steady state, the members' fiscal policies may generate a balance-of-payments deficit for the union ($\dot{R}^t < 0$), and the central bank may tighten its monetary policies sufficiently to interfere with the members' income targets. This is the more likely to occur the more ambitious is the North in its attempt to raise Northern income, and the consequences are the more likely to be serious, politically and economically, the larger the sales of the Southern bond made by the central bank in its attempt to stem the outflow of reserves. The South may be unable to stabilize its income in the face of those large sales. When fiscal and monetary policies are selected separately, conflicts can arise even when policy targets are compatible in principle.

National fiscal policies with a flexible external rate

If the members of a monetary union want its policies to influence aggregate income, they may opt for a flexible external exchange rate. In Chapter 16 we showed that monetary policy has larger short-run effects on Y^t when that rate is flexible than when it is pegged. Furthermore, its influence is permanent, not temporary, although it cannot regulate relative incomes – the distribution of the long-run changes in Y^t between North and South. Finally, a flexible external rate insulates aggregate income in the long run against the effects of goods-market disturbances; the steady-state level of Y^t is not affected by a shift in demand between one of the members' goods and the foreign good or by a change in the price of the foreign good.

It is the main aim of this section to examine the relationships between a union's monetary policies and its members' fiscal policies when the union has a flexible external rate. Before we can do so, however, we first have to show how fiscal policies function by themselves in an exchange-rate union with a flexible external rate–to retrace the analysis in the first part of Chapter 17, where we looked at the effects of various fiscal policies under pegged exchange rates. Posing the problem differently, we must look at the effects of fiscal policies conducted by the members of a monetary union whose central bank elects to stabilize the money supply by allowing the external exchange rate to float.

Balanced-budget changes in spending

The impact effects of fiscal policies do not depend on the exchange-rate regime. Even if those policies lead to budget deficits, altering supplies of bonds through time, their first effects appear only in goods markets and cannot affect the external exchange rate. Thus we can invoke our findings in the first part of Chapter 17. When all goods are gross substitutes but not perfect substitutes and goods markets are fully symmetrical, deficit spending by one country raises incomes in both countries, regardless of the good purchased by the government. A tax cut does so too, although it is less effective, given the size of the deficit generated. Finally, a balanced-budget increase in a country's spending on its own domestic good must always raise that country's income by more than it raises the other country's income. (It can indeed reduce the other country's income.)

To carry the analysis further, it is necessary to distinguish between policies that cause budget deficits and those that do not. The distinction is especially important when the external exchange rate is flexible, because changes in supplies of bonds have permanent effects on incomes. We begin, then, with a policy that does not generate a budget deficit–a balanced-budget increase in Northern spending on the Northern good.

On impact, an increase in $\bar{G}_1$ causes the North to incur a current-account deficit. The Southern current account can go either way, but even if it moves into surplus, the Northern deficit will be larger absolutely, so that the union as a whole will move into deficit. This situation is described in Figure 18.4A. The short-run income curve for the union as a whole shifts from $z^t z^t$ to $z^{t'} z^{t'}$, displacing equilibrium from v to v' at the initial external exchange rate. Aggregate income rises. The long-run curve shifts too, from $Z^t Z^t$ to $Z^{t'} Z^{t'}$. In Chapter 4, however, we showed that it shifts by less than the short-run curve, so that v' lies above the new long-run curve, indicating that the union has a current-account deficit. The situa-

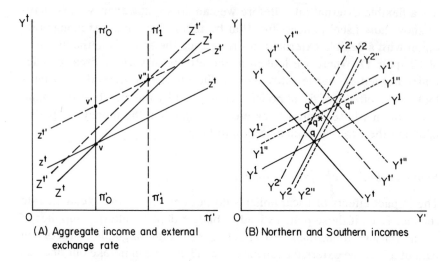

(A) Aggregate income and external exchange rate

(B) Northern and Southern incomes

Figure 18.4 Balanced-budget increase in Northern spending on the Northern good: impact and steady-state effects on aggregate and national goods markets under a flexible external rate.

tions of the North and South are described in Figure 18.4B. The aggregate income curve shifts upward from Y^tY^t to $Y^{t\prime}Y^{t\prime}$, by a distance equal to vv' in Figure 18.4A. The Northern income curve shifts upward from Y^1Y^1 to $Y^{1\prime}Y^{1\prime}$, because the increase in government spending on the Northern good exceeds the reduction in private spending caused by the corresponding increase in Northern taxes. The Southern income curve shifts from Y^2Y^2 to $Y^{2\prime}Y^{2\prime}$, because of the reduction in private spending. Goods-market equilibrium is established at g', where Northern income is higher than it was initially, but Southern income can be higher or lower, depending on the sizes of the shifts in the two countries' income curves. (It is drawn to be higher in Figure 18.4B, just as in the corresponding pegged-rate case shown in Figure 17.4B.)[4]

A current-account deficit is always accompanied by dissaving, and excess flow supplies emerge in all asset markets at the initial interest rates

[4] Figures 17.4B and 18.4B both show the relationship between income changes and depict identical impact effects. But Figures 17.4A and 18.4A are not identical. Figure 17.4A shows the relationship between Northern income and the external exchange rate, with Northern income on the vertical axis. Accordingly, the equilibrium points in Figures 17.4A and 17.4B line up horizontally. But Figure 18.4A shows the relationship between aggregate (union) income and the external exchange rate. Therefore, the changes in Y^t shown in Figure 18.4A correspond to the vertical shifts of the aggregate income curve in Figure 18.4B, but the equilibrium points in Figures 18.4A and 18.4B do not line up horizontally. The axes in Figure 18.4B refer to Y and Y', which add up to Y^t.

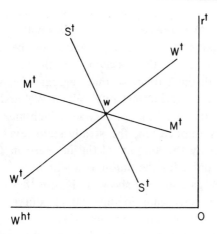

Figure 18.5 Balanced-budget increase in Northern spending on the Northern good: impact and steady-state effects on aggregate asset markets under a flexible external rate.

and initial exchange rate. The excess flow supply of the foreign bond produces a capital inflow from the outside world ($\dot{F}^t < 0$), but it is not large enough to offset the union's current-account deficit. At the initial exchange rate, then, the union would have a balance-of-payments deficit with the outside world (the counterpart of the excess supply of union currency). The union's currency must start to depreciate, switching foreign and domestic demands from the foreign good to the union's goods, and raising aggregate income. In Figure 18.4A the exchange-rate schedule moves to the right, from $\pi_0'\pi_0'$ to $\pi_1'\pi_1'$, and equilibrium is displaced gradually from v' to v'', where $Z''Z''$ intersects $z''z''$. Aggregate income is higher in the steady state than it was initially or on impact.

Before we look at the effects on the two countries' incomes, we must examine the effects on the union's asset markets and aggregate wealth. These effects are shown in Figure 18.5, which uses familiar relationships. The aggregate bond-market curve, W^tW^t, shows the combinations of r^t and W^{ht} that clear the *sum* of Northern and Southern bond markets. The aggregate money-market curve, M^tM^t, shows the combinations that clear the *sum* of money markets. Curve S^tS^t shows the combinations at which saving is zero in the union as a whole, given Y^{dt}, aggregate disposable income.

A balanced-budget increase in Northern spending cannot affect the position of W^tW^t. It does not alter the supply of Northern bonds. With a flexible external exchange rate, moreover, it cannot affect the position of

M^tM^t. The sum of money supplies is policy determined when there are no changes in aggregate reserves. As in the case of the single small economy, asset-market equilibrium remains at w. The depreciation of the union's currency is just large enough to offset the dissaving and the sales of the foreign bond that take place through time, so that aggregate wealth remains constant, as does the average interest rate. When W^{ht} and r^t are constant, however, the position of S^tS^t cannot change, which means that Y^{dt} must be constant too. By implication, the steady-state level of aggregate income, Y^t, must rise by the amount of the increase in $\bar{G}_1$ (the balanced-budget multiplier is unity for the union as a whole).

The gradual increase in aggregate income shown in Figure 18.4A is also shown in Figure 18.4B. The aggregate income curve shifts upward through time, from $Y^{t'}Y^{t'}$ to $Y^{t''}Y^{t''}$, and the countries' income curves shift too, in response to the gradual changes in π', r_1, r_2, W^h, and $W^{h'}$. The depreciation of the union's currency raises the demands for both countries' goods–and does so by equal amounts with goods-market symmetry. Taken by itself, the depreciation shifts the Northern income curve upward and the Southern curve rightward by the same amounts. But other things are happening to influence the positions of the curves. Although aggregate wealth does not change, it is redistributed from North to South, as the North has the larger current-account deficit. As Northern wealth declines, moreover, r_1 must rise to clear the Northern bond market, and r_2 must fall by the same amount, because the average interest rate remains constant. Finally, money is redistributed from North to South, because of the changes in wealth holdings and interest rates.

Because the demand for the Northern good is more sensitive to changes in r_1 and Northern wealth, and the opposite is true of the demand for the Southern good, the gradual changes in stocks of wealth and national interest rates depress the demand for the Northern good and stimulate the demand for the Southern good. And with goods-market symmetry, the changes in demands are equal absolutely. Combining these changes with those caused by the depreciation of the union's currency, there is an increase in demand for the Southern good, shown in Figure 18.4B by the rightward shift of the Southern income curve from $Y^{2'}Y^{2'}$ to $Y^{2''}Y^{2''}$. The demand for the Northern good, by contrast, can rise or fall, and it is shown to fall slightly in Figure 18.4B, where the Northern income curve shifts downward from $Y^{1'}Y^{1'}$ to $Y^{1''}Y^{1''}$. (The negative effects of the changes in wealth holdings and interest rates are assumed to dominate the positive effects of the exchange-rate change.) Goods-market equilibrium moves gradually from q' to q'', where Southern income must be higher than it was at q', but Northern income can be higher or lower. Nevertheless, both countries' incomes are higher at q'' than they were at q, before the increase in $\bar{G}_1$, and the permanent increase in Northern income must exceed the increase in Southern income.

To recapitulate and interpret these results intuitively, balance-of-payments adjustment involves a combination of exchange-rate changes vis-à-vis the outside world and money (reserve) flows between members of the union. The union's deficit with the outside world is corrected by the depreciation of the union's currency, which tends to stimulate the demands for each member's good, whatever the member's own balance-of-payments position. In the example just supplied, the demand for the Southern good rises even though the South may have a balance-of-payments surplus. Taken by itself, then, the depreciation of the union's currency creates an imbalance inside the union. It generates a Southern surplus, matched by a Northern deficit. There is thus the need for balance-of-payments adjustment within the union, involving money (reserve) flows from North to South. Deflationary pressures in the North and inflationary pressures in the South reduce the imbalance between the two countries. Although aggregate income rises through time, Northern income rises more slowly than Southern income (and can indeed decline from the level reached on impact).

Comparing the long-run effects of this fiscal policy when the external exchange rate is flexible and when it is pegged, we find that flexibility increases its influence on each country's income. In Figure 18.4B, steady-state equilibrium occurs at q'' with a flexible external rate and at q^* with a pegged external rate. (Point q^* is transcribed from Figure 17.4B.) Aggregate income grows through time with a flexible rate, so that its steady-state level exceeds its impact level; the opposite is true with a pegged rate. And although Northern income can decline through time with a flexible rate, its steady-state level is likely to be higher than it is with a pegged rate.[5]

[5] Denoting by $(dY/dG_1)_f$ the outcome with a flexible external rate, obtained from Eq. (13.23a), and denoting by $(dY/dG_1)_p$ the outcome with a pegged external rate, obtained from Eq. (13.23b),

$$
\begin{aligned}
(dY/dG_1)_f - (dY/dG_1)_p = \; & u_{20}^t\{(u_{10}^t + p_1C_1^f)(M_g + m_0M_0) \\
& + u_1^t(1 - m_1)\sigma_2'[(u_{10}^t + p_1C_1^f) - (u_{20}^t + p_2C_2^f)\} \\
& + U_\pi\{u_{12}^t[M_g + m_2\sigma_2'(u_{10}^t - u_{20}^t) \\
& + [1 - (m_1 - m_2)]\sigma_2'(M_g + m_2\sigma_2'u_{10}^t)\}
\end{aligned}
$$

This difference is necessarily positive when $u_{10}^t \geq u_{20}^t$ and $p_1C_1^f \geq p_2C_2^f$, and it need not be negative otherwise. With goods-market symmetry, of course, $u_{10}^t = u_{20}^t$ and $p_1C_1^f = p_2C_2^f$, so that the difference is positive.

How would these findings be affected by an increase of structural inter-dependence? An increase of internal asset-market integration (of $-B_{12}^t$) reduces the dispersion of national interest rates around r^t and enlarges the redistribution of wealth between North and South. But it does not affect the sizes of the income changes in the short run or the long run, as these changes are determined entirely in goods markets. For this same reason, of course, goods-market integration is quite important. An increase of internal integration (of u_{12}^t) diminishes the difference between changes in the countries' incomes, and this conclusion holds for both exchange-rate regimes. With perfect goods-market integration ($u_{12}^t \to \infty$), prices in the North and South move together, and with goods-market symmetry, so do incomes. The two countries' income curves come to coincide with a 45° line passing through q, and the other equilibria, q' and q'', must lie on that line (at its intersections with $Y^{t'}Y^{t'}$ and $Y^{t''}Y^{t''}$, respectively). Internal in-tegration, however, does not affect the size of the change in aggregate income.[6]

In the absence of full-scale goods-market symmetry, it is hard to say very much about the changes in the countries' incomes. In the long run, of course, the increase in Y^t must always equal the increase in $\bar{G}_1$. The balanced-budget multiplier has still to be unity, because Y^{dt} is constant when r^t and W^{ht} are constant. We cannot be sure, however, that an in-crease in $\bar{G}_1$ will raise Northern income by at least as much as Southern income, on impact or in the steady state. To illustrate, consider the limit-ing case of perfect goods-market integration (the case in which Y and Y' would rise by the same amounts with goods-market symmetry). Because the changes in p_1 and p_2' must be equal, the changes in incomes must be proportional to the supply responses:

$$(\delta Y/\delta Y') = (dY/dY') = (\sigma_1/\sigma_2')$$

so that Southern income will rise by more than Northern income when-ever $\sigma_2' > \sigma_1$, regardless of the government or good involved in the balanced-budget increase of government spending.

Long-run effects of changes in supplies of debt

Thus far, we have dealt with the special case in which budgets are bal-anced continuously. In Chapter 17, however, we dealt with several poli-

---

[6] The greater the degree of goods-market integration, the larger the dispersion of interest-rate changes and the larger the redistribution of wealth between North and South. As Y rises less and Y' rises more with closer integration, Y^d falls more and $Y^{d'}$ falls less. For each country's saving to be zero in the steady state, r_1 must rise farther and r_2 must fall far-ther, whereas W^h must fall farther and $W^{h'}$ must rise farther.

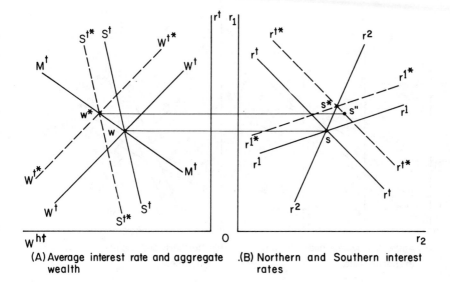

(A) Average interest rate and aggregate wealth

.(B) Northern and Southern interest rates

Figure 18.6 Increase in the supply of the Northern bond resulting from a Northern budget deficit: steady-state effects on aggregate and national asset markets under a flexible external rate.

cies that give rise to deficits–with a temporary increase of deficit spending, a temporary tax cut, and a permanent increase of government spending offset sequentially by raising taxes. When the external exchange rate is flexible, these policies involve additional effects on aggregate income and on other variables, including the exchange rate itself, because they involve changes in supplies of bonds.[7] These effects take place through time, not on impact, after the fashion described in Chapter 6, but they show up very clearly in the steady state.

In Figure 18.6A we trace the effects on asset-market aggregates of an increase in B_1 (resulting from a Northern budget deficit) and an increase in B'_2 (resulting from a Southern deficit). The aggregate bond-market curve shifts gradually outward, from $W^t W^t$ to $W^{t*} W^{t*}$, but the money-market curve remains in place, because R^t is constant with a flexible external rate. Hence asset-market equilibrium is made to move along $M^t M^t$ from w to $w*$, and $S^t S^t$ must shift to $S^{t*} S^{t*}$. As this is a leftward shift when $S^t S^t$ is steeper than $M^t M^t$ (when crowding out does not dominate in the union as a whole), it implies an increase in Y^{dt}, aggregate disposable income.

[7] If a budget deficit is brought to an end by rescinding an increase of spending or a temporary tax cut, the income changes brought about by changes in supplies of bonds are the *only* permanent income changes. If a deficit is brought to an end by raising taxes to offset an earlier increase in spending, those income changes are *additional* to the changes shown in Figure 18.4, for a balanced-budget increase in government spending.

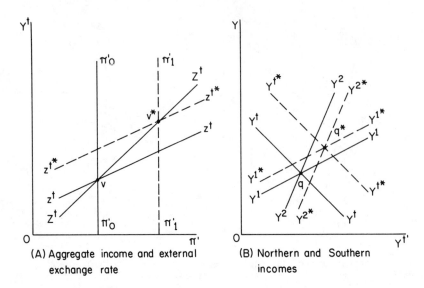

(A) Aggregate income and external
exchange rate

(B) Northern and Southern
incomes

Figure 18.7 Increase in the supply of the Northern bond resulting from a Northern budget deficit: steady-state effects on aggregate and national goods markets under a flexible external rate.

The corresponding increase in aggregate income, Y^t, is shown in Figure 18.7A. Increases in supplies of bonds have no direct effects on the positions of the income curves, but the short-run curve rises gradually from $z^t z^t$ to $z^{t*} z^{t*}$ under the influence of the increase in absorption (dissaving) induced by the changes in r^t and W^{ht}. Steady-state equilibrium is established at v^*, where $z^{t*} z^{t*}$ intersects $Z^t Z^t$. Aggregate income rises, and the union's currency depreciates.

The responses of the individual interest rates depend, of course, on the bond that is issued and on the degree of asset-market integration. Consider the effects of a Northern budget deficit, which raises B_1. In Figure 18.6B, the Northern bond-market curve shifts upward from $r^1 r^1$ to $r^{1*} r^{1*}$. The Southern curve can move either way, depending on the distribution of the increase in W^{ht} and the strength of the effects of wealth changes on the demand for the Southern bond.[8] To simplify the diagram, we show no shift at all. Asset-market equilibrium is displaced from s to s^*, and there is an increase in each country's interest rate but a larger increase in the

[8] With full-scale goods-market symmetry, the horizontal shift of the Southern bond-market curve is given by

$$dr_2 = -(1/B_{11}^t)[B_{1W}(dW^{h'}/dB_1) + B_{2W}(dW^h/dB_1)]\, dB_1$$
$$= (1/B_{11}^t)[(S_1 - S_2)(B_{1W} - B_{2W})L_{1W}(B_{11}^t + B_{12}^t) - S_W L_{11}^t B_{1W}^t(B_{11}^t - B_{12}^t)]\, dB_1,$$

which is ambiguous. If $r^2 r^2$ shifted to the left, r_2 could fall with an increase in B_1, rather than rising as it does in Figure 18.6B, but the average interest always rises.

Northern rate. An increase of internal asset-market integration would narrow the gap between the changes in the interest rates and would therefore reduce the gap between the wealth changes. The smaller the increase in r_1 relative to r_2, the smaller the increase in Northern saving relative to Southern saving and the smaller the Northern share in the increase of aggregate wealth shown in Figure 18.6A. With perfect asset-market integration, r_1, r_2, and r^t would change by the same amounts, and the increase in aggregate wealth would be divided evenly between North and South. (In Figure 18.6B, r^1r^1 and r^2r^2 would come to coincide with a 45° line passing through s, and asset-market equilibrium would be displaced to s''.) We return to this limiting case later in this chapter, when we come to fiscal unification. In a full-fledged fiscal union, Northern and Southern bonds may be replaced completely by union bonds, which means that there would be one bond market in the union.

The responses of the countries' incomes, Y and Y', depend solely on goods-market parameters, given the increase in aggregate income shown in Figure 18.7A. With full-scale goods-market symmetry, the two countries' incomes rise by the same amounts. The outcome does not depend on the bond that is issued or on the degree of asset-market integration.[9] In Figure 18.7B, both countries' income curves shift out by the same amounts, from Y^1Y^1 to $Y^{1*}Y^{1*}$ and from Y^2Y^2 to $Y^{2*}Y^{2*}$, respectively. At the same time, the aggregate income curve shifts upward from Y^tY^t to $Y^{t*}Y^{t*}$. The economies move from q to q^*, where the changes in incomes are equal. Without goods-market symmetry, of course, the changes in the countries' incomes are not likely to be equal. But the configuration of income changes will still depend entirely on goods-market responses,[10] and each country's income will still rise when, as here, crowding out does not dominate.

The effects of monetary and fiscal policies

When a monetary union has an active policy and its member governments have active fiscal policies, policy conflicts are quite likely to arise. They

---

[9] Taken by itself, the larger increase in r_1 shown in Figure 18.6B would depress the demand for the Northern good more than the demand for the Southern good. But the larger increase in r_1 is accompanied by an increase in Northern wealth relative to Southern wealth, and this redistribution, by itself, would raise the demand for the Northern good more than the demand for the Southern good. In the context of our model, moreover, the interest-rate and wealth effects cancel completely.

[10] From Eqs. (13.20a), (13.23a), and (13.24a), $(dY/dB_1)/(dY'/dB_1) = (dY/dB_2')/(dY'/dB_2') = (U_{1\pi}/U_{2\pi})$, so that $(dY/dB_1) = (dY'/dB_1)$ and $(dY/dB_2') = (dY'/dB_2')$ with goods-market symmetry.

are, in fact, more likely to occur when the external exchange rate is flexible, as monetary policy need not be assigned to safeguard reserves and may therefore be used more freely to influence the union's income. Its influence on income is permanent, moreover, so that conflicts will not disappear through time. To complicate matters, fiscal policies can have two distinct effects on incomes. If governments run budget deficits, supplies of bonds will grow, and changes in supplies of bonds have permanent effects on incomes additional to the effects of balanced-budget changes in spending.

But certain propositions continue to hold. Policy conflicts are bound to arise when the members' income targets do not add up to the union's target (when $\bar{Y} + \bar{Y}' \neq \bar{Y}^t$). As in the pegged-rate case, moreover, governments may be constrained by economic and political limitations on changes in spending and taxes, and these constraints are the more likely to be binding, the greater the degree of goods-market integration. When goods markets are closely integrated, internally or with the world market, large changes in spending, taxes, or both are needed to achieve independent income targets, even when those targets are consistent in principle.

As the impact effects of fiscal policies are not influenced by the exchange-rate regime, the policy reaction curves for deficit spending shown in Figure 17.3 apply without modification when the external exchange rate is flexible. If the Northern government seeks an increase in Northern income and the Southern government opposes any change in Southern income, the requisite changes in fiscal policies are shown at g'. The North must run a budget deficit, and the South must run a surplus. Similarly, Figure 17.5 can be reinterpreted to define the balanced-budget change in each country's spending required to achieve this same set of short-run targets. With positive spillover effects, the solution lies at g'. The North must make a balanced-budget increase in spending, and the South must make a balanced-budget cut in spending.

Through time and in the long run, however, the effects of fiscal policies come to be different with a flexible exchange rate, and the interactions with monetary policy come to differ markedly from those that we studied in Chapter 17. In Figure 18.8 we draw long-run reaction curves for balanced-budget changes in G_1 and G_2'. Curve I_U–I_U depicts the combinations of changes in the Northern and Southern budgets that will keep Northern income constant. Curve II_U–II_U is its Southern counterpart. Both curves are drawn on the (provisional) supposition that the union's central bank makes no change in policy (that B^{ct} is constant), and both curves are downward sloping, as spillover effects are necessarily positive when the external exchange rate is flexible.

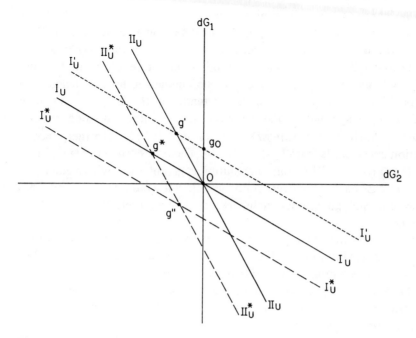

Figure 18.8 Policy interdependence: policy reaction curves for balanced-budget changes in spending required to achieve long-run income targets with an open-market purchase by the union's central bank and a flexible external rate.

Let us look now at the case that we have studied several times. The North would like to raise Northern income ($d\bar{Y} > 0$); the South would like to keep Southern income constant ($d\bar{Y}' = 0$). The new Northern target is reflected in Figure 18.8 by the shift in the Northern reaction curve from I_U–I_U to I'_U–I'_U. Absent any change in Southern fiscal policy, the North would make a balanced-budget increase in G_1 equal to the distance $0g_0$, and the joint policy solution is given at g'. The South must make a balanced-budget cut in G'_2 to keep Southern income constant, and the North must make an increase in G_1 larger than $0g_0$ to offset the effects of Southern policy and achieve its income target.[11]

---

[11] To find this solution and the one following, allowing for an open-market purchase too, we multiply by σ_1 the coefficients of dG_1, dG'_2, and dB^{ct} in Eq. (13.23a) and multiply by σ'_2 the coefficients in Eq. (13.24a). Inverting the results, we solve for dG_1 and dG'_2 in terms of the income targets, $d\bar{Y}$ and $d\bar{Y}'$, and an open-market purchase, $d\bar{B}^{ct}$, of arbitrary size:

$$dG_1 = (1/M_f)\{M_w[\sigma'_2(U_{2a} + \sigma_1 U_b)\,d\bar{Y} - \sigma_1(U_{1a})\,d\bar{Y}']$$
$$- (1/S_Y J_\pi)[(\sigma'_2 U_{1\pi} U_{2a} - \sigma_1 U_{2\pi} U_{1a})(\sigma_1 U_{1a} + \sigma'_2 U_{2a} + 2\sigma_1\sigma'_2 U_b)$$
$$+ U_{1\pi}(\sigma_1\sigma'_2 U_b)^2][(1 - B_{0W})S_1^t + S_W B_{01}^t]\}\,d\bar{B}^{ct}$$
$$dG'_2 = (1/M_f)\{M_w[\sigma_1(U_{1a} + \sigma'_2 U_b)\,d\bar{Y}' - \sigma'_2(U_{2a})\,d\bar{Y}]$$
$$- (1/S_Y J_\pi)[(\sigma_1 U_{2\pi} U_{1a} - \sigma'_2 U_{1\pi} U_{2a})(\sigma_1 U_{1a} + \sigma'_2 U_{2a} + 2\sigma_1\sigma'_2 U_b)$$
$$+ U_{2\pi}(\sigma_1\sigma'_2 U_b)^2][(1 - B_{0W})S_1^t + S_W B_{01}^t]\}\,d\bar{B}^{ct}$$

What happens when the central bank is active too? Suppose first that each government wants to keep its country's income constant (that $d\bar{Y} = d\bar{Y}' = 0$) but that the union's central bank wants to raise aggregate income (that $d\bar{Y}^t > 0$) and makes an open-market purchase that would achieve its income target if there were no changes in fiscal policies. The composition of that purchase does not matter in the long run and, with goods-market symmetry, the increase in Y^t will be divided equally between North and South ($dY = dY' = d\bar{Y}^t/2$). The Northern policy reaction curve shifts from I_U–I_U to I_U^*–I_U^*. The Southern curve shifts from II_U–II_U to II_U^*–II_U^*. The long-run solution is given at g'', where each government cuts back its budget, but by less than it would if the other did not do so too. Each government achieves its income target. The central bank does not.

To complete the argument, we have to combine the implications of the union's target with those of the Northern target, and we do so by dealing with a simple example. Suppose that the increase in Y^t sought by the central bank is exactly twice as large as the increase in Y sought by the Northern government (that $d\bar{Y} = d\bar{Y}^t/2 > 0$). If there were no need to take account of responses by the South, the North would not have to adjust its budget. Its policy reaction curve would be I_U–I_U, and the policy solution would be given at g^*, where I_U–I_U intersects II_U^*–II_U^*. The South would cut back its budget to keep Southern income constant. The North would expand its budget to offset the spillover effects of Southern fiscal policy. Comparing the solutions at g' and g^*, we see at once the consequences of the union's policy for the fiscal policies of its member governments. There is less work for Northern policy to do, because the open-market purchase raises Northern income, which is the objective of the Northern government. Conversely, there is more work for Southern policy to do, because it must combat the effects of the open-market purchase, as well as the effects of Northern fiscal policy.[12]

where

$$M_f = (\sigma_1\sigma_2'U_b)[(u_{10}^t u_{20}^t + u_{12}^t U_\pi)(\sigma_1 + \sigma_2') + \sigma_1(u_{20}^t)p_1C_1' + \sigma_2'(u_{10}^t)p_2C_2' + (\sigma_1\sigma_2'U_b)]$$
$$U_{1a} = u_{20}^t(u_{10}^t + p_1C_1') + u_{12}^t U_\pi \qquad U_{2a} = u_{10}^t(u_{20}^t + p_2C_2') + u_{12}^t U_\pi$$
$$U_b = [1 - (m_1 - m_2)]U_\pi$$

When $u_{12}^t \to \infty$, then, $dG_1 \to \infty$ and $dG_2 \to \infty$, as the numerators of the relevant expressions contain $(u_{12}^t)^2$, whereas the denominators contain only u_{12}^t. (This proves the assertion in the text that goods-market integration increases the sizes of the policy changes required to achieve independent income targets.)

[12] If the Northern income target were less than half as large as the union's target, the new Northern curve would be between I_U^*–I_U^* and I_U–I_U, and the policy solution would lie on II_U^*–II_U^* to the southeast of g^*. The budgetary changes would be smaller in both countries (and it could be necessary to reduce G_1, as it is at g'', if the Northern target were small

Even in this simple case, there is a clear-cut conflict between policy targets. The increase in Northern income at g^* is just half as large as the increase in aggregate income sought by the central bank, and Southern income has not changed at all. The central bank has not achieved its income target. In the present instance, moreover, the central bank has no way to minimize the conflict, let alone resolve it. The composition of an open-market purchase has no permanent effect on the distribution of the increase in Y^t. As usual, the outcome of the policy conflict cannot be predicted without knowing the constraints on each party's policy. If the central bank purchases additional bonds, the governments may be unable to respond; they may run up against constraints on spending and tax changes. In another case, however, the central bank can be constrained. If it seeks to stabilize aggregate income or to raise it by less than the sum of the members' income targets, the bank must make an open-market sale and could run out of bonds. (In this same case, however, other things can happen. If Southern fiscal policy is constrained, the North and the union may prevail, and the South will suffer a reduction in income as a result of the objective pursued by its partner.)

Another possibility should be mentioned briefly. Suppose that the Northern government runs a budget deficit to pursue its income target, raising the supply of Northern bonds. With goods-market symmetry, incomes in the North and South will rise by the same amounts in the long run (see Figure 18.7B), but the Northern interest rate will rise by more than the Southern rate (see Figure 18.6B). If the union's central bank wanted to cooperate with the Northern government, it could make an open-market purchase, and would be most helpful to the North if it bought the Northern bond, so as to hold down the Northern interest rate. (It would monetize part of the increase in B_1, and bond financing would give way to money financing.) If it wanted to oppose the Northern government, it could sell the Northern bond. The composition of its open-market sale would not affect the income changes in the North and South, but sales of the Northern bond would amplify the increase in the Northern interest rate, making it more costly for the North to finance its deficit. The

enough). If the Northern target were more than half as large as the union's target, the new Northern curve would be between I_U–I_U and I'_U–I'_U, and the policy solution would lie on $II^*_{\overline{U}}$–$II^*_{\overline{U}}$, to the northwest of g^*. The budgetary changes would be larger in both countries. With goods-market symmetry, however, the increase in G_1 cannot be as large as the one at g'. Using Eq. (13.20a) to replace $d\bar{B}^{ct}$ with $d\bar{Y}^t$, the union's target, setting $d\bar{Y}$ at zero, and invoking goods-market symmetry, we can rewrite the equation in the previous note as $dG_1 = (1/M_f)\{M_w[\sigma'_2(U_{2a} + \sigma_1 U_b)]\,d\bar{Y} - [U_{1\pi}(\sigma_1\sigma'_2 U_b)^2]\,d\bar{Y}^t\}$. For a given Northern target, $d\bar{Y} > 0$, dG_1 will be smaller when $d\bar{Y}^t > 0$ than when $d\bar{Y}^t = 0$.

Northern government might be compelled to reconsider its objective, because of opposition to the increase in r_1 or constraints on its ability to raise taxes sufficiently to offset the extra increase in debt-service payments. For reasons mentioned earlier, however, governments are apt to win a struggle with the central bank. They can threaten to withdraw from the monetary union or demand a change in the union's management.

If monetary policy is assigned to influence some other variable–the average interest rate, the structure of national interest rates, or the flexible external exchange rate–targets will not be inconsistent in principle, and there is less likelihood of policy conflict. But it cannot be ruled out. Under a flexible external rate, changes in the fiscal instruments have permanent effects on r_1, r_2, r^t, and π'. Fiscal policies can interfere with the work of the central bank, and it may be unable to carry out its task unless its bond holdings are very large. Conversely, monetary policy has permanent effects on Y and Y', and it may interfere with fiscal policies. Governments may be unable to achieve their income targets if they are not able to make large budgetary changes.[13] When countries opt for flexible exchange rates, moreover, it is in part to free monetary policy for the more effective regulation of domestic income, and a monetary union is apt to have the same motivation.[14] A union with a flexible external rate is thus likely to pursue an income target and come into conflict with its members' targets. The functioning and very survival of a monetary union require the harmonization of income targets, among the member governments themselves and between the members and the monetary union. The harmonization of national targets, however, calls for the coordination of fiscal instruments and, perhaps, the unification of those instruments, to make sure that the targets are pursued effectively.

Fiscal coordination and unification in a monetary union

Let us recapitulate. When a monetary union and its member governments adopt income targets, the monetary policies of the union and the fiscal

---

[13] Strictly speaking, changes in B_1 and B_2' have permanent effects on r_1, r_2, r^t, and π', but changes in G_1 and G_2' do not affect r^t. No interference would occur, then, if monetary policy were assigned to stabilize r^t at its initial level and governments pursued their income targets by changing G_1 and G_2' without ever altering supplies of debt. In all other instances, however, some form of interference can occur.

[14] See, e.g., R. Jenkins, "European Monetary Union," *Lloyds Bank Review* (January 1978), pp. 1–14, where the argument for monetary integration appeals to the need for the joint use of monetary and fiscal policies to stimulate European growth behind a flexible external rate.

policies of its members are interdependent. If those income targets are inconsistent, policy conflicts are inevitable. Outcomes will be inefficient, as policies cancel one another, and a policy failure is bound to occur somewhere in the system, if not indeed throughout the system. Three solutions are available.

1. The monetary union can give up its income target and pursue some other target. This solution is sensible when the external exchange rate is pegged, as monetary policy can be used effectively to regulate reserves. It should, in fact, be given this assignment; the central bank has custody of the union's reserves, and monetary policy is well suited to the task. The solution may not be adopted, however, when the external exchange rate is flexible, as monetary policy has powerful, permanent effects on aggregate activity, and one would expect its managers to exploit their influence. Furthermore, national fiscal policies may not be capable of regulating incomes without the assistance of monetary policy – which is why a flexible exchange rate may be chosen. The execution of fiscal policy is cumbersome and subject to constraints.

2. The member governments can give up *their* income targets and use their fiscal policies for other purposes. But this solution is not terribly attractive, because monetary policy by itself may not be powerful enough to regulate domestic activity. With a pegged external exchange rate, its influence is temporary, and it cannot be assigned to a domestic target without regard for the need to regulate the union's reserves. With a flexible external rate, its influence is larger and does not wear off, and there is no need to worry about losses of reserves. Even under this regime, however, monetary policy cannot control the long-run relationship between members' incomes. It is a blunt instrument. Finally, fiscal policies can get in the way of monetary policy, even when they are not aimed at influencing incomes. They have long-run effects on income, whether the union's exchange rate is pegged or flexible.

3. It may thus be necessary to harmonize income targets and use monetary and fiscal policies together to pursue those targets. This solution, however, raises a hard question. Should governments retain control of the fiscal instruments, or should they confer control on a fiscal union, giving it powers to tax and spend and the concomitant power to borrow? This question is too large for economists to answer. The powers to tax and spend are quintessential to national sovereignty, even more so than the power to print money. No nation can conduct an independent foreign policy if it is not free to decide how much it will spend on its armed forces. It is de Gaulle's *force de frappe,* one Frenchman said, that blocks the trans-

formation of the European Common Market into a full-fledged economic union. Nevertheless, economists have something to say about the problems and effects of policy coordination compared to those of policy unification, and this is the comparison that we shall make to wind up our work.

Fiscal coordination

What is involved in policy coordination when the North and South have formed a monetary union? First, the parties must agree on consistent income targets. Second, they must decide how to pursue those targets–on the role of the union's central bank, which controls the money supply, and the roles of the governments, which continue to control the fiscal instruments. The targets can be framed in terms of the two members' incomes, Y and Y', or equivalently in terms of aggregate income, Y^t, and its distribution, but there can be no more than two targets if they are to be consistent. The strategies, by contrast, are numerous, because they can combine open-market operations in the two countries' bonds with changes in spending, taxes, or both, by each of the two governments. Even in the long run, when the composition of an open-market operation no longer matters for the distribution of aggregate income and each government must balance its own budget, there are at least three instruments with which to pursue the two independent income targets–changes in B^{ct} and balanced-budget changes in G_1 and G_2'.[15]

In what follows, we assume that the union and its members agree to keep aggregate income constant but to raise Northern income and reduce Southern income (that $d\bar{Y} = -d\bar{Y}' > 0$, so that $d\bar{Y}^t = 0$). We also assume that they agree to make no change in B^{ct}, so that the money supply will be constant when the external exchange rate is flexible and will be determined by R^t when the rate is pegged). We make this additional assumption in aid of simplicity–to focus most directly on fiscal policies.

Suppose that the governments decide to achieve their targets by balanced-budget changes in G_1 and G_2', so that neither one will run a

[15] There are, in fact, *five* instruments, even in the long run, as each country can change its spending on its partner's good. But changes in G_1' and G_2 are not likely to be made for macroeconomic purposes, because the spillover effects are apt to exceed the domestic effects, and the latter can even be negative. Consider the long-run effects of an increase in G_2 when the external exchange rate is flexible. From Eqs. (13.23a) and (13.24a),

$$dY = (\sigma_1/M_w)[u_{20}^t(u_{10}^t + p_1C_1') + u_{12}^tU_\pi - \sigma_2'U_\pi(m_1 - m_2)] \, dG_2$$
$$d\hat{Y}' = (\sigma_2'/M_w)[u_{10}^t(u_{20}^t + p_2C_2') + u_{12}^tU_\pi + \sigma_1U_\pi] \, dG_2$$

so that $d Y' > 0$, but $dY \gtrless 0$. With goods-market symmetry, moreover, $dY - dY' = -(U_\pi/M_w)\sigma_1\sigma_2'[1 - (m_1 - m_2)] \, dG_2$, which is unambiguously negative.

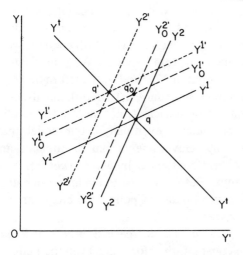

Figure 18.9 Fiscal policies to redistribute a constant aggregate income: impact effects of a balanced-budget increase in Northern spending and a balanced-budget decrease in Southern spending.

budget deficit or surplus at any time. The short-run solution does not depend on the exchange-rate regime and is shown in Figure 18.9. With full-scale goods-market symmetry, the budgetary changes must be exactly equal but opposite in sign ($dG_1 = -dG_2' > 0$). With an increase in G_1, by itself, the Northern income curve would shift from $Y^1 Y^1$ to $Y_0^{1'} Y_0^{1'}$, and the Southern curve would shift from $Y^2 Y^2$ to $Y_0^{2'} Y_0^{2'}$, moving the economies from q to q_0'. Northern income would rise and Southern income would fall, but aggregate income would rise, because an increase in G_1 raises Northern income by more than it reduces Southern income.[16] An equal decrease in G_2', however, would have symmetrical effects. The Southern income curve would shift leftward from $Y_0^{2'} Y_0^{2'}$ to $Y^{2'} Y^{2'}$ (a distance equal to the upward shift of the Northern curve from $Y^1 Y^1$ to $Y_0^{1'} Y_0^{1'}$), and the Northern income curve would shift upward from $Y_0^{1'} Y_0^{1'}$ to $Y^{1'} Y^{1'}$ (a distance equal to the leftward shift of the Southern curve from $Y^2 Y^2$ to $Y_0^{2'} Y_0^{2'}$). The economies would move from q_0' to q', where Northern income is higher, Southern income is lower, and aggregate income is unchanged.

The movement from q to q_0' will not be observable when fiscal policies

[16] In Chapter 17 we saw that the spillover effects of these policies can be positive or negative. Figure 18.9 is drawn for the case in which they are negative; q_0' lies slightly to the left of q, and q' lies slightly above q_0'. But the shifts in the income curves do not depend on the signs of the spillover effects and are not ambiguous in direction; see the table of equations at the end of Chapter 15.

are fully coordinated; the economies will move directly from q to q'. But the location of q'_0 must be known if fiscal policies are to be coordinated; it determines the sizes of the changes in G_1 and G'_2. With goods-market symmetry, of course, q'_0 is equidistant from q and q'. Without goods-market symmetry, it has to be to the right of $Y^t Y^t$ and to the left of $Y^2 Y^2$, but can be almost anywhere within those boundaries. To coordinate fiscal policies perfectly, governments must be omniscient, not merely cooperative.[17]

Although budgets must be balanced eventually in our model, they need not be balanced continuously. Governments can run deficits and surpluses for finite intervals. There are thus many ways to get from q to q', if not to stay there permanently. Before turning to the long-run counterpart of Figure 18.9, let us look at a couple of policy combinations involving temporary deficits and surpluses.

To increase Northern income and decrease Southern income while holding aggregate income constant, the North must run the budget deficit and the South must run the surplus. Consider two ways of doing so:

1. An increase of expenditure by the North and decrease of expenditure by the South, with no change in either country's taxes; i.e., $\delta(G_1, D) > 0$ and $\delta(G'_2, D') < 0$,

2. An increase of expenditure by the North combined with an equal decrease of Northern taxes, and a decrease of expenditure by the South combined with an equal increase of Southern taxes; i.e., $\delta(G_1, D) = \delta D > 0$ and $\delta(G'_2, D') = \delta D' < 0$.

These policy combinations are more powerful than the one described by Figure 18.9, where changes in spending were offset by changes in taxes. This is because a change in Northern taxes has more effect on Northern than Southern income, and a change in Southern taxes has more effect on Southern income.[18] In the illustration that follows, however, we standardize the sizes of the changes in expenditure (rather than the sizes of the income targets), in order to simplify the exposition. Therefore, the

---

[17] The presentation in the text should not be taken to imply that governments begin by choosing the change in G_1, finding q'_0, and then choosing the change in G'_2. The budgetary changes are chosen simultaneously. But they cannot be chosen at all without the information required to locate q'_0. (If the presentation were reversed, with the change in G'_2 chosen first, the counterpart of q'_0 would lie to the left of $Y^t Y^t$ and of $Y^1 Y^1$.)

[18] This might not be the case if consumption were not biased or there were significant goods-market asymmetries. From Eqs. (13.7) and (13.8),

$$\delta Y - \delta Y' = [(1 - S_Y)/M_s][M_Y(m_1 - m_2)\sigma_1\sigma'_2 + (1 - m_0)(\sigma_1 - \sigma'_2)u^t_{12} + (m_1\sigma_1 u^t_{20} - m_2\sigma'_2 u^t_{10})]\,\delta D$$

which is certain to be positive when consumption is biased ($m_1 > m_2$) and goods-market responses are symmetrical ($\sigma_1 = \sigma'_2$ and $u^t_{10} = u^t_{20}$).

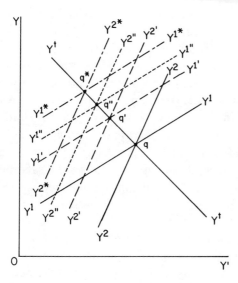

Figure 18.10 Fiscal policies to redistribute a constant aggregate income: impact effects of various policy combinations.

tax changes in combination 2 are additional to the expenditure changes in combination 1, and the second policy combination will be more powerful than the first and will also lead to larger deficits and surpluses.

In Figure 18.10 we compare three sets of fiscal policies–the balanced-budget changes in G_1 and G_2' examined earlier, and the policy combinations 1 and 2 involving Northern deficits and Southern surpluses. With balanced-budget changes in expenditures, the two countries' income curves shift from Y^1Y^1 and Y^2Y^2 to $Y^{1\prime}Y^{1\prime}$ and $Y^{2\prime}Y^{2\prime}$, as in Figure 18.9. Short-run equilibrium is displaced from q to q'. With policy combination 1, the expenditure changes are not offset by tax changes, and the curves shift further, to $Y^{1\prime\prime}Y^{1\prime\prime}$ and $Y^{2\prime\prime}Y^{2\prime\prime}$, displacing equilibrium to q''. The redistribution of income is larger. With combination 2, the expenditure changes are reinforced by tax changes, and the income curves shift all the way to $Y^{1*}Y^{1*}$ and $Y^{2*}Y^{2*}$, displacing equilibrium to $q*$. The redistribution of income is even larger. Turning these results around, suppose that the North and South want merely to move from q to q'. They can do so with smaller budgetary changes when they are permitted to run deficits and surpluses than when they are constrained to balance their budgets.

Note next that the distance $q'q''$ along Y^tY^t is equal to the distance $q''q*$ and that this would be true even without goods-market symmetry. The reason has to do with the changes in lump-sum taxes, T^h and $T^{h\prime}$, that take place in this exercise. No tax changes are involved in the movement from q to q''. With balanced-budget changes in expenditures, by contrast, the tax burden is shifted from Southerners to Northerners; there is an increase in T^h equal to the increase in G_1 and a decrease in $T^{h'}$ equal to the decrease in G_2'. This redistribution of tax burdens favors Southern income at the expense of Northern income, so that q' is southeast of q''. And with the tax changes embodied in combination 2, the tax burden is shifted from Northerners to Southerners; there is a decrease in T^h equal to the increase in G_1 and an increase in $T^{h'}$ equal to the decrease in G_2'. This redistribution favors Northern income, so that q^* is northwest of q'', and the sizes of the changes in T^h and $T^{h'}$ involved in the movement from q'' to q^* are equal absolutely to those involved in the movement from q'' to q^*.

One could concoct other combinations of policies to raise Northern income at the expense of Southern income. It is not necessary, for example, to make the same type of budgetary change in each country; the North might make a balanced-budget increase in spending, and the South might run a temporary budget surplus by raising taxes. It is not necessary, moreover, to keep B^{ct} constant. The central bank might make an open-market purchase of the Northern bond, with the short-run effect of raising both countries' incomes but Northern income by more than Southern income. The rest of the job might then be done by tightening fiscal policy in the South, by tightening it more in the South than the North, or by tightening it in the South and relaxing it in the North, depending on the size and strength of the open-market purchase and the types of budgetary changes.

But budgets must be balanced in the long run, and the number of permanent policy combinations is very much smaller. At this stage, moreover, we must pay attention to the exchange-rate regime. When the external rate is pegged, monetary policy has no role to play in pursuing permanent income targets; balanced-budget changes in G_1 and G_2' are the only instruments available to influence the steady-state level of Y^t and its distribution between North and South. When the external rate is flexible, monetary policy can play an important role in adjusting Y^t permanently, and there is another complication. If budgets are not balanced continuously, supplies of bonds will change, and any change in B^t, the sum of the supplies, will affect Y^t. When choosing permanent levels of B^{ct}, G_1, and G_2', the central bank and governments must therefore allow for changes in B^t.

If B^t and B^{ct} are constant, however, an interesting result obtains. With full-scale goods-market symmetry, the budgetary changes that are needed

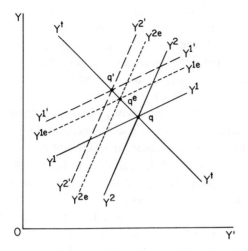

Figure 18.11 Fiscal policies to redistribute a constant aggregate income: steady-state effects of a balanced-budget increase in Northern spending and a balanced-budget decrease in Southern spending.

in the long run to redistribute aggregate income are different from the changes needed in the short run, but are the same for both of the exchange-rate regimes.

With a flexible external rate, a balanced-budget increase in Northern spending, taken by itself, causes Southern income to rise through time from the level reached on impact, and Northern income can rise too. (In Figure 18.4B, long-run equilibrium was established at q'', northeast of q'.) With goods-market symmetry, however, a balanced-budget increase in Northern spending matched by a balanced-budget decrease in Southern spending has symmetrical effects; the two policies result in a gradual increase in Northern income and an equal decrease in Southern income, with no change in aggregate income. In Figure 18.11 we reproduce the short-run solution shown in Figure 18.9 and show these long-run tendencies. The Northern income curve shifts downward gradually from $Y^{1'}Y^{1'}$ to $Y^{1e}Y^{1e}$, the Southern curve shifts rightward from $Y^{2'}Y^{2'}$ to $Y^{2e}Y^{2e}$, and long-run equilibrium is established at q^e. The fiscal policies adopted to move from q to q' must be reinforced through time. Otherwise, the actual redistribution of Y^t will fall short of the desired redistribution.

With a pegged external rate, these processes are reversed, but the outcome is the same. In Figure 18.4B, a balanced-budget increase in Northern spending led to long-run equilibrium at q^*, southwest of q'; Northern income fell through time, and so did Southern income (but by less than Northern income). Here again, however, the decrease in Southern spending has symmetrically opposite effects, so that aggregate income is unaffected, but Southern income rises and Northern income falls. It can be shown, moreover, that the long-run outcome is identical to the one in Figure 18.11; the size of the slippage in redistribution, the distance $q'q^e$, does not depend on the exchange-rate regime.[19]

This particular case has another interesting feature. When goods markets are symmetrical and governments use balanced-budget changes in spending to redistribute aggregate income, the external exchange-rate regime has no effect on the outcome for *any* variable. In Figure 18.4A, $z^t z^t$ and $Z^t Z^t$ do not shift when changes in G_1 and G_2' offset each other. This means that there can be no saving or dissaving by the union as a whole and no change in its demand for money. By implication, reserves are constant when the external exchange rate is pegged, and the rate is constant when it is flexible. Within the union, wealth, bonds, and money are redistributed gradually from North to South, but the sizes of the redistributions are not affected by the external exchange-rate regime.

Although the particular conclusions drawn from Figure 18.11 depend on the assumption of goods-market symmetry, the general conclusion does not. When goods markets are not perfectly integrated and income targets are consistent, there must always exist a combination of fiscal policies that satisfies those targets. Fiscal policies can regulate the level of aggregate income (the position of $Y^t Y^t$) and its distribution (the location of points q' and q^e). If goods markets are not symmetrical, of course, the sizes of the budgetary changes may not be equal absolutely (and may not be the same with a flexible external rate as with a pegged external rate), even in the special case described by Figure 18.11, where Y^t was not altered. When targets are consistent, however, and the requisite budgetary changes are feasible, the members of a monetary union can regulate Y^t

---

[19] With a flexible external rate, the long-run change in Northern income, obtained from Eq. (13.23a), is $dY = [1 - (m_1 - m_2)]\sigma_1(\sigma_2' U_\pi/M_w) \, d(G_1, - G_2')$, where $d(G_1, -G_2')$ denotes the pair of balanced-budget changes $dG_1 = -dG_2' > 0$. With a pegged external rate, the long-run change, obtained from Eq. (13.23b), is $dY = [1 - (m_1 - m_2)]\sigma_1[(u_{20}^t + m_0\sigma_2')/M_k]d(G_1, - G_2')$. With goods-market symmetry, however, $(u_{20}^t + m_0\sigma_2')M_w = (\sigma_2' U_\pi M_k)$, so that the income changes are identical. Furthermore, the difference between the long-run change and the instantaneous change, given by Eq. (13.7), can be written as

$$dY - \delta Y = -(2S_Y/M_s M_w)(m_1 - m_2)(u_{10}^t + p_1 C_1')[\sigma_1 u_{10}^t + u_{12}^t(\sigma_1 + \sigma_2')][\sigma_1 u_{10}^t + M_Y(\sigma_1\sigma_2')] \, d(G_1, - G_2') < 0$$

Symmetrical results can be obtained for Southern income, using Eqs. (13.24a), (13.24b), and (13.8).

and its distribution, in the short run and the long run, without the assistance of monetary policy.

Fiscal unification

What are the differences between fiscal unification and fiscal coordination? In a fiscal union, the choice of policy targets and administration of policy instruments are vested in a single, supranational authority. Accordingly, fiscal unification differs in four ways from fiscal coordination. (1) Policy targets are not chosen by haggling between governments and are less likely to be inconsistent. (2) The tasks of fiscal and monetary policies are decided centrally, at the union-wide level, and are less likely to work at cross purposes. (3) The instruments of fiscal policy can be combined more flexibly, because there is just one budget to be balanced. (4) Through time, if not at once, the union's bonds will displace the members' bonds, fostering asset-market integration.

The first and second differences are more important than the third and fourth. The largest benefits of fiscal unification derive from the prevention of policy conflict and from a more efficient division of labor between fiscal and monetary policies. The largest costs relate to the sacrifice of sovereignty involved in the transfer of decision-making power. But there is not much more to say about the first and second, as we have already shown what can go wrong when policy targets are inconsistent and policy instruments are used at cross purposes. We do have more to say about the third and fourth, especially the third, having to do with the uses of the fiscal instruments.

As before, we emphasize the influence of fiscal policy on the distribution of aggregate income, even though the level of aggregate income may come to be the more important policy target in a full-fledged fiscal union. The reason is simple. If we were to concentrate on the level of Y^t, our findings would resemble those in Parts II and III. The effects of fiscal and monetary policies on Y^t, r^t, R^t, and π' are similar to their effects on the income, interest rate, reserves, and exchange rate of a single small economy, and we need not recite them here. Furthermore, we continue to emphasize effects on gross domestic products, Y and Y', not on disposable incomes, Y^d and $Y^{d'}$, even though we concentrate on distribution, because we are interested in macroeconomic problems. In the Keynesian variant of our model, the signs of changes in Y and Y' determine the signs of changes in prices, p_1 and p_2', in real outputs, Q_1 and Q_2', and in levels of employment, E and E'. For this reason, however, our discussion is not comprehensive. A fiscal union can manipulate its budget to shift the distribution of disposable incomes without redistributing gross domestic products. It can also redistribute public goods and services without redistributing taxes or expenditures. The pattern of its purchases in the North and South bears no necessary relationship to the distribution of public goods and services. In brief, the powers of a fiscal union are far larger than those stressed in this short discussion.

We have already shown that fiscal policy is most potent when governments are not compelled to balance their budgets. In Figure 13.10, for example, policy combination 1, involving an increase in G_1 and a decrease in G_2' with no change in taxes, was shown to be stronger than its balanced-budget counterpart. In that same case, however, the North ran a deficit and the South ran a surplus, raising the supply of the Northern bond ($\dot{B}_1 > 0$) and reducing the supply of the Southern bond ($\dot{B}_2' < 0$). This state of affairs cannot be perpetuated when fiscal systems are not unified. If Northern and Southern bonds are not perfect substitutes, r_1 will rise and go on rising for as long as the North runs a deficit. Even when they are perfect substitutes, moreover, the difficulties are not overcome completely. In that instance, of course, $r_1 = r_2 = r^t$, and the latter will not change when the Northern deficit is equal absolutely to the Southern surplus. (When $\dot{B}_1 = -\dot{B}_2'$, then $\dot{B}^t = 0$, and there is no interference with convergence to a steady state.) But the two bonds may cease to be perfect substitutes if Northern indebtedness rises hugely and Southern indebtedness falls. Furthermore, the North will continue to incur an increase in debt-service costs (albeit at the rate $r^t\dot{B}_1$ rather than the higher rate $\dot{r}_1 B_1 + r_1\dot{B}_1$), and the North must raise taxes or cut spending continuously, merely to prevent its budget deficit from growing. But it cannot raise taxes or cut spending forever and has to balance its budget eventually. This requirement is relaxed when the North and South form a fiscal union.

In our work thus far, moreover, no government has changed its spending on the other country's good; changes in G_1' and G_2 have not been used as fiscal instruments. This omission was deliberate. Governments may not be willing to tax their own residents in order to pursue a fiscal policy that stimulates another country's income more strongly than it stimulates domestic income.[20] But this constraint is not binding in a fiscal union. Additional taxes can be levied on *both* countries' residents in order to purchase any combination of the two countries' goods.

[20] See note 15.

To illustrate these and other points, we return to the policy problem considered earlier. It has been decided to raise Northern income at the expense of Southern income and to make no change in aggregate income. A fiscal union can achieve these targets by methods that cannot be used when governments must balance their budgets individually.

The simplest example is the union-wide counterpart of policy combination 1. The union can increase its spending on the Northern good, decrease its spending on the Southern good, and make no change in taxes; algebraically, $dG_1^u = -dG_2^u > 0$, where $dG_1^u = \frac{1}{2}(dG_1 + dG_1')$ and $dG_2^u = \frac{1}{2}(dG_2 + dG_2')$.[21] The union does not run a budget deficit or surplus (B^t does not change), so that it can follow this policy forever. In consequence, the permanent effects of the union's policy will be larger than those of the balanced-budget changes in Northern and Southern spending that are the only permanent policies available in the absence of a union. With a flexible external exchange rate, the effects of union policy will be

$$dY = -dY' = (U_\pi/M_w)(\sigma_1\sigma_2')\, d(G_1^u, -G_2^u)$$

and those of separate national policies will be

$$dY = -dY' = [1 - (m_1 - m_2)](U_\pi/M_w)(\sigma_1\sigma_2')\, d(G_1, -G_2')$$

which are manifestly smaller.[22] With a pegged external rate, the effects of union policy will be

$$dY = -dY' = [\sigma_1(u_{20}^t + m_0\sigma_2')/M_k]\, d(G_1^u, -G_2^u)$$

and those of separate national policies will be

$$dY = -dY' = [1 - (m_1 - m_2)][\sigma_1(u_{20}^t + m_0\sigma_2')/M_k]\, d(G_1, -G_2')$$

which are likewise smaller. Under both regimes, in fact, national policies are weaker to the same degree.

The union has another option. It can cut taxes in the North and raise them in the South, and it can do so permanently if total taxes do not change ($dT^h = -dT^{h'} < 0$). This policy may not be palatable politically

[21] As dG_1 and dG_2 were defined in Part IV to be balanced-budget changes in Northern spending, whereas dG_1' and dG_2' were defined to be balanced-budget changes in Southern spending, $dG_1^u > 0$ involves an increase in both countries' taxes and $dG_2^u < 0$ involves a decrease. With goods-market symmetry, however, $dG_1^u = -dG_2^u$, and total taxes are unchanged in each country.

[22] These results are obtained from Eqs. (13.23a) and (13.24a), using the definitions of dG_1^u and dG_2^u supplied in the text. Those for the pegged-rate case are obtained from Eqs. (13.23b) and (13.24b).

but is feasible economically. It does not throw the union's budget out of balance.[23] With a flexible external exchange rate, the long-run effects will be

$$dY = -dY' = (m_1 - m_2)(U_\pi/M_w)(\sigma_1\sigma_2') \ d(T^{h'}, \ -T^h)$$

With a pegged external rate, the effects will be

$$dY = -dY' = (m_1 - m_2)[\sigma_1(u_{20}^t + m_0\sigma_2')/M_k] \ d(T^{h'}, \ -T^h)$$

A shift in the tax burden affects the distribution of aggregate income to the extent that consumption in each country is biased in favor of the domestic good $(m_1 > m_2)$. The redistribution of Y^t is smaller, however, than the one resulting from an equivalent shift in expenditure.

Finally, a word about the fourth effect of a fiscal union–the displacement of Northern and Southern bonds by union bonds. This could happen gradually, in consequence of union budget deficits financed by issuing union bonds, and displacement would be relative, not absolute. It could happen quickly and absolutely, with an agreement under which Northern and Southern bonds would be exchanged for union bonds. In the case of the United States, which began as a customs union and weak fiscal union but grew gradually into a full-fledged monetary and fiscal union, both processes occurred. The new federal government assumed the debts incurred by the state governments during the Revolutionary War, but the subsequent growth of the federal debt, especially during World War I and World War II, was more important in explaining the present situation. U.S. asset markets are closely integrated, largely because federal debt instruments are widely held and traded.

Suppose for simplicity that the fiscal union redeems its members' debts. Northern and Southern bonds are replaced by union bonds, and two important variables, B^t and r^t, come to have new meanings. The former is the stock of union bonds, not the sum of stocks of Northern and Southern bonds, and the latter is the interest rate on the union bond, not the average of r_1 and r_2. Asset markets are completely unified. This may be deemed to be disadvantageous from one point of view.

---

[23] Analytically, this policy is equivalent to a balanced-budget decrease in Northern spending on the Northern good matched by a balanced budget increase in Southern spending on the Northern good $(dG_1' = -dG_1 > 0)$, which is another reason why it was ruled out in the absence of a fiscal union. It is also equivalent, however, to a balanced-budget decrease in Northern spending on the Southern good matched by a balanced-budget increase in Southern spending on the Southern good, which might not be ruled out (because the North reduces its taxes on Northern residents as it reduces its spending on the Southern good). In any case, this is the mathematical analogy used to derive the results in the text.

When the central bank holds Northern and Southern bonds, it can influ ence Y and Y' independently. By purchasing the Northern bond and selling the Southern bond, it can raise Northern income at the expense of Southern income. Its ability to do so, however, is limited to the short run, and it may be a nuisance rather than a blessing. When the effects of monetary policy are distributed evenly, as they would be with a single bond, the central bank cannot be accused of meddling in matters best left to member governments or to the managers of a fiscal union. Monetary policy is criticized severely because its incidence by *sector* is seen to be uneven. It would be criticized even more severely if its incidence by *region* were seen to be uneven. On balance, then, the substitution of union for national bonds may be beneficial for a monetary union.

Conclusion

When two countries form a simple exchange-rate union and their asset markets are already integrated closely, much can be said for taking the next step–the formation of a full-fledged monetary union–and little can be said against it. The formation of an exchange-rate union, if deemed to be durable, will itself intensify asset-market integration, and members will not have much monetary autonomy. They will not be able to conduct independent monetary policies, even if their common external exchange rate is flexible. In the short run, each country may still have more influence on its own income than its partner's income, but that influence may be quite small. In the long run, moreover, the incidence of each country's monetary policy is determined uniquely by goods-market parameters that central banks cannot control. If the countries form a monetary union, pooling their reserves and placing the conduct of monetary policy in the hands of a single central bank, they are apt to gain, individually and collectively. Monetary policy can be conducted more efficiently, as open-market operations in one country will not be offset or duplicated by open-market operations in the other, and they will conserve reserves, as imbalances between them will be settled on the books of the single central bank.

When they form a monetary union, however, they must face the problem studied in this chapter–the harmonization of policy targets. If they adopt a pegged external rate, the problem will be minimal in principle and, perhaps, in practice. The central bank will have to safeguard the union's reserves and may devote its efforts exclusively to that objective. If they adopt a flexible external rate, by contrast, the central bank will be free to pursue some other aim, and it may seek to regulate aggregate income. It is then essential to harmonize the aims of the central bank with those of the governments, which continue to conduct their own fiscal policies. It is necessary, moreover, not only to harmonize policy targets but also to choose roles for the principal policy instruments. This was the case we made for policy coordination.

Once governments have gone *this* far, a case can be made for going farther–for the formation of a full-fledged fiscal union. It may, indeed, be necessary to go farther because sovereign governments will not go far enough. They may not be able to harmonize targets by negotiation and must therefore do so by delegation. By forming a fiscal union and giving it the task of formulating targets, as well as use of the main fiscal instruments, the members of a monetary union can avoid conflict or stalemate. A fiscal union, moreover, will enjoy more flexibility in the execution of fiscal policy and may be able to collaborate more closely with the central bank–the operating arm of the monetary union.

The logic of this argument may be impeccable, but the obstacles to its acceptance are formidable. Without the right to make fiscal-policy decisions, governments cannot carry out many of their functions. They must have at least limited powers to tax and spend in order to deliver the public goods and services demanded by their citizens, and demands may differ from country to country. For that matter, macroeconomic stability is itself a public good, and governments are loathe to relinquish control over its delivery.

When economies are interdependent, it is not easy to achieve domestic stability or any other macroeconomic aim. Fiscal policies will be interdependent and will also interact with the policies adopted by a monetary union. National autonomy may also be constrained by economic and political limitations on the sizes of spending and tax changes, and those limitations are more likely to be binding the higher the degree of market integration. But asset-market integration does not interfere with fiscal autonomy, and goods markets are not likely to be integrated as closely as asset markets. One country's bond may be a perfect substitute for another country's bond in an exchange-rate union. But one country's goods will rarely be perfect substitutes for another country's goods. The "law of one price" may apply within each and every market. It does not apply across goods markets–not even in a customs union with negligible transport costs. As a practical matter, then, the formation of a fiscal union does involve a sacrifice of national autonomy.

One last point must be made about the size of that sacrifice and the concomitant costs of fiscal unification. It cuts the other way. If labor mobility is high and labor movements are sensitive to fiscal policies–to tax rates and supplies of public goods–governments may not have as much policy independence as those in our formal model, where we have ruled out factor mobility. Firms may be footloose too, and sensitive to differences in fiscal policies. We touched on this issue in Chapter 14 but said no more about it. To deal with it systematically, however, we would have to write another book.

Equations for additional policy reaction curves and other new relationships

---

Desired long-run change in Northern income: combinations of balanced-budget changes in spending (I_U–I_U) (Eqs. 13.20a and 13.23a)

$$dG_1 = [1/(U_{1a} + U_b)]\{(M_w/\sigma_1)\, d\bar{Y} - (U_{1a})\, dG_2'$$
$$- (U_{1\pi}/S_Y J_\pi)[S_B B_{01}^t + S_1^t(1 - B_{0W})]\, d\bar{B}^{ct}\}$$

Desired long-run change in Southern income: combinations of balanced-budget changes in spending (II_U–II_U) (Eqs. 13.20a and 13.24a)

$$dG_2' = [1/(U_{2a} + U_b)]\{(M_w/\sigma_2')\, d\bar{Y}' - (U_{2a})\, dG_1$$
$$- (U_{2\pi}/S_Y J_\pi)[S_W B_{01}^t + S_1^t(1 - B_{0W})]\, d\bar{B}^{ct}\}$$

Long-run effect on aggregate reserves of balanced-budget changes in Northern spending ($T_1 T_1$) (Eqs. 13.20b and 13.22b)

$$dR^t = -(S_Y/J_K)(J_\pi/M_k)\{M_g + u_{10}^t[1 - (m_1 - m_2)]\sigma_2'\}\, dG_1$$

Long-run effect on aggregate reserves of balanced-budget changes in Southern spending ($T_2 T_2$) (Eqs. 13.20b and 13.22b)

$$dR^t = -(S_Y/J_K)(J_\pi/M_k)\{M_g + u_{20}^t[1 - (m_1 - m_2)]\sigma_1\}\, dG_2'$$

Open-market operations required to achieve aggregate reserve target given balanced-budget changes in Northern and Southern spending required to achieve long-run income targets (EE) (Eq. 13.22b)

$$dB^{ct} = -\{J_K[S_W B_{01}^t + S_1^t(1 - B_{0W})]^{-1}\}(d\bar{R}^t - d\hat{R}^t)$$

where $d\hat{R}^t$ is the change in aggregate reserves resulting from the changes in G_1 and G_2' required to achieve long-run income targets (those given by $T_1 T_1$ and $T_2 T_2$)

The equations in this table are written for the case in which the exchange rates equal unity initially. The same assumption is made in drawing the corresponding diagrams.

Appendixes

Appendix A

The supply side of the model

To obtain solutions for $*E_1$ and $*E_N$, required to solve Eqs. (2.27a), (2.28a), and (2.3a), use Eqs. (2.4) through (2.8) to write

$$(A.1) \quad [a_1(p_1/w)Q_1]\left(\frac{\delta p_1}{p_1}\right) + [a_N(p_N/w)Q_N]\left(\frac{\delta p_N}{p_N}\right)$$

$$- [a_1(p_1/w)Q_1 + a_N(p_N/w)Q_N]\left(\frac{\delta w}{w}\right) - \delta E = 0$$

where

$$a_1 = -(wE_1/p_1Q_1)(E_1Q_{1EE}/Q_{1E})^{-1} > 0$$
$$a_N = -(wE_N/p_NQ_N)(E_NQ_{NEE}/Q_{NE})^{-1} > 0$$

In the classical case, Eq. (2.9a) applies, and Eq. (A.1) becomes

$$(A.1a) \quad \left(\frac{\delta w}{w}\right) = u_E\left[(1/a_Np_NQ_N)\left(\frac{\delta p_1}{p_1}\right) + (1/a_1p_1Q_1)\left(\frac{\delta p_N}{p_N}\right)\right]$$

where

$$u_E = (a_1p_1Q_1)(a_Np_NQ_N)/(a_1p_1Q_1 + a_Np_NQ_N)$$

In the Keynesian case, Eq. (2.9b) applies, and Eq. (A.1) becomes

$$(A.1b) \quad \delta E = [a_1(p_1/w)Q_1]\left(\frac{\delta p_1}{p_1}\right) + [a_N(p_N/w)Q_N]\left(\frac{\delta p_N}{p_N}\right)$$

Equations (A.1a) and (A.1b) are employed in Chapter 3 to obtain the signs for $(\delta w/w)$ and δE. Like all other equations in this appendix, moreover, they hold without change for steady-state changes (one has only to substitute d for δ).

In the classical case, Eqs. (2.1) through (2.7) and (A.1a) imply that

$$(A.2a) \quad \delta^*E_i = (u_E/w)\left[\left(\frac{\delta p_i}{p_i}\right) - \left(\frac{\delta p_j}{p_j}\right)\right]$$

(A.3a) $p_i \, \delta Q_i = u_E \left[\left(\dfrac{\delta p_i}{p_i} \right) - \left(\dfrac{\delta p_j}{p_j} \right) \right]$

where $i, j = 1, N$ and $i \neq j$. Note that $(\delta Q_1 / \delta Q_N) = -(p_N/p_1)$; the slope of the transformation curve equals the absolute value of the price ratio. Furthermore,

(A.4a) $\delta Y = \displaystyle\sum_i (p_i Q_i) \left(\dfrac{\delta p_i}{p_i} \right)$

In the Keynesian case, Eqs. (2.1) through (2.7) and (A.1b) imply that

(A.2b) $\delta^* E_i = [a_i(p_i/w)Q_i] \left(\dfrac{\delta p_i}{p_i} \right)$

(A.3b) $p_i \, \delta Q_i = a_i(p_i Q_i) \left(\dfrac{\delta p_i}{p_i} \right)$

where $i = 1, N$. Employment and output changes depend exclusively on own-price changes. Therefore,

(A.4b) $\delta Y = \displaystyle\sum_i (1 + a_i) p_i Q_i \left(\dfrac{\delta p_i}{p_i} \right)$

In much of our algebraic work, we consolidate the classical and Keynesian cases:

(A.3c) $p_i \, \delta Q_i = [u_E + a_i(p_i Q_i)] \left(\dfrac{\delta p_i}{p_i} \right) - u_E \left(\dfrac{\delta p_j}{p_j} \right) \qquad i, j = 1, N$

(A.4c) $\delta Y = \displaystyle\sum_i \sigma_i \left(\dfrac{\delta p_i}{p_i} \right) \qquad \sigma_i = (1 + a_i) p_i Q_i \qquad i = 1, N$

Classical outcomes can then be obtained by treating the a_i as though they were zero (in which case, $\sigma_i = p_i Q_i$). Keynesian outcomes can be obtained by treating u_E as though it were zero.

Appendix B

Outcomes when bonds are consols

To illustrate the statement in Chapter 2 that the substitution of long-term bonds (consols) for short-term bonds (bills) would not change the sign of any important outcome, we reformulate our model and show some of the solutions.

Let each bond be a perpetual annuity paying continuously one unit of the currency in which the bond was issued. Denote the *numbers* of bonds by β_0 and β_1. Their market values in home currency are $(\pi\beta_0/r_0)$ and (β_1/r_1), and these terms can be substituted for πB_0 and B_1 throughout Chapter 2. (Analogous substitutions must be made for B_1^c, B_1^h, $*B_1^h$, etc.)

These substitutions do not affect the market-clearing equations for domestic goods, Eqs. (2.27a) and (2.28a). They do affect the market-clearing equations for the domestic bond and money. The former, for example, becomes

(B.1) $\quad B_1(\bar{r}_0, r_1, W^h) + (\bar{\beta}_1^c/r_1) - (\beta_1/r_1) = 0$

where the function $B_1(\cdot\ \ \cdot)$ is now to be interpreted as the demand for the annuity, that is, for the quantity $(*\beta_1^h/r_1)$. Important amendments must also be made in the counterparts of Eqs. (2.12), (2.34), and (2.38a), defining W^h, W^c, and β_1 as integrals:

(B.2) $\quad W^h = W^{hs} + \displaystyle\int_0^T \{(\beta_0^h/r_0)\dot{\pi} - [\pi\beta_0^h/(r_0)^2]\dot{r}_0 - [\beta_1^h/(r_1)^2]\dot{r}_1\}\, dt$

(B.3) $\quad W^c = \displaystyle\int_0^T \{R\dot{\pi} - [\bar{\beta}_1^c/(r_1)^2]\dot{r}_1\}\, dt$

(B.4) $\quad \beta_1 = \displaystyle\int_0^T (r_1 D)\, dt$

Under a flexible exchange rate, Eqs. (3.2a) and (3.3a) give way to

(B.2a) $\quad \delta r_1 = (1/H_\pi^v)[(B_{1W}L_{10} - B_{10}L_{1W})\,\delta\bar{r}_0 - (L_{1W} + B_{1W})(\delta\bar{\beta}_1^c/r_1)$
$\qquad\qquad + (L_{1W})(\delta\beta_1/r_1) - (0)\,\delta W^{hs}]$

(B.3a) $\left(\dfrac{\delta\pi}{\pi}\right) = (1/V_\pi^v H_\pi^v)\{[(B_{10}L_{11} - B_{11}L_{10}) + V_0(B_{11}L_{1W} - B_{1W}L_{11})$

$+ V_1(B_{00}L_{1W} - B_{0W}L_{10}) + L_{1W}(V_0V_1)]\,\delta\bar{r}_0$
$+ (B_{0W}V_1 - B_{01})(\delta\bar{\beta}_1^c/r_1)$
$+ (L_{1W}V_1 - L_{11})(\delta\beta_1/r_1) - (H_\pi^v)\,\delta W^{hs}\}$

where

$$H_\pi^v = (B_{11}L_{1W} - B_{1W}L_{11}) + L_{1W}V_1 = H_\pi + L_{1W}V_1$$

and

$V_\pi^v = (\pi\beta_0^h/r_0)$
$V_0 = [\pi\beta_0^h/(r_0)^2]$
$V_1 = [\beta_1^h/(r_1)^2]$

The terms V_π^v, V_0, and V_1 reflect the effects of changes in π, r_0, and r_1, respectively, on household wealth (the effects of capital gains and losses resulting from changes in bond prices expressed in home currency).

Under a pegged exchange rate, Eqs. (3.2b) and (3.3b) give way to

(B.2b) $\delta r_1 = (1/H^v)[(B_{1W}V_0 - B_{10})\,\delta\bar{r}_0 - (1)(\delta\bar{\beta}_1^c/r_1) - (B_{1W}V_\pi^v)\left(\dfrac{\delta\bar{\pi}}{\bar{\pi}}\right)$

$+ (1)(\delta\beta_1/r_1) - (B_{1W})\,\delta W^{hs}]$

(B.3b) $\bar{\pi}\,\delta R = -(1/H^v)\{[(B_{10}L_{11} - B_{11}L_{10}) + V_0(B_{11}L_{1W} - B_{1W}L_{11})$
$+ V_1(B_{00}L_{1W} - B_{0W}L_{10}) + L_{1W}(V_0V_1)]\,\delta\bar{r}_0$

$+ (B_{0W}V_1 - B_{01})(\delta\bar{\beta}_1^c/r_1) - (V_\pi^v H_\pi^v)\left(\dfrac{\delta\bar{\pi}}{\bar{\pi}}\right)$

$+ (L_{1W}V_1 - L_{11})(\delta\beta_1/r_1) - (H_\pi^v)\,\delta W^{hs}\}$

where

$$H^v = B_{11} + (L_{1W} + B_{0W})V_1$$

Although Eqs. (B.2a) through (B.3b) are somewhat more complicated than Eqs. (3.2a) through (3.3b), the signs of the outcomes are the same.

Equations (3.5) and (3.6), showing the effects of goods-market disturbances on p_N and p_1, are not altered by replacing bills with consols. There are new terms in the equations showing price responses to financial disturbances, the counterparts of Eqs. (3.7a) through (3.8b), but these new terms do not affect the signs of the responses. There are new terms too in the equations showing the effects on holdings of foreign bonds, in those that prove stability, and in those that describe the behavior of saving, the counterparts of Eqs. (3.11) through (3.18b). Here again, however, the signs are unaffected.

The term V_π did not appear in any steady-state solution shown in Chapter 3; neither does its counterpart, V_π^v. But the terms V_0 and V_1 do crop up from time to time, reflecting the effects of changes in interest rates. Under a flexible exchange rate, for example, Eq. (3.19a), showing the steady-state changes in r_1, is replaced by

$$(\text{B.4a}) \quad dr_1 = (1/H_\pi^v)[(L_{10}B_{1W} - L_{1W}B_{10})\, d\bar{r}_0 - (L_{1W} + B_{1W})(d\bar{\beta}_1^c/r_1) \\ + L_{1W}(d\beta_1/r_1)]$$

and V_1 enters every outcome because it figures in H_π^v. Similarly, Eq. (3.21a), showing the steady-state changes in Y^d, is replaced by

$$(\text{B.5a}) \quad dY^d = (1/H_\pi^v S_Y)\{(H_0^v)\, d\bar{r}_0 + [S_1(L_{1W} + B_{1W}) \\ - S_W(V_1 - B_{01})](d\bar{\beta}_1^c/r_1) \\ + (S_W L_{11} - L_{1W}S_1)(d\beta_1/r_1)\}$$

where

$$H_0^v = H_0 + V_1(S_W L_{10} - L_{1W}S_0)$$

so that the sign of H_0^v is ambiguous because the sign of H_0 is itself ambiguous.[1] But there are no changes in the steady-state equations for p_N, p_1, and π. As in Chapter 3, financial disturbances affect these three variables only insofar as they affect the steady-state level of Y^d, and the changes in Y^d are described completely by Eq. (B.5a). Under a pegged exchange rate, small changes crop up in the counterparts of Eqs. (3.19b) and (3.24b), showing the effects of financial disturbances on the steady-state levels of r_1 and $\bar{\pi}R$, but these changes do not alter any sign. Furthermore, no changes need be made in the income and price equations, as financial disturbances affecting r_1 and $\bar{\pi}R$ do not appear at all in those equations.

---

[1] Notice that $H_0^v > 0$ when, as in Parts III through V of this book, we impose restrictions sufficient to guarantee that $H_0 > 0$. We assume "proportionality" in certain interest-rate responses and that "crowding out" does not dominate. But when crowding out does not dominate, $S_W L_{10} > L_{1W}S_0$, so that $H_0^v > 0$ when $H_0 > 0$.

Appendix C

The specification of government spending

There are two ways to modify the specification of government spending in Chapter 2. The first is to assume that the government has a demand function for each domestic good. The second is to assume that its demands are determined exogenously, as they were in Chapter 2, but defined in real rather than nominal terms.

The first of these alternative specifications does not alter substantially any outcome in Chapter 3. In proof, let C_N^q and C_1^q be government demands for physical quantities of the two domestic goods, and let them be functions of domestic prices and of total nominal government spending. The government's demand for the traded good can be written as

(C.1) $C_1^q = C_1^q(p_N, p_1, \bar{G})$

and its demand for the nontraded good can then be written as

(C.2) $p_N C_N^q = \bar{G} - p_1 C_1^q$

Let these demands have properties identical to those of the households' demands in Chapter 2. The two goods are gross substitutes in government consumption (so that $C_{11}^q < 0$, and $C_{1N}^q > 0$); the functions have unitary elasticities with respect to $\bar{G}$ (and $p_1 C_{1G}^q$ is represented by g_1, where $0 < g_1 < 1$); and the functions are homogeneous of zero degree in p_N, p_1, and $\bar{G}$. These suppositions, taken together, say that

$$u_{11}^q = u_{1N}^q + p_1 C_1^q$$

where u_{11}^q and u_{1N}^q are price elasticities of government demand weighted by government spending [e.g., $u_{11}^q = -p_1 C_1^q(p_1 C_{11}^q/C_1^q)$].[1]

Substituting C_1^q for $(\bar{G}_1/p_1)$ in Eq. (2.27a) and C_N^q for $(\bar{G}_N/p_N)$ in Eq. (2.28a), we find only one small change in the goods-market system (3.4). The term u_{1N}^q appears in every element on the left-hand side. Thus, the

---

[1] As the government does not consume the imported good, its price, p_0, does not appear in Eq. (C.1), and there is no term u_{0N}^q analogous to u_{0N}.

552

first element is $-\{u_{0N} + (u_{1N} + u_{1N}^q) + u_E + [1 - m_N(1 - S_Y)]\sigma_N\}.$[2] It is thus easy to amend our results. Wherever u_{1N} appears in Chapter 3, we need merely substitute $(u_{1N} + u_{1N}^q)$.

The second of the two specifications, that government demands for the two domestic goods are determined exogenously in real terms, makes for larger changes in the model. It implies that nominal government expenditure is endogenous:

(C.3) $\quad G = p_1\bar{C}_1^q + p_N\bar{C}_N^q$

and this in turn implies that the lump-sum tax, T^h, must be adjusted whenever there is any change in p_1 or p_N. (Otherwise, there would be unintended changes in the budget surplus or deficit.) Finally, the definition of disposable income becomes

(C.4) $\quad Y^d = Y + \bar{D} - [p_1\bar{C}_1^q + p_N\bar{C}_N^q]$

None of these changes, however, causes very large mathematical amendments.

Substituting $\bar{C}_1^q$ and $\bar{C}_N^q$ for $(\bar{G}_1/p_1)$ and $(\bar{G}_N/p_N)$ in Eqs. (2.27a) and (2.28a), we find again just one small change in the system (3.4); the term σ_1 is replaced by $(\sigma_1 - p_1\bar{C}_1^q)$ wherever it appears, and σ_N is replaced by $(\sigma_N - p_N\bar{C}_N^q)$. Thus, the first element of the goods-market matrix becomes $-\{u_{0N} + u_{1N} + u_E + [1 - m_N(1 - S_Y)](\sigma_N - p_N\bar{C}_N^q)\}.$[3]

The new terms $(\sigma_1 - p_1\bar{C}_1^q)$ and $(\sigma_N - p_N\bar{C}_N^q)$ are unambiguously positive. Replacing σ_1 and σ_N with their equivalents, we find that

$$(\sigma_1 - p_1\bar{C}_1^q) = (p_1^*C_1 + p_1^*C_1^f) + a_1(p_1Q_1)$$
$$(\sigma_N - p_N\bar{C}_N^q) = (p_N^*C_N) + a_N(p_NQ_N)$$

In the classical case, then, the new terms are equal to household and foreign consumption of the two domestic goods (because a_1 and a_N are deemed to be zero). In the Keynesian case, the terms include the positive supply effects of changes in goods prices.

[2] There is a change in the appearance of the right-hand side. The last vector is replaced by

$$\begin{bmatrix} -m_N(1 - S_Y) & [g_N - m_N(1 - S_Y)] \\ -m_1(1 - S_Y) & [g_1 - m_1(1 - S_Y)] \end{bmatrix} \begin{bmatrix} \delta\bar{D} \\ \delta\bar{G} \end{bmatrix}$$

The same change, however, would occur if system (3.4) were rewritten to reflect the supposition we make later in Chapter 3 (that $\delta\bar{G}_N = g_N \, \delta\bar{G}$, and $\delta\bar{G}_1 = g_1 \, \delta\bar{G}$).

[3] There is again a change in the appearance of the final vector on the right-hand side. But if we assume that exogenous changes in $\delta\bar{C}_N^q$ and $\delta\bar{C}_1^q$ reflect policy-determined changes in total nominal government spending (i.e., that $p_N \, \delta\bar{C}_N^q = g_N \, \delta\bar{G}$, and $p_1 \, \delta\bar{C}_1^q = g_1 \, \delta\bar{G}$), the outcome is identical algebraically to the one shown in the previous note.

Taking the argument one step further, let us look at the case in which there are two types of government expenditure. A fraction b_N of government spending on the nontraded good is fixed in nominal terms, so that $p_N \bar{C}_N^g = (1 - b_N)G_N$, where G_N is total government spending on that good. Similarly, a fraction b_1 of government spending on the traded good is fixed in nominal terms, so that $p_1 \bar{C}_1^g = (1 - b_1)G_1$, where G_1 is total government spending on that good. In this case, we must replace σ_N and σ_1 with $\sigma_N - (1 - b_N)G_N$ and $\sigma_1 - (1 - b_1)G_1$, respectively, where G_N and G_1 are initial levels of expenditure. In other words, σ_N and σ_1 are redefined as

(C.5) $\sigma_N = P_N Q_N - G_N + (a_N p_N Q_N + b_N G_N)$

(C.6) $\sigma_1 = p_1 Q_1 - G_1 + (a_1 p_1 Q_1 + b_1 G_1)$

so that

(C.7) $\sigma_N + \sigma_1 = Y^d - \bar{D} + (a_N p_N Q_N + b_N G_N) + (a_1 p_1 Q_1 + b_1 G_1)$

These expressions can be used to generate some others that are used extensively in Chapter 5.

Under a flexible exchange rate, the steady-state changes in relative domestic prices resulting from financial disturbances and policies depend on the change in Y^d. Using Eqs. (3.22a) and (3.23a),

(C.8) $\left(\dfrac{dp_1}{p_1}\right) - \left(\dfrac{dp_N}{p_N}\right) = (1/N_t)(N_{1t} - N_{Nt})\, dY^d$

$$= (1/N_t)\{u_\pi[\sigma_N - m_N(\sigma_N + \sigma_1)] + u_{0N}[p_1 C_1^f - m_0(\sigma_N + \sigma_1)]\}\, dY^d$$

In the initial steady state, however, Eqs. (C.5) through (C.7) apply. Furthermore, $Y^d = {}^*C$, so that $m_i Y^d = p_i C_i$, and trade is balanced, so that $p_1 C_1^f = p_0 C_0$. Therefore,

(C.8a) $\left(\dfrac{dp_1}{p_1}\right) - \left(\dfrac{dp_N}{p_N}\right) = -(1/N_t)\{u_\pi[m_N(a_1 p_1 Q_1 + b_1 G_1)$

$$- (1 - m_N)(a_N p_N Q_N + b_N Q_N)]$$
$$+ m_0 u_{0N}[(a_1 p_1 Q_1 + b_1 G_1)$$
$$+ (a_N p_N Q_N + b_N G_N)]\}\, dY^d$$

Thus, there will be no such change in relative prices when two conditions are fulfilled: (1) There is no "money illusion" in the labor market (the $a_i = 0$). (2) There is no "money illusion" in government behavior (the

$b_i = 0$). Under these same circumstances, moreover, the change in the exchange rate will be proportional to the change in Y^d. Rewriting Eq. (3.24a),

$$(C.9) \quad \left(\frac{d\pi}{\pi}\right) = (Y^d N_w / N_t)(dY^d / Y^d)$$

But $(Y^d N_w / N_t) = 1$ when $a_i = b_i = 0$. In proof, write $N_t - Y^d N_w = (u_t + u_{1N}^f)\{(u_{1N} + u_E)[(\sigma_N + \sigma_1) - Y^d] + \sigma_N[\sigma_1 - (m_1 + m_0)Y^d]\} + u_{0N}\{[(u_{1N} + u_E) + (u_t + u_{1N}^f)][(\sigma_N + \sigma_1) - Y^d] + \sigma_1[(\sigma_N + p_1 C_1^f) - (m_N + m_0)Y^d]\} + (p_1 C_1^f - m_0 Y^d)N_0$. Invoking the relationships cited above, including Eqs. (C.5) through (C.7), it can therefore be shown that $N_t - Y^d N_w = [(u_t + u_{1N}^f)(u_{1N} + u_E) + u_{0N}(u_t + u_{1N}^f + u_{1N} + u_E)] \times [(a_1 p_1 Q_1 + b_1 G_1) + (a_N p_N Q_N + b_N G_N)] + \sigma_1 u_{0N}(a_N p_N Q_N + b_N G_N) + \sigma_N(u_t + u_{1N}^f)(a_1 p_1 Q_1 + b_1 G_1)]$. Thus, $N_t > Y^d N_w$ whenever $a_i > 0$ or $b_i > 0$, and $N_t = Y^d N_w$ whenever $a_i = b_i = 0$.

Under a pegged exchange rate, moreover, Eq. (3.21b) says that $(dY^d / Y^d) = (N_t / Y^d N_w)(d\bar{\pi}/\bar{\pi})$, which is symmetrical with Eq. (C.9). By implication, the size of the steady-state change in Y^d resulting from a devaluation will depend on the a_i and b_i. When $a_i > 0$ or $b_i > 0$, (dY^d / Y^d) will be larger than $(d\bar{\pi}/\bar{\pi})$. When $a_i = b_i = 0$, the two will be equal. Furthermore, Eqs. (3.22b) and (3.23b) can be combined with Eq. (3.21b) to replicate Eq. (C.8), defining the long-run change in relative domestic prices, so that Eq. (C.8a) applies in this case too. When $a_i = b_i = 0$, a devaluation can have no permanent effect on relative domestic prices.

Consider, finally, the effects of a devaluation on the terms of trade. Using Eq. (3.23b) and the fact that $p_0 = \pi \bar{p}_0^f$, the steady-state change in the terms of trade can be written as

$$(C.10) \quad \left(\frac{dp_1}{p_1}\right) - \left(\frac{dp_0}{p_0}\right) = \left(\frac{dp_1}{p_1}\right) - \left(\frac{d\bar{\pi}}{\bar{\pi}}\right) = (1/N_w)(N_{1t} - N_w)\left(\frac{d\bar{\pi}}{\bar{\pi}}\right)$$

$$= (1/N_w)\{u_{0N}[p_1 C_1^f + m_1(\sigma_N + \sigma_1) - \sigma_1] + (u_{1N} + u_E)[p_1 C_1^f - m_0(\sigma_N + \sigma_1)] + \sigma_N[(m_0 + m_1)p_1 C_1^f - m_0 \sigma_1]\}\left(\frac{d\bar{\pi}}{\bar{\pi}}\right)$$

Proceeding as before,[4]

[4] To obtain the last term of Eq. (C.10a), write $\sigma_N[(m_0 + m_1)p_1 C_1^f - m_0 \sigma_1] = \sigma_N[m_1 p_1 C_1^f + m_0(p_1 C_1^f - \sigma_1)] = \sigma_N[(m_1 p_1 C_1^f - m_0 p_1 C_1) - m_0(a_1 p_1 Q_1 + b_1 G_1)]$. In the initial steady state, however, $p_1 C_1^f = p_0 C_0$, $m_1 p_0 C_0 = m_1 m_0^* C$, and $m_0 p_1 C_1 = m_0 m_1^* C$.

(C.10a) $\left(\dfrac{dp_1}{p_1}\right) - \left(\dfrac{dp_0}{p_0}\right) = (1/N_w)\{u_{0N}[m_1(a_N p_N Q_N + b_N G_N)$

$$- (1 - m_1)(a_1 p_1 Q_1 + b_1 G_1)]$$
$$- m_0(u_{1N} + u_E)[(a_1 p_1 Q_1 + b_1 G_1)$$
$$+ (a_N p_N Q_N + b_N G_N)]$$

$$- m_0 \sigma_N (a_1 p_1 Q_1 + b_1 G_1)\} \left(\dfrac{d\bar{\pi}}{\bar{\pi}}\right)$$

When $a_i = b_i = 0$, a devaluation can have no permanent effect on the terms of trade.

Appendix D

Money financing of budget deficits

Elsewhere in this book, budget deficits are financed by issuing bonds. This is true of the model in Chapter 2, where lump-sum taxes are adjusted continuously and the budget deficit is exogenous, and of the model in Chapter 10, where taxes depend on income and the budget deficit is endogenous. Here we show what happens when budget deficits are financed by issuing money.

To represent these cases in models where money is issued by the central bank, bonds must be issued by the government and bought by the central bank, not by the public. We must define

$$\dot{B}_1^c = \dot{B}_1 = D$$

As $\dot{B}_1$ is too small to affect B_1 instantaneously, so $\dot{B}_1^c$ is too small to affect B_1^c and L_1 instantaneously. The impact effects of a tax cut are confined to goods markets and are therefore the same as those described in Chapters 5 and 10. The dynamic effects, however, differ from those that obtain when bonds are sold to the public, and so do the steady-state effects. We must thus investigate the path of the economy under the influence of a tax cut and the steady-state position to which it will tend. We work first with the model in Chapter 2, then with the one in Chapter 10.

A tax reduction with an exogenous deficit

Under a pegged exchange rate, the steady-state effects of a temporary tax cut are given by Eqs. (3.19b), (3.20b), (3.21b), and (3.24b). When $\dot{B}_1^c = \dot{B}_1$, then $dB_1^c = dB_1$, so that $dY = dY^d = dW^h = dr_1 = 0$, and $\bar{\pi} \, dR = -dB_1$.[1] Income, wealth, and the interest rate return eventually to their initial levels, and there is a permanent loss of reserves equal in size to the increase in central bank holdings of government bonds (which means that the money stock returns to its initial level). These results obtain regardless of the strength of the "crowding-out" effect or degree of

---

[1] By implication, $\pi \, dB_0^h = 0$.

substitutability between domestic and foreign bonds. (A bond-financed deficit, by contrast, raises W^h and r_1, and a loss of reserves occurs only when crowding out does not dominate.)

To derive the dynamic effects of the tax cut and to know the situation just before time $t = k$, when the government rescinds the tax cut to balance its budget, we work with these equations:

$$\dot{B}_1^h = B_{1W}\dot{W}^{hs} + B_{11}\dot{r}_1 = \dot{B}_1 - \dot{B}_1^c = 0$$
$$\dot{L}_1^h = L_{1W}\dot{W}^{hs} + L_{11}\dot{r}_1 = \dot{L}_1 = \dot{B}_1^c + \bar{\pi}\dot{R}$$

By implication,

$$\dot{r}_1 = -(B_{1W}/B_{11})\dot{W}^{hs}$$
$$\bar{\pi}\dot{R} = (1/B_{11})[(H_\pi - B_{11})\bar{D} + H_\pi(S - \bar{D})]$$
$$\dot{L}_1 = (H_\pi/B_{11})S$$

At time $t = 0$, however, $\bar{D} > S > 0$, so that $\dot{r}_1 < 0$, $\bar{\pi}\dot{R} < 0$, and $\dot{L}_1 > 0$. Finally,

$$*\dot{S}|_{\bar{Y}^d} = S_1\dot{r}_1 + S_W\dot{W}^{hs} = -(H_f/B_{11})S$$

which says that absorption rises (saving falls) during the interval $0 < t < k$, so that income rises under the influence of the tax cut (and the current-account deficit gets bigger). By inference, income will be higher at time $t = k$ than it was before the tax cut and must fall thereafter (there is dissaving and a current-account deficit after time $t = k$). The paths of income, the current-account deficit, and wealth will look much like those in Figure 6.11, but reserves decline under the influence of the tax cut and continue to decline as the economy moves to the new steady state.[2]

To describe behavior in terms of our asset-market diagram, Figure 6.12, there can be no shift in WW (because there is no change in the supply of bonds available to households) and no shift in SS (because there can be no permanent change in disposable income). In the interval $0 < t < k$, however, MM moves downward gradually (because the outflow of reserves is smaller than the budget deficit and the money supply is rising), and successive short-run asset-market equilibria take place at intersections of the moving money-market curve with the stationary bond-market curve (along WW to the southwest of w). After time $t = k$, however, the outflow of reserves is matched by a decline in the money supply, and the money-market curve retraces its path, returning eventually to MM.

[2] Furthermore, $\pi\dot{B}_0^h = \dot{F} = (1/B_{11})(B_{0W}B_{11} - B_{01}B_{1W})S$. There will be a capital outflow ($\dot{F} > 0$) prior to time $t = k$ and an inflow thereafter. The cumulative inflow, moreover, must offset the cumulative outflow, because $\pi\, dB_0^h = 0$.

Steady-state equilibrium is established at w, with no permanent change in wealth, the interest rate, or stock of money.

Under a flexible exchange rate, the steady-state effects of a temporary tax cut financed by new money are given by Eqs. (3.19a), (3.20a), (3.21a), and (3.24a). Setting $dB_1^c = dB_1$,

$$dY = dY^d = (H_f/S_Y H_\pi)\, dB_1 > 0$$
$$dW^h = (B_{11}/H_\pi)\, dB_1 > 0$$
$$dr_1 = -(B_{1W}/H_\pi)\, dB_1 < 0$$
$$\left(\frac{d\pi}{\pi}\right) = (N_w/N_t)\, dY^d > 0$$

Income and wealth rise permanently, the interest rate declines, and the home currency depreciates.[3] The crowding-out effect plays no role, but the size of the permanent increase in Y does depend on the degree of substitutability–a point to which we return below. (With a bond-financed deficit of similar cumulative size, by contrast, r_1 rises, the increase in W^h is smaller, and we have shown that Y and π rise only when crowding out does not dominate. Furthermore, Y and π are always larger in the long run with money financing than with bond financing.)

To derive the dynamic effects of the tax cut, we work with these equations:

$$\dot{B}_1^h = B_{1W}\dot{W}^h + B_{11}\dot{r}_1 = \dot{B}_1 - \dot{B}_1^c = 0$$
$$\dot{L}_1^h = L_{1W}\dot{W}^h + L_{11}\dot{r}_1 = \dot{L}_1 = \dot{B}_1^c$$
$$\dot{W}^h = \dot{W}^{hs} + V_\pi\left(\frac{\dot{\pi}}{\pi}\right)$$

Thus,

$$\dot{r}_1 = -(B_{1W}/B_{11})\dot{W}^h$$
$$\dot{W}^h = (B_{11}/H_\pi)\bar{D}$$
$$\dot{L}_1 = \bar{D}$$
$$\left(\frac{\dot{\pi}}{\pi}\right) = (1/H_\pi V_\pi)[(B_{11} - H_\pi)\bar{D} - H_\pi(S - \bar{D})]$$

At time $t = 0$, then, $\dot{r}_1 < 0$, $\dot{W}^h > 0$, $\dot{L}_1 > 0$, and $\dot{\pi} > 0$.[4] Furthermore,

$$\dot{Y} = (N_t/N_s)\left(\frac{\dot{\pi}}{\pi}\right) - (N_u/N_s)^*\dot{S}|_{\bar{Y}^d}$$

[3] There will be an increase in the home-currency value of holdings of the foreign bond (because $dW^h > dB_1$), but we cannot know if there will be an increase or decrease in the quantity held.
[4] There is a capital inflow ($F < 0$) prior to time $t = k$, when the current account is in deficit. Thereafter, however, $S \gtrless 0$, which means that there can be an inflow or outflow.

where

$$*\dot{S}|_{\bar{Y}^d} = S_1\dot{r}_1 + S_W\dot{W}^h = -(H_f/H_\pi)\bar{D}$$

Thus, income rises in the interval $0 < t < k$, because $\dot{\pi} > 0$ and $*\dot{S}|_{\bar{Y}^d} < 0$, but we cannot know what it will do thereafter. We know that $*\dot{S}|_{\bar{Y}^d} = 0$ when $\bar{D} = 0$, but do not know the sign of $\dot{\pi}$, because $S \gtrless 0$ after time $t = k$. The outcomes in this case are similar to those described at (1) in Chapter 6, where a bond-financed deficit was assumed to cause a depreciation of the home currency in the interval $0 < t < k$.[5]

Interpreting these results in terms of Figure 6.12, WW remains in place, but MM shifts downward gradually and permanently (because the money supply rises by an amount equal to the integral of budget deficits and is constant when $t \geq k$). Asset-market equilibrium is displaced gradually and permanently to a point on WW that is southwest of w, and disposable income has to be higher in the new steady state (because SS must shift to intersect the new equilibrium).

When a budget deficit is financed by issuing bonds, asset-market integration enhances the effectiveness of fiscal policy under a pegged exchange rate and reduces its effectiveness under a flexible rate. What happens when the deficit is financed by issuing money? Under a pegged exchange rate, $*\dot{S}_{\bar{Y}^d}$ rises in the interval $0 < t < k$, so that absorption and income grow more slowly.[6] In Figure 6.11, the path of income would be flattened. Under a flexible rate, $*\dot{S}|_{\bar{Y}^d}$ falls in the interval $0 < t < k$, and $\dot{\pi}$ rises, so that absorption and income grow more rapidly.[7] Furthermore, the steady-state increase of income is raised.[8] Thus, the familiar conclusion is reversed. When deficits are financed by money creation, fiscal policy comes to resemble monetary policy, in that asset-market integration reduces its effectiveness under a pegged exchange rate and enhances its effectiveness under a flexible rate.

Note finally that we can extend this comparative-static analysis to cover combinations of money and bond financing. The impact effects of a tax cut do not depend on the method of financing. The steady-state effects

[5] See pp. 182–5.

[6] Differentiating with respect to $-B_{01}$, $[\delta*\dot{S}|_{\bar{Y}^d}/\delta(-B_{01})] = (S_1/B_{11})(B_{1W}/B_{11})S > 0$ when $S > 0$.

[7] Differentiating with respect to $-B_{01}$, $[\delta*\dot{S}|_{\bar{Y}^d}/\delta(-B_{01})] = -(1/H_\pi)(S_W L_{11} - L_{1W}S_1)$ $\times (B_{1W}/H_\pi)\bar{D} < 0$ when crowding out does not dominate, and

$$[\delta(\dot{\pi}/\pi)/\delta(-B_{01})] = -(1/H_\pi V_\pi)(L_{11}B_{1W}/H_\pi)\bar{D} > 0.$$

[8] Differentiating the steady-state change in income with respect to $-B_{01}$, $[\delta(dY/dB_1)/\delta(-B_{01})] = (1/H_\pi)(S_W L_{11} - L_{1W}S_1)(B_{1W}/H_\pi) > 0$ when crowding out does not dominate.

depend only on the cumulative changes in the stocks of assets, not on the timing of those changes. Therefore, the steady-state effects of money-financed deficit are identical to those of a bond-financed deficit of the same cumulative size combined with a single open-market purchase of that same size. (And though the method of financing does affect the time path of the economy, it does not impinge on stability, because the budget is balanced exogenously.)

A tax reduction with an endogenous deficit

Turning next to the income-tax specification adopted in Chapter 10, we find that the method of financing affects the stability of the economy as well as the steady-state outcomes. As all disturbances push the budget out of balance by affecting income and income-tax collections, their steady-state effects include not only the effects of the disturbance per se but also the effects of changes in stocks of assets induced by the evolution of the budget and the method of financing.

To draw comparisons with the results in Chapter 10, where budget deficits were financed by issuing bonds, we begin by examining the implications of money financing in a closed economy. Here, stability requires that $(\delta \dot{B}_1/\delta B_1) < 0$. With money financing, however, $\dot{B}_1^c = \dot{B}_1$, so that

$$(\delta \dot{B}_1/\delta B_1) = -(1/N_n B_{11})N_b'$$

where $N_b' = [\tau H_f + S_Y(1 - \tau)V_h(B_{1W}/r_1)] > 0$ (and $N_b' > N_b$). Therefore, $(\delta \dot{B}_1/\delta B_1) < 0$. The economy is unequivocally stable with money financing. When money is issued to finance a deficit, the interest rate declines, raising absorption and income and enlarging tax revenues. Furthermore, the government's interest payments fall (because there is no change in household holdings of government bonds). The increase in tax revenues combines with the decrease in interest payments to shrink the budget deficit. (With bond financing, by contrast, there is the possibility of instability, due primarily to an increase in interest payments. As B_1 rises, r_1 rises, and crowding out tends to reduce tax revenues at the same time that there is an increase in interest payments. The budget deficit may not shrink.)

With money financing, the steady-state changes in r_1, Y, and B_1 are

$$d\hat{r}_1 = (1/N_b')\{[\tau S_W + S_Y(1 - \tau)V_h(B_{1W}/B_1^h)] \, d\bar{B}_1^c + \tau(S_Y B_{1W}) \, d(\bar{G}_1, \bar{T}_0) - (S_Y B_{1W})(-d\bar{T}_0)\},$$

$$d\hat{Y} = (1/N_b')\{(1 - \tau)V_h[(S_W/r_1) - (H_f/B_1^h)] \, d\bar{B}_1^c$$
$$+ S_Y(1 - \tau)V_h(B_{1W}/r_1) \, d(\bar{G}_1, \bar{T}_0) + H_f(-d\bar{T}_0)\}$$
$$d\hat{B}_1 = -(1/N_b')\{\tau S_1 + S_Y(1 - \tau)(V_h/r_1)[1 + r_1(B_{11}/B_1^h)]\} \, d\bar{B}_1^c$$
$$+ (1/N_b')[\tau(S_Y L_{11}) \, d(\bar{G}_1, \bar{T}_0) - (S_Y L_{11})(-d\bar{T}_0)]$$

These results bear close examination. For each disturbance, the integral of the budget deficit or surplus, $d\hat{B}_1$, is smaller than it would be with bond financing. This is because the economy adjusts more rapidly ($N_b' > N_b$), so that the budget is balanced more rapidly. Furthermore, the steady-state interest rate is lower with money than with bond financing if the disturbance causes a budget deficit and higher if it causes a surplus. (The change in the interest rate is ambiguous with an open-market purchase but cannot fall as much as it does with bond financing, because the open-market purchase generates a budget surplus and leads, therefore, to subsequent open-market sales. The interest rate rises in response to a balanced-budget increase in government spending, which also generates a budget surplus, and falls in response to a tax cut, which generates a deficit.) Finally, the steady-state level of income is higher with money financing if the disturbance induces a surplus and lower if it induces a deficit. An open-market purchase causes a decline in steady-state income under both methods of financing, but a smaller decline with money financing. A balanced-budget increase in government spending causes a gradual decline in income. With money financing, however, that decline is too small to offset completely the initial increase in income, and there is an increase in steady-state income; with bond financing, by contrast, there is a decrease in steady-state income. A tax cut raises income permanently under both forms of financing, but income rises less with money financing.

Does this last result suggest that fiscal policy is more effective with bond financing? No. A given amount of money financing is always more expansionary than the same amount of bond financing (because there is no crowding out with money financing). But when the budget is endogenous, it is balanced more rapidly with money financing. Therefore, a tax cut of given size leads to less money creation than bond creation, and there is as a result a smaller increase in steady-state income.[9]

Money financing tends also to stabilize an open economy with a flexible

---

[9] Working with a similar model, Blinder and Solow found that an increase in deficit spending led to a larger long-run increase in income with bond financing than with money financing. They concluded that "the long-run multiplier for bond-financed deficit spending exceeds that for money-financed deficit spending." [See A. S. Blinder and R. M. Solow, "Does Fiscal Policy Matter?," *Journal of Public Economics*, 2 (November 1973), p. 327.] In their model as in our own, the reason is the larger increase in the supply of bonds that takes place on account of slower adjustment. [They touch upon this point in "Does Fiscal Policy Still Matter? A Reply," *Journal of Monetary Economics*, 2 (October 1976), pp. 505–6.]

exchange rate. When $\dot{B}_1^c = \dot{B}_1$, the trace of the requisite matrix is

$$
\begin{aligned}
-(1/N_d H_\pi)\{&S_Y(1 - \tau)u_\pi \sigma_1(H_\pi/V_\pi) + \tau\sigma_1[u_\pi(B_{11}/V_\pi) + m_1 H_f] \\
&+ (1 - \tau)(u_t + N_Y\sigma_1)V_h(B_{1W}/r_1) \\
&+ \tau(u_t + \sigma_1)(V_f/\pi B_0^h)(B_{11}B_{0W} - B_{01}B_{1W})\} < 0
\end{aligned}
$$

and the determinant is

$$
(\sigma_1 u_\pi/N_d V_\pi H_\pi)N_b' > 0
$$

The stability conditions are satisfied, regardless of the strength of the crowding-out effect or the degree of substitutability between domestic and foreign bonds. There is downward pressure on the interest rate when a budget deficit is financed by issuing money, and it has the same stabilizing influence as in a closed economy. Furthermore, it removes the additional source of instability that crops up in an open economy. With bond financing and close asset-market integration, there is upward pressure on the interest rate that leads to large sales of the foreign bond; the home currency can appreciate, reducing income and tax revenues. With money financing, there is downward pressure on the interest rate that leads to large purchases of the foreign bond, with opposite effects on the exchange rate, income, and tax revenues.

The steady-state changes in r_1 are the same as those for the closed economy. The steady-state changes in Y and B_1 are

$$
\begin{aligned}
d\hat{Y} = (1/N_b')\{&(1 - \tau)V_h[(S_W/r_1) - (H_f/B_1^h)] \\
&- \tau(V_f/\pi B_0^h)(S_W B_{01} - S_1 B_{0W}) \\
&+ S_Y(1 - \tau)(V_f/\pi B_0^h)(V_h/r_1)[B_{0W} \\
&+ (r_1/B_1^h)(B_{11}B_{0W} - B_{01}B_{0W})]\} \, d\bar{B}_1^c \\
&+ (1/N_b')[S_Y(1 - \tau)V_h(B_{1W}/r_1) \\
&+ \tau S_Y(V_f/\pi B_0^h)(B_{11}B_{0W} - B_{01}B_{1W})] \, d(\bar{G}_1, \bar{T}_0) \\
&+ (1/N_b')[H_f - S_Y(V_f/\pi B_0^h)(B_{11}B_{0W} - B_{01}B_{1W})](-d\bar{T}_0) \\
d\hat{B}_1 = -(1/N_b')\{&\tau[S_1(L_{1W} + B_{1W}) + S_W B_{01}] \\
&+ S_Y(1 - \tau)(V_h/r_1)[(L_{1W} + B_{1W}) + r_1(H_\pi/B_1^h)]\} \, d\bar{B}_1^c \\
&- (1/N_b')\tau(S_Y H_\pi) \, d(\bar{G}_1, \bar{T}_0) + (1/N_b')(S_Y H_\pi)(-d\bar{T}_0)
\end{aligned}
$$

As in the closed economy, the cumulative changes in B_1 are smaller with money financing than with bond financing (for the same basic reason that adjustment is more rapid). But two of the income changes come to be ambiguous because of changes in interest income earned from foreigners. An open-market purchase can cause income to rise; it need not be deflationary in the long run. A tax cut can cause income to fall; it need not be expansionary in the long run. If holdings of the foreign bond are small initially and there is little substitutability between bonds, the steady-state changes in income will resemble those for the closed economy. (When indeed $B_{0W} = B_{01} = 0$, the income changes are the same.) We can therefore affirm our earlier conclusion: The changes in income from impact to the steady state are smaller with money financing because of more rapid adjustment. And this conclusion holds a fortiori when foreign and domestic bonds are close substitutes, because asset-market integration slows adjustment with bond financing (and can even cause instability, in which case, there are no steady-state results). But we can make no such simple statement about the effects of an increase in holdings of the foreign bond.[10]

Does money financing also serve to stabilize an open economy with a pegged exchange rate? The trace of the relevant matrix is

$$- (1/N_d B_{11})\{H_f[(u_t + \sigma_1) - m_1(1 - \tau)\sigma_1] \\ + S_Y(1 - \tau)(u_t + \sigma_1)[V_h(B_{1W}/r_1) \\ - (V_f/\pi B_0^h)(B_{11}B_{0W} - B_{01}B_{1W})]\}$$

which is ambiguous in sign. Furthermore, the determinant is zero. The conditions for stability are not satisfied. But when the trace is negative, the economy moves to what we have described as a quasi-stationary state.[11] The gradual change in wealth drives saving to zero, leaving the budget deficit equal to the current-account deficit. The money issued to finance the budget deficit is used to buy foreign currency (in order to buy foreign goods), and the foreign currency is supplied by the central bank out of its reserves. There are no further changes in income, the interest rate, the budget deficit, or the supply of money—until the central bank runs out of reserves.[12]

---

[10] Branson has analyzed a model with a flexible exchange rate and money financing but with no interest payments in the government budget. (In our notation, $D = G - \tau Y$.) He finds that an open-market purchase has no permanent effect on income and ascribes its neutrality to the endogeneity of the money supply when the resulting budget surplus is used to retire money. He goes on to draw an analogy between his finding and the familiar result that monetary policy can have no permanent effect on income under a pegged exchange rate (because the money supply is endogenous in this case too). [W. H. Branson, "The Dual Roles of the Government Budget and the Balance of Payments in the Movement from Short-Run to Long-Run Equilibrium," *Quarterly Journal of Economics*, 90 (August 1976), pp. 345–67.] His own finding, however, stems from his specification of the government budget, not from the endogeneity of the money supply. Under his specification, an open-market purchase can have no permanent effect on income even when the resulting budget surplus is used to retire bonds. If interest payments were included in the budget, there would be a permanent change in income under both types of financing.

[11] The rate of change of saving is $(\delta \dot{W}^{hs}/\delta W^{hs})\dot{W}^{hs} + (\delta \dot{W}^{hs}/\delta B_1)\dot{B}_1$. But the first term is the trace [because $(\delta \dot{B}_1/\delta B_1) = 0$], and the second term is zero.

[12] Using a model similar to ours, Turnovsky examines the problem of stability with a pegged exchange rate and no capital mobility. He finds that the sterilization of changes in reserves

Appendix E

Effects on Northern reserves

Impact effects

Differentiating totally Eq. (11.78a) and solving for the instantaneous change in Northern reserves,

$$(E.1) \quad \pi\,\delta R = L_{10}\,\delta\bar{r}_0 + L_{11}\,\delta r_1 + L_{12}\,\delta r_2 + L_{1W}(V_\pi)\left(\frac{\delta\pi'}{\pi'}\right) + L_{1W}\,\delta W^{hs}$$

$$- (\delta\bar{B}_1^c + \delta\bar{B}_2^c)$$

With a *flexible external rate*, $\delta\pi' = \delta\hat{\pi}'$, which is in turn replaced by Eq. (13.4a), whereas δr_1 and δr_2 are replaced by Eqs. (13.2a) and (13.3a). Thus,

$$
\begin{aligned}
(E.2a) \quad \pi\,\delta R = {} & [0]\,\delta\bar{r}_0 - [2(B_{11}^t - B_{12}^t)]^{-1}[(B_{11}^t - B_{12}^t) \\
& + (L_{11} - L_{12})](\delta\bar{B}_1^c - \delta\bar{B}_2^{c'}) \\
& + [2(B_{11}^t - B_{12}^t)]^{-1}[(B_{11}^t - B_{12}^t) - (L_{11} - L_{12})](\delta\bar{B}_1^{c'} - \delta\bar{B}_2^c) \\
& + [2(B_{11}^t - B_{12}^t)]^{-1}[L_{1W}(B_{11}^t - B_{12}^t) \\
& - (L_{11} - L_{12})(B_{1W} - B_{2W})](\delta W^{hs} - \delta W^{hs'}) \\
& + [2(B_{11}^t - B_{12}^t)]^{-1}[L_{11} - L_{12}](\delta B_1 - \delta B_2')
\end{aligned}
$$

With a *pegged external rate*, $\delta\pi' = \delta\bar{\pi}'$, and the two interest rates are replaced by Eqs. (13.2b) and (13.3b). Thus,

$$
\begin{aligned}
(E.2b) \quad \pi\,\delta R = {} & (1/J)(B_{11}^t - B_{12}^t)(J_\pi V_\pi)\left(\frac{\delta\bar{\pi}'}{\pi'}\right) \\
& + (1/J)(B_{11}^t - B_{12}^t)[L_{10}(B_{11}^t + B_{12}^t) - L_{11}^t B_{10}^t]\,\delta\bar{r}_0 \\
& - (1/J)[J + (B_{11}^t L_{11} - B_{12}^t L_{12})]\,\delta\bar{B}_1^c \\
& - (1/J)[B_{11}^t L_{11} - B_{12}^t L_{12}]\,\delta\bar{B}_1^{c'}
\end{aligned}
$$

---

can stabilize the economy. Specifically, his model is stable when the proportion of the budget deficit that is financed by issuing money and the proportion of the balance-of-payments deficit that is sterilized sum to more than unity. See S. J. Turnovsky, "The Dynamics of Fiscal Policy in an Open Economy," *Journal of International Economics*, 6 (May 1976), pp. 115–42. In the same special case (no capital mobility), our model will be stable when a small amount of sterilization is combined with a large amount of money financing. The outcome is not so clear, however, when capital mobility is introduced.

$$- (1/J)[J + (B_{11}^t L_{12} - B_{12}^t L_{11})] \, \delta \bar{B}_2^c$$
$$- (1/J)[B_{11}^t L_{12} - B_{12}^t L_{11}] \, \delta \bar{B}_2^{c'}$$
$$+ (1/J)[L_{1W}(J) - B_{11}^t (B_{1W} L_{11} + B_{2W} L_{12})$$
$$+ B_{12}^t (B_{2W} L_{11} + B_{1W} L_{12})] \, \delta W^{hs}$$
$$- (1/J)[B_{11}^t (B_{1W} L_{12} + B_{2W} L_{11})$$
$$- B_{12}^t (B_{1W} L_{11} + B_{2W} L_{12})] \, \delta W^{hs'}$$
$$+ (1/J)[B_{11}^t L_{11} - B_{12}^t L_{12}] \, \delta B_1 + (1/J)[B_{11}^t L_{12} - B_{12}^t L_{11}] \, \delta B_2'$$

The impact effects of $\delta \bar{\pi}'$ and $\delta \bar{r}_0$ on πR are half as large as their impact effects on πR^t, the sum of Northern and Southern reserves given by Eq. (13.4b). This is one more consequence of symmetrical asset preferences.

To analyze the responses of $\pi \dot{R}$, the Northern balance of payments, is difficult and unrewarding, as many outcomes are ambiguous. To illustrate, we show some outcomes under a flexible external rate (where $\pi \dot{R}$ is the balance of payments between North and South) and in the limiting case in which Northern and Southern bonds are perfect substitutes (a case discussed in Chapter 16).

Before imposing this limiting simplification, the instantaneous change in $\pi \dot{R}$, obtained from Eqs. (13.16) and (E.2a), is given by

(E.3a) $\quad \pi \, \delta \dot{R} = [2(B_{11}^t - B_{12}^t)]^{-1}[L_{1W}(B_{11}^t - B_{12}^t)$
$$- (L_{11} - L_{12})(B_{1W} - B_{2W})](\delta \dot{W}^{hs} - \delta \dot{W}^{hs'})$$
$$+ [2(B_{11}^t - B_{12}^t)]^{-1}[L_{11} - L_{12}](\delta \bar{D} - \delta \bar{D}')$$

where

(E.4a) $\quad \delta \dot{W}^{hs} - \delta \dot{W}^{hs'} = S_Y(\delta Y^d - \delta Y^{d'}) + (S_1 - S_2)(\delta r_1 - \delta r_2)$

With perfect substitutability, $L_{11} = L_{12}$ in Eq. (E.3a), and $\delta r_1 = \delta r_2$ in Eq. (E.4a). Therefore:

(E.5a) $\quad \pi \, \delta \dot{R} = L_{1W}(S_Y/2)(\delta Y^d - \delta Y^{d'})$

Using Eqs. (13.7) through (13.10), however, we can show that the differences between δY^d and $\delta Y^{d'}$ are ambiguous for most goods-market disturbances. The exceptions are balanced-budget changes in government spending. A balanced-budget increase of Northern spending, whether on Northern or Southern goods, worsens the Northern balance of payments (improves the Southern); a balanced-budget increase of Southern spending worsens the Southern balance of payments (improves the Northern).[1]

Using Eqs. (13.14a) and (13.15a), we can also show that the difference

---

[1] Other outcomes would be unambiguous with full-scale goods-market symmetry, which would suppress the differences in supply responses and in price elasticities that produce the ambiguities.

between δY^d and $\delta Y^{d'}$ is ambiguous for all financial disturbances, because it depends on the difference between $\sigma_1 M_{1\pi}$ and $\sigma_2' M_{2\pi}$. There is thus uncertainty about $\pi \, \delta \dot{R}$ even when Northern and Southern bonds are perfect substitutes.

Steady-state effects

The steady-state changes in Northern reserves are

(E.6) $\pi \, dR = L_{10} \, d\bar{r}_0 + L_{11} \, dr_1 + L_{12} \, dr_2 + L_{1W} \, dW^h - (d\bar{B}_1^c + d\bar{B}_2^c)$

With a *flexible external rate*, dr_1 and dr_2 are replaced by Eqs. (13.27a) and (13.28a), and dW^h is likewise replaced by an expression obtained from the bond-market and saving equations:

(E.7a) $\begin{aligned} dW^h = &(1/2J_W)[S_Y(B_{11}^t - B_{12}^t)](dY^d - dY^{d'}) \\ &- (1/J_\pi)[L_{10}(B_{11}^t + B_{12}^t) - L_{11}^t B_{10}^t] \, d\bar{r}_0 \\ &- (1/2J_\pi J_W)[J_W B_{01}^t + (S_1 - S_2)J_\pi](d\bar{B}_1^c + d\bar{B}_1^{c'}) \\ &- (1/2J_\pi J_W)[J_W B_{01}^t - (S_1 - S_2)J_\pi](d\bar{B}_2^c + d\bar{B}_2^{c'}) \\ &+ (1/2J_\pi J_W)\{(S_1 - S_2)[L_{1W}(B_{11}^t + B_{12}^t) - 2B_{1W}L_{11}^t] \\ &\quad + S_W(B_{11}^t - B_{12}^t)L_{11}^t\} \, d\bar{B}_1 \\ &- (1/2J_\pi J_W)\{(S_1 - S_2)[L_{1W}(B_{11}^t + B_{12}^t) - 2B_{2W}L_{11}^t] \\ &\quad - S_W(B_{11}^t - B_{12}^t)L_{11}^t\} \, d\bar{B}_2' \end{aligned}$

For goods-market disturbances, then, Eq. (E.6) yields

(E.8a) $\begin{aligned} \pi \, dR = &(1/2J_W)S_Y[L_{1W}(B_{11}^t - B_{12}^t) \\ &- (L_{11} - L_{12})(B_{1W} - B_{2W})](dY^d - dY^{d'}) \end{aligned}$

Thus, the sign of the steady-state change in Northern reserves is governed by the difference between the changes in disposable incomes. As shown in Chapter 13, moreover, the sign of this difference is given by the sign of dY^d, the change in Northern disposable income. For financial disturbances, the corresponding statements are very complicated, and all outcomes are uncertain. In proof, we treat the simplest case. When Northern and Southern bonds are perfect substitutes, $dr_1 = dr_2 = dr^t$, and dr^t is given by Eq. (13.19a). Thus, Eq. (E.6) yields[2]

[2] Equation (E.9a) is obtained with the aid of the fact, noted in Chapter 13, that $dY^d - dY^{d'} = [(\sigma_1 U_{1\pi} - \sigma_2' U_{2\pi})/M_w] \, dY^{dt}$ for all financial disturbances. With perfect substitutability between the two bonds, then, the wealth effects of financial disturbances, given by Eq. (E.7a), are

$\begin{aligned} dW^h = &-(S_Y/2S_W)[(\sigma_1 U_{1\pi} - \sigma_2' U_{2\pi})/M_w] \, dY^{dt} - (1/J_\pi)[L_{10}(B_{11}^t + B_{12}^t) - L_{11}^t B_{10}^t] \, d\bar{r}_0 \\ &- (1/2J_\pi)(B_{01}^t)(d\bar{B}_1^c + d\bar{B}_1^{c'} + d\bar{B}_2^c + d\bar{B}_2^{c'}) - (1/2J_\pi)(L_{11}^t)(d\bar{B}_1 + d\bar{B}_2') \end{aligned}$

Replacing dY^{dt} with Eq. (13.20a) and substituting into Eq. (E.6), we obtain Eq. (E.9a).

(E.9a) $\pi\, dR = -(1/2S_W J_\pi)[(\sigma_1 U_{1\pi} - \sigma_2' U_{2\pi})/M_w]L_{1W}\{(2J_0)\, d\bar{r}_0$
$+ [(1 - B_{0W})S_1^t + S_W B_{01}^t](d\bar{B}_1^c + d\bar{B}_1^{c'} + d\bar{B}_2^c + d\bar{B}_2^{c'})$
$+ (J_B)(d\bar{B}_1 + d\bar{B}_2')\}$
$+ (1/2)[(d\bar{B}_1^{c'} + d\bar{B}_2^{c'}) - (d\bar{B}_1^c + d\bar{B}_2^c)]$

These outcomes are uncertain because $\sigma_1 U_{1\pi} - \sigma_2' U_{2\pi} \gtrless 0$. Only when we have perfect substitutability between Northern and Southern bonds *and* full-scale goods-market symmetry can we say anything definite about the permanent changes in Northern reserves resulting from financial disturbances. Under that special combination of assumptions, an open-market purchase by the Northern central bank redistributes reserves from North to South; an open-market purchase by the Southern bank redistributes them in the opposite direction; and other financial disturbances do not affect the steady-state distribution of reserves.

With a *pegged external rate, dr_1* and *dr_2* are replaced by Eqs. (13.27b) and (13.28b), and dW^h is replaced by

(E.7b) $dW^h = (S_Y/J_W J_K)[B_{1W}(S_1 B_{11}^t - S_2 B_{12}^t) + B_{2W}(S_2 B_{11}^t - S_1 B_{12}^t)$
$- S_W(B_{11}^t + B_{12}^t)(B_{11}^t - B_{12}^t)]\, dY^d$
$- (S_Y/J_W J_K)[B_{1W}(S_2 B_{11}^t - S_1 B_{12}^t)$
$+ B_{2W}(S_1 B_{11}^t - S_2 B_{12}^t)]\, dY^{d'}$
$- (1/J_K)[S_1^t B_{10}^t - S_0(B_{11}^t + B_{12}^t)]\, d\bar{r}_0$
$- (1/J_W J_K)[B_{1W} S_1^t(S_1 - S_2)$
$- S_W(S_1 B_{11}^t - S_2 B_{12}^t)][(d\bar{B}_1^c + d\bar{B}_1^{c'}) - d\bar{B}_1]$
$+ (1/J_W J_K)[B_{2W} S_1^t(S_1 - S_2)$
$+ S_W(S_2 B_{11}^t - S_1 B_{12}^t)][(d\bar{B}_2^c + d\bar{B}_2^{c'}) - d\bar{B}_2']$

For goods-market disturbances, then, Eq. (E.6) yields

(E.8b) $\pi\, dR = (1/J_W J_K)S_Y[(B_{1W} B_{11}^t - B_{2W} B_{12}^t)(S_W L_{11} + L_{1W} S_1)$
$+ (B_{2W} B_{11}^t - B_{1W} B_{12}^t)(S_W L_{12} + L_{1W} S_2) - S_W L_{1W}(J)$
$- B_{1W}^t(B_{1W} - B_{2W})(S_1 L_{11} - S_2 L_{12})]\, dY^d$
$+ (1/J_W J_K)S_Y[(B_{2W} B_{11}^t - B_{1W} B_{12}^t)(S_W L_{11} - L_{1W} S_1)$
$+ (B_{1W} B_{11}^t - B_{2W} B_{12}^t)(S_W L_{12} - L_{1W} S_2)$
$+ B_{1W}^t(B_{1W} - B_{2W})(S_2 L_{11} - S_1 L_{12})]\, dY^{d'}$

Although each of the arguments of this equation is unambiguously positive,[3] the sign of the change in Northern reserves is not always easy to ascertain. There is, of course, an increase of Northern reserves whenever a goods-market disturbance moves the two countries' disposable incomes

---

[3] The signs of the two terms depend on the fact that $S_1 L_{11} < S_2 L_{12} < 0$ (because $S_1 > S_2$, whereas $L_{11} < L_{12} < 0$), on the assumption that crowding out does not dominate (so that $S_W L_{11} > L_{1W} S_1$, and $S_W L_{12} > L_{1W} S_2$), and on the assumption of proportionality (so that $S_2 L_{11} = S_1 L_{12}$).

in the same direction, which is what happens with shifts in demand to the foreign good and with a devaluation of the pegged external rate. But with balanced-budget changes in government spending, disposable incomes do not move together, and the problem is harder. There is, in fact, just one case in which the change in Northern reserves is unambiguous. When the Northern government raises its spending on the Northern good, Northern reserves fall.[4]

Turning finally to the steady-state effects of financial disturbances,

$$
\begin{aligned}
\text{(E.9b)} \quad \pi \, dR = {}& -(1/J_K)[J_0] \, d\bar{r}_0 \\
& - (1/J_W J_K)\{S_1^t(S_1 - S_2)[B_{1W}^t(B_{1W} - B_{2W}) + L_{1W}B_{1W}] \\
& \quad - S_W[B_{11}^t(S_1 B_{1W} + S_2 B_{2W} + S_1 L_{1W}) \\
& \quad - B_{12}^t(S_1 B_{2W} + S_2 B_{1W} + S_2 L_{1W})] \\
& \quad + S_W[B_{1W}^t(B_{12}^t + L_{12})S_1^t + B_{01}^t(S_1 B_{1W} + S_2 B_{2W}) \\
& \quad - S_W(B_{11}^t L_{12} - B_{12}^t L_{11}) - S_W B_{01}^t(B_{11}^t - B_{12}^t)]\} \, d\bar{B}_1^c \\
& - (1/J_W J_K)\{B_{1W}S_1^t L_{1W}(S_1 - S_2) \\
& \quad + S_W[B_{11}^t(S_W L_{11} - S_1 L_{1W}) - B_{12}^t(S_W L_{12} - S_2 L_{1W})] \\
& \quad - S_W[B_{1W}(L_{11}S_1 - L_{12}S_2) \\
& \quad + B_{2W}(L_{11}S_2 - L_{12}S_1)]\}(d\bar{B}_1^{c'} - d\bar{B}_1) \\
& - (1/J_W J_K)\{S_1^t(S_1 - S_2)[B_{1W}^t(B_{1W} - B_{2W}) - L_{1W}B_{2W}] \\
& \quad - S_W[B_{11}^t(S_1 B_{1W} + S_2 B_{2W} + S_2 L_{1W}) \\
& \quad - B_{12}^t(S_1 B_{2W} + S_2 B_{1W} + S_1 L_{1W})] \\
& \quad + S_W[B_{1W}^t(B_{12}^t + L_{11})S_1^t + B_{01}^t(S_1 B_{1W} + S_2 B_{2W}) \\
& \quad - S_W(B_{11}^t L_{11} - B_{12}^t L_{12}) - S_W B_{01}^t(B_{11}^t - B_{12}^t)]\} \, d\bar{B}_2^c \\
& + (1/J_W J_K)\{B_{2W}S_1^t L_{1W}(S_1 - S_2) \\
& \quad - S_W[B_{11}^t(S_W L_{12} - S_2 L_{1W}) - B_{12}^t(S_W L_{11} - S_1 L_{1W})] \\
& \quad - S_W[B_{1W}(L_{11}S_2 - L_{12}S_1) \\
& \quad + B_{2W}(L_{11}S_1 - L_{12}S_2)]\}(d\bar{B}_2^{c'} - d\bar{B}_2')
\end{aligned}
$$

The first and second outcomes are unambiguous; an increase in the foreign interest rate reduces Northern reserves (in fact, it reduces both countries' reserves), and so does a Northern open-market purchase of the Northern bond.[5] Every other outcome is uncertain, however, for the reason given in Table 13.2B, that the change in the Northern interest rate

[4] Analogously, an increase of Southern spending on the Southern good reduces Southern reserves. Even in these instances, however, it is impossible to know what happens to the other country's reserves. With an increase in Northern spending on the Northern good, for example, there is a reduction of Northern reserves, but also of R^t, the sum of Northern and Southern reserves; it is thus impossible to draw any inference about the change in Southern reserves. Furthermore, the Southern analogue to Eq. (E.8b) is no help in this instance, just as Eq. (E.8b) itself is no help in determining the change of Northern reserves when the Southern government increases its spending on the Southern good.

[5] Analogously, a Southern open-market purchase of the Southern bond reduces Southern reserves.

is uncertain. But all ambiguities are resolved when Northern and Southern bonds are perfect substitutes. In this limiting case, $dr_1 = dr_2 = dr^t$, the changes in r_1 are quite definite, and so are the changes in Northern reserves. They are given by

$$
\begin{aligned}
\pi \, dR = {} & -(1/J_K)[J_0] \, d\bar{r}_0 \\
& - (1/2J_K)[S_1^t(2B_{1W}^t + L_{1W}) + S_W(L_{11}^t + 2B_{01}^t)](d\bar{B}_1^c + d\bar{B}_2^c) \\
& + (1/2J_K)[J_B][(d\bar{B}_1^{c\prime} + d\bar{B}_2^{c\prime}) - (d\bar{B}_1 + d\bar{B}_2')]
\end{aligned}
$$

An open-market purchase by the Northern central bank causes a permanent decline in Northern reserves; an open-market purchase by the Southern bank causes an increase. These results obtain regardless of the bond bought. An increase of B_1 or B_2', reflecting a history of budget deficits, causes a permanent decline in Northern reserves. (It follows, of course, that an open-market purchase by the Northern bank raises Southern reserves, a purchase by the Southern bank reduces them, and an increase of B_1 or B_2' reduces them too.) In brief, an open-market purchase by one bank causes a bilateral transfer of reserves to the other bank, along with a loss to the outside world, whereas a budget deficit and bond issues by one country cause both countries to lose reserves.

Glossary

This Glossary lists all variables and related terms used in the text. It does not include those introduced and used exclusively in a table or appendix and those used within a single paragraph or footnote solely for illustrative purposes. Variables prefixed by an asterisk are quantities demanded. (In the text and appendixes, variables carrying a bar are exogenous or policy determined, and those carrying a dot are time derivatives. The operators δ and d designate impact and steady-state changes, respectively. The first part of the Glossary deals with terms used in the one-country model of Chapters 2 through 10; the second part deals with terms used in the two-country model of Chapters 11 through 18.

I. The one-country model

Unless otherwise indicated, all variables are measured in units of domestic currency. The first set of variables listed below are endogenous to the one-country model in Chapter 2.

B_0^h, $*B_0^h$	Households' holdings of foreign bonds, in units of foreign currency
B_1^c, $*B_1^c$	The central bank's holdings of domestic bonds
B_1^h, $*B_1^h$	Households' holdings of domestic bonds
B_1	The stock of domestic bonds outstanding
$*C$	Domestic consumption (household spending on domestic and foreign goods)
$*C^f$	Foreign consumption, in units of foreign currency
$*C_0$	Households' purchases of foreign goods, in physical units
$*C_1$	Households' purchases of traded domestic goods, in physical units
$*C_N$	Households' purchases of nontraded domestic goods in physical units

$*C_1^f$ Foreign purchases of traded domestic goods, in physical units

D The government's budget deficit

E Total employment, in physical units

E_1, $*E_1$ Employment in the production of traded domestic goods, in physical units

E_N, $*E_N$ Employment in the production of nontraded domestic goods, in physical units

$*G_1$, $*G_N$ Government spending on traded and nontraded domestic goods, respectively

L_1^h, $*L_1^h$ Households' holdings of domestic money

L_1 The stock of domestic money

p_0, p_0^f The domestic and foreign-currency prices, respectively, of traded foreign goods

p_1, p_1^f The domestic and foreign-currency prices, respectively, of traded domestic goods

p_N, p_N^f The domestic and foreign-currency prices, respectively, of nontraded goods

π The domestic price of foreign currency

Q_1, Q_N Outputs of traded and nontraded domestic goods, respectively, in physical units

R The central bank's holdings of foreign-currency reserves, in units of foreign currency

r_0, r_1 The interest rates on foreign and domestic bonds, respectively

S, $*S$ Household saving

T^f Transfers from foreigners to government

T^h Transfers from households to government (taxes)

w The money wage rate

W^c The central bank's wealth (net worth)

W^h Households' wealth (net worth)

W^{hs} The integral of household saving

Y Gross domestic product (nominal income)

Y^d Households' disposable income

These terms are also used in the one-country model:

$\dot{B}_1$ The rate of issue of domestic bonds (equal to D)

$\dot{F}$ The capital outflow measured in domestic currency

G Total government spending on domestic output

$\dot{R}$ The reserve inflow measured in foreign currency (the balance-of-payments surplus after instantaneous stock adjustments)

W^{hs} The rate of change in the stock of accumulated saving (equal to S)

τ The income tax rate

Certain partial derivatives appear many times, and it is important to know their signs. In particular, S_0, S_1, B_{00}, and B_{11} are positive; S_Y, B_{0W}, B_{1W}, and L_{1W} are positive but smaller than unity; and S_W, B_{01}, B_{10}, L_{10}, and L_{11} are negative.

The following symbols are used to denote combinations or transformations of variables:

$$a_i = -(wE_i/p_iQ_i)(E_iQ_{iEE}/Q_{iE})^{-1} \qquad i = 1, N$$

$$e_{ii} = -p_i(C_{ii}/{}^*C_i) \qquad i = 0, 1, N$$

$$e_{ii}^f = -p_i^f(C_{ii}^f/{}^*C_i^f) \qquad i = 0, 1, N$$

$$e_{ij} = p_j(C_{ij}/{}^*C_i) \qquad i, j = 0, 1, N \qquad i \neq j$$

$$e_{ij}^f = p_j^f(C_{ij}^f/{}^*C_i^f) \qquad i, j = 0, 1, N \qquad i \neq j$$

$$e_{ic} = {}^*C(C_{ic}/{}^*C_i) \qquad i = 0, 1, N$$

$$e_{ic}^f = {}^*C^f(C_{ic}^f/{}^*C_i^f) \qquad i = 0, 1, N$$

$$g_i = \bar{G}_i/\bar{G} \qquad i = 1, N$$

$$m_i = p_iC_{ic} \qquad i = 0, 1, N$$

$$\sigma_i = (1 + a_i)p_iQ_i \qquad i = 1, N$$

$$u_E = (a_1p_1Q_1 \cdot a_Np_NQ_N)/(a_1p_1Q_1 + a_Np_NQ_N)$$

$$u_{ij} = p_i{}^*C_ie_{ij} \qquad i, j = 0, 1, N$$

$$u_{ij}^f = p_i{}^*C_i^fe_{ij}^f \qquad i, j = 0, 1, N$$

$$u_t = u_{10} + u_{10}^f$$

$$u_\pi = u_t + u_{1N}^f + u_{0N} + p_1{}^*C_1^f$$

$$H_e = H_\pi V_\pi + \gamma_\pi(B_{10}L_{11} - L_{10}B_{11}) > 0$$

$$H_f = S_1B_{1W} - S_WB_{11} > 0$$

$$H_k = S_YH_\pi + S_1H_W - S_WH_Y > 0$$

$$H_W = B_{1W}L_{1Y} - B_{1Y}L_{1W} > 0$$

$$H_Y = B_{0Y}L_{11} - B_{01}L_{1Y} > 0$$

$$H_\pi = L_{1W}B_{11} - L_{11}B_{1W} > 0$$

$$H_0 = B_{1W}(S_0L_{11} - S_1L_{10}) + B_{11}(S_WL_{10} - L_{1W}S_0) - B_{10}(S_WL_{11} - L_{1W}S_1) \gtreqless 0$$

$$N_b = \tau(S_WL_{11} - S_1L_{1W}) - S_Y(1 - \tau)V_h[(L_{1W}/r_1) + (B_{11}/B_1^h)] > 0$$

$$N_c = \tau(S_WL_{11} - S_1L_{1W}) - S_Y(1 - \tau)V_h[(L_{1W}/r_1) + (H_\pi/B_1^h)] > 0$$

$$N_d = u_t + \sigma_1[N_Y + \tau m_1(1 - S_Y)] > 0$$

$$N_e = (u_t + \sigma_1N_Y) + \gamma_p(m_1)^2(S_0 + S_1) > 0$$

$$N_{\pi e} = u_\pi(B_{10}L_{11} - L_{10}B_{11}) + m_1V_\pi[H_0 + m_0(S_0 + S_1)H_\pi] > 0$$

$$N_g = (u_t + u_{1N}^f)(u_{0N} + u_{1N} + u_E) + u_{0N}(u_{1N} + u_E) > 0$$

$$N_n = S_Y + \tau(1 - S_Y) > 0$$
$$N_r = H_f(u_t + m_0\sigma_1) - S_YV_f[(B_{11}B_{0W} - B_{01}B_{1W})/\pi B_0^h](u_t + \sigma_1) > 0$$
$$N_s = (u_t + u^f_{1N})(u_{0N} + u_{1N} + u_E) + u_{0N}(u_{1N} + u_E) + N_0N_Y$$
$$+ u_{0N}[1 - m_1(1 - S_Y)]\sigma_1$$
$$+ (u_t + u^f_{1N})[1 - m_N(1 - S_Y)]\sigma_N > 0$$
$$N_t = \sigma_N N_{N\pi} + \sigma_1 N_{1\pi} = u_\pi N_0 + u_{0N}[(u_t + u^f_{1N})\sigma_N$$
$$+ (u_t + u^f_{1N} + p_1^*C_1^f)\sigma_1] > 0$$
$$N_u = \sigma_N N_{NU} + \sigma_1 N_{1U} > 0$$
$$N_w = N_s - S_Y(\sigma_N N_{NU} + \sigma_1 N_{1U}) > 0$$
$$N_Y = S_Y + m_0(1 - S_Y) > 0$$
$$N_{Nk} = a_{NP}N_Q_N + b_N G_N \geq 0$$
$$N_{1k} = a_1 p_1 Q_1 + p_1 G_1 \geq 0$$
$$N_0 = (u_{1N} + u_E)(\sigma_1 + \sigma_N) + \sigma_1\sigma_N > 0$$
$$N_{1\pi} = u_\pi[u_{1N} + u_E + m_1(1 - S_Y)\sigma_N] + (u_t + u^f_{1N} + p^*C_1^f)(u_{0N} + N_Y\sigma_N) > 0$$
$$N_{N\pi} = u_\pi[u_{1N} + u_E + m_N(1 - S_Y)\sigma_1] + u_{0N}(u_t + u^f_{1N} + N_Y\sigma_1) > 0$$
$$N_{1t} = u_\pi(u_{1N} + u_E + m_1\sigma_N) + (u_{0N} + m_0\sigma_N)(u_t + u^f_{1N} + p_1^*C_1^f) > 0$$
$$N_{Nt} = u_\pi(u_{1N} + u_E + m_N\sigma_1) + u_{0N}(u_t + u^f_{1N} + m_0\sigma_1) > 0$$
$$N_{1U} = m_1(u_{0N} + \sigma_N) + (1 - m_0)(u_{1N} + u_E) > 0$$
$$N_{NU} = m_N(u_t + u^f_{1N} + \sigma_1) + (1 - m_0)(u_{1N} + u_E) > 0$$
$$U = V_\pi[(u_t + \sigma_1 N_Y)H_\pi + \sigma_1(m_1 S_1)H_W] + \sigma_1(u_\pi - m_1 S_W V_\pi)H_Y > 0$$
$$U_f = (u_t + \sigma_1 N_Y)B_{11} - \sigma_1(m_1 S_1)B_{1Y} > 0$$
$$V_f = \bar{r}_0(\pi B_0^h) > 0$$
$$V_h = r_1 B_1^h > 0$$
$$V_\pi = \pi B_0^h$$

II. The two-country model

Unless otherwise indicated, variables without primes are measured in units of Northern currency, variables with primes are measured in Southern currency, and variables with the superscript f are measured in world (foreign) currency. The first set of variables listed below are endogenous to the two-country model in Chapter 11.

$B_1^c, *B_1^c$ — The Northern central bank's holdings of Northern bonds

$B_1^{c\prime}, *B_1^{c\prime}$ — The Southern central bank's holdings of Northern bonds, in units of Northern currency

$B_2^c, *B_2^c$ — The Northern central bank's holdings of Southern bonds, in units of Southern currency

$B_2^{c\prime}, *B_2^{c\prime}$ — The Southern central bank's holdings of Southern bonds

B_0^h, $*B_0^h$	Northern households' holdings of world bonds, in units of world currency
$B_0^{h\prime}$, $*B_0^{h\prime}$	Southern households' holdings of world bonds, in units of world currency
B_1^h, $*B_1^h$	Northern households' holdings of Northern bonds
$B_1^{h\prime}$, $*B_1^{h\prime}$	Southern households' holdings of Northern bonds, in units of Northern currency
B_2^h, $*B_2^h$	Northern households' holdings of Southern bonds, in units of Southern currency
$B_2^{h\prime}$, $*B_2^{h\prime}$	Southern households' holdings of Southern bonds
B_1	The stock of Northern bonds outstanding
B_2'	The stock of Southern bonds outstanding
$*C$, $*C'$	Northern and Southern consumption, respectively
$*C^f$	World (foreign) consumption
$*C_0$, $*C_0'$	Northern and Southern households' purchases of world (foreign) goods, in physical units
$*C_1$, $*C_1'$	Northern and Southern households' purchases of Northern goods, in physical units
$*C_2$, $*C_2'$	Northern and Southern households' purchases of Southern goods, in physical units
$*C_1^f$, $*C_2^f$	World (foreign) purchases of Northern and Southern goods, in physical units
D, D'	The Northern and Southern governments' budget deficits, respectively
$*E$, $*E'$	Northern and Southern demands for labor, respectively, in physical units
E, E'	Northern and Southern supplies of labor, respectively, in physical units
$*G_1$, $*G_2$	Northern government spending on Northern and Southern goods, respectively
$*G_1'$, $*G_2'$	Southern government spending on Northern and Southern goods, respectively
L_1^h, $*L_1^h$	Northern households' holdings of Northern money
$L_2^{h\prime}$, $*L_2^{h\prime}$	Southern households' holdings of Southern money
L_1, L_2'	The stocks of Northern and Southern money, respectively
p_0, p_0', p_0^f	The prices of world (foreign) goods in Northern, Southern, and world currencies, respectively
p_1, p_1', p_1^f	The prices of Northern goods in Northern, Southern, and world currencies, respectively

p_2, p_2', p_2^f	The prices of Southern goods in Northern, Southern, and world currencies, respectively
π, π'	The prices of world (foreign) currency in Northern and Southern currencies, respectively
Q_1, Q_2'	Outputs of Northern and Southern goods, in physical units
R, R'	The Northern and Southern central banks' holdings of foreign-currency reserves, in units of world (foreign) currency
r_0, r_1, r_2	The interest rates on world (foreign), Northern, and Southern bonds, respectively
$S, *S$	Northern household saving
$S', *S'$	Southern household saving
$T^h, T^{h'}$	Northern and Southern taxes
$T^f, T^{f'}$	Foreign transfers to the Northern and Southern governments, in units of Northern and Southern currency, respectively
w, w'	The Northern and Southern money wage rates
$W^c, W^{c'}$	The Northern and Southern central banks' wealth (net worth)
$W^h, W^{h'}$	Northern and Southern households' wealth (net worth)
$W^{hs}, W^{hs'}$	The integrals of Northern and Southern household saving
Y, Y'	Northern and Southern gross domestic products (nominal incomes)
$Y^d, Y^{d'}$	Northern and Southern disposable incomes
z	The price of Southern currency in units of Northern currency (the bilateral exchange rate)

These terms are also used in the two-country model:

B^t	The sum of stocks of Northern and Southern bonds outstanding, in units of Northern currency (i.e., $B_1 + zB_2')$[1]
B_1^{ct}	The sum of Northern and Southern central banks' holdings of Northern bonds, in units of Northern currency (i.e., $B_1^c + B_1^{c'})$
B_2^{ct}	The sum of Northern and Southern central banks' holdings of Southern bonds, in units of Southern currency (i.e., $B_2^c + B_2^{c'})$
$\dot{B}_1, \dot{B}_2'$	The rates of issue of Northern and Southern bonds in Northern and Southern currencies, respectively

[1] Sums such as B^t are always valued at a *constant* bilateral exchange rate.

R^t	The sum of Northern and Southern reserves, in units of world (foreign) currency (i.e., $R + R'$)
$\dot{R}^b$	The bilateral reserve flow from South to North, in units of world (foreign) currency
$\dot{R}^t$	The sum of Northern and Southern reserve inflows, in units of world (foreign) currency (the joint balance-of-payments surplus after instantaneous stock adjustments)
r^t	The *average* of interest rates on Northern and Southern bonds
T^b	A bilateral transfer from South to North, in units of Southern currency
W^{ht}	The sum of Northern and Southern households' wealth, in units of Northern currency (i.e., $W^h + zW^{h'}$)
$\dot{W}^{hs}, \dot{W}^{hs'}$	The rates of change in Northern and Southern stocks of accumulated saving in units of Northern and Southern currencies, respectively (equal to S and S', respectively)
Y^t	The sum of Northern and Southern incomes, in units of Northern currency (i.e., $Y + zY'$)
Y^{dt}	The sum of Northern and Southern disposable incomes, in units of Northern currency (i.e., $Y^d + zY^{d'}$)

Certain partial derivatives appear many times, and it is important to know their signs. In particular, S_0, S_1, S_2, B_{00}, B_{11}, and B_{22} are positive; S_Y, B_{0W}, B_{1W}, B_{2W}, and L_{1W} are positive but smaller than unity; and S_W, B_{01}, B_{10}, B_{12}, B_{21}, L_{10}, L_{11}, and L_{12} are negative. The same signs apply to the Southern (primed) parameters, including those that have no Northern counterparts (e.g., L'_{2W}, which is positive, and L'_{20}, L'_{21}, and L'_{22}, which are negative).

The following symbols are used to denote other combinations or transformations of variables:[2]

$$u^t_{ij} = u_{ij} + zu'_{ij} + \pi u^f_{ij} \qquad i, j = 0, 1, 2,$$
$$B^t_{11} = B_{11} + zB'_{11} = zB'_{22} + B_{22} = B_{11} + B_{22} > 0$$
$$B^t_{12} = B_{12} + zB'_{12} = zB'_{21} + B_{21} = B_{12} + B_{21} < 0$$
$$B^t_{10} = B_{10} + zB'_{10} = zB'_{20} + B_{20} = B_{10} + B_{20} < 0$$

---

[2] Terms such as a_i, e_{ii}, e_{ij}, m_i, σ_i, and u_{ij} are defined in the list for the one-country model and are not repeated here. It is necessary only to note that $i = 1, 2$ for a_i and σ_i, and that $i = 0, 1, 2$ for e_{ii}, e_{ij}, m_i, and u_{ij}. Terms without superscripts refer to Northern supplies or demands (and are denominated in Northern currency); terms with primes refer to Southern supplies or demands (and are denominated in Southern currency); terms such as u^f_{ij} refer to world (foreign) demand (and are denominated in world currency).

$$B_{01}^t = B_{01} + zB_{01}' = zB_{02}' + B_{02} = B_{01} + B_{02} < 0$$

$$B_{1W}^t = B_{1W} + B_{1W}' = B_{2W}' + B_{2W} = B_{1W} + B_{2W} > 0$$

$$J = (B_{11}^t - B_{12}^t)(B_{11}^t + B_{12}^t) > 0$$

$$J_B = S_W L_{11}^t - L_{1W} S_1^t > 0$$

$$J_F = S_1(B_{2W}B_{11}^t - B_{1W}B_{12}^t) + S_2(B_{1W}B_{11}^t - B_{2W}B_{12}^t) > 0$$

$$J_K = B_{1W}^t S_1^t - S_W(B_{11}^t + B_{12}^t) > 0$$

$$J_\pi = L_{1W}(B_{11}^t + B_{12}^t) - B_{1W}^t L_{11}^t > 0$$

$$J_0 = B_{1W}^t[(L_{11}S_0 - L_{10}S_1) + (L_{12}S_0 - L_{10}S_2)] + J_S(S_W L_{10} - L_{1W}S_0)$$
$$- B_{10}^t[(S_W L_{11} - L_{1W}S_1) + (S_W L_{12} - L_{1W}S_2)] > 0$$

$$J_R = -B_{01}^t\{2[(B_{01}^t + L_{11}^t)L_{12} + B_{12}^t L_{11}^t] - B_{01}^t(B_{11}^t - B_{12}^t)\} > 0$$

$$J_S = (B_{11}^t + B_{12}^t) > 0$$

$$J_W = (S_1 - S_2)(B_{1W} - B_{2W}) - S_W(B_{11}^t - B_{12}^t) > 0$$

$$L_{11}^t = L_{11} + zL_{21}' = zL_{22}' + L_{12} = L_{11} + L_{12} < 0$$

$$M_f = U_\pi(\sigma_1\sigma_2')[1 - (m_1 - m_2)]\{(u_{10}^t u_{20}^t + u_{12}^t U_\pi)(\sigma_1 + \sigma_2')$$
$$+ (\sigma_1 u_{20}^t)p_1 C_1^f + (\sigma_2' u_{10}^t)p_2 C_2^f$$
$$+ U_\pi(\sigma_1\sigma_2')[1 - (m_1 - m_2)]\} > 0$$

$$M_g = u_{10}^t u_{20}^t + u_{12}^t(u_{10}^t + u_{20}^t) > 0$$

$$M_k = M_g + (1 - m_1)(\sigma_2' u_{10}^t + \sigma_1 u_{20}^t) + m_0 M_0 > 0$$

$$M_\pi = \sigma_1 M_{1\pi} + \sigma_2' M_{2\pi} > 0$$

$$M_{1\pi} = (u_{10}^t + p_1 C_1^f)(M_{22} + M_{21}) + (u_{20}^t + p_2 C_2^f)M_{21} > 0$$

$$M_{2\pi} = (u_{20}^t + p_2 C_2^f)(M_{11} + M_{12}) + (u_{10}^t + p_1 C_1^f)M_{12} > 0$$

$$M_s = M_g + [1 - m_1(1 - S_Y)](\sigma_2' u_{10}^t + \sigma_1 u_{20}^t)$$
$$+ M_Y\{u_{12}^t(\sigma_1 + \sigma_2') + [1 - (m_1 - m_2)(1 - S_Y)]\sigma_1\sigma_2'\} > 0$$

$$M_u = \sigma_1 M_{1U} + \sigma_2' M_{2U} > 0$$

$$M_w = \sigma_1 U_{1\pi} + \sigma_2' U_{2\pi} = (u_{10}^t + p_1 C_1^f)(\sigma_1 u_{20}^t + M_0)$$
$$+ (u_{20}^t + p_2 C_2^f)(\sigma_2' u_{10}^t + M) > 0$$

$$M_Y = S_Y + m_0(1 - S_Y) > 0$$

$$M_0 = u_{12}^t(\sigma_1 + \sigma_2') + [1 - (m_1 - m_2)]\sigma_1\sigma_2' > 0$$

$$M_{11} = u_{10}^t + M_Y\sigma_1 > 0$$

$$M_{12} = u_{12}^t + m_2(1 - S_Y)\sigma_1 > 0$$

$$M_{21} = u_{12}^t + m_2(1 - S_Y)\sigma_2' > 0$$

$$M_{22} = u_{20}^t + M_Y\sigma_2' > 0$$

$$M_{1d} = [(m_1 S_2 + m_2 S_1)M_{22} + S_1^t(1 - m_0)M_{21}](B_{11}^t - B_{12}^t)$$
$$+ B_{11}^t(m_1 - m_2)(S_1 - S_2)M_{22} > 0$$

$$M_{2d} = [(m_1 S_2 + m_2 S_1)M_{11} + S_1^t(1 - m_0)M_{12}](B_{11}^t - B_{12}^t)$$
$$+ B_{11}^t(m_1 - m_2)(S_1 - S_2)M_{11} > 0$$

$$M_{1e} = M_{1d} - (B_{11}^t + B_{12}^t)(m_1 - m_2)(S_1 - S_2)M_{22} > 0$$

$$M_{2e} = M_{2d} - (B_{11}^t + B_{12}^t)(m_1 - m_2)(S_1 - S_2)M_{11} > 0$$

$$M_{1g} = \sigma_1 u_{20}^t[1 - m_1(1 - S_Y)] + M_Y(\sigma_1 u_{12}^t)$$
$$+ M_Y[1 - (m_1 - m_2)(1 - S_Y)]\sigma_1\sigma_2' > 0$$

$$M_{2g} = \sigma_2' u_{10}^t [1 - m_1(1 - S_Y)] + M_Y(\sigma_2' u_{12}^t)$$
$$+ M_Y[1 - (m_1 - m_2)(1 - S_Y)]\sigma_1\sigma_2' > 0$$

$$M_{1h} = \sigma_1[M_Y u_{12}^t - m_2(1 - S_Y)u_{20}^t] \gtrless 0$$

$$M_{2h} = \sigma_2'[M_Y u_{12}^t - m_2(1 - S_Y)u_{10}^t] \gtrless 0$$

$$M_{1p} = -2J_S[B_{01}^t B_{11}^t + J_S(B_{12}^t + L_{12})][(m_1 S_2 + m_2 S_1)M_{22}$$
$$+ S_1^t(1 - m_0)M_{21}] > 0$$

$$M_{2p} = -2J_S[B_{01}^t B_{11}^t + J_S(B_{12}^t + L_{12})][(m_1 S_2 + m_2 S_1)M_{11}$$
$$+ S_1^t(1 - m_0)M_{12}] > 0$$

$$M_{1q} = -B_{01}^t(m_1 - m_2)(S_1 - S_2)J_S M_{22} > 0$$

$$M_{2q} = -B_{01}^t(m_1 - m_2)(S_1 - S_2)J_S M_{11} > 0$$

$$M_{1U} = (1 - m_0)(M_{22} + 2M_{21}) > 0$$

$$M_{2U} = (1 - m_0)(M_{11} + 2M_{12}) > 0$$

$$S_1^t = S_1 + zS_1' = zS_2' + S_2 = S_1 + S_2 > 0$$

$$U_\pi = (u_{10}^t + p_1 C_1^f) + (u_{20}^t + p_2 C_2^f) > 0$$

$$U_{1\pi} = (u_{10}^t + p_1 C_1^f)[u_{20}^t + u_{12}^t + (1 - m_1)\sigma_2']$$
$$+ (u_{20}^t + p_2 C_2^f)(u_{12}^t + m_2\sigma_2') > 0$$

$$U_{2\pi} = (u_{20}^t + p_2 C_2^f)[u_{10}^t + u_{12}^t + (1 - m_1)\sigma_1]$$
$$+ (u_{10}^t + p_1 C_1^f)(u_{12}^t + m_2\sigma_1) > 0$$

$$U_{1a} = u_{20}^t(u_{10}^t + p_1 C_1^f) + u_{12}^t U_\pi > 0$$

$$U_{2a} = u_{10}^t(u_{20}^t + p_2 C_2^f) + u_{12}^t U_\pi > 0$$

$$U_b = U_\pi[1 - (m_1 - m_2)] > 0$$

$$V_\pi = \pi B_0^h = \pi' B_0^{h'} > 0$$

Index

absorption, 108, 113, 146
and current-account surplus, 158
aggregate responses, compared to a single
economy, 340, 399–400,440–3, 455–6
Alexander, S. S., 6
asset-market approach, 14, 199
and exchange-rate expectations, 242
asset-market disturbances, 30, 58
asset-market integration
criterion for optimum currency area, 383
defined, 13–14, 84
and devaluation, 148
and distribution of income changes,
445–6
effectiveness of fiscal policy, 140–2,
194, 233–7, 490–1
effectiveness of monetary policy, 118,
120, 122–4, 194, 415
external, as substitute for bilateral, 410
and foreign interest-rate changes,132
and goods-market disturbances, 84–5
instability with an income tax, 288
interdependence of fiscal policies,
490–1, 520
interdependence of monetary policies,
422, 430–1
and temporary tax cut, 185, 191, 192–3
see also bilateral integration
asset-market symmetry, 328–32
asymmetry between goods and asset markets, 16

balance of payments
flows, 60, 157, 322–3
instantaneous stock adjustments, 56
joint, 356
see also current account
balanced-budget changes, 51, 97, 349
with an income tax, 270
relative effects on two countries, 475,
518–19
balanced-budget multiplier, 101, 272, 360
Balassa, B., 380, 394
bias
toward domestic assets, 330–1
toward home goods, 327

bilateral integration
between bond markets, 410
between goods markets, 414–15
relative effects of fiscal policy, 490–1
relative effects of monetary policy, 414–
15
see also asset-market integration; goods-
market integration
Blinder, A. S., 17, 111n, 267
bond markets, 42, 317
bonds
central bank's demand, 39, 309
defined as bills, 33, 304
demand for, 38, 308
supply of, 40, 134, 270, 316
symmetric tastes, 331
Branson, W. H., 17, 268
Bryant, R. C., 297n
budget deficit
bond financing, 40, 316
defined, 40, 270, 316
endogenous, 267, 286
exogenous, 41, 316
specification, long-run implications, 279
see also lump-sum tax; income tax

capital gains on foreign bonds, 34, 46, 198,
305
and conditions for insulation, 232
as offset to dissaving, 168
reasons for overshooting and undershooting, 114
resulting from devaluation, 146
capital mobility, 28
see also asset-market integration
capital stocks, 203, 204
nontransferability, 32, 33–4
central bank, 39, 309
income, 40
classical variant, 32, 51, 303
composite-good variant, 81, 82, 88–9, 94,
124, 151
compound disturbances, 133
consumption, 36, 305–6
identical tastes, 325–7
symmetrical tastes, 327; *see also* goods-
market symmetry

581